This book about the Red Army Faction [in] Germany is one that should be read by any serious student of anti-imperialist politics. "Volume 1: Projectiles for the People" provides a history of the RAF's development through the words of its letters and communiqués. What makes the book especially important and relevant, however, is the careful research and documentation done by its editors. From this book you will learn the mistakes of a group that was both large and strong, but which (like our own home-grown attempts in this regard) was unable to successfully communicate with the working class of a "democratic" country on a level that met their needs. While the armed struggle can be the seed of something much larger, it is also another means of reaching out and communicating with the people. Students interested in this historic era would do well to study this book and to internalize both the successes and failures of one of the largest organized armed anti-imperialist organizations operating in Western Europe since World War II.

　　　　—Ed Mead, former political prisoner, George Jackson Brigade

Clear-headed and meticulously researched, this book deftly avoids many of the problems that plagued earlier attempts to tell the brief but enduring history of the RAF. It offers a remarkable wealth of source material in the form of statements and letters from the combatants, yet the authors manage to present it in a way that is both coherent and engaging. Evidence of brutal—and ultimately ineffective—attempts by the state to silence the voices of political prisoners serve as a timely and powerful reminder of the continued need for anti-imperialist prisoners as leaders in our movements today. At once informative and inspirational, this is a much-needed contribution to the analysis of armed struggle and the cycles of repression and resistance in Europe and around the world.

　　　　—Sara Falconer, Toronto Anarchist Black Cross Federation

This first volume about the RAF is about a part of WWII that did not end when the so called allies defeated the nazis. The RAF warriors come from a strong socialist history and knew they were fighting for the very life of their country. Many victories and many errors were scored which provide this important look into <u>real</u> her/history lessons. A must read for all serious alternative history students who then in turn can use it as a teaching tool towards a better future.

　　　　—b♀ (r.d. brown), former political prisoner, George Jackson Brigade

*Starting in the Sixties, a new revolutionary strategy began to
plague the capitalist metropolis—the urban guerilla. Warfare
once waged by peasant armies in the countryside of a Cuba, a
China, or a Guinea-Bissau, was suddenly transferred to small
cells of ex-students in the imperialist centers of Berlin, Rome,
and New York. No urban guerillas became more famed or more
demonized than West Germany's Red Army Faction (RAF).
We knew their signature bold actions in the headlines: from the
damaging bombing of the u.s. army V Corps headquarters in
Frankfurt in 1972, in response to Washington's mining of Hanoi's
harbor in an escalation of the Vietnam War, to the kidnapping
and later execution of the head of the West German industrialists'
association, in an effort to negotiate for the release of revolutionary
prisoners. <u>But we never heard their political voices.</u> Since the
RAF's political statements, debates, and communiqués were
untranslated and unavailable in English even within the left.*

   *Now, at last, a significant documentary history of the RAF
has come into the spotlight, complete with a readable account
of the postwar German New Left from which it emerged. Even
better, this work was done by editors/translators who reject the
obedient capitalist media's trivializing of the RAF as "pathological"
death-wishing celebrities. In their hands, the words of the RAF
are revealed as serious responses to the failure of parliamentary
reformism, trade-unionism, and pacifism, to stop the solidification of
Germany's own form of a neofascist capitalism (lightly cosmeticized
with a layer of that numbing "consumer democracy"). The young
RAF fighters hoped for liberation in their dangerous experiment
but were willing to accept tragic consequences, and their story
is emotionally difficult to read with eyes open. Controversial as
the RAF was, their systematic torture in special "anti-terrorist"
facilities stirred worldwide unease and even protest. In fact, those
special prisons were the eagerly studied forerunners for the u.s.
empire's own latest human rights abuses, from Guantanamo to
the domestic "maxi-maxi" prisons. We all and the RAF are much
closer than the capitalist public wants to believe. It is all here, in
this first volume of the Red Army Faction documentary histories,
and we should thank all those who worked on this book.*

   —J. Sakai, author of Settlers: Mythology of the White Proletariat

THE RED ARMY FACTION:
A DOCUMENTARY HISTORY

VOLUME I

PROJECTILES
for the PEOPLE

THE RED ARMY FACTION:
A DOCUMENTARY HISTORY

VOLUME I

PROJECTILES

for the PEOPLE

forewords by Bill Dunne and Russell "Maroon" Shoats

introductory texts and translations by
André Moncourt and J. Smith

the red army faction: a documentary history
volume 1: projectiles for the people

introductory texts and translations by André Moncourt and J. Smith

The opening epigram on page v is from Karl-Heinz Dellwo "Kein Ankommen,
kein Zurück" in *Nach dem bewaffneten Kampf*, Angelika Holderberg ed. (Gießen:
Psychsozial-Verlag, 2007).

ISBN: 978-1-60486-029-0
Library of Congress Control Number: 2008929110

Many of the translated texts in this book
are available online at www.germanguerilla.com

Kersplebedeb Publishing and Distribution
CP 63560
CCCP Van Horne
Montreal, Quebec
Canada H3W 3H8
www.kersplebedeb.com
www.leftwingbooks.net

PM Press
PO Box 23912
Oakland, CA 94623
www.pmpress.org

Layout and Index by Kersplebedeb

Cover Design: Josh MacPhee/Justseeds.org
The photo used on the front cover is of the funeral of Andreas Baader, Gudrun Ensslin,
and Jan-Carl Raspe in 1977.

Printed in the USA

dedicated to the memory of Jim Campbell

"We are a projectile," Andreas Baader wrote to the group, thereby articulating an ethical point of view in which the subject and his objective became a single thing. It also meant that if no further separation existed between the "subject" and "object" it was obvious how it would end: in death.

Karl-Heinz Dellwo

CONTENTS

FOREWORD BY BILL DUNNE

Projectiles for the People, Volume One of *The Red Army Faction: A Documentary History,* is an important exposition of what it means to wage armed struggle as an urban guerilla in the post WWII western imperial-capitalist paradigm. Via the fast-turning pages of *Projectiles,* Smith and Moncourt usher us through the RAF's emergence in Germany from a moribund and constrained left opposition misdirected and suppressed by U.S. imperialism and a quisling bourgeoisie. The RAF's "projectiles for the people" documented their political, practical, intellectual, and emotional trajectory into taking up and using the gun in service of revolutionary communist class war. *Projectiles* brings us their voices and links their context to ours.

Projectiles shows us how the RAF engaged in people's warfare without descending into adventurism. It reveals how the guerilla was able to work with apparently unlikely allies and eschew involvement with ostensibly likely ones based on sophisticated analysis of the demands of conditions, time, and place. It illustrates how the comrades were able to internalize the trauma of frequently fatal mistakes and defeats as well as the euphoria of correct practice and victories. It explains how the organization recognized and responded to the enemy's slanderous campaign of vilification aimed at creating a false opposition to the underground. *Projectiles,* in this exploration of these and many other elements of RAF praxis, thus illustrates that and how the RAF developed arguably the highest expression of armed struggle in the late capitalist first world.

Projectiles for the People is more than a dry historical treatise, however; it is a highly accessible rendition of a story of struggle that puts us into both the thought and the action. That placement conveys more than a sense or understanding of the RAF's praxis. It transmits a connection in a visceral way. Not since reading *Ten Days that Shook the World* have I been so drawn into a political narrative. Reading like a historical thriller notwithstanding, *Projectiles* lets us see a rare confluence of theory and practice of which anyone who aspires to make revolution should be aware. The RAF may no longer be with us, but it has prepared the ground for and can yet aid the current movement for the most equitable social reality in which all people will have the greatest possible freedom to develop their full human potential. Nowhere else has the RAF's life, times, and legacy been so clearly laid out.

A WORD FROM
RUSSELL "MAROON" SHOATS

In today's world ANYONE who dares to raise their voice against ANYTHING being heaped on them by those in power needs to read this book. The repressive methods that the West German state brought to bear against the RAF—detailed by the authors—have been adopted, universalized, and refined, and can be found in use in a prison, jail, detention center or other "holding facility" not far from you.

In the throes of the worst economic crisis since the Great Depression, world-wide capital—led by U.S. imperialism—is possibly in the end-game struggle, not of Marx's "Socialism or Barbarism," but of what is beginning to be understood by a majority of our planet's humans: 21st century capitalism/imperialism... equals EXTERMINISM!

The prison isolation and torture methods detailed in this volume are one of the repressive forces' last ditch efforts to arrest the global material forces that signal their demise.

After being subjected to similar methods of isolation and torture for decades, I can only offer one piece of advice: either stand up and struggle against this monster—and face the horrors detailed in this book— or lay down and accept the idea (and reality) that 21st century capital/ imperialism—unchecked—will destroy EVERYTHING it comes into contact with.

Bill Dunne was captured on October 14, 1979. He had been shot three times by police, and according to the state had been involved in an attempt to break a comrade out of the Seattle jail, as part of an unnamed anarchist collective. In 1980, he received a ninety-five-year sentence, and in 1983 had a consecutive fifteen years with five concurrent added due to an attempted escape. As he has stated, "The aggregate 105 years is a 'parole when they feel like it' sort of sentence."

In 1970, Russell "Maroon" Shoats was accused of an attack on a Philadelphia police station in which an officer was killed. He went underground, functioning for eighteen months as a soldier in the Black Liberation Army. In 1972, he was captured and sentenced to multiple life sentences. He escaped twice—in 1977 and 1980— but both times was recaptured. Most of his time in prison, including at present, has been spent in isolation conditions, locked down 22 to 24 hours a day.

ACKNOWLEDGEMENTS

Many, many people were very helpful to us as we worked on this book.

Many, many more had already laid the basis for our study through years of hard work providing a voice for the underground. In the days before the internet, a number of movement publications took responsibility for translating and distributing texts by illegal groups like the Red Army Faction. In this regard, we would like to thank those who worked on *Resistance* (based in Vancouver, Canada in the 1980s), *Arm the Spirit* (based in Toronto, Canada in the 1990s), and *l'Internationale* (based in France, 1983-1984). While it did not specifically focus on the guerilla, the Toronto-based newspaper *Prison News Service*, which appeared in the 1980s and early 1990s, is worth also mentioning in this regard.

We must certainly thank Maspero, the French publisher, several of whose books were of great use to us, as well as Nadir, Extremismus, Zeitgesichte, and the Marxist Internet Archive, all of which maintain excellent websites.

Anthony Murphy translated the RAF's *The Urban Guerilla Concept* in 2003; while we did not end up using his version, we are nevertheless grateful for his work and assistance.

This project would have been impossible in its present form if not for the excellent Rote Armee Fraktion Collection of the International Institute of Social History, Amsterdam, maintained online as an archive by former RAF member Ronald Augustin. We are grateful to both the IISH, and to Augustin in particular.

Many of the graphics in this book come from the book and CD *Vorwärts bis zum nieder mit,* compiled by Sebastian Haunss, Markus Mohr, and Klaus Viehmann from a variety of archives and published by Verlag Assoziation A. The interested reader can view the entire contents of this CD online at http://plakat.nadir.org/. All those involved in producing this artwork, and the book and website in question, have our thanks.

Dan Berger and Matthew Lyons provided very useful feedback to earlier drafts of our text. Henning Böke, Jutta Ditfurth, comrades from the Parti Communiste Marxiste-Léniniste-Maoïste, members of the Leftist Trainspotters and Marxmail email lists, all provided very useful answers to questions regarding the West German radical left and the guerilla. Muhammad Abu Nasr provided helpful insight into the Palestinian resistance, specifically around the Black September action in Munich. Romy Ruukel provided much needed help and advice, proofreading the text and teaching us how to compile a bibliography. Many others provided great assistance to us in this project, yet would rather not be named here. They too have our thanks.

It should go without saying that none of these individuals or groups are likely to agree with everything we have stated in this book, nor do they necessarily approve of the conclusions we have drawn. It goes without saying that they have no responsibility for any errors contained herein.

Finally, and with our tongues planted firmly in our cheeks, we would like to thank the U.S. military for creating the internet, without which this project might not have been possible.

TRANSLATORS' NOTE

In preparing these texts, we consulted the many existent versions in both French and English. However, in each case these translations were found to have serious shortcomings. Not surprisingly, many of them, the work of committed activists whose grasp of German was limited, were marred by erroneous translation—usually these errors were predictable given the complexity of the German language. In no few cases, segments of the original text were found to be missing from the available translations. It was also not uncommon to encounter what might best be called transliteration—the translator "adjusted" concepts to suit the milieu for which he or she was translating the document. The end result of this latter phenomenon was often, however unintentional, the ideological distortion of the original document—usually only slight in nature, but occasionally egregious. Perhaps the oddest thing we encountered on more than a few occasions was the existence of accretions in the translated documents we referred to; usually only a phrase or a sentence or two, but occasionally entire paragraphs.

After several months of poring over the existing translations, hoping to tweak them into publishable shape (about two thirds of the documents in this book existed in some form of translation in the two languages accessible to us), we were obliged to accept the inevitable: all of the documents we hoped to use would have to be checked against the originals before going to publication. Then began the task of hunting down the originals, a process greatly facilitated by the existence of several online sources, including an indispensible website maintained by former RAF prisoner Ronald Augustin.[1] Of no less importance was the discovery, in pdf form, of the entire 1997 ID-Verlag book, *Texte und Materialien zur Geschichte der RAF* on the Nadir website.[2] With these two resources in hand, we had all the documents we needed to complete this book save a small handful that we tracked down elsewhere.

The process of translation we used was to some degree unique. Only one of the two "translators" was actually conversant in German, and so it fell to him to prepare the translations. Once a document was translated, he would forward it to the other "translator" who would meticulously

---

1 http://labourhistory.net/raf/

2 http://www.nadir.org/nadir/archiv/PolitischeStroemungen/Stadtguerilla+RAF/RAF/raf-texte+materialien.PDF

examine it and make suggestions for improving (de-Germanizing) the English used. These suggested changes—always numerous—would then be checked against the original to assure that the intent was not being skewed. This process would usually involve two or three rounds of the document going back and forth between the translators, before a finalized version acceptable to both of us was arrived at. On three occasions, each involving a single sentence, neither of us was happy with the other's proposal and so a compromise had to be arrived at—this would affect in total approximately a half a page of the book you are holding. The end result was that no document in this book was examined fewer than three times and most of the major ones were examined at least five or six times.

Are we saying that these translations are perfect? Undoubtedly not. In a project of this grandeur, involving the translation of between four and five hundred pages, disagreements about decisions we made and interpretations we arrived at are de facto inevitable, as are errors—hopefully none of them significant.

That said, we are confident that the documents in this book accurately represent the history and the ideology of the Red Army Faction and provide the reader with a resource unparalleled elsewhere in English.

Before closing one other issue cries out to be addressed. We refer to this work as the complete texts of the Red Army Faction. The meaning of that statement seems indisputable, but that is not the case, and so we must explain what we mean by "complete." To the best of our knowledge, we have included every document issued by the RAF in its close to thirty-year history in either this volume (1968-1977), the second volume (1978-1984), or the forthcoming third volume (1985-1998). By this, we mean every theoretical manifesto, every communiqué accompanying an action, and every letter sent by the organization to the media.

After some discussion we decided not to include *Über den bewaffneten Kampf in Westeuropa* (Regarding the Armed Struggle in West Europe) penned by Horst Mahler. This 1971 document, a sprawling theoretical text, was rejected by the other members of the RAF and played no small role in the decision to expel Mahler from the group—making him the only member ever publicly expelled. (The interested reader proficient in German will have no difficulty finding this document online, including in the aforementioned ID-Verlag book.)

We also did not include, with several exceptions, letters written by imprisoned RAF members. There are literally thousands of them, a significant selection of which have been published in German in a book entitled *Das Info*, edited by former lawyer to RAF prisoners Pieter Bakker Schut. This book can be found in its entirety on the site maintained by Augustin, as can Bakker Schut's invaluable historical analysis of the Stammheim trial, simply entitled *Stammheim*. Nor did we publish, with the exception of a handful, any of the hundreds of court statements, often of epic length, made by RAF defendants over the years. In the cases where we did choose to publish a letter or a court statement, it was because the document in question filled out some theoretical or historical aspect of the RAF's history that we felt was not adequately addressed elsewhere. This is also true of the open letter from the RZ to the RAF that we publish in this volume—a number of similar documents from other German and European guerilla groups will appear in the second and third volumes of this work.

PREFACE

The book you hold in your hands, along with its companion volumes, constitute the most complete works and history of the Red Army Faction ever published in the English language.

The Red Army Faction was formed in 1970 when a small group of West German revolutionaries decided to go underground and carry out armed actions against U.S. imperialism. Within a few years, almost all of the original members were either dead or captured, yet the harsh treatment the latter received as prisoners garnered them a degree of sympathy, and their own unflagging resistance earned them the respect of many.

Indeed, it would not be an exaggeration to say that they captured the imagination of a generation of West German youth. Certainly, before they fell, they had already succeeded in inspiring others to pick up their banner.

In fact, the RAF was to remain a factor in German politics for almost thirty years as successive waves of radicals extended the struggle, carrying out increasingly sophisticated and daring campaigns of assassination and bombings against key members of the West German ruling class and American armed forces stationed in the Federal Republic. On more than one occasion, they shook their society to its core, baiting its ruling class into dictatorial reactions that shocked the consciences of even their own supporters. Eventually, the RAF became emblematic of the "euro-terrorism" of the 1970s and 80s, yet like so many things that are emblematic, it was never typical of that which it represented.

In its halcyon days, many people considered the guerilla a legitimate political force, and one can read reports of soccer fans wearing RAF insignia and of young people secretly keeping photos clipped from wanted posters in their wallets. As this naïve and romantic honeymoon period faded, the group became the object of mass hatred and hysteria, the most egregious example of things going "too far," of people "losing their moral compass."

As with any powerful symbol, for much of its history what seemed most important about the RAF was what people thought about it. For many, fascination with the group grew out of a fascination with its founding members. In the 1960s, Ulrike Meinhof was already a well known journalist who seemed able to combine radical politics with an increasingly successful career. At the same time, Andreas Baader had a reputation for being the charming rogue of the Berlin hipster scene, his panache enhanced as he and a group of his friends were brought to trial for firebombing a Frankfurt department store.

People may not have agreed with what they did next, or with why they did it, but if nothing else, the misnamed "Baader-Meinhof Gang" had style, and as the media played up every detail and the old fogies in power got more and more freaked out, they were briefly loved for simply being the most hardcore urban guerillas around.

Much could be written about this bizarre fascination, this production of *guerilla cachet*, but to do so would be to write a cultural history, and we intend something else altogether.

Except in passing, these books will not deal with the private lives or personalities of the RAF combatants. How the guerillas got along with their parents, friends, or each other is not really our concern. We will not concentrate on the kind of cars they liked or their taste in music or what kind of childhood they had. We will not guess at who was "nice" and who was a "prick," or go over who slept with whom, or catalog the names people called each other when they were arguing.

To have to provide such a disclaimer may seem absurd, for most political histories pass over such details as a matter of course. Yet, a brief survey of the few books available about the RAF will show that these questions have been the major preoccupation of almost anyone who has approached this subject. Nor are we unaware of the point that the RAF prisoners themselves would make on more than one occasion: that efforts to explain their actions in psychological terms were part of a conscious state strategy of pathologizing them and their politics, or at least shifting people's attention onto trivial and often fabricated personal details. While there are things we consider mistaken in the RAF's broader analysis, on this question they appear to have been 100% correct.

While the personal may be political, we believe that the RAF's greatest significance is not to be found in the part it played in the individual lives of its members or supporters. Rather, to appreciate what it was and what it meant, and as a first step towards being able to evaluate its praxis, the RAF must be placed within the context of left-wing revolutionary struggle in the First World at a very particular point in time. As such, we are most interested in the group's ideas, its line as established in its communiqués and other documents, how it put this line into practice through its actions and campaigns, and the relationship the group enjoyed with its supporters and other leftists.

Some may accuse us of being uncritical, or of even supporting the RAF's politics and their practice. We would answer that in order to be critical one must first be in possession of the facts. While we consider questions of morality and means and ends to be very important, given that this is the first time most of this material has been made available to English-readers, we prefer not to muddy the waters by condemning or praising the guerilla every step of the way.

Certainly we will offer no blanket denunciation—nor will we indulge in cheap praise. What has been written so far is replete with judgment, and often contains very little factual content or political analysis. We hope with these books to do our small part in correcting this imbalance.

In order for the guerilla's actions and statements to be at all comprehensible, they need to be placed in the context of their times and of the wider left-wing movement in West Germany. Even as these events were unfolding, this context was not well understood by many of us in North America; now, decades later, it is even harder to grasp. For that reason, we have provided two background chapters providing an overview of postwar West Germany, as well as a series of introductory texts to the different documents from the guerilla. These are overviews and as will be clear, they have been written from a particular perspective. It is here that our analysis most obviously departs from that of the RAF, our sympathy for many of its aims notwithstanding.

We offer these documents to the comrades of today—and to the comrades of tomorrow—both as a testament to those who struggled before and as an explanation as to how they saw the world, why they made the choices they made, and the price they were made to pay for having done so.

ACRONYM KEY

2JM   *Bewegung 2. Juni* (2nd of June Movement); West Berlin-based guerilla group formed in early 1972, its name comes from the date of the police shooting of protester Benno Ohnesorg in 1967.

APO   *Außerparlemtarische Opposition* (Extra-Parliamentary Opposition); the name given to the broad-based militant opposition with its roots in the student movement that encompassed the left-wing anti-imperialist and social revolutionary movements of the late sixties and early seventies.

ARD   *Arbeitsgemeinschaft der öffentlich-rechtlichen Rundfunkanstalten der Bundesrepublik Deutschland* (Syndicate for Publicly Regulated Radio Stations in the Federal Republic of Germany); state-funded radio.

BAW   *Bundesanwaltschaft* (Federal Prosecutors Office); noted for its aggressive prosecution of cases against the guerilla and the left.

BGS   *Bundesgrenzschutz* (Federal Border Patrol); border security police.

BKA   *Bundeskriminalamt* (Federal Criminal Bureau); the German equivalent of the FBI, particularly active in police activities against the guerilla and the left.

BND   *Bundesnachrichtendienst* (Federal Intelligence Service); the FRG's foreign intelligence service.

CDU   *Christlich Demokratisches Union Deutschlands* (Christian Democratic Union of Germany); Germany's mainstream conservative party.

CSU   *Christlich-Soziale Union in Bayern* (Bavarian Christian-Social Union); Bavaria's mainstream conservative party, the Bavarian partner to the CDU.

DGB   *Deutscher Gewerkschaftsbund* (German Union Federation); the largest union federation in the FRG.

DKP   *Deutsche Kommunistische Partei* (German
         Communist Party); the pro-Soviet communist party
         founded in 1968, in effect the rebranding of the
         KPD (Communist Party of Germany), which was
         banned in 1956.

FAZ   *Frankfurter Allgemeine Zeitung;* a high-quality,
         national, moderate conservative, German daily
         newspaper.

FDP   *Freie Demokratische Partei* (Free Democratic Party);
         Germany's mainstream liberal party.

GIM   *Gruppe Internationale Marxisten* (International
         Marxist Group); West German section of the
         Trotskyist Fourth International active in the FRG in
         the seventies and eighties, fused with the KPD/ML to
         form the VSP in 1986.

GSG-9   *Grenzschutzgruppe 9* (Border Patrol Group 9);
         officially part of the BGS, in practice Germany's
         antiterrorist special operations unit.

KB   *Kommunistischer Bund* (Communist League); a
         small Maoist group active in the seventies.

KBW   *Kommunistischer Bund Westdeutschland* (West
         German Communist League); founded in Bremen in
         1973. A Maoist organization originally associated
         with China, subsequently shifted their support to
         Albania and Pol Pot's Cambodian regime. Dissolved
         in 1985.

KPD   *Kommunistische Partei Deutschlands* (Communist
         Party of Germany); pro-Soviet communist party
         founded in 1919, banned under Hitler in 1933
         and under Adenauer in 1956, rebranded as DKP
         (German Communist Party) in 1968.
         Also a Maoist party founded by the KPD/AO in
         1971 and dissolved in 1980.

KPD/AO   *Kommunistische Partei Deutschlands/
         Aufbauorganisation* (Communist Party of Germany/
         Pre-Party Formation); a Maoist organization
         founded in 1970, became the KPD in 1971.

KPD/ML	*Kommunistische Partei Deutschlands/Marxisten-Leninisten* (Communist Party of Germany/Marxist-Leninist); a Maoist party founded on December 31, 1968. It fused with the Trotskyist GIM in 1986 to form the VSP.
KSV	*Kommunistische Studentverband* (Communist Student Association); student wing of the KPD/AO and later the KPD, founded in 1971 and dissolved in 1980.
ID	*Informationsdienst;* a left-wing news service published weekly from 1973 until 1981. In 1988, its archives were used to launch the left-wing publisher, Verlag Edition ID-Archiv, specializing in books about the German far left.
LG	*Landesgericht* (*Land* Court); each of the *Länder* had it's own court system.
LKA	*Landeskriminalamt* (*Land* Criminal Bureau); the equivalent of the BKA functioning at the level of a state or province.
LAW	*Landesanwaltschaft* (*Land* Prosecutors Office); the equivalent of a state or provincial prosecutors office.
NPD	*Nationaldemokratische Partei Deutschlands* (National Democratic Party of Germany); far-right political party, supported by many neo-nazis.
OLG	*Oberlandesgericht* (*Land* Court of Appeal); each of the *Länder* had it's own Court of Appeal.
ÖTV	*Gewerkschaft öffentliche Dienste, Transport und Verkehr* (The Public Service, Transport, and Communication Union).
PFLP	Popular Front for the Liberation of Palestine; founded in 1953, secular nationalist and Marxist, the second largest tendency within the PLO after Fatah.
PFLP (EO)	Popular Front for the Liberation of Palestine (External Operations); originally a section of the PFLP, expelled in the early seventies for conducting controversial actions outside of Israel, effectively dissolved in 1978 after the death of its leader Waddi Haddad, who had been poisoned by the Mossad.
RAF	*Rote Armee Fraktion* (Red Army Faction).

RH	*Rote Hilfe* (Red Aid); an important prisoner support network which came out of the APO.
RH E.V.	*Rote Hilfe e.v.* (Red Aid registered association); a Red Aid network set up by the KPD/AO in 1970.
RZ	*Revolutionäre Zellen* (Revolutionary Cells); founded in 1973, most groups within its structure ceased activity in 1991, with the final action occurring in 1994.
SDS	*Sozialistischer Deutscher Studentenbund* (Socialist German Students Federation); founded by the SPD in 1946. By the late sixties it was an independent left-wing student federation and the most significant organization in the APO. It dissolved in 1970.
SHB	*Sozialdemokratischer Hochschulbund* (Social Democratic Student Federation); founded in 1960 by the SPD, dissolved in 1992.
SPD	*Sozialdemokratische Partei Deutschlands* (Social Democratic Party of Germany); Germany's mainstream social democratic party.
SPK	*Socialistiches Patientenkollektiv* (Socialist Patients' Collective); founded in 1970, part of the antipsychiatry movement. It dissolved under extreme state pressure in 1971, many of its core members later joining the RAF.
VSP	*Vereingte Sozialistische Partei* (United Socialist Party); formed in 1986 through the fusion of the KPD/ML and the GIM, splintered into various groups in 1993.
ZDF	*Zweites Deutsches Fernsehen* (Second German Television); German publicly regulated television, Europe's largest broadcasting corporation.

GERMAN TERMS

This is by no means a complete list of German words and terms used in this volume, most of which are explained in the text or by means of footnote. What follows are simply some of the more frequently recurring words the reader will encounter.

Bundestag: The federal parliament of West Germany.

Bundeswehr: The armed forces of West Germany, re-established in 1954.

Jusos: Arbeitsgemeinschaft der Jungsozialistinnen und Jungsozialisten in der SPD (Workers Association of Young Socialists in the SPD); the SPD's youth wing.

Kripo: Short for *Kriminalpolizei* (Criminal Police); the principal German police force.

Land/Länder: The singular and plural for the German equivalent of states or provinces.

Ostpolitik: the FRG's official policy towards the GDR and the East bloc.

Rote Zora: the independent feminist affiliate of the RZ. Its members were originally active as the Women of the Revolutionary Cells in 1975. The last Rote Zora action occurred in 1995.

Stasi: The *Ministerium für Staatssicherheit* (Ministry for State Security), better know as the *Stasi,* was the East German secret police force that tracked both internal dissent and foreign threats. It was similar in some ways to the FBI or the BKA, but played a more central role in policy decision-making.

Verfassungsschutz: Literally "Protection of the Constitution" or Guardians of the Constitution; the German internal intelligence service, primary police force for intelligence actions against the guerilla and the left.

PROJECTILES
for the PEOPLE

AUTOBAHNS ••••

MILES
0   50   100

"Democracy" Comes to Deutschland: Postfascist Germany and the Continuing Appeal of Imperialism

IT IS IMPOSSIBLE TO REALLY understand the rise of the New Left or the development of armed struggle in West Germany in the late sixties and early seventies without understanding the nature of the country and the role it played within the hegemonic, anticommunist strategy developed by the United States in the period following World War II.

The Federal Republic of Germany was a hybrid state, some elements—its institutions, some legislation, many personnel—seamlessly persisting from the Nazi period, and others grafted on by the Americans. As a nation almost constitutionally defined as a junior partner of U.S. imperialism, West Germany remained subordinate to it in the first postwar decades in a way that even Britain or France were not. Making matters even worse, in return for their allegiance, the West German ruling and professional classes were given free reign to negotiate their own stiflingly conservative and authoritarian post-Nazi culture and identity.

All of this was built on a post-genocidal basis; dead Jews remaining the elephant in the corner, alternately ignored or explained away as a tragic consequence of the "lack of morals" under Hitler. Many Germans growing up after the war would not know any Jews personally, and would be only vaguely aware of the horrors that had befallen them: bitter testimony to the way in which the dead, precisely because they are dead, have no say over how their murderers explain or ignore their absence.

At first, the defeat of Nazism in May 1945 seemed to spell the end of Germany's national sovereignty, its territory occupied by France, Britain, and the United States in the West, and the Soviet Union in the East.

In this Soviet Zone, which would eventually become the German Democratic Republic (GDR), the Socialist Unity Party (SED) held power. The Soviet Union and other Eastern Bloc countries had borne the brunt of Germany's war, and so for many years rehabilitation took second place to reparations in the GDR. Throughout its existence, East Germany bore many of the hallmarks of "real existing socialism": compared to the capitalist West, there was less abject poverty and less involvement in the pillage of the Third World; at the same time, there was next to no room for political dissent or protest. Even communists suspected of differing from the dominant party line could find themselves arrested and tortured by the *Stasi*, the secret police. Society and culture were not frozen, yet they were certainly chilled, creating a distinctly "socialist" kind of conservatism.

Yet more than a few lifelong Communists felt that this was an unfortunate but acceptable price to pay to fetter the German aggression that had defined the first half of the century. As Markus Wolf, head of the dreaded *Stasi* during the period covered by this book, would explain in his post-wall apologia:

> *We East German Socialists tried to create a new kind of society that would never repeat the German crimes of the past. Most of all, we were determined that war should never again originate on German soil.*[1]

In the Western Zone too, initially the United States had toyed with the idea of deindustrializing the country, so as to cripple its development and preclude any future German wars. Very soon, however, this approach was rejected, the American Joint Chiefs of Staff Directive of June 1947 finding that, "An orderly, prosperous Europe requires the economic contributions of a stable and productive Germany."

It didn't hurt that corporations such as Ford, General Motors, Chase Manhattan Bank, IBM, and Standard Oil had had huge prewar investments in Germany and were all lobbying for a rapid resumption of business-as-usual.[2]

---

1 Markus Wolf and Anne McElvoy, *Man without a Face: The Autobiography of Communism's Greatest Spymaster* (New York: Times Books, 1999), xi.
2 Charles Higham, *Trading with the Enemy: An Exposé of the Nazi-American*

The geopolitical goals of the United States, always foremost amongst the Western occupiers, combined with the interests of the German middle and upper classes, effectively sabotaging any real efforts at denazification in the West. In no time at all, important sections of the establishment that had helped maintain the Third Reich were being welcomed into the new pro-American administration. As the late William D. Graf observed:

> Almost all the representatives of big business labeled as war criminals by the American Kilgore Commission in 1945 were back in their former positions by 1948; and of roughly 53,000 civil servants dismissed on account of their Nazi pasts in 1945, only about 1,000 remained permanently excluded, while the judiciary was almost 100% restored as early as 1946.[3]

The result, much as desired, was a political system which remained significantly tilted to the right.

This period marked the beginning of the American "Cold War" against the Soviet bloc, in which Germany was to become an important chip. In keeping with the Truman Doctrine, the zone occupied by the Western Allies was built up as an anticommunist bulwark. The vehicle for this project was the European Relief Program, a blueprint for the economic and military reconstruction of Western Europe, which U.S. Secretary of State George C. Marshall convinced the U.S. Congress to pass in 1948. Almost one-and-a-half billion dollars were pumped into West Germany through the Marshall Plan, its economy rebuilt in such a way as to guarantee the expansion of U.S. economic influence in Europe, to serve as the foundation for the military and political integration of West Europe into the anticommunist bloc, and to facilitate the cultural and technological Americanization of European societies, especially West Germany itself.[4]

In short, demolished by war and in social and economic chaos, West Germany was offered reconstruction, rapid economic growth, and integration into the Allied Bloc in exchange for offering its support to

---

Money Plot, 1933-1949 (New York: Delacorte Press, 1983).

3 William D. Graf, "Anti-Communism in the Federal Republic of Germany," *Socialist Register* (1984): 167.

4 Women Against Imperialist War (Hamburg), "War on Imperialist War," in Prairie Fire Organizing Committee, *War on the War Makers: Documents and Communiqués from the West German Left* (San Francisco: John Brown Book Club n.d.), 21.

international capitalism and the use of its territory as a front line position in the Cold War with the USSR. This was an appeal aimed not only at the ruling class, but also at "ordinary" Germans, who may have benefited from the Third Reich's policies of plunder and genocide, but who now, in defeat, found themselves thrown into economic insecurity.[1] An early propaganda document from the Western occupation government, issued just weeks after a pro-Soviet coup in neighboring Czechoslovakia, explained what was at stake:

> The fate of the Marshall Plan will determine who is to be the victor in the great ideological conflict of democracy versus totalitarianism. Unless the Germans can get enough to eat and decent homes to live in, no amount of fine words about the benefit of democracy and no amount of repression will prevent them from going over to Communism.[2]

Former Nazis, provided they were not personally too notorious or unwilling to play by the new rules, appeared to the Americans as far preferable to communists or their presumed fellow travelers. Indeed, it has been noted that for much of the West German establishment, "anti-communism provided a point of common cause with the Western victors and hence... a means of avoiding being called to account for their complicity" with the Hitler regime.[3]

By the time the Federal Republic of Germany (FRG) was granted semi-sovereign statehood in 1949, this set of common interests had become embodied in the Christian Democratic Union (CDU), under the iron fist of Chancellor Konrad Adenauer. Ruling for almost twenty years, normally in coalition with the much smaller liberal Free Democratic Party (FDP) and the slightly more rabid Christian Social Union (CSU) in Bavaria, the CDU soon became almost synonymous with the state itself.

---

1 There has been much written over the past thirty years about the ways in which the non-Jewish German working class benefited from the Third Reich's policies, enjoying the position of a labor aristocracy. The most noteworthy book on this subject is Götz Aly's *Hitler's Beneficiaries: Plunder, Racial War, and the Nazi Welfare State*; translated by Jefferson Chase, 1st U.S. ed. (New York: Metropolitan, 2007).

2 "How to Fight Communism," March 25, 1948, OMGUS in Patrick Major, *The Death of the KPD: Communism and Anti-Communism in West Germany, 1945-1956* (Oxford: Clarendon Press, 1997), 247.

3 Graf, "Anti-Communism," 169.

West Germany was to be more than just a shield against the "encroaching red menace"; it was to be Western imperialism's visible model of economically and socially "progressive" capitalism, serving as an example to other West European states and as a taunt to the working class on the other side of the "wall."

As an anticommunist showpiece, the FRG soon payed for itself in a time honored capitalist fashion—on the backs of the proletariat, especially the most desperate and oppressed layers.

Heightened levels of exploitation combined with the financial assistance offered by the Marshall Plan made the FRG the envy of other Western capitalist states. By every measure of the ruling class, the West German economy shone. Real wages in the period 1948-1958 were at the level already established by the fascist regime,[4] roughly 25% below that of workers in the United States,[5] while the working week in 1955 could go as high as fifty hours, longer in key sectors like the steel industry. In that year, West German industrial workers had a work-week two-and-a-half hours longer than their counterparts in Britain and eight hours longer than industrial workers in the United States and Canada.[6]

The profits made possible by this arrangement encouraged an extremely high rate of investment, which grew from 19.1% in 1950 to 26.5% in 1965; even with the recessions of the seventies, it wasn't until 1976 that it had fallen back to 20%. In 1960, when France was showing a rate of investment of 17.4% and both Britain and the U.S. only registered 16%, West Germany was already showing an investment rate of 24%.[7]

As Werner Hülsberg notes:

> The 'economic miracle' merely indicated the existence of ideal conditions for the exploitation of wage labor and, as such, is somewhat of a cynical myth. The long-term upswing in the economy, however, did lead to a continuous rise in the living standards of the West German population. While net wages and

---

4 Werner Hülsberg, *The German Greens: A Social and Political Profile*. Translated by Gus Fagan. (London: Verso, 1988), 22.

5 Karl Heinz Roth, *L'autre movement ouvrier en Allemagne 1945-78*. Translated by Serge Cosseron. (Paris: Christian Bourgois Editeur, 1979), 50.

6 Hülsberg, 22-3.

7 Ibid., 23.

*salaries during the period 1950 to 1962 grew by 143 per cent,
the income of independent entrepreneurs during the same period
grew by 236 per cent.[1]*

This boom was also based on real divisions in the working class, with German men in their prime being lifted into higher status and better paying jobs than the "pariah layers" which included young and older German men, but were fundamentally built around immigrant and female labor.

In the immediate aftermath of German defeat, working-class women had borne the brunt of reconstruction unpaid and off the books, but absolutely necessary for survival, to the point that the term *Trümmerfrauen* ("women of the rubble") was coined for those who hauled away the debris of bombed out buildings with their bare hands. At the same time, in October 1945, the Allied Control Council had declared it a duty of all women between the ages of fifteen and fifty to also work in the official economy: the female labor force, which had already earned only 86 cents to the male dollar under the Nazis, now saw its relative wages dropping, until in the 1950s and 60s women's wages were on average just 60% of those of their menfolk.[2]

Throughout the 1950s, seven million refugees and displaced persons, many of whom were highly skilled, streamed into the country from the East. The German industries which had been structured around the use of forced labor during the Nazi period soon found they could fill this same niche with immigrant labor.

As New Left historian Karl Heinz Roth has remarked, from the point of view of big business, "this exceptionally mobile subproletariat compensated completely for the loss of the slaves condemned to forced labor in the Nazi era."[3] Yet, with a crucial difference: unlike the slave labourers, who were literally worked to death under Nazism, these new immigrants were to be highly favored. They were overwhelmingly loyal and politically reliable in the eyes of the ruling class, seeing as they came from the "Communist East" where more than a few of them had lost real privileges as ethnic Germans when the Nazi occupation came to an end. Indeed, these expellees and refugees from the East, exploited as they were, were naturally drawn towards the most virulent

---

1 Ibid., 24.
2 Ibid., 22.
3 Roth, 47.

anticommunism, and catalyzed shopfloor and grassroots resistance to the left within the working class.[4]

Following this initial wave of cheap labor, which was regimented by its own political sympathies, came guest workers, many of whom were politically active on the left, and who were thus subjected to greater external regimentation and control. As the source of this labor switched from the East to Southern Europe, these workers would be politically screened before entry, and targeted with deportation if identified as "troublemakers."

So, at the same time as the German working class was highly exploited, it was also deeply divided. An inevitable consequence of this was that its more privileged layers would develop a different political orientation from the more oppressed.

To quote Hülsberg once again:

> It is against this background that we must see the tragedy of the integration of the West German working class into the capitalist system and the loss of political strength. Class struggle was replaced by the "American way of life". Even the king of rock'n'roll, Elvis Presley, paid tribute to it while on his tour of military duty in Germany... For the German petit-bourgeois soul this was the purest balm.[5]

Greek workers in a West German bottling factory: by the end of the 1960s, women constituted almost a third of all "guest workers" in West Germany.

---

4 Major, 174, 192.

5 Hülsberg, 25.

These hierarchies within the working class resonated within its supposed institutions, the trade union movement and the Social Democratic Party (SPD).

In the first years of the Federal Republic, the trade unions were reorganized by the Allied victors with the express goal of avoiding the "economic chaos" the bourgeoisie feared most. These unions focused on *Mitbestimmung* (co-management, whereby workers would have some token representation in corporate boards of directors), thus further guaranteeing that the official labor movement would remain hostile to revolutionary politics. This degeneracy reached such a point in the 1960s that union members formed the backbone of the "factory militias" whose job it was repress wildcat strikes and unruly workers,[1] and one foreign journalist began an article on the German labor market with the question, "What is a country to do when its trades unions decline to ask for more money?"[2]

As a complement to this sad political trajectory, the SPD "led the less class-conscious workers and the petit bourgeoisie into the arms of the reactionaries," with a program that "in the immediate postwar period consisted of a crude mixture of nationalism and anti-communism garnished with a meaningless proclamation of the actuality of socialism."[3] Left-wing trade unionists were expelled from the party, as were the editors of the socialist newspaper *Die Andere Zeitung*,[4] while the SPD leadership used its position as the official opposition to repeatedly mislead and sabotage any grassroots revolt.

Needless to say, neither the SPD nor the trade union leadership had any interest in bridging the divide between their (increasingly privileged) base and the growing "pariah layers" of the proletariat:

> As a consensus-producing mechanism that united the most powerful interests in the corporate and labour organizations, Social Democratic corporatism consciously excluded the weaker elements: foreigners, women, youth and older workers, thus converting class struggles to group struggles and doing nothing to reduce racism, sexism and anti-welfarism within the subordinate classes.[5]

---

1 Roth, 121.

2 David Haworth, "Why German Workers Don't Ask For Raises," *Winnipeg Free Press,* December 11, 1968.

3 Hülsberg, 25.

4 Graf, "Anti-communism," 183.

5 William Graf, "Beyond Social Democracy in West Germany?" *Socialist Register*

Of course, the Marshall Plan was not simply a local economic project: from the very beginning it was intended that West Germany also be a European outpost of U.S. imperialism. This is indicated not only in the virtually simultaneous foundation of both NATO and the FRG in 1949, but in the very nature of the Federal Republic as a state: when it was granted formal sovereignty in 1955, it was only on condition that it allow the Western powers to station their armed forces within its borders, and within four days of achieving its new condition, it had joined the Atlantic Alliance.[6] Perhaps most significantly, in the event of a military conflict, the commanding officer in NATO—always an American—would also become the Commander-in-Chief of the West German armed forces.

As Rudolph Augstein, the editor of the influential liberal magazine *Spiegel*, stated in 1955: "The new German army has not been founded to guarantee the safety of Bonn; rather the new state has been founded to be able to build up an army against the Soviet Union."[7]

The result was a West Germany with more than one hundred U.S. bases on its territory and a ruling class eager to support American imperialism around the world. This was achieved by (1) acting as a conduit for financial and military support to anticommunist regimes opposing the national liberation movements, (2) establishing neocolonial penetration of former colonies on behalf of the West, and (3) providing logistical support for American military interventions around the world.

Some important examples of this first role—that of being a conduit to repressive regimes—could include West Germany's support for the South African apartheid regime, for the fascist Salazar dictatorship in Portugal in its continuing war against freedom fighters in Mozambique and Angola, military and political support for the killers of Patrice Lumumba and for imperialist intervention in the Congo, massive financial aid (disguised as reparations) to the state of Israel, imperialism's new colonial beachhead in the Middle East, and economic support for the South Vietnamese puppet regime.

Apart from loans, economic investment, military sales, and eventually the sharing of nuclear technology, these reactionary regimes would

---

(1985/86): 118.

6 "Die Integration der Bundesrepublik ins westliche Bündnissystem," http://www.kssursee.ch/schuelerweb/kalter-krieg/kk/integration.htm.

7 Women Against Imperialist War, 22.

also benefit from the occasional intervention of German soldiers[1] and mercenaries, including veterans of the Nazi SS.[2]

The task of entangling the former colonies in the Western sphere was accomplished primarily through "development aid," much of which took the form of weapons shipments to the new so-called "national states." While such aid was often used to pressure the new national states to join pro-American military alliances, or else to refuse recognition to the GDR, it was equally important simply as a method of maintaining and entrenching the ties between Western capitalism and Third World elites.

By the late 1950s, the FRG had established itself as an important "donor" nation, for a while providing more "aid" than any Western government other than the United States.[3] It was a logical candidate for this role given the fact that it had lost its own colonies decades earlier; as the *Stuttgarter Zeitung* noted in 1963:

> *It is clear why African states turn to Bonn and not to Paris or London… They turn to a country which is not tainted by colonialism.*

Or, as the American *Evening Star* wrote that same year:

> *West Germany has been specifically authorized by the Atlantic Alliance to grant military aid to Africa and other countries; the simple reason is that no other western country is as well suited for these tasks. West Germany is free from the blemish of colonial rule…[4]*

The prime examples of the FRG's third role—providing direct support for American military forces—were the many U.S. military bases scattered throughout the country. These served both as a threat to the East Bloc countries, as well as staging areas for special operations. As

---

1 Regarding all these, see *The Neo-colonialism of the West German Federal Republic* (German Democratic Republic: Afro-Asian Solidarity Committee, 1965), 20-35, 39-45, 62-65, 82-85.

2 Madeleine G. Kalb, *The Congo Cables: The Cold War in Africa from Eisenhower to Kennedy* (New York: Macmillan, 1982), 193.

3 Frieder Sclupp, "Modell Deutschland and the International Division of Labour: The Federal Republic of Germany in the World Political Economy," in *The Foreign Policy of West Germany: Formation and Contents*, ed. Ekkert Kruippendorf and Volker Rittberger (London: SAGE Publications, 1980).

4 Quoted in *The Neo-colonialism of the West German Federal Republic*, 96-7.

military strikes against Third World targets became increasingly important to Western imperialism, the Federal Republic's airbases were all the more appreciated.

All U.S. bases had extra-territorial status and functioned under American law. They were, of course, also sites for CIA interventions in the FRG and in Western Europe in general, not only against Soviet influence, but also against independent left opposition. According to Operation Plan 101-1, the U.S. Commander-in-Chief in Europe was legally entitled to intervene in cases of internal unrest in West Germany. Furthermore, in cooperation with both former Nazis and a new generation of neo-nazis, the CIA established "stay behind" networks which were to carry out terrorist attacks should communists ever come to power in Germany.[5]

BETTER DEAD THAN RED

While both the economic and military aspects of the Federal Republic were, to a greater or lesser degree, formulated in the public forum, and in some cases faced public opposition, the model had another equally important aspect, one which was never up for debate, and yet it bears directly on the topic under discussion here: anticommunism, described as the third pillar of West German society.[6]

"All Marxist Roads Lead to Moscow": election poster for the CDU, 1953.

As we shall see, this anticommunism was far more than a mere ideological construct; rather, the legal structure of West German "constitutional democracy" was from its earliest days intended to prevent and/or eliminate all revolutionary left-wing opposition. This found its legal basis in the way that

---

5 Daniel Ganser, *NATO's Secret Army: Operation Gladio and Terrorism in Western Europe* (London: Frank Cass, 2005), 190-211.
6 Hülsberg, 15.

personal rights were framed in the Federal Republic's Constitution, the *Grundgesetz* (Basic Law), which came into effect in 1949. While the Basic Law established the same personal rights and freedoms normally found in bourgeois democracies, it did this with one recurrent caveat: these rights could be withdrawn from those designated as enemies of the state.

This qualification was stated unambiguously in Article 18:

> *Whoever abuses the freedom of expression, in particular the freedom of the press (paragraph (1) of Article 5), the freedom of teaching (paragraph (3) of Article 5), the freedom of assembly (Article 8), the freedom of association (Article 9), the privacy of correspondence, posts and telecommunications (Article 10), the rights of property (Article 14), or the right of asylum (Article 16a) in order to combat the free democratic basic order shall forfeit these basic rights. This forfeiture and its extent shall be declared by the Federal Constitutional Court.*[1]

The following restriction to Article 21, limiting the right to form political parties, was added to this already ominous provision:

> *Parties that, by reason of their aims or the behavior of their adherents, seek to undermine or abolish the free democratic basic order or to endanger the existence of the Federal Republic of Germany shall be unconstitutional. The Federal Constitutional Court shall rule on the question of unconstitutionality.*[2]

These passages were marked by the experience of political instability that had traumatized the Weimar Republic. Their design owed very much to the desire to prevent any future such upheaval. Constraints on political freedoms were further rationalized by some observers as necessary to prevent a resurgence of Nazism, a credulous argument which would soon be disproved by the fact that the chief target of these exclusions would be the left.

In 1951, the CDU moved to further tighten the legal framework of repression with a volley of state security legislation, defined in the following five sections: High Treason, Dangers to the State, Offenses against Constitutional Organs, Resistance to the Authority of the State, and

---

1 German Bundestag, Administration, Public Relations section, *Law for the Federal Republic of Germany* (Berlin, 2001), 22.
2 Ibid., 23.

Offenses against Public Order.[3] Minister of Justice Thomas Dehler explained that these laws would be used to combat "ideological high treason," "ideological subversion," and "ideological sabotage."[4] In short, thought crime.

The immediate target of all these statutes and constitutional restrictions became clear with due haste. On November 23, 1951, the federal government applied to the Constitutional Court to have the Communist Party of Germany (KPD) proscribed, on the basis of the aforementioned Article 21 of the Basic Law. This was at a time when the party held fifteen seats in the *Bundestag*.

The Communists had opposed integration into NATO and as late as 1952 paid lip service to the revolutionary overthrow of the Adenauer regime. While it clearly didn't have mass political support—it had garnered only 2.2% of the vote in the 1952 elections[5]—the KPD nevertheless constituted a potential nuisance as the only political institution to speak up for a number of popular interests which were poorly represented by the major parties:

> *Its continued advocacy of an anti-fascist, socialist front, its opposition to rearmament and atomic weapons, its resistance to authoritarian trends such as restrictions on free speech and emergency laws, and its demands for a greater measure of economic democracy were aims shared by members of a great range of groups, including neglected interests within the established parties. It was evident... that to discredit or even criminalize the KPD would also be to reduce the appeal of all groups that shared any of its aims.[6]*

The trial of the KPD began on November 11, 1954. Sensing the direction things were going in, the party distanced itself from revolutionary politics in public statements in early 1956. It was already too late: on August 17 of that year, the KPD was declared illegal. Hundreds of arrests followed; not only party members, but also their families, members of alleged front groups, and anyone suspected of communist sympathies, were targeted, and a comprehensive apparatus developed

---

3 Sebastien Cobler, *Law, Order and Politics in West Germany* (Harmondsworth, Eng.: Penguin Books, 1978), 76.

4 Ibid., 74.

5 Wolfgang Abendroth, Helmut Ridder and Otto Schonfeldt, eds., *KPD Verbot oder mit Kommunisten leben* (Hamburg: Rororo Taschenbuch Verlag, 1968), 38.

6 Graf, "Anti-communism," 179.

to undertake surveillance of all these individuals and organizations.[1]

The suppression of the KPD was just the most obvious volley in a broader process of constitutional repression. On August 2, 1954, the Supreme Court ruled that the organization and promotion of demonstrations, meetings, and strikes could also constitute treason. A few months later, the Federal Supreme Court ruled that, "No action in a strike which goes beyond the cessation of work and violates interests protected by the law is justified by the so-called strike law."[2] In 1955, the essential nature of the Basic Law was further confirmed by a general ban on all political strikes.[3]

At the same time, ample use was made of Dreher's new security measures. By the 1960s, thousands of cases of treason were being brought before the courts:

> ...in 1963 10,322 actions were started against people alleged to have committed treasonable offenses of one kind or another. In many cases these actions were against more than one person. In 1961 a total of 442 people were sentenced for various categories of "treason". Admittedly, of these 36 were only fined and 212 only got between 9 months and 5 years and 5 were sentenced to between 5 and 15 years. Many others had their careers ruined by court actions in which the State failed to prove its case.[4]

With its culture sterilized and its traditions of worker militancy broken, the postfascist, post-genocidal society provided an ideal foundation for a new authoritarian and technocratic capitalist state.

---

1 Ibid., 180.

2 Cobler, 183-184.

3 Ibid., 80.

4 David Childs, *From Schumacher to Brandt: The Story of German Socialism 1945-1965* (New York: Pergamon Press, 1966), 49.

Not Wanted In The Model: The KPD

Immediately after the war, the KPD benefited from an unambiguous anti-Nazi track record, but this strong position quickly crumbled due to a variety of factors. Patrick Major of Warwick University has provided a valuable overview of this decline in his book *The Death of the kpd: Communism and Anti-Communism in West Germany, 1945-1956*.

According to Major, the postwar Party leadership found itself frequently at odds with its more radical rank and file. It was ill placed to connect with its supposed constituency—the proletariat—as many working-class grievances took aim at the occupying powers, one of which was the Soviet Union. Indeed, as Major notes, "the earliest proponents of strikes tended to be Social Democrats, whereas, like their French comrades, the German Communists placed national reconstruction before wage increases or even denazification of management."[1]

The Party was further handicapped by its ties to East Germany's ruling Socialist Unity Party (SED). The SED encouraged the KPD's conservative tendencies, insisting that it prioritize forging a progressive nationalist opposition to the Western occupiers, relegating class struggle to the back burner. Not only was it still hoped that the "Western Zone" could be pried out of the hands of imperialism, but it was also recognized that the KPD's chief competition—the SPD—was winning support with its own "nationalistic rabble rousing."[2]

During this patriotic phase, anticapitalist rhetoric was toned down; in some *Länder,* Party members were instructed to stop singing the *Internationale* in public, and the hammer and sickle and Soviet star emblems were removed from their paraphernalia.[3] To the disgust of many comrades who had barely survived the Third Reich, the KPD even briefly attempted to establish a broad "anticolonialist" National Front, appealing to

---

1 Patrick Major, *The Death of the KPD: Communism and Anti-Communism in West Germany, 1945-1956* (Oxford: Clarendon Press, 1997), 170.

2 Ibid., 115.

3 Ibid., 116.

middle-class elements, patriotic capitalists, and even former Nazi supporters.[1]

Although the KPD was banned in 1956, this dubious "anticolonialism" represented real class forces, and a significant section of progressive opinion. While these gestures failed to win the Communists any significant nationalist support, the politics they represented remained visible in the future campaigns against rearmament and nuclear weapons. Though overwhelmingly left-wing, these campaigns were still able to attract (and accept) support from conservatives and even fascists who opposed integration within the Western bloc as "unpatriotic."

The connection to East Germany's SED became an ever-greater liability as the Cold War descended: while Western communists opposed rearmament in the FRG, they had to make excuses for it in the GDR; while they decried exploitative work conditions in the West, they had to defend piece work policies in the East; while they complained of "colonization" of the FRG by the Americans, they had to remain pointedly silent about "integration" of the GDR into the Soviet Bloc.

Thus, even as the Party played an important role in articulating opposition to the authoritarian Adenauer regime, it faced an uphill battle, not only because of right-wing repression, but also due to the contradictory demands of struggling in the Western Zone while its counterpart ruled in the East.

These political weaknesses, combined with the deep changes to Germany's class structure that occurred during the Hitler period, prevented the KPD from ever mounting a serious challenge to the new FRG. So much so that according to Major, "In some ways the KPD leadership was 'saved by the bell', banned before an internal party discussion could look for scapegoats for the disastrous policies of the past decade."[2]

---

1 Ibid., 133.
2 Ibid., 226.

The Re-Emergence of Revolutionary Politics in West Germany

IN THE YEARS BEFORE THE Hitler regime, Germany was home to one of the strongest and most militant left-wing movements in Europe, firmly based in the country's large and well organized working class. The years after World War I saw insurrections in Bavaria and the Ruhr region, and had it not been for errors and betrayals on the left, many still believe that communist revolution in Germany could have succeeded in giving birth to a radically different twentieth century.

That, of course, is not what happened, and as events unfolded the left that had impressed generations of European socialists was decimated by the rise of German fascism, forced into exile, reduced to inactivity, or sent off to the camps.

When the organized institutions of the left reappeared in the postwar period, they were incapable of overcoming their own historical weaknesses, weaknesses that were actively reinforced by the Allies' corrupt and repressive policies. Those few independent antifascist groups which had formed in the last days of the war quickly found themselves banned, unwelcome intruders on the victors' plans, this Allied suppression of any autonomous workers' or antifascist revolt constituting the flipside to the charade of denazification.

The eclipse of any authentic left-wing opposition continued in the years following the division of Germany. The Christian Democratic Union, the concrete expression of the alliance between the German ruling class and American imperialism, experienced little in the way of opposition as it helped implement the Marshall Plan and establish the legal machinery with which to fight any resurgence of left-wing militancy.

Yet, while the political aspects of the Marshall Plan were carried out with little difficulty, the rearming of West Germany, not surprisingly when one considers the outcome of both World Wars, met with intense opposition.

In the immediate postwar period, West Germans were overwhelmingly opposed to rearmament. By 1952, this sentiment had coalesced into a broad movement, including the not-yet-banned KPD, trade unions, socialist youth groups, Protestant church groups,[1] pacifists, and, at times, sections of the SPD. This progressive alliance was flanked on its right by small numbers of nationalists and even fascists who objected to the way in which rearmament would anchor the country in the Western bloc.[2] Despite this, the "Without Us Movement" (as it was known) was a predominantly left-wing amalgam. It was the first large protest movement in the new Federal Republic,[3] and while it may appear timid and ineffectual in retrospect, it represented a real break in the postwar consensus at the time.

The response from the Adenauer regime revealed the limits of CDU democracy: in 1951, a KPD referendum initiative on the question was

---

1 Paul Hockenos has noted that for some Protestants, their religion may have made them particularly receptive to the first postwar protest movements, due to feelings of marginalization within the new truncated state: whereas Protestants had outnumbered Catholics by nearly two to one in prewar Germany, there was rough parity between the two religions in the FRG. See Paul Hockenos, *Joschka Fischer and the Making of the Berlin Republic: an Alternative History of Postwar Germany* (Oxford: Oxford University Press, 2008), 22. Despite this fact, the churches remained overwhelmingly anticommunist and hostile to left-wing politics.

2 As one deputy from the neo-nazi Socialist Reich Party put it, "First we were told that guns and ammunition were poison and now this poison has turned to sweets which we should eat. But we are not Negroes or idiots to whom they can do whatever they want. It is either they or us who should be admitted to the insane asylum." [Martin Lee, *The Beast Reawakens* (Boston: Little, Brown and Company, 1997), 65.]

3 For the sake of clarity, it should be remembered that in the years between the Nazi defeat and the establishment of the FRG, there was a large strike movement in favour of nationalization of the country's largest industries. This movement, which initially seemed to have the wind in its sails, was opposed by the Allied occupiers. Its fate was sealed when the new trade unions obediently redirected it towards token co-management and de-cartelization. As such, it provides a stark example of workers' political activity sabotaged by their putative left-wing representatives even before the occupation had ended. (Roth, 50-51; Hülsberg, 29-32; Childs, 67-84.)

banned, as according to the Basic Law only the federal government was empowered to call a plebiscite. The Communists decided to go ahead anyway, polling people on street corners, through newspaper questionnaires, and at popular meeting places. The "referendum" was more agit prop than a scientific study; at one movie cinema in the town of Celle, for instance, there is a report that just as the feature film ended an eager pollster asked everyone opposed to rearmament to stand up—100% opposition was recorded. Little surprise that the KPD eventually found that almost six million West Germans had "registered" their opposition to the government's plans.[4]

Suffice it to say that Adenauer was not amused, and polling people soon became a risky endeavor: there were a total of 7,331 arrests, and the KPD Free German Youth front group was banned simply for engaging in what amounted to a glorified petition campaign.[5]

At the same time, as if to make matters crystal clear, on May 11, 1952, a peace rally in the city of Essen was attacked by police, at first with dogs and clubs, and then with live ammunition. Philipp Müller, a member of Free German Youth, became the first person to be killed in a demonstration in the new Federal Republic. As a sign of things to come, no police officer would ever face charges for Müller's death, but eleven demonstrators were subsequently jailed for a total of six years and four months for disorderly conduct and "crimes of treason against the Constitution."[6]

*Philipp Müller,
April 5, 1931–
May 11, 1952*

Not that repression was the only tool against incipient revolt: misdirection also remained an important weapon in the ruling-class arsenal. Throughout 1953, there were almost one hundred strikes at different factories to protest against the CDU's rearmament policies. As the politicized sections of the working class were moving aggressively against Adenauer's plans, the SPD and trade union leadership lined up to rein things in. All energy was now funneled into one big rally in Frankfurt. However, the initiative was removed from the rank and file, and in the

---

4 Major, 145.

5 Ibid., Hülsberg, 33.

6 Bernd Langer, *Art as Resistance*. Translated by Anti-Fascist Forum. (Göttingen: Aktiv-Dr. und Verl., 1998), 8.

end the rally was simply used to drum up support for the SPD.[1] As the CDU moved ahead regardless, the Social Democrats withdrew organizational support, and the movement (now robbed of any autonomous basis) dissipated almost immediately.[2]

With its most steadfast opponents kept in disarray by their "leaders," the Adenauer regime easily ratified rearmament through the Treaty of Paris in 1954. The next few years saw the establishment of voluntary military service, universal male conscription, and the production of war materials, further sealing the ties between big business and the state. Demoralized by their failure to prevent any of this, the opposition began to melt, a 1955 poll finding that almost two thirds of the population now considered remilitarization to be a "political necessity."[3]

For the CDU, rearmament, like the Basic Law, was simply part of the Federal Republic acquiring the powers of a "normal" state, part of West Germany's integration into the imperialist bloc. While there were numerous such state powers bestowed during this period, one which will bear some relevance to our study is the 1951 establishment of the *Bundesgrenzschutz*, the Federal Border Guard, also known as the BGS. Under the jurisdiction of the Federal Ministry of the Interior, the BGS was initially a paramilitary force of 10,000, its activity restricted "to the border area to a depth of thirty kilometres."[4]

In 1951, most leftists had feared that the BGS was a roundabout way to establish a standing army. As we have seen, such a ploy did not prove necessary (although many border guards would be integrated into the new armed forces). Rather, the Border Guard would eventually serve as the basis for a national semi-militarized police force.

Despite these discouraging beginnings, antimilitary sentiment remained high, and when, in 1956, the Adenauer government responded favorably to a U.S. "offer" of tactical nuclear weapons, this set off a series of spontaneous mobilizations across the country. In 1957, members of West Germany's second largest union, the Public Service, Transport, and Communication Union (ÖTV) voted 94.9% in favor of a strike against nuclear armament, a call which was echoed by the president of the powerful IG Metall trade union. In Hannover, 40,000 people

---

1 Hülsberg, 34.

2 Hockenos, 42-3.

3 Nick Thomas, *Protest Movements in 1960s West Germany: A Social History of Dissent and Democracy* (New York: Berg, 2003), 33.

4 Cobler, 134.

demonstrated against nuclear arms, while in Munich there was a turn-out of 80,000, and in Hamburg 120,000 people took to the streets.[5] Opinion polls showed 52% of the population supporting an antinuclear general strike.

The SPD and trade union brass moved to quash this mass move-ment, which was spinning out of control, by redirecting the campaign away from the streets and factories and into the ballot boxes, proposing a referendum instead of a general strike. Predictably, the government challenged this referendum proposal before the Constitutional Court, where it was ruled unconstitutional in 1958.

The ploy worked, the momentum was broken, and the antinuclear weapons movement entered a period of sharp decline. For years to come, its only visible legacy would be the annual peace demonstrations held every Easter Weekend, the so-called Easter Marches.

Of great relevance to the future history of the West German left, and our story in particular, an important counterpoint to the disreputable machinations of the SPD emerged from its own youth wing: the Socialist German Student Union (SDS).

The SDS had been founded in 1946 as a training ground from which to groom the future party elite (Helmut Schmidt, West Germany's future Chancellor, was the group's first president). In the context of the anti-rearmament movement, though, a shift began to occur, and at its 1958 conference, the leadership of the SDS was won by elements significantly to the left of the SPD:

> Their main interest was in the development of socialist policies and, in particular, they wanted to build the campaign against nuclear weapons, a campaign which the SPD had already deserted. The resolutions of the SDS conference were a "declaration of war" on the SPD leadership. The SDS first of all developed an anti-imperialist position and demanded the right of national self-determination for the Algerians and the withdrawal of French colonial troops. After this there were congresses against nuclear weapons, for democracy and in opposition to militarism. The SPD strongly condemned this development.[6]

In May of 1960, to counter this leftwards drift, students loyal to the SPD leadership formed the Social Democratic Student Union (SHB).

---

5 Thomas, 35.
6 Hülsberg, 38.

This move by the right was answered in October 1961 by SPD left wingers forming the Society for the Promotion of Socialism (SF). Unable to neutralize this growing left-wing revolt, the SPD leadership decided to do what it could to isolate it, purging the SF and SDS in a move which completed the alienation of the critical intelligentsia and youth from the party for years to come. (Ironically, the SHB itself continued to be pulled to the left, forced to tail positions staked out by the SDS, until it too would find itself expelled in the 1970s.)[1]

Things were brewing beneath the surface, and a new generation was finding itself increasingly miserable within this suffocating and conservative Cold War West Germany. American expatriate Paul Hockenos

---

1 Graf, "Beyond Social Democracy," 104-5.

The Old Left and the New Reality

Under the postwar occupation regime, various intellectuals who had been exiled under Nazism returned home, while others who had remained silent found their voices.

While this was a broader phenomenon, two groups in particular stand out: the Frankfurt School and the *Gruppe 47*.

The Frankfurt School had emerged from the Institute for Social Research, founded at the University of Frankfurt in 1924 under the tutelage of one of its prominent members, Max Horkheimer. Critical of the narrow intellectual nature of traditional Marxism, members integrated new ideas from the fields of sociology, philosophy, and psychiatry to produce a highly influential and intellectually rigorous theoretical platform, eventually known as "Critical Theory." Key members, almost all of them men, many of them Jewish, included Horkheimer, Herbert Marcuse, Erich Fromm, Theodor Adorno, and Jürgen Habermas. Going into exile in 1933, the Frankfurt School was based out of Columbia University in New York City until 1943. While Horkheimer and Adorno chose to return to Germany after the war, many others remained in the United States.

The *Gruppe 47* was a literary circle founded in 1947 to help give expression to a new generation of German writers who had lived

describes the fifties cultural climate that surrounded these young people:

> *Corporal punishment in schools… was still routine, and at universities students could be expelled for interrupting a lecture. The Federal Republic still had "coupling laws" on the books that forbade single men and women under twenty-one to spend the night together—or even to spend time together unchaperoned. Parents who allowed their children to stray could face legal penalties. In contrast to the GDR's school curricula, in which the churches had no say, in the West German schools there weren't sexual-education programs until the 1960s.[2]*

---

2 Hockenos, 31.

---

through the war, and who hoped to use their craft as a way to reckon with the Nazi experience. Key members included Heinrich Böll, Günter Grass, Alexander Kluge, Ilse Aichinger, and Erich Fried. There were few Jews or women involved, and amongst the Germans, some were later revealed to have previously been active Nazis. Yet, despite these shortcomings, the *Gruppe 47* established itself as an important progressive influence on postwar German culture.

While they may have all initially sympathized with the sixties revolt, many of these intellectuals soon felt alienated by the younger generation's goals and methods of direct action and violent protest.

Ironically, while the Frankfurt School influenced many of the sixties revolutionaries, it also provided the strongest negative reaction, with Jürgen Habermas going so far as to accuse student radicals of flirting with "left-wing fascism." Though an inability to agree about the meaning of the student revolt led to the precipitous decline of the *Gruppe 47*, some of its members remained vocal critics of the political establishment. Heinrich Böll and Erich Fried in particular continued to denounce the state's penchant for authoritarian solutions, even in regards to its war against the guerilla.

In the words of Detlev Claussen, who would later participate in his generation's revolt, "They try to make it look better than it was but it really was that bad! It was a terrible, terrible time to grow up."[1]

Another indication of what life was like in the post-genocidal society came in the winter of 1959-60, as a wave of antisemitic graffiti and attacks on Jewish cemeteries swept over the country. This prompted some Frankfurt School sociologists to carry out a study which revealed that behind an apathetic 41% who remained indifferent, a hardcore 16% of the population was openly antisemitic, supportive of the death penalty (banned under the Basic Law), and expressing "an excessive inclination for authority."[2]

One of the projects most responsible for challenging this reactionary and stultifying culture was the magazine *konkret*, published in Hamburg by Klaus Rainer Röhl. An increasingly important forum for progressive youth who rejected the CDU consensus and the country's conservative cultural mores, the magazine was widely read within the SDS. As Karin Bauer notes, "the magazine thrived from the happy union of intellectual, aesthetic, and popular appeal..."[3] Decidedly political, "Recurrent themes were Cuba, anticolonialism, German fascism, the antinuclear struggle, human rights, and social justice."[4]

Unbeknownst to its public, *konkret* was actually funded and in part controlled by one of the remaining clandestine KPD cells which had gone into exile in East Germany.[5] The magazine's chief editor was Röhl's wife, a woman who had been active in the SDS since 1957, and had secretly joined the illegal KPD in 1959. Her name was Ulrike Meinhof.

Another radicalizing event for many young people at the time was the Auschwitz trials, held in Frankfurt between 1963 and 1965. Largely a propaganda exercise to cover up the far greater number of Nazis who had found their way into the new West German establishment, twenty-two former SS-men and one *Kapo* were tried for murder or complicity in murder. Regardless of the hypocritical aspect of the trial, the fact that for two-and-a-half years almost three hundred witnesses came and

---

1 Ibid., 29.

2 Jean-Paul Bier, "The Holocaust and West Germany: Strategies of Oblivion 1947-1979" *New German Critique* 19, Special Issue 1: Germans and Jews Winter (1980): 13.

3 Karin Bauer, *Everybody Talks About the Weather... We Don't: The Writings of Ulrike Meinhof* (New York: Seven Stories Press, 2008), 27.

4 Ibid., 30.

5 "My Mother, The Terrorist", *Deutsche Welle* [online], March 14, 2006.

testified, and had their testimony reported in the media, gave an inkling of what Auschwitz meant to a generation of German youth, who—quite understandably—now saw their teachers, civic leaders, and even their parents in a horrible new light.

These trials, and the general "discovery" of the Holocaust, were a radicalizing event for many young people at that time;[6] as one veteran of the New Left would later recall:

> *That the Germans could kill millions of human beings just because they had a different faith was utterly inexplicable to me. My whole moral world view shattered, got entwined with a rigorous rejection of my parents and school. If religion had not prevented this mass destruction of human beings, then it is no good for anything, then the whole talk of love of your neighbor and of meekness... was just a lie.[7]*

Despite what in retrospect may seem to have been a growing potential for revolt, during these early years, the SDS was silent, turned inward, engaging in "seminar Marxism" as it found its bearings outside of the SPD and struggled to elaborate a consistent analysis and strategy. When it did return to the public arena, it was as a small, consciously anti-imperialist organization influenced by the experiences of China, Cuba, Algeria, and Vietnam, advancing the analysis that "liberation movements in the Third World, marginal groups in society, and socialist intellectuals now constituted the revolutionary subject in society and the appropriate strategy was direct action."[8] (It is worth noting that the German Democratic Republic was pointedly *not* one of the ideological reference points for the new SDS.)

A line was crossed when Moise Tschombe visited Berlin in December 1964. To the applause of the West German ruling class, and with the help of German mercenaries, Tschombe had led a bloody, anticommunist secession in the Congolese province of Katanga. He was considered responsible for the 1961 murder of Patrice Lumumba, the first president of the Congo and a beloved symbol of the anticolonial struggle in Africa.

---

6 Hockenos, 34-35. See also Dagmar Herzog, "'Pleasure, Sex, and Politics Belong Together': Post-Holocaust Memory and the Sexual Revolution in West Germany," *Critical Inquiry* 24, 2: Intimacy, (Winter 1988): 402-403.

7 Eberhard Knodler-Bunte, in Herzog, 416.

8 Hülsberg, 39.

Hundreds of protesters turned out against Tschombe, and when the police tried to clear them away, they fought back in what would later be described as the starting point of the antiauthoritarian revolt in West Germany.[1]

The SDS played a prominent part in this protest. Based on university campuses, it was becoming the most important organization in the growing and increasingly militant protest movement against imperialist domination of the global South, most especially against the war in Indochina. Demonstrations ceased to be the timid rituals they had been; for the first time in decades, student protests escalated into street fighting.

1964 was also a year of change for *konkret*. The communist world was at the time deeply divided by the falling out between the Soviet Union and the People's Republic of China. Over the years, this split would only become more bitter until each side came to see the other as being objectively as bad as—or even worse than!—the imperialism represented by the United States. Despite its ties to the KPD, *konkret* was taking an increasingly pro-Chinese line, going so far as to support China's acquiring nuclear weapons. At this, its East German patrons lost patience, and after failing to browbeat Meinhof into submission at a secret meeting in East Berlin, they cut off all funding.[2] In their turn, Meinhof and Röhl resigned from the KPD. As a solution to this new lack of money, Röhl made drastic changes to the magazine's presentation, turning it into a glossy publication which now featured scantily-clad women in every issue—its circulation almost tripled.[3]

Far from suffering as a result of their separation from the SPD, the SDS, *konkret*, and others on the left were now particularly well placed to benefit from a series of economic and political developments, even though these were not of their doing and lay well beyond their control.

In 1966-67, a recession throughout the capitalist world pushed unemployment in the FRG to over a million for the first time in the postwar era, a situation the ruling class attempted to exploit to tip the balance of

---

1 Thomas, 94. See also Gretchen Dutschke, *Wir hatten ein barbarisches, schönes Leben* (Köln: K&W, 1996), 60-61.

2 Jutta Ditfurth, *Ulrike Meinhof: Die Biographie* (Berlin: Ullstein, 2007), 180-181.

3 David Kramer, "Ulrike Meinhof: An Emancipated Terrorist?" in *European Women on the Left: Socialism, Feminism, and the Problems Faced by Political Women, 1880 to the Present*. Jane Slaughter and Robert Kern, eds. Contributions in Women's Studies. (Westport, Conn.: Greenwood Press 1981), 201.

power even further in its favor. As Karl Heinz Roth explains:

> *Threats of job losses and elimination of all the groups of workers*
> *who would have been able to initiate advanced forms of struggle*
> *laid the basis for a general anti-worker offensive.*[4]

Furthermore:

> *The bosses freely admitted that they were using the crisis to intensify*
> *work conditions amongst all layers of the global working class.*
> *From their point of view, the temporary investment strike was*
> *necessary to create the basis for a recovery through a "cleansing of*
> *the personnel." Three hundred thousand immigrant workers and*
> *almost as many German workers were thrown out into the street.*[5]

In a move to consolidate support amongst more privileged German workers and thus exploit the divisions within the proletariat, the SPD was brought into a so-called "Grand Coalition" government alongside the Christian Democratic Union and Christian Social Union. This created a situation in which former resistance fighter and SPD chief Willy Brandt was now vice-chancellor alongside former Nazi Georg Kiesinger of the CDU, and the CSU's far-right Franz Josef Strauß was Minister of Finance alongside the SPD's young luminary, Karl Schiller, who held the Economics portfolio.

The SPD was completely discredited by its open embrace of these reactionaries, and it now appeared that any real change could only come about outside of government channels. Disenchantment struck at West Germany's youth in the universities, in the factories and on the street, as younger workers were increasingly marginalized by the new corporatist compact. The *Außerparlamentarische Opposition* (APO), or Extra-Parliamentary Opposition, was born.

The revolt was focused in West Berlin, an enclave that was a three-hour drive into East Germany, and which remained officially under Western Allied occupation, and so enjoyed the bizarre status of being a de facto part of the Federal Republic even though it remained legally distinct.[6] In a sense, West Berlin afforded the personal freedoms of the

---

4 Roth, 101.

5 Ibid., 100.

6 There was one autobahn through the GDR connecting the city to the Federal Republic, which the East Germans were obligated by international agreements to keep open. The highway ran through desolate countryside, and was flanked by East German armed forces at all times.

capitalist West while its odd diplomatic status provided its residents with extra room to maneuver outside of the West's constraints.[1] This had many important consequences, not the least of which was that young men who moved to West Berlin could avoid the draft, as they were technically living outside of the FRG.

Not surprisingly, the city became a magnet for the radicals and counterculture rebels of the new generation. In the words of one woman who lived there, it was "a self-contained area where political developments of all kinds... become evident much earlier than elsewhere and much more sharply, as if they were under a magnifying glass."[2]

Thus, it was in West Berlin that a group of students, gathered around Hans-Jürgen Krahl and the East German refugees Rudi Dutschke and Bernd Rabehl, began questioning not only the economic system, but the very nature of society itself. The structure of the family, the factory, and the school system were all challenged as these young rebels mixed the style of the hippy counterculture with ideas drawn from the Frankfurt School's brand of Marxism.

Andreas Baader, Dorothea Ridder, and Rainer Langhans, dancing in the streets of West Berlin (August, 1967)

---

1 For many examples of just how careful the Federal Republic had to be in imposing itself in West Berlin, see Avril Pittman, *From Ostpolitik to reunification: West German-Soviet political relations since 1974* (Cambridge, England & New York: Cambridge University Press, 1992), 32-62.

2 Hilke Schlaeger and Nancy Vedder-Shults, "West German Women's Movement," *New German Critique* 13 (Winter 1978): 61.

Communes and housing associations sprung up. Women challenged the male leadership and orientation within the SDS and the APO, setting up daycares, women's caucuses, women's centers, and women-only communes. The broader counterculture, rockers, artists, and members of the drug scene rallied to the emerging political insurgency. Protests encompassed traditional demonstrations as well as sit-ins, teach-ins, and happenings. So called "Republican Clubs" spread out to virtually every town and city as centers for discussion and organizing, bridging the divide between the younger radicals and veterans of the earlier peace movements.

As one historian has put it:

> *Everywhere it could, the 1960s generation countered the German petit bourgeois ethic with its antithesis, as they interpreted it: prudery with free love, nationalism with internationalism, the nuclear family with communes, provincialism with Third World solidarity, obedience to the law with civil disobedience, tradition with wide-open experimentation, servility with in-your-face activism.*[3]

Or, as one former SDS member would recall, it was a time when "everything"—hash, politics, sex, and Vietnam—"all seemed to hang together with everything else."[4]

Despite its growing popularity on campus and amongst hipsters, this new radical youth movement was not embraced by the population at large, and demonstrations would often be heckled or even attacked by onlookers. This widespread hostility was a green light for state repression, with results which would soon become clear for all to see.

On June 2, 1967, thousands of people turned out to demonstrate outside the German Opera against a visit by the Shah of Iran, whose brutal regime was a key American ally in the Middle East. Many wore paper masks in the likeness of the Shah and his wife; these had been printed up by Rainer Langhans and Holger Meins of the K.1 commune,[5] "So the police couldn't recognize us [and so] they only saw the face of the one they were protecting."[6] Thus adorned, the protesters greeted the

---

3 Hockenos, 80.

4 Eckhard Siepmann in Herzog, 427.

5 Kommune 1 in German.

6 G. Conradt and H. Jahn, *Starbuck Holger Meins*, directed by G. Conradt. (Germany: Hartmut Jahn Filmproduktion, 2002).

Iranian monarch and his wife with volleys of rotten tomatoes and shouts of "Murderer!"

(As Ulrike Meinhof would later write in *konkret*: "the students who befouled the Shah did not act on their own behalf, but rather on behalf of the Persian peasants who are in no position to resist under present circumstances, and the tomatoes could only be symbols for better projectiles...")[1]

The June 2 rally would be a turning point, as the protesters were brutally set upon by the police and SAVAK, the Iranian secret service. Many fought back, and the demonstration is reported to have "descended into the most violent battle between protesters and police so far in the post-war period... It was only around 12:30 AM that the fighting came to an end, by which time 44 demonstrators had been arrested, and the same number of people had been injured, including 20 police officers."[2]

Most tragically, a young member of the Evangelical Student Association, Benno Ohnesorg, attending his first demonstration, was shot in the back of the head by Karl-Heinz Kurras, a plainclothes police officer with the Red Squad. Even after Ohnesorg was finally picked up by an ambulance, it was another forty minutes before he was brought to a hospital. He died of his wounds that night.

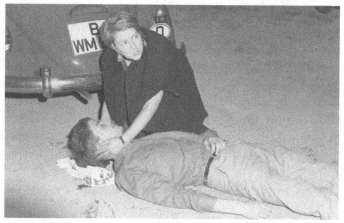

Benno Ohnesorg, shot by police, lies dying in the arms of fellow student Fredericke Dollinger.

---

1 "Women in the SDS; or, On Our Own Behalf, (1968)" in *German Feminist Writing*, eds. Patricia A. Herminghouse and Magda Mueller (New York: Continuum, 2001), p. 160.

2 Thomas, 111-112.

This police murder was a defining event, electrifying the student movement and pushing it in a far more militant direction. It has been estimated that between 100,000 and 200,000 students took part in demonstrations across the country in the days immediately following Ohnesorg's death. For many, especially those outside of West Berlin, it was their first political protest. As has been noted elsewhere, "Although two-thirds of students in the period before the shooting declared themselves to be apolitical, in the immediate aftermath of the shooting a survey found that 65 per cent of students had been politicized by Ohnesorg's death."[3]

The murder catapulted the SDS into the center of student politics across the Federal Republic. As one student activist would recall years later:

> The SDS didn't have more than a few hundred members nationwide... and then all at once there was such a huge deluge that we couldn't cope. Our offices were overrun. So we just opened SDS up and decentralized everything. We let people in different cities and towns organize themselves into autonomous project groups and then we'd all meet at regular congresses to thrash things out. More or less by chance it turned out to be an incredible experiment in participatory democracy.[4]

Initially, the state and the newspapers owned by reactionary press magnate Axel Springer[5] tried to justify this murder, repeating lies that the protesters had had plans to kill police and that Kurras had shot in self-defense. Springer's *Bild Zeitung* ominously warned that "A young man died in Berlin, victim of the riots instigated by political hooligans who call themselves demonstrators. Riots aren't enough anymore. They

---

3 Ibid., 114.

4 Christian Semler in Hockenos, 69.

5 The Springer chain consisted of conservative tabloids, among them *Bild, Berliner Zeitung*, and *Berliner Morgenpost*. They led a campaign to smear progressive students as "muddle heads," East German spies, and storm troopers—at times even crossing the line and advocating vigilante violence. As Jeremy Varon notes, "Springer publications accounted for more than 70 percent of the West Berlin press and more than 30 percent of the national daily newspaper market. As the press fed a climate of anti-student hysteria, the reaction of the media to the New Left itself became a major object of protest." [Jeremy Varon, *Bringing the War Home: The Weather Underground, the Red Army Faction, and Revolutionary Violence in the Sixties and Seventies* (Berkeley: University of California Press, 2004), 38-39.]

want to see blood. They wave the red flag and they mean it. This is where democratic tolerance stops."[1]

On June 3, the Berlin Senate banned demonstrations in the city—twenty-five year old Gudrun Ensslin was one of eight protesters arrested for defying this ban the next day[2]—and the chief of police Duensing proudly explained his tactics as those he would use when confronted with a smelly sausage: "The left end stinks [so] we had to cut into the middle to take off the end."[3] As for the Shah, he tried to reassure the Mayor of Berlin Heinrich Albertz, telling him not to think too much of it, "these things happen every day in Iran..."[4]

Nevertheless, given the widespread sense of outrage and the increasing evidence that Ohnesorg had been killed without provocation, Duensing was forced out of his job, and Senator for Internal Affairs Büsch and Mayor Albertz were eventually made to follow suit.

If June 2 has been pointed to as the "coming out" of the West German New Left mass student phenomenon, the international circumstances in which this occurred were not without significance. Just three days after Ohnesorg's murder, West Germany's ally Israel attacked Egypt, and quickly destroyed its army—as well as Jordanian and Syrian forces—in what became known as the Six Day War.

In the FRG, the Six Day War provided the odd occasion for a broad-based, mass celebration of militarism. To some observers, it suddenly seemed as if the same emotions and social forces that had supported German fascism were now expressing themselves through support for the Israeli aggressors, described (approvingly) as the "Prussians of the Middle East."[5] Although the SDS was already pro-Palestinian, most leftists had previously harbored sympathies for the Jewish state. The 1967 war put a definite end to this, establishing the New Left's anti-Zionist orientation; as an unfortunate side effect of this turn, it also discouraged attempts to grapple with the gravity of Germany's antisemitic past from a radical, anticapitalist point of view. (For more on Germany's relationship to Israel, see Appendix III—The FRG and the State of Israel, pages 550-553.)

---

1 Hockenos, 68.

2 Stefan Aust, *The Baader-Meinhof Group: The Inside Story of a Phenomenon.* Translated by Anthea Bell. (London: The Bodley Head Ltd., 1987), 44.

3 Thomas, 115.

4 Aust, 44.

5 George Lavy, *Germany and Israel: Moral Debt and National Interest* (London: Frank Cass, 1996), 154.

An uneasy calm reigned in the wake of the June 2 tragedy, and yet the movement continued to grow. More radical ideas were gaining currency, and at an SDS conference in September Rudi Dutschke and Hans-Jürgen Krahl went so far as to broach the possibility of the left fielding an urban guerilla. This was the first time such an idea had been mentioned in the SDS or the APO, and for the time being, such talk remained a matter of abstract conjecture.

On February 17 and 18, 1968, the movement reached what was perhaps its peak when 5,000 people attended the International Congress on Vietnam in West Berlin, including representatives of anti-imperialist movements from around the world. Addressing those present, Dutschke called for a "long march through the institutions," a phrase with which his name is today firmly associated.[6] (By this, the student leader did not mean joining the system, but rather setting up counterinstitutions while identifying dissatisfied elements within the establishment that might be won over or subverted.)[7] The congress closed with a

INTERNATIONALE VIETNAM-KONFERENZ WESTBERLIN
Koordinierung anti-imperialistischer Aktionen in Westeuropa

ES LEBE DIE VIETNAMESISCHE REVOLUTION!

17. Februar 1968, 11.00 Uhr, Auditorium Maximum der TU

DER KAMPF DES VIETNAMESISCHEN VOLKES UND DIE GLOBALSTRATEGIE DES IMPERIALISMUS

Forum I   Die vietnamesische Revolution
Forum II   Vietnam und die Revolution in der Dritten Welt
Forum III Der anti-imperialistische und anti-kapitalistische Kampf in den kapitalistischen Ländern

Sozialistischer Deutscher Studentenbund

18. Februar 1968, ł
vom Rathaus Sch

GROSSKUNDGEBUNG mit

S. de Beauvoir (Frankreich), D. Dillinger (USA), R. Dutschke (SDS), C. L. Guggomos (Kampagne für Demokratie und Abrüstung), Melva Hernandez (ZK der KP Kuba), E. Mandel (Belgien), O. Smith (Black Power SNNC, USA), Peter Weiss und Vertretern der FNL

Sozialistischer Deutscher Studentenbund
Kampagne für Demokratie und Abrüstung (Regional-Ausschuß Berlin)

---

6 Tariq Ali, *Street Fighting Years: An Autobiography of the Sixties* (New York: Verso, 2005), 243.

7 While one cannot mention Dutschke today without referring to the "long march," the phrase is interpreted wildly differently by different writers. The description offered here is Herbert Marcuse's, as it appeared in his 1972 essay "The Left Under the Counterrevolution" in which he endorsed the concept while crediting it to his former student Dutschke. [Herbert Marcuse, *Counterrevolution and Revolt* (Boston: Beacon Press, 1989), 55-57]

demonstration of more than 12,000 people, and would be remembered years later as an important breakthrough for the entire European left.[1]

The establishment mounted its response on February 21, as the West Berlin Senate, the Federation of Trade Unions, and the Springer Press called for a mass demonstration against the student movement and in support of the U.S. war against Vietnam. Eighty thousand people attended, many carrying signs reading "Rudi Dutschke: Public Enemy Number One" and "Berlin Must Not Become Saigon."

Increasing polarization was leading to a definitive explosion: less than one year after Ohnesorg's murder, another violent attack on the left served as the spark.

On April 11, 1968, Josef Bachmann, a young right-wing worker, shot Rudi Dutschke three times, once in the head, once in the jaw, and once in the chest. Dutschke, who was recognized as the leading intellectual in the SDS and the APO, had been the target of a massive anticommunist smear campaign in the media, particularly the Springer Press, which would be widely blamed for setting the stage for the attack. Indeed, Bachmann would later testify in this regard, saying, "I have taken my daily information from the *Bild Zeitung*."[2]

The shooting occurred one week after Martin Luther King had been assassinated in the United States, and to many young German leftists, it appeared that their entire international movement was under attack. One young working-class rebel, like Dutschke a refugee from the East, summed up how he felt as follows:

> Up to this point they had come with the little police clubs or Mr Kuras (sic) shot; but now it had started, with people being offed specifically. The general baiting had created a climate in which little pranks wouldn't work anymore. Not when they're going to liquidate you, regardless of what you do. Before I get transported to Auschwitz again, I'd rather shoot first, that's clear now. If the gallows is smiling at you at the end anyway, then you can fight back beforehand.[3]

Bachmann had carried out his attack on the Thursday before Easter, and the annual peace demonstrations were quickly transformed into

---

1 Ali, 246.

2 Thomas, 170.

3 Bommi Baumann, *Terror or Love? The Personal Account of a West German Urban Guerilla* (London: John Calder Publications, 1979), 41.

protests against the assassination attempt; it has been estimated that 300,000 people participated in the marches over the weekend, the largest figure achieved in West Germany in the 1960s.[4] Universities were occupied across the country, and running battles with the police lasted for four days. "Springer Shot Too!" became a common slogan amongst radicals, and in many cities, the corporation was targeted with violent attacks. Thousands were arrested, hundreds were hospitalized, and two people (a journalist and a protester) were killed, most likely by police. On May 1, 50,000 people marched through West Berlin.

"The Revolution Won't Die of Lead Poisoning"

Unprecedented numbers of working-class youth took part in these battles, with university students constituting only a minority of those arrested by police, a development that worried the ruling class.[5]

By the time it was over, there had been violent clashes in at least twenty cities. Springer property worth 250,000 DM (roughly $80,000) was damaged or destroyed, including over 100,000 DM worth of window panes.[6]

This rebellion and the police repression pushed many radicals' thinking to an entirely new level. Bommi Baumann, for instance, credited the riots with opening his eyes to the possibility of armed struggle:

> On the spot, I really got it, this concept of mass struggle-terrorism; this problem I had been thinking about for so long became clear to me then. The chance for a revolutionary movement lies in this: when a determined group is there simultaneously with the masses, supporting them through terror.[7]

Ulrike Meinhof was clearly thinking along similar lines, only she put her thoughts in print, sharing them with the public in a groundbreaking

---

4 Thomas, 171.

5 Ibid., 176.

6 Ibid.

7 Baumann, 41.

konkret article entitled "From Protest to Resistance." Arguing that in the Easter riots "the boundaries between protest and resistance were exceeded," she promised that "the paramilitary deployment of the police will be answered with paramilitary methods."[1]

On May 31, the *Bundestag* passed the *Notstandsgesetze*, or Emergency Powers Act, which besides providing the state with tools to deal with crises such as natural disasters or war, was also intended to open the movement up to greater intervention. The CDU had been trying to pass such repressive legislation for years, and short-circuiting opposition to it had been one of the advantages of forming a Grand Coalition along with the SPD. Coming as it did on the heels of the April violence, the legislation passed easily. (The fact that, just across the Rhine, France seemed also on the brink of revolution, enjoying its defining rebellion of the sixties, certainly didn't hurt matters.)

Under the new Act, the Basic Law was amended to allow the state to tap phones and observe mail unhindered by previous stipulations requiring that the targeted individual be informed. Provisions were introduced in particular for the telephone surveillance of people suspected of preparing or committing "political crimes," especially those governed by the catch-all §129 of the penal code, criminalizing the "formation or support of a criminal association." The Emergency Powers Act also officially sanctioned the use of clandestine photography, "trackers" and *Verfassungsschutz* informants and provocateurs.

Throughout the month of May, as the Act was being passed into law, universities were occupied, students boycotted classes, and tens of

Poster for a demonstration against the Emergency Powers Act, organized by the Munich Board for the Emergency Facing Democracy: "The Emergency Powers Act Plans for War, Not Peace!"
Amongst those who gave closing speeches was one Rolf Pohle, at the time a law student prominent in the Munich APO.

---

1 Thomas, 180.

thousands of people protested in demonstrations across the country, while a similar number of workers staged a one-day strike. To its critics, the Act represented a dangerous step along the road to re-establishing fascism in the Federal Republic, and this fear was simply reinforced by the way in which the Grand Coalition could pass the legislation regardless of the widespread protests against it.

Anti-*Notstandsgesetze* activities were particularly impressive in Frankfurt, the financial capital of West Germany, which had also become something of an intellectual center for the student movement. On May 27, students occupied the Frankfurt University, and for several days held seminars and workshops addressing a variety of political questions. It took large scale police raids on May 30 to clear the campus.

All this notwithstanding, the Act was passed into law.

The failure of the anti-*Notstandsgesetze* movement was experienced as a bitter defeat by the New Left. Many entertained alarmist fears that the laws would be used to institute a dictatorship, in much the same way as Hindenburg had used similar powers in 1930 and 1933 to create a government independent from parliament, which had facilitated the Nazi dictatorship. In the words of Hans-Jürgen Krahl:

> *Democracy in Germany is finished. Through concerted political activism we have to form a broad, militant base of resistance against these developments, which could well lead to war and concentration camps. Our struggle against the authoritarian state of today can prevent the fascism of tomorrow.*[2]

In this heady climate, matters continued to escalate throughout 1968, sections of the movement graduating to more organized and militantly ambitious protests. The most impressive examples of this were probably those that accompanied attempts to disbar Horst Mahler.

Mahler was a superstar of the West Berlin left, known as the "hippy lawyer" who defended radicals in many of the most important cases of this period. He had been involved with the SDS, and was a co-founder of the West Berlin Republican Club and the Socialist Lawyers Collective.[3] He had been arrested during the anti-Springer protests that April, and in what would prove to be a foolish move, the state had initiated proceedings to see him disbarred.[4]

---

2 Hockenos, 88.

3 Aust, 65-6.

4 Ibid., 64.

Mahler's case became a new lightning rod for the West Berlin left, which felt that the state was trying to muzzle their most committed legal defender. The student councils of the Free University and the Technical University called for protests the day of his hearing, one organizer describing the goal as "the destruction of the justice apparatus through massive demonstrations."[1]

The street fighting which broke out on November 3 would go down in history as the "Battle of Tegeler Weg."[2] On the one side, the helmet-wearing protesters (roughly 1,500) attacked with cobblestones and two-by-fours, on the other the police (numbering 1,000) used water cannons, tear gas, and billy clubs:

> *Several lawyers and bystanders were hit by cobblestones ripped from the sidewalks and hurled by the youths, most of them wearing crash helmets, as they moved forward in waves directed by leaders with megaphones.*
>
> *Injured demonstrators were carried to waiting ambulances marked with blue crosses and staffed by girls wearing improvised nurses' uniforms.[3]*

Nor were the police spared. As another newspaper reported:

> *The demonstrators caused a heavy toll of police casualties with their guerrilla style of battle: thrusting at police, withdrawing, consolidating and then thrusting again from another angle.*
>
> *At one stage they managed to beat back a 300-man police force a distance of 150 yards... Police counted 120 injured in their own ranks. Ten of them had to be treated at a hospital. A police spokesman said seven of 21 injured demonstrators were taken to a hospital. The number of arrests was placed at 46.[4]*

That same night a horse was injured when several molotov cocktails were thrown into the police stable.[5] It would later be suggested that

---

1 Associated Press, "Student 'Army' Battles With Berlin Police," *Fresno Bee,* November 4, 1968.

2 Tegeler Weg is a fashionable street in West Berlin where the Bar Association was located.

3 Associated Press, "Student 'Army'."

4 George Thomson, "Berlin police, leftists battle," *Lowell Sun,* November 4, 1968.

5 Ibid.

this attack was the work of an agent provocateur by the name of Peter Urbach.[6]

The court declined to disbar Mahler. Within a few days, the firebrand lawyer was once again making headlines with his latest case: the defense of the young antifascist Beate Klarsfeld, who had smacked CDU Chancellor—and former Nazi—Kurt Georg Kiesinger, hitting him in the face.[7] Mahler would eventually win Klarsfeld a suspended sentence, at which point he counter-sued Kiesinger on her behalf, arguing that the very fact that a former Nazi was chancellor constituted an insult to his client.[8]

The Battle of Tegeler Weg was another milestone, representing a willingness to engage in organized violence the likes of which had not been seen for decades. This period also saw the first experiments with clandestine armed activities, a subject to which we will soon return.

Thus, we can see that even as the spectre of increased repression haunted sections of the militant left, there existed both the desire and the capacity to rise to the next level.

At the same time, however, other developments offered the tempting promise that change might come about in a more comfortable manner by backing down and working within the system.

In October 1969, the Grand Coalition came to an end, and under the slogan "Let's Dare More Democracy!" an SPD government (in coalition with the FDP) was elected. SPD leader Willy Brandt was now Chancellor, and FDP leader Walter Scheel became Foreign Minister. The largely symbolic post of president went to political old-timer Gustav Heinemann, widely considered one of the Federal Republic's most liberal politicians, despite the fact that he had been the Grand Coalition's SPD Minister of Justice.[9]

For the first time in its history, the Christian Democrats had lost control of the West German parliament.

---

6 Aust, 145.

7 Associated Press, "Woman gets Jail for Slapping Bonn Chief," *Fresno Bee*, November 8, 1968.

8 Associated Press, "Hit Kiesinger; Term Suspended," *European Stars and Stripes*, August 26, 1969.

9 Heinemann had in fact held a cabinet position for the CDU as early as 1949, a post he left, along with the CDU, in the early fifties in protest against Adenauer's rearmament policies. When Ulrike Meinhof was sued for slander by CSU leader Franz Josef Strauß in 1961 as a result of a *konkret* article, Heinemann agreed to take on her case, successfully defending her—the two had become allies if not friends during the peace movements of the 1950s.

The new SPD government announced a series of measures which partially fulfilled the students' more "reasonable" demands: there were new diplomatic overtures to East Germany, it was made easier to be declared a conscientious objector, the age of consent and the legal voting age were lowered from twenty-one to eighteen, no fault divorce legislation was passed, and a series of reforms aimed to modernize and open up the stuffy, hierarchical German school system.

For many, it seemed like a brand new day.

At the same time, Brandt announced an "immediate program to modernize and intensify crime prevention," which included:

> *strengthening of the Criminal Investigation Bureau, the modernization of its equipment and the extension of its powers, the re-equipping and reorganization of the Federal Border Guard as a Federal police force, together with the setting up of a "study group on the surveillance of foreigners" within the security services.*[1]

Nevertheless, these measures would not affect most activists, and the government shift away from the anachronistic conservatism of the CDU helped confuse and siphon off less committed students, draining potential sources of support for the radical left.

At the same time, the movement itself was beginning to fragment.

Problems of male supremacy in the APO had become increasingly difficult to bear for radical women inspired by the feminist movements in the United States, France, and England. In September 1968, things had come to a head at an SDS conference in Frankfurt, where Hans-Jürgen Krahl found himself being pelted by tomatoes after he refused to address the question of chauvinism in the SDS. While many (but not all) of the women from the APO would continue to identify as being on the left, their political trajectory became increasingly separate, both as a result of dynamics internal to the women's movement and of the continuing sexism outside of it.

The decline of the APO also occurred alongside renewed attempts to build various workers' parties in line with the "correct" Marxist analysis. In 1968, the banned KPD ("Communist Party of Germany") had been re-established under a new name as the DKP ("German Communist Party"), but boasting the same program and leadership. To most young radicals, though, this "new" Communist Party was of little

---

1 Cobler, 154-155.

interest, not only because of its association with the clearly unattractive East German regime, but also because of what was seen as its unimpressive and timid track record in the years before Adenauer had had it banned.

Rather, there followed a veritable alphabet soup of Maoist parties, most of which were as virulently anti-Soviet as they were anti-American. These were joined by a much smaller number of Trotskyist organizations, and together all these would eventually become known as the "K-groups," in a development roughly analogous to the New Communist Movement which developed at the same time in North America.

Those who remained to the left of the SPD while not joining any of these new party-oriented organizations included the *sponti* ("spontaneous") left which had grown out of the APO's anti-authoritarian camp, anarchists, and assorted independent socialists. Together, these were referred to as the "undogmatic left," their bastions being the cities of Frankfurt, Munich, and—of course—West Berlin.

The movement continued to struggle, but with increasing difficulty, fragmenting in all directions, as the APO seemed to be coming apart at the seams.

The different tendencies to emerge from the APO tapped into different aesthetic traditions—above: a call-out from the radical magazine Agit 883 for a demonstration against the Vietnam War.

below: "Everybody Out to the Red May 1st; Resist Wage Controls; Resist Wage Slavery; A United Working Class Front Against the Betrayal of the SPD Government"

In March 1970, following a chaotic congress at the Frankfurt Student Association Building, the SDS was dissolved by acclamation. In a brilliant ploy, two months later the government decreed an amnesty for protesters serving short sentences, thereby winning many of these middle-class students back to the establishment. The student movement in West Germany was particularly vulnerable to this kind of recuperation, being overwhelmingly comprised of young people for whom there was a place in the more comfortable classes; in 1967, for instance, only 7% of West German students were from working-class families (by comparison, in England the figure was almost one in three).[1]

Despite the APO's inability to meet the challenges before it, one cannot deny that in just a few years it had thoroughly transformed West German society:

> Among the consequences were the reform of education; a new Ostpolitik;[2] the deconstruction of the authoritarian patriarchal relations in the family, school, factory and public service; the development of state planning in the economy; a greater integration of women into professional life and a reform in sexual legislation... the APO also provided the impetus to a socio-cultural break with the past. There was a very rapid change in social outlook and behavior patterns. The old ascetic behavior based on the notion of duty came to an end. Along with a different conception of social roles came a new set of sexual mores and a dissolution of the old respectful and subservient attitude towards the state and all forms of authority. There developed, in other words, a new culture which was to pave the way for the new social movements of the 1970s and 1980s.[3]

---

1 Thomas, 144.

2 *Ostpolitik*: the FRG's official policy towards the GDR and the East bloc.

3 Hülsberg, 42-43.

3

Taking up the Gun

As the APO foundered, the majority of those to the left of the SPD remained committed to legal, aboveground activism. Nevertheless, a section of the movement had begun testing the waters with another kind of praxis, and for the purposes of our study, it is to this that we will now turn.

The first experiments with armed struggle developed out of the counterculture, as individuals around the K.1 commune in West Berlin began carrying out firebombings and bank robberies. Coming from a milieu where drugs and anarchism mingled freely, these young radicals hung out in a scene known as "the Blues," and would take on the purposefully ironic name of the "Central Committee of the Roaming Hash Rebels." As Bommi Baumann later explained, with perhaps a tongue in his cheek:

> Mao provided our theoretical basis: "On the Mentality of Roaming Bands of Rebels." From the so-called robber-bands, he and Chu-Teh had created the first cadre of the Red Army. We took our direction from that. We directed our agitation to make the dopers, who were still partly unpolitical, conscious of their situation. What we did was mass work.[4]

---

4 Baumann, 50.

The Hash Rebels carried out actions under a number of different names, but became best known as the Tupamaros-West Berlin, after the urban guerillas in Uruguay.[1] Initially, this antiauthoritarian, pre-guerilla tendency suffered from anti-intellectualism, unquestioned male chauvinism, and a lack of any coherent strategy. It has also been criticized for tolerating and engaging in antisemitism under cover of anti-Zionism, one of its first actions being to firebomb a cultural center housed in a synagogue on the anniversary of a Nazi pogrom.[2]

On the other hand, it did seem to enjoy an organic relationship with its base, such as that was.

As the APO fell apart and many of the Hash Rebels' leading members were arrested or simply had a change of heart, what remained of this tendency would crystallize into a guerilla group known as the 2nd of June Movement (2JM—a reference to the date when Benno Ohnesorg had been killed in 1967). Rooted in West Berlin, this group eventually overcame many of its initial weaknesses while retaining an accessible and often humorous rhetorical style that resonated with many in the anarchist and *sponti* scenes throughout the country.

The second guerilla tendency, with which we are more directly concerned, brought together individuals who were peripheral to the countercultural milieu of the Hash Rebels, and of a somewhat more serious bent. As Bommi Baumann would later explain, they "formed at about the same time as we did, because they considered us totally crazy."[3] This second tendency was much more theoretically rigorous (or pretentious, to its critics), and heavily influenced not only by Marx, Lenin, and Mao, but also by New Left philosophers ranging from Nicos Poulantzas to the Frankfurt School.

This nascent Marxist-Leninist guerilla scene had its earliest manifestation in the firebombing of two Frankfurt department stores on April 3, 1968, one week before Rudi Dutschke was shot. Petrol bombs with rudimentary timing devices were left in both the Kaufhaus Schneider and Kaufhof buildings, bursting into flames just before midnight. The fires caused almost 700,000 DM ($224,000 U.S.) in damage, though nobody was hurt.

---

1 Ibid., 59.

2 Tilman Fichter, interview by Philipp Gessler and Stefan Reinecke, "The anti-Semitism of the 68ers," *die tageszeitung*, October 25, 2005. The action was intended to show solidarity with the Palestinian struggle. See Baumann, 60-61 and 67-68.

3 Baumann, 76.

A cartoon from the radical counterculture magazine *Agit 883* shows a young man bearing a striking resemblence to Holger Meins (who was a member of the newspaper's editorial collective) throwing an incendiary device of some sort out of a car. He gets busted because he forgot to change the car's license plates, but luckily some of his friends are willing to vouch for him and the police are forced to release him, even though they know he did it.

On April 5, Horst Söhnlein, Thorwald Proll, Gudrun Ensslin, and Andreas Baader, who had all traveled from West Berlin to carry out the action while attending an SDS conference, were arrested and charged with arson.

The four had taken few precautions to protect their identities and avoid arrest. They had issued no communiqué, and in retrospect, the action appears almost flippant in its execution. Indeed, some of those arrested initially denied their participation, and later tried to minimize it all, Baader claiming, "We had no intention of endangering human life or even starting a real fire."[1]

In court, the four had no united strategy; apparently without bitterness or recrimination, Baader and Ensslin at first tried to present a legal defense, and then switched to accepting full responsibility while insisting that Proll and Söhnlein were both completely innocent.[2] For their part, these two did not deny their involvement, yet chose not to defend themselves, though Proll did offer an eloquent denunciation of the court and judicial system (see pages 66-78).

In the end, there was no denying that this was a political action, albeit an ill-defined one. In court, Ensslin explained that the arson was "in protest against people's indifference to the murder of the Vietnamese," adding that "We have found that words are useless without action."[3]

Then, in a statement that could only be appreciated in retrospect, she told a television reporter, "We have said clearly enough that we did the wrong thing. But there's no reason for us to discuss it with the law or the state. We must discuss it with people who think as we do."[4]

While the four were repudiated by the SDS, they were embraced by others for whom the step into illegality seemed both appropriate and timely. "They were like little media stars for the radical left," Thorwald's younger sister Astrid Proll would recall years later.[5]

One of these admirers was Ulrike Meinhof, who had divorced *konkret* publisher Klaus Rainer Röhl and moved to West Berlin with their twin daughters in 1967. Meinhof visited Ensslin in prison, and would approvingly write about the case in her magazine column. "[T]he

---

1 Aust, 51, 58.
2 Ibid., 58.
3 Ibid., 58.
4 Ibid., 62.
5 Astrid Proll, *Baader Meinhof: Pictures on the Run 67-77* (Zurich: Scalo, 1998), 8.

progressive moment of arson in a department store does not lie in the destruction of goods," she opined, "but in the criminality of the act, the breaking of the law..."[6]

Publicly, the arsonists' friends from the K.1 commune declared their solidarity, Fritz Teufel paraphrasing Bertolt Brecht to the effect that "It's always better to torch a department store than to run one."[7] Privately, however, they wondered at how clumsily the whole thing had been carried out, some even supposing that the four might suffer from some "psychic failure," a subconscious desire to go to jail.[8]

In October 1968, the four were each sentenced to three years in prison.

As the judge read out the verdict a familiar figure stood up: "This trial belongs before a student court," Daniel Cohn-Bendit[9] shouted, at which point the gallery erupted into pandemonium, spectators swarming the guards as two of the accused attempted to make a break for it. Three people, including Cohn-Bendit, were arrested as a result of this melee, and all four young arsonists remained in custody.[10]

The next day, persons unknown lobbed three molotov cocktails into the Frankfurt courthouse.[11] Again, no one was hurt.

The arsonists had been represented by Horst Mahler, whom the state failed to have disbarred just days after this defeat, in the hearings which would provoke the aforementioned Battle of Tegeler Weg. The four would not be able to participate in that historic rout of the West Berlin police: despite appealing their sentence, they remained imprisoned until June of 1969. Only then were they finally released on

---

6 Aust, 60.

7 Andreas Elter "Die RAF und die Medien: Ein Fallbeispiel für terroristische Kommunikation," *Bundeszentrale für politische Bildung* [online], August 20, 2007. Brecht, the famous communist playwright, had stated that "Small timers rob banks, professionals own them."

8 Aust, 51-2.

9 A law student at the University of Frankfurt, "Danny the Red" had been barred from France in 1968 for his symbolic leadership role in the May events of that year (it was his expulsion which had provoked students to occupy Nanterre University). Today, a respectable politician in the German Green Party, in 1969, he was (in)famous around the world, the very personification of anarchist student revolt. As we shall see in Section 11, (Meanwhile, Elsewhere on the Left...), he would play an important role in deradicalizing a section of the movement in the mid-seventies.

10 Associated Press, "Cohn-Bendit Jailed; Court Brawl Follows," *European Stars and Stripes*, November 1, 1968.

11 *European Stars and Stripes*, "New Violence Hits Frankfurt," November 2, 1968.

their own recognizance until such a time as the court finally reached its decision.

As the summer of 69 turned to fall and the court continued to deliberate, the recently released Ensslin, Baader, and Proll would busy themselves working in the "apprentices' collectives" scene. These collectives consisted of young runaways from state homes, and were at the time the object of political campaigning from the disintegrating APO. As Astrid Proll would recall:

> When Andreas Baader and Gudrun Ensslin were released from custody they knew exactly what they wanted. Unlike the drugged "communards" they radiated great clarity and resolve... Gudrun and Andreas launched a big campaign in Frankfurt against the authoritarian regimes in young offender institutions. We lived with youths who had escaped from closed institutions, joined them in fighting for their rights, and managed to achieve some successes. Ulrike Meinhof, as a commited (sic), critical journalist, joined us and became friends with Gudrun and Andreas.[1]

In November 1969, the court denied their appeal and ordered the four back to prison: only Söhnlein turned himself in. Ensslin and Baader went underground and set about establishing the contacts that would be necessary for a prolonged campaign of armed struggle. Thorwald Proll was soon abandoned—he was not considered serious enough—but his sister Astrid joined them.

Over the next months, the fugitives would cross into France and Italy and back to West Berlin again, laying the groundwork for the future organization. At this point, they resumed contact with their lawyer Horst Mahler,[2] who was still facing criminal charges stemming from the April 1968 revolt.[3] While enduring these legal battles, Mahler had himself been trying to set up a "militant group" in Berlin,[4] and so joining forces with his former clients simply seemed like a wise strategic decision.

At the same time, the serious Marxist-Leninists considered—and rejected—the idea of joining forces with the anarchist guerilla groups that were coalescing within the Roaming Hash Rebels scene. The reasons

---

1 Proll, 8.

2 Aust, 73.

3 Associated Press, "West Berlin Publisher is Sentenced," *Danville Bee,* February 16, 1970.

4 Aust, 77.

for this decision to continue following separate paths are not clear-cut, and the consequences were more nuanced than might be expected. It is important to remember that many of the figures involved knew each other from the APO, in some cases were friends, and certainly would have had opinions about each other's politics and personalities. It has been said that Dieter Kunzelmann, a prominent figure in the Hash Rebels scene, was wary of Baader claiming leadership.[5] It has also been suggested that the RAF as a whole had a haughty manner, and was made up of middle-class students who didn't fit in with the supposedly more proletarian 2JM.[6]

While none of the guerillas have ever said as much, one cannot help but wonder what RAF members might have thought of the counter-cultural scene out of which the Hash Rebels had developed, specifi-cally the sexual arrangements. The K.1 commune was not only famous for its brilliant agit prop, its radical cultural experiments, and its phe-nomenal drug consumption, but also for its iconic role in the sexual revolution which swept the Federal Republic in the years of the APO. At the same time as K.1's sexual politics constituted a reaction to the oppressive conservatism of Christian Germany, it was also very much a macho scene built around the desires of key men involved. Polygamy was almost mandatory, and women were passed around between the "revolutionaries"—as one male communard put it, "It's like training a horse; one guy has to break her in, then she's available for everyone."[7] As Bommi Baumann would later admit regarding the Hash Rebels, "They were just pure oppressors of women; it can't be put any other way."[8]

There were always many women playing central roles in the RAF. It is difficult to imagine Ulrike Meinhof, Gudrun Ensslin, or Astrid Proll putting up with the kind of sexist libertinage which has been docu-mented in the West Berlin anarchist scene. Indeed, during her own pe-riod in the wild depths of the counterculture, Proll had not gone to K.1 but had chosen to live in a women-only commune, helping to form a short-lived female version of the Hash Rebels, the Militant Black Panther Aunties.[9]

---

5 Ibid.
6 Baumann, 77-78.
7 Herzog, 425.
8 Baumann, 75.
9 Eileen MacDonald, *Shoot the Women First* (London: Arrow Books Ltd., 1991), 209-210.

These various explanations, however, are not only difficult to evaluate, they also risk obscuring the fact that cooperation between the anarchist guerilla scene and the Marxist-Leninists would continue throughout the seventies, many members of the former eventually joining the RAF, while a few individuals continued to carry out operations with both organizations. Certainly, from what can be seen, a high level of coordination and solidarity existed between the groups at all times. While their supporters might occasionally engage in unpleasant disputes, the actual fighters seem to have maintained good relations even as they traveled their different roads.

Ultimately, in the early 80s, the 2nd of June Movement would publicly announce that it was joining the RAF en masse. This provided the opportunity for some 2JM political prisoners who opposed the merger to give their own explanation as to why they had always chosen to fight separately. Although these observations were made over ten years later, they help shed light on relations in these early days:

> The contradiction between the RAF and the 2nd of June at that time was the result of the different ways the groups had evolved: the 2nd of June Movement out of their members' social scene and the RAF on the basis of their theoretical revolutionary model. And, equally, as a result of the RAF's centralized organizational model on the one hand, and our autonomous, decentralized structures on the other. Another point of conflict was to be found in the question of cadre going underground, which the RAF insisted on as a point of principle.
>
> As such, the immediate forerunners to the 2nd of June Movement were always open to a practical—proletarian—alternative; an alternative that had nothing to do with competition, but more to do with different visions of the revolutionary struggle.
>
> There was strong mutual support and common actions in the early period of both groups... At the time both groups proceeded with the idea that the future would determine which political vision would prove effective in the long run.[1]

---

1 Ralf Reinders, Klaus Viehmann, and Ronald Fritzsch, "Zu der angeblichen Auflösung der Bewegung 2. Juni im Juni 1980," http://www.bewegung.in/mate_nichtaufloesung.html. This is an excerpt from a much longer document which, along with the 2JM's declaration of the merger, appear (translated) in our second volume: André Moncourt and J. Smith, *The Red Army Faction, a Documentary History, Vol. II: Dancing with Imperialism* (Montreal/Oakland: Kersplebedeb and PM Press, 2013), 141-142.

So, during this germinal period, friendly contacts were maintained even as differences were clarified between the various activists who were choosing to take the next step in the struggle.

For shelter and support, those who were underground became dependent on the goodwill and loyalty of friends and allies who maintained a legal existence. One of those who occasionally sheltered Baader and Ensslin was Ulrike Meinhof, who was already feeling that their commitment and sense of purpose contrasted sharply with what she experienced as her own increasingly hollow existence as a middle-class media star, albeit one with "notorious" left-wing politics. At the same time, Meinhof continued to work with young people in closed institutions, specifically girls in reform school, with whom she began producing a television docudrama.

While Meinhof eventually became world famous for what she did next in life, it is worth emphasizing that her time as a journalist was far from insignificant. As her biographer Jutta Ditfurth has argued:

> *With her columns, and above all with the radio features about things like industrial labor and reform school children, Meinhof had an enormous influence on the thinking of many people. Much more than she realized. She took on themes that only exploded into view years later. For instance, the women's question. When women in the SDS defended themselves from macho guys, they did it with words and sentences from Meinhof's articles. She could formulate things succinctly.*[2]

Baader was captured in West Berlin on April 3, 1970, set up by a police informant.[3] Peter Urbach had been active around the commune scene for years, all the while secretly acting on behalf of the state. He was particularly "close" to the K.1 commune, and had known Baader since at least 1967. While the bombs and guns Urbach supplied to young rebels never seemed to work, the hard drugs he provided did their job nicely, showing that even as theories of the "liberating" effects of narcotics were being touted in the scene, the state knew on which side its bread was buttered.[4]

While it has always been stressed that there were neither hierarchies

---

2 Jutta Ditfurth, interview by Arno Luik, "Sie war die große Schwester der 68er," *Stern* 46 (2007).

3 Aust, 81.

4 Ibid., 47.

nor favorites amongst the various combatants, Baader seemed to bring with him a sense of daring and possibility which would always make him first amongst equals, for better or for worse. As such, following his capture, all attention was focused on how he could be freed from the state's clutches.

A plan was hatched, whereby Meinhof would use her press credentials to apply for permission to work with Baader on a book about youth centers, an area in which by now they both had some experience. The prison authorities reluctantly agreed, and on May 14 Baader was escorted under guard to meet her at the Institute for Social Issues Library in the West Berlin suburbs.

This provided the necessary opportunity. Once Baader and Meinhof were in the library, two young women entered the building: Irene Goergens, a teenager who Meinhof had recruited from her work with reform school kids, and Ingrid Schubert, a radical doctor from the West Berlin scene. They were followed by a masked and armed Gudrun Ensslin, and an armed man. Drawing their weapons, these rescuers moved to free Baader. When an elderly librarian, Georg Linke, attempted to intervene, he was shot in his liver.[1] The guards drew their weapons and opened fire, missing everyone, and all six jumped out of the library window and into the getaway car waiting on the street below.[2]

Barely a month after his arrest, Baader was once again free.

The library breakout made headlines around the world, both Meinhof and Ensslin being identified as likely participants. Journalists tried to outdo each other in their sensationalist tripe, describing the one as a middle-class poseur and the other as a former porn actress.[3] Headlines continued to be made when a neofascist arms dealer, Günther Voigt, was arrested and charged with selling the guerilla their guns.[4] Then, French journalist Michele Ray declared that she had met with Mahler, Meinhof, Ensslin, and Baader in West Berlin—she promptly sold the extensive interviews she had taped to *Spiegel*.[5]

---

1 According to several accounts, Linke was accidentally shot by the man at the scene. Apparently, he had two weapons, an air gun and a real gun, and he intended to scare him with the former, but got confused as to which was which. (MacDonald, 213.)

2 Aust, 6-9.

3 Neil Ascherson, "Leftists Disturbed by Violence of Berlin Gunmen," *Winnipeg Free Press*, July 4, 1970.

4 Ibid., Becker, 125.

5 Aust, 15-16.

The group had made an impression. Its first action had struck a chord. Yet this was very much a mixed blessing, as Astrid Proll, who had driven the getaway car during the jailbreak,[6] would later explain:

> *I think we were all very nervous; I remember some people throwing up. Because we weren't so wonderful criminals, we weren't so wonderful with the guns, we sort of involved a so-called criminal who could do it so much better than we, and... he was so nervous that he shot somebody. He didn't kill him, but he shot him very very badly, and that was really really very bad for the whole start of it.[7]*

As she elaborated elsewhere:

> *After a man had been severely hurt... we found ourselves on wanted lists. It was an accident that accelerated the development of the underground life of the group. Ulrike Meinhof, who had so far been at the fringes of the group, was all of a sudden wanted on every single billpost for attempted murder against a reward of DM 10,000... When we were underground there were no more discussions, there was only action.[8]*

In what would be a recurrent phenomenon, the state made use of the media frenzy around the prison-break to help push through new repressive legislation—in this case the so-called "Hand Grenade Law," by which West Berlin police were equipped with hand grenades, semi-automatic revolvers, and submachine guns.[9]

This was all hotly debated on the left, prompting the fugitives to send a letter to the radical newspaper *883*, in which they explained (somewhat defensively) the action and their future plans. At the insistence of the radical former film student Holger Meins who was working at *883* at the time and who would later himself become a leading figure in the RAF, the newspaper published the statement, making it the first public document from the guerilla. (Even without Meins's support, it would have been odd for *883* to not publish the text: Baader, Meinhof, Mahler, and Ensslin had all formerly served in the

---

6 Ben Lewis and Richard Klein, *Baader Meinhof: In Love With Terror* (United Kingdom: a Mentorn production for BBC FOUR, 2002).

7 Ibid.

8 Proll, 10.

9 Ascherson, "Leftists Disturbed."

editorial collective, as had several other individuals who would go on to join the guerilla.)[1]

The Red Army Faction had been born.

The next year was spent acquiring technical skills, including a trip to Jordan where more than a dozen of the aspiring German guerillas received training from the PLO. While this first trip may not have had great significance for the group, given the subsequent importance of its connection with certain Palestinian organizations, it may be useful to examine the context in which it occurred.

At the time, Jordan contained a very large Palestinian refugee population, one which had swollen since the 1967 Israeli Occupation of the West Bank and the Gaza Strip; by 1970, the Palestinians constituted roughly 1,000,000 of the country's total population of 2,299,000.

Based in the refugee camps, the PLO managed to constitute itself as a virtual parallel state within the country. Indeed, many considered that revolution in Jordan could be one step towards the defeat of Israel, an idea expressed by the slogan, "The road to Tel Aviv lies through Amman"—a sentiment which worried King Hussein, to say the least— as did the increasing use of Jordanian territory as a rear base area for all manner of Palestinian radical organizations.[2]

In September 1970, the left-wing Popular Front for the Liberation of Palestine skyjacked three Western aircraft, landing them in Dawson's Field, a remote desert airstrip in Jordan. This provided Hussein with the excuse he needed, and the PLO soon came under attack from the monarch's armed forces, supported by Israel. By the time a truce was brokered, between 4,000 and 10,000—Yassir Arafat would claim as many as 20,000—Palestinians had been killed, including many non-combatants. (This would be remembered as "Black September," and it was in memory of this massacre that the PLO's unofficial guerilla wing would adopt that name.)

Prior to this, the Palestinians' Jordanian bases were important sources of inspiration and education for revolutionaries, not only in the Arab world, but also in many European countries. While the largest number of visitors came from Turkey[3]—many of whom would stay and fight

---

1 Datenbank des deutschsprachigen Anarchismus: Periodika, "Agit 883," http://projekte.free.de/dada/dada-p/P0000921.HTM.

2 Helen Chapin Metz, Library of Congress Federal Research Division, *Israel, a Country Study* (Whitefish, Montana: Keesinger publishing 2004), 110.

3 Cengiz Candar, "A Turk in the Palestinian Resistance," *Journal of Palestine Studies* 30, no. 1. (Autumn, 2000): 68-82.

alongside the Palestinians—there were also Maoists, socialists, and aspiring guerillas from France, Denmark, Sweden, and, of course, West Germany. (It would be claimed that members of the Roaming Hash Rebels scene had already received training from the Palestinians, and Baumann has pointed to this as a turning point in its transformation into a guerilla underground.)[4]

Even during their Middle Eastern sojourn, the RAF continued to make headlines in Germany, Horst Mahler sending a photo of himself waving a gun and dressed like a fedayeen to a radical newspaper with the message, "Best wishes to your readers from the land of A Thousand and One Nights!"[5]

Juvenile theatrics aside, this trip signaled the very public beginning of an aspect of the RAF which would bedevil the police, namely, their proficient use of foreign countries as rear base areas. As has been discussed elsewhere:

> *Rear base areas are little discussed, but essential to guerillas. This is something precise: a large area or territory, bordering on the main battle zone, where the other side cannot freely operate. Either for reasons of remoteness or impenetrable mountain ranges, or because it crosses political boundaries.*[6]

The RAF would make extensive use of various Arab countries as rear base areas throughout their existence, places where one could go not only to train, but also to hide when Europe got too "hot." During the 1970s at least, it does not seem to have been the governments of these countries which provided the group with aid and succor, but rather various revolutionary Palestinian organizations which were deeply rooted in the refugee populations throughout the region. In this way, in the years following the Palestinians' defeat at the hands of Jordan's armed forces in 1970, Lebanon and the People's Democratic Republic of Yemen emerged as homes away from home for more than one West German revolutionary.

---

4 Baumann, 59: "There was a split when people got back from Palestine. The Palestinian faction said, 'things don't make sense the way they're going now. We have to really start with the armed struggle.' That meant giving up the Blues, the whole broad open scene."

5 Ascherson, "Leftists Disturbed."

6 Butch Lee, *Jailbreak Out Of History: The Re-Biography of Harriet Tubman* (Montreal: Kersplebedeb Publishing, 2000), 25.

Another source of foreign support, of course, was the "communist" German Democratic Republic—East Germany—from which the RAF and other guerilla groups would receive various forms of assistance over the years. As far as the RAF is concerned, it is unclear exactly how or when this relationship began. Certainly if it existed in the early seventies, this was very secret, and indeed unimagined on the radical left, for which the "other" German state remained a corrupt and authoritarian regime, alternately "Stalinist" or "revisionist," but in any case one from which little good could come.

And yet it is known that, as early as 1970, the GDR did choose to knowingly allow the guerilla to pass through its territory, for instance on flights to and from the Middle East. After the first trip to Jordan, it even detained one member—Hans-Jürgen Bäcker—and questioned him about the underground for twenty-four hours, but then released him.[1] Clearly, by the end of the decade, this policy had been extended to provide other sorts of assistance. It has also been claimed that even at the time of the 1970 training expedition, there were plans to relocate Meinhof's twin daughters to East Germany if their father won custody away from her sister.[2]

Given the unpopularity of the GDR, why was this aid accepted, and what effects did it have on the RAF?

The answer to the first of these questions is easy enough to guess: at first, East German "aid" seems to have been very limited in scope, really little more than turning a blind eye to what was going on.[3] Who could complain about that?

Eventually, as we will see, more substantial favors would be forthcoming: shelter, training, even new identities—and yet, for most of its history, there is absolutely no indication that the RAF was choosing its targets or formulating its ideology to please foreign patrons. Certainly in the 1970s, the RAF-*Stasi* connection seems to have been casual if

---

1 Aust, 99-100. Bäcker would claim that based on their questions, it was clear the East Germans were already well informed about the group's activities. In November 1972, Bommi Baumann was similarly detained at the East German border while in possession of false identification papers; he was similarly questioned, and provided information on almost one hundred people in the West German underground before being released. Jan-Hendrik Schulz "Zur Geschichte der Roten Armee Fraktion (RAF) und ihrer Kontexte: Eine Chronik," *Zeitgeschichte Online*, May 2007.

2 Ditfurth, 290. See Appendix V—Strange Stories: Peter Homann and Stefan Aust, pages 557-558.

3 *Deutsche Presse-Agentur*, "Stasi soll RAF über Razzien informiert haben," September 29, 2007.

not ephemeral.

At most, one might perhaps argue a case of the GDR egging the guerilla on as a way to get at the Americans, in the context of the ongoing conflagration in Vietnam.

Certainly, throughout the 1970s, the Palestinian connection was of far greater importance, and yet the guerilla's first visit to the Middle East ended on an unpromising note: according to several reports, the West Germans were far from ideal guests, and the Palestinians eventually sent them on their way.

They returned to West Berlin—via the GDR—as the summer of 1970 came to an end.[4]

The group now set about obtaining cars and locating safehouses. New contacts were made, and new members were recruited, among them Ilse Stachowiak, Ali Jansen, Uli Scholze, Beate Sturm, Holger Meins, and Jan-Carl Raspe, this last being an old friend of Meinhof's, and himself a founding member of Kommune 2.[5] Some of these individuals would soon think better of their decision and drop out at the first opportunity, others would determine the very course of the RAF, and in some cases give their lives in the struggle.

But first, the young guerilla needed to acquire funds, and to this end a daring combination of bank raids was planned in cooperation with members of the Roaming Hash Rebels scene.[6] Within ten minutes, on September 29, three different West Berlin banks were hit: the revolutionaries managed to make off with over 220,000 DM (just over $60,000) without firing a shot or suffering a single arrest.[7] As Horst Mahler's former legal assistant Monika Berberich, who had herself joined the RAF, would later explain, "It was not about redistributing wealth, it was about getting money, and we weren't going to mug grannies in the streets."[8]

The "triple coup" was a smashing success. Things were looking good.

Then, on October 8, police received an anonymous tip about two safehouses in West Berlin: Mahler and Berberich, as well as Ingrid

---

4 Aust, 99, 101.

5 Kommune 2 was another West Berlin commune, one with a more "serious" and "intellectual" reputation than the yippiesque K.1.

6 Reinders, Viehmann, and Fritzsch.

7 Aust, 108.

8 *Baader Meinhof: In Love With Terror.*

Schubert, Irene Goergens, and Brigitte Asdonk, were all arrested. (It was suspected that Hans-Jürgen Bäcker had snitched to the police. He was confronted and denied the charge, but quickly parted ways with the guerilla. The fact that he was left unmolested should be taken into account when evaluating later claims that the RAF executed suspected traitors or those who wished to leave its ranks.)[1]

Following these arrests, the RAF moved to transfer operations outside of West Berlin, and members of the group began crossing over into West Germany proper. During this period, the fledgling guerilla burglarized the town halls of two small towns, taking blank ID cards, passports, and official stamps for use in future operations.

On December 20, Karl-Heinz Ruhland and RAF members Ali Jansen and Beate Sturm were stopped by police in Oberhausen. Ruhland, who was only peripheral to the group, surrendered while Jansen and Sturm made their getaway. The next day Jansen was arrested along with RAF member Uli Scholze while trying to steal a Mercedes-Benz. (Sturm soon left the guerilla, as did Scholze when he was released one day after his capture. Ruhland cooperated with police, helping to reveal the location of safehouses and testifying in court against RAF members. Jansen received a ten year sentence for shooting at police.)

On February 10, 1971, Astrid Proll was spotted by Frankfurt police along with fellow RAF member Manfred Grashof. The police opened fire in a clear attempt to kill the two as they fled; luckily, they missed. Subsequently, the cops involved would claim that they had shot in self-defense, yet unbeknownst to them the entire scene had been observed by the *Verfassungsschutz*, who filed a report detailing how neither of the guerillas had even drawn their weapons. This fact would remain suppressed by the state for years.[2]

The alleged "firefight" with Proll and Grashof was added to a growing list of propaganda stories used by the police to justify a massive nationwide search, with Federal Minister of the Interior Hans-Dietrich Genscher declaring the RAF to be "Public Enemy Number One." Apartments were raided in Gelsenkirchen, Frankfurt, Hamburg, and Bremen, yet the guerilla managed to elude capture.

Meanwhile, the trial of Horst Mahler, Ingrid Schubert, and Irene Goergens opened in West Berlin on March 1. Schubert and Goergens were charged with attempted murder and using force in the Baader

---

1 Aust, 111-112.
2 Ibid., 140.

jailbreak, while Mahler (who had arranged to be in court during the action, and so had an alibi) was charged as an accessory, and with illegal possession of a firearm.

This first RAF trial would set the tone for twenty years of collusion between the media, the police, and shadowy elements intent on presenting the guerilla in the most horrific light. The term "psychological warfare" was eventually adopted by the left to describe the phenomenon.

Already in February, police had announced that the RAF had plans to kidnap Chancellor Willy Brandt in order to force the state to release Mahler.[3] The guerilla would subsequently deny this charge, claiming it was intended to make them look like "political idiots."[4]

Then, on February 25, a seven-year-old boy was kidnapped. Newspapers announced that his captors were demanding close to $50,000 ransom as well as the release of "the left-wing lawyer in Berlin," which journalists quickly explained must be a reference to Mahler.[5]

Clearly horrified, Mahler made a public appeal to the kidnappers to release the child.[6] At the same time the provincial government of North Rhine-Westphalia agreed to pay the ransom—the boy was from a working-class family that could not afford such a sum.[7]

Arrangements were made, a well-known lawyer agreeing to act as the go between. The money was delivered on Saturday February 27 and a young Michael Luhmer was released in the woods outside Munich, suffering from influenza but otherwise unharmed. According to the lawyer who personally delivered the money to the kidnappers, they denied being in the least bit interested in Mahler or anyone else from the RAF. Indeed, he came away with the impression that they were in fact "a rightist group like the Nazi party."[8] Police later announced that they suspected the son of a former SS officer of being involved in the plot.[9]

---

3 Associated Press, "Paper reports plot to kidnap Willy Brandt," *European Stars and Stripes*, February 13, 1971.

4 See page 84.

5 Associated Press, "Terrorists Take Child as Hostage," *Troy Record*, February 25, 1971.

6 Associated Press,"Wrong Boy Kidnaped, Released; Ransom Paid," *Panama City News Herald*, February 27, 1971.

7 Ibid.

8 Associated Press, "Kidnaped German Boy, 7, Freed After Ransom," *European Stars and Stripes*, February 29, 1971.

9 Associated Press, "Police Hunting SS Member's Son in Kidnapings," *European Stars and Stripes*, March 2, 1971.

This first kidnapping occurred just as Mahler, Schubert, and Goergens were about to go on trial. This is what could be called a "false flag" action, a term referring to an attack carried out by certain parties under the banner of another group to which they are hostile in order to discredit them. As we shall see, false flag attacks were to plague the RAF throughout the 1970s, as all manner of antisocial crimes would be carried out or threatened by persons pretending to be from the guerilla.

The RAF repeatedly denied its involvement in these actions, and yet the slander often stuck.

Doubly vexing is the fact that in most of these false flag actions, no firm evidence has ever come to light proving who in fact was responsible. Suspicions have ranged from some secret service working for the state, or for NATO, or else perhaps neofascists, or some combination thereof. Or perhaps these were "normal" criminal acts, and it was the media or police who were fabricating details to tie them to the RAF.

Judging from experiences elsewhere in Europe, it is entirely possible that elements within the state, within NATO, and within the far right collaborated in some of these attacks. Such scenarios are known, for instance, to have played themselves out in France, Italy, and Turkey. The goal for such operations was generally not simply to discredit the left-wing guerilla, but rather to create a general climate of fear in which people would rally to the hard right.

In most cases, we may never know, but amazingly enough, there was a second false flag kidnapping during the first RAF trial, and the authors of this second crime actually ended up admitting the ruse.

On Sunday April 25, newspapers reported that a university professor and his friend had been kidnapped by the guerilla, which was threatening to execute them if Mahler, Schubert, and Goergens were not released. The kidnappers were allegedly demanding that the three be allowed to travel to a country of their choosing, and insisted that this be announced on television.[1]

Two days later, the men were found, one of them tied to a tree. The kidnappers, however, were nowhere in sight. After some questioning, the "captives" broke down and admitted that they had staged the entire thing in the hopes of scaring people into voting against the "left-wing"

---

1 United Press International, "Professor Endangered by Kidnapper's Threat," *Dominion Post*, April 25, 1971.

SPD in the provincial elections in Schleswig-Holstein.[2] The mastermind behind this plan, Jürgen Rieger,[3] was active in neofascist circles; he would eventually be sentenced to six months in prison as a result.

As a corollary to these staged actions, the police were happy to oblige by setting the scene at the trial itself:

> *The criminal court in the Moabit prison had been transformed into a fortress for the trial. There were policemen armed with submachine guns patrolling the corridors, the entrances and exits; outside the building stood vehicles with their engines running and carrying teams of men, there were officers carrying radio equipment, and more units waited in the inner courtyard to go into action if needed.*[4]

Far-right hoaxes were helping to justify shocking levels of police militarization and repression. One did not need to be a paranoid conspiracy theorist to think that the state was more than willing to play dirty in order to get rid of its new armed opponents and that the talk of a "fascist drift" was more than mere rhetoric.

Not that the radical left was unwilling to fight for the captured combatants, though kidnapping innocent children or academics would never feature amongst its strategies. When kidnappings would eventually be carried out, the targets were always important members of the establishment, men with personal ties to the system against which the guerilla fought.

In 1971, however, nobody was in a position to carry out such an operation, and so the struggle for the prisoners' freedom took place largely in the streets. As the trial wrapped up, rioting broke out for two days in West Berlin: "youths blocked traffic, and smashed store and car windows," all the while shouting slogans like "Free Mahler!" and "Hands off Mahler!"[5]

---

2 United Press International, "West German Professor Admits Kidnaping Hoax," *European Stars and Stripes*, April 27, 1971.

3 Jürgen Rieger is a lawyer whose career has been devoted to defending those charged under Germany's anti-Nazi laws. Ironically, in 2006, both Rieger and Mahler, the latter by this time a Holocaust denier himself, would end up working on the legal defense team of neo-nazi publisher Ernst Zundel, who was charged in connection with the publication of Holocaust denial literature.

4 Aust, 144.

5 Associated Press, "Berlin Cops, Leftists Clash for 2nd Night," *European Stars and Stripes*, May 17, 1971.

Clearly, although its capacities were not yet developed, a section of the left was willing to carry out militant actions in support of the guerilla, while itself preferring to remain aboveground.

In late May, after twenty-two days in court, the verdicts came down. Goergens was sentenced to four years youth custody, and Schubert received a six-year sentence.[1]

It should be noted that both women would soon have additional years tacked on, as they also faced charges relating to various bank robberies.[2]

As for Horst Mahler, he was found not guilty, but was kept in custody as the state appealed the verdict. He was also facing additional charges stemming from the bank robberies.[3]

Throughout the trial, other combatants had been picked up by the state.

On April 12, 1971, Ilse Stachowiak was recognized by a policeman and arrested in Frankfurt. Known by her nickname "Tinny," Stachowiak was probably the youngest member of the guerilla, having joined in 1970 at the age of sixteen.

The next day, Rolf Heißler was arrested trying to rob a bank in Munich. Heißler had previously been active in the Tupamaros-Munich (a Bavarian group inspired by the Tupamaros-West Berlin),[4] but had followed his friend Brigitte Mohnhaupt into the RAF.

Then, on May 6, not three months after her narrow escape in Frankfurt, Astrid Proll was recognized in Hamburg by a gas station attendant who called the police—she tried to escape by car, but was surrounded by armed cops and arrested.[5]

Two documents appeared about this time, each allegedly produced by the RAF. The first of these, *Regarding the Armed Struggle in West Europe,* was published under the innocent title "New Traffic Regulations" by the radical West Berlin publishing house of Klaus Wagenbach.[6] Not only did this lead to Wagenbach receiving a suspended

---

1 Jillian Becker, *Hitler's Children: The Story of the Baader Meinhof Gang* (London: Panther Granada Publishing, 1978), 307.

2 When Goergens was finally released in May 1977, she did not return to the guerilla. Schubert, as we shall see, never made it out of prison alive.

3 Becker, 307

4 Baumann, 63.

5 Macdonald, 214-215.

6 Aust, 142.

nine-month sentence under §129[7]—the catch-all "supporting a criminal organization" paragraph of the Orwellian 1951 security legislation—but the document was quickly disavowed by the RAF itself: it had been written by Mahler in prison, without consultation with any of the others, and did not sit well with the rest of the group.

While Mahler would remain in the RAF for the time being, this was the first visible sign of an ongoing process of estrangement between the former attorney and the rest of the guerilla.

Almost at the same time as Mahler's document began to circulate, a second text, one which enjoyed the approval of the entire RAF, was released. On May 1, at the annual May Day demonstrations, supporters distributed what became known as the RAF's foundational manifesto, emblazoned with a red star and a Kalashnikov submachine gun: *The Urban Guerilla Concept*. This text was widely reprinted, not only in radical publications like *883*, but in the mainstream *Spiegel*, the result of a deal whereby the liberal weekly agreed to "donate" 20,000 DM to youth shelters.[8]

Drawing heavily on the guerillas' experiences in the APO, and what they saw as the weaknesses of the New Left, *The Urban Guerilla Concept* tried to answer some of the questions people were asking about the RAF, while critiquing both the anarchist scene and the K-groups (referred to respectfully as "the proletarian organizations"). It also constituted an open invitation to join with the guerilla in the underground.

It was a document aimed at the seasoned activists of the left, speaking to their sense of frustration with the legal struggle in the hope that they might be won over to clandestinity.

7 Cobler, 113.
8 *tageszeitung* "30 Jahre Deutscher Herbst 'Die RAF war nicht ganz so schlicht,'" *Deutschlandradio*, October 17, 2007.

Faced With This Justice System, We Can't Be Bothered Defending Ourselves

This was Thorwald Proll's closing statement in the Frankfurt Department Store Firebombing Trial. (M. & S.)

The trial for conspiracy to commit arson followed the trial for committing arson. But that's obviously another question. Justice is the justice of the ruling class. Faced with a justice system that speaks in the name of the ruling class—and speaks dishonestly—we can't be bothered defending ourselves. Faced with a justice system that forced a student couple underground by using laws regarding breach of the public peace and causing a disturbance from the year 1870/71 to sentence them to 12 months without parole, we can't be bothered defending ourselves (breachers of the public peace, torch their ramshackle peace).

Faced with a justice system that uses laws from 1870/71 and then talks about what's right—and speaks dishonestly—we can't be bothered defending ourselves. Faced with a justice system that gave Daniel Cohn-Bendit[1] (*lex Benda, lex Bendit*) an 8-month suspended sentence for jumping over a security fence, we can't be bothered defending ourselves. Faced with a justice system that, on the other hand, only pursued most Nazi trials in order to ease their own guilty right-wing conscience, trials in which they charge anyone that swore the Führer Oath[2] as a criminal, an act which the entire justice system quite willingly engaged in itself in 1933; faced with a justice system like that, we can't be bothered defending ourselves.

Faced with a justice system that prosecutes the minor murderers of Jews and lets the major murderers of Jews run around free, we can't be bothered defending ourselves. Faced with a justice system that in 1933 shamelessly plunged into fascism and in 1945 just as shamelessly deserted

---

1 Earlier that summer, Daniel Cohn-Bendit had received an eight-month suspended sentence for getting through security at a protest against the German Book Trade's "Peace Prize" being bestowed upon President Léopold Sédar Senghor of Senegal.

2 An oath of fealty to Hitler and the NSDAP that all people working in the public sector were obliged to swear. Millions of people swore this oath for no other reason than to retain their employment.

it, we can't be bothered defending ourselves. Furthermore, faced with a justice system that already in the Weimar Republic always sentenced leftists more heavily (Ernst Niekisch,[3] Ernst Toller[4]) than right wingers (Adolf Hitler[5]), that rewarded the murderers of Rosa Luxemburg and Karl Liebknecht[6] (and in so doing became complicit in their deaths), we can't be bothered defending ourselves. Comrades, we want to take a moment to remember Rosa Luxemburg and Karl Liebknecht—stand up!—the eye of the law sits in this court.

Faced with a justice system that never dismantled its authoritarian structure, but constantly renews it, we can't be bothered defending ourselves. Faced with a justice system that says might makes right and might comes before right (might is always right), we can't be bothered defending ourselves. All power to freedom! Faced with a justice system that defends property and possessions better than it does human beings, we can't be bothered defending ourselves. Faced with a justice system that is an instrument of social order, we can't be bothered defending ourselves.

Faced with a justice system that makes laws against the people rather than for them, we can't be bothered defending ourselves. Human rights only for the right humans (the state that leans to the right). Right is what the state does, and it's always right. The state is the only criminal activity allowed. In a capitalist democracy such as this, in an indirect democracy such as this, it is possible for anyone to end up ruling over anyone, and that's how it should stay, and don't ask for how much longer. The ruling morality is bourgeois morality, and bourgeois morality is immoral. Bourgeois morality is and will remain immoral. If it is reformed, it will only result in a new form of

---

3 Ernst Niekisch, briefly involved in the Bavarian Soviet Republic of 1919, went on to become a leader of German chauvinist "National Bolshevism"—it is unclear why Proll singles him out as an example of the Weimar regime persecuting leftists, although under the Nazis he would be sentenced to life imprisonment for "literary high treason" in 1937.

4 Ernst Toller was a Bavarian Jew and an anarchist who was imprisoned for his role on the short-lived Bavarian Soviet Republic of 1919. (He subsequently went into exile, eventually committing suicide in his hotel room in New York City in 1939.)

5 On April 1, 1924, Hitler was sentenced to five years for his November 8, 1923, attempted fascist coup, known as the Beer Hall Putsch. He was pardoned and released in December of 1924, having served less than a year of his sentence.

6 Luxemburg and Liebknecht were leading figures in the failed 1918 German communist uprising. They were both captured, tortured, and murdered by right-wing militias, the *Freikorps*.

immorality (and nothing more). Faced with a justice system that undermines the ethical underpinnings of the people (whatever they may be), we can't be bothered defending ourselves. This state prosecutor is nothing more than a piece of the criminal justice system. He requested 6 years of prison time.

Furthermore, faced with a justice system that says it represents the people, but means that it represents the ruling class, we can't be bothered defending ourselves. Faced with a justice system that works to assure the ongoing reproduction of existing relationships, we can't be bothered defending ourselves. Faced with a justice system for which the (so-called) criminal class is and will remain the criminal class, we can't be bothered defending ourselves. What does return to society mean? Back to which society? Back to the capitalist society where you will have the opportunity to re-offend? Back to the bourgeois, capitalist society that is itself a prison, which amounts to going from one hole to another.

Every reform to criminal law only reforms the existing criminal injustice; criminal law is criminal injustice; the sentence is the injustice. I wouldn't again offend against society, if they didn't give me another reason to do so. How am I supposed to return changed to an unchanged society, and so on, and so forth. It is not the laws that need to be changed; it's the society that must be changed. We want a socialist society. Faced with a justice system that plays homage to an abstract concept of law (Roman law is Bohemian law) and does not see individuals as the result of their society, we can't be bothered defending ourselves. Faced with a justice system that treats defendants as second-class citizens, we can't be bothered defending ourselves.

Furthermore, faced with a justice system that is a system of the ruling class, we can't be bothered defending ourselves. (And furthermore) faced with a justice system that doesn't reduce delinquency, but creates ever more of it (guilty verdicts and acquittals), we can't be bothered defending ourselves (the outcome can only serve their interests). In an authoritarian democracy like this one, it can never amount to more than an assessment of guilt or innocence. The judge sentences the individual, not the society and not himself. What's the magic word? The magic word is power, and it means the death of freedom! What do we have here that does not come from Nietzsche, that sociopath? For example, the will to power. You should think about power, but do not think that power thinks about disempowering itself at some point; ergo: destroy power (the question of power, the power of the question). Faced with a justice system that wants power and not freedom, we can't be bothered defending ourselves (what freedom do you mean—bourgeois freedom is servitude, and socialist freedom is a long way off).

Furthermore, faced with a justice system that seeks to criminalize Kommune 1 and has persecuted them with an endless series of trials, we can't be bothered defending ourselves. Such a justice system should itself be put on trial. Faced with a justice system that seeks to criminalize a section of the SDS, we can't be bothered defending ourselves. How can the public peace of 1870/71 be broken in 1967/68? Yet again: torch this ramshackle peace!

Furthermore, faced with a justice system with a concept of law—a deceitful concept—that is shaped by the opinions of the ruling class (already the case with Franz von Liszt[1] in 1882) we can't be bothered defending ourselves. Furthermore, faced with a justice system that doesn't see crime as a social phenomenon and which passes sentences that serve no social function (Franz von Liszt), we can't be bothered defending ourselves. Faced with a justice system that speaks of punishment—meaning oppression, meaning repression—helping the offender, while in fact defending bourgeois society, always defending it, defending it to the end; faced with such a justice system, we can't be bothered defending ourselves.

Quotes from the first draft of the reforms to the criminal code: "The bitter necessity of punishment." "Responsibility lies with the law breakers" (and not the representatives of the law), "given the flawed nature of people" (and so it will remain in a capitalist society such as this, in which antiauthoritarian structures that promote perfection don't exist and there are no examples of moral perfection—the principle of guilt, which guarantees the continuation of the principle of punishment, lives on, spelling the death of freedom and assuring the integrity of power). Another quote from the first draft of the criminal law reforms (this will be the last one): "(W)hat the principle of punishment presupposes is a virtually unchallenged standard of criminal law, etc., etc." When will this stop?

Faced with a justice system that holds that the irrational standards of criminal law and criminology are appropriate, that denies the reality of the capitalist social order, that denies and suppresses psychology and

1 Franz von Liszt (not to be confused with his cousin, the composer Franz Liszt) was a Prussian law professor whose work heavily influenced the 1882 Marburger Program, a conservative document that influenced the 1933 Nazi German Prevention of Crime Act.

the study of crime in a particularly nauseating way, constantly imped-
ing them, that treats criminology as a science of social relationships;
faced with such a justice system, we can't be bothered defending ourselves. Furthermore, faced with a justice system that represents the law
of the ruling class—represents duplicity—we can't be bothered defending ourselves.

Furthermore, bourgeois morality is and remains immoral, and if
reformed, it is only as a new immorality. All attempts at reform are
pointless, because they are inherent to the system. We demand the resignation of Minister of Justice Heinemann (also a pointless demand).
Where is the judge who will turn his back on this crap and join the
general strike, instead of remaining eternally stuck up to his armpits
in this shit? Where are the antiauthoritarian judges? I can't see them.
This is your chance, Herr Zoebe,[1] to be the first. I wrote that before I
knew you. Later, you responded to the word democracy like it was lep-
rosy, which is to say, you shrunk away from the concept. And for you,
resocialization sends you into a rage; it's the final blow. And for you it
should be the final blow. Always: the final blow.

Faced with a justice system that has completely authoritarian judges,
like the judge Schwalbe,[2] we can't be bothered defending ourselves (but
one Schwalbe doesn't make for an authoritarian summer). Faced with
a justice system that has judges like the judge in Hamburg, who on
August 15 of this year, following a 2½ minute hearing, sentenced a
young worker to 4 months with the possibility of parole, beginning at
Easter, with the comment that the young worker should be happy—in
spite of the brevity of the hearing—that he was given a chance to clarify
his political motivations, and then went on to tell this young worker
that he should stop worrying about things that don't concern him; faced
with a justice system that is made up of such judges, we can't be bothered defending ourselves. Yet again: torch this ramshackle peace.

Faced with a justice system that has judges like those that presided
over the Timo Rinnelt trial,[3] once more extending the reach of the
German billy club, we can't be bothered defending ourselves.

And finally, faced with a justice system that has judges like the judge

---

1 Gerhard Zoebe was the judge in this case.

2 A judge in Frankfurt who often presided over trials against left-wing defendants.

3 In 1964, seven year-old Timo Rinnelt of Wiesbaden was kidnapped and murdered.
Some years later, his neighbour, a twenty-seven year-old man, was arrested for the
crime. In 1968, he received a life sentence.

presiding in the case against Jürgen Bartsch,[4] who was sentenced to life imprisonment on the grounds that if he had wanted to he could have struggled to control his abnormal appetites (whatever that means), with the judge saying in conclusion, "And may God help you to learn to control you appetites"—so God and not society—and for such a judge it would be preferable if he had never been born or had died long ago; faced with such a justice system, we can't be bothered defending ourselves.

It has been said that the trial of Jürgen Bartsch was the trial of the century. It was actually a trial against this century, and the sentence spoke for this century, which is to say, it spoke for the morality of the preceding century (it will only get worse), which in this trial was celebrated as a barbaric triumph. When the judgment was read, the spectators, a petit bourgeois gathering, clapped and cheered. Nobody forbid that. The teeth of justice were chattering, but nobody heard that. Child murderers are useful. They eliminate all consciousness that criminals were once themselves children (the authoritarian upbringing). A hundred children of West German families are beaten to death every year. Beaten to death. Child murderers work to ease our conscience about this slaughter. And what of the daily murder of children in Vietnam (with its breathtaking body-count)? What do respectable people pray for? Today we get our daily ration of murder (The Springer papers are the centerpiece of every breakfast).

Furthermore, bourgeois morality is the ruling morality, and bourgeois morality is immoral. Faced with a justice system that has state prosecutors like state prosecutor Griebel,[5] who told me "under four eyes"[6] that he holds Marx's teachings in the highest regard (but what does he do about it?), that he is as much a prisoner of a labyrinthine bureaucracy as I (but what does he do against it?). He accuses the left here of only wanting to change superficial things, but nothing beyond that (but he bears the mark of Cain of repression on his forehead), and he had the effrontery to bare his broken bourgeois heart to me, saying that on the one hand he is troubled by the rigidity of the ruling conditions, while on the other—how grotesque—he continued to speak of the legitimacy of the laws of 1870/71—speaking deceptively—faced

---

4 Jürgen Bartsch, a German serial killer, who as a child suffered both emotional and sexual abuse, was responsible for four brutal child murders in the 60s.

5 Walter Griebel was the prosecutor in the case at hand.

6 In German *"unter vier Augen"*; this is an obvious reference to the Nazi term for a meetings involving only Hitler and one of his close associates. The content of these discussions was meant to stay between the two men.

with such a justice system, I can't be bothered defending myself, and we can't be bothered defending ourselves. Imprison the state prosecutors. Where is the state prosecutor who will indict the state?

Faced with a justice system that is charging us with life-threatening arson, we can't be bothered defending ourselves. Faced with a justice system, in the eyes of which, we have every reason to believe, we are politically tainted from the outset, we cannot defend ourselves (all the charged are arsonists and all judges are honest men). Yet again: torch this ramshackle peace.

And furthermore, faced with a justice system that speaks for the ruling class—and speaks deceptively—we can't be bothered defending ourselves.

Faced with a justice system with custodial judges as authoritarian as judge Kappel, who gave every impression of being convinced of the guilt (whatever that is) of all of the accused before the trial even started. Amongst other things, his macho aggressiveness is such that he said to me, "Take your hand out of your pocket." When I put my other hand in my pocket (obviously not the same one), he didn't say anything, he just laughed, and my laughter caught in my throat at the thought that he and I could ever laugh at the same thing for the same reason—a question of consciousness. Faced with such a justice system, I can't be bothered defending myself, and we can't be bothered defending ourselves.

Faced with such a decadent justice system, we can't be bothered defending ourselves (a legal right is only what is right legally). Faced with a justice system that grotesquely misuses detention, I can't be bothered defending myself. If you have a fixed address, the justice system holds on to you until you lose it, which is to say, until you're tossed out. Then the justice system says, "Ah, you don't have one. In any event, if you're released you will no longer have one. That essentially makes you a flight risk." Faced with a justice system that grotesquely abuses preventive detention, we can't be bothered defending ourselves. In this way they reveal the abyss that is the justice system. If you have a fixed address, the police make sure you lose it, so they can take you into custody. It happened to August Klee, who like me has been held in detention for some months now. While all of this has not been enough to convince me that life is a theatrical drama, I do believe that the remand centre can be. When Klee was detained in this way, the police assured him that it was not the first time they had done this; making the criminal police potential criminals.

Risk of flight always offers the necessary excuse. For instance, August Klee is also classified a flight risk because his closest relatives, first and foremost among them his wife, live outside of Germany. He must divorce her (what's that about?) if he wants to get out. On the other hand, if you live in Germany, but do not live with your wife (what's that about?), if you have no family ties (because you're not chained to that structure), then you're a flight risk. If you lived outside the country 40 years ago, you're a flight risk. If you've recently come back from a trip (and not from some crappy tourist trip), in that case you're a flight risk. If you're a foreigner, then you're a flight risk. (I can recite all of this by heart). If there is a mix-up of some sort in your arrest, as occurred recently on *Hammelsgasse* (bourgeois freedom is a *Hammelsgasse[1]*), there's no need for concern, phony paperwork will be prepared. Here the danger is that one will be silenced.

Following conviction, it may be the case that you will be released for good behavior. He, however, has been refused this, because he has behaved so well that he has become institutionalized, and will surely be unable to find his bearings on the outside. He must remain inside until the end. This is an example of the risk of unadorned reconstruction. If you happen to be an arsonist, there is the danger of evidence being suppressed, etc.; faced with such a justice system, we can't be bothered defending ourselves.

Faced with a justice system that supports a prison system that attacks and violates the personal freedom and dignity of 365 people every second—first the attack, then the violation—we can't be bothered defending ourselves.

What is permissible and what is not permissible in remand: prisoners in remand are permitted to do what the justice system—acting as administrators—permits them to do. You are not permitted to be afraid. You are not permitted to lie around in bed, but you can lie under the bed. You are not permitted to play ping-pong with multiple balls; you are only permitted one ball. You are not permitted to refuse dinner; you are not permitted to show any kind of defiance. As a revolutionary socialist, you can never show defiance.

---

1 *Hammelsgasse*, a street in an upper class neighbourhood in Frankfurt, could be translated literally as Mutton Alley; a play on words referencing sheeps being led to the slaughter is intended.

A rate of 1.23 DM[1] per day is designated for meals (what a fantastic amount). You are not permitted to throw your dinner in the guard's face, or he's not responsible for what happens next. The guards are prisoners just like you, and most of them know it. The guards are only the little warlords.

You are not permitted to smoke outside of your cell, only in it. You are permitted to experience the hell of it all inside your cell. You are not permitted to light fires, because you can't use the fire alarm, because you can't reach it, because you can't leave your cell, because the door is locked.

You are not permitted to take the opportunity to engage in discussion with the other prisoners, the so-called criminals, whatever might come out of it. Let's be perfectly clear, they are staple products of the capitalist social order. You need to be clear about this.

Furthermore, you are not permitted to hang anything on the walls, but you are permitted to hang up the memo that tells you that you are not permitted to hang anything on the walls. You are not permitted to loiter. You are not permitted to lean against the wall. You are not permitted to just hang around. You should spend every day formulating a more thorough understanding of the justice system.

If you go to see the minister, don't forget it's just a crutch. Don't go to church; God is dead, but Che lives. Study the rudiments of socialism, and you will have everything you need.

You are only permitted a half-hour a day to walk. You are not permitted to yell out the window. You are not permitted to have as many comrades as you like. You are permitted to spend 35 DM[2] per week. That's how it goes in Hessen. And don't forget, Hessen has the most liberal penal system. You are not permitted to drink as much coffee as you wish. You are not permitted to drink any alcohol. You are not permitted to smoke hash. You are not permitted to consume in the way you wish, and you are not permitted to consume what you wish, and all of that in a society based on consumption. Note that in prison consumption becomes a treat.

Correspondence is monitored. Sexual intercourse is not monitored, but then there's not much of it. Adultery is not permitted (what's that about?), but it is not permitted to consummate a marriage (what's that about?). All of those in the hole who still cling onto bourgeois existence

---

1 Roughly forty cents.
2 Roughly $11.20.

(woe be it to those who see no alternative), and that's most of them, will be driven crazy by the bourgeois social order. That's how it is. How, for instance, are they to maintain their marriages? They will all fail, and that's good.

Every citizen should go to prison to gain a real understanding of the situation.

Every socialist should go to prison to gain a real understanding of the situation.

Every citizen should go to prison so that he develops a correct relationship to socialism.

Yet every individual capitalist or socialist has the opportunity to be the first to blow up a prison. Don't read any of the Springer papers; burn them. Then blow Springer up.

You are not permitted to beat off or masturbate if that's what you want to do. You can do what you want with your body. The duality of homosexuality exists. If new sexual laws are passed, will you still be permitted to fuck chicks; not to speak of other prisoners. In Butzbach penitentiary there was a flourishing trade in bras. Forced sodomy (what's that all about?). Rape the guards that torment you.

You aren't permitted to commit a break-in, but you are permitted to break out. Out of prison I mean. Attempted escape is not an indictable offense. You are not permitted to receive photos 1-3 from the Kommune 1 book, *Klau Mich*,[3] because their obscene content is a threat to the moral order of the remand centre.

The way Glojne, alias Globne, the Regional Court Judge explained it to me in a letter—who asked?—you are not permitted to hang anything in your cell or hang yourself in the cell. You are not permitted to hide in your cell. Try it some time. You are not permitted to take anything from the library. You are not permitted to lose your mind. You are permitted to buy food and specialty items, as well as other items you require in keeping with a reasonable lifestyle. You are not permitted to violate these conditions. The administrators decide what reasonable means (each individual administrator in this mental asylum).

If for reasons of order they want to reduce the number of newspapers and magazines you receive, you must attempt to have them delivered to you by means of disorder—in the sense of antiauthoritarian order. You must pull them out of the guard's hands, just as he pulled them out of yours. You have to try. You can't give up without trying. If the warden

---

3 Steal Me.

addresses you with *du*, you must also address him with *du*.[1] You mustn't work—for 80 pfennig[2] a day. You can't let yourself be exploited. The justice system practices the most secretive, most efficient and most disgraceful exploitation possible. It fattens itself by using primitive capitalist techniques in a modern capitalist system. Grievances are pointless, particularly as you are not permitted to file common grievances. Grievances are suppressed at will. Grievances are pointless, because you must submit them to the ruling structure. Common dispositions are common dispositions, and solitary dispositions are solitary dispositions. You can't give in to loneliness. You can't lose the dialogue. You can't lose the socialist dialogue. In prison you have nothing to lose and lose nothing. You have everything to win.

Note that the rights and responsibilities of remand prisoners mentioned here are an introduction to inequality and bondage; you're a first class citizen, you're a second class citizen, you're a fourth class citizen, you're a fifth class citizen, etc., and that's what you'll remain. You're a criminal and that's what you will remain. Conduct regarding the attendants: the prisoner must immediately disengage himself from the attendants; he must immediately disengage.

Life in the penal institution is one in which work time, free time, and quiet time are carefully divided, and the prisoner is bound to this division. Life in the penal institution is life in barracks. It consists of sitting around. Life in the penal institution is divided into time for oppression, time for bondage, and time of dead silence. The time of unconsciousness is over. The time for realism has begun. Bourgeois life is its own kind of remand. If you didn't already know that, now you do. You are not permitted to live and you are not permitted to die; you are not permitted to die and you are not permitted to live. Exactly. You are not permitted to run amok in the house. You are not permitted, of your own free will, to leave your assigned place. You are not permitted to break out. You are not permitted to scream, yell, or speak out the window. You aren't allowed to speak to your cellmates (what's that about?). You are not permitted to threaten the security of the institution. You are not permitted to withhold, store, or use anything. You are not permitted to retain anything, etc.

---

1 German has two forms of the singular you; *du*, which is used with social inferiors, younger people, and very close friends, and *Sie*, which is the polite form of address. What the writer is saying is that patronizing behaviour should be answered with patronizing behaviour.

2 Roughly thirty cents.

You must do everything that you are not permitted to do, and you must not let your guard down. Always think about it. Send every state prosecutor to prison. You are not permitted to defend yourself. Never. Those who defend themselves incriminate themselves. Do not forget that. You are not permitted to have unauthorized telephone contact. Your correspondence is monitored. Letters you send from prison cannot be sealed. You are not permitted to seal them yourself. You are not permitted to... You are not permitted to...

You cannot give in to fatigue. You cannot, at risk of retribution, pass parliamentary representative Güde[3] in the street without pushing him around. He brings out the best in you. But beforehand you must paint your hand red. The left one, obviously.

Yet again (in the hole), you cannot give in to fatigue. Concentrate. You're sitting in bourgeois capitalism's concentration camp. Beyond that, the prisoner has a cell to keep clean. The most oppressive power in prison is the power of cleanliness. Cleaning is the major form of torture. You are not permitted to get dirty while cleaning things. Only clean up when it suits you. Otherwise you aren't in prison; prison is in you. Keep in mind: the cleaner the cell, the more complete the hell. Furthermore, the prisoner and his seven suitcases[4] and his cell can be searched at any time. When you are searched, ask them if they're looking for new people, etc., etc.

I can't continue talking about this. Faced with a justice system that has such an indescribable prison system, we can't be bothered defending ourselves. Such a justice system must itself be indicted. Such a justice system must be exposed by the revolutionary process. It is the responsibility of every antiauthoritarian judge to take legal action against this justice system. We encourage the antiauthoritarian segment of the justice system to use its strength to call a general strike. We particularly encourage antiauthoritarian interns to call a general strike.

I declare my solidarity with Gudrun Ensslin and Andreas Baader, although they have chosen to defend themselves here, which was obviously a decision that no one really understood. This solidarity will continue through the next period while they are in prison and the penitentiary. I have, in any event, every reason to do so. I declare my solidarity

---

3 Max Güde, a former Nazi, and at the time a member of parliament for the CDU.
4 A reference to a poem by Soviet poet Samuel Marschak about a woman bringing her valued possessions with her to the train station, the title of which in German is *Die Sieben Sachen* (which would translate as "Seven Suitcases" in English).

with Horst Söhnlein. And if I do so, although he chose not to defend himself, it is as much *prollidarisch*[1] as it is in solidarity. And with that, I stop.

We declare our solidarity with all of the actions that the SDS has undertaken in response to the recent attempts to undermine their public support. We demand the abolition of judicial unaccountability, because they use their power to assure the rule of some people over other people.

We demand the abolition of the power of some people over other people.

Workers of the world unite!

Venceremos!

Thorwald Proll
October 14, 1968

---

1 A neologism combining the author Thorwald Proll's last name and *solidarisch*, the German word for solidarity.

Build the Red Army!

Comrades of *883*,

It is pointless to explain the right thing to the wrong people. We've done enough of that. We don't want to explain the action to free Baader to babbling intellectuals, to those who are freaked out, to know-it-alls, but rather to the potentially revolutionary section of the people. That is to say, to those who can immediately understand this action, because they are themselves prisoners. Those who want nothing to do with the blather of the "left," because it remains without meaning or consequence. Those who are fed up!

The action to free Baader must be explained to youth from the Märkisch neighbourhood, to the girls from Eichenhof, Ollenhauer, and Heiligensee, to young people in group homes, in youth centers, in Grünen Haus, and in Kieferngrund.[2]

To large families, to young workers and apprentices, to high school students, to families in neighborhoods that are being gentrified, to the workers at Siemens and AEG-Telefunken, at SEL and Osram, to the married women who, as well as doing the housework and raising the children, must do piecework—damn it.

They are the ones who must understand the action; those who receive no compensation for the exploitation they must suffer. Not in their standard of living, not in their consumption, not in the form of mortgages, not in the form of even limited credit, not in the form of midsize cars. Those who cannot even hope for these baubles, who are not seduced by all of that.

Those who have realized that the future promised to them by their teachers and professors and landlords and social workers and supervisors and foremen and union representatives and city councilors is nothing more than an empty lie, but who nonetheless fear the police. It is only necessary that they—and not the petit bourgeois intellectuals—understand that all of that is over now, that this is a start, that the liberation of Baader is only the beginning! That an end to police domination is in sight! It is to them that we want to say that we are building the

---

2 Places where disenfranchised youth could be found. RAF members had previously worked with such marginalized youth in the "apprentices collectives." Some of these young people became members of the RAF and were involved in the action to free Baader.

red army, and it is their army. It is to them that we say, "It has begun." They don't pose stupid questions like, "Why right now precisely?" They have already traveled a thousand roads controlled by the authorities and managers—they've done the waiting room waltz; they remember the times when it worked and the times when it didn't. And in conversations with sympathetic teachers, who are assigned to the remedial schools that don't change anything, and the kindergartens that lack the necessary spaces—they don't ask why now—damn it!

They certainly won't listen to you, if you aren't even able to distribute your newspaper before it is confiscated. Because you don't need to shake up the left-wing shit eaters, but rather the objective left, you have to construct a distribution network that is out of the reach of the pigs.

Don't complain that it's too hard. The action to free Baader was hardly a walk in the park. If you understand what's going on (and your comments indicate that you do understand, so it's opportunism to say that the bullet also hit you in the stomach[1]—you assholes), if you understand anything, you need to find a better way to organize your distribution. And we have no more to say to you about our methods than we do about our plans for action—you shitheads! As long as you allow yourselves to be brought in by the cops, you aren't in a position to be giving anyone else advice about how to avoid being brought in by the cops. What do you mean by adventurism? That one only has oneself to blame for informers. Whatever.

What does it mean to bring conflicts to a head? It means not allowing oneself to be taken out of action.

That's why we're building the red army. Behind the parents stand the teachers, the youth authorities, and the police. Behind the supervisor stands the boss, the personnel office, the workers compensation board, the welfare office, and the police. Behind the custodian stands the manager, the landlord, the bailiff, the eviction notice, and the police. With this comes the way that the pigs use censorship, layoffs, dismissals, along with bailiff's seals and billy clubs. Obviously, they reach for their service revolvers, their teargas, their grenades, and their semi-automatic weapons; obviously, they escalate, if nothing else does the trick.[2] Obviously,

---

1 A reference to Georg Linke, the sixty-four-year-old librarian at the Institute for Social Studies who was shot during the action to free Baader. This shooting led to substantial criticism, even from otherwise sympathetic leftists.

2 A reference to the Hand Grenade Law passed shortly after Baader's prison break, whereby police in West Berlin were equipped with hand grenades, semi-automatic revolvers, and submachine guns.

the GIs in Vietnam are trained in counterguerilla tactics and the Green Berets receive courses on torture. So what?

It's clear that prison sentences for political activities have been made heavier. You must be clear that it is social democratic bullshit to act as if imperialism—with all its Neubauers[3] and Westmorelands,[4] with Bonn, the senate, *Länder* youth offices, borough councils, the whole pig circus—should be allowed to subvert, investigate, ambush, intimidate, and suppress without a fight. Be absolutely clear that the revolution is no Easter March. The pigs will certainly escalate their means as far as possible, but no further than that. To bring the conflict to a head, we are building the red army.

If the red army is not simultaneously built, then all conflict, all the political work carried out in the factories and in Wedding[5] and in the Märkisch neighborhood[6] and at Plötze[7] and in the courtrooms is reduced to reformism; which is to say, you end up with improved discipline, improved intimidation, and improved exploitation. That destroys the people, rather than destroying what destroys the people! If we don't build the red army, the pigs can do what they want, the pigs can continue to incarcerate, lay off, impound, seize children, intimidate, shoot, and dominate. To bring the conflict to a head means that they are no longer able to do what they want, but rather must do what we want them to do.

You must understand that those who have nothing to gain from the exploitation of the Third World, of Persian oil, of Bolivian bananas, of South African gold, have no reason to identify with the exploiter. They can grasp that what is beginning to happen here has been going on for a long time in Vietnam, in Palestine, in Guatemala, in Oakland and Watts, in Cuba and China, in Angola and in New York.

They will understand, if you explain it to them, that the action to liberate Baader was not an isolated action, that it never was, but that it is just the first of its kind in the FRG. Damn it.

Stop lounging around on the sofa in your recently-raided apartment counting up your love affairs and other petty details. Build an effective

---

3 Kurt Neubauer was a member of the SPD and the Berlin Senator for Youth and Sports.

4 General William Westmoreland was Commander of the U.S. troops in Vietnam from 1964 to 1968 and army Chief-of-Staff from 1968 to 1972.

5 A neighborhood in West Berlin.

6 A working-class suburb of West Berlin.

7 The women's prison at Plötzensee.

distribution system. Forget about the cowardly shits, the bootlickers, the social workers, those who only attempt to curry favor, they are a lumpen mob. Figure out where the asylums are and the large families and the subproletariat and the women workers, those who are only waiting to give a kick in the teeth to those who deserve it. They will take the lead. And don't let yourselves get caught. Learn from them how one avoids getting caught—they know more about that than you.

DEVELOP THE CLASS STRUGGLE
ORGANIZE THE PROLETARIAT
START THE ARMED STRUGGLE
BUILD THE RED ARMY!

RAF
June 5, 1970

The Urban Guerilla Concept

We must draw a clear line between ourselves and the enemy.

Mao

I hold that it is bad as far as we are concerned if a person, a political party, an army or a school is not attacked by the enemy, for in that case it would definitely mean that we have sunk to the level of the enemy. It is good if we are attacked by the enemy, since it proves that we have drawn a clear dividing line between the enemy and ourselves. It is still better if the enemy attacks us wildly and paints us as utterly black and without a single virtue; it demonstrates that we have not only drawn a clear dividing line between the enemy and ourselves but have achieved spectacular successes in our work.

Mao tse Tung
May 26, 1939[1]

I. CONCRETE ANSWERS TO CONCRETE QUESTIONS

I still insist that without investigation there cannot possibly be any right to speak.

Mao[2]

Some comrades have already made up their minds about us. For them, it is the "demagoguery of the bourgeois press" that links these "anarchist groups" with the socialist movement. In their incorrect and pejorative use of the term anarchism, they are no different than the Springer Press. We don't want to engage anyone in dialogue on such a shabby basis.

Many comrades want to know what we think we're doing. The letter to 883, in May 1970, was too vague. The tape Michele Ray had, extracts of which appeared in *Spiegel*, was not authentic and, in any event, was drawn from a private discussion. Ray wanted to use it as an

---

1 This version is close to that in *Quotations from Chairman Mao Tse Tung* (Peking: Foreign Languages Press, 1966), 15. Please note, however, that in keeping with the German translation, the ending here differs slightly from the standard English translation, which reads simply "achieved a great deal in our work."
2 Ibid., 230.

aide-mémoire for an article she was writing. Either she tricked us or we overestimated her. If our practice was as hasty as she claims, we'd have been caught by now. *Spiegel* paid Ray an honorarium of $1,000.00 for the interview.

Almost everything the newspapers have written about us—and the way they write it—has clearly been a lie. Plans to kidnap Willy Brandt are meant to make us look like political idiots, and claims that we intend to kidnap children are meant to make us look like unscrupulous criminals. These lies go as far as the "authentic details" in *konkret #5*, which proved to be nothing more than unreliable details that had been slapped together. That we have "officers and soldiers," that some of us are slaves of others, that comrades who have left us fear reprisals, that we broke into houses or used violence to take passports, that we exercise "group terror"—all of this is bullshit.

The people who imagine an illegal armed organization to be like the *Freikorps* or the Feme,[1] are people who hope for a pogrom. The psychological mechanisms that produce such projections, and their relationship to fascism, have been analyzed in Horkheimer and Adorno's *Authoritarian Personality* and Reich's *Mass Psychology of Fascism*. A compulsive revolutionary personality is a *contradictio in adjecto*— a contradiction in terms. A revolutionary political practice under the present conditions—perhaps under any conditions—presumes the permanent integration of the individual's personality and political beliefs, that is to say, political identity. Marxist criticism and self-criticism has nothing to do with "self-liberation," but a lot to do with revolutionary discipline. It is not the members of a "left organization," writing anonymously or using pen names, who are just interested in "making headlines," but *konkret* itself, whose editor is currently promoting himself as a sort of left-wing Eduard Zimmermann,[2] producing jack-off material for his market niche.

Many comrades spread untruths about us too. They brag that we lived with them, that they organized our trip to Jordan, that they know about our contacts, that they are doing something for us, when, in fact, they are doing nothing. Some only want to make it look like they are

---

1 The *Freikorps* were right-wing paramilitary groups that sprang up in the period following World War I; many were later integrated into the Nazi rise to power. The Feme was a secret medieval court which meted out the death sentence, the bodies of its victims generally being left hanging in the streets.

2 Eduard Zimmermann was TV moderator for the German equivalent of Crimewatch. This program was used in the search for RAF members.

"in the know." Günther Voigt[3] had to pay for puffing himself up in a conversation with Dürrenmatt,[4] claiming he was the one who freed Baader, which he regretted when the cops showed up. It's not easy to clear things up with denials, even when they're true. Some people want to use these lies to prove that we're stupid, unreliable, careless, or crazy. By doing so, they encourage people to oppose us. In reality, they are irrelevant to us. They are only consumers. We want nothing to do with these gossipmongers, for whom the anti-imperialist struggle is a coffee klatch. Many are those who don't gossip, who have some understanding of resistance, who are pissed off enough to wish us luck, who support us because they know that there is no point spending life implicated in and adapted to this crap.

What happened at the Knesebekstr. 89 house (Mahler's arrest) was not due to carelessness on our part, but to betrayal. The traitor was one of us. There is no guarantee against that for people who do what we do. There is no certainty that comrades will not break under extreme police pressure, or will hold up in the face of the terror that the system uses against us, with which it attacks us. The pigs wouldn't have the power if they didn't have these tools.

Our existence makes some people feel pressured to justify themselves. To avoid political discussion with us, to avoid comparing their practice to ours, they distort even the smallest details. For example, the rumor is still circulating that Baader had only three or nine or twelve months to serve, though the correct length of time is easily ascertained: three years for arson, a further six months on probation, and approximately six months for falsifying documents. Of these 48 months, Andreas Baader had served 14 in ten different Hessian prisons—nine times he was transferred because of bad behavior, for example, organizing mutinies and resistance. Reducing the remaining 34 months to three, nine or twelve is intended to reduce the moral justification for the May 14 breakout. In this way, some comrades rationalize their fear of the personal consequences of entering into a political discussion with us.

The question frequently asked, as to whether we would have proceeded with the breakout if we had known that Linke would be shot, can only be answered with a no. The question of what we would have

---

3 Günther Voigt was a West Berlin arms dealer. A pistol that could be linked to him was dropped during the Baader liberation. Voigt fled to Switzerland where he gave an interview that led to his arrest, claiming he was involved in the liberation of Baader.
4 Friedrich Dürrenmatt was a Swiss playwright and essayist.

done if... is ambiguous—pacifist, moralistic, platonic, and detached. Anyone who thinks seriously about the breakout would not pose this question, but would think it through for himself. In asking this question, people only want to see if we are as brutal as the Springer Press claims. It's like an interrogation in catechism class. It is an attempt to trivialize the question of revolutionary violence, by treating revolutionary violence and bourgeois violence as the same thing, which leads nowhere. In anticipating all the possible developments, there was no reason to believe that a civilian would intervene. It is suicidal to think that one can conduct a jailbreak unarmed.

On May 14, the cops fired the first shots. This was the case in Frankfurt as well, where two of us ran for it, because we are not going to just let ourselves be arrested. The cops shot to kill. Sometimes we didn't shoot at all, and when we did, we didn't shoot to kill. In Berlin, in Nuremburg, in Frankfurt.[1] It can be proven, because it is true. We do not "use firearms recklessly." The cop who finds himself in the contradiction of being a "little man" and a capitalist pawn, a low paid employee and monopoly capitalism's agent, is not obliged to follow orders. We shoot back if someone shoots at us. The cop who lets us go, we let him go as well.

It is clear that the massive hunt for us is really directed against the entire socialist left in the Federal Republic and West Berlin. This circus cannot be justified by the small amount of money or the few cars and documents we are alleged to have stolen, or by the attempted murder they're trying to pin on us. The ruling class has been scared out of its skin. They thought that they had this state and all of its inhabitants, classes, and contradictions under control, right down to the last detail: the intellectuals reduced to their magazines, the left isolated in its own circles, Marxism-Leninism disarmed, and internationalism demoralized. However fragile it may pretend to be, the power structure is not so easily damaged. One should not be tricked by this hue and cry into contributing to all this noise.

We are not saying that the organization of armed resistance groups can replace the legal proletarian organizations, that isolated actions can replace the class struggle, or that armed struggle can replace political work in the factories or neighborhoods. We are arguing that

---

1 Berlin refers to the Knesebeckstr. arrest mentioned above. On December 21, 1971, RAF member Ali Jansen was arrested following a shootout at a police roadblock in Nuremberg. On February 10, 1971, police in Frankfurt opened fire on Astrid Proll and Manfred Grashof, who escaped unharmed.

armed struggle is a necessary precondition for the latter to succeed and progress, that armed struggle is "the highest form of Marxism-Leninism" (Mao), and that it can and must begin now, as without it there can be no anti-imperialist struggle in the metropole. We are not Blanquists nor are we anarchists, though we think Blanqui was a great revolutionary and the personal heroism of many anarchists is certainly above reproach.

We have not even been active for a year yet. It is too soon to draw conclusions. The extensive publicity that Genscher, Zimmermann[2] and Co. have given us opens up a propaganda opportunity which we are using to share a few thoughts.

2. THE METROPOLE: THE FEDERAL REPUBLIC

> *The crisis isn't the result of the stagnation of development, but of development itself. Since the aim is to increase profit, development encourages parasitism and waste, harming whole social sectors, multiplying needs that it cannot satisfy, and accelerating the disintegration of social life. A monstrous apparatus is necessary to control, by means of manipulation and open repression, the tensions and revolts which it itself often provokes. The crisis in American political unity caused by the student rebellion and the Black Movement, the spread of the student struggle in Europe, the vehement renewal and the growth of worker and mass struggles leading to the "May" explosion in France, the tumultuous social crisis in Italy, and the rebirth of dissatisfaction in Germany all indicate the nature of the situation.*

Il Manifesto:
The Necessity of Communism, extract from Thesis 33[3]

The comrades from Il Manifesto rightly place the Federal Republic of Germany last in their analysis, vaguely describing the situation here as

---

2 Friedrich Zimmermann (CDU) was, at this time, the Chairman of the CDU/CSU parliamentary faction.

3 Expelled from the Italian Communist Party in 1969, *Il Manifesto* was an influential group in the Italian autonomist movement, having 6,000 members in 1972. They advocated council communism, whereby decisions would be made by workers' councils, not by a vanguard party or state. *Il Manifesto* was extremely influential for the entire European New Left. The quote comes from a manifesto of 200 theses issued by the group in 1971.

dissatisfaction. West Germany, which Barzel[1] described six years ago as an economic giant but a political dwarf, has not lost any of its economic power since, while its external and internal political power has increased. With the formation of the Grand Coalition in 1966, the political danger posed by the coming recession was forestalled. With the Emergency Laws the instrument was created to secure unified ruling-class action in the event of future crises—the unity of political reactionaries and all those who cling to legality was established. The Social-Liberal coalition succeeded, neutralizing the "dissatisfaction" that had become evident in the student revolt and the extra-parliamentary movement. Insofar as the SPD's supporters have not broken with reformism, this section of the intelligentsia has been prevented from embracing a communist alternative; in this way reformism acts as a brake on the anticapitalist struggle. *Ostpolitik* is opening new markets for capitalism, while at the same time it represents the German contribution to an accommodation and alliance between U.S. imperialism and the Soviet Union, which the U.S.A. requires in order to have a free hand for its wars of aggression in the Third World. This government seems to have managed to separate the New Left from the old antifascists, cutting off the New Left from its own history, the history of the working class movement. The DKP, which can thank the new collusion between U.S. imperialism and Soviet revisionism for its new legal status, has organized demonstrations in favor of this government's *Ostpolitik*. Niemöller—a symbol of antifascism—is shilling for the SPD in the upcoming election.

Using the smokescreen of "the common good," the government has established state control and curbed the union bureaucracy with its wage guidelines and its notion of concerted action. The strikes of September 69 showed that things have been overwhelmingly skewed to the benefit of profit; and the fact that these strikes only addressed economic issues indicates how firmly the government holds the reins.

The system shows its strength in the way that the Federal Republic, with its 2 million foreign workers and unemployment approaching 10%, can make use of the looming recession to develop the terror and the disciplinary measures that unemployment implies for the proletariat, without having to deal with any political radicalization of the masses.

In exchange for development aid and military support for the U.S.A.'s wars of aggression, the Federal Republic profits from the exploitation of

---

1 Rainer Barzel was, at this time, the party Chairman of the CDU.

the Third World, without having to take responsibility for these wars, and without having to struggle against internal opposition. While it is no less aggressive than U.S. imperialism, the Federal Republic is less vulnerable.

The political options open to imperialism here have not been exhausted in either their reformist or their fascist forms, and imperialism has not exhausted its ability to either integrate or repress the contradictions that it produces.

The RAF's urban guerilla concept is not based on an optimistic evaluation of the situation in the Federal Republic and West Berlin.

3. THE STUDENT REVOLT

> *The conclusion that it is impossible to separate the revolution in the "heartland" from that in "underdeveloped areas" is based on an analysis of the unique character of the capitalist ruling system. Without a revival of revolution in the West, the imperialists, with their logic of violence, will be able to develop their exit strategy through a catastrophic war, and it will be impossible to prevent the world's superpowers from imposing crushing oppression.*
>
> Il Manifesto: from Thesis 52

To dismiss the student movement as a petit bourgeois revolt is to reduce it to the grandiose claims that accompanied it, to deny its roots in the contradiction between bourgeois society and bourgeois ideology; it means recognizing its obvious shortcomings while ignoring the theoretical level that this anticapitalist protest managed to achieve.

The pathos with which the student movement became aware of its mental immiseration in the knowledge factories was certainly exaggerated, as was the identification of this with the situation of the exploited peoples of Latin America, Africa, and Asia. The comparison between the mass circulation of *Bild Zeitung* here and the massive bombing of Vietnam was a grotesque oversimplification, just as it was arrogant to compare the ideological critique of the system here and the armed struggle over there. The students' belief that they were the revolutionary subject, insofar as it was based on the appeal of Marcuse, betrayed their ignorance as to the actual nature of bourgeois society and the mode of production which it has established.

The student revolt in the Federal Republic and West Berlin—with its street fighting, its arsons, its use of counterviolence, its pathos, as well as its exaggerations and ignorance... in short, with its practice—has the merit of having reconstructed Marxism-Leninism, at least in the consciousness of the intelligentsia, as that political theory without which the political, economic, and ideological factors and their outward manifestations cannot be combined into an overall analytical perspective. Without this, internal and external relationships cannot be described.

The student movement was based on the contradiction between the theory of academic freedom and the reality of monopoly capitalism's control of the universities. Precisely because it was based on this, and not merely on ideology, it didn't run out of steam before it had established the relationship between the crisis in the universities and the crisis of capitalism, if only in theory. Not before it was clear to the student movement and their public that "liberty, equality, and fraternity" would not be achieved by appeals to human rights or the UN Charter, that what was occurring here was what had always occurred in the colonialist and imperialist exploitation of Latin America, Africa, and Asia: discipline, subordination, and brutality for the oppressed and for those who take up their struggle by protest, those who resist and wage the anti-imperialist struggle.

In its ideological critique, the student movement viewed almost all aspects of state repression as expressions of imperialist exploitation: in the Springer campaign, in the demonstrations against American aggression in Vietnam, in the campaign against class justice, in the *Bundeswehr* campaign,[1] in the campaign against the Emergency Laws, and in the high school student movement. Expropriate Springer! Smash NATO! Resist Consumer Terror! Resist Education Terror! Resist Rent Terror!—these were all correct political slogans. They aimed to expose the contradiction between new needs which could be satisfied through the development of productive forces, on the one hand, and the pressure of irrational subordination to class society, on the other. Their identity was not based on class struggle here, but rather on the knowledge that they were part of an international movement, that they were dealing with the same class enemy as the Viet Cong, the same paper tigers, the same pigs.

The second merit of the student movement was that it broke through the old left's parochialism: the old left's popular front strategy in the form of the Easter Marches, the German Peace Union, the *Deutsche*

---

1 An SDS campaign encouraging soldiers to desert from the *Bundeswehr*, the West German Army.

Volkszeitung, an irrational hope for a "massive landslide" in some election or another, a parliamentary fixation on Strauß here or Heinemann there, their pro- and anticommunist vacillation about the GDR, their isolation, their resignation, and their moral conflicts: ready for every sacrifice, incapable of any practice. The socialist section of the student movement developed its consciousness, in spite of theoretical errors, from the correct recognition that "the revolutionary initiative in the West can be based on the crisis in the global balance of power, and on the development of new forces in old countries." (Il Manifesto, Thesis 55) They based their agitation and propaganda on what can be considered the most important aspect of German reality. They opposed the global strategy of imperialism by internationalizing national struggles, by creating a connection between the national and international aspects of the struggle, between traditional forms of struggle and international revolutionary initiatives. They managed to turn their weakness into strength, because they recognized that continuing resignation, parochialism, reformism, and popular front strategies could only lead to a dead-end for socialist politics in the post- and pre-fascist conditions existing in the Federal Republic and West Berlin.

The left knew that it was correct to link the distribution of socialist propaganda in factories with actually preventing the distribution of *Bild Zeitung.* It was correct to link propaganda against GIs being sent to Vietnam with actual attacks on military planes targeting Vietnam, and the *Bundswehr* campaign with attacks on NATO airports. It was correct to link the critique of class justice with the blowing up of prison walls, and the critique of the Springer Corporation with the disarming of its private security services. It was correct to set up radio stations, to demoralize the police, to have safehouses for *Bundeswehr* deserters, to combine agitation amongst foreign workers with the production of false documents, to prevent the production of napalm by sabotaging factories.

It was an error, however, to make their own propaganda dependent on supply and demand: to have no newspaper if the workers could not yet finance it, no car if the "movement" could not afford it, no transmitter because they had no license for it, no sabotage because capitalism wouldn't collapse immediately as a result.

The student movement fell apart when its typically student and petit bourgeois form of organization, "antiauthoritarianism," proved itself ill-suited to achieving its goals. Its spontaneity proved ineffective in the factories, nor could it create a functioning urban guerilla movement or a socialist mass organization. Unlike in Italy and France, the spark of the student movement here failed to ignite the prairie fire of class struggle, and it was at that point that it collapsed. It could enumerate the aims and contents of the anti-imperialist struggle, but it could not be the revolutionary subject, could not offer the necessary organizational structure.

Unlike the proletarian organizations of the New Left, the Red Army Faction doesn't deny its roots in the history of the student movement, a movement that reshaped Marxism-Leninism into a weapon of class struggle and established the international basis for revolutionary struggle in the metropole.

4. THE PRIMACY OF PRACTICE

> *If you want to know a certain thing or a certain class of things directly, you must personally participate in the practical struggle to change reality, to change that thing or class of things, for only thus can you come into contact with them as phenomena; only through personal participation in the practical struggle to change reality can you uncover the essence of that thing or class of things and comprehend them.*
>
> *Marxism emphasizes the importance of theory precisely and only because it can guide action. If we have a correct theory but merely prate about it, pigeonhole it and do not put it into practice, then that theory, however good, is of no significance.*
>
> Mao tse Tung: *On Practice*[1]

The decision of leftists and socialists, the student movement's authority figures, to turn to the study of scientific socialism and transform the critique of political economy into a self criticism of the student movement, was at the same time a decision to retreat into the classroom. Considering their paper output, their organizational models, and their bombastic statements, one might think that these revolutionaries were leading a violent class struggle, as if 1967/68 was the 1905 of socialism in Germany. In 1903, Lenin pointed out, in *What Is to Be Done*, that the Russian workers needed a specific theory, and postulated, in opposition to the anarchists and the Social Revolutionaries, the necessity

---

1 *Selected Works of Mao Tse-tung* (Peking: Foreign Languages Press, 1967). The first of these two paragraphs comes from pages 299-300, the second from page 304.

of class analysis, organization, and all-encompassing propaganda, because a broad-based class struggle was unfolding:

> *The fact is that the working masses are roused to a high pitch of excitement by the social evils in Russian life, but we are unable to gather, if one may so put it, and concentrate all these drops and streamlets of popular resentment that are brought forth to a far larger extent than we imagine by the conditions of Russian life, and that must be combined into a single gigantic torrent.*
>
> Lenin: *What Is to Be Done?*[2]

Under the existing conditions in the Federal Republic and West Berlin, we doubt it will be possible to create a strategy to unify the working class or to create an organization that could simultaneously express and initiate the necessary unifying process. We doubt that the unity of the socialist intelligentsia and the proletariat can be "molded out of" the political programs or the declarations coming from the proletarian organizations. The drops and streamlets based on the horrors have long been collected by the Springer Corporation, to which they then add new horrors.

We believe that without a revolutionary initiative, without the practical revolutionary intervention of the vanguard, the socialist workers and intellectuals, and without concrete anti-imperialist struggle, there will be no unifying process. Unity can only be created through the common struggle of the conscious section of the working class and the intellectuals, one which they do not stage-manage, but which they model, or else it will not happen at all.

The paper output of these organizations shows their practice to be mainly a contest between intellectuals for the best Marx review before an imaginary jury, which couldn't possibly be the working class, as the language used excludes their participation. They are more embarrassed when they are caught misquoting Marx than when they are caught lying in their practice. Talking is their practice. The page numbers in their footnotes are almost always correct, the membership numbers they give for their organizations seldom are. They fear the accusation of revolutionary impatience more than corruption by bourgeois careers. It's more important to them to spend years pursuing a degree

---

2 Marxists Internet Archive "Lenin's What is to be Done? Trade-Unionist Politics and Social Democratic Politics," http://www.marxists.org/archive/lenin/works/1901/witbd/iii.htm.

with Lukacs[1] than to allow themselves to be spontaneously inspired by Blanqui. They express internationalism in the form of censorship by favoring one Palestinian guerilla organization over another. White masters who claim to be the true guardians of Marxism, they express themselves through patronage, begging their rich friends for alms in the name of the Black Panther Party—not with a view to "victory in the people's war," but to soothe their consciences. That's not a revolutionary method of intervention.

Mao, in his *Analysis of the Classes in Chinese Society* (1926), contrasted the revolution and the counterrevolution in this way:

> *Each has hoisted a huge banner: one is the red banner of revolution held aloft by the Third International as the rallying point for all the oppressed classes of the world, the other is the white banner of counterrevolution held aloft by the League of Nations as the rallying point for all the counterrevolutionaries of the world.*[2]

Mao differentiated between classes in Chinese society based on the positions they took towards the red and white banners. It wasn't enough for him to analyze the economic situation of different classes in Chinese society. Part of his class analysis involved the relationship of different classes to the revolution.

There will be no leadership role for Marxist-Leninists in future class struggles if the vanguard doesn't hold up the red banner of proletarian internationalism, if the vanguard can't answer the question of how to establish the dictatorship of the proletariat, of how to develop the power of the proletariat, of how to break the power of the bourgeoisie, if it isn't prepared to do anything to answer these questions. The class analysis we require cannot be developed without revolutionary practice or revolutionary initiative.

The "provisional revolutionary demands" put forward by the proletarian organizations throughout the country—such as the struggle against the intensification of exploitation, for a shorter work week, against the squandering of social wealth, for wage parity for men, women, and foreigners, against production quotas, etc.—are nothing but trade union economism as long as they don't address the question of

---

1 George Lukacs was an influential Hungarian Marxist philosopher and art critic. His work greatly influenced the New Left of the 60s and 70s.
2 Mao Tse-Tung "Analysis of the Classes in Chinese Society," Marxists Internet Archive, http://www.marxists.org/reference/archive/mao/selected-works/volume-1/mswv1_1.htm.

how to break the political, military, and propaganda power that always stands firmly in the way of these demands when they are put forward in mass class struggles. If these demands stay the same, one can only call them economistic shit, because they are not worth the revolutionary energy wasted in fighting for them, and they won't lead to victory if "victory means to accept the principle that life is not the most precious thing for a revolutionary" (Debray[3]). Trade unions intervene with demands like these—but "the trade union politics of the working class are bourgeois working class politics" (Lenin). That's not a revolutionary method of intervention.

The proletarian organizations failed to pose the question of armed struggle as a response to the Emergency Laws, the army, the BGS, the police, or the Springer Press. This shows that the proletarian organizations differ in their opportunism from the DKP only in that they are even less rooted in the masses, even if they are more verbally radical and theoretically advanced. In practice, they function at the level of civil rights and are concerned with gaining popularity at any price. They support the lies of the bourgeoisie by supporting the idea that with this state it is still possible to correct social problems by parliamentary means. They encourage the proletariat to engage in struggles that have no chance of success, given the state's capacity for violence and its barbaric ways. "These Marxist-Leninist factions or parties," Debray writes of the communists in Latin America, "move within the political environment as if they were controlled by the bourgeoisie. Rather than challenging the political status quo, they reinforce it...."

These organizations don't offer any alternatives to the thousands of apprentices and young people who, as a result of being politicized by the student movement, became determined to put an end to exploitation in their workplaces. They simply advise them to adapt to capitalist exploitation. Concerning youth crime, when it comes down to it they share the position of prison wardens. Regarding the comrades in prison, they share the point of view of the judges. And regarding the underground, they share the point of view of social workers.

Without political practice, reading *Capital* is nothing more than bourgeois study. Without political practice, political programs are just so much twaddle. Without political practice, proletarian internationalism

---

3 Regis Debray is a French Marxist intellectual who was a proponent of foco theory, the theory that a small group of guerillas could act as an inspiration to revolutionary activity. He joined Che Guevara on his ill-fated Bolivian adventure.

is only hot air. Adopting a proletarian position in theory implies putting it into practice.

The Red Army Faction asserts the primacy of practice. Whether it is right to organize armed resistance now, depends on whether it is possible, and whether it is possible can only be determined in practice.

5. THE URBAN GUERILLA

Hence, imperialism and all reactionaries, looked at in essence, from a long-term point of view, from a strategic point of view, must be seen for what they are—paper tigers. On this we should build our strategic thinking. On the other hand, they are also living tigers, iron tigers, real tigers which can devour people. On this we should build our tactical thinking.

Mao tse Tung, January 12, 1958[1]

If it is true that American imperialism is a paper tiger, this means it can, in the final analysis, be defeated. And if the thesis of the Chinese communists is correct, then victory over American imperialism is possible, because struggles against it have erupted all over the world, and as a result imperialism's power is divided. It is this division that renders its defeat possible. If this is true, then there is no reason to exclude or leave out any country or any region from the anti-imperialist struggle simply because the forces of revolution are especially weak, and the forces of reaction are especially strong.

If it is incorrect to demoralize the revolutionary forces by underestimating them, it's equally incorrect to push them into confrontations that can only lead to defeat. In the conflicts between the honest comrades in the proletarian organizations—let's leave the big talkers out of it—and the Red Army Faction, we accuse them of demoralizing the revolutionary forces, whereas they feel we are leading the revolutionary forces down a blind alley. There is an attempt to bridge this divide between the comrades in the factories and the neighborhoods and the Red Army Faction, and if we succeed in doing so, we will arrive at the truth. Dogmatism and adventurism are typical deviations in any country during periods in which the revolutionary movement is weak. Since the anarchists have always been the strongest critics of opportunism,

---

1 *Quotations from Chairman Mao Tse Tung* (Peking: Foreign Languages Press, 1966), 74.

everyone who criticizes opportunism is called an anarchist—this is nothing more than fashionable nonsense.

The concept of the urban guerilla comes from Latin America. There, like here, it is the method of revolutionary intervention by generally weak revolutionary forces.

The urban guerilla struggle is based on an understanding that there will be no Prussian-style marching orders, which so many so-called revolutionaries are waiting for to lead the people into revolutionary struggle. It is based on the analysis that by the time the conditions are right for armed struggle, it will be too late to prepare for it. It is based on the recognition that without revolutionary initiatives in a country with as much potential for violence as the Federal Republic, there will be no revolutionary orientation when the conditions for revolutionary struggle are more favorable, as they soon will be given the political and economic developments of late capitalism.

The urban guerilla is the consequence of the long since complete negation of parliamentary democracy by the elected representatives themselves. It is the inevitable response to the Emergency Laws and the Hand Grenade Law. It is the willingness to struggle with the very means that the system appropriates for itself to neutralize its enemies. The urban guerilla is based on facing facts, not making excuses for them.

The student movement already had a partial understanding of what the urban guerilla could achieve. It can give concrete form to the agitation and propaganda work to which the left has been reduced. For instance, in the Springer campaign, in the Carbora Bassa campaign of the Heidelberg students,[2] in the squatting movement in Frankfurt, in the context of the military aid that the Federal Republic gives the comprador regimes in Africa, and in the security measures and the in-house justice in the factories. The urban guerilla can make verbal internationalism concrete by providing weapons and money. It can blunt the system's weapons and the banning of communists by organizing an underground that can elude the police. The urban guerilla is a weapon of class struggle.

---

2 A campaign to stop the building of a massive dam in Mozambique, then a Portuguese colony. The right-wing Portuguese government had plans to settle over one million European colonists in the African country. By 1969, five German companies were implicated in the project. There were protests in the FRG, particularly in Heidelberg, against the project when the U.S. Secretary of Defense Robert McNamara visited the country.

The urban guerilla struggle is armed struggle in a situation in which the police use their weapons recklessly and in which class justice finds Kurras not guilty and buries comrades alive. The urban guerilla struggle means not being demoralized by the violence of the system.

The urban guerilla aims to destroy certain aspects of the state structure, and to destroy the myth of state omnipotence and invulnerability.

The urban guerilla requires the organization of an illegal structure, including safehouses, weapons, cars, and documents. What one needs to know about this, Marighella describes in his *Minimanual of the Urban Guerilla*. What needs to be known beyond that, we are always ready to tell anyone who wants to participate in the guerilla struggle. We don't know that much yet, but we know a little bit.

Before deciding to take up the armed struggle, it is important that one first experience the legal struggle. When one's connection to the revolutionary left is based on just wanting to follow the latest fad, then it is better not to start anything you will not be able to get out of later on.

The Red Army Faction and the urban guerilla represent the only faction and practice which draws a clear line between ourselves and the enemy, and is therefore subject to the sharpest attack. This requires that one have a political identity, and it presumes that a learning process has already occurred.

Our original organizational concept implied a connection between the urban guerilla and the work at the base. We wanted everyone to work in the neighborhoods, the factories, and the existing socialist groups, to be influenced by the discussions taking place, to have some experience, to learn. It has become clear that that doesn't work. The degree to which the political police can monitor these groups, their meetings, their appointments, and the contents of their discussions is already so extensive that one has to stay away if one wants to escape this surveillance.

The urban guerilla struggle requires that one be totally clear about one's motivations, that one not be put off by the attacks from *Bild Zeitung*, the antisemitic-criminal-subhuman-murderer-arsonist label that they apply to revolutionaries. All that shit they spit out and are willing to say, and which still influences what many comrades think about us, must have no effect.

Naturally, the system doesn't give any ground, and there is nothing they will not do and no slander they will not use against us.

There are no publications that have any goals that can be distinguished from those that serve the interests of capital. There is still no socialist publication that reaches beyond itself, its circle, the people handed copies, and its subscribers, and which does not exist primarily in an incidental, private, personal, bourgeois context. All forms of media are controlled by capital, through advertising sales, as a result of the ambitions of the writers, who want to write their way into the establishment, through the radio stations' boards of directors, and through the market control of the press corporations. The leading publications are the publications of the ruling class. They divide the market opportunities between themselves, developing ideologies for specific milieus, and what they publish serves to assure their market domination. Journalism is about one thing: sales. News is a commodity; information is a consumer product. Whatever isn't suitable for consumption is vomited back out. The need to retain the readership for advertisement-heavy publications, and point system ratings for television, prevent antagonistic contradictions from developing between these media and the public; no antagonism, nothing of consequence. Whoever wants a place in the market must maintain connections with these extremely powerful opinion shapers. This means that dependence on the Springer Corporation grows in step with the Springer Corporation itself, which has also started to buy up local papers. The urban guerilla can expect nothing but bitter hostility from this public. It has to orient itself around Marxist criticism and self-criticism, and nothing else. As Mao said, "Whoever is not afraid of being drawn and quartered, can dare to pull the emperor from his horse."

Long-term, meticulous work is crucial for the urban guerilla, insofar as we want to go beyond discussion to action. If the option of retreating to a bourgeois profession is not kept open, if the option of leaving behind the revolution for a townhouse is not maintained, if none of this is even desirable, then, with the full pathos of Blanqui's statement, "The duty of the revolutionary is to always struggle, in spite of everything to struggle, to struggle until death." There is no revolutionary struggle, and there has been no revolutionary struggle, in which this hasn't shown itself to be true: Russia, China, Cuba, Algeria, Palestine, Vietnam.

Some say that the political possibilities of organization, agitation, and propaganda are far from being exhausted, and only when they have been exhausted should one consider armed struggle. We say that the political possibilities will not be fully utilized until armed struggle is recognized as the political goal, as long as the strategic conclusion that all reactionaries are paper tigers is not grasped despite the tactical conclusion that they are criminals, murderers, and exploiters.

We will not talk about "armed propaganda": we will do it. The prison breakout didn't take place for reasons of propaganda, but to get the guy out. The bank robberies they try to lay at our doorstep, we'd only do that to grab the money. The "spectacular successes" that Mao tells us we must have scored if "the enemy paints us as utterly black" are not our successes alone. The big clamour that has been made about us is due more to the Latin American comrades—given the clear line they have already drawn between themselves and the enemy—which has led the ruling class here, suspecting us of some bank robberies, to "energetically oppose" us, because of what we have begun to build here: the urban guerilla in the form of the Red Army Faction.

6. LEGALITY AND ILLEGALITY

Revolution in the West, the challenge to capitalist power in its strongholds, is the order of the day. It is of decisive importance. The current world situation offers no place and no power that is in a position to guarantee peaceful development and democratic stability. The crisis is intensifying. Parochialism or the decision to postpone the struggle would mean being sucked into the abyss of complete collapse.

Il Manifesto, extract from Thesis 55

The anarchists' slogan, "Destroy what destroys you," is aimed at mobilizing the base, young people in prisons and reformatories, in high schools and training centres. It reaches out to all of those in the shittiest situations. It is meant to be spontaneously understood, and is a call for direct resistance. Stokely Carmichael's[1] Black Power slogan, "Trust your own experience!" means just that. And the slogan is based on the insight that in capitalism there is absolutely nothing that oppresses, tortures, constrains, and burdens that does not have its origin in the capitalist mode of production, and that each oppressor, in whatever form he may appear, is a representative of the class interests of capital, which makes him the class enemy.

To this extent the anarchists' slogan is correct, proletarian, and in line with the class struggle. It is incorrect insofar as it leads to false

---

1 Stokely Carmichael was a prominent militant in the Black Liberation Movement in the United States, playing a leading role in the Student Non-Violent Coordinating Committee (SNCC) and then the Black Panther Party.

consciousness. One goes on the offensive simply to give them a kick in the teeth, and organization then takes second place, discipline becomes bourgeois, and class analysis superfluous. If you don't work out the dialectic of legality and illegality in terms of organization, you will be defenseless against the heavy repression that will follow your actions, and you will be legally arrested.

The statement of some organizations, "Communists are not so stupid as to get themselves banned," renders them a mouthpiece for class justice, that is to say, for no one. The statement is correct insofar as it means that the legal possibilities for communist agitation, propaganda, and organizing for a political and economic struggle must be fully utilized and cannot be carelessly jeopardized—but that is not what they mean. They mean that there is no way of getting around the limits that the class state and its justice system establish for the socialist project, that one must stop at these limits, that one must retreat from the state's illegal encroachments as these encroachments are legalized—legality at any price. Illegal imprisonment, terroristic sentences, police harassment, blackmail and coercion on the part of the BAW—eat shit or die—Communists are not that stupid....

This statement is opportunist. It shows a lack of solidarity. It abandons the comrades in prison. It excludes the organization and politicization in a socialist context of anyone who, as a result of their social background and situation, has no choice but to survive through crime: the underground, the subproletariat, innumerable proletarian youth, and guest workers. It facilitates the theoretical criminalization of all those who are not members of these organizations. It expresses complicity with class justice. It is stupid.

Legality is a question of power. The relationship between legality and illegality has to be determined by examining the contradiction between reformist and fascist domination, whose representatives in Bonn are, on the one hand, the Social-Liberal coalition, and on the other, Barzel and Strauß. Their media representatives are, for the former: the *Süddeutsche Zeitung*, *Stern*, the WDR[2] Third Program, SFB, and the *Frankfurter Rundschau*. And, for the latter: the Springer Corporation, the *Sender Freies Berlin*, the *Zweites Deutsches Fernsehen*, and the *Bayernkurier*. The Munich police line here, and the Berlin model there. Here the justice of the Federal Administrative Court and there that of the Federal Supreme Court.

---

2 *Westdeutscher Rundfunk*, West German Radio.

The reformist line attempts to avoid conflicts by using institutional options (co-management) and promises of improvements (in prison conditions, for example), by addressing obsolete sources of conflict (the Chancellor's genuflection in Poland, for example), by avoiding provocation (the soft line of the Munich police and the Federal Administrative Court in Berlin, for example), and by airing grievances (regarding public education in Hessen and Berlin, for example). As part of this reformist line of avoiding conflict, they move a bit further inside and a bit less outside of legality. They do this to look legitimate. With the Constitution in hand, they intend to neutralize contradictions and leave left-wing criticism dead in the water and empty of content, thereby keeping the *Jusos* within the SPD.

There is no doubt that, in the long run, the reformist line is the more effective way of stabilizing capitalist domination, but it relies on certain conditions being met. It requires economic prosperity, because the soft line of the Munich police, for example, is much more expensive than the hard line of Berlin—as the Munich police chief pointed out: "Two officers with machineguns can hold a thousand people in check. 100 officers with truncheons can control a thousand people. Without weapons of this sort, 300 or 400 police officers are necessary." The reformist line requires a situation in which no organized anticapitalist opposition exists, as one can see by the Munich example.

Camouflaged by political reformism, the concentration of state and economic power accelerates. What Schiller has achieved with his financial policy and Strauß has pushed through with his financial reforms is an increase in exploitation through the intensification of work and heightened division of labor in the productive sector, and through long-term rationalization in the administrative sector and the service industries.

The concentration of violent power in the hands of the few can occur unopposed if it is done quietly, if unnecessary provocation, which can set a process of solidarity in motion, is avoided—that is something that was learned as a result of the student movement and the Paris May. Therefore, the Red Cells[1] are not yet banned. Therefore the KP can exist as the DKP without the ban on the KP being lifted. Therefore there are still some liberal television programs. And, therefore, some organizations can get away with thinking that they are not as stupid as they really are.

---

1 The Red Cells were an independent university-based Marxist organization.

The margin of legality that reformism affords is capital's response to the attacks of the student movement and the APO—the reformist response is the more effective one, so long as they can manage it. To rely on this legality, to count on it, to perpetuate it metaphysically, to base statistical projections on it, to want to defend it, means repeating the errors of the Latin American self-defense zones. It means you haven't learned anything and have provided the reactionaries with time to regroup and reorganize, creating a situation in which they won't ban the left, they'll smash it.

Willy Weyer[2] doesn't play at tolerance. When the liberal press complains that his highway breathalyzers treat all drivers like potential criminals, he maneuvers and audaciously responds, "We will carry on!"—and in so doing he demonstrates the irrelevance of the liberal public. Eduard Zimmermann creates a whole nation of police agents, and the Springer Corporation has taken on the role of leading the Berlin police—*Bild Zeitung* columnist Reer recommends arrest warrants to the custodial judges. The mass mobilization in favor of fascism, of crackdowns, of the death penalty, and for more and better-armed police carries on unabated—the New Look of the Brandt-Heinemann-Scheel administration is a facade for Bonn's policies.

The comrades who only deal with the question of legality and illegality superficially have obviously misunderstood the amnesty with which the student movement was to be tamed. In lifting the criminalization of hundreds of students, they sent them away with just a fright, preventing further radicalization and impressing upon them the value of the privileges that come with being a bourgeois student—that in spite of the nature of the knowledge-factory, the universities are helpful to social climbers. This deepens the class divide between students and the proletariat, between their privileged everyday life and the everyday life of those who do the shit work and who were not offered the same amnesty by the same class enemy. So once again the division between theory and practice is maintained. The equation: amnesty equals pacification.

The social democratic voter initiative involving some respected writers—not only that fuck-up, Grass[3]—is an attempt at a positive, democratic mobilization, and is a form of resistance against fascism, and

---

2 Willy Weyer (SPD) was, at this time, the Minister of the Interior for North Rhine-Westphalia and a key proponent of the militarization of the police force.

3 At the time a member of *Gruppe 47*, Günter Grass is one on the most significant German post-World War II authors and a noted liberal.

therefore should not be dismissed lightly. It is having some effect on the reality presented by certain publishers and some radio and television editorial departments, those that have not yet capitulated to the logic of the monopolies and have not yet been absorbed into the superstructure, with its overarching political reality. The areas of increasing repression are not those with which writers are normally concerned: prison, class justice, intensified work, work-related accidents, installment plans, schools, *Bild* and the *Berliner Zeitung*, barrack-style housing in the suburbs,[1] and ghettos for foreigners—all of this troubles these writers aesthetically, not politically.

Legality is the ideology of parliamentarianism, of social partnership, and of a pluralistic society. Legality becomes a fetish when those who insist upon it ignore the fact that phones are legally tapped, mail is legally monitored, neighbors are legally interrogated, and informants are legally paid. The organization of political work, if it is not to be under constant observation by the political police, must be simultaneously conducted both legally and illegally.

We don't count on terror and fascism provoking a spontaneous antifascist mobilization, nor do we think that legality is always corrupt. We understand that our work offers pretexts, just as alcohol does for Willy Weyer, just as the increase in crime does for Strauß, just as *Ostpolitik* does for Barzel, just as a Yugoslav running a red light does for a Frankfurt taxi driver, just as a tool in the pocket does for the murderers of car thieves in Berlin. Regarding other pretexts that result from the fact that we are communists, whether communists organize and struggle will depend on whether terror and repression produce only fear and resignation, or whether they produce resistance, class hatred, and solidarity, and whether or not everything goes smoothly for imperialism. It depends on whether communists are so stupid as to tolerate everything that is done to them, or whether they will use legality, as well as other methods, to organize illegality, instead of fetishizing one over the other.

The fate of both the Black Panther Party and *Gauche Prolétarienne*[2] resulted from an incorrect understanding of the contradiction between the constitution and legal reality and the increased intensity of this

---

1 Unlike North America, suburbs in Northern Europe are generally occupied by the subproletariat and poorly paid immigrant workers.

2 *Gauche Prolétarienne* was a French Maoist organization that, in 1968, began attempts to build a factory-based guerilla group. They were banned in 1970.

contradiction when organized resistance occurs. And this incorrect understanding prevents people from seeing that the conditions of legality are changed by active resistance, and that it is therefore necessary to use legality simultaneously for political struggle and for the organization of illegality, and that it is an error to wait to be banned, as if it were a stroke of fate coming from the system, because then the banning will constitute a death blow, and the issue will be resolved.

The Red Army Faction organizes illegality as an offensive position for revolutionary intervention.

Building the urban guerilla means conducting the anti-imperialist struggle offensively. The Red Army Faction creates the connection between legal and illegal struggle, between national struggle and international struggle, between political struggle and armed struggle, and between the strategic and tactical aspects of the international communist movement. The urban guerilla means intervening in a revolutionary way here, in spite of the weakness of the revolutionary forces in the Federal Republic and West Berlin!

Cleaver said, "Either you're part of the problem or you're part of the solution. There is nothing in between. This shit has been examined and analyzed for decades and generations from every angle. My opinion is that most of what happens in this country does not need to be analyzed any further."[3]

SUPPORT THE ARMED STRUGGLE!
VICTORY TO PEOPLE'S WAR!

Red Army Faction
April 1971

---

3 Eldridge Cleaver was the Minister of Information for the Black Panther Party. When the party splintered into warring factions, he went into self-imposed exile in Algeria. He is the author of several books, including *Soul on Ice*, from which this quote is drawn.

ERSCHOSSEN:

VERFAHREN EINGESTELLT!

Flier denouncing the murder of Petra Schelm, who was shot in the head by police. Hamburg Red Aid 1971.

Building a Base and "Serving the People"

WITH SAFEHOUSES AND SUPPORTERS IN several cities, and dozens of guerillas living underground, the RAF patiently built up its organization over two years, a period during which there occurred several clashes with police, leaving two members dead and many more in prison.

The state's first serious attempt to eradicate the RAF had begun shortly after the publication of *The Urban Guerilla Concept* in 1971. Named *Aktion Kobra* ("Operation Cobra"), it involved three thousand heavily armed officers patrolling cities and setting up checkpoints throughout Northern Germany.

On July 15, 1971, a new line was crossed when RAF members Petra Schelm and Werner Hoppe were identified by police in the port city of Hamburg. A firefight ensued, and while Hoppe managed to surrender,[1] Schelm was shot dead. A working-class woman who had entered the guerilla though the commune scene, moving on from the Roaming Hash Rebels to the RAF,[2] she was nineteen at the time.

There was widespread outrage at this killing, and in an opinion poll conducted shortly thereafter by the respected Allensbach Institute,

---

1 He would eventually receive a ten year sentence for allegedly shooting at police. (Associated Press, "German Draws 10-year term," *European Stars and Stripes*, July 27, 1972.)
2 Baumann, 53.

"40 percent of respondents described the RAF's violence as political, not criminal, in motive; 20 percent indicated that they could understand efforts to protect fugitives from capture; and 6 percent confessed that they were themselves willing to conceal a fugitive."[1]

In the wake of the APO, the RAF began to take on the aura of folk heroes for many young people who were glad to see someone taking things to the next level. As one woman who joined the group in this period put it, "For the first time, I found a theoretical foundation for something that, until then, I had only felt."[2]

Or in the words of Helmut Pohl, who stole cars for the guerilla at this time:

> What was clear was the drive, the resolve, quite simply, the search for something new—something different from the shit here. That was what made it attractive and created the base of support. This existed from the beginning, and there is no way it could have been otherwise.[3]

Thousands of students secretly carried photographs of RAF members in their wallets, and time and time again, as the police stepped up their search, members of the young guerilla group would find doors open to them, as they were welcomed into people's homes, including not a few middle-class supporters—academics, doctors, even a clergyman.[4] Newspapers at the time carried stories under headlines like "Celebrities Protect Baader Gang" and "Sympathizers Hamper Hunt for Baader Group."[5]

The guerilla continued to attract new members, including several former members of the Socialist Patients' Collective (SPK), a radical therapy group that had carried out some armed actions before its leading members were arrested in July 1971 (see sidebar on next page).

On October 22, there was another shooting in Hamburg, but this time a police officer was killed. Margrit Schiller, a former SPK member who had joined the RAF, was being pursued by two policemen when Gerhard Müller (also formerly of the SPK) and a female RAF member

---

1 Varon, 199.

2 Margrit Schiller in *Baader Meinhof: In Love With Terror*.

3 Helmut Pohl's Testimony at the Stammheim Trial, July 29, 1976. This testimony is available on the internet at http://www.germanguerilla.com/red-army-faction/documents/76_0708_mohnhaupt_pohl.html#22.

4 Philip Jacobson, "Show Trial," *Sunday Times Magazine*, February 23, 1975, 17.

5 Aust, 141.

The Socialist Patients' Collective

While the RAF was forming, other groups in the Federal Republic were also experimenting with armed politics. One of these, the Socialist Patients' Collective (SPK), started as a radical therapy group based at Heidelberg University in Southwest Germany. Under the leadership of psychiatrist Wolfgang Huber, the group adopted the slogan, "The system has made us sick: let us strike the death blow to the sick system!"

In tying together political radicalism and psychotherapy, the SPK were not as odd as they might be considered today. As already mentioned, the student left was deeply indebted to the Frankfurt School's brand of Marxism, and the Frankfurt School in turn was deeply influenced by psychoanalysis, as were philosophers like Jean-Paul Sartre and Simone de Beauvoir and revolutionary theorists like Frantz Fanon, all of whom greatly influenced sixties radicals. As such, there was much enthusiasm about psychology, psychoanalysis, and psychotherapy within the New Left, and this was nowhere more true than in West Germany.

According to government officials, the SPK held that only the maladjusted can survive in modern society, and the insane are actually too sane to live under present social conditions.[1] The SPK members began carrying out armed attacks after Huber was fired from his post at the university in February 1970, burning down the State Psychiatric Clinic, robbing banks, and even trying (unsuccessfully) to plant a bomb on a train in which the president of the Federal Republic was traveling. In July of 1971, Huber, his wife, and seven SPK members were arrested on charges of having formed a criminal association and illegally procuring arms and explosives.[2]

Many of the SPK members who remained at large would go on to join the RAF.

---

[1] United Press International, "U.S. Hunts German Terrorists," *Pacific Stars and Stripes*, July 23, 1978.

[2] Becker, *Hitler's Children: The Story of the Baader-Meinhof Gang*. Please note that this book, written by a right-wing South African journalist, is counterinsurgency tripe. Nevertheless, it has been used for specific details like dates and places,when no other source is available.

came to her defense: in the ensuing melee, officer Norbert Schmid was shot dead.

Schiller was nevertheless captured, and a macabre scene played out as police called a press conference to display their trophy. Millions of television viewers watched, amazed, as the young woman—clearly unwilling to play the part assigned to her—was carried in front of the cameras by a pack of cops, her head pulled back by her hair so that all could see her face as she struggled to break free.[1]

Police searches and checkpoints increased as the hunt for the guerilla continued. On December 4, police in West Berlin stopped a car carrying Bommi Baumann and Georg von Rauch, leading figures in the nascent 2nd of June Movement anarchist guerilla. Von Rauch was immediately shot and killed, which many people took as proof that the cops had adopted a policy to "shoot first, ask questions later." Thousands participated in demonstrations protesting this killing, and an abandoned nurses' residence at the Bethanien Hospital was occupied and renamed the Georg von Rauch House.[2]

Georg von Rauch, murdered by police in West Berlin.

(Subsequent to leaving the guerilla, Baumann told an interviewer from *Spiegel* that von Rauch had fired his weapon first, though he later backtracked, claiming instead, "I no longer know who first pulled the trigger."[3] All of this was viewed with some suspicion, many observers feeling that

---

1 LA Times—Washington Post Service, "West Germany's 'Bonnie and Clyde' Have Country in an Uproar," *The Lawton Constitution*, December 3, 1972. Margrit Schiller could not in fact be tied to any RAF actions, and so was simply charged with illegal possession of a firearm and false identification papers. In February 1973, she received a twenty-seven-month sentence, but was released pending an appeal, at which point she went back underground, only to be captured again in 1974. (United Press International, "Raided Flat is Suspected Anarchist Hq." *European Stars and Stripes*, October 28, 1971; *European Stars and Stripes* "Released from Custody," February 11, 1973; Associated Press, "Raids in German Cities Smash New Terror Ring," *European Stars and Stripes*, February 5, 1974.)

2 The Georg von Rauch House still exists today, housing approximately forty itinerant youth at any given time.

3 Baumann, 95.

Die PoLizei

Genscher's KiLLer – ELite, oder die neue SA?

"The Police: Genscher's Killer Elite or the New Stormtroopers?"

Baumann's move to an anti-guerilla position rendered it tantamount to counter-insurgency propaganda.)

The "shoot first" hypothesis would be given further credence on March 1, 1972, when Richard Epple, a seventeen-year-old apprentice, was mowed down by police submachine gun fire after a car chase through Tübingen. Epple had run a police checkpoint because he was driving without a license—he had no connections to the RAF or any other guerilla group.[4] Later that year, in Stuttgart, a Scottish businessman, Ian McLeod, was similarly killed by police fire as he stood naked behind a bedroom door. Depending on who one believes, Macleod was either completely unconnected to the RAF, or else was himself a British intelligence agent intent on infiltrating the group—in either case it was clear the police shot without cause or provocation. Hundreds of people took to the streets to protest this police murder.[5]

The next bust occurred as 1971 came to a close: on December 17, Rolf Pohle was arrested in a gun shop in Neu-Ulm attempting to buy thirty-two firearms which the police claimed were meant for the RAF.[6] Pohle had been a young law student in Munich in the days of the APO. He had organized legal aid during the 1968 Easter riots,[7] and had been subjected to heavy police harassment ever since, eventually pushing him to join the underground.

---

4 Vague, 42-43.

5 United Press International, "Paper Says Macleod was a British Spy," *European Stars and Stripes*, July 3, 1972.

6 Associated Press, "Trial starts in Munich for accused Meinhof-gang munitions supplier," *European Stars and Stripes*, September 26, 1973. Pohle went to trial in 1973, charged with possession of firearms and support for a criminal organization under §129; during the trial, he spat at reporters and refused to acknowledge his court appointed lawyers. While he denied the charges against him, and repeatedly claimed that he was not a member of the RAF, he maintained solidarity with the guerilla. In 1974, he was sentenced to six-and-a-half years in prison, a term which he did not serve without some interruptions.

7 Freie Arbeiterinnen- und Arbeiter-Union, "Nachruf auf Rolf Pohle," https://www.fau.org/artikel/art_040308-182546.

On December 22, exactly two months after officer Schmid's demise, another cop was killed. Several RAF members were robbing a bank in the small military city of Kaiserslautern—the nearest police station had literally been blocked from interfering, guerilla helpers barricading its entrance with cars. By plain bad luck for all concerned, police officer Herbert Schoner spotted the parked getaway van as he passed by the bank, just as it was being relieved of its funds. When Schoner knocked on the van's window, he was shot twice—he managed to draw his gun before he was finished off by a third bullet.[1]

In the immediate aftermath of December 22, there was no publicly available evidence to tie the robbery or Schoner's death to any political organization. To all appearances, this was simply a "normal" crime. Nevertheless, the very next morning, the *Bild Zeitung* led the charge: "Baader-Meinhof Gang Strikes Again. Bank Raid: Policeman Shot," screamed the headline.

The Springer Press was merely doing what was by now a tradition, tarring the radical left with any and all crimes and misdemeanors. (Except, of course, that in this case they were right.)

The progressive *Gruppe 47* intellectual Heinrich Böll, perhaps the most important author in postwar Germany, was flabbergasted, and publicly accused the anti-RAF smear campaign of bearing all the hallmarks of fascism. While condemning their violence, he tried to put the RAF into perspective, famously describing their struggle as a "war of six against sixty million."

Böll's words may have been appreciated by the RAF, but he was certainly no supporter. Of course, this was not the way the right saw things, and he became the target of a hate campaign, branded an apologist for murder and a terrorist sympathizer,[2] to which he replied that those accused of sympathizing were simply "people who have committed the criminal sin of making distinctions."[3] He and his family would experience unusual levels of police harassment for years to come. At one point, for instance, as he was entertaining guests from out of town, police with submachine guns raided his home, claiming they suspected Ulrike Meinhof of being on the premises. (To the cop in charge, Böll declared that if Meinhof ever did show up he would

---

1 Aust, 190.
2 Ibid., 190-191.
3 Cobler, 41.

shelter her, but only on condition that she not bring any guns into his house. In his words, it would be the Christian thing to do.)[4]

It wasn't only the streets that were being policed, but also the cultural and political parameters of debate, and the RAF was being placed clearly beyond the pale.

A second, and at least initially less successful move to solidify public opinion against the RAF was the trial of Karl-Heinz Ruhland, which came to a close in March 1972.

Ruhland had been peripheral to the RAF when he was captured in December 1970. Soon after his arrest, he started providing the police with information, the location of safehouses and the names of those who had sheltered the guerilla.[5] When brought to trial on charges relating to a RAF bank robbery, much was made of his class status as a manual worker who was never fully accepted by the other members of the group, all in a fairly transparent ploy to show the guerilla up as hypocritical middle-class revolutionaries with no real affinity for the proletariat.

Ruhland provided the police with their first real break, however slight, into the world of the RAF, a service for which he received a relatively lenient sentence of four-and-a-half years. Although even the corporate press had to admit that he did not make a very convincing witness, often changing his testimony to fit the latest police theory, he would remain a fixture in future RAF trials[6] until someone more convincing could be turned. In retrospect, his significance appears to be as a template for future state witnesses to come.[7]

In the meantime, guns continued to blaze as the police and guerilla played an increasingly deadly game of hide and seek. Following a narrow escape, Andreas Baader even sent off a letter to the non-Springer press that he authenticated with his thumbprint, essentially to thumb his nose at the cops, and to prove that he was still alive.[8]

---

4 Robert Spaemann, "Kaffee, Kuchen und Terror," *Die Zeit* [online], 19 (1998).

5 Aust, 140.

6 Ruhland testified against Horst Mahler, Ali Jansen, and Astrid Proll amongst others. Several years later, after the Stammheim deaths, Ruhland was once again trotted out as an "old comrade" of the prisoners in order to explain how they must have felt suicidal. (United Press International, "Suicide Victim Died of Despair—Comrade," *Raleigh Register*, November 14, 1977).

7 Heinrich Hannover, "Terrorsitenprozessen," http://www.freilassung.de/div/texte/kronzeuge/heinhan1.htm.

8 Andreas Eichler, "Die RAF und die Medien." This document is reprinted in this volume: Andreas Baader: Letter to the Press, see pages 120-121.

*Thomas Weissbecker,
murdered by Augsburg
police on March 2, 1972.*

Then, on March 2, police in the Bavarian city of Augsburg killed Thomas Weissbecker and captured Carmen Roll (a former SPK member). Weissbecker was the son of a Jewish concentration camp survivor,[1] and had cut his teeth in the Hash Rebels scene before gravitating to the RAF. Twenty-three years old, he was never given a chance to surrender.

The killing took place as the two left Weissbecker's apartment. It was later revealed that the police had had him under surveillance since February, renting an apartment above his, and had been listening in on him just before he went out. This would suggest to many not a chance identity check, but a carefully staged murder.

In retaliation, the 2nd of June Movement bombed the police headquarters in West Berlin and, as in the case of Georg von Rauch, an empty building in Berlin was occupied and renamed the Tommy Weissbecker House.

While in custody Roll was drugged, apparently in the hope that she would provide police with information; as part of this chemically assisted interrogation, on March 16 the prison doctor gave her such a large dose of ether that she almost died.[2]

News of Weissbecker's murder spread quickly. In Hamburg, RAF members Manfred Grashof and Wolfgang Grundmann feared this meant the safehouse they were staying at—which had been rented by Weissbecker—might also be compromised. RAF policy in such situations was to simply leave the house and never return, but Grashof, whose speciality was producing false documents, decide to risk one trip back to gather some items he needed. When he and Grundmann returned, three cops were sitting inside in the dark. As soon as the guerillas opened the door, even before they turned on the lights, a cop panicked and started shooting.[3] Grashof was shot three times. He

---

1 Tilman Fichter, interview by Philipp Gessler and Stefan Reinecke, "The anti-Semitism of the 68ers."

2 Komitees gegen Folter, *Der Kampf Gegen die Vernichtungshaft* (n.p.) (n.d.), 131.

3 Gabriele Goettle, "Die Praxis der Galaxie," *die tageszeitung*, July 28, 2008.

returned fire, aiming blindly in the dark, and hit police commissioner Hans Eckardt, fatally wounding him.[4]

Grundmann had come to the RAF from *Schwarze Hilfe*, or Black Aid, a support group for anarchist political prisoners in West Berlin.[5]

As for Grashof, he had come to West Berlin in 1968 as an army deserter, and had joined with Horst Mahler in the Republican Club arguing that the semi-city be turned into an official refuge for others fleeing military service.[6] He had been with the guerilla from the beginning, being particularly close to Petra Schelm and especially upset by her death.

Despite his injuries, Grashof was moved from the hospital to a regular prison cell by Federal Supreme Court Judge Wolfgang Buddenberg, who had been put in charge of all RAF arrests. After two months, he was moved into isolation, only allowed to exercise for a half hour each day, and even then only with his wrists handcuffed behind his back. As a result of this treatment, his wounds opened up again, but he did not die.[7]

All of this unfolded within a context of increasing and increasingly visible police control and new repressive legislation. After having offered the carrot of amnesty and limited reforms, Brandt's SPD-FDP coalition was now showing that it also knew how to wield the stick.

In September 1971, a new Chief Commissioner was appointed to the BKA (Federal Criminal Bureau): Horst Herold, former Chief of the Nuremberg police, and an expert on the new methods of using computerized data processing as a law enforcement tool. Under Herold's leadership, the BKA was transformed from a relatively unimportant body into the West German equivalent of the FBI. Over the next decade, he would oversee a six-fold increase in the BKA budget, and a tripling of its staff as he personally pushed West Germany to the worldwide forefront of computerized repression.[8]

By 1979, Herold's computers contained files on 4.7 million names and 3,100 organizations, including the photos of 1.9 million people and 2.1

---

4 In 1977, Grashof received a life sentence for murder and other offenses; Grundmann received four years on lighter charges (Associated Press, "2 German Terrorists Given life," *European Stars and Stripes*, June 3, 1977.)

5 Becker, 273.

6 David Binder, "'Republic of West Berlin' Suggested by Radical Group," *Charleston Gazette*, November 7, 1968. Whereas young men living in West Berlin were already exempt from the draft, those who lived elsewhere and had already been drafted were liable to prosecution if they deserted.

7 Aust, 203.

8 Ibid., 181.

million sets of fingerprints.[1] While today it is routine for such data to be available at the touch of a police keyboard, in the 1970s this represented a simply unheard of level of surveillance and technical sophistication.

One of Herold's first moves was to set up a "Baader-Meinhof Special Commission," and hunting for the RAF remained his utmost priority throughout his tenure.

The significance of these changes in the BKA was overshadowed, though, by a new clampdown on the legal left, arguably the greatest since the ban on the KPD, as the Interior Ministers Conference passed the *Radikalenerlass* (Anti-Radical Act) on January 28, 1972. The new legislation was supported by all three major political parties, as well as all the major trade unions.[2] Known as the *Berufsverbot* (Professional Ban) by its opponents, its intention was to bar leftists from working in the public sector. The potential targets of this ban included some 14% of the workforce, not only government bureaucrats, but also anyone employed by the post office, the railways, public hospitals—and most importantly university professors and school teachers.[3]

The decree also dramatically increased the visibility of the *Verfassungsschutz* political police—the so-called "Guardians of the Constitution"—as the names of all applicants for public sector jobs were now sent to this agency, which determined on the basis of its own files whether a special hearing was necessary to gauge the applicant's loyalty to the state. Not only did the *Verfassungsschutz* comb open sources—speeches, pamphlets, doctoral theses, etc.—for names, but it also engaged in covert surveillance, telephone taps, and a network of informers which was said to include students hired to note who among their classmates held radical views.[4] (Little surprise that the agency's president until 1972 was Hubert Schrübbers, who had spent the early forties as a Nazi prosecutor notorious for seeking harsh sentences against antifascists, which would certainly have meant confinement in a concentration camp.)[5]

---

1 Ibid.

2 Gerard Braunthal, *Political Service and Public Loyalty in West Germany: the 1972 decree against radicals and its consequences* (Amherst: University of Massachusetts Press, 1990), 36-37.

3 Monica Jacobs, "Civil Rights and Women's Rights in the Federal Republic of Germany Today," *New German Critique* 16 Special Feminist Issue (Winter 1978): 166.

4 Braunthal, 42.

5 Ibid., 43.

As Georgy Katsiaficas has noted, "the decree resulted in loyalty checks on 3.5 million persons and the rejection of 2,250 civil service applicants. Although only 256 civil servants were dismissed, the decree had a chilling effect."[6] So much so that according to one survey carried out in the city of Mannheim, "84 percent of university students there refrained from regularly checking leftist materials out of public libraries for fear of being blacklisted."[7]

Obviously, those students who had refused the SPD's amnesty in 1971 found themselves among the first to be targeted. While most of these people would no doubt have rejected the RAF's politics, fears about the guerilla were exploited to help push through the legislation. As Heinz Kühn, SPD President of North Rhine-Westphalia, put it, "We could hardly have Ulrike Meinhof employed as a teacher, or Andreas Baader in the police force."[8]

In the wake of the sixties student movement, the state was establishing the conditions under which erstwhile rebels would be allowed to join the establishment. As its corollary, this rollback included ongoing attacks on the universities themselves. For instance, in early 1972, the Free University hired the Trotskyist Ernest Mandel as professor of economics: the Berlin Senate responded by vetoing this appointment,[9] and despite student strikes, Mandel was barred from entering the FRG. (This ban was only lifted in 1978.)[10]

In this context, in April 1972, the RAF released its second theoretical statement, *Serve the People: The Urban Guerilla and Class Struggle*. As with *The Urban Guerilla Concept*, this text was distributed in magazine form at the May Day demonstrations that year.

In a text almost twice as long as the previous one, the RAF was trying to provide an analysis of the previous year's events, both within the left and within the Federal Republic as a whole. Considerable energy was spent analyzing the unsuccessful workers' struggles in the chemical sector in 1971 and the failure of the legal left to respond to class

---

6 Georgy Katsiaficas, *The Subversion of Politics: European Autonomous Social Movements and the Decolonization of Everyday Life* (Oakland: AK Press, 2006), 64.

7 Ibid.

8 Aust, 192.

9 *Time Magazine* [online], "Battle of Berlin," July 3, 1972.

10 Rote Armee Fraktion, *Texte und Materialien zur Geschichte der RAF*, (Berlin: ID-Verlag, 1997), 82.

oppression within the FRG. These weaknesses were pointed to as so many factors underscoring the necessity for armed politics.

A real attempt to find a strategic connection between class oppression, working-class struggle (outside of the unions, of course) and the guerilla is apparent in all the RAF's theoretical documents in this period.

This will not always be the case. In contradistinction to its anti-imperialism, this class orientation at times approximated left-communism in its focus on working-class self-activity and alienation. Partly, the explanation for this can be found in the political experiences and trajectories of the core members of the RAF at this point: the sixties revolt and the APO, with their grounding in not only Marxism-Leninism and anti-imperialism, but also Frankfurt School Marxism, the "apprentices collectives," and, via the SPK, radical therapy.

At the same time, the period between 1969 and 1973 was one of heightened class conflict in the FRG, beyond and at times against the trade union leadership, with wildcat strikes often being led by women, youth, and immigrant workers. Combined with the sudden turn of many former APO comrades to the new "proletarian" K-groups, this created a context in which it would have been difficult to elaborate a revolutionary strategy without dealing with the question of the working class.

As we shall see later on, some of the ideas in this document were soon qualified, if not rejected, while others were sharpened, finding their place in the centre of the RAF's worldview.

Finally, *Serve the People* provides the RAF's response to Karl-Heinz Ruhland, who had been turned into an instrument of police propaganda. Similarly, two drop-outs from the guerilla, Beate Sturm and Peter Homann, were also excoriated as traitors.

Unlike Ruhland, Sturm's main crime seems to have been that, subsequent to leaving the RAF, she contacted the media, providing *Spiegel* with a highly unflattering portrait of the group.

Homann's story, on the other hand, was more complex; some controversy about his falling out with the group remains even today. While there are radically different versions of the circumstances, it is clear that he was on very bad terms with his erstwhile comrades upon his return from the Jordan training trip in 1970. Immediately after this, he and his friend Stefan Aust traveled to Sicily where Meinhof's seven-year-old twin daughters were being cared for by comrades. Pretending to be members of the RAF, the two men took Meinhof's girls with them, delivering them to their father, *konkret* editor Klaus Rainer Röhl.

It seems likely that this direct intervention to thwart Meinhof's plans for her children played some part in provoking his denunciation as a traitor in *Serve the People*. There are contradictory versions as to why Homann did what he did,[1] but regardless of the facts surrounding this initial "treason," he would fully earn the sobriquet later that year, going so far as to provide the police with information, and to testify against the guerilla in court.[2]

In retrospect, *Serve the People* is significant not so much in its contents, but in its timing, by which it serves as the end of a chapter. With its explanations of the bank robberies and the painstaking preparations undertaken, it allowed the guerilla to deal with some preliminary questions before moving on to grander schemes.

It would be the last theoretical document produced by the RAF outside of prison for almost ten years.

---

1 See Appendix V—Strange Stories: Peter Homann and Stefan Aust, on pages 557-58.

2 United Press International, "Meinhof-Al Fatah Ties Described," *European Stars and Stripes*, October 19, 1972.

Andreas Baader:
Letter to the Press

The cops will continue to fumble about in the dark, until circumstances oblige them to see that the political situation has become a military situation.

Marighella

The truth of the matter is that no further information has come out about the group since the first twenty were trained in Jordan. The RAF's work is clandestine. The "security forces," the security agencies, the police, the BND, the *Verfassungsschutz*, the BAW, *Spiegel*, and the Springer Press know nothing.

They know nothing about the size, the number of members, the organization, the firepower, or the tactics of the group. Everything written about us by the police state for public consumption over the past year-and-a-half is false, is speculation, or is counterpropaganda with the objective of discrediting the theory and practice of the urban guerilla and driving a wedge between us and our base.

I haven't considered turning myself in. No RAF members have considered turning themselves in. So far no RAF prisoner has provided testimony. Announcements of successes against us have only been about arrests or killings. The guerilla's strength lies in the determination of each of us. We are not on the run. We are here organizing armed resistance against the regime of the propertied classes and the ongoing exploitation of the people.

The RAF's current activities are directed towards the formation of politico-military cadre, acquiring better arms and training for revolutionaries, and the anchoring of the group in a sympathetic scene that is ready to support armed resistance. The tactical line that we are currently following is to develop the propaganda of the urban guerilla through the revolutionary organizations that are still legal and to develop broad-based logistical support amongst all layers of the population.

None of us see any subjective or objective basis for betraying the struggle to which we have committed ourselves; not Genscher's dirty amnesty deal, not Ruhland, the Social Democrats' van der Lubbe,[1]

---

1 Marinus van der Lubbe, a Dutch council communist, confessed to the 1933

not the extensive militarization of the police, not prison, not torture, and not the police terror against the population. "The stones they have thrown will fall at their own feet."[2]

If the price for our lives or our freedom is to be the betrayal of the anticapitalist struggle, there is only one response: we won't pay it.

The armed struggle does not develop from one headline to the next. The politico-military strategy of the urban guerilla is based in the resistance to parliamentary democracy's fascist drift and the organization of the first regular units of the Red Army in the people's war. The battle has just begun.

Andreas Baader
January 24, 1972

A. Baader

Reichstag fire under Gestapo torture. It remains unclear if he was, in fact, guilty. Karl-Heinz Ruhland, a fringe member of the RAF, under pressure from the BKA and with coaching from the BAW, provided clearly fabricated testimony against RAF prisoners during a series of trials.

2 This phrase, which will reoccur in a number of different forms in RAF documents over the years, comes from a speech Mao gave at the Meeting of the Supreme Soviet of the USSR in Celebration of the 40th Anniversary of the Great October Socialist Revolution on November 6, 1957: "'Lifting a rock only to drop it on one's own feet' is a Chinese folk saying to describe the behaviour of certain fools. The reactionaries in all countries are fools of this kind. In the final analysis, their persecution of the revolutionary people only serves to accelerate the people's revolutions on a broader and more intense scale. Did not the persecution of the revolutionary people by the tsar of Russia and by Chiang Kai-shek perform this function in the great Russian and Chinese revolutions?"

Serve the People:
The Urban Guerilla
and Class Struggle

Everyone dies, but death can vary in its significance. The ancient Chinese writer Szuma Chien said, "Though death befalls all men alike, it may be heavier than Mount Tai or lighter than a feather." To die for the people is heavier than Mount Tai, but to work for the fascist and die for the exploiters and oppressors is lighter than a feather.

Mao tse Tung

"The armed struggle is a technical issue and therefore requires technical knowledge: training, morale and last of all practice. In this area, improvisation has cost many lives and led to failed attacks. The 'spontaneity' that some people romanticize, speaking vaguely about the people's revolution and 'the masses,' is either simply a dodge or it indicates that they have decided to rely upon improvisation during a critical phase of the class struggle. Every vanguard movement must, if they want to remain true to themselves at the decisive moment in the class struggle, analyze and understand the violence of the people, so as to correctly direct it against oppression, thereby achieving the goal with the least sacrifice possible."[1]

ALL POWER TO THE PEOPLE!

---

1 Although not referenced as such by the RAF, this is a quote from *30 Questions to a Tupamaro* (see page 128, fn 1).

20,000 die every year because the stockholders of the automobile industry only care about profit and, therefore, don't stop to consider technical safety issues for automobiles or road construction. 5,000 people die every year at their workplace or on their way to or from it, because the owners of the means of production only consider their profits and don't care about an increase or a decline in the number of accidental deaths. 12,000 commit suicide every year, because they don't want to die in the service of capital; they'd rather just get it over with themselves. 1,000 children are murdered every year, as a result of living in low quality housing, the only purpose of which is to allow the landlord to pocket a large sum.

People treat death in the service of the exploiter as normal. The refusal to die in the service of the exploiter leads to what people think of as "unnatural deaths." The desperate actions of people, coping with the working and living conditions that capital has created, are perceived as crimes. People feel there's nothing to be done about the situation. To ensure that the incorrect perspective of the people is not replaced with a correct perspective, the Federal Minister of the Interior, the *Länder* Ministers of the Interior, and the BAW have set up police death squads. Without this incorrect perspective about crime and death, the ruling class could not maintain its rule.

Petra, Georg, and Thomas died in the struggle against death at the hands of the exploiters. They were murdered so that capital could continue killing undisturbed, and so that people would continue to think that nothing can be done about the situation. But the struggle has begun!

"Murdered—The Struggle Continues": poster protesting the police killings of Petra Schelm, Georg von Rauch, and Thomas Weissbecker.

I. PERSIA AND THE
CONTRADICTION WITHIN THE NEW LEFT

Brandt has flown to Tehran to visit the Shah and calm his remaining distress about the greeting he received from West German and West Berlin students during the summer of 67; to inform him that the left in the Federal Republic and in West Berlin is dead, that what remains will soon be liquidated, that the Confederation of Iranian Students[1] is effectively isolated, and about the Foreigners Act that is in the works and that will allow for their legal liquidation.

In this way Brandt has revealed the true nature of his foreign and domestic policies; they are the foreign and domestic policies of the corporations meant to control foreign and external markets and to determine who holds political power

In Tehran Brandt said, "The foreign policy of the Federal Republic must be based on its own interests and must remain free of ideological bias." The interests of the Federal Republic in Persia are the interests of the German enclave in Tehran, which is to say Siemens, AEG-Telefunken, Bayer, BASF, Hoechst, Daimler-Benz, Deutsche Bank, Mannesmann, Hochtief, Klöckner-Humboldt-Deutz, Merck, Schering, Robert Bosch, the Bayerische Vereinsbank, Thyssen, Degussa, and others. They are the ones that had the greetings to the Chancellor published in Tehran's newspapers.

The Shah also contributed a statement to the daily press celebrating the Chancellor as a Nobel Peace Prize laureate, because the Shah also has no ideological biases; concerning cheap labor in Iran, concerning stable political conditions in Iran, not to mention raw materials and certain nearby markets.

Under "ideological biases," the Chancellor and the Shah subsume the interests of the German and Persian peoples regarding the relationship between their two countries. Three days before Brandt's arrival, four comrades were murdered in Tehran and Thomas Weissbecker was murdered in Augsburg. A week after Brandt's return, nine death penalties were carried out against comrades in Tehran. Meanwhile, Attorney General Martin[2] praised the police officers for so impressively proving their worth in the manhunts in Augsburg and Hamburg.

---

1 The Confederation of Iranian Students (CIS) was a Maoist student organization based in the refugee communities and active on university campuses throughout the Western world.

2 Ludwig Martin, Attorney General from 1963 until 1974, when he was replaced by Siegfried Buback.

German capital in Persia is taxed at a lower rate than other capital in Persia. German development aid credit finances German projects in Persia; and the imperial arsenal in Persia is to be modernized with the help of the German military. A 22 million DM[3] investment in the Persian arms industry in 1969 meant 250 million DM[4] in follow-up orders for the German arms industry. The Shah's regime plans to use G-3s and MG-3s[5] in the struggle against "crime" in Persia, so that in the future wages will remain low, political conditions will remain stable and the conditions of exploitation will remain favorable for German capital. Meaning that pressure for increased wages at home can be handled with threats to move production out of the country. Pressure will also be applied to the public at home, because antifascist protest against the Shah threatens the foreign policy interests of the Federal Republic of Germany.

After prostrating himself in Poland,[6] the Chancellor now prostrates himself before the murderous Shah. The repression of the Polish, Russian, Czech, and Hungarian peoples by German fascism is no longer gong on. The repression of the Persian people under German imperialism is what is going on now. The Nuremberg Conventions are no longer in effect, but laws against Iranian students, against Greek, Turkish, and Spanish workers, who all come from countries with fascist regimes, are a current reality. German corporations profit from the fascism in these countries, controlling foreign workers here with the threat of what the fascism at home means for them. They are safe from the death penalty, which imprisoned comrades here are spared, but which is enforced in Persia, Turkey, Greece, and Spain.

The West German left met Brandt's Persian trip with silence. They left him free to babble twaddle. They let Howeida[7] babble twaddle about how the death penalty is only used against common criminals. Given that the Shah is sensitive, given that the 2nd of June disturbed the relationship between Germany and Iran, given that the Shah's reputation is hardly stellar, as would have to be the case, given that, as

---

3 Roughly $6 million.

4 Almost $69 million.

5 The G-3 is an assault rifle and the MG-3 is a machinegun.

6 This is a reference to the so-called *Warshauer Kniefall*, the "Warsaw Genuflection," Brandt's December 1971 public atonement at the monument commemorating the Warsaw Ghetto Uprising.

7 Amir Abbas Howeida, Prime Minister of Iran during the rule of Shah Reza Pahlavi. He was executed in 1979 following the Islamic revolution.

everyone knows, enemies of the people dread being called enemies of the people, given that one can presume that even Brandt wasn't all that comfortable with the hypocrisy, given that German capital is predisposed to fascism, and given that it's relatively easy to demonstrate the connection between fascism in Iran and German capital in Iran... given all these things, nobody can defend the relationship without presenting themselves in a poor light.

The intellectual left came to the conclusion that only the proletarian masses can change the current situation, that only the West German masses can expropriate the profits that the corporations make from the Shah's fascism—a situation from which the Shah's fascism also profits. With this realization, the left stopped criticizing the Shah's fascism and the domination imposed by West German capitalism in the Third World. With the realization that the resistance of the West German masses against the rule of capital would not be sparked by the problems of the Third World, but only by the problems developing here, they stopped posing the problems of the Third World as a factor in politics here.

This shows both the dogmatism and the parochialism of a section of the left. The fact that the working class in West Germany and West Berlin can only think and act in the national context, while capital thinks and acts in a multinational context, is first and foremost an example of the splitting of the working class, as well as of the weakness of a left that only focuses on capital's domestic policies in its critique and ignores capital's foreign policy, thus internalizing the split in the working class. They tell the working class only half of the truth about the system, about what capitalist policy means for the working class on a daily basis and what it means for wage demands in the foreseeable future.

The contradiction facing the New Left is that their basic economic analysis and political assessment is more radical and incisive than anything produced by the West German left prior to the 66/67 recession. This left experienced the end of the postwar reconstruction phase and the strengthening of West German imperialism and understood that they had to base themselves on the extraordinary class struggle, which led to them restricting their propaganda and organizational efforts to the national context. As a result, they have an unimaginative and narrow view of what revolutionary methods of intervention are possible.

In their efforts to give a scientific orientation to the anticapitalist protest—which reaches into the schools, the unions and the SPD— to maintain and develop their position in the high schools, they used

Marxism to make the history of the working class more accessible to teachers and students. They hoped in this way to gain a foothold in the factories and schools.

Through these activities they show a willingness to act and to intervene that stands in contradiction to their actual methods of intervention, which remain those that were appropriate for the working class during the phase of competitive capitalism and parliamentarianism. They were appropriate in the period when Rosa Luxemburg, looking at the mass strikes in Russia in 1905, recognized the immense importance of strikes in the political struggle and Lenin recognized the importance of union struggles. It is the contradiction between their use of the German working class as their historical reference point, and the increasing tendency today of West German capitalism to organize itself in the form of West German imperialism.

A section of the left still sees the RAF as Baader and Meinhof's personal thing and—like Howeida, the *Bild* and the *BZ*—discusses armed struggle as if it were a form of criminal activity. In a similar vein, they also attribute our activity to faulty reasoning and misrepresent our positions. As a result, they will fail to resolve the contradiction between what they know to be the state of the class struggle, and what they perceive to be the revolutionary methods of intervention. They transform the objective problem that we all face into our subjective problem alone. They conduct themselves as if they fear the difficult task ahead of them—they bury their heads in the sand and refuse to think about it. The denunciation of the concept of the urban guerilla within a section of the left succeeds far too easily and without much thought, thereby allowing us to see the growing distance between their theory and their practice, a distance that we do not believe can be closed by our efforts alone. Their claim that they are actually involved in this debate proves, we think, that we and they have different self-perceptions.

A year ago, we said that the urban guerilla unites the national and international class struggle. The urban guerilla makes it possible for the people to become aware of the interconnectedness of imperialist rule. The urban guerilla is the revolutionary form of intervention suited to an overall position of weakness. An advance in the class struggle only occurs if legal and illegal work are connected, if political propaganda has a perspective that includes armed struggle and if political organization includes the possibility of the urban guerilla. This was made clear through the concrete example of the chemical workers strike in 1971, which showed the objective reality of the social question, the subjective reality of the question of capitalist ownership, and the militarization of the class struggle in West Germany and West Berlin.

> *In the current phase of history no one can any longer deny that an armed group, however small it may be, has more of a chance of becoming a people's army than a group that has been reduced to spouting revolutionary rhetoric.*
>
> 30 Questions to a Tupamaro[1]

2. THE CHEMICAL WORKERS STRIKE OF 1971

The widespread strikes in the chemical and metal industries in 1971—among the most developed industries in West Europe—made it clear what the problems facing the working class will be in the coming years. They exhibited a widespread readiness to struggle on the part of the workforce, while simultaneously showing the economic and political advantages the chemical and metal industries have vis-à-vis the working class; they showed the complicity of the union bureaucracies with the Social-Liberal government and the role of the government as the executive organ of this "corporate state."

The workers lost the strikes. They struck for 11 and 12 percent, and the unions settled with the employers for 7.8 and 7.5 percent. The situation that socialists in the Federal Republic and West Berlin will face in coming years was certainly clarified by this strike: subjectively, an increase in readiness to struggle on the part of the working class and, objectively, the reduced capacity to struggle; objectively, a decrease in wages and the loss of "vested social rights," subjectively, increased class antagonism and class hatred.

Economically speaking, the strength of the chemical industry was the result of the trends towards concentration and the export of capital which have been forced upon the entire West European economy by North American competition. Politically, it was the result of the lessons that West German industry drew from May 68 in France and the wildcat strikes of September 69. Their counteroffensive against the September strikes here certainly increased class consciousness.

---

1 The Tupamaros were a guerilla group in Uruguay at the time. This short interview started circulating as an internal document in 1967, and was first made public in a Chilean journal in mid-1968. Within a few years, it had become a text of some importance to the revolutionary edge of the New Left in the metropole.

Concentration

Due to their size and technological advantages, the large American industrialists can achieve lower production costs despite paying higher wages. Hugh Stephenson of *Time* magazine:

> *the problem of size is not essentially one of the size of factory installations, rather the key is understanding the grandeur of the financial and economic factors that stand behind this. A large volume of business means almost nothing. However, it does have advantageous implications regarding dominant market position. And that is an advantage that can't be achieved without substantial investment in modern industry, even if it is not in the area of developing technologies. The type of competition between industrialists in developing branches of industry, such as the automobile, chemical, and oil industries, has completely changed. The cost of new investments is so high for the enterprises involved that as stable a future market as the intense competition allows for must be guaranteed. Under these circumstances, it is inevitable that European industry must in the future enter a phase of concentration into fewer and larger groups.*
>
> *Die Welt*, February 23, 1972

Public Funds

Concentration is the first reality. The influx of public funds to cover the costs of research and development is the second. North American industries have access to greater funds of this variety as a result of their size and the U.S.A.'s permanent war economy. In 1963-64, the U.S.A. used 3.3 percent of its gross national product for research purposes—compared to an average of 1.5 percent in West Europe. Hugh Stephenson:

> *In the area of developing technologies, Europe will never be able to deal with the immense and ever-growing research and development costs if a constant flow of public funds is not guaranteed.*

If not, then it would be better to just sign deals with American firms right away. That is the pressure that today's economy places on the state. Concentration and state subsidies have become a question of survival for capitalist West Europe.

The Export of Capital

The third thing is the export of capital. This entails cooperation with foreign industries and building factories in foreign countries, with the aim of profiting from the cheaper raw materials and lower wages available in these countries, and of reducing transportation costs by buying from foreign markets.

Because the chemical industry stands at the forefront of this development, the chemical workers strike of 1971 had a central significance. It serves as an example of an entire trend, from the chemical companies' strike preparations in December 1970, through the purge of teachers who are members of the DKP from the public service and the incorporation of the BGS into the federal police force, from the first signs of fascism in the Federal Republic to the CSU seizing control of *Bayerischen Rundfunk*,[1] from the refusal to allow Mandel to teach at the Free University to the application of the death penalty to the Red Army Faction.

As a result of this, in the coming years increasing numbers of people from all levels of society, with the exception of the owners of capital, will find themselves dissatisfied with the structure of ownership. It therefore follows that it is tactically and strategically incorrect not to treat the question of ownership, which is now addressed with trivial and wishy washy arguments about co-management[2] and "protecting what we've begun," as the general and ongoing central issue. The situation has also led to a development whereby anyone who profits from these circumstances can conceal that fact.

Bayer – BASF – Farbwerke Hoechst

The chemical industry is among the industries with the highest levels of concentration in West Germany. The market share of just three, IG Farben-Nachfolger Bayer, Farbwerke Hoechst, and BASF, makes up 50 percent of the industrial sector. These three chemical corporations are among the four largest companies incorporated in the Federal Republic.

Of the 597,000 employed in the sector, 200,000 work for the big three. They control over 50 percent of the funds for research and

---

1 *Bayerischen Rundfunk*: Bavarian Broadcasting, the public radio station in Bavaria.

2 The practice of union representatives having a vote on the corporate boards dates from the late 1940s. Also referred to as co-determination.

development in the chemical industry. In the years 1965-70 alone, BASF gained control of business and corporate concerns that conducted 4 billion DM³ worth of business, which was more than it had itself been conducting in 1965.

Regarding the cooperation between the state and the chemical corporations, the 1969 Federal Research Report states:

> *In the chemical industry one can speak of a genuine division of labor between state-funded basic research and industrial research. The chemical industry can only continue their recent rate of growth and retain their international importance if a high level of (state-supported) basic research continues.*

What export of capital means in the chemical industry is that while in 1970 West German industry did 19.3 percent of their business outside of Germany, for Farbwerke Hoechst it was 44 percent, for BASF 50 percent, for Bayer 56 percent. South Africa, Portugal, Turkey, Iran, and Brazil are some of the places where they have production facilities.

The Federal Republic also provides military aid to Portugal, Turkey, and Iran. Obviously, this military aid serves to ensure conditions of exploitation beneficial to West German capital in these countries, which is to say, holding down wages and gunning down workers who resist. It is also clear that since the mid-60s this military aid has also served to build up "security forces," which is to say the police, who conduct the anti-guerilla war under the guise of fighting crime, saying whatever is necessary to support that position: there is no resistance, the masses are completely satisfied, it's only a question of criminals and crime.

American military aid to Iran was given to support the campaign against drug dealing and smuggling, and Brandt has no "ideological biases" if the execution of revolutionaries is disguised as sentences carried out against criminals. Scheel spoke recently—in the context of the signing of a contract, in which the Federal Republic secured future Brazilian uranium discoveries—of the common interest of the Federal Republic and the Brazilian military junta in resisting "terrorism and subversive activities," which is in reaction to the Latin American guerillas who laid bombs at the BASF installation.

Together with American corporations, the West German chemical corporations control almost the entire chemical and pharmaceutical market in Iran. Iran is the site of the greatest rate of expansion

---

3 Roughly $1.45 billion.

of Western interests; South Africa offers the highest rate of profit—Volkswagen for example averaged dividends of 30 percent last year, and in 1968 they were as high as 45 percent. Between what they produce and what they sell, the West German chemical and pharmaceutical industry controls 10 to 12 percent of the South American market.

Pressure on wages and the reduction of the wage-cost ratio in production was achieved through the exploitation of lower wage standards in foreign countries, through guest workers, and through investments at home, all of which the chemical industry has used in recent years to achieve a 75 percent increase in capacity, as well as rationalization and redundancy in the labor force.

The figures: between 1950 and 1970, the number of people employed in the chemical industry increased by only 100 percent, compared to an increase in sales of 636 percent. In general, the tendency is for the number of people to decrease. The closing of Phrixwerke made the headlines. Hüls announced this February that in 1972 the number of people it employs will decrease by 3 to 4 percent. The chemical industry speaks of "the increasing importance of labor costs." This indicates that they intend lay-offs and wage rollbacks. They entered the 1971 round of negotiations with the aim of asserting their concept of "labor costs," which is to say, with the hope of putting the working class on the defensive through a massive attack.

The Strength of the Capitalist Class

Concentration as the precondition for a strong negotiating position for capital requires nothing more than a unified position on the part of the employers, in a situation where the Employers Association is controlled by the corporations that control the market: Bayer, BASF, and Hoechst. Export of capital is a source of strength for the chemical industry, given that it creates a situation in which the working class that confronts it is not the industry's only source of profit. In the workers' struggle, the elimination of competition between wage workers always finds its practical limits within national borders, and so a strike only stops a part of capital's profitable production. While the workers gamble everything, capital only gambles part of what it has.

Just because the chemical industry ruthlessly uses its strengths to gain the upper hand politically is absolutely no reason for whining. It is an error to see the chemical companies as especially evil because they make use of slave labor in Africa, Asia, and Latin America to put pressure on wages, because they use investments to get the labor force off their backs, and because they use concentration to secure economic and political mobility and flexibility. The brutality of their exploitative behavior—in the form of political repression and pressure to reduce the costs of social reproduction—indicates the effect of North American competition on West Europe's economy, as well as the rationalization of the sector, its products, and the market. It is an integral part of the inhumanity and criminality of the system and will only be eliminated when the system is eliminated, or it will not be eliminated at all.

The chemical industry prepared meticulously for the strike; it was they and not the unions that wanted the strike, and they and not the unions that won the strike. The workers suffered a setback. Everybody played different roles against them: capital, the government, and the union bureaucracy.

Preparing for the Strike

In February 71, the unions called for a wage increase beginning March 31 in Hessen, North Rhine and Rhineland Palatinate, demanding 11 to 12 percent, and for Hessen a flat 120 marks,[1] which for Hessen meant the same wage increase for all wage levels, the freezing of wage cuts and a step forward in the unity of the working class. The chemical industry refused to make any deal.

In December 70, the chemical industry had already created "mutual support systems" between their companies in case of a strike. This took the form of transferring money related to wage payments to the development and conversion of raw materials, to the production of primary and intermediate products, and to the setting aside of capital for production facilities and transportation. They also provided their customers with an 8-week stock of their products, including the smaller clients such as drugstores and universities—the rector of Düsseldorf University, for example, called upon the institutes and seminars to stock up as a precautionary measure.

Operating measures were worked out in detail: instruction manuals for strike breakers, secure plant telephone systems, a list of the names of union representatives, facilities to print leaflets, contacts with the local press and opinion-makers such as teachers, ministers, and associations.

---

1 Roughly $43. Regarding the flat rate: wage increases in many German industries were indexed by workers' "skill category," which meant that every wage increase in fact served to increase the divide between different layers of the working class. The demand for a flat wage increase was meant to counter this trend, as such an increase would benefit all workers equally. On this, see Roth, 116-117.

Lists were drawn up of supposed members of an "underground political force" to be forwarded to the *Verfassungsschutz* and the police. Contacts with the police, government departments, and Interior Ministers. A line of argument was also developed about the "danger to the workplace posed by the strike," etc.

In December 70, the union representatives at Farbwerke Hoechst polled their members regarding the proposed wage demands. The Wage Commission—made up of representatives from the IG Chemie trade union and the larger companies—refused the demands. The vote with which the demands were rejected wasn't even close: 4 to 1. The union representatives from Merck in Darmstadt demanded 160 marks[1] or 12 percent. They also had little luck with the Wage Commission.

State Support for the Capitalist Class

The Employers Association received state support. The basic 9 percent wage increase projected in the government's wage guidelines was reduced to 7.5 percent at the beginning of the year. Brandt, on May 11 in parliament: "In the current phase, wage costs that are too high risk causing underemployment." The experts in their opinions supported the chemical industry, stating that "a very slow reduction in the rate of wage increases" is not enough, but that "extreme measures are necessary." (May 71)

In May, the chemical industry made an offer of 5 percent, and IG Chemie issued a press release stating that they wouldn't insist upon 11 or 12 percent, but would accept 8 or 9 percent

The Betrayal of Rhineland Palatinate

On May 24, however, Rhineland Palatinate—to great public surprise—signed a wage contract for 7.8 percent over ten months, which on the basis of a real duration of twelve months is 6.5 percent, less than that suggested in Schiller's[2] reference data. Rhineland Palatinate is controlled by BASF. BASF won't accept strikes.

Bayer and Hoechst also later avoided strikes. The employees of the large companies don't want the humiliation of a setback during a strike; they have been disciplined by a broad and diverse system of pacification:

---

1 Roughly $58.

2 Karl Schiller was the SPD's Federal Minister of Economic Affairs and Minister of Finance at the time. His reference data would presumably have determined the government's wage guidelines.

company housing, purported profit sharing, training grants, a body of company representatives alongside the unions, the organization of the workplace whereby the employees are split into hundreds of separate factory units, a wage system split into different wage levels, separate low wage groups for men and women.

The chemical industry in Hessen circulated to its own employees the leaflet that the IG Chemie trade union had prepared for its members regarding this outcome. The Wage Commission in North Rhine and Hessen bristled at the outcome in Rhineland Palatinate. They talked about options for struggle, but didn't prepare them. IG Chemie simply demanded that their members get their dues in order and recruit new members.

The Strike
In the face of the chemical industry's resistance, federal government arbitration eventually failed in North Rhine and Hessen, and later in Westphalia and Hamburg. Following the failure of federal government arbitration, the strike began. From the beginning of June until the beginning of July, a total of 50,000 workers in these four areas were on strike and 150,000 were involved in support actions. In North Rhine they struck for 9 percent, in Hessen for a flat increase of at least 120 marks,[3] or 11 percent, and in the other areas for 11 or 12 percent. It was the first strike in the chemical industry in 40 years, since the wage struggles at the beginning and end of the 1920s.

The organizational initiative didn't come from the unions; it came from the workers. At Glanzstoff in Oberbruch, it started with 120 skilled workers, who spontaneously walked out on June 3. Later, when the union called for a work stoppage in the key sectors, other workers spontaneously joined the strike. At Dynamit Nobel in Troisdorf, the action began with a spontaneous walkout on the part of skilled workers in the explosives factories. At Clouth-Gummiwerken in Cologne, where the strike lasted 4 weeks, it began with the mill workers. At Degussa in Wolfgang, small groups of skilled workers walked out of the various production centres, calling for a demonstration against the factory committee and the union representatives. At Braun in Melsungen, it began with workers in the engineering building. In Glanzstoff in Kelsterbach, the action began with a sit-down strike by some Spanish workers. In Merck, at Farbwerken Hoechst, the action began with

---

3 Roughly $43.

different small groups. In some factories the strike lasted for the entire month of June.

On June 8, 10,000 workers took part in a mass IG Chemie trade union demonstration at the Cologne Arena. On June 14, there was a day of action in North Rhine; 19,000 workers from 38 factories joined the strike. On June 16, 10,000 workers again participated in a second mass IG Chemie demonstration in Cologne. Simultaneously, 16,000 took part in actions in Hessen—4,000 workers from Farbwerke Hoechst participated in a union demonstration; it was the first time in 50 years that there was a strike at Hoechst—even if it only lasted a few hours. At the end of June, 38,000 workers were on strike in Hessen, North Rhine, Hamburg, and Westphalia. If one considers the dubious behavior of the union bureaucracy, and the fact that the strike initiative came from small groups, these are impressive numbers.

At Merck, the employees were pressured by the chairman of the factory committee to back the union's demands. The strike motion put forward by strike leaders at Bayer in Leverkusen wasn't accepted by the regional strike headquarters. Many didn't want to strike, because they felt not enough was being demanded. Many didn't want to strike, because they feared it would end in a rotten compromise. That activities were restricted to isolated actions at Farbwerken Hoechst and at Bayer in Leverkusen—the largest factories in Hessen and North Rhine— demoralized many people. The corporations' system of pacification paid off.

During the strike, the chemical industry took every possible step to remain on the offensive—and to keep the unions on the defensive. Pressure was kept on the workers by claims that the strike was illegal because no strike vote had been held—at IG Chemie, a strike vote is not required, as is also the case at IG Metall. At Hoechst, the argument that there could be "no strike without a strike vote" prevented the strike. The strike leadership at Merck treated the issue of rights as an issue of power in the class struggle: "In the workers' struggle, and everything is in the wording, we are governed first and foremost by the opinion of the majority, or more specifically the strikers." IG Chemie can only conceive of things in terms of their own bylaws.

The chemical industry made equal use of legal and illegal methods; Merck spread rumors about injuries; they claimed that stones had been placed on the tracks of the factories' rail system, that "anticorporate elements" had engaged in sabotage and that strike centres were defended with bicycle chains and brass knuckles. At Glanzstoff in Oberbruch, rumors were spread about shootings. Police units ensured that strike breakers could gain access to the factories at Merck and Glanzstoff. The *Kripo* photographed and attacked strike centres. Buses carrying strike breakers drove into strike centres (Glanzstoff). Company management at Merck disrupted radio communication between strike centres and increased plant security. Riot police stood at the ready. Outside workers were brought in as strike breakers. An encampment was forced off the factory premises. At Glanzstoff, the police units were so vicious that young police officers were crying and older ones had to be replaced before the police could clear a path for the strike breakers.

Class Justice

An injunction issued by the Labor Court ensured strike breakers access to the factories, sanctioned the use of police units, and criminalized strike actions. In Merck, following this injunction, IG Chemie accepted a settlement, the contents of which did not respect the work stoppage— the entry for strike breakers—and held that if anything the injunction sanctioned the unions. As a result, union strike leaders of Merck in Rükken said regarding the injunction, "The eyes of the law look out from the face of the ruling class." (Ernst Bloch)[1] "We accuse society's leaders of violence; the violence begins and ends with society's leaders." Regarding the injunction, they said, "The injunction makes a mockery of the right to work, using it to permit strike breakers. But the employers refuse to protect the real right to work. Where was the right to work during the crisis of 1966-67?"

The mayor of Darmstadt followed a declaration of state and police neutrality with the threat that surely no one wanted a vacation in the hospital.

The workers at Merck, resisting the police, sometimes with the support of students, continued to block the entry of strike breakers. The fact that they conducted their strike aggressively indicates that the workers had no doubts about the legitimacy of their actions. In response to this, 17 apprentices and young workers from Merck were illegally terminated after the strike ended.

As the unions gradually scaled back their demands, and while the workers were still striking, the chemical industry announced without

---

1 Ernst Bloch was an important 20th century German Marxist theorist and art critic who counted the much younger Rudi Dutschke among his friends and intellectual peers.

further ado that, as of June 1, wages would be increased by 6.5 percent. Corruption proceedings launched by the workers were an overall failure. The workers were no match for the machinations of the union leadership. The latter released a Communiqué on Concerted Action in what amounted to a call for the workers to accept defeat and end the strike: "The language of the Common Concerted Action was completely the work of the employers and the unions, to make sure that not everyone will benefit from the anticipated rise in prices and incomes being created by the boom, but rather that everyone will be subjected to the dictates of a phase of macroeconomic consolidation."

At the beginning of July, the Board of Directors of IG Chemie reached an agreement with the chemical industry: 7.8 percent = wage guidelines = the outcome at Rhineland Palitinate. The Merck strike leadership sent a protest telegram to the board requesting that the decision be rescinded. At Clouth-Gummiwerken, the union traitors were shouted down when the outcome was announced. The strike was over.

The chemical industry had achieved its goal. They wanted the first strike in the chemical industry, the first strike by chemical workers of this generation, to end in defeat, because "given the increasing importance of labor costs, they must consider the possibility that in future wage negotiations in the chemical industry, serious confrontations, possibly even labor disputes, may prove unavoidable" [from: *Hilfeleistung im Arbeitskampf*[1]]—because for the chemical industry this strike was not an isolated incident, but rather one step in a long term strategy of struggle against the working class. In the words of the Deutsche Bank's spokesman, Ulrich, "It requires many steps, each of which must be large enough to reach the goal—rates of increase of only two or three percent." (February 72)

The workers didn't achieve what they hoped for: more unity—that was the objective of the 120 mark demand in Hessen; wage increases that do not lag behind price increases—that was the objective of the entire strike movement; close relations—unity and not separation between the workers from Bayer, BASF, and Hoechst; success.

This wage agreement is an expression of the actual power relations between the classes. One could say that capital has almost all of it and the workers almost none: capital has closed ranks and "concentrated," while the working class suffers from numerous divisions; capital has powerful organizations that are firmly in control, while the workers

---

1 Support During Labor Disputes.

have unions that are out of their control, with a bureaucracy and a leadership that, like the current government, advance anti-worker policies; capital has the state, and the state is against the working class; capital is organized internationally, while the working class is still only able to organize in the national context; capital has a clear, long term strategy and uses propaganda to promote it at every opportunity, with the goal of attacking the working class; the workers can counter this only with their rage—that is all they have.

The Militarization of the Class Struggle
In spite of capital's strength and the weakness of the working class, the state is arming itself and preparing for the militarization of the class struggle. The political means correspond with the economic facts: capital's aggression. The political facts signal the extent and the strength of the attack.

The less the common good—which is to say general affluence, increasing income, and improved living conditions for all—is addressed by capitalist policy, the more it must be promoted, so as to reduce possibilities for criticizing the methods employed by capital. Therefore, critical journalists have been fired everywhere; therefore the schools have been cleared of leftists; therefore, the CSU has seized control of the *Bayerischen Rundfunk,* which can only signal the beginning of the acquisition of ARD stations by the ZDF[2]—even if the process can't proceed as quickly in other *Länder.*

To the extent that the system can no longer purchase the loyalty of the masses, they must be coerced. As it will no longer be given willingly, it will be gained through threats of violence; the BGS will be transformed into a federal police force and increased from a force of 23,000 to a force of 30,000; the police will be armed with submachine guns, and the citizenry should become as accustomed to seeing submachine gun-armed police on street corners as they are of paying taxes;[3] penal law will be stiffened; emergency exercises will be conducted using

2 The ARD is the *Arbeitsgemeinschaft der öffentlich-rechtlichen Rundfunkanstalten der Bundesrepublik Deutschland* (Consortium of Public-Law Broadcasting Institutions of the Federal Republic of Germany); *Bayerischen Rundfunk* is a member of the ARD. ZDF is the *Zweites Deutsches Fernsehen* (Second German Television), owned by Deutche Telekom; it is commercial TV, partially funded through advertising.

3 This is a reference to a statement by Willy Weyer, Interior Minister of North Rhine-Westphalia, who stated that "Citizens must get as used precisely to the sight of policemen with machine pistols as they are to paying tax." (Cobler, 141).

sharpshooters; comrades will be taken into preventive custody; RAF suspects will be subject to the death penalty.

To the extent that people have no further reason, once capitalism is finally enforced in West Germany, to continue being anticommunist, communists must be forcibly separated from the people. Therefore, the left is being pushed out of the factories. Therefore the price the DKP must pay to remain legal will get higher and higher (and it is apparent that they'll pay any price). Therefore, the chemical industry threatens the Free University; they will not hire Free University graduates if peace and order are not re-established at the Free University.

To the degree that the ideas of the communist alternative win ground as a result of the system's own contradictions, the liberated spaces from which such ideas can be propagated must be closed; therefore Mandel should not be permitted to teach at the Free University; therefore the president of the university in Frankfurt calls in the police to make sure that exams supported by industry are written; therefore Löwenthal[1] rants about the Spartacus Youth,[2] and Löwenthal's cameramen attack students to get photos of as many violent scenes that can be used to incite the people as possible.

After ten years of employing foreigners in the Federal Republic—since the wall in 1961[3]—the accident rate of foreigners has reached a level double that of German workers, which is already high enough, and they still live in ghettos and discrimination is still prevalent in the factories and neighborhoods. As foreign workers have now begun to organize to better protect themselves, the Basic Law is to be changed to make it easier to monitor foreigners' organizations, so as to make it easier to dismantle them, something that is already possible with the fascist laws governing foreigners and the anticommunist law governing association.

Capitalist propagandists use the narrow opportunity that the Red Army Faction affords them to argue that their core problem, the escalation of the class struggle, is caused by us, and that the rise of right-

---

1 Gerhard Löwenthal was a German journalist and a ZDF news anchor from 1969 until 1988.

2 "Spartacus Youth": the DKP's student section, by far the largest self-styled communist organization active on campuses during this period.

3 The construction of the Berlin Wall cut off the flow of refugees from the East that had been providing a reservoir of cheap labor up until that time. This signaled the beginning of a guest worker policy of recruiting cheap labor from Southern Europe, Turkey, and elsewhere.

wing radicalism is a response to us. This is objectively the argument of the class enemy and subjectively an entirely shallow approach based on nothing more than the superficial assessment of the issues found in the bourgeois press.

The Legal Left and Public Enemy No. 1

In the face of capital's offensive, the legal left is not just on the defensive, it is objectively helpless. They respond with their leaflets and their newspapers and their agitation among the workers, in which they say all the blame lies with capital, which is true, that the workers must organize themselves, that the social democratic line must be overcome in the factories, that the workers must learn to conduct economic struggles so as to regain their class consciousness—all of which is important work. But proposing it as the only form of political work it is shortsighted.

They see semi-automatic pistols and say, "Organize the economic struggle." They see the emergency exercises and say, "Class consciousness." They see fascism and say, "Don't bring the class struggle to a head." They see war preparations and say, "Develop a policy of unity with the middle class." They see Labor Court and Federal Labor Court decisions that will ban future strikes and say, "Legality."

The counterrevolution believes that it is possible to get rid of all of the problems that it itself produces, and no means is too dirty in achieving that goal. But they can't wait until fascism has really been established and the masses have been mobilized in their service. They need the security offered by a monopoly of weapons and armed violence—so that the rage of the working class, which they did so much to provoke, does not lead the working class to the idea, and with the idea, the means: the idea of the revolutionary guerilla's armed struggle, striking from the shadows and not easily caught, imposing accountability, demoralizing the police, and resisting their violence with counterviolence.

Genscher would not be the Minister of the Interior of the ruling class if he were not prepared to use unimaginable measures to take us "out of circulation," if he hadn't declared us Public Enemy No. 1 even before we did anything, if he hadn't indicated that he was prepared to do anything, to engage in any action, to isolate us from the left, the labor force and the people, if he wasn't prepared to murder us. This situation will surely get worse.

But they can no longer continue their war preparations covertly, and they cannot continue to act within their own legal parameters. They are obliged to violate their own system, and in so doing they show their true colors as enemies of the people—and the left creates accurate propaganda at a high dialectical level, as ought to be the case, when they say: this terror is not directed against the RAF, but rather against the working class. Obviously its target isn't the RAF, but rather the development of the coming class struggle. This is why the idea of armed struggle is met with all the violence the system is currently capable of, in order to prevent the working class from embracing it.

We're not feeling edgy; the system is feeling nervous.

Capital can't wait until it has established fascism because American competition won't wait. The hysteria of the system doesn't make our strategy or tactics incorrect. And the system is not incorrect in making it incredibly difficult for us to anchor the guerilla in the masses. Knowing this, it is not incorrect to develop resistance, given that the war will be a protracted war.

What could comrades be waiting for in a country that allowed Auschwitz to occur without resistance? Doesn't the current workers' movement bring with it the history of the German workers' movement and this police force the history of the SS?

> *Communists struggle for the satisfaction of the goals and interests of the working class immediately at hand, but they also show the way forward for the movement as well as its future.*
>
> *Communist Manifesto*

That is what we mean by SERVE THE PEOPLE.

3. THE QUESTION OF OWNERSHIP
AND THE MILITARIZATION OF THE CONFLICT

The argument that the Federal Republic is not Latin America obscures local conditions more than it clarifies them. This is indicated by (and the debate is liberally seasoned with these): "The same horrifying poverty doesn't exist here as does there"; "Here the enemy is not a foreign power"; "Here the state is not so hated by the people"; "We are not ruled by a military dictatorship here as is the case in many Latin American countries."

Meaning: conditions there are so intolerable that violence is the only option—here things are still good enough that the conditions are not ripe for violence.

In the Rowohlt[1] volume *Zerschlagt die Wohlstandsinseln der iii. Welt,*[2] which includes Marighella's *Minimanual of the Urban Guerilla*, it says in the preface that the decision to publish his text is a protest against arrests and torture in Brazil, not a guide for action here, "however weak parliamentary democracy may be and whatever threat is posed by its own economic system."—"To use counterviolence (the Latin American urban guerilla model) which is meant to be used against a terrorist capitalist ruling class, in a country where one can discuss workers' participation, is to make a mockery of the wretched of the earth."

Following this logic, to bomb BASF in Ludwigshafen would be to mock the people who bombed BASF in Brazil. The Latin American comrades feel differently. BASF does as well.

The argument that the Federal Republic is not Latin America is advanced by people who speak about current affairs from a perspective in which their monthly income is secure, and who speak in a way which keeps it secure; it is an example of human coldness and intellectual arrogance in the face of the problems of people here. Reality in the Federal Republic is in this way factually and analytically removed from the table. An analysis of questions here must be based on the objective relevance of social questions, on the subjective relevance of the question of ownership, and on the militarization of the class struggle.

Poverty in the Federal Republic
The objective relevance of social questions means the reality of poverty in the Federal Republic. The fact that this poverty is largely hidden doesn't mean that it doesn't exist. The fact that there is no chance that this poverty will lead to social revolution is no reason to act as if it doesn't exist.

Jürgen Roth,[3] in his book *Armut in der Bundesrepublik*[4] has assembled almost everything that needs to be said on this topic. 14 million people in the Federal Republic and West Berlin are living in poverty today. 1.1 million people living in rural areas must get by on 100 to 400 marks[5] per month; these are the families of small farmers and people retired from sharecropping. 4.66 million households with

---

1 A prominent German publishing company.
2 Destroy the Islands of Wealth in the Third World.
3 Jürgen Roth is a German investigative journalist.
4 Poverty in the Federal Republic.
5 Roughly $35 to $140.

an average of three members must get by on a monthly net income of less than 600 marks;[1] that is 21 percent of all households. Over 5 million pensioners have a monthly pension of around 350 marks.[2] To this add 600,000 people in low-income housing projects, 450,000 in homeless shelters, 100,000 institutionalized children, 100,000 in mental asylums, 50,000 adults in prison and 50,000 youth in reform schools. Those are the official figures. Everyone knows that official figures in this area are always underestimates. In Bremen, 11,000 people receive heating subsidies because they can't afford to buy coal. The Munich Housing Bureau calculates that the number of homeless will increase from 7,300 to 25,000. In Cologne, in 1963, 17,000 lived in low-income housing projects.

In the Nordweststadt neighborhood in Frankfurt one pays 460 marks[3] rent for two rooms totaling about 60 square metres. In Nordweststadt the electricity metres are found in the basement. In almost every high-rise at least one electricity metre is turned off, regardless of whether there are small children in the apartment and regardless of whether it is winter. The city of Frankfurt turns off the electricity to 50 homes every day; approximately 800 families a month have their electricity cut.

Approximately 5,000 vagrants live in Frankfurt. At night, water is used to drive them from the area where they sleep on the B level of the Hauptwache pedestrian mall. When the police leave, they come back, lie newspapers on the wet ground, and go back to sleep.

7 million homes in the Federal Republic have neither a bath nor a toilet. 800,000 families live in barracks. In Frankfurt, 20,000 people are searching for homes. In Düsseldorf, it's 30,000.

600,000 people in the Federal Republic suffer from schizophrenia. If schizophrenia is not treated it is debilitating. 3 percent of the population is unable to work or pursue a career. 5 to 6 million people require some form of psychological support. Some psychiatric institutions have only 0.75 square metres of space per patient.

High school teachers estimate that 80 percent of working class children do not attend classes.

Poverty in the Federal Republic is not decreasing; it is increasing. Demand for housing is increasing. The need for schools is increasing. Child abuse is increasing. At the end of 1970, 7,000 cases were reported;

---

1 Roughly $220.

2 Roughly $127.

3 Roughly $167.

it is estimated that in reality there were 100,000. It is also estimated that 1,000 children are beaten to death each year.

"To describe the school system in the Federal Republic is to describe poverty in a rich country," says Luc Jochimsen[4] in her book *Hinterhöfe der Nation,*[5] which provides the necessary details:

> The public education system is a slum with the characteristics of any slum: deprivation, budget shortfalls, shortages, obsolescence, crowding, disrepair, discontent, resignation, indifference, and ruthlessness.
>
> What occurs today with six- and seven-year-olds in the primary schools of the Federal Republic reflects a conscious plan to use compulsory education to later deny these children the right to education and training. It is a crime against education. A crime for which no punishment exists. A crime that will never face prosecution.

In 1970, 35,000 people lived in the Märkisch neighborhood in Berlin. It is projected to reach 140,000 by 1980. The people are saying, "It's brutal here, totally squalid; in any event, it destroys the will to live— but inside the houses are well laid out." Everything is available in the Märkisch neighborhood: playgrounds, a transportation system, schools, cheap shopping, doctors and lawyers; and they are cesspools for poverty, child abuse, suicide, criminal gangs, bitterness, and need. The Märkisch neighborhood shows the future of social conditions.

(Bourgeois authors, faced with the conclusions we are drawing here, make no effort to place their observations within a context which recognizes that poverty is caused by the mobility of capital and the concentration of capital by banks, insurance companies, and home and property owners. They come to terms with the research data through verbal protests.)

The reality of poverty is not the same thing as revolutionary reality. The poor are not spontaneously and of their own accord revolutionary. They generally direct their aggression against themselves rather than against their oppressors. The objects of their aggression are usually other poor people, not those who benefit from their poverty. Not the real estate companies, the banks, the insurance companies, the

---

4 Lukrezia Jochimsen was a sociologist and TV journalist. Today she is a member of parliament for the left-wing *Partei des Demokratischen Sozialismus* (PDS).

5 Backyards of the Nation.

corporations and the city planners, but rather other victims. Inactive, truly depressed, a discouraging example providing material for the fascism of *Bild* and ZDF.

The ZDF showed the following scene: in the slums of Wiesbaden, ZDF had children play in the dirt, beating on each other and screaming. The adults had to scream at them to let each other be. The television voice-over says, "The Federal Republic is not Latin America"; the poor in the Federal Republic have only themselves to blame; they are criminals; there are very few poor people—this is the concrete evidence. The Springer Press prints stuff like this. The material of fascism.

The Reality of Ownership Conditions

But the objective reality of poverty has in no small way clarified the subjective fact that capitalist ownership since the early postwar years— the CDU's Ahlener Program[1]—has provided nothing. No gains came spontaneously, all were won through negotiations. Little was developed for the poor, but in the rest of society Citizens Initiatives with their platitudes became more widespread, albeit very poorly organized and vague, not worth repressing.

The 20,000 sacrificed in car accidents to the automobile industry's lust for profit has not led to any consideration of the future of the highway system; the insurance aristocracy that represents capital guarantees illness, the downside of which being miserable hospital stays; the contradiction between community debt and the dividends enjoyed by the corporations that engage in production on their territory; between the exploitation of guest workers and the accommodations provided to guest workers; between the misery of children and the profits of toy companies; between profit made by landlords and miserable housing conditions—all of this is common knowledge. It is covered at length in *Spiegel* every week, and daily in *Bild*, in most cases as isolated incidents. But this state of affairs has been worsening so quickly that it can no longer be covered up. Deutsche Bank spokesman Ulrich babbles about "the demonization of profit," "the attack against our economic system," and the "criticism of profit": "We are insufficiently committed to broadly clarifying the nature of employers' profits, without which development and progress are impossible in a free market system"—that

---

1 The Ahlener Program, adopted by the CDU on February 3, 1947, in the town of Ahlen, stated in its opening that the interests of capitalism and those of the German people were identical.

a part of this should also be for the common good is rejected by almost all owners of capital.

Eppler[2] hopes to secure support for the unpopular sales tax increase by using the taxation of higher income brackets for propaganda purposes. The CDU is afraid that the Moscow and Warsaw Treaties[3] could lead to an ideological softening within the Federal Republic—Schröder's[4] key argument is that the demonization of communism could lose credibility, because communism has come to represent expropriation and collectivization of the means of production. The CDU does not attack the contents of the Moscow and Warsaw Treaties, they struggle against ideological tolerance of the thinking of sworn enemies of capitalism.

The initiatives of the left after 1968, when they had a broad base everywhere, addressed the question of ownership and created a consensus behind their criticism. They did this in a way that constituted an attack against capitalist ownership and acted as a brake on capitalist profiteering. This took place in the squats in cities throughout the Federal Republic, in the Citizens Initiatives opposed to gentrification, in the initiatives for non-profit development in the suburbs—the Märkisch neighborhood, Nordweststadt in Frankfurt—and in the Citizens Initiatives opposed to the development of industrial sites in residential neighborhoods.

The Heidelberg SPK, through collective study and action, developed such a persuasive critique of the connection between illness and capitalism that SPK cadre have been detained in prison under §129 since July 71. The struggle of the students against the standardized testing which capital has imposed, and the campaign of the *Jusos* against private property development on public lands in the countryside, both have capitalist ownership as their target.

The most important strikes occurred in September 69, and were sparked by the year's high profits. The most powerful campaign of the student movement was that against the Springer Corporation: "Expropriate Springer." The most brutal police action was against the

---

2 Erhard Eppler, a member of the SPD and left-leaning Federal Minister for Economic Cooperation. He resigned in 1974.

3 Signed in August and December 1970, these two treaties were milestones in the SPD's *Ostpolitik*, normalizing the FRG's relations with Poland and the Soviet Union for the first time since World War II.

4 Gerhard Schröder was a CDU politician, Minister of the Interior from 1953 until 1961, Minister of Foreign Affairs from 1961 until 1966, and Minister of Defense from 1966 until 1969.

Belgian community's squats in Kassel, where women and children were beaten with clubs, and against the squats in Hannover, which were destroyed through trials for damages. After Georg's murder, a sticker appeared in Berlin that read: "Killer cops murdered our brother Georg because they were worried about their loot."

Social Democracy and Reformism

Promise of reform has become the ersatz religion, the opium of the people. Promises of a better future have only one function, to provide a motivation for patience, endurance, and passivity. With all the efforts that are required to push reforms through, one could have a revolution. The people who say otherwise—like the *Jusos*, and like those who believe that the *Jusos* have the power to push through meaningful reforms—misunderstand the system's ability to resist change. They misunderstand its determination to adapt society to the exploitative conditions of capitalism and not the other way around. They do not understand that the system no longer feels constrained to act "within the bounds of the constitutional state." Above all, they fail to understand that the *Jusos* are the cream of the younger generation of social democrats.

There is, however, a difference between the SPD and the CDU. They despise the working class and the people in different ways. The SPD believes in the carrot and the stick. The CDU is only interested in the stick. The SPD is more experienced at leading the working class around by the nose. Wehner[1] is more experienced in deceiving and purging the left. Brandt is more experienced in the way to take over the leadership of a movement so as to neutralize it (e.g., the antinuclear movement in Berlin in 1958). They are more imaginative than the CDU in their tactics against the people.

The SPD pushed the amnesty through to defuse the solidarity that was developing around the trials of students, to disrupt the criticisms of the justice system, to break the solidarity the left was receiving against the justice system and the administration, thereby eliminating the rebellion without involving state security.

With their *Ostpolitik*, they beat back the criticism that their reform policies were in disarray. The Berlin Senate didn't send in the police in response to the occupation at the Bethanien Hospital and the establishment of the Georg von Rauch House, instead they chose to shut

---

1 Herbert Wehner was leader of the SPD's parliamentary group from 1958 until 1983, and Deputy Chairman of the SPD from 1958 until 1973.

off the water and take over administration of the building. Because of the protests against his Persian trip, Heinemann is still gun-shy about diplomacy. Under Brandt's leadership, the ban on foreigners' organizations was already in the works. It is the SPD that has influence with the unions and the workers, while the CDU distrusts the unions and their method of functioning: accumulation of capital through voluntary membership donations instead of through the extraction of profits. And Posser[2] in many ways avoids lying: Mahler is a "fellow human being," and in his impact report he says Brigitte Asdonk had been mistreated.

The difference between the SPD and the CDU has been defined by some comrades as the difference between the plague and cholera. That's the choice the West German people face when they vote.

The system is taking the steps necessary to preserve the social status quo. Preserving the status quo requires: the concentration of European businesses to resist American competition; tax funded basic research to maintain high rates of profit; supplying weapons to the Third World through capital export markets so as to keep the liberation movements in check and using foreign production to keep wages down at home; keeping Siemens Annual General Assembly free from criticisms about Carbora Bassa investments;[3] protecting the Shah from criticism about the death penalty in Persia.

Preserving the status quo requires: keeping anyone who is poor away from people who are addressing the issue of ownership; keeping the working class divided; using the accumulation of wealth and promises of reform to rein in the working class; keeping up a steady flow of propaganda: consumer ownership is the same as ownership of the means of production; all attacks against private property are the same; all attacks against private property are criminal; capitalist production is the natural state of affairs; capitalism is the best option available and the best that humans have come up with; criticisms of capitalism serve particular, selfish agendas of individuals and groups; wages are responsible for inflation; employers' profits serve the common good; whoever has a different perspective is making problems and stands alone and is, in the final analysis, a criminal.

---

2 Diether Posser, SPD Minister of Justice in the *Land* of North Rhine-Westphalia from 1972 until 1978.

3 The project to build a massive dam in Mozambique, then a Portuguese colony. The right-wing Portuguese government had plans to settle over one million European colonists in the African country. By 1969, five German companies were implicated in the project.

It is a status quo of relations of ownership and ideas that cannot be preserved without the militarization of the class struggle and the criminalization of the left.

The Springer Press
The role of the Springer Press in the militarization of the class struggle was well described in 1968 during the "Expropriate Springer" campaign:

> *One can see the way in which the Springer Press's public is produced following a simple formula: The Springer Press treats every attempt by people to free themselves from the constraints of late capitalism as a crime. Political revolutionaries are assigned the attributes of violent criminals. Political struggle is presented as individual, abstract terror, and the campaign against imperialism as pointless destruction.*
>
> *The Springer Corporation represents the propaganda vanguard of aggressive anticommunism. The Springer Press is the enemy of the working class. They undermine its ability to act freely and in solidarity. They transform the reader's desire for equality into a lynching instinct and the longing for a free society into hatred against everybody who wants to build a free society. The Springer Press serves the interests of war preparations. Their construct of the enemy is a way of saying, "If you're ever disruptive, if you don't leave your divorce to the divorce lawyers, the question of wage increases for contract negotiations, the issue of housing in the hands of the Housing Office, injustice in the hands of the judges, your security with the police, and your destiny to the vicissitudes of late capitalism, the response will be murder, torture, rape, and criminal attacks."*
>
> from: *Destroy Bild*

The situation has gotten increasingly critical since the Molotov Cocktail Meeting in February 68.[1] *Bild* has launched the column *"Bild* Fights for You!" and reports daily successes in the struggle against exorbitant rents, against the criminalization of foreigners, against denunciations

1 In February 1968, a film by Holger Meins showing how to make a molotov cocktail was presented at a meeting held in Berlin to discuss the campaign against the Springer Press.

of large families, against forced retirement and the impoverishment of retirees. Before the oppressed masses turn their backs on the institutions of the constitutional state, *Bild* turns them against themselves; before their dissatisfaction with the institutions of the class state can become class consciousness, *Bild* takes the lead in expressing this dissatisfaction, and just as was the case with the Nazis in 1933, *Bild* speaks for capital, not for the proletariat.

Böll called this fascist, by which he meant, so there is no misunderstanding, the "agitation, lies, dirt."[2] In this he, analytically and politically, hit the nail on the head. The reaction showed how sensitive the system really is, how unstable the status quo, how fascistic *Bild*, and how agitated the climate at the Springer Corporation.

The Dialectic of Revolution and Counterrevolution

> *It isn't a question of whether we want the reactionary militarization or not; it is a question of whether we have the conditions necessary to transform the fascist militarization into a revolutionary mobilization, whether we can transform the reactionary militarization into a revolutionary one, whether it is better to lay down and die or to stand up and resist.*
>
> Kim Il Sung

Most people say, "It's unacceptable." Most people say, "The masses do not want this." Many people say, "Fighting now will provoke fascism." Böll says, "Six against 60,000,000—capital has everything, we have nothing."

They see only the status quo. They see in the system's violence only the violence, not the fear. They see in the militarization only the weapons, not the crumbling mass base. They see in *Bild*'s hatred only the hatred, not the dissatisfaction of *Bild* readers. They see cops with semi-automatic pistols and see only cops with semi-automatic pistols, not the lack of mass support for fascism. They see the terror against us and see only the terror, not the fear about the social explosiveness of the RAF, which must be "nipped in the bud." They see in the political apathy of the proletariat only the apathy, not the protest against a system that has nothing to offer them. They see in the high level of suicide amongst

---

2 On December 20, 1971, Heinrich Böll famously said that *Bild*'s news coverage "isn't crypto-fascist anymore, nor fascistoid, but naked fascism, agitation, lies, dirt."

the proletariat only the act of desperation, not the protest. They see in the proletariat's disinterest in economic struggle only a disinterest in struggle, not the refusal to struggle for a paltry percentage and the right to idiotic consumption. They see in the proletariat's lack of union organization only the lack of organization, not the mistrust of union bureaucrats as accomplices of capital. They see in the population's hostility towards the left only the hostility towards the left, not the hatred against those who are socially privileged. They see in our isolation from the masses only our isolation from the masses, not the insane lengths to which the system will go to isolate us from the masses. They see in the long periods comrades spend in preventive custody only the long periods in preventive custody, not the system's fear about the free members of the RAF. They see in the exclusion of DKP teachers only the end of the march through the institutions,[1] not the beginning of the adoption of revolutionary politics by children and their parents, which must be choked off. They see everything in terms of the existing movement, not the future one, only the bad, not the good: the dialectic of revolution and counterrevolution.

We're not saying it will be easy to build the guerilla, or that the masses are just waiting for the opportunity to join the guerilla. However, we do, above all, believe that the situation will not change by itself. We don't believe that the guerilla will spontaneously spring forth from the mass struggle. Such illusions are unrealistic. A guerilla that developed spontaneously out of the mass struggle would be a bloodbath, not a guerilla group. We do not believe that the guerilla can be formed as the "illegal wing" of a legal organization. Such an illegal wing would lead to the illegalization of the organization, i.e., its liquidation, and nothing else. We don't believe that the concept of the guerilla will develop by itself from political work. Therefore, we believe that the options and the specific role of the guerilla in the class struggle can only be collectively perceived and understood, that the guerilla stands in opposition to the consciousness industry.

We have said that any talk of their defeating us can only mean our arrests or deaths. We believe that the guerilla will develop, will gain a foothold, that the development of the class struggle will itself establish the idea of armed struggle only if there is already an organization in existence conducting guerilla warfare, an organization that is not easily demoralized, that does not simply lie down and give up.

---

1 A reference to Rudi Dutschke's proposed strategy. See p. 35, fn 7.

We believe that the idea of the guerilla developed by Mao, Fidel, Che, Giáp, and Marighella is a good idea that cannot be removed from the table. If one underestimates the difficulties in establishing the guerilla, if one is scared off by the difficulties against which we must struggle, this also shows that one underestimates the difficulties which the guerilla had to face even in those places where it has made a good deal of progress and is now anchored in the masses. We believe that these reservations are an indication of how far capital is prepared to go when it's a question of securing exploitative conditions, an area where they have never hesitated: not with the Paris Commune, not in Germany in 1918, not in 1933, not in Algeria, Vietnam, the Congo, Cuba, Latin America, or Mozambique, not at Attica, not in Los Angeles, Kent State, Augsburg or Hamburg.

MAKE THE QUESTION OF OWNERSHIP THE KEY QUESTION FOR ALL MOVEMENTS!

ADVANCE THE REVOLUTIONARY GUERILLA AGAINST THE REACTIONARY MILITARIZATION!

No party can call itself revolutionary if it fails to prepare for armed struggle, and that is true at all levels of the party. That is the way to most effectively confront the reactionaries at every step of the revolutionary process. Any disregard for this factor can only lead to missed revolutionary opportunities.

30 Questions to a Tupamaro

That's what we mean by SERVE THE PEOPLE!

4. ON CURRENT ISSUES

The Ruhland Trial

There is still a liberal press in the Federal Republic for whom the trial was a scandal. Ruhland was never as close to the Red Army Faction as he claims. His fawning, his reliance on evidence from the investigation rather than his own memory, the fact that Mahler's lawyer Schily was prevented from attending his trial, the fact that from the beginning of the trial it was established that there would be a verdict based on negotiations that neither the federal prosecutor nor the defense attorney would challenge (the *FAZ* reported this). As the *Frankfurter Rundschau* describes it, "like a nice teacher delivering a worn out speech to a sympathetic student" —proving very clearly that discovering the truth and due process have nothing to do with anything anymore.

The assurance that Ruhland is certainly telling the truth, the fulminations that those he has incriminated are not telling the truth, the assumption that anyone who doesn't cooperate with the justice system is guilty... that is exactly what class justice means, show trials, making them an—effectively ornamental—component of capital's general offensive against the left as the vanguard of the working class in the Federal Republic and West Berlin.

One cannot offer up *Verfassungsschutz* informants, as in earlier communist trials or as with Urbach, to a public increasingly polarized by the growing class contradictions. They expect the left-wing public to be dazzled by state witnesses presented by the Bonn Security Group, and it'll probably work. The person who's really screwed in this situation is Ruhland himself, since he no longer knows his friends from his enemies, up from down, the revolution from the counterrevolution. The poor pig doesn't understand how they're using him.

Urban guerilla struggle requires that one not be demoralized by the system's violence. One certainly should not be demoralized by a trial that shows us to be morally and politically in the right. Demoralization is in fact their goal. The Ruhland trial is only a very superficial event in the unfolding of history, the development of class struggle, and the question of whether the urban guerilla is legitimate.

On Traitors

There are people who believe there might be some truth in the things Homann and the like are spreading around. At least, they say, Homann is no idiot. They take him to be what he presented himself as in *Spiegel*, a "political scholar"; from a vocabulary that encompasses both hunter and prey.[1] These terms have nothing to do with class antagonism. The assertion that you are a scholar doesn't make you one when you deal in the techniques used by *Spiegel* journalists. The substance of Marxism, the dialectic of being and consciousness, excludes the possibility that police statements can contribute to the revolutionary strategy. Marxism can only be taught by Marxists, as Margharita von Brentano[2] told *Spiegel*. What Mandel has to say, Schwan[3] couldn't spell.

Anybody who shares the interests of the status quo cannot possibly have anything to say about social change. But it is the nature of traitors to share the interests of the status quo, to want to return to their hereditary place in class society, to not feel right in unfamiliar circumstances, to only have a sense of identity in their own milieu, and to remain the object of their own development.

Ruhland only really feels comfortable in his old role as a criminal proletariat, handcuffed and oppressed, and Homann in the role of the lost son of the lumpen proletariat, ever at the beck and call of the bourgeoisie—in *Spiegel* and *konkret*—in his heart of hearts he has no interest in matters of the market. Sturm had an adventure and then fled back home to the bosom of her family.

Ruhland remains a victim and Homann a consumer, the overpaid illiterate and the profiteering academic—the class balance is re-established, legality is obviously the natural state of affairs. Regarding Homann, *FAZ* wrote: "...a journalist and visual artist, with a politically untrained but sensitive intelligence"; about Ruhland: "...he doesn't want to be a villain, he is perhaps an honest man with a guileless mind. Facing his guards in the court room, two young security police officers, he exhibits a completely natural and comradely bearing."

The psychological makeup of traitors is venal and conservative. The conservative *FAZ* sympathizes with these sons and servants.

We suffered from a false fascination and have underestimated illegality. We've overestimated the unity of some groups. That is to say that we have not taken into account all of the implications of the student movement being a relatively privileged movement, that we have failed to

---

1 Peter Homann had previously worked as a journalist for the *Spiegel*.

2 Margharita von Brentano was a sociology professor at the Free University, where a prize and a building are now named in her honour.

3 A. Schwan, a West Berlin professor and a member of the *Bund Freiheit de Wissenshaft* (Alliance for Free Scholarship). The BFW was an organization of right-wing university professors who accused the student movement of attempting to establish a left-wing educational system to the exclusion of free thought.

observe that for many people much of the politics of 67/68 is no longer relevant, as it offers them no way of increasing their own privilege. It can be pleasant to know a little Marxism, to have some clarity about the conditions of the ruling class's economic domination and their psychological techniques, to shed the self-imposed pressure to perform of a bourgeois overachiever, to embrace an alienated form of Marxism, acquired by privilege, as an item for one's intellectual wellbeing and benefit and not directed towards serving the people.

A preference for certain actions because they are illegal is an expression of bourgeois self-indulgence. The student movement, given its suppositions, could not be free of blind followers and people with a mercenary mentality. The tedious, long-term drudgery that must first of all be undertaken to lay the basis for the urban guerilla must seem to these people, who are so falsely programmed, like a scene from a horror show. Anyone who arrives with criminal fantasies, anyone who only wants to improve their personal situation, will certainly and inevitably improve their situation through treason.

We believed if someone said he had worked in this or that organization for such and such a period of time, then he must know what political work entails, what organization means, or else they would already have tossed him. We now know that we should ourselves have established the political organization necessary for the urban guerilla, that we made a mistake when we relied so readily upon others.

Above all, we think that on our own it would have been very difficult for us to have avoided this error and prevented the treason. We think that a false understanding of the police and the justice system, a false understanding of what SERVE THE PEOPLE means, and a false approach to contradictions within the New Left made the treason inevitable.

As long as traitors still find a place with comrades, not even receiving a single punch in the face, but rather finding understanding as to why they must quickly resume their bourgeois existence and do away with their other existence—because they can't tolerate another day in prison, they send others inside for years or deliver them up to the police death squads—as long as political cooperation with the armed power of capital continues to be tolerated as a political difference of opinion, as long as something that has long been politically condemned is treated as a private matter, treason will continue to exist. Without criticizing liberalism within the left, we cannot eliminate treason.

Traitors must be excluded from the ranks of the revolution. Tolerance in the face of traitors produces more treason. Traitors in the ranks of the revolution cause more harm than the police can without traitors. We believe that is a general rule. It is impossible to know how much they will betray if they are threatened. Given that they are little pigs, one cannot permit them to be in a situation where they can be blackmailed. Capital will continue to turn people into little pigs until we overthrow its rule. We are not responsible for capital's crimes.

On Bank Robberies

Some people say robbing banks is not political. Since when is the question of financing a political organization not a political question? The urban guerilla in Latin America calls bank robberies "expropriation actions." Nobody is claiming that robbing banks will be all it takes to change the oppressive social order. For revolutionary organizations, it mainly represents the solution to their financial problems. It makes logical sense, because there is no other solution to the financial problem. It makes political sense, because it is an expropriation action. It makes tactical sense, because it is a proletarian action. It makes strategic sense, because it finances the guerilla.

A political concept that bases itself on parliamentary democracy, the political concept of competitive capitalism, a concept that understands class antagonism to be nothing more than a power struggle, that perceives the institutions of the class state to be institutions of a constitutional state, thereby definitely turning its back on progress and humanity... such a political concept cannot condone bank robbery. In the imperialist metropole, where the organization of the anti-imperialist struggle must have both legal and illegal components, the political struggle and the armed struggle, bank robbery cannot be dispensed with. It is, in practice, expropriation. And it points to the necessary method for establishing the dictatorship of the proletariat against the enemy: armed struggle.

On Logistics and Continuity

Many comrades are impressed by the Tupamaros'[1] actions. They don't understand why, instead of carrying out popular actions, we're preoccupied with logistics. They can't be bothered with going to the trouble

---

1 Most likely a reference to the *West German* Tupamaros, not to be confused with their South American namesake. These groups had existed in West Berlin and Munich at the beginning of the decade, part of the same amorphous scene as the Roaming Hash Rebels. The 2nd of June Movement grew out of this scene, although several members would instead join the RAF.

to consider what the urban guerilla is and how it functions.

It is most likely maliciously intended when comrades recite the position of the Düsseldorf judge in Ruhland's trial: Ruhland was a handyman and the gang's mascot. The concept of the capitalist division of labor has proven to be an abstraction for them. In practice, they still conceive of proletarian comrades as jack-of-all-trades prefiguring some Silesian idyll. That the technical means can only be developed by working and learning collectively, that the urban guerilla must abolish the division of labor so that the arrest of one individual is not a disaster for us all—these comrades' imagination can't get that far. Not having the logistical problems at least partially resolved, not having oneself learned how to resolve logistical problems, not engaging in a collective learning and working process, would mean leaving the outcome of actions to chance technically, psychologically, and politically.

Resolving logistical problems assures the ongoing security of a revolutionary organization. We place great importance in the tactical requirements necessary to secure the continuity of the Red Army Faction. It is in the interest of capital to divide, to destroy, to break down solidarity, to isolate people, and to deny the historical context—in the area of production as well as that of housing, of commerce, of opinion making, of education—so as to guarantee ongoing profits. It is in the interest of capital to guarantee that conditions remain the opposite of those necessary for proletarian revolution: unity, continuity, historical consciousness, class consciousness. Without organizational continuity, without guaranteeing the organizational permanence of the revolutionary process, the revolutionary process is left to the anarchy of the system, to chance, to historical spontaneity.

We consider disregard for the question of organizational continuity to be a manifestation of opportunism.

On Solidarity

The revolutionary process is revolutionary because it makes objects out of the laws of capitalist commodity production and exchange, rather than being their object. It cannot be measured by market criteria. It can only be measured by criteria that simultaneously destroy the power of market criteria for success.

Solidarity, insofar as it is not based on market criteria, destroys the power of those criteria. Solidarity is political, not so much because solidarity is based on politics, but because it is a refusal to be subservient to the law of value and a refusal to be treated like a mere aspect of exchange value. Solidarity is the essence of free action ungoverned by the ruling class; as such it always means resistance against the influence of the ruling class over relationships between people, and as resistance against the ruling class, it is always correct.

In the view of the system, people whose behavior is not guided by the system's criteria for success are lunatics, halfwits, or losers. In the view of the revolution, all those who conduct themselves with solidarity, whoever they may be, are comrades.

Solidarity becomes a weapon if it is organized and is acted upon in a consistent way against the courts, the police, the authorities, the bosses, the infiltrators, and the traitors. They must be denied any cooperation, afforded no attention, denied access to evidence, offered no information, and afforded absolutely no time and energy. Solidarity includes struggling against liberalism within the left and addressing contradictions within the left as one addresses contradictions amongst the people, and not as if they were a class contradiction.[1]

All political work is based on solidarity. Without solidarity, it will crumble in the face of repression.

"We must prevent the possibility of unnecessary victims. Everybody in the ranks of the revolution must take care of each other, must relate to each other lovingly, must help each other."

SERVE THE PEOPLE!

MAKE THE QUESTION OF OWNERSHIP
A KEY QUESTION EVERYWHERE!

SUPPORT THE ARMED STRUGGLE!

BUILD THE REVOLUTIONARY GUERILLA!

VICTORY IN THE PEOPLE'S WAR!

RAF
April 1972

---

1 In his 1957 "On the Correct Handling of Contradictions Among the People," Mao differentiated between two kinds of conflict or contradiction—"those between ourselves and the enemy and those among the people." While the former should be dealt with by attacking the class enemy, the latter should be dealt with through criticism with the goal of bringing about unity.

a note from the editors:
On the Treatment of Traitors

There have been insinuations, always vague on details or proof, that the RAF was an intensely authoritarian organization, particularly in regards to people not being allowed to leave. Claims have been made that Baader murdered Ingeborg Barz, a young woman who had joined the RAF from the anarchist Black Aid, simply because she wanted to quit the underground. These claims have been contradicted by other witnesses.[1]

Some have pointed to *Serve the People* as evidence that the RAF endorsed the assassination of drop-outs, one passage in particular being mentioned in this regard:

> *Traitors must be excluded from the ranks of the revolution. Tolerance in the face of traitors produces more treason. Traitors in the ranks of the revolution cause more harm than the police can without traitors. We believe that is a general rule. It is impossible to know how much they will betray if they are threatened. Given that they are little pigs, one cannot permit them to be in a situation where they can be blackmailed. Capital will continue to turn people into little pigs until we overthrow its rule. We are not responsible for capital's crimes.[2]*

This position should be evaluated in light of the RAF's documented practice, and the realities of armed struggle.

No clandestine organization can tolerate informants, nor should any revolutionary movement do so, regardless of its legal or illegal status. Yet many observers are wary, and rightly so, of such calls to "exclude" traitors; the reason for this unease is the strong tendency for factions or entire organizations to end up using such a line as cover to attack any and all dissidents, drop-outs, critics or even rivals, accusing them all of "treason." Examples abound

---

1 See page 352.
2 Serve the People: The Urban Guerilla and Class Struggle, cf 156-7.

of revolutionary movements gutting themselves and doing inestimable damage to their cause and their political integrity through this error.

Despite allegations to the contrary, there is no substantive evidence of the RAF ever going down that road. The RAF was criticized throughout its existence, yet none of the critics were ever targeted. What is striking about the cases of Sturm, Homann, and Ruhland is not that they were insulted or berated, but that no harm befell them even after they all took public stands against the guerilla. Another guerilla member, Hans-Jürgen Bäcker, suspected of being an informant, was not targeted by any attack even after testifying in court against the RAF.

Stefan Aust and Jillian Becker have both claimed that members of the guerilla made what can only be described as half-hearted attempts to exact vengeance, but their stories are difficult to gauge. Both authors claim that Baader and Mahler were trying to find Homann and Aust to kill them, but if so, they evidently gave up the search quickly.[3] This is just one aspect of the story that casts doubt on its veracity. Becker furthermore claims that Astrid Proll shot at Bäcker but missed; the way in which she phrases the allegation, however, indicates the source may be Karl-Heinz Ruhland, himself far from reliable.[4] No charges were ever laid against Proll for this.

There is one, and only one, documented case of the RAF doing violence to an informant. In 1971, a friend of Katharina Hammerschmidt's, Edelgard Graefer, was arrested on bogus charges and threatened with having her five-year-old son permanently taken away from her. Under pressure, Graefer gave information to the police. In early 1972, she was abducted by the RAF and had a bucket of tar poured over her. Following this attack on her person, she stopped working with the police.[5]

While unpleasant, such a violent warning is not on the order of a death sentence. Indeed, as Brigitte Mohnhaupt later argued in Stammheim, the fact that a known informant was assaulted and

---

3 Aust, 104; Becker, 255-256.

4 Becker, normally not shy about stating that various combatants actually *did* various things, in this case merely writes, "Astrid Proll ('Rosi') was to claim later that she shot at him from a car but missed." (Becker, 228)

5 Aust, 170-172.

not killed should suffice to discredit claims that other members were executed merely for dropping out.[1]

Certainly, given the guerilla's ability to carry out attacks against even heavily guarded targets, the fact that all of those who testified against them remained unscathed should tell us something.

As for the many others who left over the years, if they did not cooperate with the police or run with tall tales to the media, there is no indication that the guerilla bore them any ill will.

DAS IST EDELGARD GRAEFER

DIESE DENUNZIANTIN STECKT MIT DEN KILLERSCHWEINEN UNTER EINER DECKE

ES LEBE DIE R A F !

THIS IS EDELGARD GRAEFER

THIS COLLABORATOR IS IN BED WITH THE KILLER-PIGS

LONG LIVE THE RAF!

March 27, 1972

---

1 The relevant excerpts from Mohnhaupt's testimony are included in this volume, see page 357.

5

The May Offensive:
Bringing the War Home

This decision, this project, was arrived at through collective discussions involving everyone in the RAF; in other words, there was a consensus of all the groups, of the units in each of the cities, and everyone clearly understood what this meant, what the purpose of these attacks was.

Brigitte Mohnhaupt
Stammheim Trial
July 22, 1976

I N MAY 1972, SHORTLY AFTER the release of *Serve the People*, the RAF left the stage of logistics and preparation, launching a series of attacks that were to go down in history as the "May Offensive."

On the evening of May 11, the day the United States mined the harbors of North Vietnam, the RAF's "Petra Schelm Commando" bombed the U.S. Army V Corps headquarters and the site of the National Security Agency in Frankfurt. At least three blasts went off, killing Lieutenant Colonel Paul A. Bloomquist and injuring thirteen others. As one military police officer noted, the toll would have been much worse had the bombs gone off during duty hours. Damage to property was estimated at $300,000.[2]

---

2 Dan Synovec, "Security Beefed Up at U.S. installations," *European Stars and*

"We expected things like this in Saigon," a captain just back from Vietnam was quoted as saying. "Not here in Germany."[1]

One can imagine that words like that put smiles on many a face, and within twenty-four hours, U.S. military officials reported receiving a number of threats promising all kinds of follow-up attacks. These quickly snowballed, and by early June, the *Frankfurter Allgemeine Zeitung* was reporting that thousands of such calls had been made by "high school students, drunks, psychopaths, and criminals."[2]

"These calls," complained the American Lieutenant General Williard Pearson in a similar vein, "were made by mentally unbalanced or irresponsible individuals seeking to create tension or panic within our community."[3]

Given that the RAF always issued proper communiqués, these threats were most likely the work of people who were simply glad to see the Americans finally being hit. The state was far from amused, and it was noted that the financial consequences of false bomb threats were substantial for warehouses, newspapers, factories, and banks. More importantly, the wave of political prank calls helped create a signal-to-noise situation that can only have helped the guerilla. Nor was the activity without some risk: prison sentences for these false bomb threats ran from a couple of months to as high as three years.[4]

The day after the first bombing, on May 12, attacks were carried out in two Bavarian cities in response to the March 2 shooting of Weissbecker. In Augsburg, bombs were planted inside the police headquarters, and one cop suffered mild injuries. In the state capital Munich, a car bomb was parked just outside the six-storey police building; when it went off, it blew out the windows up to the top floor. A nearby pay station had received a telephone warning, but by the time the police got wind of it, there was not enough time to evacuate—twelve people were injured, and damages were estimated at $150,000.[5] These bombings were claimed by the RAF's "Thomas Weissbecker Commando."

Stripes, May 13, 1972; Dave Lams, "Police Trace Leads in V Corps Blasts," *European Stars and Stripes*, May 13, 1972.

1 Synovec, "Security Beefed Up."

2 Thomas Kirn, "Bombendrohungen werden schnell geahndet," *Frankfurter Allgemeine Zeitung*, June 9, 1972.

3 "General Pearson seeks community help in solving Frankfurt bombings," *European Stars and Stripes*, May 16, 1972.

4 Kirn, "Bombendrohungen werden schnell geahndet."

5 *European Stars and Stripes*, "German Facilities Struck by Bombs," May 13, 1972.

On May 16, in Karlsruhe, the RAF's "Manfred Grashof Commando" placed a bomb in the car of Federal Supreme Court Judge Buddenberg, who had been put in charge of all RAF cases. However, it was not the judge who was behind the wheel, but his wife on her way to pick him up from work. Gerta Buddenberg sustained serious injuries, but survived.

On May 19, the Springer Press building in Hamburg was bombed in retaliation for the constant red baiting and counterinsurgency propaganda published in its newspapers. One bomb went off in the proofreaders' room, and two in the toilets. Three telephone warnings were ignored and, as a result, seventeen employees were injured, two of them seriously. The attack was claimed by the RAF's "2nd of June Commando."

A Springer editor was later quoted saying, "I was only surprised that if they wanted to hit a Springer Building they'd go for the proofreaders, whose views are rather left of centre. I'd have thought there were more rewarding targets if they wanted to strike a real blow. If they'd picked the computer centre, that would have done the building much more damage."[6]

As many workers had been injured, this attack caused some consternation on the left, and it was subsequently alleged that it caused dissension within the RAF itself.[7] An anonymous tip the next day led to the discovery of three more bombs in the building, which were all safely defused.[8]

On May 24, the RAF bombed the Heidelberg headquarters of the U.S. Army in Europe. Two cars loaded with explosives had been parked 140 meters apart near a data processing center and the officers' club at Campbell Barracks. They were timed to go off after most people had finished work for the day,[9] but nevertheless three soldiers were killed[10] and six others were injured. This was the work of the "July 15th Commando," commemorating the date Petra Schelm had died in a firefight with police.

---

6 Aust, 211.

7 See the RAF's interview with *Le Monde Diplomatique,* on page 422 of this volume. See also Brigitte Mohnhaupt's testimony at the Stammheim trial, cf. 357-58.

8 Aust, 211.

9 Dan Synovec, "Bombs kill 3 at USAREUR Hq," *European Stars and Stripes,* May 25, 1972.

10 They were: Clyde Bonner of El Paso, Texas, Ronald Woodward of Otter Lake, Michigan, and Charles Peck of Hawthorne, California. (Associated Press, "W. Germans Sentence 3 Guerrillas to Life for Bomb Deaths," *Tri-City Herald,* April 28, 1977.)

This was a more daring attack than any of the others so far: unlike the V Corps headquarters in Frankfurt, the Campbell Barracks were fenced off and military police were always stationed at the gates. Any person in civilian clothes or in a vehicle without U.S. military plates was supposed to show identification before entering.[1]

The computer destroyed in this attack had been used to make calculations for carpet-bombing sorties in South and North Vietnam with the aim of achieving the highest possible number of deaths. This at a time when, though it was clear the war had been lost, the United States had stepped up bombings of Hanoi, Haiphong, and Thanh Hoa province.[2] The RAF would later claim that their pictures had gone up on walls in Hanoi as a result of this action,[3] and this clearly remained a point of pride among guerilla veterans even decades later.

Regarding the May Offensive, it has been noted:

> *Although people were injured or killed in most of these bombings, with the exception of the Buddenberg bombing, they differ from later RAF attacks in not being directed against specific individuals, a point that should be kept in mind when examining the RAF's history.[4]*

Despite the many anonymous bomb threats called in during this period, and the fact that the RAF's actions coincided with a global wave of protest against ongoing American military aggression in Southeast Asia, some observers have claimed that the May Offensive alienated many of the RAF's liberal sympathizers. Those who had seen them as modern day Robin Hoods, or as romantic idealists, took a step back once they realized that this was for real.

It would be more true to say that the 1972 bombing campaign polarized the left, and, in a healthy way, provided direction and inspiration to numerous activists who had been considering armed politics, while clarifying the disagreements which existed with opponents of the guerilla struggle. Indeed, the period in question showed a marked rise in newspaper articles describing molotov cocktail attacks and other low-

---

1 Synovec, "Bombs Kill."

2 *Internazionale Kommission zum Schutz der Gefangenen une Gegen Isolationshaft*, October 1980, 2.

3 "Wir waren in den Durststreik treten," *Spiegel* 4/1975, translated in this volume on pages 300-318.

4 Arm The Spirit, "A Brief History of the Red Army Faction," http://www.hartford-hwp.com/archives/61/191.html.

Alienating Which Masses?

"When we heard about the RAF bombing the American Headquarters in Frankfurt and Heidelberg, we jumped with joy. At last someone had done something against the imperialist bases in the Federal Republic of Germany."

These were not the words of a petit bourgeois sect, but rather come from the report of a freedom fighter fighting for national liberation in a land occupied by Portugal. He and his comrades had heard the news while he was in a guerilla base. For years the people there had heard of the FRG being one of the worst enemies of the African people—as a source of arms for Portuguese colonialism—and now for the first time the guerillas could see something happening in the Federal Republic which they considered to be an effective form of resistance to imperialism.

I remarked that their reaction was quite different from that of Marxist groups in the Federal Republic, to which the African comrade responded, "When you are struggling, you see things differently."

Christian Sigrist

Christian Sigrist, "De Heidelberg au Cap Vert" in *à propos du procès Baader-Meinhof, Fraction Armée Rouge: de la torture dans les prisons de la RFA*, Klaus Croissant (ed.) (Paris : Christian Bourgeois Éditeur, 1975), 53-54.

level actions against symbols of state power, encouraged by the context the guerilla's bombs had helped create. Years later, the Revolutionary Cells (another West German guerilla group) would explain the long-term effect of the May Offensive in this way:

> At the time, these actions drew the widespread anti-imperialist movement together, causing the further development of an idea that had been rattling around in the heads of thousands of people. We saw that what had long been thought about was in fact possible. Without the RAF, there wouldn't be an RZ today, there wouldn't be groups that understand that resistance doesn't stop where the criminal code starts.[1]

One thing is certain: the RAF's bombing campaign was strongly criticized by the Maoist K-groups who were enjoying their heyday and rejected such attacks as infantile adventurism. The KB (Communist League), whose newspaper *Arbeiterkampf* would later distinguish itself by offering some of the most intelligent commentary on the guerilla in Germany, even went so far as to suggest that the Springer attack might have been the work of right-wing extremists.

For its part the KSV (Communist Student Association), the youth section of the Maoist KPD,[2] complained about the RAF's violence:

> [It is] neither practiced by the masses... nor is it understood by the masses as an expression of their interests. The masses, on the contrary, perceive the actions as a threat, and therefore identify with the reactions of the state apparatus... The violence is not revolutionary. It sabotages the struggle against state repression in that it helps to conceal the class character of this repression and encourages the isolation of communists.[3]

These comments were delivered at a Teach-In Against State Repression, which was held at Frankfurt University on May 31, just a couple of weeks after the Springer Building in that city was bombed. Organized by *Rote Hilfe* (Red Aid), a network of autonomous prisoner support collectives which had their roots in the antiauthoritarian wing of the APO, the event attracted hundreds of people, not all of whom were

---

1 RZ Letter to the RAF Comrades, reprinted in this volume on pages 457-463.

2 Not to be confused with the pro-Soviet KPD that was banned in the 50s and later reconstituted as the DKP.

3 Varon, 213.

as negative as the Maoists.[4] Indeed, one leaflet produced for the event argued that, "If imperialism is a worldwide system, and that it is, then the struggle against it must be waged worldwide. It will and must be a violent and armed struggle, or it will not be waged at all."[5]

The RAF itself sent a statement to the Red Aid Teach-In in the form of a tape recording by Ulrike Meinhof in which she once again encouraged the radical left to organize armed struggle, arguing that increasing repression and popular resentments were providing the potential which, properly exploited, could lead to a revolutionary situation. As was typical of the RAF at this time, Meinhof was attempting to engage directly with the guerilla's left-wing critics.[6]

Remarkably, the Teach-In brought together Maoists and *spontis*, and as such was representative of the revolutionary left. As for the tamed left, in its eyes the RAF remained well beyond the pale. The pro-Soviet DKP made a point of condemning "anarchist demonstrations" in Frankfurt, pontificating that, "The anarchist groups have clearly made hysteria the order of the day. We are making the struggle to win the solidarity of the people of Frankfurt for the Vietnamese liberation struggle the order of the day."[7] Various labor leaders also took turns condemning the "political adventurists," "terror," and "murder." The chairman of the Public Service, Transport, and Communication Union explained that his union supported the government, for, while it was independent, it shared many common concerns with employers.[8]

Clearly not reassured by claims that the RAF was driving people away from left, the state recognized that if it did not move quickly, the May bombings could easily inspire renewed resistance. "The longer the Baader-Meinhof gang remains at large," Attorney General Ludwig Martin worried, "the easier it will be for the public to gain the impression that the powers of the state have broken down."[9]

An essential feature of the campaign against the RAF consisted of psychological operations, meant to discourage any solidarity or

---

4 Hockenos, 114.

5 Varon, 213.

6 Statement to the Red Aid Teach-In, reprinted in this volume on pages 183-85.

7 *Frankfurter Allgemeine Zeitung*, "DKP verurteilt anarchistische Demonstrationen in Frankfurt," May 26, 1972.

8 *Frankfurter Allgemeine Zeitung*, "Keine Solidarisierung mit Abenteurern," May 29, 1972.

9 Dan Synovec, "Terrorists: odd solidarity prompts aid to the Baader-Meinhof gang," *European Stars and Stripes*, June 3, 1972.

identification with the guerilla, while legitimizing the state's own repressive response. As an example of this, on the heels of the May Offensive, communiqués attributed to the RAF, but most likely penned by the secret services or police, were received claiming that on June 2 (the anniversary of Benno Ohnesorg's murder) three car bombs would be set off in random locations in Stuttgart "as a reminder of the bombing war of the U.S. imperialists in Vietnam."[1]

The RAF promptly issued its own communiqué repudiating this as a false flag provocation.[2] Nevertheless, this denial was largely ignored, and on the day in question, "Stuttgart presented the appearance of a beleaguered city. Thousands of police checked all access roads, vehicles, and 'suspicious persons.'"[3]

Thousands of cops were mobilized, supported by both West German and U.S. intelligence units, in a determined effort to hunt down the guerilla. A $59,000 reward was offered for their capture, and Chancellor Willy Brandt warned the public that any solidarity shown would be treated as criminal complicity.[4] At the same time, Genscher announced that supporters could hope for light sentences if they turned themselves in and helped in the hunt;[5] there do not seem to have been any takers.

Nevertheless, the wave of arrests was not long in coming.

On June 1, RAF members Holger Meins, Jan-Carl Raspe, and Andreas Baader were cornered as they arrived at a safehouse in Frankfurt that had been identified by police. Raspe tried to make a run for it, but was quickly apprehended. Meins gave himself up, following police orders to strip down to his underwear before he did so.

Three hundred cops surrounded the warehouse where Baader was holed up, and eventually an armored vehicle tried to enter the building; Baader shot out its wheels. At that point, a sniper took aim and shot the eponymous guerilla fighter in the leg and the police moved in quickly to take him into custody.

---

1 Associated Press, "Bombers Threaten 3 Blasts Friday in Stuttgart Area," *European Stars and Stripes*, May 29, 1972.

2 Regarding the Fascist Bomb Threats Against Stuttgart, reprinted in this volume on pages 181-82.

3 Cobler, 169.

4 Dan Synovec, "Anarchist gang blamed," *European Stars and Stripes*, May 27, 1972.

5 "Bescheidene Mitgliederzahlen radikaler Organisation," *Frankfurter Allgemeine Zeitung*, June 7, 1972.

Holger Meins was the only one of the three who had surrendered without resistance, a fact that did not stop the police from beating him so severely that he required hospitalization. "I didn't squeal or scream," he would later tell his father. "They kicked me black and blue with their big boots. It's a thing you just can't describe."[6]

It later came out that the RAF had intended to kidnap the three U.S. Army City Commanders in Berlin, but called off this action due to security concerns following the June 1 arrests.[7]

On June 7, Gudrun Ensslin was arrested in Hamburg when a store clerk noticed a gun in her handbag. (The government's somewhat farcical Mainz report would later explain this bust in memorably sexist terms: "The arrest of her boyfriend Baader affected this deviant woman to such a degree that she simply had to buy something new, like any normal woman does when something is wrong.")[8]

On June 9, Brigitte Mohnhaupt and Bernhard Braun were arrested in West Berlin; they were both former SPK members. Mohnhaupt had gravitated to the RAF via the Tupamaros-Munich. Braun, who was also close to 2JM, had come to the RAF via the Tupamaros-West Berlin.

On June 15, Ulrike Meinhof and Gerhard Müller were arrested in Hannover, turned in by a left-wing trade unionist who had agreed to put them up for the night.[9] Police found forged passports, gun oil, a four-and-a-half-kilo homemade bomb, two homemade hand grenades, a semi-automatic pistol, two 9mm handguns, numerous fully loaded magazines, and more than three hundred rounds of ammunition in Meinhof's luggage, which weighed over twenty-five kilos.[10] With her capture, some observers felt that the guerilla's entire leadership was now in custody, and yet there were more arrests to come.

On June 30, Katharina Hammerschmidt, who had fled to France, was convinced to turn herself in by her lawyer Otto Schily. The police

---

6 Aust, 219.

7 Brigitte Mohnhaupt's Testimony at the Stammheim Trial, July 22, 1976, http://www.germanguerilla.com/red-army-faction/documents/76_0708_mohnhaupt_pohl.html.

8 Clare Bielby, "'Bonnie und Kleid': Female Terrorists and the Hysterical Feminine," *Forum* 2, http://forum.llc.ed.ac.uk/issue2/bielby.html.

9 They were turned in by Fritz Rodewald, who evidently did not know if he was coming or going: he would donate the reward money to the prisoners' defense fund (Vague, 49). For more details on Rodewald's motivations, see page 201.

10 Wolfgang Tersteegen, "Mit der Bombe im Handgepäcke," *Frankfurter Allgemeine Zeitung*, June 19, 1972; *Frankfurter Allgemeine Zeitung*, "Erst nach Stunden identifiziert," June 19, 1972.

suspected Hammerschmidt of setting up safehouses and perhaps having a role in the recent bombings.[1]

Finally, on July 7, Klaus Jünschke and Irmgard Möller were arrested in Offenbach, set up by a nineteen-year-old who had been recruited by the guerilla earlier that year, and who had since been identified and turned by the police. Jünschke was a former SPK member sought in relation to the December 22, 1971, bank robbery, in which police officer Herbert Schoner had been killed.[2] Irmgard Möller was sought in connection to the 1971 killing of police officer Schmid in Hamburg, and was suspected of participating in the May bombings.[3] (With typical hype, *Stars and Stripes* described her as "the gang's new chief, replacing jailed Ulrike Meinhof and Andreas Baader.")[4]

The RAF was decimated, and what few members remained at large could do little more than concentrate on their own survival.

Following the successes of this counterinsurgency campaign, the West German government felt confident it had snuffed out its fledgling armed opposition. Even sympathetic observers felt that the RAF might have met its end.

They were all wrong.

---

1 United Press International, "Ends French Stay: Member of Gang Turns Self In," *European Stars and Stripes,* July 1, 1972.

2 He was sentenced to life in prison in 1977. Associated Press, "2 German terrorists given life," *European Stars and Stripes,* June 3, 1977.

3 Four years later, she was sentenced to four-and-a-half years for forging documents, resisting arrest, possession of an unlicensed firearm, and membership in a criminal organization. In 1979, she was found guilty of three counts of murder and sentenced to life for planting the bombs in the Augsburg and Heidelberg attacks. By the time she was released in 1994, she had survived 22 years behind bars, making her Germany's longest held female prisoner at that time.

4 United Press International, "8 Terrorist gang suspects still sought," *European Stars and Stripes,* July 10, 1972.

"The objective of these actions was clear..."

The RAF was at the time organized in the following way: there were eight groups established in six cities, and of these there were two strong groups in two cities. There was one group in Munich. The groups, the different units, were integrated into a logistical system. There was contact between the different groups for discussions, but they were autonomous in their decisions regarding how to carry out operations. That was left to the individual groups—and it couldn't have been otherwise. We didn't know anything in advance about these actions. However, even if we had known, we wouldn't have prevented them, because, yeah, it's not a simple thing to stop a group from doing what it has decided to do. In fact, we couldn't have prevented it, both because of the underlying perspective and for practical reasons; it would have been impossible given the circumstances. The objective of these actions was clear: they were a response to the fact that fighters were shot in the street, for example, Petra and Tommy. It would never have been our intention to prevent them.

Brigitte Mohnhaupt
Stammheim Trial
July 22, 1976

For the Victory of the People of Vietnam

On Thursday May 11, 1972—the day the U.S. imperialist mine blockade of North Vietnam began—the Petra Schelm Commando detonated three bombs containing 80kg of TNT at the Frankfurt Headquarters of the V Army Corps of the U.S. Forces in West Germany and West Berlin. West Germany and West Berlin shall no longer be a safe hinterland for the strategy of extermination against Vietnam. They must understand that their crimes against the Vietnamese people have created new and bitter enemies for them, and there is nowhere left in this world where they will be safe from the attacks of revolutionary guerilla units.

We demand an immediate stop to the bomb blockade against North Vietnam.

We demand an immediate end to the bombing of North Vietnam.

We demand the withdrawal of all American troops from Indochina.

VICTORY TO THE VIET CONG!
BUILD THE REVOLUTIONARY GUERILLA.
DARE TO STRUGGLE—DARE TO WIN!
BUILD TWO, THREE, MANY VIETNAMS!

Petra Schelm Commando
May 14, 1972

Attacks in Augsburg and Munich

On Friday, May 12, 1972, the Thomas Weissbecker Commando detonated three bombs at the police headquarters in Augsburg and in the LKA office in Munich.

On March 2, Thomas Weissbecker was murdered in a well-planned surprise attack by a death squad of the Munich *Kripo* and the Augsburg police; he had absolutely no chance to defend himself. The police had no intention of taking Thomas Weissbecker prisoner; they intended to shoot him.

The authorities responsible for the manhunt must understand that they can't liquidate any of us without having to anticipate that we will strike back. The security services, the special squads, the *Kripo*, the BGS and their organizational and political employers must be made aware that their attempts to "solve" the problems of this fascist country by arming the police, by militarizing the class struggle, and by the ruthless and vicious use of guns will provoke resistance. This is also true of the police operations in response to the Munich bank robbery, in response to the Cologne bank robbery, against the Tübingen apprentice Epple, and against foreign workers.

The tactics and tools that we use are the tactics and tools of guerilla warfare. The Minister of the Interior and the BAW assess the situation incorrectly if they think that they can rule with their death squads. It is in the nature of the guerilla—because they struggle in the interests of the people—that they cannot be wiped out by military actions, because their freedom of action can be developed anew whenever it suffers temporary setbacks. Faced with the brutal arrogance of the authorities responsible for the manhunt and the "short cuts" of the fascists, our response is the steady development of the revolutionary guerilla and the long, protracted process of the struggle for liberation from fascism, from capitalist exploitation, and from the oppression of the people.

RESIST THE POLICE DEATH SQUADS!
RESIST THE SS PRACTICES OF THE POLICE!
STRUGGLE AGAINST ALL EXPLOITERS AND ENEMIES OF THE PEOPLE!

Thomas Weissbecker Commando
May 16, 1972

Attack on Judge Buddenberg

On Monday, May 16, 1972, the Manfred Grashof Commando carried out a bomb attack against Judge Buddenberg of the Karlsruhe Federal Supreme Court. Buddenberg is the judge at the Federal Supreme Court responsible for the arrests and investigations in the current political proceedings under §129.

Buddenberg, the pig, allowed Grashof to be moved from the hospital to a cell; the transfer and the risk of infection in the prison put his life at risk. He attempted to murder Grashof. The police having failed, he tried again to kill the defenseless Grashof.

Buddenberg, the pig, is responsible for Carmen Roll being drugged in order to get her to talk. The foreseeable effect of the drug indicates that this was attempted murder.

Buddenberg, the pig, doesn't give a shit about existing laws and conventions. The strict isolation in which prisoners are held to destroy them psychologically: solitary confinement, isolated yard time, the ban on speaking to other prisoners, constant transfers, punitive confinement, observation cells, the censoring of mail and the confiscation of mail, books, and magazines. The means used to destroy them physically—the glaring cell lights at night, frequent interruption of sleep for searches, chaining during yard time, and physical abuse—are not the bullying of insignificant, frustrated prison wardens; these are Buddenberg's decrees, meant to force the prisoners to make statements. It is institutionalized fascism in the justice system. It is the beginning of torture.

We demand the immediate application of laws governing remand prisoners, the Geneva Human Rights Convention, and the United Nations Charter regarding the use of remand custody for political prisoners. We demand the justice system call off the systematic destructive attacks upon the lives and health of the prisoners.

We will carry out bomb attacks against judges and federal prosecutors until they stop violating the rights of political prisoners. We are, in fact, demanding nothing that is impossible for this justice system. We have no other means to compel them to do so.

FREEDOM FOR THE POLITICAL PRISONERS!
RESIST CLASS JUSTICE! RESIST FASCISM!

Manfred Grashof Commando
May 20, 1972

Attack on the Springer Building

Yesterday, Friday May 19, at 3:55 PM, two bombs exploded in the Springer Building in Hamburg. Despite prompt and early warnings, the building wasn't evacuated and 17 people were injured. At 3:29 PM, the first warning was given to number 3471, who was told to evacuate the building within 15 minutes because a bomb would detonate shortly. The answer was, "Stop this nonsense." The call was cut off. With a second call at 3:31 PM, we said, "If you don't evacuate immediately, something horrible will happen." But the telephone operators obviously had instructions not to pay attention to such calls. The third call, at 3:36 PM, was to the cops saying, "Goddamn it, see to it that the building is immediately evacuated." Because the Springer Corporation can't cover up the fact that they were warned, they distort it, stating, "There was only one call and it came too late." Two telephone operators and the police can confirm that the Springer Press is lying once again.

Springer would rather risk his workers and staff being injured by a bomb than risk losing a couple of hours of work time, and therefore profit, as a result of a false alarm. For capitalists, profit is everything, and the people who make it for them are dirt. We regret that workers and staff were injured.

Our demands of Springer: that his newspapers stop the anticommunist hysteria against the New Left, against working-class solidarity actions such as strikes, and against communist parties here and in other countries; that the Springer Corporation stop the hysteria against liberation movements in the Third World, especially against the Arab people who struggle for the freedom of Palestine; that he stop his propagandistic support for Zionism—the imperialist politics of the Israeli ruling class; that the Springer Press stop spreading lies about foreign workers here.

We demand that the Springer Press print this communiqué.

We demand nothing impossible. We will stop our attacks on the enemies of the people if our demands are met.

EXPROPRIATE SPRINGER!
EXPROPRIATE THE ENEMIES OF THE PEOPLE!

2nd of June Commando
May 20, 1972

Attack on the Heidelberg Headquarters of the U.S. Army in Europe

Every form of monstrosity will be abolished

Mao

Yesterday evening, May 24, 1972, two bombs with an explosive capacity of 200 kg of TNT, were detonated in the Heidelberg Headquarters of the American Armed Forces in Europe. The attack was carried out after General Daniel James, Department Head at the Pentagon, said, on Wednesday in Washington, "For the U.S. Air Force, no target North or South of the 17th parallel in Vietnam will be exempt from bombing attacks." On Monday, the Minister of Foreign Affairs in Hanoi again accused the United States of bombing densely populated areas of North Vietnam. In the last 7 weeks, the American Air Force has dropped more bombs on Vietnam than were dropped on Germany and Japan during World War II. Many millions of additional bombs is the response the Pentagon intends to use to stop the North Vietnamese offensive. This is genocide, the slaughter of a people; this is "the final solution"; this is Auschwitz.

The people of the Federal Republic don't support the security service in its search for the bombers, because they want nothing to do with the crimes of American imperialism and the support it receives from the ruling class here, because they haven't forgotten Auschwitz, Dresden, and Hamburg, because they know that the bomb attacks against those who commit mass murder in Vietnam are just, and because they know from experience that demonstrations and words are of no use against the crimes of imperialism.

WE DEMAND AN END TO BOMB ATTACKS ON VIETNAM!
WE DEMAND A HALT TO THE MINE BLOCKADE AGAINST
NORTH VIETNAM!
WE DEMAND THE WITHDRAWAL OF AMERICAN TROOPS
FROM INDOCHINA!

July 15th Commando
May 25, 1972

To the News Editors
of the West German Press

On May 26, Willy Brandt said in his television broadcast that the bombings of recent weeks have no logical political basis, and that they have endangered innocent lives.

The Federal Chancellor can deceive the people with these assertions because the West German press has almost completely suppressed the communiqués of the urban guerilla commandos.

Instead the *Frankfurter Rundschau* published a letter created out of cut out letters—which, when compared to authentic RAF communiqués, can clearly be seen to be a fake—to create the impression that the bombers are brainless twits who act chaotically in an effort to create fear amongst the people.

The Chancellor's statement does not differ from similar statements by General Franco, General Patakos, von Howeida, the followers of Salazar, or the Turkish military dictator: the reasons for the actions are ignored, and only the condemnation of the Chancellor and the pundits is presented. The reasons for this conduct are obvious:

- The communiqué of the Thomas Weissbecker Commando was intended to bring every individual police officer to the point where he must think about whether or not he wants to be an active part of the hunt for the RAF;
- An investigation would have proven that the 2nd of June Commando warned the Springer Corporation on time and that Springer, as always, has lied;
- The people, who know from their own experience all about genocide and the terrorist bombing of civilian populations, can draw their own conclusions about the bomb attacks against those who commit mass murder in Vietnam and against the fascism of the Springer Corporation;
- And because of this, there can be no doubt that the bomb attacks were directed solely against the enemies of the people, the enemies of the working class, the enemies of the Vietnamese people, the imperialists.

"We're all in the same boat" has always been the motto of the exploiters and fascists.

Springer has, under threat of further bomb attacks, published the demands made of him, albeit in a mutilated form.

The rest of the press must understand that they themselves will be provoking actions against Springer if they, as a result of economic pressure coming from Springer, submit voluntarily and opportunistically to this practice of censorship. We therefore demand that they no longer deceive the people about the political reasons behind the bomb attacks, that is to say, that they not aggravate the situation unnecessarily. We demand that they print in full the following communiqués: the communiqué of the Thomas Weissbecker Commando, the communiqué of the 2nd of June Commando, and the communiqué of the July 15th Commando.

SERVE THE PEOPLE!
EXPROPRIATE SPRINGER!

RAF
May 28, 1972

Regarding the Fascist Bomb Threats Against Stuttgart

The two bomb threats pasted together out of letters cut from newspapers for next Friday, June 2, in Stuttgart don't come from the Red Army Faction. Genuine communiqués of the urban guerilla commandos can easily be authenticated by comparing their contents with other RAF communiqués. And they are typewritten, as the cops well know.

The fake communiqués, given their contents, their purpose, their essence, and their style, more likely come from the cops themselves.

The cops know this. The Springer journalists, who have published the false communiqués without reservation, know this. Filbinger,[1] Krause,[2] and Klett[3] know this. They are taking precautions only as a pretext to prepare new police actions and to drive the war of nerves to the extreme.

Because the authorities leading the manhunt are receiving no help from the people, they are seizing upon fascist provocation. It is possible that if by Friday they haven't had any success in their hunt—if they haven't met their kill quota—they will carry through on the crimes they have threatened. Just as Springer didn't allow his building to be evacuated, although he himself said he could foresee the attacks coming. Just as the Nazis set the Reichstag on fire and attacked the Gleiwitz transmitter. One must assume that they intend similar communiqués and attacks in the future.

Fake communiqué threatening random bombings in Stuttgart.

---

1 Hans Filbinger (CDU) was, at this time, the *Land* Chairman of Baden-Württemberg, of which Stuttgart is the capital.

2 Walter Krause (SPD) was, at this time, the Minister of the Interior and acting President of Baden-Württemberg.

3 Arnulf Klett was, at this time, the Mayor of Stuttgart.

We are not responsible for the crimes of fascists.

The actions of the urban guerilla are directed against the institutions of the class state, imperialism, and capital. They are never directed against working people or against people who have nothing to do with the crimes of imperialism. They are directed against those who plan vicious attacks against the people, such as those announced in the false communiqués, and those carried out daily by U.S. imperialism against the Vietnamese people.

FIGHT FASCISM!
DESTROY AND OBLITERATE THE POWER OF IMPERIALISM!
EXPROPRIATE SPRINGER!

RAF
May 29, 1972

Statement to the Red Aid Teach-In

Comrades, some of you still believe that you don't have any reason to dialogue with the Red Army Faction.

Some of you still believe that the cops will soon have a handle on the armed struggle in the metropole. Some of you still believe what you read in the newspapers: that the RAF is on the run, that there are splits in the RAF, that the RAF has a hierarchical structure, that the RAF is isolated. You aren't seeing reality.

The KB in Hamburg believed that the attack against the Springer Corporation was the work of right-wing extremists. Instead of engaging us in debate, they assure the police that they themselves are not guilty. And the Frankfurt KSV asserts, in agreement with the *Rundshau*, that the recent bomb attacks have nothing to do with the class struggle in West Germany and Berlin. These comrades no longer understand what's going on.

Although they now understand that Genscher didn't call out the police for show, that the murders of Petra, Georg, and Thomas were not mistakes on the part of the system, that the *Kripo* was responsible for the destruction of strike centrals during the strikes last year, that the Emergency Laws weren't adopted just for the fun of it, that the banning of foreigners' organizations isn't just for show, and that over sixty prisoners are being abused in prison—although they know all of this full well, they still believe it is too early to begin to resist.

They protest the death penalty in Persia and in Turkey; they wish the Palestinian resistance success; they protest the terror in Greece and Spain; they protest the complicity of the system with fascist regimes— but they are afraid to intervene or to act. They are clearly afraid to arrive at the obvious conclusion. They hide behind the masses and present their problem as one located outside of themselves.

We see things differently than these comrades. We are of the opinion that the hateful assembly-lines and piecework in the factories have gotten so bad that hardly anyone has any illusions any more about the fact that corporate profits require irreparable damage to the health of the workers. The masses already know that in the Federal Republic they must work themselves to death because that is the source of their employers' profits, that the factory workers already know who they're working for—soon it will be for themselves.

We are of the opinion that the problem these comrades see as lying elsewhere is their own subjective problem, that they project onto the masses their own lack of clarity. They want to identify their own inability—an inability to express solidarity with the masses because of their own privileged class position—as lying with the masses, to present it as an objective problem based in the masses' need to develop a higher level of consciousness.

If, as occurred recently in Frankfurt, some women comrades say, for example, that they want to take to the streets if another one of us is murdered, then that indicates it would be easy to spontaneously intervene. Which is to say: the problem of agency is, as Springer journalists put it in a headline, one of marketing and competition. Political content as the commodity, the masses as the market. So they are ready to moan about imperialist crimes, but not to prevent them with clubs and bombs. For the imperialists, the assembly lines are still not going fast enough and the time required must be further reduced. They will consume as much as they can extract.

There is no reason for further delay in addressing the problem of armed struggle and resistance. Reduced hours, lay-offs, strikes, two million foreign workers, "*Bild* fights for you!", "the extortionist of the week" in *Stern*, Citizens Initiatives, squatted houses—there is hardly any area in which the system can maintain its facade. The people's desires must be unified and transformed into an organized leap forward.

This greed-driven system is ravaging the cities. Teachers must learn to muzzle themselves or they are fired. The mass media has been purged of decent critical journalists. Riot police are mobilized against strike centrals. Rulings of the Federal Labor Court prepare the way to criminalize future strikes. The BKA hopes to eliminate the remaining press freedoms. They are not waiting for the legal left to take up the armed struggle before proceeding with this. It's happening now; it has begun. Is this the point when you will start to resist—or are you still waiting for something?

Comrades, stop hiding behind the masses! Stop shifting the question of resistance to the masses! Stop rationalizing your fear of the system's excessive violence as a problem of agency! Stop presenting your confusion as erudition and your helplessness as a broad perspective!

The system is now producing contradictions at such a rate that they can no longer be integrated, and the masses no longer believe talk of reforms. It is equally true that the guerilla can only be anchored in the people to the degree that we carry out appropriate actions and you make effective propaganda. For this to happen, the revolutionary process and revolutionary consciousness must be developed further; the consciousness that action is justified—and possible!

When we build the revolutionary guerilla, we are creating an instrument that is beyond the reach of the system's repression, that does not depend on the system's tolerance for its capacity to act, that does not have its room to maneuver determined by the *Verfassungsshutz*. If you are domesticated like Müller's[1] demonstrators in Frankfurt on May 18, you can continue to demonstrate for some time to come, and you can celebrate it along with the KSV as the most powerful and most insular demonstration in a long time. Under the watchful eye of the police and funneled between two water cannons and rows of batons, you can go on celebrating successes long into the future. But the price to be paid is the distance people took from Tuesday's demonstration, the denunciation of the comrades who broke free from the Hauptwache;[2] the price in the end was betrayal of the goals in exchange for permission to walk in the streets.

Today, everyone understands our actions against the extermination strategy in Vietnam. Everybody should be able to understand our actions to defend the lives and health of the prisoners and of the RAF comrades still at large. That the media no longer publishes our communiqués about our bomb attacks, but publishes false statements of fascist origin, that they downplay attacks on U.S. imperialism and play up fascist provocations such as that against the citizens of Stuttgart, demonstrates how things really are, demonstrates what they are afraid of and how far they'll go to hide the truth from the masses, to prop up their facade.

Dare to struggle; dare to win! Attack and smash the power of imperialism! It is the duty of every revolutionary to make the revolution! We call on all militants in the Federal Republic to make all American establishments targets of their attacks in their struggle against U.S. imperialism!

Long live the RAF!

Ulrike Meinhof
for the RAF
May 31, 1972

---

1 Frankfurt police chief at the time.
2 The Hauptwache is the central point on a major pedestrian mall in Frankfurt.

6

Black September: A Statement from Behind Bars

I N THE FALL OF 1972, operationally devastated, the RAF issued its first document from behind bars: *The Black September Action in Munich: Regarding the Strategy for Anti-Imperialist Struggle.* Written by one or several of the captured combatants, the text was first made public in West Berlin at Mahler's second RAF trial, during which he faced charges of conspiracy and establishing a terrorist organization. The former lawyer worked it into the court record by using it as the basis for questions to Ulrike Meinhof, whom he had called as a witness. By November, it was being distributed by outside supporters in magazine format as the RAF's third major publication.

In this paper, the RAF re-examined the geopolitics of anti-imperialism and the class base for revolution in the First World while responding angrily to Frankfurt School intellectual Oskar Negt, who had recently emerged as a vocal critic of armed struggle in the FRG. What caught people's attention most was the RAF's expression of warm solidarity with the Palestinian group Black September, which had carried out a daring, and ultimately tragic, hostage-taking during the Munich Olympics just months earlier.

DEN ANTIIMPERIALISTISCHEN KAMPF FÜHREN!

DIE ROTE ARMEE AUFBAUEN !

Die Aktion des Schwarzen September in München -
Zur Strategie des antiimperialistischen Kampfes

"The guerillas took part in a courageous action," Mahler explained, "in which they were ready to sacrifice themselves. The only fault the Black September guerillas can be reproached for is that they did not take Interior Minister Hans-Dietrich Genscher as a hostage."[1]

At this point, the courtroom full of left-wing supporters erupted into cheers, prompting the judge to order it cleared.

There is no indication that the RAF played any part in the Black September operation; it was effectively out of action at the time, gutted by the arrests it had suffered following the May Offensive. Even so, given the group's public statement of solidarity, it may be best to revisit the events at the Munich Olympics that year. (For more about the relationship between the West Germany and Israel, and how this affected the New Left, see Appendix III—The FRG and the State of Israel, pages 550-53.)

Black September had its origin in the aftermath of the civil war between Palestinian forces and the Jordanian state in September 1970. Formed by militants within Arafat's Al Fatah, its first action had been the assassination, on November 28, 1971, of Jordan's Prime Minister Wasfi Tel.[2] Not one month later, the group had attempted its second assassination, wounding Zaid el Rifai, Jordan's ambassador to England, as he drove through the streets of London.[3] By September of 1972, Black September had carried out a number of operations in Europe, including skyjacking a Sabena Belgian World Airlines plane en route from Vienna to Tel Aviv. The plane was flown to Lod airport, where Israeli Defense Minister Moshe Dayan sent in a squad of paratroopers disguised as maintenance workers, who carried out a successful assault. Two of the hijackers were killed and two others captured.[4]

Meanwhile, opening on August 26, the 1972 Olympic Games were supposed to be a symbolic graduation ceremony for the FRG. The last time the Olympics were held on German soil had been the 1936 Berlin games, which became a propaganda vehicle for the Hitler regime. Commentators were not shy to admit that the 1972 Munich Olympics were meant to signal a moving on, a testament to how well West Germany had gotten over its fascist past.

---

1 United Press International, "Baader-Meinhof lawyer praises guerillas," *European Stars and Stripes,* October 10, 1972. As we shall see, this was not moot criticism.

2 Christopher Dobson, *Black September: Its Short, Violent History* (New York: Macmillan, 1974), 1.

3 Ibid., 12.

4 Ibid., 65-79.

As an unrecognized portent of things to come, that June, the International Olympic Committee refused requests to allow a Palestinian team to participate in the games.[5]

Early on September 5, midway through the games, an eight-man Black September commando entered the "Olympic Village" housing athletes from around the world. The commando made directly for the Israeli dorms, which they secured, in the process killing two sportsmen who tried to resist. They seized nine other Israeli athletes as hostages and issued their demands: the release of 234 Palestinians and non-Arabs from Israeli prisons, the release of Andreas Baader and Ulrike Meinhof in the FRG, and safe passage to Egypt for all concerned.[6]

Black September named this its "Operation Iqrith and Kafr Bir'im."[7]

Golda Meir, the Israeli Prime Minister, informed the West German authorities that Israel would not release any of the prisoners. At that point, the West Germans developed a plan to pretend to arrange for the safe passage of the commando and the hostages out of the FRG, while in fact preparing an ambush.

At 10:20 PM, the guerillas and their captives were flown to the military airfield at Fürstenfeldbruck, halfway between Munich and Augsburg. A Lufthansa Boeing 727 waited on the tarmac, ostensibly to fly the group to Tunis. But the area was crawling with cops, and five snipers had been positioned with orders to take the "terrorists" out as soon as the signal was given.

Two members of the commando checked out the Boeing to make sure that all was as had been promised. They then started back to the helicopters where the hostages and the other commando members had

---

5 Simon Reeve, *One Day in September: The Full Story of the 1972 Munich Olympics Massacre* (New York: Arcade Publishing, 2000), 40.

6 Black September would later tell Voice of Palestine radio that they had demanded the release of five "revolutionary German girls belonging to the Baader-Meinhof organization," which five being left open to conjecture. (United Press International, "Other Arab guerrilla demand told," *Hayward Daily Review*, September 8, 1972.)

7 Iqrith (also spelled Ikrit) and Bir'im were two Christian villages in the upper Galilee. In 1948, shock troops from the Zionist *Hagana* expelled the towns' inhabitants at gunpoint. "The pogrom-like expulsion was carried out without the Israeli government approval," writes Palestinian journalist Khalid Amayreh. "However, the democratic Israeli state never allowed the Christian inhabitants to return, despite several rulings to the contrary by the Israeli High Court." (Khaled Amayreh, "Christians, too, suffer the evilness of the occupation," at http://www. thepeoplesvoice.org/cgi-bin/blogs/voices.php/2007/12/26/christians_too_suffer_ the_evilness_of_th).

remained. At this point, the police sharpshooters opened fire: they missed, and there ensued intermittent volleys of bullets lasting over an hour. Finally, unable to subdue the Palestinians with gunfire, just after midnight police in armored vehicles moved in to try and storm the helicopters.

Seeing this, the commando executed the nine hostages.

By the time the cops were in control, five members of the Palestinian commando and a police officer also lay dead. The entire hostage-taking had lasted barely twenty hours.

It was later revealed that the Bavarian police had seriously bungled their ambush. A team that had been designated to overpower the commando inside the Boeing had voted (!) to desert their posts just twenty minutes before the helicopters landed at Fürstenfeldbruck—they considered the proposed ambush "suicidal."[1] This put all the pressure on the marksmen, and yet there were only five deployed, they were not equipped with the recommended rifles for such an operation, nor had they received infrared sights, bulletproof vests, or walkie talkies.[2] They were not even informed of each other's positions, which led to one police sniper shooting another, whom he mistook for a member of the commando![3]

The authorities had obviously underestimated the Palestinian guerilla. "At the moment we fired there were not enough terrorists exposed," explained Bruno Merck, the Bavarian Minister of the Interior. "We had expected, nevertheless, that those who had not been shot would surrender in the shock of the gun battle. That didn't happen... All we could do was hope for a mistake. But these people are not amateurs."[4]

The distinction between "amateurs" and "professionals" is an odd one. Two of the commando members were teenagers, and the others mostly in their early twenties; obviously, none had participated in other actions of this sort. Their determination most likely came from their own personal experiences. They had all grown up in refugee camps, their families forced to endure extreme poverty, hunger, and the constant threat of Israeli violence, while most of the world happily ignored their existence.[5]

---

1 Aaron J. Klein, *Striking Back: the 1972 Munich Olympics Massacre and Israel's deadly response* (New York: Random House, 2005), 72-73.

2 Reeve, 116.

3 Ibid., 121-122.

4 Dobson, 85.

5 Reeve, 41-42.

In the words of Abu Daoud, who claims to have organized the operation, "They were people who had left their homes in '48, forced to flee, and then languished in the Lebanese camps since then. They were people whose houses were now the homes of Polish, French and American Jews who had replaced them in their own country, living as citizens there without any right to."[6]

The three survivors from the commando—Sammar 'Adnan 'abd al-Ghani al-Jishshi,[7] 'Abd al-Qadir ad-Dinnawi, and Samer Muhammad 'Abdallah[8]—were taken into West German custody. Less than two months later, on October 29, a second Black September commando skyjacked a Lufthansa jet en route from Beirut to Ankara, threatening to blow up the plane if the three were not released. Still licking its wounds from the Fürstenfeldbruck fiasco, the West German government agreed: the Munich survivors were granted safe passage to Libya.[9]

Operation Iqrith and Kafr Bir'im sent shockwaves around the world. To Israel and its supporters, Black September had massacred innocents, and the Germans had been criminally incompetent. In the words of one Israeli diplomat, "The human mind fails to grasp the barbaric depravity of the cruel murderers of the Israeli athletes."[10]

The response was not long in coming and took the form of collective punishment:

> [On September 8] Israeli Skyhawk planes attacked villages and refugee camps in Lebanon and Syria... killing a total of 59 people and wounding 40 others, all of whom were civilians. Among the victims were 19 children.[11]

Eight days later, a second exercise in collective punishment was carried out:

> The Israeli army, supported by tanks, armored cars and jet aircraft, crossed into Lebanese territory, and for 36 hours attacked a

---

6 Ibid, 42.

7 The FRG press reported his name as Ibrahim Badran.

8 Mahmud Abdallah Kallam, *Sabra wa-Shatila, dhakirat ad-Damm* (Beirut: Beisan Publishing), 40-41.

9 *Time Magazine* [online], "Return of Black September," November 13, 1972.

10 Associated Press, "Bay Area service for slain Jews," *Hayward Daily Review*, September 8, 1972.

11 Sami Hadawi, *Crime and No Punishment: Zionist-Israeli Terrorism 1939-1972* (Beirut: Palestine Research Centre, 1972), 83.

number of Lebanese villages within an area of some 250 square kilometers, killing people at random and destroying houses and blowing up bridges...

The refugee camp at Nabatiya was attacked from the air by napalm bombs, wounding eight of its inmates...

By the time the Israelis withdrew, they left behind a trail of death and destruction. About 200 civilians, including women and children, were killed or wounded, and over 200 houses destroyed or damaged. In addition, 18 Lebanese soldiers died in defense of their homeland.[1]

The United States vetoed a United Nations resolution condemning these massacres, and in doing so put Israel's policy of carrying out reprisals against Palestinian civilians on a firm international footing for decades to come.[2]

Not only did the Munich operation provoke attacks against Palestinian civilians, it also spelled the beginning of the end of Black September as an organization. On the one hand, Israeli secret services embarked on a bloody campaign of retribution, letter bombs and targeted assassinations, which would eventually claim dozens of lives.[3] At the same time, various Arab regimes which supported the PLO began to worry that the Palestinians' struggle might endanger their relationship with the imperialist West. The final turning point for these regimes occurred just six months later when a Black September commando took over the Saudi embassy in Khartoum, Sudan during a farewell party for the U.S. Chargé d'Affaires[4]—one Belgian and two American diplomats were executed before the commando surrendered.[5] The pressure from conservative Arab states increased, and the PLO and Fatah withdrew their support for hijackings and hostage-takings, which caused Black

---

1 Ibid., 84.

2 Henry Cattan, *The Palestine Question* (London: Croom Helm, 1987), 122-123.

3 Reeve, 160-169, 175-195. For more on Israel's reaction, see Brad E. O'Neill, *Armed Struggle in Palestine: A Political-Military Analysis* (Boulder, Colorado: Westview Press, 1978), 87-88.

4 Black September was demanding the release of Sirhan Sirhan, who had assassinated Bobby Kennedy, a number of Palestinians held in Jordan, all Arab women held in Israel, as well as Ulrike Meinhof and Andreas Baader in the FRG.

5 Patricia McCarty, "The Terrorist War," *European Stars and Stripes,* August 9, 1973.

September operations to rapidly taper off.[6] Within a few years, the organization was no more.

As for the West German reaction to the events at the Munich Olympics, the whole mess was seen as a great embarrassment. One result was the decision to establish a crack special operations unit, the *Grenzschutzgruppe 9* (literally, "Border Protection Group 9" but shortened to GSG-9), announced within weeks of the Fürstenfeldbruck blunder. Led by Ulrich Wegener, Genscher's liaison officer with the BGS, who had been present on the scene at the airfield, it would receive its initial training from Britain's SAS and Israel's *Sayeret Mat'kal*. As its name implies, the GSG-9 fell under the umbrella of the Border Police, not the armed forces, legally enabling it to attempt long-term "deep cover" infiltration of the radical scene. The GSG-9 would eventually win international recognition as one of the most fearsome "counterterrorism" units in the world, some of its operatives receiving additional training in NATO's International Long Range Reconnaissance Patrol (LRRP) School.[7]

Of more immediate consequence was the crackdown against the FRG's small Arab population.

Earlier that year, Black September had already carried out less dramatic attacks in West Germany. On February 6, the group had assassinated five Jordanians, believed to be intelligence officers who had been active in the civil war, near Cologne.[8] Then, on February 8, a bomb had gone off in a factory belonging to the Strüver Corporation near Hamburg. The factory produced electrical generators for Israeli aircraft.[9] On February 22, the Esso Oil pipeline near Hamburg had been similarly damaged.[10]

Now, with the Munich attack passing under the glare of the Olympic spotlight, the state moved into action; raids were carried out, and the FRG's 4,000 Arab students and 37,000 Arab "guest workers" came under intense scrutiny. In short order, approximately one hundred Palestinian activists were expelled, and two Fatah front groups—the

---

6 O'Neill, 151.

7 "Terrorism 101—Counter-Terrorism Organizations: Germany - GSG-9," http://www.terrorism101.org/counter/Germany.html.

8 Edgar O'Balance, *Arab Guerilla Power* (London: Faber and Faber, 1974), 215.

9 MIPT Terrorism Knowledge Base, "Black September Attacked Business Target (Feb. 8, 1972, Federal Republic of Germany)," http://www.tkb.org/Incident.jsp?incID=790.

10 Dobson, 65.

General Union of Palestinian Students and the General Union of Palestinian Workers—found themselves banned.[1]

At the same time, within the radical left, some saw the events of September 5 quite differently. To anti-imperialists and others who sympathized with Black September, the operation had been a legitimate one, even if it had ended in tragedy. Some would even argue that the operation had been a success, for although no prisoners had been freed and so many people had died, the world could no longer pretend it did not know about the plight of the Palestinians.[2] Furthermore, it was argued that blame for the Israeli athletes' death lay squarely with the West German police, who had attempted a double-cross which simply blew up in their faces.

Sympathetic observers pointed out that the Palestinians had certainly not wanted to kill their hostages. They hoped rather to free their own comrades. This argument was more difficult to dismiss in 1972 than it would be today, as skyjackings and exchanging hostages for prisoners had not yet exhausted their utility for guerillas at that time, and often did meet with success (as the October 29 skyjacking would demonstrate).[3]

Furthermore, although the athletes were noncombatants, they were nonetheless representatives of a colonial state, one which was for all intents and purposes waging war against the Palestinian people. Certainly, far bloodier actions had been carried out in anticolonial campaigns around the world. No less than Carlos Marighella, the

---

1 Ibid., 132.

2 Decades later, Abu Daoud remained adamant on this point. "I would be against any operation like Munich ever again," he told *Sports Illustrated* magazine in 2002. However, "[a]t the time, it was the correct thing to do for our cause. ... The operation brought the Palestinian issue into the homes of 500 million people who never previously cared about Palestinian victims at the hands of the Israelis." (Alexander Wolff, "Thirty years after he helped plan the terror strike, Abu Daoud remains in hiding—and unrepentant," *Sports Illustrated*, August 26, 2002.)

3 Indeed, the years 1969-1972 can be considered the golden age of political hostage takings. While kidnappings were a particularly prevalent tactic for the South American guerilla, skyjackings in this period were pioneered by various Palestinian organizations. Whereas there had been only twenty-seven aircraft hijacked between 1961 and 1968, and most of these had been non-political acts, between 1969 and 1972, two hundred seventy-seven aircraft were hijacked, many of them successfully, i.e. the hijackers got away and their demands were met. During this period, seventy-eight political prisoners were released as demanded by various skyjackers. [Alona E. Evans, "Aircraft Hijacking: What is Being Done?" *American Journal of International Law* 67 (1973): 641-645].

Brazilian guerilla leader, had argued in his famous *Minimanual* that "non-political" celebrities could constitute legitimate targets:

> *The kidnapping of personalities who are well-known artists, sports figures or who are outstanding in some other field, but who have evidenced no political interest, can be a useful form of propaganda for the guerrillas, provided it occurs under special circumstances, and is handled so the public understands and sympathizes with it.*[4]

Whether the operation was understood or enjoyed public sympathy depended very much on who one thought of as constituting the "public." Certainly, in the Arab world, the action was widely understood, and met with a large measure of sympathy. When the bodies of the slain commando members were brought to Libya, for instance, over 30,000 mourners followed their funeral procession from Tripoli's Martyr's Square to the Sidi Munaidess Cemetery.[5]

It is equally true that in the imperialist countries, most people neither understood nor sympathized with the aims of the Palestinians. The commando's public testament, released shortly afterwards, met with simple incomprehension. Thus the outrage, not only at Black September, but also at anyone who dared to speak up in defense of the Palestinian guerilla action.

If it has been necessary to our study to consider these events in such detail, it is precisely because of this outrage.

Critics of the RAF have zeroed in on the *Black September* document, scandalized at this support for the Munich operation. The guerilla's penchant for purposefully shocking formulations (i.e. "Israel burned their own athletes just as the Nazis had burned the Jews") did not help matters. Likewise, a strong argument could be made that the RAF, like much of the revolutionary left, did a poor job at acknowledging and analyzing the specifically antisemitic dimensions of German fascism.

What is important to stress in the context of our study is that this is not why the RAF was criticized. Rather, the fact that the captured combatants dared to stand in solidarity with Black September has been

---

4 Carlos Marighella, "Kidnapping," Minimanual of the Urban Guerilla, http://www.marxists.org/archive/marighella-carlos/1969/06/minimanual-urban-guerrilla/ch28.htm.

5 Reeve, 147.

construed as "proof" that they were antisemites, not in the sense of having a weak analysis or oppressive blindspots, but in the sense of "hating Jews." According to the state, various "terrorism experts," and some right-wing and liberal pundits, it was in this sense that the RAF was accused of being an antisemitic organization.

Yet regardless of whether one finds it to have been correct or ill-conceived, justified or egregious, it is plainly evident that the Munich hostage taking had nothing to do with antisemitism. It was simply part of the struggle of the Palestinian people against colonial oppression. There may be plenty of moral and political arguments with which to object to the targeting of the Olympic athletes, but opposition to antisemitism is not one of them. Indeed, while anti-Jewish racism may well have led some bigots to applaud the action, anti-Arab racism seems to have led far more to automatically condemn it, and with it all those who would not turn their backs on the Palestinian people.

Yet the accusation did not stop there: some liberal and right-wing critics have gone further, accusing Meinhof of making antisemitic comments as the RAF text was being delivered. This story has gained some currency in recent years, especially on the internet, so it is worth extending this already lengthy examination in order to establish the facts of the matter.

As already mentioned, the *Black September* document was read out in court by Horst Mahler, taking the form of a "cross examination" of Ulrike Meinhof, who had been called to the witness stand. At one point, Meinhof interrupted the reading with an impromptu observation of her own, specifically regarding the nature of German antisemitism and the Holocaust. The only record of what Meinhof said is in an article from the *Frankfurter Allgemeine Zeitung*, in which many of her words were paraphrased. Here is what the *FAZ* reported Meinhof as saying:

> *"Auschwitz meant that six million Jews were murdered and carted off to Europe's garbage heap, dispensed with as money Jews." Finance capital and banks, "the hard core of the system" of imperialism and capitalism deflected the hate of the people for money and oppression from itself and transferred it to the Jews.*[1]

---

1 Peter Jochen Winters, "Ulrike Meinhof läßt sich nur die Stichwort geben," *Frankfurter Allgemeine Zeitung*, December 15, 1972. Our translation. Note that those sections not in quotes consist of the summary by Winters. The entire relevant portion of the FAZ article is reproduced in German and English in Appendix I, pages 544-47.

The *FAZ*, like all initial observers, seems to have understood Meinhof as saying that the Nazis took advantage of anticapitalist sentiment, using stereotypes about "rich Jews" to mobilize gentiles behind a program of genocide. That Meinhof saw herself as opposed to this, and therefore opposed to antisemitism, was taken for granted.

Such an analysis of Nazism may be criticized for being facile, economistic, or simply incorrect. Nevertheless, it has an established place on the left, and is not in and of itself in any way anti-Jewish. Rather, it can trace its lineage directly back to the early 20th century social democrat, August Bebel, who famously described antisemitism as "the socialism of fools."

Even so, Meinhof's words were to be turned against her, especially in the English-speaking world. One of the first translations of the *FAZ* quote into English appeared in an article by one George Watson in the British literary magazine *Encounter*, a CIA-funded publication, which had as its aim the winning over of "progressive" intellectuals to the American side in the Cold War.[2] This translation had a curious wording, though, one which seemed to give new meaning to what Meinhof had said. According to Watson, the guerilla leader had stated that "Auschwitz means that 6 million Jews were killed, and thrown onto the waste heap of Europe, *for what they were*: money-Jews."[3] (emphasis added)

The clear implication here is that Meinhof approved of their murder—that she approved of the Holocaust and Nazism and also Auschwitz. This would flatly contradict everything Meinhof and the RAF had stated both before and after this point, and this fact alone should suffice to cast doubt on Watson's translation. As should the fact that those who have gone back to the original German *FAZ* article have disputed Watson's interpretation with apparent unanimity.[4]

---

2 In the words of Andrew Roth, a friend of the magazine's editor Melvin Lasky: "*Encounter*'s function was to combat anti-Americanism by brainwashing the uncertain with pro-American articles. These were paid for at several times the rate paid by the *New Statesman* and offered British academics and intellectuals free U.S. trips and expenses-paid lecture tours. There was no room for the objective-minded in this cold war to capture intellectuals." (Andrew Roth, "Melvin Lasky, Cold Warrior who Edited Encounter Magazine," *The Manchester Guardian* [online], Obituaries, May 22, 2004.)

3 George Watson, "Race and the Socialists," *Encounter* 47 (Nov. 1976): 23.

4 Scholar Diane Paule, for instance states: "Watson's translation and analysis make Meinhof's point appear to be much clearer than in fact it is, and his charge that she 'spoke up publicly in the Good Old Cause of revolutionary extermination' is not

However, most people do not return to the original, and this conveniently damning translation has subsequently found its way into all sorts of studies and discussions, not only of the RAF, but of the left in general. Saul Bellow quoted it as he accepted the Nobel Prize in Literature in 1976,[1] and it has been featured in books "proving" that revolutionary anticapitalism is antisemitic.[2] All over the internet it appears as "evidence" that not only the RAF, but indeed the entire German New Left, was anti-Jewish, if not crypto-Nazi.

We are not claiming that there are no legitimate criticisms to be made of how the West German left dealt with—or failed to deal with—the question of antisemitism. It has been noted that many radicals' fierce antifascism rested on an analysis which saw the persecution of Jews as merely incidental to Nazism. Some radicals, including the RAF, often did seem to view the Third Reich as nothing more than a case of hyper-capitalism, the solution to which could be as simple as hyper-anticapitalism.

Combined with a persisting lack of clarity regarding the status of Germany—imperialist? or colonized?[3]—and a keen awareness of Israel's role in world imperialism, these weaknesses pushed sections of the left to occasionally espouse positions which belied a certain antisemitism. This was a serious error at times in the 1970s, and coming to grips with it would eventually acquire some importance for some individuals within both the K-groups and the undogmatic left.

Despite these facts, being a left-wing German anti-Zionist was in no way tantamount to being an antisemite. Far from it. In the precise case of the RAF, those who would accuse the group of antisemitism have yet to make their case.

As to Ulrike Meinhof's words in question, Watson's translation is simply wrong. Whether this was an "honest mistake," or whether it had something to do with the CIA funding the magazine for which he wrote is a question readers had best ponder for themselves. Certainly, the timing is suspect: his article appeared in November 1976. As detailed in

---

obviously supported by the text." ["'In the Interests of Civilization': Marxist Views of Race and Culture in the Nineteenth Century," *Journal of the History of Ideas* 42, no. 1. (January-March, 1981): 128.]

1 Nobel Foundation "Saul Bellow—Nobel Lecture," http://nobelprize.org/nobel_prizes/literature/laureates/1976/bellow-lecture.html.

2 Paul Lawrence Rose, *Revolutionary anti-Semitism in Germany from Kant to Wagner* (Princeton: Princeton University Press, 1990).

3 For more on this, see Not Wanted in the Model: the KPD, pages 17-18.

Section 10, Meinhof had been found dead—with convincing evidence pointing to murder—in her prison cell earlier that year, and this had elicited much sympathy for the RAF within the left. In this context, discrediting the guerilla leader took on great importance for the state and counterinsurgency forces.

(For more on the original *FAZ* article, Watson's loose translation style, and our own translation, see Appendix I—Excerpts from the Frankfurter Allgemeine Zeitung, pages 544-47.)

As has already been mentioned, the RAF did not limit itself to dealing with the Munich events in its *Black September* document. For the RAF, these merely provided a starting point from which to launch into a discussion of imperialism and anti-imperialism in the Arab world, including the possible use of petroleum as a weapon. This was a year before the OPEC nations carried out their partial oil embargo as retaliation against Western support for Israel in the 1973 Yom Kippur war.

From the question of oil, the RAF went on to consider the problem of opportunism within the imperialist countries, the "metropole." This discussion focused on Oskar Negt, a former assistant of Jürgen Habermas and a professor of sociology at the Technical University in Hannover, who following the May Offensive had publicly called on socialists to deny the RAF any solidarity or support.

In the early seventies, Negt was considered a leading left-wing intellectual. In 1973, for instance, in the first issue of *New German Critique*, he would be described as "the most innovative theorist in Germany today."[4] He was particularly prominent in the West German campaign to provide solidarity for the Black Liberation Movement militant Angela Davis. Accused of complicity in a failed hostage taking which had been meant to free imprisoned Black revolutionaries (the Soledad Brothers), Davis was incarcerated in the United States for eighteen months between 1970 and 1972. For Negt, the connection was both political and personal, as he had gotten to know Davis when she had spent time studying in Frankfurt in the 1960s.[5] It was only natural for him to now support her as a political prisoner.

Davis's trial wound up in San Jose, California, in the late spring of 1972, and the jury began its deliberations on Friday, June 2. That same weekend, as a show of solidarity, an Angela Davis Congress had been

---

4 Horst Mewes, "The German New Left," *New German Critique* 1,
(Winter 1973): 39.
5 "The Angela Davis Case," *Newsweek* [online], October 26, 1970, 20.

organized in Frankfurt by the *Sozialistisches Büro*, a loose network that had emerged out of the APO in 1969, and had since established itself as an important force within the undogmatic left.[1] Keynote speakers included Frankfurt School personalities Herbert Marcuse and Wolfgang Abendroth, and, of course, Oskar Negt. Close to ten thousand people attended, and one can only imagine what the scene must have been when news arrived on the Sunday that Davis had been found not guilty.[2]

While the conference was scheduled perfectly to coincide with this victory across the Atlantic, it also occurred at a very particular moment in the FRG. As we have seen, the entire month of May had been filled with bombings carried out by the RAF. Just days before the Congress opened, also in Frankfurt, Red Aid had held a Teach-In Against Repression at which a tape-recorded statement from Ulrike Meinhof had been played. The very next day, the first of the arrests came: Andreas Baader, Holger Meins, and Jan-Carl Raspe were captured.

At this critical juncture, at what should have been an ideal occasion to make the connection between revolutionary movements in West Germany and the United States, Negt dropped his own bombshell. His address at the Congress took aim not at imperialism or racism or state repression, but at the RAF, and at those who supported its strategy of armed struggle in the FRG.

According to Negt, the RAF's politics were disconnected from the experiences of most citizens of the FRG, and for that reason could only be self-defeating. Whereas he believed the Black Liberation Movement was justified in using political violence in the United States, and he fully supported the Black Panther Party and similar groups, he argued that people were not particularly oppressed in the FRG, and, as such, the guerilla could only alienate the working class there. Armed politics in such a context were vanguardist, counterproductive, and doomed to fail, as anyone who robbed banks or planted bombs would only cut themselves off from the very people whose support they should be seeking.

Perhaps worst of all, Negt accused the RAF of being simple "desperadoes" trying to put a political veneer on apolitical crimes. Arguing that "uncritical solidarity" ran contrary to socialist organizing principles,

---

1 Mewes, 32-35.

2 Jürgen Schröder,"USA Black Panther Party (BPP) und Angela Davis Materialien zur Analyse von Opposition," http://www.mao-projekt.de/INT/NA/USA/USA_Black_Panther_Party_und_Angela_Davis.html.

Negt called on leftists to refuse the RAF any support—be it safehouses or IDs or whatnot—smugly adding that if this was done, the guerilla would simply not be able to survive.[3]

It has been reported that his words did not go over so well with everyone at the Congress, and he was vigorously denounced by many in attendance, notably members of Frankfurt's *sponti* scene.[4]

It might have been enough that he speak out against the guerilla in order for the RAF to take him to task, but Negt would be accused of doing far more than that.

Apparently the Hannover sociology professor was friends with Fritz Rodewald—the same Fritz Rodewald who set Ulrike Meinhof and Gerhard Müller up to be captured within a few weeks of the Frankfurt conference. According to Meinhof's biographer Jutta Ditfurth, Rodewald, uneasy about his prior decision to aid the fugitives, had turned to Negt for advice. Negt repeated his position that nobody owed anyone "mechanical" or "automatic" solidarity, and as a result, the police were contacted.[5]

In Negt's hard line, one can discern the first clear rejection of the guerilla by a section of the undogmatic left. While this position can't have done the guerilla any good, the evidence seems to indicate that in 1972, and for several years thereafter, it failed to achieve hegemony. Which is not to say that the undogmatic left was pro-guerilla, but rather that different people held different opinions, and it would have taken more than the ravings of one left-wing intellectual to cause a definite repudiation. When such a move away from political violence did eventually occur, it would be as a result of former street fighters, guerillas, and semi-legal activists re-examining the question. It would take militants like Daniel Cohn-Bendit and Joschka Fischer, and former combatants like Bommi Baumann and Hans-Joachim Klein, to do what Negt could not.

If the RAF saw a thread connecting its negative evaluation of Negt to its glowing appraisal of Black September, it was the question of the labor aristocracy. It is surely no accident that the *Black September* document provides the guerilla's most detailed examination of this concept.

Specifically, the "labor aristocracy" refers to those more well-to-do layers of the working class, people who no longer have any material

---

3 Linksnet "Rede zum Angela-Davis-Kongress 1972," http://www.linksnet.de/artikel.php?id=374.

4 Schröder, "USA Black Panther Party."

5 Jutta Ditfurth, interview by Arno Luik, "Sie war die große Schwester der 68er."

incentive to engage in the dangerous, grueling task of carrying out a revolution against capitalism. Lenin had argued that the labor aristocracy was a product of imperialism, as the profits earned from exploitation in the developing countries were used to pay for the elevated position of certain sections of the working class in the metropole. This concept has been accepted by almost all strains of the Marxist-Leninist tradition, though often accorded little actual importance in practice.

To the first wave of the RAF, however, the question of the labor aristocracy had by this point become central. The labor aristocracy was not seen simply as a section of the West German working class, but as the dominant section, almost to the exclusion of any classical proletariat. As such, the idea of using popular support in the FRG as a barometer of political legitimacy—which is what Negt seemed to propose—was not simply wrong, it reeked of opportunism.

This analysis was hinted at in *Serve the People* earlier in 1972, but *Black September* spelled it out clearly, while also exploring what this might imply.

In the RAF's view, in 1972, there was no material basis for revolution in the FRG: the crumbs from the imperialist table were enough to win most people's loyalty for the system. Yet the RAF did not see this as a reason to give up on revolutionary politics, or to abandon armed struggle; instead, they argued that "the situation is 'ripe' to take up the anti-imperialist struggle in the metropole—not 'ripe' for revolution, but 'ripe' for the anti-imperialist offensive."

The RAF emphasized the alienation which persisted even in an affluent consumer society, zeroing in on people's individual dissatisfaction and misery in the midst of plenty. Much was made of the way in which consumerism distorted and manipulated people's desires, "the exploitation of their feelings and thoughts, wishes, and utopian dreams."

This psychological misery—insufficient, perhaps to carry out a revolution, but enough to establish a revolutionary tradition—was seen as providing a subjective basis for armed resistance to imperialism within the metropole. As the capitalist system would find itself increasingly besieged by the liberation struggles in the Third World—or so the theory went—this base could grow, and then, "the masses here will eventually find their political identity on the side of the liberation struggles, and will eventually free themselves from the grip of the system, with its lies, its glitziness, its election promises, and its lotteries."

Black September provides the RAF's most explicit attempt to link the concepts of imperialism, the labor aristocracy, and the subjective basis for revolt in the metropole. In hindsight, it is clear that the optimistic notion that the West German masses might rally to an anti-imperialist position has not been borne out. Nevertheless, this should not detract from the fact that the RAF was at least trying to deal with questions that most leftists in imperialist societies preferred—and still prefer—to ignore.

As we have seen, Black September was a document firmly embedded in the context of its time. Perhaps for this reason, it did not "age" well, and would be increasingly ignored by those sympathetic to the guerilla in years to come. Yet it was an important document, and the relationship to the national liberation struggles in the Third World and to the working class in Germany as elaborated here would not be revisited by subsequent waves of guerilla fighters for years to come.

The Appeal of the Fedayeen: To All the Free People of the World

On Monday, September 11, 1972, the Palestinian Press Agency published a group statement from the Black September members who were killed in Munich. This statement was drafted before the operation in Munich began. (M. & S.)

We do not intend to kill any innocent people with our action. We are struggling above all against injustice. We do not want to disturb the peace, rather we want to draw the world's attention to the filthy Zionist occupation and the real tragedy our people are suffering.

We ask that the free people of the world understand our action, the goal of which is to thwart imperialism's international interests, to expose the relationship between imperialism and Zionism, and to clarify for our Arab nation what "Israel" is and who its allies are.

We are a significant element in the armed Palestinian revolutionary movement, which is itself part of the Arab revolution. We ask you, in spite of the enemy's conspiracy and the difficulties presented by the struggle, not to lay down your weapons. The earth can only be freed with blood.

The world only respects the strong. Our strength does not lie in speeches, but in action.

We apologize to the young athletes of the world if their sensibilities are disturbed by our undertaking. But they should know that there is a people whose homeland has been occupied for 24 years. This people has suffered anguish at the hands of an enemy that moves amongst them in Munich.

It is irrelevant where we are buried; the enemy can defile our corpses. What we hope is that Arab youth are ready to die in the service of the people and the fatherland. We call upon the "Black September" fedayeen and the Palestinian revolutionary movement to carry the struggle forward.

LONG LIVE OUR PEOPLE!
LONG LIVE THE WORLDWIDE REVOLUTION FOR FREEDOM!

The Black September Action in Munich: Regarding the Strategy for Anti-Imperialist Struggle

Proletarian Revolutions… are constantly self-critical, repeatedly come to a standstill, return to past undertakings to begin them anew, pitilessly and thoroughly mocking their own half-measures, and the weakness and shabbiness of their own preliminary efforts. They seem to throw down their adversary only in order that he may draw new strength from the earth and rise again, more gigantic, before them. They shrink time and again from the unimaginable enormity of their own goals, until they reach a time which makes all turning back impossible, and the conditions themselves call out: hic rhodus, hic salta.[1]

Karl Marx

THE STONES YOU HAVE THROWN AT US
WILL FALL AT YOUR OWN FEET.

The Black September action in Munich has simultaneously clarified both the nature of the imperialist ruling class and of the anti-imperialist struggle, in a way that no revolutionary action in West Germany or West Berlin has. It was simultaneously anti-imperialist, antifascist, and internationalist. It indicated an understanding of historical and political connections, that are always the province of the people—that is to say, those from whom profit is sucked, those who are free from complicity with the system, those who have no reason to believe the illusions fostered by their oppressors, no reason to accept the fantasy their oppressors pass off as history, no reason to pay the slightest attention to their version of reality. It revealed the rage and the strength that these revolutionaries get from their close connection to the Palestinian

---

1 A quote from Karl Marx's *The Eighteenth Brumaire of Louis Bonaparte.*

people, a connection resulting in a class consciousness that makes their historical mission to act as a vanguard perfectly clear. Their humanity is firmly based in their knowledge that they must resist this ruling class, a class which as the historical endpoint of this system of class rule is also the most cunning and the most bloodthirsty that has ever existed. It is based in the knowledge that they must resist this system's character and its tendency towards total imperialist fascism—a form which has many fine representatives: Nixon and Brandt, Moshe Dayan and Genscher, Golda Meir and McGovern.

The West German left can reclaim their political identity—antifascism—antiauthoritarianism—anti-imperialist action—if they cease to embrace the Springer Press and opportunism, if they begin to once again address Auschwitz, Vietnam, and the systemic indifference of the masses here.

BLACK SEPTEMBER'S STRATEGY IS THE REVOLUTIONARY STRATEGY FOR ANTI-IMPERIALIST STRUGGLE, BOTH IN THE THIRD WORLD AND IN THE METROPOLE, GIVEN THE IMPERIALIST CONDITIONS CREATED BY MULTINATIONAL CORPORATIONS.

I. IMPERIALISM
Anti Imperialist Struggle
<u>The action was anti-imperialist.</u>
The comrades from Black September, who had their own Black September in 1970 when the Jordanian army massacred 20,000 Palestinians,[1] went back to the place that is the origin of this massacre: West Germany—formerly Nazi Germany—now at the centre of imperialism. Back to the site of the power that forced the Jews of both West and East Europe to emigrate to Israel. Back to those who had hoped to profit from the theft of Palestinian land. Back to where Israel got its reparation payments and, until 1965, officially, its weapons. Back to

---

1 In the wake of the 1967 Six Day War, hundreds of thousands of Palestinians had fled to Jordan, where they lived in ramshackle refugee camps. On September 16, 1970, alarmed at the growing power of Palestinian revolutionaries, King Hussein declared martial law, and the Jordanian armed forces attacked suspected militant strongholds: according to most sources, between four and ten thousand Palestinians, including many non-combatants, were slaughtered. This is the source of the group's name.

where the Springer Corporation celebrated Israel's 1967 Blitzkrieg in an anticommunist orgy. Back to the supplier who provided Hussein's army with panzers, assault rifles, machine-pistols, and munitions. Back to where everything possible was done—using development aid, oil deals, investments, weapons, and diplomatic relationships—to pit Arab regimes against each other, and to turn all of them against the Palestinian liberation movement. Back to the place from which imperialism launches its bombers when other means of repressing the Arab liberation movement fail: West Germany—Munich—the NATO airport at Fürstenfeldbruck.

Vietnam

Do people think Vietnam is a joke? Guatemala, Santo Domingo, Indonesia, Angola are all just jokes? Vietnam is an atrocious example for the people of the Third World, an example of how determined imperialism is to commit genocide against them if nothing else achieves the desired results—if they don't agree to being markets, military bases, sources of raw materials and cheap labor.

And the opportunistic left in the metropole behaves idiotically—being the labor aristocracy of imperialism (Lenin) who benefit from this theft, they sit on their arses. They only take to the streets if something affects them, if the war escalates, if some of them are shot—like during Easter 1968 in Berlin or May 1970 at Kent State.[2] If the system does something against them like what is always being done in the Third World, all of a sudden they get upset, they run to the police, they chase after that rat-catcher McGovern, they run for a post on the labor council, and they write a bunch of poems against the war.

The Imperialist Centre

Black September has brought its war from the Arab periphery of imperialism into the centre. The centre means: central to the multinational corporations, the market's command centre, where they determine the laws of economic, political, military, cultural, and technological development for all countries within their market. The centre is the U.S.A., Japan, and West Europe under the leadership of the FRG. The volume

---

2 On May 4, 1970, the National Guard opened fire on students demonstrating at Kent State University in Ohio against the escalation of the war in Vietnam. Four students were killed and nine others were wounded. Of the wounded, one was permanently paralyzed, and several were seriously maimed.

of business, the numbers employed by the corporations, these are only the formal, quantitative data—their weapons production is only one of the sectors of their productive capacity that is directed against the liberation movements, their price controls for raw materials constitute just one of the many ways they ensure their rule over the Third World.

The Aggressive Character of Imperialist Investment Policy

Marx analyzed machinery as a weapon that led workers in the 19th century to destroy machines. Marx:

> Machinery is the most powerful weapon for repressing strikes, those periodical revolts of the working class against the autocracy of capital. It would be possible to write quite a history of the inventions made since 1880[1] for the sole purpose of supplying capital with weapons against the revolts of the working class.

This was the machinery that created unemployment for the working class, that created the wageworker, at the same time offering the proletariat no choice but starvation or overthrowing the dictatorship of capital.

It is now time for someone to write a history of the imperialist investment strategy and in their analysis to demonstrate that it was "made for the sole purpose" of eliminating the liberation movements in the Third World.

Multinational Corporations

The multinational corporations control everything in the countries that imperialism has deprived of the opportunity to develop. They use this control against them. At one and the same time, capital creates divisions, skims profits, and then uses these same projects, investments, and profits to play the countries dependent on them off against each other—they use the very raw materials they rely upon the Third World for to oppress the people of the Third World.

Weapons

Their weapons consist of the potential of capital, technology, the means of communication and information control, and the means

---

1 In the correct version of this quote (*Capital* Volume I, chapter 15, volume 5), this year is 1830. An error was made either as this document was being written by the RAF or when it was transcribed by supporters, and the year became 1880.

of transportation. Their strategy for conquest is based on investments, transfer of profits, information policy, diversification, marketing, sales planning, and stockpiling. Their occupier or colonial ideology means controlling currency and creating work. Their goal is to assimilate, repress, and rob—the alternative offered is starvation and extermination.

Oil Investments

Oil is the primary issue in the states that support the Palestinian liberation movement. 70% of Western Europe's oil imports come from there. Western Europe's demand for oil will double by 1985 (1970: 647 million tons). The corporations and their governments are determining their oil policy based on the spectre of revolutionary Arab regimes using this demand for oil to carry through their own industrialization. This would mark the end of oil corporations making profits of more than 100%.

Algeria's Natural Gas

American corporations are investing millions of dollars in profit liquefying Algerian natural gas and shipping it by sea, so as to play Algerian natural gas off against that of Libya and against Arab oil: Kuwait, Libya, Syria, Iraq, Saudi Arabia.

Pipelines

West European consortiums (Bayerngas—Saarferngas—Gasversorgung Süddeutschland) invest billion-DM sums to build pipelines (1 km costs between 1 and 2 million DM)[2] to transport Algerian natural gas so as to partially reduce their dependence on Middle Eastern oil.

North Sea Oil

Oil companies and governments invest billions in oil and natural gas extraction in the North Sea. With regards to development costs, North Sea oil is ten times as expensive as oil from the Persian Gulf—only every sixth drill point is successful, construction and installation expenses for platforms, underwater pipelines. (North Sea oil makes up an estimated 1% of the world reserves; reserves in the Middle East make up 60%.) This is considered preferable to having a flexible approach to the Middle East. According to the European Economic Community (EEC) Europe

---

2 Roughly between $364,000 and $728,000.

Committee, "The increasing pressure on Western societies from some oil countries could lead to supply problems in the case of a political crisis"—meaning the problems that corporations will have maintaining their current high rates of profit.

Australia and Canada
Regarding raw materials available in Australia and Canada, the economic edition of *FAZ* wrote with cynical, capitalist bluntness, "The developing countries' position has deteriorated as a result of the discovery of enormous natural resource reserves in Canada and Australia. The geologically favorable sites in these countries, with their stable governments, lower taxes, and developed industry, have attracted the attention of multinationals from all over the world."

The Conference in Santiago de Chile
In April and May 1972, at the conference in Santiago de Chile, the "developing countries" attempted to establish fixed prices for raw materials. In response to their powerlessness, the *FAZ* writes, with the condescension and consciousness of a corporate bulletin, "The developing countries overlook the fact that natural resource reserves alone do not constitute wealth. In the final analysis, development, transport, and technical research are more important, and we control an ample share of the world's reserves of those. It is no accident that the powerful multinational corporations, with their restrictive policies, exercise substantial restraint in their investments in the developing countries."

Overexploitation and Stockpiling
For one thing, the corporations over-exploit the raw materials of the Third World. In Kuwait, for example, the fear is that in 16 years—the oil boom in Kuwait began in 1934—the oil could be exhausted. 95% of Kuwait's income comes from oil—800 million dollars per year for 740,000 residents. Kuwait, with 12.8% of the world's annual oil income, has built up the royal treasury—a sort of nest egg. What will they do when the oil and the money is all used up, return to herding sheep? Libya and Venezuela have already reduced their oil production to safeguard their reserves.

At the same time, a policy of stockpiling has been developed in the EEC and the FRG, increasing stocks from 85 to 90 days—Iran's portion of that is 10 million tons—the FRG needs approximately 133 million tons of oil per year.

The U.S.A. has undertaken a massive conservation program—by 1980, 365 million tons of oil will have been saved—however 770 million tons will still be required. The conservation measures will include shifting commercial transportation from trucks to the railroad, passenger traffic from the air to the ground, and city traffic from automobiles to mass transit.

Oil and Traffic-Related Deaths

In the FRG, to give one example, the automobile industry has demanded a tribute of 170,000 traffic-related deaths over the past ten years—in the U.S.A., 56,000 deaths are projected for 1972, in the FRG it's 20,000—all in the service of greater profits for oil and automobile corporations.

This idiotic automobile production will be reduced to create a situation suitable to corporate interests: the wiping out of the liberation movements in the Third World. In this way the obstacle presented by the people of the Third World will be eliminated.

The fear and the circular logic of consumption—the anarchy of capitalist commodity production, which is governed by the market and not the needs of the people—can exceed the limits of the human psyche, especially with the drivel about "quality of life," for instance. In a situation where everything has been reduced to consumption—"shitty products"—the decline of the masses' loyalty has already begun. The mass mortality in the streets through the alienation and brutalization of the people is hitting the system in the pocketbook in a way they don't like.

Boycott

The goal is another oil boycott like that of the early 50s against Mossadegh's[1] nationalization of Persian oil, which cleared the way for the Shah, that puppet of U.S. imperialism. In response to the nationalization measures in Iraq at that time, Iran quickly stated its willingness to increase annual production from 271 million tons to 400 million tons. This is the kind of government that suits imperialism.

In the 60s, it was hoped that atomic energy would allow for the gradual reduction of dependence on oil as the most important source of

---

1 Mohammed Mossadegh was elected Prime Minister of Iran in 1951. He quickly began to nationalize Iranian assets including oil. In 1953, he was removed from power by the Shah of Iran Mohammad Reza Pahlavi, in a CIA-backed coup. He died in prison in 1967.

energy. By that time—or so it was hoped—high temperature ovens with which coal could be converted to oil would also exist—which was the basis for the talk of the comeback of coal.

The objective of imperialist energy policy is not only to guarantee the continuing theft of oil from the oil-producing nations for all time to come, but also to prevent them from industrializing and establishing their political independence.

Encirclement Policy

Regarding the rest of the Middle East, imperialism is hoping its policy of quiet encirclement will succeed.

In the West, they are thoroughly implanted in the Maghreb—Algeria, Tunisia, and Morocco. West German corporations have invested in mining (raw materials), in the clothing industry (cheap labor), in dam projects (electrical power), and in the automobile industry. Tunisia and Morocco are the main recipients of West German development aid among the Arab states—both countries also receive West German military aid.

In the East and the North, it's Turkey and Iran. Both countries are also the sites of American military bases. In the context of NATO, the FRG supplies weapons to Turkey. In the context of the free market economy, Siemens has recently been supplying television relay stations, with which the government's message—"This is the criminal police speaking"—can reach Eastern Turkey.[1] The German enclave in Tehran is well known—the quantity of weapons being provided by West Germany is not.

Military Bases

There should be no illusions about the desire to transform the Maghreb in the West and Turkey and Iran in the East from markets into military bases.

And there should certainly be no illusions about what conditions will be like in Algeria in three years if natural gas development by American corporations—that is to say, by big money—has begun and Algeria still attempts to maintain its principled solidarity with the other Arab states. It could only end in disaster.

---

1 Turkey's East is home to the oppressed Kurdish minority, and also bordered on the Soviet Union.

Imperialism is the Weapon

Imperialism is the weapon that the multinational corporations use to address the contradictions between developed countries and the desire for development in the countries they plunder, between states with elected governments and states with CIA-backed governments, between rich and poor countries. Imperialism unifies North and South as the centre and the periphery of a single system.

It is a system that allows the constitutional state to function in much the same way as fascism. It doesn't eliminate the contradictions, it simply coordinates them, plays them off against one another, integrates them as various interrelated profit-making conditions for their various subsidiaries.

"Slaves of the System"

Outwardly, they adjust to the existing conditions—making use of them where possible—creating domestic capital reserves, surrendering middle management to the local population, learning the local language, respecting local laws, all the time using their normative power to establish their control of the market.

The *FAZ* condescendingly informs "developing countries" that are attempting to protect their mineral resources by reducing mining that they misjudge the marketplace. It informs them that they are actually establishing themselves as slaves of the system if they fail to take note of the "dilemma" created by their own foreign currency needs, on the one hand, and the necessity to protect their natural resources, on the other: "The developing countries, in implementing policies against international natural resource companies, are tying their own hands."

This imperialism avoids provocation. Where possible, they absorb Third World governments into the facade of their system. They operate within the "confines of their means"—and they have more means at their disposal than any ruling class before them.

The Means at Their Disposal

They use illiteracy and hunger to control the people of the Third World; in the metropole, people are made stupid and alienated and are brutalized by television, Springer, and automobile accidents. They saw to the liquidation of the McGovern left. They use torture against the Persian, Turkish, and Palestinian comrades; against the anti-imperialist left in West Germany and West Berlin, they use the BAW. In November, following on the heels of the September massacre of

Palestinian freedom fighters, they will hold free elections here, having used the spectacle of the Olympic Games to divert attention away from the horror.

This imperialism only reveals its fascist character when it encounters resistance—it has no need for a late capitalist seizure of power. Its historical tendency is towards fascism, towards exploitation and oppression, annihilation, waste, defoliation, the destruction of people, and the plundering of natural resources. It has a greater potential for destruction than any ruling class in history, the potential to leave a wasteland in its wake—wherever there is nothing more to be gained, where everything is devastated, the country and the people—shattered and crippled—Vietnam.

Black September's Strategy

The bomb attack on the Strüver Corporation in Hamburg was an attack on one of Israel's military suppliers.

With their action at the Olympic Village, they brought the conflict between the imperialist metropole of Israel and the Palestinians from the periphery of the system into its centre—they tore off the FRG's "constitutional" mask and revealed the true objective nature of imperialism's facade: that they are waging war against the liberation movements of the Third World and that their final objective is strategic extermination and fascism.

Through this action, the Arab people were mobilized for anti-imperialist struggle. They celebrated the revolutionaries as heroes, and their will to struggle received an enormous boost.

That it would have been better to take Genscher hostage is something that Black September itself knows full well.[1] Functioning as it does at a very high level of Marxist theory combined with revolutionary practice, Black September doesn't need to be told this. The fact is that it would have been better to exchange the Israeli athletes for people who make up the facade of the Social-Liberal Coalition, as this would have destroyed the complicity between Israeli and West German imperialism and isolated Israel. It would have forced the contradiction between the fascism of the developing imperialist system

---

1 During negotiations with the Palestinian commando, Minister of the Interior Hans-Dietrich Genscher is reported to have offered himself as a hostage in exchange for the Israeli athletes. The commando is said to have refused this offer. Given Horst Mahler's comments at his October 1972 trial (see page 188), it seems likely that the RAF was attempting an oblique criticism of this decision.

and Israeli Nazi fascism (see the chapter on National Socialism) into the open. It would have made use of the system's contradictions to split the imperialist forces!

These observations are not meant as a criticism of the action, but rather as an expression of our appreciation of the action. These observations are an excellent example of how practice leads to theoretical development and how theory leads to developments in practice—of the dialectic of theory and practice.

2. OPPORTUNISM
Opportunism in the Metropole
The Marxist bible thumper—equipped with quotes and not thinking any further—will argue that Marx himself said that smashing machines was "stupid." Marx:

> *Machinery, considered alone, shortens the hours of labor, but, when in the service of capital, lengthens them; since in itself it lightens labor, but when employed by capital, heightens the intensity of labor; since in itself it is a victory of man over the forces of Nature, but in the hands of capital, makes man the slave of those forces; since in itself it increases the wealth of the producers, but in the hands of capital, makes them paupers...[2]*

So it is not machinery that should be resisted, but its capitalist application.

On the face of it, it is not clear that everything about imperialist investment policy is intended to eliminate of the Third World liberation movements. "Considered alone" and not as a waste of raw materials and labor power, or as a means of war, one might even speak of military production as being a part of the civilian sector. However, it is meant to reinforce the unequal development between the imperialist centre and the countries of the Third World, which is to say, to reinforce the ongoing rule of the imperialist system.

Sabotage
The rejection of sabotage in the metropole, based on the argument that it would be better to take things over instead of destroying them, is

---

2 Karl Marx, *Capital* Volume I, chapter 15, volume 5.
http://www.marxists.org/archive/marx/works/1867-c1/ch15.htm#S5.

based on the dictum: the people of the Third World should wait for their revolution until the masses in the metropole catch up.

This ignores the problem of the labor aristocracy within imperialism, first addressed by Lenin. Furthermore, this demands that the people of the Third World allow all sectors of the world proletariat—most of whom form part of the backbone of the imperialist system—to ride on their coattails. It is the rallying cry of opportunism.

The Opportunistic Concept of Solidarity

It's no surprise that the opportunists no longer know what to do with the concept of solidarity—they betray their claim to leadership with an incorrect analysis of imperialism. They must exclude a section of the disempowered from their concept of solidarity. This is the section that rejects their leadership, and instead turns to the people of the Third World. They must exclude anyone who by "serve the people" doesn't mean sucking up to the people disempowered by imperialism, but rather means by this that one must struggle against the imperialism which is disempowering people.

Negt—The Pig

Negt, who in Frankfurt resurrected Noske's[1] axiom "One must be a bloodhound," thereby formulated the opportunistic position, with all the jargon, all the contempt for the masses, all the appeals to "the politicians," and all the pleas for sound, common sense that are fundamental to it. However—like Bernstein[2]—without the slightest hint of an economic analysis.

Given, however, that the problem of opportunism is not objectively a question of the theoretical level he has expressed, it is necessary to engage him in debate. Objectively, it is the result of unequal development within the system, of the inequality in forms of oppression employed by the system and of the inequality of experiences of exploitation under this system.

That Negt has generally been applauded, in spite of the feeble theoretical level of his work, is an objective indication of the pressure that exists here for people to take an opportunistic position. We are dealing

---

1 Gustav Noske, the SPD Minister responsible for the military during bloody suppression of the November Revolution of 1918, during which communist leaders Karl Liebknecht and Rosa Luxemburg were killed.
2 Eduard Bernstein, a leader of the German Social Democratic Party, who helped instigate that party's rejection of revolutionary Marxism in the late 19th century.

with Negt in the hope that his supporters will see what a crock of shit they're being fed.

Negt on Solidarity

Negt: "Mechanical solidarity will destroy socialist politics. It is the worst aspect of the legacy of the protest movement."

People like to "mechanically" paw for their wallets if they come across someone playing harmonica on the Hauptwache,[3] and Bertold Beitz[4] feels good about writing a cheque for the *Bodelschwinghschen Anstalten in Bethel*.[5] Solidarity is not a reflex action, as anyone who has ever acted in solidarity knows. Or does Negt, with his concept of "mechanics," also intend to address in a backhanded way the concept of spontaneity?—"spontaneous solidarity"...?

One cannot surpass Negt when it comes to dragging the concept of solidarity through the mud, while at the same time expressing solidarity for all of those who, lacking the necessary courage and psychological stamina, out of fear for themselves, fail to act in solidarity.

Negt's Fairy Tale

"Unbidden and often anonymous" they stood at the door—a total lie, nobody ever stood at Negt's door, at least not without having sent their business card in advance or having used the phone to fill a *Verfassungsschutz* tape with babble. There they stood completely unshaven, and then they came in and made a mess of the bathroom. Is that what being revolutionary means? Where do we fit in?

Opportunistic Arrogance

Instead of offering an analysis of the connection between wealth here and poverty there—that is to say, an analysis of the system as a unitary whole—Negt renders a judgment based on the alleged power structure, in which he proclaims: "...that political morality is indivisible"—oh, you don't say—"that those who tolerate or condone the genocide in Vietnam lose the right to speak in the name of democracy"—the Federal Constitutional Court read him the riot act for that one—that should clear that up for him.

---

3 The Hauptwache is a popular pedestrian mall in Frankfurt.
4 Bertold Beitz, Krupp manager and a member of the National and International Olympic Committee.
5 *Bodelschwinghschen Anstalten in Bethel* is a large Bielefeld-based charity.

The Principle of Separation

Negt makes it his primary task to prevent any awareness of the connection between poverty here and poverty there—to prevent solidarity based on an awareness of this connection. Localizing conflicts is an objective that the system pursues in every way it can.

Negt: "The politicized masses that make up the solidarity movement, the university students, the high school students, and the young workers who have broken with family drudgery and the enforced discipline of the work world and the educational institutions"—(not are emancipated, not are in the process of breaking free, not are going forward, not of wanting more, but "have broken with")—"gradually lose the ability to have their own experiences"—(the gall of a social worker)—"always putting themselves in a position to be in touch with the most radical positions, thereby establishing a fragile and superficial identity"—(where does he get off attacking those he is talking about with socio-psychological, Youth Authority jargon?)— "based on a shameless identification with the experiences of others."

So, the people at *Bild Zeitung* should only report on what they themselves feel, and only the Viet Cong should celebrate Viet Cong victories. The validity of bombs against the U.S. Headquarters depends on who lays them—or what?

"The Self-Proclaimed Vanguard"

Negt: "Self-proclaimed vanguards"—(not appointed by the Minister of Culture, not a legitimate market niche—or what?)—"lay claim to social and historical experiences"—(so the anti-imperialist struggle is not in fact occurring)—"that individual high school students, workers, apprentices, and university students can neither reconcile with their own work environments nor use as the basis for political decisions."

How then are they supposed to develop an identity? Does Negt believe that ideas develop on their own within the mind? Apparently.

Dialectical Materialism
Mao:

> Dialectical materialism regards external reality as the condition for change and internal reality as its basis—and in this way external reality conditions internal activity.

Meaning: Negt—as external reality—gained applause for his idiotic blather in Frankfurt, because opportunism has deep roots in the metropole. People want "Freedom for Angela Davis"—but they don't carry out the struggle as relentlessly as the Viet Cong, or as Black September—never that—so great is their despair about the system, so uncertain are they about their cause, that they abandon the cause and embrace hopelessness. Enter Negt, saying that none of that is necessary; we're already doing what needs to be done—they are relieved, they applaud.

In opposition to this stands the RAF—as sure of our cause as the people of the Third World, because they accept their leadership role, because they know that the struggle must be carried out relentlessly, and that is how they carry it out.

The RAF—as external reality—has found increasing support among high school students, university students, and apprentices. Negt has seen this, even biased "polls" have noted it; the leaflets, slogans, demonstrations, teach-ins, etc.

How could this occur, other than through "internal reality"? If not their own everyday working and living conditions, what else could make them see that only with this perseverance, the same perseverance with which the people of the Third World conduct their struggle, can they achieve the goal—their freedom?

Negt's scolding proves the opposite of what he asserts; precisely because their experience of living and working conditions—internal reality—leads high school students, apprentices, and university students to begin to understand the situation of the people of the Third World, they identify with the struggle the RAF has conducted in the metropole on their behalf—as external reality.

Were it otherwise, one would not have heard a peep about the RAF, not from Genscher or Ruhnau,[1] and Negt would have had to be satisfied in Frankfurt with taking a cheap shot out of the side of his mouth at the RAF—or being and consciousness have nothing to do with each other and dialectical materialism is a pipe dream.

We know that it will be an extremely slow, difficult and exhausting process to get things underway in even a few places. That they are, however, in motion indicates that the situation is "ripe" to take up the anti-imperialist struggle in the metropole—not "ripe" for revolution, but "ripe" for the anti-imperialist offensive.

Already, at this early stage of "ripeness," there are comrades who disgrace themselves by losing sight of the realities of their lives and their liberation. Seeing this process at work, we see the system's continuing appeal in the metropole. That there are comrades who cannot see any

1 Heinz Runau, SPD Senator for Internal Affairs in Hamburg at the time.

purpose to life outside of the liberation struggle attests to how great the appeal of revolution is. Insofar as there is not a single idea, not a thought that does not have its origin in life and in society—positive thoughts, ideas, and people have been thoroughly locked away, cast aside, excluded and treated as insane.

The metropolitan left is beginning to split into a revolutionary, anti-imperialist wing and an opportunistic wing. This is not because opportunism has won the struggle on the ground, but because they've lost it. They still hope to win this struggle on the ground, even as the left wing gains in strength. Negt's attacks were a rearguard action. Given that the argument he mounted can only be described as disgraceful, he has helped to unmask opportunism. He has made our work easier.

Negt as Alexander the Great

"The knots" of "mechanical solidarity," "inferiority complexes," "fear of isolation," "overblown perceptions of reality," and "self-delusion" "must be cut" (he's right about that)—and can no longer be resolved "through polite engagement."

Which means: allowing the fascists to liquidate the growing left wing of the socialist movement. Which means: Marxist theory and serious discussions constitute "polite engagement"—one is spared socialist discussion with Negt's fatherly advice and his seminar pedagogy.

Marx and Freud could only say in response to all this: Pardon me?

A complete nut, a truculent, self-confessed petit bourgeois—this Negt. If one did not know that being determines consciousness, one might begin to think that through these thoroughly corrupted rats "corruption has claimed the day."

The Objective Role of the Opportunists

Regarding his own profession, Negt—bluntly—stated: "One should beware of attempts to push left professors and teachers out of the high schools and universities" they being the only ones who, "through routine overtime and small organized groups," keep this catastrophic institution "running." The students of the *Berliner Gegenuniversität*[1] fought tooth and nail against exactly this system-stabilizing integration of their work as "overtime"—in this way the opportunistic cat comes out of the seminar Marxist bag.

---

1 *Berliner Gegenunivesitaät*, literally Berlin Counter-University, refers to presentations organized by students independent of formal lectures.

The Core: Scholarship for the Bourgeoisie
Bourgeois scholarship still remains the practical core: "If a fraction of the money spent fighting crime was used to fight the causes of crime, one could count on a long-term impact; a society that cannot guarantee this minimum has lost its authority"—(leave it to Negt and everything will soon be running smoothly).

The investment strategy of multinational corporations is based on this kind of long-term use of money rather than on military adventures.

And to finally accomplish his true goal, Negt tosses the entirety of Marxism-Leninism overboard: "There is no clear and objective criteria for the distinction between right and left." Why is this stupid pig still called a "socialist"?

Rosa Luxemburg on Bernstein:

> *What? Is that all you have to say? Not the shadow of an original thought! Not a single idea that was not refuted, crushed, reduced into dust by Marxism several decades ago! It was enough for opportunism to speak out to prove it had nothing to say.*[2]

Negt need only come out into the open for all to see that he is in bed with the fascists—his "qualification," most probably an "unqualified tool." (R.L.)

Lenin:

> *The most dangerous people are those who do not want to understand that the struggle against imperialism is empty and meaningless if it is not unreservedly connected to the struggle against opportunism.*

Just as the oppressed themselves could smash this entire "catastrophic institution," the system could well collapse under the weight of its own contradictions. The consciousness that says we're all in the same boat, ties opportunism and the system together. They prattle on about socialism, but they mean the system. They ask no questions; they miss the answers. Setbacks for revolutionaries fill them with glee; once again they've backed the right horse.

---

2 This quote is from Rosa Luxemburg's 1900 text, *Reform or Revolution*, Chapter X: Opportunism and Theory in Practice, available from http://www.marxists.org/archive/luxemburg/1900/reform-revolution/ch10.htm.

The Revolutionary Subject

The problem with opportunism is that by making use of it Negt reveals things about himself, but nothing about the world. Having analyzed the system, the revolutionary subject bases his identity on the knowledge that the people of the Third World are the vanguard, and on an acceptance that Lenin's concept of the "labor aristocracy" regarding the masses in the metropole cannot be discounted or dismissed. On the contrary: everything starts from that point.

The exploitation of the masses in the metropole has nothing to do with Marx's concept of wage labourers from whom surplus value is extracted.

It is a fact that with the increasing division of labor, there has been a tremendous intensification and spread of exploitation in the area of production, and work has become a greater burden, both physically and psychologically.

It is also a fact that with the introduction of the 8-hour workday—the precondition for increasing the intensity of work—the system usurped all of the free time people had. To physical exploitation in the factory was added the exploitation of their feelings and thoughts, wishes, and utopian dreams—to capitalist despotism in the factory was added capitalist despotism in all areas of life, through mass consumption and the mass media.

With the introduction of the 8-hour workday, the system's 24-hour-a-day domination of the working class began its triumphal march—with the establishment of mass purchasing power and "peak income" the system began its triumphal march over the plans, desires, alternatives, fantasies, and spontaneity of the people; in short, over the people themselves!

The system in the metropole has managed to drag the masses so far down into their own dirt that they seem to have largely lost any sense of the oppressive and exploitative nature of their situation, of their situation as objects of the imperialist system. So that for a car, a pair of jeans, life insurance, and a loan, they will easily accept any outrage on the part of the system. In fact, they can no longer imagine or wish for anything beyond a car, a vacation, and a tiled bathroom.

It follows, however, that the revolutionary subject is anyone that breaks free from these compulsions and refuses to take part in this system's crimes. All those who find their identity in the liberation struggles of the people of the Third World, all those who refuse, all those who no longer participate; these are all revolutionary subjects—comrades.

This is the reason we have analyzed the 24-hour-a-day imperialist system, why we have addressed all of the living and working conditions in this society, the role that the production of surplus value plays in each of them and the connection to factory exploitation, which in any case is really the point. With the supposition: the revolutionary subject in the imperialist metropole is the person who recognizes that a life under the mandatory 24-hour-day is a life under the system's control—here we have only sketched the outline of the parameters necessary for a class analysis—we are not claiming that this supposition constitutes such an analysis.

The fact is that neither Marx nor Lenin nor Rosa Luxemburg nor Mao had to deal with *Bild* readers, television viewers, car drivers, the psychological conditioning of young students, high school reforms, advertising, the radio, mail order sales, loan contracts, "quality of life," etc. The fact is that the system in the metropole reproduces itself through an ongoing offensive against the people's psyche, not in an openly fascist way, but rather through the market.

Therefore, to write off entire sections of the population as an impediment to anti-imperialist struggle, simply because they don't fit into Marx's analysis of capitalism, is as insane and sectarian as it is un-Marxist.

Only by integrating the 24-hour workday into our understanding of imperialism and anti-imperialism can we get a picture of the actual problems facing the people, so that they will not only understand our actions—and thereby understand the RAF—but also our propaganda, our speech, our words. Serve the people!

If the people of the Third World are the vanguard of the anti-imperialist revolution, then that means that they objectively represent the greatest hope for people in the metropole to achieve their own freedom. If this is the case, then it is our duty to establish a connection between the liberation struggle of the peoples of the Third World and the longing for freedom in the metropole wherever it emerges. This means in grade schools, in high schools, in factories, in families, in prisons, in office cubicles, in hospitals, in head offices, in political parties, in unions—wherever. Against everything that openly negates, suppresses, and destroys this connection: consumerism, the media, co-management, opportunism, dogmatism, authority, paternalism, brutality, and alienation.

"This means us!" We are revolutionary subjects.

Whoever begins to struggle and to resist is one of us.

The answer to the question of how and at what level to struggle against the system, where best to apply pressure when one is at one's weakest point—we've answered this question—is not to be found in a stream of slogans, but rather in the dialectic of theory and practice.

3. FASCISM
The Black September action was antifascist.
They established the connection between Nazi fascism and the direction in which imperialism is developing.

The Olympic Games
They clearly established this connection by attacking the Olympic Games, from which all reminders of 1936, Auschwitz, and Kristallnacht[1] were to be excluded. The games were meant to serve as a spectacle distracting attention from what is currently going on in Vietnam, in Palestine, in Israel's prisons, in Turkey, in Uruguay, in Brazil, in Greece, and in Persia. Insofar as these grueling contests have only winners and losers, they are the opposite of liberation struggles, of acts of solidarity. Instead they are competitions/struggles to reinforce imperialist consciousness in the industrialized nations—games of aggression.

Bild
"GOLD-GOLD-GOLD," *Bild* panted, badgered, wheezed, and nagged during the first days of the Olympic Games. "I saw you fade away at 11:00 PM—how will the games continue," was *Bild*'s headline on September 7.
Do you want total victory—Yesssss!

The Athletes
This is not directed against the athletes. Those who hope to win the competitions have trained for years. They are not the ones who give the Olympic Games the character of an imperialist event. They are connected to the games like a wage laborer to capitalism—without them nothing happens, but they are objects in a spectacle, objects of

---

1 Kristallnacht, or the Night of Broken Glass, was an enormous pogrom against German Jews on the part of the Nazis and their supporters on the night of November 9/10, 1938.

Neckermann's *Sporthilfe*.[2] That the athletes enjoy what they're doing changes nothing.

National Socialism

National Socialism was nothing other than the political and military precursor to the imperialist system of the multinational corporations.

The ruling class—and especially the German ruling class—is so rapacious that, lead by the Flick, Thyssen, Krupp, and IG Farben corporations,[3] it hoped to achieve, in conditions that were not yet ripe, that which they managed to achieve later anyway. They formed an uneasy alliance with the old, declining petit bourgeoisie, and they bought into the irrational and deadly antisemitism. Instead of relying on their shareholders, as should have been the case, they developed the imperialist middle class to meet the corporations' extreme demand for capital—they formed an alliance with the retrograde and ideologically backwards Nazi Party. Instead of waiting to grow strong enough to subjugate peoples and countries without military adventures, they started the Second World War. Antisemitism and war compromised German fascism in the long run, once again completely unmasking the ruling class in the eyes of the masses—and making possible an antifascist alliance between communists and a section of the bourgeoisie.

Antifascism

It was this domestic and foreign antifascism that effectively prevented the expansion of West German imperialism. It is antifascist sensitivity to injustice, transgression, state brutality, and executive arrogance that has forced this state to maintain a constitutional form.

Just as imperialism has a fascist tendency, antifascism has an anti-imperialist tendency.

For a section of antifascist sympathizers, the RAF has brought the anti-imperialist struggle up to date. The §129 trials at the beginning of the 50s and the ban on the KPD had the effect of separating the KP from their own antifascism and of dismantling their alliance with a section of the bourgeoisie. Liquidating what remained of antifascism in the SPD and amongst the intelligentsia was a significant challenge for the

---

2 Josef Neckermann was a successful Frankfurt-based businessman and horse trainer and founder of the *Stiftung Deutsche Sporthilfe* (German Benevolent Sports Association).

3 All are major corporations that participated in and profited from National Socialism's reign in Germany. All of them continue to flourish.

Brandt/Scheel/Heinemann administration. Antifascism was still a part of the 1967-1968 APO, and was supported by the student movement, in the Republican Clubs, at Vietnam demonstrations, and in the movement against the Emergency Powers legislation and police terror.

The Antiauthoritarian Position

That the leaders of the student movement are themselves shying away from their anti-imperialist consciousness is a reflection of their revisionism. The positions of the antiauthoritarian movement were clearly anti-imperialist: June 2, Vietnam, Springer, and opposition to the development of West German imperialism, of which the final step in the postwar FRG was the formation of the Grand Coalition.

This movement proved itself to be primarily petit bourgeois when it stripped its political theory of anti-imperialist consciousness, as soon as the first shots were fired. Shots which were not just fired by a single private fascist (Kurras), but rather were the result of systematic imperialist terror—directed at Dutschke, cheered on by Springer.[1]

They began to compensate for their obvious powerlessness through organizational fetishism—their decline into a dogmatic and pathologically competitive closed circle that only reproduced the structures of the ruling system, alienation, a know-it-all attitude, and indifference to oppression. They express a hatred of spontaneity equal to that of the system itself, and with their "party chairmen"—Marxism's guardians of the grail—they turn the proletariat into an object of their leadership aspirations. They see in the masses nothing but what the system has made them: *Bild* readers, television viewers, car nuts, tourists, SPD voters, Germans—as the squares (already a classic) always ask: "What do the people say?"

The narrow-minded nation-state perspective of the opportunist left is petit bourgeois. It fails to recognize or acknowledge that the people of the Third World are the vanguard and that the struggle in the metropole is the struggle of international brigades of the people's war in Quang Tri and Hue,[2] Palestine, Lebanon, Angola, Mozambique, and Turkey, without which no advances will be made. It is also petit bourgeois and

---

1 This is a retort to Negt, who at the Angela Davis Congress in Frankfurt had referred to Kurras as a lone gun-nut, and to the June 2, 1967, shooting as an isolated tragedy that did not represent state policy.

2 Refers to areas in the far North of the former Republic of Vietnam (South Vietnam) that became important staging points for communist guerillas from the North during the Vietnam War.

un-Marxist to not recognize that the masses here will eventually find their political identity on the side of the liberation struggles, and will eventually free themselves from the grip of the system, with its lies, its glitziness, its election promises, and its lotteries.

Petit bourgeois impatience led to them giving up their anti-imperialist position after one disappointing year in which the student movement failed to win the support of the proletariat and discovered that Springer could not be expropriated quickly and without further ado.

Anarchism—A Reproach

Some dismiss the antiauthoritarian movement as anarchist and the international anti-imperialist struggle as anarchist internationalism. In so doing the system's only objective is denunciation—when people mount this sort of dogmatic argument, they are not drawing their conclusions from an analysis of the system and its process of development, but from a chemical analysis of explosives—from historical analogies based on nothing—a case in point: Harich.[3]

Neither the actual socio-economic conditions nor the conception of the state held by earlier anarchists—from Blanqui to Kropotkin—(the Makhno movement[4] and Spanish anarcho-syndicalism are not targeted as such in this critique) have the slightest thing to do with the objective conditions or subjective positions of the antiauthoritarian movement or the RAF. And this is equally true in the case of comrades who refer to themselves as anarchists. They are clearly anti-imperialist—overflowing with distrust for all the "Marxists" who patronize them and hope to subjugate them on the basis of nothing more than bourgeois educational advantages. Their antiauthoritarian characteristics allow them to keep their distance from this paternalism.

The old anarchist concepts are no longer useful—not in the form they had when Marx, Engels, Lenin, and Rosa Luxemburg purged them from the Social Democratic movement—and correctly so. Not in the form that Blanqui, Bakunin, Most, and Kropotkin developed them—immature ideas in an unripe situation.

The legal left completely lacks any critical self-awareness if it compares its tiny mass base to the mass base behind the anti-imperialist

---

3 Wolfgang Harich, an academic from the GDR, who for a time in the late 70s lived in Austria and the FRG, where he worked with the Green Party before returning to the GDR.

4 An early twentieth century anti-Soviet, anarchist guerilla army active in Ukraine.

struggle. No progress can be made this way. They hope to force us into a discussion by raising the issue of anarchism, but with the problems we have before us, this is just a distraction.

Whether the old anarchists' understanding of the authority structure anticipated capital's rule over the people that first developed with imperialism—their understanding of work certainly anticipated the concept of freedom put forward in the anti-imperialist struggle—should be subject to analysis—it could be the case.

Integration

To integrate the KP, it was necessary only to ban them, and for the integration of the bourgeois antifascists, the Moscow and Warsaw Treaties sufficed—the student movement required only an amnesty—a cheap bribe.

The Foolishness of the Left

The petit bourgeois, spiteful, nit-picking blather that comrades are engaging in about Munich is an example of this foolishness, and Genscher will turn it against them. So it goes. What is expressed here is not the political consciousness of Marxists, but rather the pique of bit players— "It's all about me!"

Fürstenfeldbruck and the Moscow and Warsaw Treaties

The Fürstenfeldbruck massacre would not have been possible without the Moscow and Warsaw Treaties, without the complete demoralization of the old antifascists and extreme opportunism in those sections of the New Left that let themselves be sidetracked by the ML and AO[1] deviation—completely blind now, as compared to their terrible clarity in 1967/68.

Not even Strauß, but only Schmidt,[2] could have committed the crimes at Fürstenfeldbruck: sending the fire brigade of West German imperialism onto an American NATO base to offer Israel support—for their

---

1 AO is an acronym for *AusBildung Organisation,* roughly translating as "formation organization," and was used by Marxist-Leninist organizations in Germany that did not yet consider themselves to be parties, but held the goal of eventually forming a party. In North America, such groups were called pre-party formations.

2 Franz Josef Strauß was head of the right-wing CSU in Bavaria, where the Munich events took place. Helmut Schmidt, who would become Chancellor in 1974, was at this point the SPD Minister of Defense.

torture, their murders, the oppression, the napalm, the land stolen from the Palestinian people.

Not even Dregger, but only Scheel's party comrade Genscher,[3] could arrange for the mass expulsion of Palestinians from the FRG; Palestinians who are here because of the nationalist extermination policy, which has become the Israeli extermination policy. A public policy couldn't be more clearly morally bankrupt, devoid as it is of historical content, acquiescing without once reflecting upon how extreme the hate will be on the part of those who once again must suffer the retaliation.

The Social-Liberal Coalition and Strauß
Since the SPD entered the government coalition in 1966, more elements of "democracy" have been eliminated than under all of the CDU governments of the previous 17 years; the Emergency Powers Act, the Hand Grenade Law, the *Verfassungsschutzgesetz*,[4] the Presidential Decree,[5] Federal Labor Court rulings against strikes, and the Federal Border Patrol Law.

Disoriented by their fear of Strauß, a section of the left will only realize that they have already had their vocal cords—which they require for whining—ripped out should Strauß take over these instruments which have in fact been crafted by the Social-Liberal coalition.

But Strauß couldn't knock off more people than the comrades[6] have: McLeod's liquidation, the deportation of Arabs, Prinzregentenstraße,[7] Löwenthal, *Bild*, show trials, police operations. The policies of the Social-Liberal Coalition are the policies of the corporations; their opinion is the opinion of the Springer corporation; their foreign policy is the foreign policy of Wolff von Amerongen, Beitz, Messerschmidt, Bölkow-Blohm, Siemens, Hochtief, Schickedanz, and Gelsenberg AG; their

---

3 Alfred Dregger was a CDU politician from the conservative and nationalist section of the party. At the time, Genscher was the Minister of the Interior from the small liberal FDP.

4 The *Verfassungsschutzgesetz* was a law passed by the SPD-FDP coalition in 1972; it extended the purview of the *Verfassungsschutz*, the police organization central to the struggle against the guerilla.

5 The Presidential Decree referred to here is the statute that established the *Berufsverbot*.

6 A sarcastic reference to the SPD, which was the leading party in parliament when each of the events listed occurred.

7 In 1971, police opened fire on bank robbers holding hostages at a bank on Prinzegerntenstraße in Munich. Two hostages were killed. Strauß was personally present when this occurred.

domestic policy is the domestic policy of Daimler-Benz, Glanzstoff, Klöckner, Bayer in Leverkusen; their high school education policy comes from BASF.[1]

It's not a question of parliamentary democracy (Brandt) on one side and fascism (Strauß) on the other, but rather it is a question of the imperialist centre on one side and on the other side the revolutionary liberation struggle of the people of the Third World along with the anti-imperialist struggle in the metropole—not to give this or any other government a kick in the ass, but rather to serve the people.

Acceptable Imperialism

The Social-Liberal Coalition has made West German imperialism acceptable for the bourgeois left, with its obsession with form—they see the application of imperialist policy as responding to the people's wishes—they work within "reasonable parameters," they speak the national language, they make use of parliamentary debate in the same way that they make use of BGS terror troops—they use constitutional means in the same way that they use fascism.

The anti-imperialist left had it easier with Strauß. He at least wore the disconcerting garb of colonial and Nazi imperialism, not the friendly mask of the corporate manager. He had the fucked relationship to power of Thyssen, Flick, and Krupp in 1933,[2] not the evolved self-consciousness of a multinational corporation. He would have been heckled had he entered the factories. He not only sowed hatred, he reaped it.

THE "RIGHT-WING TAKEOVER"

The "right-wing takeover" is a bugaboo created out of thin air by the left of the SPD, the chant of brainless opportunists devoid of theory, directed against the anti-imperialist left—their way of covering up the fact that Brandt and Strauß are simply two different masks on the same imperialist system.

The flipside of this is the ideology that considers the masses to be hopeless and stupid—the best example being the filthy journalism of the Springer corporation and the organization of the newsstands, which is to say, the concentration of the media.

---

1 All the companies mentioned in this paragraph are major German corporations.
2 Major German corporations that supported the Nazi rise to power.

4. ANTI-IMPERIALIST ACTION

The Massacre

Brandt, Genscher, Merck, Schreiber, Vogel, Daume, Brundage,[3] and all the others who make up imperialism's cast of characters didn't pause for a moment to consider agreeing to the revolutionaries' demand for the release of prisoners. Even before Golda Meir was informed and had taken a position, they had already on their own considered how best to massacre the revolutionaries—with gas or storm troopers or a precision strike or whatever else.[4]

All delays to the ultimatum, reached through lies and false promises, served to allow them to reach their sole objective, to win time to plan the massacre. They had only one goal, not to prove in any way inferior to the fascism of Moshe Dayan—Israel's Himmler.

The September 7 reports from the Bavarian Ministry of the Interior—the first reports were less clear than what followed—consisted of nothing but rhetoric and assertions that it is in fact possible to be a pig just like Moshe Dayan, that everything was planned to resemble his underhanded action against the hijackers in Tel Aviv,[5] that everything had been done to spring the same kind of brutal trap on the revolutionaries—truly tragic, tragic...

That Genscher went so far as to guarantee the exchange of hostages on September 6 at 8 in the morning in Cairo is concealed in the West German reports—this was first made public by the leader of the Egyptian Olympic delegation.

Foreign imperialist countries were horrified by the Germans' incompetence. Once again they had failed to liquidate the communists without also liquidating the Jews.

Israel cried crocodile tears. Isreal burned their own athletes just as the Nazis had burned the Jews—kindling for the imperialist policy of extermination. They won't even bother to use Munich as a pretext if they now bomb Palestinian villages—they will do what the imperialist

---

3 Leading politicians and police representatives who participated in the decisions that led to the massacre at the Fürstenfeldbruck airport.

4 Genscher in consultation with police chief Schreiber had considered sending in tear gas through the Olympic Village air conditioning, and also storming the Israeli dorms with regular police officers. Both plans were rejected as unlikely to succeed.

5 A reference to the fact that the paratroopers Dayan had led in May at Lod airport had been disguised as maintenance workers, whereas the assault team which had been ordered to take out the commando at Fürstenfeldbruck (see page 234, fn 1) were to be disguised as flight attendants.

system always does: they will bomb the liberation movement. They bomb because the Arab people have embraced the Black September action, because the masses understand the action; their enemy is not only Israel, their enemy is imperialism. It is not only Israel that is bloodthirsty, nor is it only the U.S. in the case of Vietnam, but rather it is all of imperialism against all of the liberation movements. They understand that without an anti-imperialist struggle there can be no victory for the people's war.

The Establishment Unmasked
The West German establishment has unmasked itself—the more they assert themselves, the more the system's inherent contradictions have proven what this means in the context of developing imperialism: phony campaigns, the social substance of which is a lot of blah blah blah.

The *Rundschau* demands the immediate dissolution of all Palestinian organizations in the FRG and the expulsion of all members, again making liberal use of old *Bild* arguments from the days of the student movement—"our taxes." The formulation from the *FAZ* references to Habash[1]—frothing at the mouth—in the style of the *Mainzer Baader Meinhof Report*[2]—he is obviously a cynical man suffering from an inferiority complex. Wischnewski[3] wants to expel "all Arabs" whose governments support the Palestinians. Augstein[4] demands painful "sanctions." Nannen[5] presents *Stern* readers with the order of the day: immediate expulsion, a Lufthansa boycott of Arab airports, "not a penny" of development aid or trade credit. Scheel speaks for the "civilized section" of humanity. Heinemann demands that Arab governments act as representatives of the World Court.

In the long run, this overblown outburst in the Springer Press will prove to be as useless as the authorities' information strategy before

1 George Habash, Secretary General of the Popular Front for the Liberation of Palestine (PFLP) at the time.
2 A farcically hysterical "study" of the RAF produced in 1972 by the BKA, the Bonn Security Group, and the Baader-Meinhof Special Commission. The *Allgemeinen Zeitung Mainz,* a German regional newspaper based in Mainz, serialized it in its pages.
3 Hans-Jürgen Wischnewski was a long-time SPD politician, known for his good relations with many Arab leaders, one result of his having firmly supported the Algerian National Liberation Front at a time when Adenauer had firmly supported the French.
4 Rudolph Augstein, founder and editor of *Spiegel* magazine.
5 Henri Nannen, editor of the German newsweekly *Stern.*

and in the first hours following the massacre.[6] When Brandt telephoned Sidki, the Egyptian President, he still believed he could screw around with the revolutionaries in the same way he does with the West German left. He didn't understand what they wanted. He claimed he didn't need to know, as everyone must surely agree that they were criminals, anarchists, subhumans, sick, or whatever else. They would be disposed of with no questions asked. Sidki hung up.[7]

Genscher, Merck, Schreiber did not think they would have to admit the embarrassing truth, that they themselves caused the death of the hostages. They thought they would have time to make up a story and people would quickly lose interest, as was ultimately the case with the self-defense version of the assassinations of Petra Schelm, Georg von Rauch, and Thomas Weissbecker.

Right from the start, Genscher thought he could shift the blame to the Bavarians, repeating the approach used to shift the blame for McLeod's death onto the Stuttgart cops.

The Munich Prosecutors Office thought they would be able to raise a smokescreen to block investigations and deny journalists information. They intended to draw upon the counterpropaganda they've been using against the RAF for two years, claiming that there really is no anti-imperialist struggle, that it is only an illusion—to the left of the Social-Liberal Coalition, there is nothing but crackpots, anarchists, criminals, and sick people.

Eppler[8]

The tactically appropriate position, the position required to serve the immediate interests of the FRG, was developed by Eppler: no blanket judgment, no sanctions, continuing development aid, though only in the Maghreb in keeping with the imperialist policy of encirclement, undermining through investments, etc. Those who are prepared to allow

---

6 Immediately following the Fürstenfeldbruck showdown, the government announced that all of the Israeli athletes had been rescued unharmed. This news was then broadcast around the world. The rationale for this escapes our comprehension.

7 Sidki had been contacted to see if the Egyptian government would agree to receive the hostages and the Palestinian commando, the FRG's goal being to get them out of the country. Sadat's government later explained that to do so would have done nothing to resolve the crisis, and would have meant simply making it Egypt's problem.

8 Erhard Eppler, SPD member and left-leaning Federal Minister of Economic Cooperation from 1968 until 1974.

the theft of their oil, their mineral resources, and their labor force, will benefit from friendship between nations and partnership.

Their Unmasking

Black September stripped the mask off of the Social-Liberal Coalition and their propagandists by forcing the system's real, rather than the purported, contradiction out into the open. The contradiction between imperialism and the people of the Third World forced them at a certain point to abandon their original goals and intentions, because they could clearly no longer be achieved. The cops wouldn't play along, refusing to carry out the massacre on the plane.[1] The news media wouldn't play along. Foreign powers wouldn't play along. The West German masses weren't consulted. The Arab people for the most part grasped what West Germany represented: the imperialist policy of extermination.

Unmasking them means forcing them to take the step after next before they have time to take the next one, forcing them to abandon their goals, so that everyone can see what has been going on for a long time now. Pressure must be brought to bear while the revolutionary left is still able to mount a counterstrategy, not after everyone has been banned and fired and is sitting in prison. Unmasking them means forcing the contradictions out into the open, clarifying laws governing trade, seizing the initiative while it's still possible, not waiting until it becomes impossible.

It is childish to imagine or to assert that the system can once again use ruling-class control of the press and the fundamental unity of the establishment to hide behind a smokescreen, and that lacking a smokescreen it might actually collapse, and that therefore whoever contributes to the smokescreen contributes to the system's preservation. The anti-imperialist struggle doesn't take place at the level of election campaigns and detergent ads.

Anti-Imperialist Consciousness

The propaganda target of anti-imperialist action is the dialectical relationship between being and consciousness, because the masses' loyalty to the system is based on their accepting its pretty exterior, its promises, and its lies. Their loyalty to the system is based on its capacity

---

1 Twenty minutes before the Palestinian commando arrived at Fürstenfeldbruck, police abandoned their posts inside the Boeing plane, claiming that the mission they had been given was suicidal.

to discourage all spontaneity in its quest to completely assimilate the masses into the "silent bondage of the relationship" (Marx), which it forces the masses to accept as if it were only natural. Anti-imperialist action rips apart the system's facade and manipulation, along with the loyalty of the masses, and forces it to admit the truth, about which the masses say, as always, "This is not what we wanted." That they would then act to put an end to the horror of the system, which has long been apparent, is not the madness the opportunists make it out to be.

Who wanted the Fürstenfeldbruck massacre? The athletes who were dragged away from the Olympics didn't want it. The aggrieved and frightened people who experienced the aftermath and who felt the enormous cold-bloodedness of the IOC and the Springer Press didn't want it. It would be idiotic to believe that the revolutionaries wanted it. They wanted the release of the prisoners. They wanted what millions in this country still want: not to be tortured—just as political prisoners here don't want to be tortured—and an end to the theft of land, the murder, the napalming and the bombing terror Israel carries out against the Palestinian refugees. And that is why they were massacred. Because success would have meant an unimaginably higher level of identification with them and their revolution—with their "humanity," their rage, their solidarity—which would have been a setback.

Anti-imperialist consciousness attempts to prevent the perfection of imperialist rule from being firmly established. The masses are assaulted by *Bild* everyday. They are swamped on every side with prefabricated positions and postulations, making it difficult for them to express their actual pain and suffering.

"Terror"
The RAF's actions are directed towards developing anti-imperialist consciousness. The system's cast of characters understand that. They have understood that this form of struggle gradually builds a mass base, because resistance that grows slowly more powerful and more courageous cannot easily be defeated.

With the tactic of phony bomb threats—used against Stuttgart—they have turned their full attention to addressing this problem. They do this after failing to achieve any breakthroughs, even though they have raided hundreds of houses, scoured thousands of kilometres of streets, and released a million media appeals directed at RAF sympathizers. With the tactic of phony bomb threats and the simultaneous banning of statements from RAF prisoners from the media, the cops themselves are trying to create chaos, which is intended to lead to calls for greater law and order. The socialist left proved incapable of telling the difference between genuine and false bomb threats, although all of the genuine ones were directed against the ruling class and aimed to clear buildings and disrupt the ruling class's establishments, cultural venues, communication structures, and media outlets—only the Stuttgart threat was directed against the people and was openly fascist and hostile to the masses.

The anti-imperialist war turns the system's weapons against the system itself—the counterrevolutionary terrorizes the people. The legal left—confused by the police actions—has ceded the issue to the opportunists (Negt).

(What needs to be said in detail about the June and July arrests, the imprisoned comrades must say themselves.)

Black September
The Black September action in Munich leaves no room for misunderstanding. They took hostages from a people who are carrying out an extermination policy against them. They put their lives on the line to free their comrades. They didn't want to die. They put off their ultimatum. In the face of the uncompromising attitude advocated by Israel, they held the Israeli hostages prisoner. The Israeli hostages understood that this was a last resort. They were betrayed by the German authorities just as the revolutionaries were. The German police massacred the hostages and the revolutionaries.

The Black September action in Munich will live on in the memory of the anti-imperialist struggle.

The death of the Arab comrades weighs as heavily as Mount Tai.

THE STONES THAT THESE BEASTS THREW AT
FÜRSTENFELDBRUCK WILL FALL AT THEIR OWN FEET!

SOLIDARITY WITH THE LIBERATION STRUGGLE
OF THE PALESTINIAN PEOPLE!

SOLIDARITY WITH THE VIETNAMESE REVOLUTION!

REVOLUTIONARIES OF ALL COUNTRIES UNITE!

RAF
November 1972

Staying Alive:
Sensory Deprivation, Torture,
and the Struggle Behind Bars

By 1972, practically the whole founding generation of the RAF
were behind bars. Yet there was still a second generation and a
third generation. Why? Primarily because of the conditions of
imprisonment and state-organized terror.

Dieter Kunzelmann
former K.1 Communard[1]

HAVING CAPTURED THE IDEOLOGICAL LEADERSHIP of the RAF, the
West German state set in motion the second element of their counterinsurgency project: one which would eventually become known as the
"Stammheim Model." The mere incarceration of the guerilla was insufficient. Those captured were to be rendered ineffective not only as
combatants, but also as spokespeople for the anti-imperialist resistance.
If at all possible, they were to be deconstructed as human beings and reconstructed as representatives of the counterinsurgency project. If this
was not possible, at a bare minimum, they were to be destroyed.

The state's weapon on this terrain was complete and total isolation of
the prisoners, both from each other and from the outside world.

As early as June 7, 1972, the importance of isolation was enunci-
ated by Horst Ehmke, the SPD minister responsible for coordinating

---

1 *Baader Meinhof: In Love With Terror.*

intelligence operations. "We all... have an interest in completely breaking all solidarity [with the RAF], to isolate them from all others with radical opinions in this country," Ehmke told the *Bundestag*. "That is the most important task."[1]

The prisoners were scattered around the country.[2] While they would all be targeted by the state, particular pains were taken to attack those who were considered the five ringleaders: Andreas Baader, Ulrike Meinhof, Gudrun Ensslin, Holger Meins, and Jan-Carl Raspe.

Andreas Baader was held in total isolation from the day of his arrest on June 1, 1972, until November 11, 1974. In that entire time, he did not see another prisoner.

As of April 11, 1973, Holger Meins was held in Wittlich prison in solitary isolation, with the cells above, below, to the left, and to the right of him kept empty. His cell was searched daily, he was denied all group activities, including church services,[3] and he was shackled whenever he left his cell.

Ulrike Meinhof was put in the so-called "dead wing" at Cologne-Ossendorf prison,[4] where Astrid Proll had previously been held. In order to ensure the women remained separate, Proll was transferred to the men's wing.

The "dead wing" was intended not only to isolate, but also to induce a breakdown through sensory deprivation torture. It consisted of a specially soundproofed cell painted bright white with a single grated window covered with fine mesh, so that even the sky could not be viewed properly. The cell was lit twenty-four hours a day with a single bald neon light. It was forbidden for the prisoner to hang photographs, posters, or anything else on the walls. All other cells in the wing were kept

---

1 Statement to the *Bundestag*, June 7, 1972, quoted in *Texte des prisonniers de la "fraction armée rouge" et dernières lettres d'Ulrike Meinhof*, Draft Version, Cahiers Libres 337 (Paris: François Maspero).

2 For instance, Andreas Baader was in Schwalmstadt (Düsseldorf), Gudrun Ensslin in Essen, Holger Meins in Wittlich (Cologne), Irmgard Möller in Rastatt (Baden), Gerhard Müller in Hamburg, Jan-Carl Raspe in Cologne, and Horst Mahler in Moabit (West Berlin). (Aust, 231.)

3 RAF members' desire to attend church services was not due to any religiosity, although in their youth Meinhof, Ensslin, and Meins had all been quite devout. Rather, these services provided one of the only places where they could meet with and be amongst other prisoners.

4 The formulation used in Germany is to put the city name first, and then the name of the prison. So Cologne-Ossendorf refers to Ossendorf prison in the city of Cologne.

vacant, and when other prisoners were moved through the prison—for instance, to the exercise yard—they were obliged to take a circuitous route so that even their voices could not be heard. The only minimal contact with another human being was when food was delivered; other than that, the prisoner spent twenty-four hours a day in a world with no variation.

The use of sensory deprivation had been studied by doctors in Canada and the United States since the late 1950s, the line of research being taken up in the FRG by Dr. Jan Gross of Hamburg's Eppendorf University Hospital. Studies carried out by Gross found that sensory deprivation consistently caused feelings of unease ranging from fear to panic attacks, which could progress to an inability to concentrate, problems of perception (including hallucinations), vegetative disorders including feelings of intense hunger, chest pains, disequilibrium, trouble sleeping, trembling, and even convulsions.[5]

(It is worth noting that just as research into isolation was not limited to the FRG, many prisoners in the United States today are also subjected to various forms of isolation clearly intended as a form of torture.)[6]

Astrid Proll had been held in the dead wing for two periods, from November 1971 to January 1972 and from April 1972 to June 1972. She would later describe this experience:

> ...I was taken to an empty wing, a dead wing, where I was the only prisoner. Ulrike Meinhof later called it the "Silent Wing". The shocking experience was that I could not hear any noises apart from the ones that I generated myself. Nothing. Absolute silence. I went through states of excitement, I was haunted by visual and acoustic hallucinations. There were extreme disturbances of concentration and attacks of weakness. I had no idea how long this would go on for. I was terrified that I would go mad.[7]

---

5 Sjef Teuns, "La Torture par Privation Sensorielle," in *à propos du procès Baader-Meinhof, Fraction Armée Rouge : de la torture dans les prisons de la RFA*, Klaus Croissant (ed.) (Paris : Christian Bourgeois Éditeur, 1975), 65-66.

6 Committee to End the Marion Lockdown, "The People's Tribunal to Expose the Crimes of the Control Units"; Dr. Mutulu Shakur et al., "Genocide Waged Against the Black Nation Through Behavior Modification/Orchestrated by Counterinsurgency and Low-Intensity Warfare in the U.S. Penal System." Both reprinted in Matt Meyer, ed. *Let Freedom Ring: A Collection of Documents from the Movements to Free U.S. Political Prisoners* (Montreal/Oakland: Kersplebedeb-PM Press, 2008.) Also: Russell Maroon Shoatz, *Death by Regulation: Pennsylvania Control Unit Abuses* (Montreal: Kersplebedeb 2008).

7 Proll, 11.

After four-and-a-half months of this torture, Proll's physical and mental health were so badly damaged that she could hardly walk. When she was brought to trial in September 1973, the court ordered her examined by a heart specialist, a man who happened to be a former POW from Russia: he testified that her condition reminded him of the prisoners interned in Siberia.[1] The state was obliged to release her to a sanitarium in the Black Forest where she stayed for a year and then escaped, making her way to England.

Even when recaptured years later, she remained scarred by her ordeal, as she wrote in 1978:

> During the 2½ years of remand I was 4½ months completely isolated in the Dead Wing of Cologne-Ossendorf. Not even today, six years later, have I completely recovered from that. I can't stand rooms which are painted white because they remind me of my cell. Silence in a wood can terrify me, it reminds me of the silence in the isolated cell. Darkness makes me so depressive as if my life were taken away. Solitude causes me as much fear as crowds. Even today I have the feeling occasionally as if I can't move.[2]

Ulrike Meinhof was held in these conditions for 237 days following her arrest on June 15, 1972, and for shorter periods in December 1973 and February 1975. After eight months of this torture, she wrote:

> I finally realized I had to pull myself out of this, I myself had no right to let these frightful things keep affecting me—it was my duty to fight my way out of it. By whatever means there are of doing that in prison: daubing the walls, coming to blows with a cop, wrecking the fitments, hunger strike. I wanted to make them at least put me under arrest, because then you get to hear something—you don't have a radio babbling away, only the bible to read, maybe no mattress, no window, etc.—but that's a different kind of torture from not hearing anything. And obviously it would have been a relief to me...[3]

Through it all, she would remain unbroken.

---

1 Ibid., 12.

2 Friends of Astrid Proll, *Astrid Proll: The Case Against Her Extradition* (London: 1978), 8. It is worth remembering that she was being charged with attempted murder for shooting at police, an incident that the state already knew had not happened, thanks to the surveillance reports of its own intelligence agents. Cf 60.

3 Aust, 246.

Having failed to destroy Meinhof through such severe isolation, the state moved to directly and medically attack her brain. On the basis of an operation she had undergone in 1962 to correct a swollen blood vessel in her brain, Federal Prosecutor Peter Zeis theorized that her political behavior might be the result of some neurological problem.

In a letter dated April 18, 1973, Zeis asked the right-wing[4] director of the University of Homburg-Saar's Institute for Forensic Medicine and Psychiatry, Dr. Hermann Witter, to ascertain what interventions might prove necessary. In a letter dated May 10, Witter responded that he felt both x-rays and a scintigraphy—a routine and normally harmless diagnostic test which involves the injection of radioisotopes—would be required to establish a diagnosis. On July 13, Federal Supreme Court Judge Knoblich ruled that the state could proceed with these tests, even against Meinhof's will, and with the use of constraining devices or anesthesia if she resisted.[5] Correspondence between Witter and the Attorney General indicates that an appropriate diagnosis would have been used to mandate neurosurgery, regardless of the prisoner or her relatives' wishes.[6]

All of this was a transparent attempt to discredit the RAF by pathologizing Meinhof: "It would be so embarrassing," Zeis mused at the time, "if it turned out that all the people began to follow a mad woman."[7]

It was only through public protests organized by the prisoner support group Red Aid, which mobilized many doctors, that the government was forced to drop its plan.[8] Yet as we shall see, this was not the last time that the state would seek to score a propaganda victory by attacking and discrediting the woman who was routinely described as the RAF's chief theoretician.

On top of imposing internal isolation, the state did all it could to cut the prisoners off from the outside world. They were limited to visits from lawyers and family members. Visits from family members were overseen by two state security employees who recorded all conversations, the contents of which could be introduced at trials, sometimes

---

4 Formerly associated with the Nazi regime, Witter had publicly opposed the payment of reparations to victims of the Holocaust.

5 Commission internationale d'enquête sur la mort d'Ulrike Meinhof. *La Mort d'Ulrike Meinhof: Rapport de la Commission international d'enquête* (Paris: Librairie François Maspero, 1979), 78-79.

6 In this volume see the interview with *Le Monde Diplomatique*, pages 410-412.

7 "Political Internment in the FRG," in *War on the War Makers*, 27.

8 Komitees gegen Folter, 131, 133.

followed by analysis from a psychologist. Political letters, books, and packages were routinely withheld.

Starting in 1975, everyone arrested under §129 in connection with "political crimes" would be held under the so-called "24-Point Program." This formalized many of the conditions that had been imposed unevenly up until then, while also adding new restrictions. The program specified, among other things, that the prisoners were banned from all common activities. The prisoners now received one hour of solitary yard time each day, which was immediately interrupted if they failed to heed an order, insulted a staff person, or caused any damage. The prisoners were permitted to keep twenty books in their cells. Visits were limited to people cleared by the authorities, and could only last a maximum of thirty minutes (the standard was two such visits a month). It was prohibited to discuss activities of the so-called "terrorist scene" or its support groups (the latter was a grab bag for all revolutionary organizations), prison revolts, or hunger strikes. All visitors were searched, and this included lawyers.[1]

In a statement regarding such isolation, Till Meyer and Andreas Vogel, both 2nd of June Movement prisoners who were subjected to these conditions for years, wrote:

> With the isolation wings, years of isolation have been carried to the extreme and the process of extermination has been perfected: the perfection of spatial limitation and the total isolation, electronic observation with cameras and microphones (openly in each cell)—and we are guarded by special corps (corps who are trained in psychology and conditioned through BKA training).[2]

RAF prisoner Helmut Pohl would express himself similarly:

> Isolation represents a more intense version of the situation which dominates on the outside, which led us to engage in clandestine armed struggle in the first place. Isolation represents its pure state, its naked reality. Whoever doesn't find a way to struggle against this situation is destroyed—the situation controls him and not the other way around.[3]

---

1 "24-Punkt-Haftstatut." http://www.nadir.org/nadir/archiv/ PolitischeStroemungen/Stadtguerilla+RAF/RAF/brd+raf/053.html.
2 Bewegung 2. Juni (2nd of June Movement), *Der Blues: Gesammelte Texte der Bewgung 2. Juni*, Vol. 2, self-published illegally in the FRG, n.d. (1982?), 680.
3 Helmut Pohl's Testimony at the Stammheim trial, July 29, 1976.

As Andreas Baader described it:

> Isolation aims at alienating prisoners from every social relationship including their history, their history above all... It makes the prisoner unconscious or kills him or her.[4]

Professor Wilfried Rasch of the Institute of Forensic Psychiatry at the Free University of Berlin, who was called upon to examine the RAF prisoners, had this to say about the isolation conditions in which they were held:

> The high security wing has simply the quality of torture, that is to say, an attempt to use special measures to achieve something amongst the prisoners through difficult or unbearable conditions, specifically, a change of heart, a defection.[5]

Even those visits that were permitted were designed to add to the prisoners' stress-level. Eberhard Dreher, held on charges of supporting the 2nd of June Movement, described the closed visiting conditions:

> [T]he screen offers a pretense of contact, simultaneously limiting the contact to visual contact and making the contact unfamiliar due to the reflective quality of the glass... Further pain is created by the lack of air and the particular acoustics. The construction of ventilators would rectify this problem... To make oneself understood, one must speak very loudly. One's own voice within the aquarium-like cabinet is amplified into an acoustic mountain crashing down directly onto one's own head.[6]

Dreher further described the effect of one such visit with his lawyer as follows:

> After... forty minutes, I had a splitting headache and, with the consent of my lawyer, had to break off the visit. I had a headache, needed air, was fed-up, wanted to be in my cell in peace.[7]

---

4 Bakker Schut (ed.), *Das Info: brief von gefangen aus der raf aus der discussion 1973-1977* (Neue Malik Verlag, Plambeck & Neuss, 1987), 218.

5 Bewegung 2. Juni (2nd of June Movement), *Der Blues: Gesammelte Texte der Bewgung 2. Juni, Vol. 1*, self-published illegally in the FRG, n.d. (1982?), 341.

6 Ibid., 320.

7 Ibid., 321.

In 1978, the European Commission of Human Rights would observe that their prison and trial conditions had contributed to Gudrun Ensslin, Jan-Carl Raspe, and Andreas Baader all developing "problems of concentration, marked fatigue, difficulties of expression or articulation, reduced physical and mental performance, instability, diminished spontaneity and ability to make contacts, depression."[1]

If the results of imprisonment in the isolation wing were horrifying, isolation combined with sensory deprivation was even more destructive, as is indicated in Ulrike Meinhof's harrowing description of her ordeal in Cologne-Ossendorf (see Ulrike Meinhof on the Dead Wing, pages 271-73).

Early on, it became clear to the prisoners that their only hope lay in resistance, and so on January 17, 1973, forty captured combatants from the RAF and other guerilla groups began a hunger strike, demanding access to independent doctors and transfer to the general population.[2]

This first hunger strike lasted four-and-a-half weeks, and was only called off when Attorney General Ludwig Martin agreed to move Meinhof out of the dead wing—a promise which was not kept, and was likely never meant as anything but a ploy.[3]

Nevertheless, even though the hunger strike did not achieve any immediate victory, it did manage to break through the wall of silence surrounding prison conditions, galvanizing support from a section of the far left. In a way that was perhaps impossible to foresee, it marked the beginning of a strategy which would give the RAF a new lease on life.

Support had so far come mainly from the Red Aid network, a situation which was less than satisfactory in the eyes of the prisoners, as Red Aid offered solidarity while remaining critical of the RAF's politics. Furthermore, within Red Aid, the focus on the RAF prisoners had begun causing dissension, especially in Munich, as Bavaria held a large number of prisoners from the antiauthoritarian scene, and it was felt that they were being neglected, too much energy being spent defending the Marxist-Leninist RAF.

Thus, following the first hunger strike in April 1973, several lawyers came together with some of the RAF's closest political sympathizers to

---

1 European Commission of Human Rights, *Decisions and Reports 14*, Strasbourg, June 1979, 96-97.
2 Rote Armee Fraktion, 181.
3 Vague, 50.

set up the *Komitees gegen Folter* (Committees Against Torture) that would take over support work for the prisoners in the future, while promoting the RAF's particular brand of anti-imperialist politics. This political orientation was no great liability for the legal left, as even many liberals were not yet ready to completely repudiate those who engaged in armed struggle.[4]

Several lawyers took leading roles in the Committees, Hans-Christian Ströbele, Klaus Croissant, Otto Schily, Siegfried Haag, and Kurt Groenewold being their most prominent members. It was Groenewold who took the lead in establishing the Committees, their Hamburg headquarters being a block away from his office.[5]

As it turned out, the decision to set up the Committees proved fortuitous. Due in part to ongoing tensions between antiauthoritarians and others, the Maoist KPD/ML managed to take control of Red Aid at a national conference in April 1974. This was the second successful attempt by a K-group to move in on the network: the KPD/AO had already formed a rival "Red Aid registered association" to capitalize on its reputation. While the KPD/ML and KPD/AO may have been occasionally sympathetic to the RAF prisoners, they were definitely hostile to their politics, and so the RAF would have been at a disadvantage had they remained dependent on either Red Aid network for support.

Committees Against Torture were established in West Berlin, Frankfurt, Hamburg, Kassel, Cologne, Munich, Münster, Stuttgart, Tübingen, and Heidelberg[6]—the latter in particular being a magnet for former SPK members.[7] Backed by many progressive intellectuals, they worked to focus public attention on the prisoners' struggle and the destructive conditions in which they were held, setting up information tables, issuing leaflets, and holding teach-ins.[8] The hope was to win the support of people with their roots in the sixties antiwar movement, people who shared much of the RAF's analysis and could be expected to express political solidarity, particularly for the idea that the captured combatants were political prisoners who had acted in the context of an international anti-imperialist movement.

---

4 Karl-Heinz Dellwo, *Das Projektil sind wir* (Hamburg: Nautilus, 2007), 95.

5 Ibid., 93-94.

6 Komitees gegen Folter, 97.

7 Dellwo, 94.

8 Komitees gegen Folter, 97-98.

The Lawyers

Hans-Christian Ströbele had helped to found the West Berlin
Socialist Lawyers Collective along with Horst Mahler in 1968.[1] He
was an SPD member in the early seventies, and, in 1978, would be
a founding member of the Alternative List, a forerunner to the left
wing of the Green Party, in which he would also be active as an
elected member of the *Bundestag* from 1985 to 1987 and again
from 1992 on.

Klaus Croissant was a member of the Stuttgart Socialist
Lawyers Collective; he had been under surveillance by the state
from at least May 1972, suspected of having himself located
safehouses for the RAF.[2] Over the years, he became one of the
prisoners' most ardent and notorious advocates—disgusted at
what he saw of West German "justice," he would eventually begin
working with the East German *Stasi* in the 1980s. He would
unsuccessfully run for mayor of Berlin-Kreuzberg on the Alternative List ticket, before joining the *Partei des Demokratischen
Sozialismus* (Party of Democratic Socialism)—the successor to
East Germany's SED—in 1990.

*Lawyers Klaus Croissant, Otto Schily, and
Hans-Christian Ströbele at a press conference in 1974.*

---

[1] Aust, 66.
[2] Aust, 207; Becker, 306.

Otto Schily was a committed civil libertarian, deeply concerned about the rule of law. He had befriended Rudi Dutschke while studying in West Berlin, and had been active in circles around the SDS.[3] Probably the only one of the lawyers to take pride in referring to himself as "bourgeois," Schily would join Ströbele in the Green Party in the 1980s, before crossing over to the Social Democrats in 1989. In 1998, years after he had left our story, Schily was appointed Minister of the Interior, the former civil libertarian now in charge of domestic repression. As such, he was personally responsible for the highly repressive "anti-terrorist" legislation that was passed in the FRG in the wake of September 11, 2001.[4] The legislation earned him a "Big Brother Award", a negative prize presented to those who excel in rolling back civil liberties.

Siegfried Haag had not been prominent in the APO or the political left previously, but was so moved by the prisoners' plight that he would eventually make their struggle his own.

Kurt Groenewold, the son of a wealthy property owner, had previously represented Ulrike Meinhof in her divorce from Klaus Rainer Röhl in 1968. He was active in the Hamburg Socialist Lawyers Collective, defending cultural radicals like the composers Ernst Schnabel and Hans-Werner Henze for their oratorio to Che Guevara, *Floß der Medusa*. He also defended the poet Erich Fried, who was accused of slandering the West Berlin police when he described the shooting of Georg von Rauch as a "preventive murder" in a letter to *Spiegel*.[5] In recent years, Groenwold has written extensively about the legal and civil rights ramifications of the state's response to the armed movements in West Germany in the 70s and 80s.

---

[3] Hockenos, 119.

[4] Ibid., 290.

[5] "Kurt Groenewold," http://www.literaturhaus.at/autoren/F/fried/gesellschaft/mitglieder/groenewold/.

While the Committees welcomed support from many intellectuals and celebrities who still rejected the prisoners' politics, by and large militants were expected to toe the RAF line. While some involved did have their own quiet reservations in this regard, it is equally clear that many others were sincerely won over to the guerilla's politics. The state certainly contributed to this process, as activists would find themselves the object of police surveillance, raids, and even in some cases criminal charges, simply for disseminating information about the conditions in West German prisons.[1]

In subsequent years, the underground would include several veterans of this prisoners' support scene, and even some from their legal team, a fact which the state would exploit time and again to attack the RAF's lawyers. While most of the legal support team never did join the guerilla despite their increasing horror at the Kafkaesque trials and inhumane prison conditions, it is clear in retrospect that work in the Committees did constitute a rite of passage into the RAF for an astonishing number of future guerillas.

It is, of course, equally true that the overwhelming majority of those who were active in this scene never joined the guerilla, and while they remained operational, the Committees Against Torture always limited themselves to nonviolent forms of protest and popular education.

Before long, they got their first opportunity for such public activity: on May 8, 1973—the anniversary of the defeat of the Third Reich—sixty prisoners throughout the Federal Republic began a second hunger strike. The Committees stepped up their activities, organizing for lawyers to engage in a solidarity hunger strike and holding a demonstration outside the Federal Court in Karlsruhe.[2]

The Committees' most significant event occurred on May 11, when they held a teach-in where several high-profile supporters spoke out against isolation torture. Heinz Brandt, an official from the IG Metall

---

1 In 1975, for instance, two activists received respective sentences of six and nine months in prison under §129, simply for handing out pamphlets with information about isolation conditions. The Supreme Court's decision made clear the object of such prosecutions: "The accused did not limit themselves to speaking to individuals in private, but by means of the leaflets sought to make contact with large numbers of people, and principally with young people, who are easily influenced in this way... Nor should the possibility of imitation by potential criminals be ignored. Whether the sentence of the accused will remain largely unknown is not important; what is important is the effect it will inevitably have on people who do know of it." (Cobler, 114-115)

2 Komitees gegen Folter, 86-87.

trade union, described the isolation conditions that the prisoners were subjected to as even worse than what he had suffered during four years in a Nazi concentration camp:

> As crass and paradoxical as it may sound, my experiences with strict, radical isolation were worse than my time... in a Nazi concentration camp... [I]n the camp, I still had the bases for human life, namely, communication with my fellow inmates... We were able in the camps to see, not only outrageously fascistic and sadistic mistreatment, but also the possibilities of resistance and collective life among the prisoners, and, with this, for the fulfillment of the fundamental need of a human being: social existence.[3]

Dutch psychologist Dr. Sjef Teuns described isolation and sensory deprivation as programmed torture. Dr. Christian Sigrist, who had worked alongside anticolonial freedom fighters in Africa, described the West German torture system as part of the worldwide counterstrategy against anti-imperialist combatants.

This last point was certainly as important to the prisoners as the former two. The RAF viewed human rights campaigns as being worse than useless; indeed, they viewed such humanitarianism as an attack on their fundamental principles. When Red Aid had put out leaflets accusing the state of denying the prisoners' basic human rights, Baader had angrily objected that, "Because our comrades are half-dead they can't think we're anything else ourselves. They're twisting the thing the same way the pigs twist it worldwide: Violence is taboo..."[4]

Similarly, Baader would later find it necessary to criticize defense attorney Otto Schily in this regard:

> We certainly can't agree with the argument regarding torture as it is developed by Schily in his petition [...] In reacting to revolutionary politics, the state does not know what to do except torture, and in doing so it exposes itself as an imperialist state. The indignation of degenerate bourgeois antifascism only masks this. The latter is already so weak, corrupted by social democracy, and locked in revisionism, that it can no longer express itself in a meaningful way.[5]

---

3 Varon, 218.
4 Aust, 242.
5 Andreas Baader Regarding Torture, reprinted in this volume on pages 319-323.

On May 24, 1973, fourteen days into the second hunger strike, the prison authorities began withholding water from Baader, despite a court decision two days earlier forbidding such tactics, as even short term water deprivation under a doctor's supervision can seriously damage one's health.[1] Indeed, after several days without water and in critical condition—suffering kidney pains, a sore throat, and difficulty seeing—Baader was forced to end his hunger strike. Apparently pleased with their success, the authorities targeted Bernhard Braun next, attempting to have him placed in the so-called "dry cell," but his lawyer managed to intervene and have this blocked.[2]

The hunger strike continued until June 29, when the District Court in Karlsruhe ordered the release from isolation of two prisoners.[3] (Although accounts are vague on this point, there is some indication that the two were former SPK members Carmen Roll and Siegfried Hausner.)[4]

Yet, soon after these two prisoners had their conditions relaxed for health reasons, another was effectively sentenced to death by medical neglect.

Katharina Hammerschmidt had fled to France in 1971, but when the May Offensive had ended in a wave of arrests, she had turned herself in, returning to face the relatively minor charges relating to her having located safehouses for the guerilla. Despite the fact that she had surrendered voluntarily, she was remanded to the West Berlin Women's Prison while awaiting her trial.

In August 1973, Hammerschmidt underwent a routine medical exam, which included some x-rays. These revealed an abnormal growth in her chest, but the prison doctors took no steps to evaluate whether this was benign or malignant. In fact, they did not even inform her of the results.[5]

In September, Hammerschmidt began to complain of intense pain in her chest and throat. She had difficulty breathing and it hurt to swallow, yet the prison doctors simply told her that if the symptoms continued, more x-rays would be taken in another three months.

---

1 Klaus Croissant, "La justice et la torture par l'isolement," in Croissant, 120-121.
2 Ibid., 120.
3 Rote Armee Fraktion, 181.
4 Hausner had been arrested in 1972 for building bombs and sentenced to three years in a youth facility; he was released from prison in 1974, at which point he made contact with other former SPK members and returned to the underground with the RAF.
5 "Des medecins portent plainte," in Croissant, 104-107.

Press Release from Baader's Lawyers

Even though Baader was doing well, at noon on May 22, 1973, the prison doctor, Dr. Degenhardt from Kassel, came to his cell with a squad of ten guards in order to force him to swallow a solution through a tube as thick as of one's thumb. Three times Baader requested a spoon so that he could take the solution on his own. Despite this fact, the doctor ordered the guards to hold him down. Pinching his nose, he then forced the tube into his mouth, down his throat and into his digestive tract. Baader vomited and almost suffocated. The tube opened up his throat and his digestive tract and he vomited blood. After this torture Dr. Degenhardt gave him three intravenous injections and he then lost consciousness for eight hours.

On the morning of May 22, Baader had been visited by one of his lawyers, Koch, from the Frankfurt Legal Collective. The lawyer was able to see that Baader's state of health was relatively good. When he came back that afternoon to continue his visit, a guard told Koch that the doctor had instructed that Baader should remain in bed. It was not possible for him to visit with his lawyer. The lawyer asked to see the warden Metz, but this was refused.

As attorneys of Andreas Baader we note: Andreas Baader is not only subjected to psychological torture in the Ziegenhain prison (Hessen), but he is also being tortured physically by methods which are carbon copies of those practiced in Greece, Spain, Portugal, Turkey, and Brazil. Force-feeding, when the prisoner has agreed to feed himself, is a form of torture.

We demand that Dr. Degenhardt and his helpers be punished.

Andreas Baader's lawyers
Golzem, von Plonitz, Riedel and Koch
May 23 1973

Klaus Croissant, "La justice et la torture par l'isolement," in Croissant, 119.

In October, the pain was so great that Hammerschmidt could not sleep; she was told by medical staff that her throat hurt from "too much yelling." As her condition deteriorated to the point that her tumors became visible to the naked eye, the doctors simply prescribed water pills.[1]

In November, her lawyers finally won a court judgment forcing the prison authorities to allow her to be seen by an independent physician. This specialist immediately issued a letter indicating that Hammerschmidt needed follow-up tests as soon as possible. These were not carried out, and she was returned to prison.

Two weeks later, on the night of November 28/29, Hammerschmidt almost suffocated from difficulty breathing. She was brought directly to a hospital, where it was found she had a cancerous tumor as large as a child's head in her chest. It was determined that the tumor was inoperable, although it was also stated that this might not have been the case just weeks earlier.[2]

An independent physician would later remark that the fact that Hammerschmidt had cancer should have been obvious from the x-rays taken in August, and yet six different prison doctors were all seemingly unable to notice that anything was wrong. Or perhaps they simply did not want to: in a public accusation signed by 131 doctors, it was suggested that she was denied necessary medical care because this would have required an end to the isolation conditions that she, like all other RAF prisoners, was being subjected to at the time.

Katharina Hammerschmidt

It was January 1974 before the court adjourned her trial, ruling that she was too sick and needed to be released to a clinic for treatment. If anything could have been done, it was now too late: Katharina Hammerschmidt struggled on for the next year-and-a-half, finally succumbing to her illness on June 29, 1975—three years to the day after she had turned herself in.

Many observers considered Hammerschmidt's death to be a case of "judicial murder." Independent physicians who examined her upon her release declared that the prison doctors' findings had been "medically

---

1 Soligruppe Christian S., "Der Spiegel, 1975, BAADER/MEINHOF Müdes Auge," http://www36.websamba.com/Soligruppe/data/spiegel1975.htm; "Les democraties face à la violence" *la Lanterne Noire* 5 (December 1975).

2 Viktor Kleinkrieg, "Les combattantes anti-impérialistes face à la torture," in Croissant, 47.

incomprehensible," evidence of "incredible medical shortcomings."[3] A court would eventually award her family the measly sum of 5,000 DM, admitting that the prison administration bore some responsibility for her death.[4]

The RAF and its supporters would lay Katharina Hammerschmidt's death at the door of the West German prison authorities. Yet, by the time she had died, hers was not the first such case of "judicial murder."

On September 13, 1974, forty prisoners led by the RAF had begun their third collective hunger strike against prison conditions.[5] The Committees Against Torture sprang into action, and Amnesty International had its Hamburg offices occupied in an attempt to pressure the liberal organization to take a stand in support of the prisoners. (Notably, several of those involved in this occupation would join the guerilla within a few years.)[6]

Not only had the previous hunger strikes failed to achieve integration of all RAF prisoners into the general population, in situations where they had been able to have contact with social prisoners, the latter often found themselves harassed or transferred. The prisoners had come to the conclusion that the demand for integration, while it had undeniable appeal given the high esteem in which the New Left held marginalized groups like social prisoners, was simply not going to work. As a

---

3 Ibid.

4 Peters Butz, *RAF Terrorismus in Deutschland* (Stuttgart: Deutsche Verlags Anstalt, 1991), 454, quoted in "Katharina Hammerschmidt," http://de.wikipedia.org/wiki/Katharina_Hammerschmidt.

5 Apart from the declaration included in this section on pages 274-78, Ulrike Meinhof used the occasion of her testimony in court to announce the strike. See Ulrike Meinhof Regarding the Liberation of Andreas Baader, page 370.

6 For instance: Susanne Albrecht, Karl-Heinz Dellwo, Lutz Taufer, Günter Sonnenberg, Christian Klar, and Knut Folkerts. (Becker, 340-341)

result, integration was dropped, and the struggle was now defined as one against isolation and for the association of political prisoners with each other.

As Karl-Heinz Dellwo, who was active in the Committees Against Torture at the time, explains:

> Up until then the hunger strikes were carried out with the goal of achieving "equality" with the other prisoners. I had long been critical of this. I thought it absolutely could not work. Either one would be placed somewhere where the prisoners changed every day, or with prisoners with whom one could not, for various reasons, talk. I was pleased when the RAF prisoners changed their line and chose the demand for association. That created some conflicts on the outside, for instance with the Frankfurt Committee,[1] which had a social revolutionary line: they were of the opinion that all prisoners were frustrated social rebels. I seriously doubted that.[2]

This new demand for association became a rallying point for the prisoners and their supporters for the next two decades. Years later, 2nd of June Movement prisoner Till Meyer, writing from the dead wing, would express the goal this way:

> Our demand—association of all prisoners—is the opposite of what the pigs offer us. Association means, above all, survival, collective political imprisonment, political identity, self-organization—while the dead wing means annihilation.[3]

In practical terms, association meant bringing together political prisoners in groups large enough to be socially viable, fifteen being the minimum number normally suggested. Political prisoners in some other European countries, such as Italy and Northern Ireland, had already won such conditions for themselves, and so it was hoped that this might prove a realistic goal.

As a brief aside, it should be noted that this reorientation, along with the third hunger strike, provided the occasion for a very public split amongst the prisoners, as Horst Mahler not only refused to participate,

---

1 Throughout the 1970s, Frankfurt was the bastion of the *spontis*, who would have been critical of such a separation from social prisoners.

2 Dellwo, 98-99.

3 Bewegung 2. Juni (2nd of June Movement), *Der Blues: Gesammelte Texte der Bewegung 2. Juni*, Vol. 2, 684.

Rote Hilfe e.v. poster demanding freedom for Horst Mahler

but also took the opportunity to publicly repudiate armed struggle and break with the RAF. It has been suggested that one reason for this was his refusal to abandon the demand for integration, though clearly he had had other disagreements with the rest of the guerilla for some time now.[4]

In point of fact, Mahler had joined Red Aid e.v., the network that had been set up by the KPD/AO in 1970. He would explain that this was intended as an attempt to "close ranks and organize a criticism of the RAF's sectarian line in the spirit of solidarity."[5] Mahler's move into orthodox Maoism would win him some support: that October, Red Aid e.v. organized a demonstration, during which, according to the *Verfassungsschutz*, 5,000 people rallied to demand his freedom.[6] Nevertheless, it failed to do any good in court, where Mahler was now facing his third RAF-related trial, the second time he would face charges relating to Baader's 1970 jailbreak. Despite his break with the guerilla, he would eventually be sentenced to fourteen years in prison; Ulrike Meinhof, who also stood accused in these proceedings, would receive an eight-year sentence, while Hans-Jürgen Bäcker, who had testified against the guerilla, would be acquitted.[7]

The other prisoners considered Mahler's public split to be serious enough to warrant a public reply, and on September 27 Monika Berberich delivered a statement at the Mahler-Meinhof-Bäcker trial

---

4 Otto Billig, "The Lawyer Terrorist and his Comrades," *Political Psychology* 6, no. 1 (March 1985): 35.

5 Rote Hilfe e.v. "Zwischen RAF-Solidarität und „linker Caritas" - Teil 1 / 1 / 2007 / Die Rote Hilfe Zeitung / Publikationen / Rote Hilfe e.V. - Rote Hilfe e.V.," http://www.rote-hilfe.de/publikationen/die_rote_hilfe_zeitung/2007/1/zwischen_raf_solidaritaet_und_linker_caritas_teil_1.

6 Ibid.

7 *European Stars and Stripes*, "Meinhof: Female German Guerrilla Leader gets eight-year term for role in murder plot," November 30, 1974.

Horst Mahler After the RAF

Horst Mahler left the RAF for the KPD (previously the KPD/AO) in 1974, but remained a Maoist for only a few years: in 1977 he publicly announced that he was now "internally freed from the dogmatic revolutionary theory of Marxism-Leninism."[1] As a repentant guerilla, he was supported on humanitarian grounds by *Jusos* chairman Gerhard Schröder, who began acting as his lawyer in 1978.

With time off for good behavior, Mahler was released from prison in 1980, at which point his only real political activity was to cooperate with government propaganda programs and appear before young people to condemn political violence.[2]

In the 1990s, however, a new Horst Mahler emerged as the former guerilla-lawyer publicly repositioned himself on the far right of the German political spectrum. Mahler had crossed the Rubicon, and has since earned international renown as a "third position" fascist, and legal defender of Holocaust Deniers and neo-nazis, racists whose opinions the former communist now shares.

His expulsion in 1974 does not stop journalists from routinely describing Mahler as a founding member of the RAF, implying a connection between his previous views and those he holds today. Indeed, Mahler the neo-nazi has attempted to exploit this smear himself, arguing dishonestly that were Meinhof alive today, she, too, would have crossed over to the neofascist camp.

While several leading lights from the sixties APO generation have indeed moved to the far right, these represent only a small minority. In the case of the RAF itself, Mahler is the only former member to have followed this sad trajectory.

---

[1] German Law Journal, "Federal Constitutional Court Issues Temporary Injunction in the NPD Party Ban Case," *German Law Journal* [online] 2, no. 13, (August 1, 2001).

[2] United Press International, "Parting shots," *European Stars and Stripes*, October 4, 1980.

formally expelling her former comrade, accusing him of being a "filthy, bourgeois chauvinist" who had attempted to "transfer his ruling-class arrogance... into the proletarian movement."[1]

This split, and tensions around the new demand for association, may explain the RAF's "Provisional Program of Struggle for the Political Rights of Imprisoned Workers," which was also released that September. An attempt to explain how the struggle against isolation could relate to a wider radical prisoners' movement, the Provisional Program left the door open to the possibility of struggle alongside other prisoners. While this strategy seems to have borne no fruit, it may have assuaged the dissatisfaction felt by some of those who were unhappy at the new orientation away from integration.

Despite this rocky beginning, the RAF's third hunger strike was a momentous event, rallying support in a way no previous hunger strike had and serving as a major radicalizing experience for various tendencies of the left.

"Solidarity with the RAF Comrades' Hunger Strike": poster for a public meeting organized by the sponti left, with Rudi Dutschke, Johannes Agnoli, and Peter Brückner. September 1974.

At first, however, little attention was paid to the striking prisoners, especially in the media, which barely mentioned the strike. The main solidarity activity remained public outreach. Students at the West Berlin Technical University staged a solidarity hunger strike,[2] and supporters in that city occupied a Lutheran Church demanding an end to isolation, extermination imprisonment, and "clean torture"—they were greeted with support by the Church's superintendent and several clergymen.[3]

---

1 The Expulsion of Horst Mahler, see pages 288-91.

2 Peter Jochen Winters, "Unklarheit über die Rolle der verhafteten Pfarrersfrau," *Frankfurter Allgemeine Zeitung*, November 23, 1974.

3 Peter Jochen Winters, "Die Verquickung in Machenschaften der Meinhof-Bande began mit einer Kirschenbetzung," *Frankfurter Allgemeine Zeitung*, Nov. 25, 1974.

Notable among the prisoners' Lutheran supporters were Undine Zühlke, a clergyman's wife, and Vicar Cornelius Burghardt. Both Zühlke and Burghardt organized a public assembly at their church on November 4, where they spoke alongside a number of the prisoners' lawyers, and where resolutions were passed against isolation torture. Burghardt also publicly admitted having sheltered Meinhof in 1971, explaining that he did so in "the Christian tradition."[1] (Zühlke and Burghardt were soon sentenced under §129—he for sheltering Meinhof and she for smuggling a letter out from Meinhof in early November.[2] Later that month, the Lutheran Church Council attempted to clamp down on radical church members, issuing a "Statement Against Terrorism" and calling on unnamed clergymen to "reorient themselves" accordingly.[3])

At the same time, another noteworthy source of support was the KPD/ML, which had successfully taken over the main Red Aid network in April of that year. The KPD/ML remained hostile to the RAF's politics, especially to what it viewed as their soft line on the East German and Soviet revisionists. Yet, on the basis of opposing state repression, it and the Red Aid network would provide substantial support, issuing leaflets and organizing demonstrations throughout the hunger strike.

During the strike's first month, two prisoners—Ronald Augustin and Ali Jansen—were both deprived of water for days at a time.[4] Jansen had been sentenced in 1973 to ten years in prison on two counts of attempted murder for having shot at cops when they caught him and other RAF members stealing a car in 1970. Augustin was a graphic artist from Amsterdam, who had joined the RAF after meeting members in that city in 1971; he was arrested on July 24, 1973, attempting to enter the FRG, and charged under §129, as well as for resisting arrest and possession of false documents.[5]

---

1 Winters "Unklarheit über die Rolle der verhafteten Pfarrersfrau."

2 *Frankfurter Allgemeine Zeitung,* "Verdacht der Unterstützung von Terroristen beunruhigt die Berliner evangelische Kirche," November 12, 1974. The letter in question, likely about prison conditions, was in fact never delivered—losing her nerve, Zühlke destroyed it rather than pass it on to Burghardt. This did nothing to help her following the Drenkmann action, when police accused her of acting as a courier of a letter which allegedly had to do with his killing, and she was unable to produce said letter to prove that it was about nothing of the sort.

3 *Frankfurter Allgemeine Zeitung,* "Erklärung der Kirche gegen Terrorismus," November 29, 1974.

4 Komitees gegen Folter, 28, 30.

5 He was sentenced to six years, and received another six months "coercive detention" for refusing to testify in the Stammheim trial. He was finally released

While these two applications of the "dry cell" alarmed the prisoners and their supporters, the strike did not falter, and, in the end, this tactic was not repeated.[6] Rather, the state sought to keep things defused; as part of this strategy, in early October, the president of the Federal Supreme Court, Theodor Prinzing, ruled in favor of force-feeding Holger Meins, Jan-Carl Raspe, and Andreas Baader. The purview of this ruling was soon extended to the other prisoners.

Force-feeding has been used since at least the early twentieth century by governments and penal authorities wishing to break hunger strikes: not only does this countermeasure seem to diminish what is at stake, as it suggests hunger strikers may no longer die from their protests, but the entire ordeal is designed to be excruciatingly painful, in large part to discourage strikers from continuing. Holger Meins described the procedure:

> A red stomach pipe (not a tube) is used, about the thickness of a middle finger… The slightest irritation when the pipe is introduced causes gagging and nausea and the cramping of the chest and stomach muscles, setting off a chain reaction of extremely intense convulsions throughout the body, causing one to buck against the pipe…

He concluded that, "The pipe is, regardless of circumstances, torture."[7]

Adelheid Schulz, a RAF member imprisoned in the 1980s, described the effects of force-feeding as hours of nausea, a racing heartbeat, pain, and effects similar to fever—"At times one experiences hot flashes; then one is freezing cold."[8]

In the words of Margrit Schiller: "I was force-fed every day for a month. Each time was like a rape. Each time, I felt totally humiliated and destroyed."[9]

The prisoners insisted that force-feeding was never meant for any purpose other than torture. Events soon convinced many that they were right.

---

and extradited back to Holland in 1980.

6 It is possible that this reticence to use water deprivation was at least partly due to the RAF prisoners' threat to escalate to a thirst strike if such measures were adopted. See Ulrike Meinhof Regarding the Liberation of Andreas Baader, cf 370.

7 Holger Meins's Report on Force-Feeding, see pages 292-95.

8 *Von der Zwangernährung zur "Koma-Losung,"* West Germany, Sept. 1985, 25.

9 *Baader Meinhof: In Love With Terror.*

On Saturday, November 9, Holger Meins died of starvation in Wittlich prison. Supporters and lawyers had already argued that this prison lacked the facilities for force-feeding to be of any medical benefit, yet the Bonn Security Group—the section of the BKA charged with protecting political figures (much like the American secret service) and also combating enemies of the state[1]—had blocked Meins from being transferred anywhere else.

For the last two weeks of his life, Meins only received between 400 and 800 calories daily, and in the last four days of his life, never more than 400 calories a day.[2]

Meins was never hospitalized, despite a court decision ordering such a transfer, and the prison doctor had gone on vacation without leaving any replacement at his post.[3] Scandalously, before Dr. Hutter left, he sought assurances that he would not be disciplined should Meins die.

Siegfried Haag, one of the RAF's attorneys, was with Meins just before he died. The prisoner had to be brought in on a stretcher as he

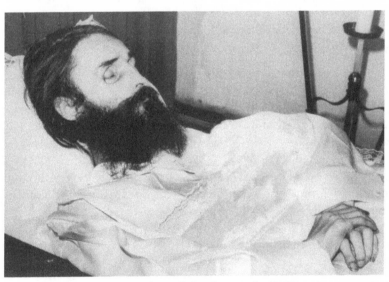

Over six feet tall, by the time he died
Holger Meins weighed less than one hundred pounds.

---

1 Cobler, 52. Many aspects of isolation were "suggested" to prison administrators by the Bonn Security Group. See, for instance, Aust, 245-246.
2 Pieter Bakker Schut, *Stammheim* (Kiel: Neuer Malik Verlag, 1986), 119.
3 Aust, 265.

could no longer walk. The visit lasted two hours, Haag would later explain, "because I realized this was his last conversation, and he knew it too."[4]

The lawyer, who would himself be moved to join the guerilla, later recalled that, "I shall never be able to forget this experience all my life. I was so intensely involved [with his situation] at the time and I felt that as a lawyer I could not defend him the way he needed to be defended... [nor] do anything to prevent [his] death."[5]

Over six feet tall, Meins weighed less than 100 pounds at the time of his death: for the RAF and their supporters, this was quite simply a murder in the context of a state security war against the prisoners. Indeed, long before the hunger strike, Meins himself had written in his will, "If I should die in prison, it was murder. Whatever the pigs say... Don't believe the murderers' lies."[6]

As word spread that a prisoner had died, hundreds of people took to the streets of West Berlin, engaging in clashes which sent five cops to the

Obituary: After 2 years of isolation, 6 weeks of hunger strike and 2 weeks of force-feeding, he died at the age of 33—we will not forget him nor will we forget his guards and force-feeders.

---

4 Ibid., 264.
5 Varon, 231.
6 Aust, 265.

hospital.[1] Stefan Wisniewski, who would be moved by Meins's death to eventually join the RAF, remembers the day well:

> *Everything was about the hunger strike. We had mobilized everyone from Amnesty International to Father Albertz, everyone it seemed possible to mobilize. I was standing on a table in the youth center—there was no podium—and was giving a speech. Suddenly someone came in and said, "Holger is dead." Tears welled up in my eyes—and I was not the only one. Some people who had been critical of the RAF up to that point immediately began to assemble molotov cocktails and head to the Ku'damm.[2]*

The next day, November 10, the 2nd of June Movement carried out its own action in solidarity with the prisoners, attempting to kidnap Günter von Drenkmann, the president of the West Berlin Supreme Court. When the judge resisted, he was shot dead.

As the 2JM explained in its communiqué for this action:

> *When the prisoners' hunger strike began, we said: if the system's extermination strategy takes the life of another revolutionary, we will hold the system responsible and they will pay with their lives.[3]*

In the already tense context of Meins's death, this action raised the struggle to a whole new level. Electrifying the radical left, it also outraged all those who identified with the state.

Security was immediately stepped up for prosecutors and judges throughout the country.[4] The CDU mayor announced a demonstration against "Terror and Violence,"[5] while the federal government offered a 50,000 DM reward for the killers.[6] Meanwhile, Beate Sturm was trot-

---

1 *Frankfurter Allgemeine Zeitung*, "Beshuldigungen nach dem Tod von Holger Meins," November 10, 1974.

2 Stefan Wisniewski, *We were so terribly consistent... A Conversation About the History of the Red Army Faction* (Montreal: Kersplebedeb, 2008), 7-8.

3 in bewegung bleiben "Wer Gewalt sät,"
http://www.bewegung.in/mate_saehen.html.

4 *Frankfurter Allgemeine Zeitung*, "Verstärkte Sicherheitsmaßnahmen im gesamtem Bundesgebiet," November 12, 1974.

5 *Frankfurter Allgemeine Zeitung*, "Berliner CDU ruft zu einer Demonstration," November 16, 1974.

6 *Frankfurter Allgemeine Zeitung*, "Empörung nach den tödlichen Schüsssen von Berlin," November 12, 1974.

ted out to the media, whom she obligingly told about how Meins "had political ideas, but behind them lay the problems he had. He always wanted to be an authority figure. He was fascinated by Baader's authority, but also intimidated by it—that's why he always tagged along." All of this led one major newspaper to opine that the fallen guerilla "perhaps did not only die as a result of his own irrationality, but as a result of manipulation by his associates as well."[7]

After having pointedly ignored the strike in the period prior to November 9, the media now engaged in disinformation like this in an attempt to undercut the widespread sympathy that this death had garnered the prisoners. For instance, it was claimed that Meins was offered contact with other prisoners, but declined, as he "did not feel he was a criminal."[8] While this claim was ludicrous considering that the demand of both the previous hunger strikes had been precisely such integration, it can also be viewed as a clever attempt to exploit divisions within the left regarding the strategies of association versus equality with social prisoners.

Meanwhile, there was an explosion of actions and demonstrations in support of the prisoners. A bomb went off (harmlessly) outside the Hamburg residence of another judge, Geert Ziegler,[9] and there were eight firebombings in the university town of Göttingen.[10] Within days, protests had spread to cities across the Federal Republic. In Frankfurt and Mannheim, courthouse windows were smashed, while the KPD/ML handed out fliers stating what everyone felt: "Holger Meins Murdered."[11] In West Berlin, a November 11 Red Aid demonstration was banned by city authorities, which did not deter roughly one thousand people from taking to the streets, demanding that those responsible for Meins's death be punished and that all political prisoners be

---

7 Jürgen Busch, "Die letzte Waffe des Anarchisten," *Frankfurter Allgemeine Zeitung*, November 11, 1974.

8 *Frankfurter Allgemeine Zeitung*, "Die Vollzuganstalt Wittlich," Nov. 10, 1974.

9 Deutsche Presse Agentur, "Wieder Anschlag auf einen Richter," *Frankfurter Allgemeine Zeitung*, November 21, 1974.

10 *Time Magazine* [online], "Guerrillas on Trial," December 9, 1974.

11 United Press International, "Gunmen kill German judge," *Hagerstown Morning Herald*, November 11, 1974. The article in question refers simply to the "Communist Party." However, it was almost certainly not the conservative DKP, but the KPD/ML, which had earned itself the distinction of being the only K-group to organize support of the hunger strike.

freed, while fighting with stones and bottles against the cops' clubs and teargas. Thirty-two people were arrested.[1]

As giant pictures of an emaciated Meins were carried through the cities of the FRG, more than one observer was reminded of the victims of the concentration camps.[2] To some on the radical left, this was yet more evidence of the "fascist drift," of the real and not rhetorical "extermination" that more and more people saw the prisoners facing.

On November 13, there was an historic meeting at Frankfurt University, where several thousand people gathered in solidarity with the hunger strike. A leaflet supporting the RAF was distributed, signed by a number of *sponti* organizations—*Revolutionärer Kampf* (Revolutionary Struggle), the *Häuserrat* (Housing Coucil), and the *Sozialistische Hochschulinitiative* (Socialist Student Initiative)—as well as Red Aid and the Committees Against Torture, expressing unambiguous solidarity not only with the RAF, but also with the killing of Drenkmann:

> *The Red Army Faction was a political group committed to struggling against oppression and exploitation, guns in hand. At a time when millions of people in Vietnam, South America, and South Africa struggle against large landowners, factory owners, and their armies, they decided to call to account the ruling class in the FRG and to integrate themselves into this struggle against imperialism...*
>
> *A successor organization to the RAF understood the death of Holger Meins as a signal. They took control of their sorrow and their hatred and shot the President of the Berlin Supreme Court, Drenkmann. No threat of torture and imprisonment could deter them.[3]*

---

1 Ibid.; *Frankfurter Allgemeine Zeitung*, "Zweihundert Studenten der Freien Universität im Hungerstriek Demonstrationen und Krawalle in Berlin," November 13, 1974.

2 Salvator Scalzo, Steffi de Jong, and Joost van den Akker, *Terror, Myth and Victims: The Historical Interpretation of the Brigate Rosse and the Rote Armee Fraktion*, October 26, 2007, 18.

3 Jürgen Busch, "Viele Gruppen—viele führende Leute" *Frankfurter Allgemeine Zeitung*, November 14, 1974. One can see from this declaration how it was assumed by not only journalists, but also by the revolutionary left, that the RAF had been finished off by the arrests in 72. Even those "in the know" were unclear about the relationship between the 2nd of June Movement and the RAF itself.

Daniel Cohn-Bendit, who had yet to leave his street fighting days behind him and was at the time one of the leading members of the *sponti* organization Revolutionary Struggle, had this to say about the Drenkmann killing:

> *Whether it was tactically correct is open to discussion. In any event, we'll discuss it. We'll make our newspapers and magazines available to the Berlin comrades if they want to use them to explain the reasoning behind their actions. We will not distance ourselves from them.*

"Danny the Red" went on to argue that the shooting had not split the left, but that it put the ruling class on notice that even in Germany there were groups prepared to take up arms.[4] (Heinrich Böll, on the other hand, accused Cohn-Bendit of speaking irresponsibly, stating for himself that, "I hold the basic concept of the Red Army Faction to be nonsense.")[5]

While not many took as strong a position as those in Frankfurt, the rapid escalation also pushed liberal organizations to speak out. The PEN Centre held a forum regarding the use of torture by police and prison officials, and Amnesty International demanded an inquiry into the circumstances surrounding Meins's death, torture in the prisons and the conditions in which the RAF prisoners were being held.[6] At the same time, prominent writers, including *Gruppe 47* authors Ernst Bloch, Erich Fried, and Martin Walser, signed a statement protesting prison conditions.[7]

Five thousand people attended Meins's funeral in Mannheim a week later, including Rudi Dutschke. The former APO leader, standing over the grave as Meins's casket was lowered, famously gave the clenched fist salute, crying, "Holger, the fight goes on!"

The state, meanwhile, was busy trying to keep up with events. Almost immediately following Drenkmann's killing, the eleven *Länder* Interior Ministers were summoned to Bonn for an emergency meeting to discuss ways to contain the growing rebellion.[8] On November 13, Federal Minister of Justice Hans-Jochen Vogel (SPD) announced that charges

---

4 Ibid.

5 *Frankfurter Allgemeine Zeitung*, "Todesfälle eingeplant?" November 14, 1974.

6 Busch, "Die letzte Waffe des Anarchisten."

7 *Frankfurter Allgemeine Zeitung*, "Beshuldigungen nach dem Tod von Holger Meins."

8 Associated Press, "Bonn fears more violence," *Syracuse Post-Standard*, November 12, 1974.

were being brought against seventeen people, and thirty-five were being held in remand while investigations were conducted. Ominously, he also noted that seven lawyers would be investigated for supporting a criminal organization,[1] and in short order, charges were laid against attorneys Croissant, Schily, Groenewold, and Haag for statements they had made describing Meins's death as a premeditated murder.[2]

But the real crackdown had yet to come.

On November 26, the state moved into action, police and border guard units setting up checkpoints and carrying out predawn raids across the country.[3] Dozens of left-wing publishers, bookstores, law firms, and activists' homes were searched. Many victims were not even seriously suspected of any ties to the guerilla. Frankfurt police, for example, admitted that their targets "included general problem houses, where the occupants were organizing rent strikes or stirring up other sorts of trouble."[4] All in all, roughly forty people were arrested,[5] several eventually facing charges of supporting a "criminal organization" under §129.[6]

Despite their efforts, dubbed *Aktion Winterreise* ("Operation Winter Trip"), the police failed to apprehend a single guerilla fighter. Nevertheless, the raids gave the new Minister of the Interior, Werner Maihofer,[7] the opportunity to shock the public with claims that police had uncovered radio transmitters, explosives, chemicals, narcotics, weapons, and ammunition, not to mention plans for kidnappings and jailbreaks.[8]

The real targets of this crackdown were in fact the sympathizers and supporters: the goal of Winter Trip was to break the back of the growing

---

1 *Frankfurter Allgemeine Zeitung*, "Maihofer: 'Brutale Strategie' der Baader-Meinhof-Bande," November 14, 1974.

2 *European Stars and Stripes*, "German terrorist is hospitalized," November 14, 1974.

3 Associated Press, "West German police round up anarchist groups," *Greeley Tribune*, November 27, 1974.

4 Cobler, 141.

5 Associated Press, "West German police round up anarchist groups."

6 The frustrating fact of the matter is that no two sources seem to agree on either the exact number of arrests, the nature of all the charges, or the numbers actually prosecuted.

7 In a cabinet shuffle after Helmut Schmidt replaced Willy Brandt as Chancellor earlier that year, Werner Maihofer replaced Hans-Dietrich Genscher as Minister of the Interior. (Genscher became Minister of Foreign Affairs.)

8 "Meinhof," *European Stars and Stripes*, November 30, 1974.

movement while preparing public opinion for a new round of repressive legislation. As defense attorney Klaus Croissant wrote soon after:

> *In the Attorney General's own words, the action was aimed at what they call "the sympathizers": that means the prisoners' family members, the lawyers, the members of Red Aid, the writers who have publicly taken a stand against isolation torture, brainwashing and detention-extermination.*
>
> *By means of this police action, public opinion was prepared so as to allow special legislation to be passed in fifteen days, just before Christmas.*[9]

Most importantly in regards to the RAF's legal team, the defense attorneys were now accused of organizing an illegal communication network to transmit messages between prisoners, as well as between prisoners and "active commandos" on the outside. The state supplemented evidence from Winter Trip with a series of cell raids, the contents of letters and documents seized being manipulated in the media to present the image of a far-reaching "terrorist conspiracy."

Croissant was not alone in his belief that the real goal of this crackdown was to deprive the remaining four alleged ringleaders (Holger Meins now being dead) of any effective defense as their trial approached. This was a matter of some importance, for while the accused did not deny responsibility for the RAF's attacks, their lawyers had marshaled compelling evidence that the isolation conditions in which they were held had rendered them unfit to stand trial. As SPD deputy Fritz-Joachim Gnädinger would later tell the *Bundestag*:

> *It is clear to anyone in the know that without the changes in procedure already agreed the trial of the Baader-Meinhof terrorists in Stammheim would have got into even greater difficulties. It might even have had to be abandoned. Only a change in the law made last year... made the continuation of the trial possible. I therefore ask all the critics to consider for a moment what disastrous consequences for our citizens' sense of law and order would have resulted if the trial in Stammheim had had to be abandoned without a verdict.*[10]

---

9 Klaus Croissant, "Le procès de Stuttgart," in Croissant, 16-17.
10 Cobler, 206.

Indeed, these Winter Trip raids prepared the public for a barrage of new laws, "refinements" to existing legislation, and restrictions on defense attorneys. Through these, the state largely achieved a condition in which the upcoming trial in Stammheim prison could proceed with the prisoners ill- or undefended, often even without their personal participation.

There was one final, and controversial, effect that Winter Trip had on the radical left: soon afterwards several key activists left the Committees Against Torture.[1] While this could be interpreted as a retreat, the truth of the matter was more complex: many of those who had banded together to provide legal support now thought better of that strategy.

With some prompting from the prisoners, they had decided to go underground, to take up arms themselves, and to renew the RAF.

---

1 The Committees themselves disbanded over the next year-and-a-half.

Right from the start, I did not speak to the guards; afterwards, I had even less to desire to. I couldn't speak to them. I know all of the brilliant analyses— "their situation is also contradictory," etc.—and those analyses are correct. But they have their limit: these analyses don't take into account that their contradictions amount to being instruments of terror—at least in some situations. They disarm you. It is obvious: contradictions which are institutionalized, set up to weaken the institution's victim, to disarm her, to take away her hatred. And hatred of the pigs is the only form that life takes in jail.

You realize how important it is to not speak when you see how they celebrate every one of your words like a victory—in reality something to ease their conscience, their knowledge that they are torturers and assassins. You help them to carry the burden of their responsibility, you make yourself into their accomplice. You are supposed to show them that you consent to the torture you are being subjected to. They want a total victory—and in this way they will have it. And in this way, perhaps for the first time, you know and you understand exactly what the brilliant analyses do not.

a RAF prisoner's letter to her lawyer

"Témoignages de Prisonniers," in Croissant, 135-6.

Ulrike Meinhof

Ulrike Meinhof on the Dead Wing

From the period between June 16, 1972, and February 9, 1973:

The feeling, one's head explodes (the feeling, the top of the skull will
    simply split, burst open)—
the feeling, one's spinal column presses into one's brain
the feeling, one's brain gradually shrivels up like, like dried fruit, for
    example—
the feeling, one is constantly, imperceptibly, flooded, one is remote-
    controlled—
the feeling, one's associations are hacked away—
the feeling, one pisses the soul out of one's body, like when one cannot
    hold water—
the feeling, the cell moves. One wakes up, opens one's eyes: the cell
    moves; afternoon, if the sun shines in, it is suddenly still. One
    cannot get rid of the feeling of motion. One cannot tell whether one
    shivers from fever or from cold—
one cannot tell why one shivers—one freezes.
To speak at a normal volume requires an effort like that necessary to
    speak loudly, almost like that necessary to shout—
the feeling, one falls silent—
one can no longer identify the meaning of words, one can only guess—
the use of sibilants—s, ß, tz, z, sch is absolutely unbearable
guards, visits, the yard seems to be made of celluloid—
headaches—
flashes—
sentence construction, grammar, syntax—can no longer be controlled.
When writing: two lines—by the end of the second line, one cannot
    remember the beginning of the first—
The feeling, internal burnout—
the feeling, if one must say what's wrong, if one wants to let it out, it's
    like a rush of boiling water in the face, like, for example, boiling
    water that scalds forever, that disfigures—
Raging aggressiveness, for which no outlet exists. That's the worst.
    Keen awareness that one cannot survive; a complete breakdown of
    the capacity to deal with this;
Visits leave no trace. A half an hour later one can only mechanically
    reconstruct whether the visit was today or last week.

Compared to this, bathing once a week means: a momentary thaw, a
   moment of rest—to stop for a couple of hours—
The feeling, time and space reconnect—
the feeling of finding oneself in a house of mirrors, like in an
   amusement park—to stagger—
Afterwards: incredible euphoria, that one heard something—
beyond the acoustic day and night differentiation—
The feeling, time now flows, the brain expands again, the spinal
   column sinks down after some weeks.
The feeling, as if one's skin is thickening.

The second time (December 12, 1973, until January 3, 1974):

Ears buzzing. Waking up, one feels as if one has been beaten.
The feeling, one moves in slow motion.
The feeling, finding yourself in a vacuum, as if you're encased in lead.

Afterwards: Shock. As if an iron plate had fallen on your head.

Comparisons, concepts that invade one's mind:
(Psycho) shredding—
The feeling of traveling through space packed into a barrel so that the
   acceleration causes your skin to flatten—
Kafka's penal colony—The version with a bed of nails—
A non-stop rollercoaster ride.

The radio: it offers minimal stress reduction, like when one, for
   example, reduces one's speed from 240 to 190.

That everything exists in a cell that makes it in no obvious way
   different from any other cell—radio, furniture, plus newspapers,
   books—is actually by its implication rather aggravating: making
   any understanding between the prisoners and people who do not
   know what silent isolation is impossible.

Also disorienting to the prisoner. (That it is white like a hospital cell, for example, only increases the terror, but mainly it is the silence. If one lived there, one would paint the walls.) Clearly, one who is in there would rather be dead.

Peter Milberg, who was in one of these things in Frankfurt-Preungesheim ("an empty medical wing") subsequently accused his judge of "attempting" to kill him. This indicates that what is going on in these places is simply a type of "execution."
That is to say: A process of inner disintegration occurs—like something being dissolved in acid, which one attempts to slow down by concentrating on resistance, but nothing can stop it

The complete destruction of the personality is insidious. Nobody exists outside of oneself in these completely extraordinary circumstances.

As means/method, it can quite clearly be compared, for instance, to that which they use against the Tupamaros: to create in them a state of nervous agitation and agony, shortly before administering pentothal—which suddenly creates a feeling of relaxation and euphoria. One expects the prisoner to lose self-control.
To babble.

Second Hunger Strike

Our January/February hunger strike was unsuccessful. The BAW's promise to end our isolation was bullshit. We are again on hunger strike.

We demand:

> THAT POLITICAL PRISONERS BE PLACED WITH ALL OF THE OTHER PRISONERS!

and

> FREE ACCESS TO POLITICAL INFORMATION FOR ALL PRISONERS—INCLUDING FROM THE MEDIA OF THE APO.

No more, no less. Now.

Enough of the dirty dealing—time is on your side; we won't be duped.

Eat shit or die! That's the law of the system. There's profit to be made. Every child, every woman, every man must be threatened, intimidated, and terrified into submission. Every option in this system ends in evil.

Either be integrated into the existing capitalist system—

the assembly line chews up people and spits out profits—
the office chews up people and spits out bosses—
the schools chew up people and spit out a labor force—
the universities chew up people and spit out robots—

or face starvation, marginalization, suicide.

Whoever doesn't accept the available options, doesn't internalize them; whoever, after 10, 15, 20 years of being socialized to conform to the capitalist system of exploitation, still has dreams, still speaks up to protest, still has the strength to resist—can no longer keep up with the tempo of work—cracks—is sick—beats his boss instead of his wife and kids—would rather himself rob and beat, than let himself be subjected to the laws of thieves and murderers—(really people, Springer makes 100 million in profits every year!)—or develops ideas about workers' power—counterviolence—organizes revolutionary politics and resistance—will be criminalized or declared insane.

It's been like that since your great-grandfather's time, since the beginning of bourgeois society: workhouses, poorhouses, prisons, reform schools, judges, cops, doctors, psychiatrists, priests.

Whoever doesn't accept the hidden relationship of war—the bourgeoisie against the people—as a natural state of affairs, as the only possible reality—will be ground down in chains in the system's prison camps. Those who can be resocialized, that is to say, those who can be stripped of their will to resist and adapted to the capitalist production process, will be spit back out—those who can't will be destroyed.

Amongst them are the prisoners who serve as the system's alibi: the white-collar criminals and a few convicted SS pigs.

The more the people's revolt shakes the system's morale and its concept of property rights, the greater the existing crisis, the more the people's dreams for the future are replaced with desires for material rewards... the more important prisons will be for a system that has always candidly recognized the need to terrorize and destroy a section of the proletariat—Treblinka, Maidanek, and Sobibór are extreme examples—to break the resistance against the exploitation of a large majority of the people—prisons and extermination camps as the next-to-final and final measures against all forms of resistance—as effectively, systematically, and intentionally as ever.

The pigs have the prisons firmly in their grip. With every reform the prison system is made more extensive.

They have everything necessary: violence, isolation, transfers, corruption, privileges, partially open, two-thirds open, and fully open prisons, infiltrators, torture, clemency—and the closed structure: justice/police/ prisons/psychiatry/media (newspapers, TV, radio); for greater efficiency: disgusting conditions and toilet-size cells; against prison breakdown: murder/"suicide"; for less grotesque coercion: clubs/bread and water/ bondage/silent cells; for friendly brainwashing: psychiatry/police therapists/valium; for slicker and blander structural violence: removing the prisoners' remaining contact with reality (e.g., the exercise cages on the 5th and 7th floors of the new building at Frankfurt-Preungesheim)—in lieu of the terrible screams of broken prisoners.

The pigs' humanism in a word: hygiene.

The Social Democrats' reform program in a sentence: nip revolt in the bud through flexible measures.

The political prisoners, those who have developed a political understanding of their reality and have acted upon it and embraced it—who understand the inhumanity of their situation and of the system—who feel hate and outrage—who, in this all out war, resist the pigs, the prison authorities, the social ideologues, the dilettantes and jerk-offs, the green fascists[1]—who act in solidarity and ask for solidarity in return: they are kept in isolation, which is to say, they are socially exterminated.

On the other side, the entire justice system talks endless shit about human rights and the Constitution—and to the degree that those can't be manipulated, don't count out the shot to the back of the head.

Resocialization means manipulation and training. Prisoners are obliged to live with walls, cops, regulations, compulsion, threats, fear, hope, and restricted movement until they have internalized this shit and are only capable of behaving as if they are behind bars.

That is the training.

The prisoners' cooperation is obviously desirable—it shortens the process and makes it irreversible. There is one thing the prisoners completely forget about in this process, in fact, they must forget about it: self-esteem.

That is the manipulation.

The more liberal the approach taken to this shit—the more discreet—the more casual—the more pleasant—the more underhanded—the more slick—in short, the more psychological—the more effective and the more profound the destruction of the prisoner's personality.

The political prisoners are the deadly enemies of the psycho-cops—because the psycho-pigs don't want the prisoners to see through it all—through the therapeutic and helpful facade, past the little shits, the piglets, to the thugs—and the political prisoners do see through it all.

The central point in modern imprisonment is: a political and psychological orientation to prisons—our isolation now and concentration camps later—whether administered by green or white[2] terror troops—the end result: extermination camps—reform Treblinkas—reform Buchenwalds—the "final solution." That's what's happening.

We demand free access to political information for all prisoners, because consciousness is necessary for politicization. We're not demanding anything from them that is not already available in prison—standardized wages for work, education/training, protection for families, autonomy—because this is not some prisoner-organized reformist

1 A term for the police, whose uniforms were green.
2 Greens being police, whites are presumably psychiatrists.

claptrap that can be demobilized and politically neutralized with promises of reform, that is integrated into the prison pigs' dictatorship and made into a kind of *"Kraft durch Freude."*[3] What we want is political solidarity—not just ideas, but real solidarity.

Our hunger strike is simply our only option for collective resistance in isolation. Without power, the violence of the streets, without the mobilization of antifascist citizens to intercede for human rights and against torture, presuming they have not already sworn allegiance to the pigs—our hunger strike will not be enough to break through our powerlessness.

Our demands are as such an appeal to you, comrades.

The pigs only win if one of us eventually buys the farm. We are depending on you to support our demands and to force them through—now while you still can: before you yourselves become prisoners.

And comrades: simply talking about torture without struggling will serve neither our interests nor your own—meaning: you will only be helping the pigs to build up their defenses.

Your actions in January/February[4]—the demonstration in Karlsruhe, attacking Jessel, the go-ins at *Norddeutschen Rundfunk*[5] and at the offices of a few pigs from the justice system, a few examples of stone throwing—good. No teach-in, no go-in at the PEN Club,[6] nothing at the writers' union, nothing addressing the churches, which have since taken up the question of torture and human rights, no demonstrations in Hamburg, Munich, Berlin, Frankfurt, Heidelberg, no sign of militant actions—bad.

We are confronting the pigs with their own laws—we are rubbing their noses in the contradiction between what they say: defense of humanity—and what they do: extermination.

Every moment hangs between life and death—us or them—they for themselves or us for ourselves.

---

3 *Kraft durch Freude* (Strength through Happiness) was a Nazi organization within the *Arbeitsfront* (Work Front), the Nazi "company" union. *Kraft durch Freude* organized vacations and leisure activities for the working class.

4 The period during which the RAF was on its first hunger strike—what follows is a list of solidarity actions about which the editors of this volume sadly have no further details.

5 North German Radio, a chain of radio stations serving North-Western Germany and headquartered in Hamburg.

6 PEN is an international organization promoting literacy and defending literary works from censorship. It's president between 1971 and 1974 was Heinrich Böll.

On February 22, 1973, the federal Attorney General Pig Martin[1] stated that there was no solution to this contradiction, which could only end in death:

"Prison conditions will be adjusted to the specific physical and psychological needs of the various prisoners!"—that's for sure. Oxygen levels will be automatically adjusted—there's food three times a day—and there's the tactic of allowing visits from relatives when one has reached a point of ice-cold clarity, to throw sand in one's eyes. The final word from the highest level of the oppressive authority clique: extermination.

Everything is clear. The program is in motion.

Pressure the pigs from the outside, and we will pressure them from the inside.

Solidarity will determine the balance of power.

ALL POWER TO THE PEOPLE!

UNITED PEOPLE'S POWER AGAINST THE SYSTEM BASED ON
PROFIT/POWER/VIOLENCE
FAMILY/SCHOOL/FACTORY/OFFICE
PRISON/REFORM SCHOOL/THE PSYCHIATRIC ASYLUM

60 political prisoners on hunger strike!
May 8, 1973

---

1 Ludwig Martin, Attorney General from April 7, 1963, until April 30, 1974.

Provisional Program of Struggle for the Political Rights of Imprisoned Workers

WHOSE FAULT IS IT
IF OPPRESSION CONTINUES?
OURS!

WHOSE FAULT IS IT
IF OPPRESSION IS NOT SMASHED?
OURS AS WELL![2]

Prisons, the military, and the police are the basic tools of the imperialist state. They are the basic tools of the state with which the bourgeoisie asserts, protects, and achieves its ruling-class power—and they always have been. Without its monopoly of violence, its armed structures—the cops, the prisons, the army—the ruling class is nothing. Its historical role was played out long ago. We represent the step that will bring down this house of cards and the facade that is holding the system together. They can no longer make us—we socialists, communists, workers chained to the assembly line, offices, schools, universities—believe that the time is not ripe for the struggle until victory, the struggle to free the proletariat from exploitation, oppression, alienation, and from material and psychological deprivation—the struggle until victory and liberation from imperialism and capitalism.

The problem in the metropole is that, although the system is politically and economically ripe for abolition, the revolutionary strength of the people remains weak. There is more resignation, lethargy, depression, agony, more illness and suicide, more people who are ready to lie down and die—because one can no longer live with this system—than there are people who are ready to stand up and fight. Although imperialism is only a paper tiger, many only see that at this moment it remains a man-eating monster, and they say, "We'll never get what we want." However, that is incorrect—it is nondialectical thinking. The darker the night that we believe we have sunk into, the closer the morning is.

---

2 This is a quote of Bertolt Brecht, the communist playright.

Nowhere is it clearer than in prison, in the very way it operates, that the pig system and its very structure—forced labor, pressure to perform, alienation—is at an end. In 1865, Marx wrote,

> The blunt force of the economic conditions assures the rule of capitalism over the working class. As well as economic means, unlimited violence will admittedly always be applied, but only exceptionally. For the normal unfolding of events, the workers need only remain subject to the "the natural laws of production."

Today, the system can no longer rely on the "blunt force of these conditions." And in prison, they can no longer simply rely on "unlimited violence." To enforce the loyalty of the people, to maintain it, to discourage them from struggling against the system, the pigs coerce them with prison, tricks, and manipulation. With sales pitches and psychological warfare, they make the prisoners go along with it: they win their collaboration, their cooperation in their own destruction through psychiatry, through brainwashing, which results in the destruction of their consciousness. They do this because they can no longer see any other way to get the unrest in the prisons back under control.

The system can no longer survive without its weapons, its riot squads, its bunkers and alarms, its punishments—without its material tools. The militarization of the state and the psychological aspects of its functioning are two aspects of the same pervasive reality. The cops use the media to develop their psychological warfare on the outside. This is accompanied on the inside by the development of managerial methods based on new, widespread security measures; the construction of dead wings, grates on the cell windows, isolation units and special wings in every prison, guards in watchtowers armed with semiautomatic handguns, close circuit cameras and monitors.

The costs that imperialism obliges its ruling class to bear: a military alliance that encompasses the world, the extension of police power in each individual state, the psychological programs, the bullshit reforms in the prisons, the attempts to extend strategic aspects of the deterrent and destructive capacity of its prisons, the fortified villages in Third World countries where anti-imperialist wars of liberation are being waged. These costs express the need to develop the pig system's strength. All of these measures also show their fear, their hollowness, their corruption, their stagnation, the very fact that they have nothing more to offer—beyond violence, fascism, oppression, manipulation—that they have no future besides barbarism. They have nothing left to offer except destruction, fragmentation, pathology, counterinsurgency—and for billions of people in the countries of the Third World: hunger, hardship, illness, illiteracy, and death.

WHAT ARE WE WAITING FOR?

Numerically and intellectually, the people are superior to the fascists. What cripples us is the fact that all the resistance in the prisons that has occurred so far has occurred in isolation. There was no communication, no plan, no cooperation, and those on the outside who were prepared to support us in our struggle against the imperialist structures were also muddling along with no idea of how to proceed.

Many also failed to understand the political prisoners' struggle against isolation, that is to say, the struggle of those prisoners taken in the armed struggle against the imperialist state—the corporations, the cops, the military, the justice system, the prison system—and the prisoners who have begun to struggle collectively against prison conditions. Isolation is the weapon the system uses to finish off the so-called disruptive elements—i.e., the rebels—to physically and psychologically destroy them, thereby removing the "political" from the flow of things—to nip every expression of autonomous organization in the bud, to liquidate from the outset the struggle for prisoners' collective power and for their basic political and human rights, to use isolation against spokesmen, cadre, and those who have something organizational and political to offer and who have already decided to use all of their power in the service of the people's liberation, the anti-imperialist struggle, and the initiation of a revolutionary prisoners' movement.

The struggle of the political prisoners being held in isolation—isolation from the outside and from others on the inside—is about the revolutionary prisoners' movement achieving the conditions necessary for survival. As long as the pigs can isolate every combatant, everyone who begins to organize resistance, who opens his yap—and not only them, but also all those who work for prisoners' autonomous organization—it will be difficult to develop continuity in the work for autonomous organization and collective counterpower in the prisons.

If the political prisoners take advantage of the publicity around their trials, that only means they are using the market value that exists in many comrades' bewildered minds as a weapon. In reality, you won't find us in the media that spews out headlines against us; instead, you'll find us downstairs in the prison, in the cell, in the special wings, in the bunkers, in isolation. And we're not struggling for privileges, but for the IMPROVEMENT OF THE CONDITIONS OF STRUGGLE FOR A REVOLUTIONARY PRISONERS' MOVEMENT WITHIN THE PRISONS! Anything else amounts to standing things on their head, ass backwards, seeing things from the outside through the eyes of the pig media, and thereby overlooking the simple, real, undeniable facts. To again explain what we're struggling for, what we're struggling against, and why we struggle:

We are struggling for PRISONER AUTONOMY, for the elementary rights of imprisoned workers, and for the strengthening of prisoners' collective power. In this sense, the action program is more than the material contents of a prison survival program; it is also an instrument—one that allows everyone to understand what's going on, because the imperialist state will not be able to fulfill these simple demands, which according to their own dishonest propaganda they obviously must fulfill. In spite of the immense sums of tax money, which they extract from the people to funnel into their oppressive apparatus, our own need to struggle to get these points put on the agenda means nothing other than the struggle for social revolution, through which our needs will be placed on the agenda. And if the pigs give in on one or another point—all the better. Our hunger for freedom will only grow as a result. What we're struggling against is the imperialist system's prison system, against the psychiatric and psychological programs, against the way we are treated, against the brainwashing techniques which are sold as reform, against the complete disenfranchisement of prisoners in the metropole's prison camps, against all of the system's efforts to play prisoners off against each other, using increased repression or perks to drive a wedge between the different initiatives undertaken by imprisoned workers.

We are also struggling against the reformist organizations that attempt to skim the cream on the outside, while they try to establish themselves on the inside by hindering our capacity to struggle. They do this through paternalism, tactical maneuvers, splits, factional bickering, dogmatism, and pacifism—taking control of everyone who is struggling in the prisons, because they are colonialist pigs who hope to colonize every step towards a revolutionary prisoners' movement—for their own goals that have nothing to do with us. Through their appeals to the imperialist media and through their demands that one character mask replace another as Minster of Justice, these reformists make the class state socially acceptable, trustworthy, and once again credible in the eyes of the people—and they do this at a point in time when every prisoner can now see that nothing is to be expected from this class, that we can only achieve what we want by our own means—in the struggle against the ruling class and class justice. These reformists propagate and practice class conciliation and collaboration with the imperialist state at a time when the imperialist state's main problem is that its legitimacy is crumbling and its authority—its apparent role as a peacekeeping force between the classes, although it has always been an instrument of the ruling class against the people—is in tatters. It can only be maintained through the massive use of psychological warfare against the people. Instead of escalating the class struggle, instead of supporting the prison struggle against the structural apparatus and the justice system, instead of supporting the collective power of autonomously organized prisoners, they cobble together arguments for a more efficient reorganization of the repressive apparatus.

The most important point overall—the abolition of prisons—can't be a demand. We're the only ones who can achieve that. Only the revolution—e.g., the destruction of the capitalist state apparatus—can bring about the abolition of prisons. In other words, the liberation of imprisoned workers can only be won through the liberation of all workers. Whoever advances such a demand either hasn't thought it through or else only wants to pull one over on us, giving the struggle a realistic scope by discrediting unrealistic demands.

We call on all prisoners to organize around this program of action both openly and conspiratorially. All those who have nothing left to lose but their chains—take up, organize, and lead the struggle in the prisons.

We are struggling for:

1. freedom for prisoners to organize themselves.
2. wages established in law, the right to training and work, a workers' association and the right to strike.
3. retirement benefits and health insurance.
4. health care provided in hospitals by doctors who are not prison employees; a free choice of doctors.
5. self-government with the right to fulfill any function.
6. unlimited right to visitors—without observation.
7. freedom to assemble unobserved.
8. abolition of the use of force, all special treatment, and isolation.
9. abolition of youth detention.

10. mixed institutions.
11. abolition of house arrest.
12. abolition of mail censorship.
13. abolition of forced medication.
14. free access to political information from all national and foreign publications and media available outside of prison.

FOR A REVOLUTIONARY PRISONERS' MOVEMENT!
VICTORY TO THE PEOPLE'S WAR!

The RAF Prisoners
September 1974

Third Hunger Strike

IF SOMEONE UNDERSTANDS THEIR SITUATION— HOW CAN THEY BE STOPPED?

This is our third hunger strike against special conditions and the extermination strategy being used against political prisoners in the Federal Republic and West Berlin; against the counterinsurgency program of imperialism's machinery of destruction, the BAW, the BKA's Bonn Security Group/State Security Division for the annihilation of revolutionary prisoners and prisoners who have begun to organize and struggle in the prisons.

We can only be kept down if we stop thinking and struggling. People who refuse to stop struggling cannot be kept down—they win or they die, rather than losing and dying.

Resistance against the extermination strategy, the special conditions and the counterinsurgency program means resistance against:

- dehumanization through years of social isolation;
- the torturous re-education program and the pressure to cooperate in the brainwashing units—Ronald Augustin has been held in the Hannover prison dead wing since early May;
- the new acoustically sealed cells in Berlin-Tegel, Berlin-Lehrter Strasse, Bruchsal, Essen, Cologne, and Straubing, based on the model of the Hamburg DFG Research Project,[1] which are constantly watched by cameras and are always overheated, and where one is under constant acoustic and video surveillance;
- delays during every visit, total isolation, eliminating even the possibility of shouting to other prisoners in the Berlin-Moabit dungeon, the Essen dungeon, the Straubing dungeon, the Preungesheim dungeon, the Fuhlsbüttel dungeon, and the Mannheim dungeon, or being under video observation in the soundless bell jar at Hamburg remand centre—where one is kept in restraints for days on end;
- attempted murder by withholding water during hunger strikes in Schwalmstadt, Munich, Hamburg, and Cologne;

---

1 The *Deutsche Forschungsgesellschaft*, the FRG's science funding agency, began supporting experiments in sensory deprivation in federal institutions in 1967.

- concentration units for political prisoners in Lübeck, Stuttgart, and Berlin;
- being shackled during yard time in Hamburg and Lübeck;
- being placed in special cells directly beside the main prison entrance in Cologne-Ossendorf for the past two years—there is never silence; the same is the case in Berlin-Moabit;
- psychiatric research and the threat and use of forced drugging in order to carry out further investigations;
- cells with plexiglass dividers for meetings with lawyers in Hannover, Stuttgart, and Straubing, making any political discussion impossible;
- periodic confiscation of defense materials—records and mail— by the Bonn Security Group/State Security Division;
- the Bonn Security Group's cell raids tied to media hate campaigns against the lawyers representing political prisoners;
- criminalizing lawyers who represent political prisoners;
- the withholding and manipulation of files by the BKA;
- the prompt relaxation of isolation conditions only once the prisoner is in the clutches of the police and is being groomed as an infiltrator or a crown witness; in Cologne-Ossendorf, Jan Raspe has refused yard time, because he is only permitted yard time with an ever-changing selection of prisoners, which is disorienting and prevents communication. All these special rules continue to be applied so as to allow the police (Security Group) to structure and control the prisoners' contacts.
- the terrorizing of relatives with house searches, spies, verbal abuse and surveillance before and after visits, to pressure them into behaving with the prisoners in a way that serves the interests of the police.

In isolation, the hunger strike is our only possible form of collective resistance to imperialism's counterstrategy. Revolutionary prisoners and prisoners who have begun to organize themselves to fight are to be psychologically and physically, that is to say politically, destroyed. Disarmed, imprisoned, isolated, this is our only option for asserting our psychological and spiritual strength, our identity as people, so that the stones the ruling class has thrown at us may land on their own feet.

To struggle is to turn weakness into strength.

Isolation is the favored weapon for executing prisoners who decide not to let themselves be destroyed by prison, who struggle against the human experiments, the brainwashing, the imperialist extermination program. Most of all, they hope to use prison isolation to liquidate political awareness and resistance. As to the other prisoners, they still don't understand how completely oppressed they are, although they are just as poor and downtrodden as we and have nothing to lose but their chains.

We encourage all prisoners being held in isolation to join us in the struggle against isolation.

The abolition of isolation is the condition that we must all struggle for if prisoners' self-organization, revolutionary politics, and prison liberation struggles are to have any real possibility of expressing proletarian counterviolence—in the context of the class struggle here, in the context of the liberation struggles of the peoples of the Third and Fourth Worlds, in the context of proletarian internationalism and a united anti-imperialist liberation front in the prisons and in the stockades developed for political prisoners in those parts of the world controlled by imperialism.

ALL POWER TO THE PEOPLE THROUGH VIOLENT CONQUEST!

FREEDOM THROUGH ARMED ANTI-IMPERIALIST STRUGGLE!

The RAF Prisoners
September 13, 1974

The Expulsion of Horst Mahler

At this point, we have nothing more to say about Horst Mahler's attempt to buy his freedom with denunciations of the RAF (Baader liberation trial). The problem with Horst Mahler has always been that he is a filthy, bourgeois chauvinist, who has transferred the ruling-class arrogance which he picked up as a lawyer within the imperialist system—an arrogance that he made his own—to the proletarian revolutionary movement, and this well before the RAF. Already, in connection with the militant student movement in Berlin in 1967/68, he could only understand the political solidarity he received as a left-wing lawyer in terms of it being a cult of personality devoted to him.

He imagined that he could continue his previous bourgeois life in the guerilla—issuing orders, manipulating the weaknesses of others, and demanding privileges, much as the oppressor deals with the oppressed in a lawyer's chambers. So—because he hadn't learned anything and didn't want to—he remained incapable of collective, protracted, patient work. He was not prepared to crawl out of the careerist slime. He never really understood the RAF's collective learning, working, and discussion process: the intensity of work in a fighting group, the unity of physical and intellectual labor, the abolition of the separation between private and professional life, the determination to act, to struggle—in a word, the way in which the guerilla works. For him, all that signified the loss of his privileges, which he found—because of his smug self-image; the caricature of the professional bourgeois politician—unacceptable.

Mahler never participated in the RAF's practice, in its concrete politics, in its tactical decisions, in its structure—nor did he participate in much else either. With his arrogant politics, he simply didn't get it. In 1970, he was already little more than a bourgeois wreck, tolerated—because of his illegal status—by the RAF's nascent politico-military organization. Yet he remained a liability to our practice, in part because of his vanity, his ignorance, his class-specific subjectivity, and his carelessness.

He himself made his expulsion from the RAF, which had been a long time coming, inevitable. He did this with his authoritarian and possessive claims to a leadership position over the other RAF prisoners, with his elitist inability to understand criticism and self-criticism as anything but power tactics, and with his ongoing, revisionist, empty, private writings. With these writings he attempted to go behind the backs of the RAF and the RAF prisoners, and sought to acquire some prestige for himself in the eyes of the left, prestige that does not reflect his true role in the RAF. His writings read like a legal argument with a confused structure, and do not reflect the politics, action, practice, experience, or tactical concepts of the RAF.

The RAF only found out about Mahler's publication when it turned up on the market. He knew he could not speak for the RAF. The guerilla expresses its theory, its strategy, and its internationalism through its actions. Nothing but theoretical discussions that do not address concrete action will be marketed under the conditions enforced by imperialism. Given the existence of the political police, the *Verfassungsschutz* and the intelligence services, the theory and practice of armed struggle cannot be discussed in public. That would only provide the government's counterinsurgency units with grist for the mill. And Mahler doesn't deal with this issue—with armed struggle—except in the form of a parlor debate, as he himself has written often enough.

Mahler will continue to be unable to offer any information about the RAF that is anything other than an example of his infantilism, his ambition, and his careerism. And he will doubtless exploit his association with the RAF's politics in his relationship with Red Aid e.v. and the *Roter Fels*[1] group, an e.v. branch in Tegel.

Our understanding of the RAF prisoners' relationship with these groups—KPD/AO, Red Aid e.v.—will remain unchanged as long as they restrict themselves to questions of solidarity. (Because their solidarity does not lie with the offensive politico-military strategy, but rather— and even this only rhetorically—with the fundamentally defensive position of the RAF prisoners: the struggle against extermination in prison.) For instance, the KPD/AO denounced the 1970 liberation of Baader as CIA-orchestrated and practically delivered us up during the manhunt of 1972. This situation will not change until this party understands that the urban guerilla constitutes a stage in the protracted people's war.

The justice system and the media have associated Mahler with the RAF, and Mahler is trying to use this association with the urban guerilla, and with the actions and practice of the RAF, and the example it sets for these groups, in an effort to obstruct and prevent his expulsion. In a fit of pique, this consistent revisionist and opportunist is simply doing this to get back at us.

---

1 Red Rock.

The fact of the matter is that, with his recent publication, he is trying to use his experiences with the RAF in order to aid state security's psychological warfare campaign within the legal left—just like Ruhland, Sturm, and Homann—and he is doing this with material provided by the cops—because he himself knows nothing about the RAF and its discussions. He quotes from BKA reports about the raids of RAF prisoners' cells, and in so doing he associates himself with the false allegations and lies found in the Bonn Security Group's reports. What he provides as quotes from the RAF are almost all quotes from himself. Like any filthy criminologist, he plays around with notes that offer no information about the RAF's politics—but which denounce, personalize, and falsify the RAF's politics, treating them as a psychological issue.

In his opening statement at the Baader liberation trial, he put his new persona on public display. He could not have come up with a more obvious method of using this trial to side with the justice system and to distance himself from armed politics, the guerilla in the metropole, and the RAF, given that state security and the BAW do not want this trial to focus on the evidence, but on destroying the RAF politically, destroying the urban guerilla concept in the Federal Republic. That is to say, they want this trial to focus on psychological warfare.

He, who has found a way to get out of isolation, says that there is no extermination imprisonment, and this at a time when more than 40 political prisoners in West Germany and West Berlin have begun a hunger strike, with which we are determined to smash the imperialist states' extermination strategy: the use of isolation against the prisoners of the RAF and other anti-imperialist social revolutionary groups, as well as against all those prisoners who have begun to organize resistance and have therefore been placed in isolation. Because he doesn't want to struggle, because he is afraid of this hunger strike, he attempts to liquidate it, making a political program out of his miserable egotism and attempting to stir up the legal left against the RAF, all to serve his own interests. And he does this at a time when the RAF's prison struggle—against the extermination of political prisoners, for the right of prisoners to organize and to launch a revolutionary prisoners' movement—requires solidarity from the legal movement. Not paternalism and not just words on paper, but solidarity through which they themselves might develop a genuine anti-imperialist practice.

Horst Mahler has consciously chosen to collaborate with the BKA and the Berlin justice system, and to act as a puppet for the political police in Wiesbaden and Bonn. He remains what he has always been:

a cynic, a chauvinist, and a mandarin, now acting openly on behalf of state security—a politically inconsequential and essentially ridiculous figure.

Monika Berberich
for the RAF Prisoners
September 27, 1974

Holger Meins's Report on Force-Feeding

Since September 30 (12 days) force-feeding has been occurring here daily. It takes place in the sickbay (in a one-storey building in B wing—a sort of annex—I am celled in A wing, in the middle of the first floor). I am escorted by 5-6 of the greens.[1]

During the first week, I attempted different forms of *active resistance* every day. Selective and timely.

5-6 greens, 2-3 medics, 1 doctor. The greens grab, push, and drag me to an operating chair. Really it's an operating table with all the bells and whistles: it can be swiveled in any direction, etc., and can be folded into an armchair with a headrest and foot- and armrests.

Strapped down: two pairs of handcuffs and foot shackles, a 30 cm wide strap around the waist, two leather straps with 4 belts from the elbow to the wrist on the left arm, on the right arm another two at the wrist and elbow, and one across the chest. Behind me a green or a medic who holds my head firmly against the headrest with both hands on my forehead. (In the case of active resistance at head level, two others, one on the left, one on the right, hold on to my hair, my beard, and my neck. In this way, my entire body is immobilized, and if it's necessary another holds my knees or shoulders. The only possible motion is muscular movement "inside" the body. This week they tied the belts and straps very tightly, so that blood accumulated in my hands, which turned bluish, etc.).

The mouth: On the right the doctor on a stool with a small crowbar about 20 cm long, one end a curved needle, the other a curved spatula wrapped with adhesive tape. This goes between the lips, which are pulled apart with fingers at the same time, and then between the teeth (that's pretty easy in my case, given that I'm missing three teeth) forcing them apart, either by applying pressure or by pushing the spatula against the gums.

(Biting the teeth together is still relatively difficult—a strong point of resistance—and leads to minor injury to the teeth or gums. Against the strength of the jaw they use three different grips: forcing them apart with fingers under the lips while simultaneously pulling on the beard both above and below the mouth; applying heavy pressure below the ears and the jaw joint, which really hurts; sharply pressing a stiffened

---

1 German police wear green uniforms.

finger against the muscles that run forward from under the ears, while using a stiffened finger to push the carotid artery, the windpipe, and the vagus nerve against the muscle and kneading and squeezing them against each other, which, in fact, was not the most painful method, but took more than a day to heal.)

When the jaws are pulled far enough apart, the medic on the left sticks—shoves—the clamp between the teeth. It is a shear tongue-like rubber-coated object, 2 fingers thick with a wingnut at its joint, with which the jaws are pried open. The tongue is pulled forward and forced down with forceps, or the doctor uses a finger with a steel sheath on the fingertip.

Force-feeing: A red stomach pipe (not a tube) is used, about the thickness of a middle finger (in my case between the joints). It is greased, but doesn't manage to go down without causing me to gag, because it is only between 1 and 3 mm narrower than the digestive tract (this can only be avoided if one makes a swallowing motion and remains completely still). The slightest irritation when the pipe is introduced causes gagging and nausea and the cramping of the chest and stomach muscles, setting off a chain reaction of extremely intense convulsions throughout the body, causing one to buck against the pipe. The more extreme and the longer this lasts, the worse it is. A single gag or vomiting reflex is accompanied by waves of cramps. They only abate or decrease if one is very focused and remains very still, forcing oneself to breathe deeply and normally. Under the circumstances, resistance makes this completely impossible. It is only possible through quiet concentration and self-control, which in these conditions of direct compulsion always means self-repression and self-discipline. This is the reason for the restraints used in this form of force-feeding, because the body "naturally" reacts.

When the pipe is in the stomach, a wider funnel is attached to it and a normal cup (about a quarter-litre capacity) is used to gradually force down small amounts of the sludge. It is some type of meat slop, murky, slimy, and fatty—in any event, it contains vitamins, glucose, eggs, and finely chopped stuff—with a thick, brownish, greasy residue (about 1 or 2 tablespoons). The intake lasts about 1½ to 3 minutes. A full cup is always poured in, even when the gagging is extreme, causing the entire body to cramp for at least 5 to 6 minutes each time without any relief. The funnelling is only possible with "relative calm." During heavy gagging and/or cramping, the slop pours out of the funnel at the top. When the pipe bucks up in the throat—and in the digestive tract as a result—it can lead to choking fits, which have occurred twice so far (but didn't pose a serious health risk). The gagging, the cramping, and the swallowing are of course painful, particularly to the larynx, which is pressed against the pipe with every swallow and gag. The iron lever has led to small injuries to the gums, the inside of the lip looks as if it has been bitten in one place and has a whitish inflammation as a result of the clamp, and the back of the throat is "irritated." The larynx constantly hurts a little bit, and I have a sore throat.

It is about 3 to 5 minutes before the pipe is taken back out, all depending. (With extreme resistance, I can make it last as long as 20 to 30 minutes, but I am not strong enough to prevent the force-feeding altogether.)

Afterwards, I remain strapped in with my head pressed down for at least 10 minutes (sometimes it is longer), "to calm me down."

The doctor has up to this point refused to give his name (his name is Freitag). A green (he's named Vollmann) generally holds my head

and presses it with all his strength against the leather headrest (until his hands start to tremble from the effort)—yeah, a real sadist—this takes place inside a 190 cm cubicle. Another one—he's named Gomes or Komes—tightens the straps so much that they cut into

my ankles and leave marks on my wrists that are still visible over an hour later. As I have, from the first day, offered occasional and partial resistance, I have a few bruises on my legs, arms, etc. The whole thing is always conducted rigorously so as to be over in 10 minutes.

As of this week (since Tuesday, October 8) I have offered almost no further active resistance, only passive resistance—no voluntary movement.

In this way it is more bearable. I can control myself so there is no gagging, etc., like today, for example, but that depends on me, not on the style of force-feeding. The pipe is, REGARDLESS OF CIRCUMSTANCES, TORTURE.

As they are now generally conducting force-feeding with a tube through the nose, I favor a public statement against the doctor (P. should do this, as he has already prepared a motion for a ban on the pipe, which can serve as an ultimatum: "If you don't ... by ... then ..." It should also definitely be raised at the press conference, but only briefly, and only against the doctor, nothing against the greens.)

Shit: Today, after the force-feeding I had a brief short circuit, nothing extreme, only 5 minutes, total flickering, but fully conscious, only the eyes and ears.

Holger Meins
October 11, 1974

Holger Meins's Last Letter

In a July 2008 interview with the Berlin left-wing daily, taz, Manfred Grashof acknowledged that he was the RAF prisoner addressed in this letter. In the interview, he explained that he had decided to break off the hunger strike because he felt that it was the result of a decision taken by a small number of prisoners who had not adequately discussed it with the others. (M. & S.)

You stupid idiot.

Start again immediately and carry on—if you haven't already done so. That and nothing else. Today is the day for it.

It must be clear what it means for the pigs and against us—in the fray. If you were fully conscious when you gobbled that up—as a step away from this—then bon appetit. Then this is the end.

If it was a flip-out, a breakdown, disorientation—enough said.

Did you make a mistake—correct it.

Have you spun out—come back.

Although. That is naturally of a somewhat different order—because it's honest. That must be clear to you—by now. If so, you must *clearly* say so, and immediately. "Simply couldn't think," etc. says nothing about you.

There is no guilt in the guerilla and no punishment in the collective. Only decisions and consequences, and I say it yet *again*.

The only thing that matters is the struggle—now, today, tomorrow; whether you eat or not, what matters is that you make a leap forward. Do better. Learn from your experience. That is what must be done. All the rest is shit. THE STRUGGLE CONTINUES. Each new fight, each action, each battle brings new and unprecedented experiences, and that is how the struggle develops. That is the only way it develops. The subjective side of the dialectic of revolution and counterrevolution: what makes the difference is knowing how to learn.

Through the struggle, for the struggle. As a result of the victories, but even more as a result of the errors, the reversals, the defeats.

That is one of the laws of Marxism.

Struggle, defeat, struggle anew, again defeat, again take up the struggle, and so on until the final victory. That is the logic of the people. So said the Old One.[1]

In any event, matter. The human being is nothing but matter, like everything else. The human being in his totality. The body and consciousness are "material," and that which makes the human what he is, his freedom—is consciousness dominating matter—THE SELF and external nature, and, above all: being oneself. One of the pages of Engels: completely clear. The guerilla materializes in struggle—in revolutionary action, that is to say: without end—precisely: the struggle until death, and, of course: the collective.

It isn't a question of matter, but of politics. Of PRAXIS. As you said: before as after, it's all the same. Today, tomorrow, and so forth. Yesterday is past. A criterion doubtless, but above all a FACT. What is—now—depends primarily on you. The hunger strike is far from over.

And the struggle never ends.

But

There is obviously only one point: if you know that with each of the PIG'S VICTORIES the concrete objective of killing gets more concrete—and that you no longer want to take part, thereby protecting yourself—then that is a victory for the PIGS, meaning you hand us over to them, and it is you who is the pig that divides and encircles us for your personal survival, so shut your mouth, "As has been said: praxis. Long live the RAF. Death to the pig system."

Because—if you don't want to continue the hunger strike with us—it would be better to be more honorable (if indeed you still know what that means: honor): "In short, I am alive. Down with the RAF. Victory to the pig system."

> Either a human or pig
> Either to survive at any price or
> to struggle until death
> Either part of the problem or part of the solution
> Between the two there is nothing

---

1 A reference to Mao.

Victory or death—the people everywhere say that and that is the language of the guerilla—even given our tiny size here. Live or die, it is all the same:

"The people (meaning: us), who refuse to stop struggling—either they win or they die, instead of losing and dying."

It's very sad to have to write you again about this sort of thing. Of course, I don't know either what it is like when a person dies or when they kill you. How would I know? In a moment of truth, the other morning, for the first time it crossed my mind: this is it (obviously I still don't know)—and afterwards (facing the gun aimed between the eyes), it's all the same, that's it. In any case, on the right side.

You too must also know something about this. Whatever. No matter what, we all die. It's only a question of how, and of how you lived, and one thing is completely clear: STRUGGLING AGAINST THE PIGS as A PERSON STRUGGLING FOR THE LIBERATION OF THE PEOPLE. As a revolutionary in struggle—with an absolute love for life: with contempt for death. That means for me: serve the people—RAF.

October 31, 1974

It's obviously bullshit, just like Berlin (previously, it sounded a lot better—a leap forward)—because I believed it to be her strategy as well: let her do it, it will soon come to a crisis, a few notable acts of swinishness in that regard: Stuttgart, Berlin starved out, Hamburg fattened up, testing and timely attack, otherwise the calculated fostering of contradictions—"to crack them."

So far.

Uh huh, it's up to us. Anyway it is also OUR STRUGGLE. The key is the unwavering struggle of each guerilla individually and within the ranks of the collective. Victory or death—really.

Then

Everything is very easy—to say. Because it's the TRUTH: whatever one has not experienced/endured/overcome—one cannot know—if it has not been EXPERIENCED/ENDURED/OVERCOME—only thought, said, known. Simply the difference between consciousness and being. That is a FACT. One should not forget it.

First and foremost, we are victorious when we win.

To make it crystal clear: I did not give a report about force-feeding to *Informationsdienst*. Not a word from me in that direction. For the ad. SO WHO? I want to know now.

Regarding the claim about the ban on the tube and this appointment of a certified doctor for force-feeding that I've heard about in the same way as you in Hamburg: previously, I had no idea. It suddenly cropped up.

That is exactly the problem with the lawyers: that they have no idea what we want or how to get it, WE and the STRUGGLE, for example, they ABOVE ALL don't understand the hunger strike, their advocacy has a limited horizon: office/court, etc.

And on the other hand, I mainly think that they block it out. So I really don't see the point, and that is the problem if one doesn't really pay attention.

The tube issue is, of course, complete bullshit. It is really unnecessary. So it changes nothing.

Beyond that, the hunger strike: here things are really moving quickly—faster than I can write. Now I'm 46.8. 140-150 g daily (I've been weighing myself since the 28th—naturally, only when only I will know the outcome). I ingest 400 calories daily. The doctor-pig claims 1200: three tablespoons per 400—that is the case: three tablespoons = 400 (I have seen a copy of the original with my own eyes).

But otherwise: he feels certain—one must distinguish—SW—will be relocated, he knows he's not part of it.

Holger Meins
November 1, 1974

Interview with Spiegel Magazine

This interview with Baader, Ensslin, Meinhof, and Raspe was published in the January 20, 1975, edition of the liberal news magazine Spiegel, under the title "Wir waren in den Durststreik treten" (We are escalating to a thirst strike). The fact that attorney Klaus Croissant worked as an intermediary between Spiegel and the prisoners to facilitate this interview would be cited as a reason to bar him from representing Andreas Baader at the Stammheim trial later that year—see page 346. (M. & S.)

Spiegel: Has the RAF adopted a new tactic? Have the campaigns that you prepared and led from within the prisons attracted the same interest amongst the people as the bombs and grenades you used in 1972?

RAF: It is not a matter of empty talk about tactics. We are prisoners, and we are currently struggling with the only weapon we have left in prison and in isolation: the collective hunger strike. We are doing this in order to break through the process of extermination in which we find ourselves—long years of social isolation. It is a life and death struggle: if we don't succeed with this hunger strike we will either die or be psychologically and physically destroyed by brainwashing, isolation, and special treatment.

Spiegel: Is it really a matter of "isolation torture" or even "extermination through prison conditions"? You read a lot of newspapers; if you like you can listen to the radio or watch television. For example, at one point Herr Baader had a library of 400 books. You are in contact with other members of the RAF. You exchange secret messages between yourselves. You receive visits and your lawyers come and go.

RAF: One might wonder about these things if all they had to go by was *Spiegel* and the information put out by the state security services.

If one only has access to *Spiegel* or state security information, one might ask that. Two, three, four years of social isolation—certainly no more than that—is enough for you to realize that you are in a process of extermination. You can deal with it for months, but not years. Breaking through the institutional brainwashing-by-isolation is a question of survival for us; this is the reason why the trials will go on without us.[1] To claim that we are using the hunger strikes to make ourselves unfit for prison or unfit to appear in court—when everyone knows that the only political prisoners who are considered unfit for prison are those who are dead—is a countertactic, it is counterpropaganda. The BAW has already postponed these trials for three-and-a-half years, so that the prisoners could be broken by isolation, by the dead wings, by brainwashing, and psychiatric reconstruction. The BAW is no longer interested in these trials taking place. Or, if they are to take place, it should only be without the accused and without their defense attorneys, because these are meant to be show trials to discredit revolutionary politics—imperialist state power is to be put on display, and Buback can only achieve this if we are not there.

Spiegel: Such lies don't become more convincing, no matter how many times you repeat them; and the public understood long ago that these lies are put out in bad faith in order to sow doubts about the justice system, a goal in which you have achieved some success.

RAF: Because these are facts, you can't eliminate their political importance simply by denying them.

Spiegel: You are being held in remand, having been charged with serious crimes such as murder and attempted murder. Aren't you being held in the same conditions as other prisoners in remand?

RAF: We are demanding an end to special treatment, and not only for those in remand, but for all political prisoners—and by this we mean all proletarian prisoners who understand their situation politically, and who organize in solidarity with the prisoners' struggle, regardless of why they are in prison.

The justice system also keeps prisoners who have already been sentenced in isolation, some for as many as four years, for example: Werner Hoppe, Helmut Pohl, Rolf Heißler, Ulrich Luther, and Siegfried Knutz. There are thousands of people here who are abused by the prison system, and the moment they begin to resist they are broken by isolation. This is what we are fighting against with this strike; it is a collective

---

1 §231a and §231b had just become law, part of the *Lex Baader-Meinhof*, allowing for trials to continue in the absence of the defendants. See page 345.

action against institutionalization and isolation. In the older prisons, where previously there were no "isolation facilities"—separate wings for "troublemakers"—meaning for those who disrupt the inhumanity which victimizes them—they will be built; for instance in Tegel, Bruchsal, Straubing, Hannover, Zweibrücken, etc.

In their architectural design, the new prisons incorporate isolation as a form of incarceration. In the FRG, these design principles are not in line with the Swedish model, but rather with the American methods and experiments with fascist rehabilitation programs.

Spiegel: In concrete terms, tell us what you mean by special treatment. We have looked into the actual prison conditions of the RAF collective. We found no evidence of "special treatment," other than a series of privileges.

RAF: You have not looked into anything. You got your information from the state security services and the BAW.

When we say special treatment, we are referring to:[1]

- Eight months in the dead wing for Ulrike and Astrid;
- Years of isolation for all the RAF prisoners;
- Forced drugging ordered by the court "as an investigation technique";
- Years of being chained during yard time;
- Ongoing court-ordered "immediate use of force," which means cruel treatment in pacification cells, during transportation, during interrogation, as a result of confrontations, and during visits;
- Newspaper censorship;
- Special legislation;
- Special buildings for the trials of RAF prisoners in Kaiserslautern and in Stammheim—the 150 million DM,[2] bloated state security budget for the Stammheim trial to take place in a concrete fortress, which will require the relocation of police units from three *Länder*, even though it looks like neither the accused nor their lawyers will even be allowed to be present—assuming, that is, that the justice system will let the accused live that long;

---

1 In the original, this list appeared in one long paragraph; we have reformatted it for greater readability.
2 Roughly $60 million at the time.

- Interfering with the defense, publishing defense materials, sections of files and state security documents and using them in government campaigns to determine the verdicts and have the defense barred.

The Springer Press has access to defense files and to files that the BAW has withheld from the defense. The defense attorneys are watched day and night. Their mail is opened, their telephones are bugged, and their offices are searched. They receive disciplinary sanctions from the bar for their public work. Relatives and visitors are harassed by the state security services, even at their jobs. They have been terrorized with open surveillance. Anyone who wants to write to us or visit us is spied on and ends up in the state security services' files.

Because of the pressure from the hunger strike, they have made cosmetic changes, small things, details, which the Ministry presents to film crews. In reality, nothing has changed.

The reality right now is that isolation is organized within the prisons with deadly technical precision—now with prisoners allowed to be together in groups of two for a few hours at a time. This doesn't interfere with the destructive process; it remains a closed system. This means that the brainwashing is to continue and any social interaction will remain impossible. In regards to the outside, isolation is perfected by excluding the lawyers, or else by limiting their number to three at a time.

Given Posser's[3] conditions—for example our six years of remand—and the role of the BAW in postponing the trial, it's clear what we mean by "extermination through prison conditions." Disprove even one of these "privileges"!

Spiegel: First you said that force-feeding was a fascist tactic, then after Holger Meins died of starvation, you described his death as a "murder by installment." Isn't that a contradiction?

RAF: We're not the ones who said that, but force-feeding is a tactic used to diminish the effect of the hunger strike—how it appears—on the outside world; in short, to camouflage the murder. This is why intensive care units were set up in the prisons, so that it could be said that "they did everything they could," although they didn't do the

---

3 Diether Posser was the SPD Minister of Justice in of North Rhine-Westphalia at the time.

simplest thing they could have done: abolish isolation and special treatment.

Holger Meins was intentionally executed by systematic undernourishment. From the beginning, force-feeding in Wittlich prison was a method of assassination. At first, it was carried out by brutal and direct violence to break his will. After that, it was only done for show. With 400 calories a day, it is only a matter of time, certainly only days, before one dies. Buback and the Security Group arranged for Holger Meins to remain in Wittlich prison until he died. On October 21, the Stuttgart Supreme Court ordered that Holger Meins be transferred to Stuttgart by November 2 at the latest. On October 24, Buback informed the Stuttgart court that the state security services would not be able to respect this timetable—a fact that was only made public after Holger's death. Finally, Hutter, the prison doctor, completely cut off the force-feeding and went on vacation.

It must also be pointed out that throughout the hunger strike the BKA received "reports" from the prison administration as to the prisoners' condition. It must be emphasized that in an effort to protect himself, because he could see that Holger was dying, before Hutter left he asked Degenhardt to guarantee that he would not face charges, in the same way that all of the charges against Degenhardt had been dropped. Degenhardt was the doctor who, in the summer of 1973, during the second hunger strike, deprived prisoners at Schwamstadt of water for nine days "for medical reasons," until a coma was induced. He is the doctor who Buback described, in comparison to Frey, who was dealing with the prisoners in Zweibrücken, as having what it takes.

Holger was assassinated according to a plan by which the scheduling of his transfer was manipulated to create an opening that the BAW and the Security Group could use to target the prisoner directly. The fact that so far no journalist has looked into this and nobody has written about it doesn't change the facts, but does say everything that needs to be said about the collaboration, complicity, and personal ties between the media conglomerates and state security: the BAW, the BKA, and the intelligence services.

Spiegel: There is no way we can accept your version of the so-called "murder by installment" of Meins. It seems to us that you have a persecution complex, which would make sense after years spent underground and in prison. We at *Spiegel* criticized Dr. Hutter's behavior, and the BAW launched an investigation into his actions.

RAF: It's not about Hutter or any other prison doctor—they decide practically nothing. The medical system in prison is organized hierarchically, and at most Hutter is an expendable figure. He's a pig, but only a little one, who in the long run might be held accountable, although nobody who knows anything about prison or prison medicine would believe it. When you say you "criticized" him, you are referring to the old trick of talking about "mistakes," so that the actual mistake will not be understood: class society, its justice system, and its prison camps.

Given the situation in the prisons, the media's fascist demagogy around the hunger strike, the chorus of professional politicians—the uncontrollable outburst against a nonviolent action carried out by a small group of people, imprisoned and isolated, who have been pushed into a position of extreme defensiveness, as if the hunger strike were a military attack—Strauß spoke of the rules of war—all of this shows to what point the system's political and economic crises have eroded its facade of legitimacy. That's where you should look for the sickness, in the state's real interest in exterminating the RAF prisoners, instead of babbling about persecution complexes.

Spiegel: The British recently stopped the use of force-feeding, for instance in dealing with the terrorists from the IRA. The hunger strikes stopped right away. How would you react if this was done here?

RAF: It's not our problem. The CDU calls for an end to force-feeding, in the same way that it leans openly towards a state of emergency and fascism, while the SPD uses its electoral base and its history towards the same end—fascism. State control of every aspect of life, total militarization of politics, media manipulation, and indoctrination of the people, all to promote the domestic and foreign policies of West German imperialism. And public policy amounts to disguising "social shortcomings" and selling them as reforms. So the CDU openly advocates murder, while the SPD passes off the murders as suicides, being unable to openly embrace the state security hard line, which in the final analysis determines our prison conditions.

Spiegel: Isn't this another case of your tilting at windmills? Is it not true that everything we have heard from the RAF so far is based on a patently false analysis of the state, society, the SPD, the CDU, and the justice system?

RAF: What you're serving up here is a bit foolish. That which you describe as "patently false" is not some kind of scam or simply a position held by us alone: proletarian counterpower in response to your imperialist power—analytical and practical antagonism.

It is analytically empty to take a journalistic approach, to talk about the weaknesses, the effects and the basis of revolutionary politics—which it is your job to dispute—as journalism has long been recognized as playing a supportive role for the state, which is to say, it negates proletarian politics. For us, the question—as a question coming from *Spiegel*—is pointless. Theory and practice are only united in struggle—that's their dialectic. We are developing our analysis as a weapon—so it is concrete, and has only been properly presented in cases in which we have control of its publication.

Spiegel: You won't end your hunger strike until your demands have been met. Do you think you have any chance of success? Or will you escalate matters and, for instance, begin a thirst strike if the demands are not met? What further actions are you preparing inside and outside of prison?

RAF: Buback still believes that he can break the hunger strike and use it to destroy us. He hopes to do this by using murder, psychological warfare, and counterpropaganda—and forced psychiatric treatment, which is to be intensified in prison, with us strapped down 24 hours a day and disoriented by psychiatric drugs and sleep deprivation, so as to provoke our complete physical and psychological stagnation.

Buback received the help he needed from, amongst other places, the Heinemann Initiative, but also from the precisely worded fascism of the *Spiegel* essay written by Ditfurth,[1] for whom murder and forced psychiatric treatment are fair game for his cynical distortions, meant to increase the brutality of the political climate around the hunger strike. When, in mid-November, Carstens[2] began to produce propaganda openly calling for our murder it created public shock, antagonism, and horror.

It was Heinemann's role to eliminate any lingering doubts—among intellectuals, writers and the churches—regarding Buback's hard line.

---

1 Christian von Ditfurth, historian and journalist.
2 Karl Carstens, a former Nazi who was at this time the Leader of the Opposition for CDU in parliament.

It has always been the role of this character to dress up the aggressive policies of West German imperialism in a language and form that makes them seem humane. Heinemann's letters amounted to an appeal for us to submit to brainwashing or murder. In the same way that he, as President, pardoned Ruhland, with his letters he promoted the death sentences the BAW wanted to impose on us, with humanist gestures that soothe the conscience of his supporters. What he wanted was to clear the way for murder—just like in Easter 1968, during his Presidency, when he hoped to integrate the students, the old antifascists, and the New Left into the new fascism.

We are going to escalate to a thirst strike, but imprisoned and isolated as we are, we are not planning actions either inside or outside of prison.

Spiegel: Did Holger Meins's death provide the RAF collective with an opportunity?

RAF: That is fascist projection, an idea from someone who can no longer think except in the terms of the market—the system that reduces all human life to money, egotism, power, and one's career. Like Che, we say, "The guerilla should only risk his life if this is absolutely necessary, but in such a case, without a moment's hesitation." Holger's death most certainly has "the resonance of history," meaning that what started with the armed anti-imperialist struggle has become a part of the history of the people of the world.

"An opportunity" in this case could only mean that it broke through the news blackout about the strike. You yourself bear some responsibility for the fact that lots of people only woke up when someone was finally murdered, and only then began to realize what was going on. For eight weeks *Spiegel* did not say a word about the hunger strike of forty political prisoners, in order to prevent solidarity and leave them vulnerable. Your first report on it appeared on the 53rd day of the strike, five days before Holger's death.

Spiegel: Are you prepared to see other people die?

RAF: Buback is sitting at his desk waiting for that.

Spiegel: You must know that we think that's a monstrous suggestion.

RAF: Oestereicher, the Chairman of Amnesty England, a professional human rights activist, following a conversation with Buback in his efforts at mediation with the state, was "shocked" by the "ice-cold" way that Buback "was gambling with the prisoners' lives." That's a quote.

Spiegel: How do you analyze the situation in the Federal Republic?

RAF: An imperialist center. A U.S. colony. A U.S. military base. The leading imperialist power in Western Europe and in the European Community. Second strongest military power in NATO. The representative of U.S. imperialist interests in Western Europe.

The position of the Federal Republic vis à vis the Third World is characterized by the fusion of West German and American imperialism (politically, economically, militarily, ideologically based on the same interests in exploiting the Third World, as well as on the standardization of their social structures through the concentration of capital and consumer culture): in terms of its participation in the wars which imperialism wages, as well as being a "city" in the worldwide revolutionary process of cities being encircled by the countryside.

So the guerilla in the metropole is an urban guerilla in both senses: geographically, it emerges, operates, and develops in the big cities, and in the strategic and politico-military senses, because it attacks imperialism's repressive machinery within the metropole, from the inside, like partisans operating behind enemy lines. That is what we mean by proletarian internationalism today.

To sum up: the Federal Republic is part of U.S. imperialism's system of states, not as one of the oppressed, but rather as an oppressor.

In a state like this, the development of proletarian counterpower and the liberation struggle to disrupt the ruling power structure must be internationalist right from the beginning, which is only possible through a strategic and tactical relationship with the liberation struggles of the oppressed nations.

Historically, since 1918-1919, the German imperialist bourgeoisie and its state has held the initiative in an offensive against the people, from the complete destruction of the proletariat's organizations under fascism, through the defeat of the old fascism, not by armed struggle here, but by the Soviet army and the Western Allies, and onward up until today.

In the 1920s, there was the treachery of the Third International,[1] with the communist parties all totally aligned with the Soviet Union, which prevented the KPD from advancing the revolution and conquering power through a policy oriented around armed struggle, through which it could have developed a class identity and revolutionary energy. After 1945, U.S. imperialism tried to brainwash the people with anticommunism, consumer culture, and the political, ideological, and even military restoration of fascism in the form of the Cold War. Nor did the GDR develop communist politics through a liberation war. Unlike France, Italy, Yugoslavia, Greece, Spain, and even Holland, there was no mass, armed antifascist resistance here. What conditions there were for that were then destroyed by the Western Allies after 1945.

What this means for us and for the legal left here is that we have nothing to hold on to, nothing to base ourselves on historically, nothing that we can take for granted in terms of proletarian organization or consciousness, not even democratic republican traditions. In terms of domestic policies, this is one of the factors which makes the drift towards fascism possible, with the exaggerated runaway growth of the police apparatus, the state security machine as a state within the state, the de facto concentration of power, and the proliferation of fascistic special legislation in the framework of "internal security"—from the Emergency Laws to the current special laws that allow show trials to be held in the absence of the accused and their lawyers, permit the exclusion of "radicals" from the public service, and extend the jurisdiction of the BKA. A democracy that is not won by the people, but is imposed on them, has no mass base, cannot be defended, and won't be.

All this sums up the specific conditions within the borders of the Federal Republic.

Spiegel: So far, all of your bombs and slogans have only attracted very small groups of intellectuals and anarchist fellow travelers. Do you think you'll be able to change this?

RAF: The Third World peoples' liberation wars have economic, political, military, and ideological repercussions within metropolitan society,

---

1 The Third International was a worldwide organization of communist parties under the leadership of the USSR.

which Lin Biao[1] referred to as "cutting the feet out from under imperialism." They accentuate the contradictions within the metropole. The techniques the system depends on to cover up these contradictions cease to work. Reform turns into repression. In areas where people lack social necessities, the military and police budgets are enormously bloated. Inevitably, the system's crisis unfolds: impoverishment of the people, militarization of politics, and increased repression. The historic, politically defensive intervention into this process of disintegration forms the basis for revolutionary politics here.

Spiegel: You are often criticized for having absolutely no influence on the masses or connections to the people. Do you think this might be because the RAF collective is out of touch with reality? Have you sharpened your perspective? Many now feel that the only people paying attention to you are those who feel sorry for you, and that even the far left does not approve of you. Where do you think your supporters are?

RAF: The politics of the RAF have had an impact. Not supporters, not fellow travelers, not successor organizations, but the RAF and its political effect is apparent in the fact that—as a result of the measures the government has taken against us—many people are seeing this state for what it is: the repressive tool of the imperialist bourgeoisie against the people. To the degree that they identify with our struggle, they will become conscious—the system's power will eventually show itself to be relative, not absolute. They will discover that one can do something, that the feeling of powerlessness does not reflect objective reality on the level of proletarian internationalism. They will become conscious of the connection between the liberation struggles in the Third World and here, conscious of the need to cooperate and work together legally and illegally. On the level of practice, it's not enough to talk. It is both possible and necessary to act.

Spiegel: Do you intend to remain a cadre organization and bring down the system all by yourselves or do you still think you will be able to mobilize the proletarian masses?

---

1 Lin Biao was a close associate of Mao, and second in command during the Cultural Revolution.

RAF: No revolutionary wants to "bring down the system on his own," that's ridiculous. There is no revolution without the people. People said things like this about Blanqui, Lenin, Che, and now they say it about us, but they only ever say this to denounce revolutionary initiative, appealing to the masses in order to justify and sell reformist politics.

It is not a matter of struggling alone, but of creating a politico-military vanguard, through everyday struggles, mobilizations, and organizing on the part of the legal left, of creating a political-military core that can establish an illegal infrastructure, which is necessary in order to be able to act. In conditions of persecution, an illegal practice must be developed and can provide continuity, orientation, strength, and direction to the legal struggles in the factories, the neighborhoods, the streets, and the universities. In this way it indicates what is necessary at this point in the imperialist system's economic and political crisis: seizing political power.

Our political objective, what we are struggling to develop, is a strong guerilla movement in the metropole. This is a necessary step, in this phase of U.S. imperialism's definite defeat and decline, if the legal movements and the movements that develop in response to the system's contradictions are not to be destroyed by repression as soon as they appear. In this age of multinational capital, of transnational imperialist repression at home and abroad, the guerilla organizes proletarian counterpower, and in so doing represents the same thing as the Bolshevik cadre party did in Lenin's day. It will develop through this process—nationally and internationally—into a revolutionary party.

It is stupid to say that we are acting alone, given the actual state of anti-imperialist struggle in Asia, Latin America, and Africa, in Vietnam, Chile, Uruguay, Argentina, and Palestine. The RAF is not alone in Western Europe: there is also the IRA, the ETA, and the armed struggle groups in Italy, Portugal, and England. There have been urban guerilla groups in North America since 1968.

Spiegel: It seems that right now your base consists of forty RAF comrades in prison and about three hundred anarchists living underground in the FRG. What about your sympathizer scene?

RAF: Those are the constantly-changing numbers issued by the BKA. They are incorrect. It is not so simple to quantify the process by which people become conscious. At the moment solidarity is spreading internationally. At the same time, international public opinion is becoming increasingly aware of West German imperialism and of the repression that goes on here.

Throughout the RAF's existence, there has been an increasing process of discussion and polarization on the legal left regarding the question of armed struggle. A new antifascism is taking shape, one which is not based on any apolitical pity for the victims and the persecuted, but on an identification with the anti-imperialist struggle, directed against the police, the state security services, the multinational corporations, and U.S. imperialism.

Helmut Schmidt wouldn't have listed the RAF in his New Year's speech under the five things/developments of 1974 that are most threatening to imperialism—worldwide inflation, the oil crisis, Guillaume,[1] unemployment, and the RAF—if we were fish out of water, if revolutionary politics here had as limited a base as you and the psychological warfare campaign claim.

Spiegel: It is said that one of your main sources of support is the dozen or so lawyers who are in charge of coordinating things for you inside and outside of the prisons. What role do your lawyers play?

RAF: Committed lawyers, those who are involved in our cases, are inevitably politicized, because quite literally at every turn, right from their very first visit with a RAF prisoner, they experience the fact that nothing they took for granted about the legal system holds true. The body searches, the mail censorship, the cell raids, the hysteria, the paranoia, the Disciplinary Committee rulings, the criminalization, the psychological warfare, the legislation custom-made to exclude them, on top of what they see of the special conditions we are subjected to, and their utter powerlessness to change anything in the normal way, that is to say, by using legal arguments in court, and the fact that every step of the way they see that it is not the judges who are making the decisions regarding us, but the Bonn Security Group and the BAW. The discrepancy between the letter of the law and the reality of the law, between the pretense of the rule of law and the reality of a

---

1 This refers to the "Guillaume affair." Günter Guillaume was an East German spy who worked as SPD Chancellor Willy Brandt's personal assistant. He was uncovered in late 1973 and arrested on April 24, 1974. The crisis forced Willy Brandt to step down, making room for the more bluntly right-wing and pro-American Helmut Schmidt to take over the party and the chancellorship. Guillaume was released to the GDR in 1981.

police state, turns them into defenders of the constitutional state, into antifascists.

It is part of the counterstrategy of the BAW and the BKA to claim that these lawyers are our "auxiliary forces," which they are not. To a large degree, the justice system has been taken over by state security, in order to serve the goals of the counterinsurgency campaign and to aid in the BAW's extermination strategy. In this context, defense attorneys who insist on the separation of powers are considered obstacles to the drift towards fascism and must inevitably be targeted.

Spiegel: Do you have political disagreements with other underground anarchist groups?

RAF: Not about *Spiegel*.

Spiegel: What about the 2nd of June Movement, which murdered the West Berlin Supreme Court Judge Drenkmann?

RAF: You should ask the 2nd of June about that.

Spiegel: What do you think: did Drenkmann's murder accomplish anything?

RAF: Drenkmann didn't become the top judge in a city of almost three million without ruining the lives of thousands of people, depriving them of their right to life, choking them with laws, locking them away in prison cells, destroying their futures.

What's more, just look at the fact that despite calls from the highest West German authorities, the President of the Republic and the President of the Constitutional Court, only 15,000 Berliners came out to the funeral, and this in a city where 500,000 to 600,000 people used to come out for anticommunist demonstrations. You yourselves know that all the indignation about this attack on the Berlin judge is nothing but propaganda and hypocrisy, nobody mourns a character mask. This whole exercise was just a way for the bourgeoisie and the imperialists to send a message. The indignation was just a reflex action in one particular political climate, nothing more.

Those who, without themselves being from the ruling elite, automatically identify with such a character mask of the justice system simply make it clear that wherever exploitation reigns, they can only imagine themselves on the side of the exploiter. In terms of class analysis, leftists and liberals who protested the Drenkmann action simply exposed themselves.

Spiegel: We know something quite different. We know that Drenkmann was shot, and we consider the RAF's justification of this murder to be outrageous, nothing but lynch mob justice for a so-called "crime" that was committed collectively by what you refer to as a "fascist" justice system. Even if one accepts the maxim that the ends justify the means, as you obviously do, one can see by the public's reaction that Drenkmann's murder constituted a setback for the RAF.

RAF: The logic behind the means lies with the ends. We are not justifying anything. Revolutionary counterviolence is not only legitimate, it is our only option, and we expect that as it develops it will give the class that you write for many more opportunities to offer up ignorant opinions, and not just about the attempted kidnapping of a judge. The action was powerful—as an expression of our love and our mourning and rage about the murder of an imprisoned combatant. If there are to be funerals—then they will be on both sides.

Your indignation has to be seen in the light of your silence regarding the attack in Bremen, where a bomb went off in a vending machine shortly after a football game had been cancelled.[1] Unlike the action against Drenkmann, this bomb was not aimed at a member of the ruling class, but at the people; it was a CIA-style fascist action, and it met with a much less heated reaction. How do you explain that in this case the Bremen Railway Police were already on alert the morning of December 8—the day that the bomb went off at 4:15 PM—because they had been warned by the Hessian Criminal Bureau to expect an attack in the station or on a train. How do you explain the fact that at 3:30 PM the Civil Protection Service in Bremen-North had already received the order to send five ambulances to the central station because a bomb was going to explode, while the police, who were there immediately after the explosion, claimed that they had only received word of the bomb threat at 3:56 PM, and that they had thought it was going to go off in a downtown department store? The Bremen authorities not only knew

---

1 The Bremen bombing and other false flag attacks are discussed in Section 9. Shadow Boxing: Countering Psychological Warfare. The RAF's statement on this attack in particular can be found on page 371.

the exact time and place of this attack, but immediately afterwards they had this statement prepared to conceal, manipulate, and deflect any investigation away from what they had actually been doing. So where is your indignation now?

Spiegel: We will look into your allegations. While underground, you yourselves emphasized violence. When the bombs went off in Munich, Heidelberg, and Hamburg, the RAF saw these as political acts and claimed them as such. Since then have you recognized that violence against property and people is ineffective—that it doesn't attract solidarity, but rather repels it—or do you intend to continue along this path?

RAF: The question is, who does it repel? Our photos were hung in the streets of Hanoi, because the RAF attack in Heidelberg destroyed the computer that was used to program and guide U.S. bombers deployed in North Vietnam. The American officers and soldiers and politicians found this repellent, because, in Frankfurt and in Heidelberg, they were suddenly confronted by Vietnam, and could no longer feel safe.

Today revolutionary politics must be both political and military. This is a given because of the structure of imperialism, which must guarantee its sphere of control both internally and externally, in the metropole and in the Third World, primarily by military means, through military pacts, military interventions, and counterguerilla programs, and through "internal security," i.e. building up the internal machinery for maintaining power. Given imperialism's capacity for violence, there can be no revolutionary politics without resolving the question of violence at each organizational stage as the revolution develops.

Spiegel: How do you see yourselves? Do you consider yourselves to be anarchists or Marxists?

RAF: Marxists. But the state security image of anarchists is nothing more than an anticommunist hate campaign aimed at portraying anarchists as only being interested in blowing stuff up. In this way, the necessary terminology is established for the government's counterinsurgency campaign, meant to manipulate those anxieties which are always lurking just below the surface. Anxieties about unemployment, crisis, and war, which feed the insecurity about living conditions that people experience in a capitalist society, and which are used to sell the people "internal security" measures as peace and security measures in the form of the state's military machine—the police, the intelligence services, and the army. It aims at a reactionary, fascist mass mobilization of the people, thereby manipulating them into identifying with the state's machinery of violence.

It is also an attempt to turn the old quarrel between Marxism and revolutionary anarchism to the advantage of the imperialist state, to use the bland opportunism of contemporary Marxism against us: "Marxists don't attack the state, they attack capital," and "It is not the streets, but the factories that are key to class struggle," and so on. Given this incorrect understanding of Marxism, Lenin must have been an anarchist, and his work, *The State and Revolution*, must have been an anarchist work. Whereas it is, in fact, the strategic guide of revolutionary Marxism. The experience of all the guerilla movements is simple: the tool of Marxism-Leninism—what Lenin, Mao, Giáp, Fanon, and Che took from Marxist theory and developed—was for them a useful weapon in the anti-imperialist struggle.

Spiegel: So far as the people are concerned, it would seem that the "people's war" as conceived of by the RAF has become a war against the people. Böll once spoke of six against sixty million.

RAF: That's just the wishful thinking of imperialists. In the same way that in 1972 the newspaper *Bild* turned the idea of people's war into "a war against the people." If you think that *Bild* is the voice of the people... We don't share Böll's contempt for the masses, because NATO, the multinational corporations, state security, the 127 U.S. military bases in the Federal Republic, Dow Chemical, IBM, General Motors, the justice system, the police, and the BGS are not the people. Furthermore, hammering into the people's consciousness the idea that the policies of the oil companies, the CIA, the BND, the *Verfassungsschutz*, and the BKA are in the interests of the people and that the imperialist state represents the common good is the function of *Bild, Spiegel,* and the psychological war waged by state security against the people and against us.

Spiegel: Vox populi, vox RAF? Haven't you noticed that nobody takes to the streets for you anymore? When there is a RAF trial, hardly anyone shows up in court. Haven't you noticed that from the moment you began throwing bombs nobody has been willing to shelter you? All of which goes some way to explaining the successes in the hunt for the RAF since 1972. It is you and not Böll who have contempt for the people.

RAF: It's nice of you to repeat Hacker's clichés, but the situation is this: a tactically weak and divided legal left, facing heavy repression in the national context, cannot transform the reactionary mobilization into one that is revolutionary. This is not on their agenda. It is precisely because of this contradiction that proletarian politics must be armed politics.

The understanding of strategy and class analysis contained in your silly polemic can be repudiated by examining these facts.

The RAF, its politics, its line, and its actions are proletarian, and are the first stages of proletarian counterviolence. The struggle has just begun. You talk about the fact that some of us are prisoners—this is only a setback. You don't talk about the political price the imperialist state has paid hunting this little unit, the RAF. Because one of the goals of revolutionary action—its tactic at this point in its development—is to force the state to show itself, to force a reaction from the repressive structure, so that the tools of repression become obvious and can be transformed into the basis for struggle in a revolutionary initiative. Marx said: "Revolution progresses by giving rise to a powerful, united counterrevolution, by the creation of an opponent through which the party of revolt will ripen into a real revolutionary one."[1]

The surprising thing is not that we suffered a defeat, but that five years later the RAF is still here. The facts to which the government alludes have changed. In answer to a poll in 1972, 20% of adults said that they would hide one of us at their home for a night, even if it meant risking criminal charges. In 1973, a poll of high schools found that 15% of high school students identified with the RAF's actions. Of course the value of revolutionary politics cannot be measured through opinion polls, as one cannot quantify the processes of becoming conscious, of gaining knowledge, and of becoming politicized. But this does show how the concept of armed insurrection develops into protracted people's war—this shows that through the struggle against the imperialist power structure, the people will eventually recognize their role and will break free from media brainwashing—because our battle is a realistic

---

1 This is a rough quote from "The Class Struggles in France," a series of articles which Marx wrote in 1850 about the 1848-1849 revolution and counter-revolution in France. These articles can be read online at http://www.marxists.org/archive/marx/works/1850/class-struggles-france/index.htm.

one, it is a battle against the real enemies of the people, whereas the counterrevolution is obliged to stand facts on their head.

At the same time, there is the problem of metropolitan chauvinism in the people's consciousness, which is poorly addressed by the concept of labor aristocracy as an economic category. There is the problem that national identity can only be reactionary in the metropole, where it implies an identification with imperialism. This means that right from the beginning, popular revolutionary consciousness is only possible in the form of proletarian internationalism, by identifying with the anti-imperialist liberation struggles of the people in the Third World. It cannot develop simply through the class struggle here. It is the role of the metropolitan guerilla to create this connection, to make proletarian internationalism the basis for revolutionary politics here, to connect the class struggle here and the liberation struggles of the people of the Third World.

Andreas Baader
Regarding Torture

*This statement was made after the testimony by Henck
(the Stammheim prison psychiatrist), who concluded by
declaring that isolation intensifies the impact of torture
and, as such, constitutes a "philosophical problem."
Prinzing and the BAW interrupted Andreas seventeen
times to prevent him from developing a coherent argument
connecting isolation torture to his political perspective,
to which it is directly related. This explains the blanks.
This is an example of what it was like every day.[1]*

Events unfolded exactly as follows: the dead wing—and when that
didn't work as they had hoped, when no confession was forthcoming
despite the effects of isolation becoming apparent—at the BAW's request they locked Ulrike in an isolated psychiatric unit for eight weeks,
"for observation," as Götte said. And when that didn't work either—
they tried to arrange for forced drugging and a forced scintigraphy.
The Federal Supreme Court's idea being to open her head to see where
human thought comes from; the BAW's concrete project was stereotactical intervention in her brain. Witter was to be in charge of the drugging and scintigraphy; Loew was proposed for the brain surgery (note:
both are connected to the University of Homburg/Sarre).

After the mobilization prevented this project, the dead wing was
used again. The hunger strike and the smear campaign. Following the
smear campaign came the law that makes it possible to exclude defense
attorneys and to continue the trial in the absence of the accused,[2] which
signifies the elimination of what remained of public accountability.
Because the *hearing* to establish the prisoner's inability to appear
wasn't public, the hearing was held in the special section—just like in
Stammheim.

---

1 This introductory paragraph comes from the book *Karlek med forhinder* ("Love
with Impediments") published in Sweden in 1978 by independent publisher Bo
Cavefors. The intent was to smuggle the RAF writings in a book with a phony cover
into West Germany where publication and distribution of RAF material was illegal.
2 This legislation, part of the *Lex Baader-Meinhof*, was passed in December 1974.
For more on this see page 345.

In Zweibrücken last week, in the case of Manfred Grashof, it was demonstrated how these obligatory medical examinations could be used to prevent a prisoner from testifying.

We certainly can't agree with the argument regarding torture as it is developed by Schily in his petition. That is to say, we refuse to be the object of his analysis. For the torture victim, arriving at a conception of torture is an ambiguous and impossible endeavor, because we can only appeal—and it's pointless—to an indignation based on a liberal conception of the state confronted with the deformation of that state, a deformation which is unavoidable for it is conditioned by the contradictions resulting from the movement of capital itself. In reacting to revolutionary politics, the state does not know what to do except torture, and in doing so it exposes itself as an imperialist state. The indignation of degenerate bourgeois antifascism only masks this. The latter is already so weak, corrupted by social democracy, and locked in revisionism, that it can no longer express itself in a meaningful way.

An example of this same old miserable situation. So bourgeois antifascism puts itself at the service of the state in the hope of changing it, and is itself changed by the state, becoming an instrument of the state, serving to prevent radicalization, before it is finally liquidated for being an expression of bourgeois ideology, of bourgeois humanism, of traditional bourgeois liberties, that disrupts the broader process of capital's ideological reproduction.

It makes no sense to talk about torture without at the same time talking about the perspective and strategy that will abolish it: those of *revolutionary* politics. The bourgeois antifascist blather on this subject ends up denouncing the torture victims themselves.

Certainly isolation is torture. No matter how those who suffer it experience it, it is a slow process that leaves one with lots of time to reflect on the destruction of one's political identity and is more horrifying than any physical pain we have experienced. Political consciousness falls into the trap set by consumer society, the trap of alienated production and alienated consumption, with all its complex cultural and psychological mediations. It is only in opposition to all this that one's identity can be developed—it is a process that can only be realized in struggle. In the agony of isolation, it is this process that they want to break down by depriving us of its basis: political practice and conscious social interaction. The prisoner is deprived of his political history, *his own* history to the degree that his conscious history is a political history.

It is also the end of one's personality.

To the degree that history is the process that creates the personality, if history is lost the personality is lost. Not because one forgets it (even if that is one manifestation), but because the ability to reconstruct it, to reflect upon it, to *recognize* it, is destroyed. One becomes unable to relate to what has been accomplished and what one has oneself accomplished.

It is the system that creates the relationship. One regresses and flounders about aimlessly amidst the ubiquitous mystifications of bourgeois socialization, because one is *alone* and can no longer see that these mystifications are utterly destructive.

The moment one ceases to fight—*can* no longer fight—one becomes a blank slate, as we have said, a *victim* (and, in this way, maybe one becomes innocent as well).

One's misery is fundamentally connected to the fact that it could be foreseen for some time, and to the fact that one knows that spending years in isolation is the equivalent of being shot. It is just harder to comprehend—this is part of what it's all about—and much more cruel.

> The human being is in the most literal sense a *"zoon politikon"* not merely a gregarious animal, but an animal which can individuate itself only in the midst of society. Production by an isolated individual outside society—a rare exception which may well occur when a civilized person in whom the social forces are already dynamically present is cast by accident into the wilderness—is as much of an absurdity as is the development of language without individuals living together and talking to each other.
>
> Grundrisse[1]

It took us quite some time in the special section to recognize the method and the goal of isolation. I would say that to make sense of isolation it must be considered as part of the system as a whole: the fact that the system must respond with extermination to the contradictions that it produces, because it sees in these contradictions the possibility of its own definitive extermination. One who is re-educated is effectively destroyed by the special section. While this isn't the objective of forced

---

1 The *Grundrisse* by Karl Marx was a book of notes for future work on economics that was cut short by the author's death. This passage comes from Karl Marx, *Grundrisse*, Foundations of the Critique of Political Economy, trans. Martin Nicolaus (New York: Random House, 1973), 83-84, available at http://www. marxists.org/archive/marx/works/1857/grundrisse/ch01.htm.

socialization, even the problem that it exposes, social dissatisfaction, can only be addressed by the destruction of the prisoners.

The attempt to clarify this and to justify the torture comes from Klug, who has since become Senator for Justice in Hamburg. This comes as no surprise, because he provides a corrupt liberal facade, disguising his filthy work with the pretence of morality—the need for re-education—although this society no longer has any morals.

Its basic problem, even in this respect, lies in an antagonism, in that re-education or brainwashing, as a project, must be legitimized by the system. That is to say, to use it, the system must be able to create the subject. But the thing the repressive state apparatus shares with the revolutionary (the prisoner) is that both know very well that they are, in their irreconcilable antagonism (as in their relationship), the expression of the very process by which the bourgeois state's legitimacy is disintegrating. The fact that the state has sensed the extent of this disintegration leads it to develop its extermination strategy against us.

Posser, as a Social Democrat, knows this—(and acts accordingly, in spite of his ineffective and panicked denials). What he has foremost in his mind is not re-education, but the destruction of Ulrike and the propaganda value of presenting a destroyed prisoner in the trial, all of which would be made even more powerful if she confessed: the collapse. As an official in a party that props up the state, he is pragmatic: the smooth ritual of power is what he wants to orchestrate in order to plug the hole at the edge of the abyss his clique is hovering over. When problems arose—because the lawyers managed to mobilize people to break through the silence his plan required—he had a sick idea, typical of social democracy's version of the truth: buy them off. After all, the entire leadership of the Brandt/Schumacher party was bought off in 1945 by American capital, turning against the German proletariat in the process, so why not buy a witness? The government faction, of course. (…"against"… is not precise enough. The strategic function of social democracy is to safeguard the initiative of capital during the crisis.)

Witnesses for the crown, witnesses for the state: while this is an institution to guarantee overall ideological continuity and, above all, to affirm the constitutional state, it is also used to address our politics. Even if it is only a passing expression of the rupture on which we base our understanding of the state's reaction to armed politics.

Because the strategic necessity in this phase (the crisis of capital and the economic crisis of the state), of which each guerilla action is a political interpretation, is to finally transform the state's political crisis into a rupture. This must be done through an ongoing offensive, in what will certainly be a long and contradictory process.

We will return to this subject.

I cannot talk about the person who has been tortured. What is proven with him, through what in the end constitutes the open liquidation of his fictional status as a subject—because he is the object of state repression—is simply the fact that from the moment they are no longer of use to capital, the values of bourgeois legal ideology appear as outdated fetters to the imperialist state.

What should be talked about is the source of torture—the state—and the process by which the state's entire counterrevolutionary strategy is reduced to torture, developing a new fascism within the state apparatus, its technology, its structures, and, always lagging a bit behind, its laws (and, finally, the structural and organizational means of mass communication, which dull the senses)—everything which torture presupposes at an institutional level.

We repeat here: torture is not a concept of revolutionary struggle.

Information about torture fulfils a protective function, but a mobilization based on such information must eventually turn against the very politics that the state is targeting with torture (and, in the final analysis, against the prisoners themselves). This will be the case as long as such a mobilization's politics are based on the moral reflexes of those who still feel comfortable with this state—and this is because they want to address it as revisionists. This means the mobilization must eventually turn against us if it is not combined with propaganda for armed politics, if it doesn't propagate the morals and strategy of armed struggle, which would mean that it hasn't itself accepted armed action yet.

Andreas Baader
June 18, 1975

8

A Desperate Bid to Free the Prisoners: the Stockholm Action

Nᴏᴛ ᴀʟʟ RAF ᴍᴇᴍʙᴇʀs ʜᴀᴅ been arrested in 1972. Furthermore, there was no real evidence against many of those who had been captured, meaning they could only be charged with belonging to a "criminal organization" under §129. Even when found guilty of this crime, they could not be held for more than a maximum of six years, and in practice, often had to be released before that.

These remnants of the RAF's first wave did seem to carry on an underground existence of sorts, but failed to carry out any actions after May 1972. Still in the preparatory stages of acquiring documents and weapons, many of them were picked up on February 4, 1974, in simultaneous predawn raids in Frankfurt and Hamburg. Ilse Stachowiak, Margrit Schiller, Helmut Pohl, and Wolfgang Beer (who had all been active prior to 1972) were captured along with former SPK attorney Eberhard Becker, Christa Eckes (from RAF lawyer Kurt Groenewold's legal office), and Kay-Werner Allnach.

Police claimed that they had had these individuals under observation for months, bugging their phones and opening all mail before it was delivered without their being any the wiser. When they did move in, they claimed it was because they had recently learned of plans to rob a bank in the North German port city of Kiel.[1]

---

1 Associated Press, "New Terror Ring Smashed By Raids in German Cities," *European Stars and Stripes*, February 5, 1974.

Stachowiak had been sought in connection with the May Offensive; she would be released in 1978. Pohl and Schiller each received five-year sentences; they were released in September 1979. Beer was released one year earlier, in 1978. Allnach was kept in isolation for two years after his arrest, during which time he broke with the RAF while still refusing to testify against anyone. He was convicted under §129 and sentenced to three years. The others, sentenced for possession of guns, explosives, and phony papers, similarly spent years behind bars.

As we have seen, capture did not spell the end for the guerilla. Despite these ongoing setbacks, the intense confrontation between vulgar state brutality and the steadfast determination of the captured combatants enabled the latter to inspire a new militant support movement on the outside. In the face of the brutal prison conditions, the RAF prisoners did, at least initially, seem to succeed in exposing the violence inherent in the system, as the state's actions lent credence in some circles to the accusation that the Federal Republic had an "extermination policy" regarding the revolutionary left.

Indeed, according to one leading British news magazine in 1975:

> During the past year... there has been a discernible return of support—or at least sympathy—for imprisoned members of the group among politically uncommitted West Germans. It is founded upon growing concern at the apparent determination of the authorities not to put Meinhof and her comrades on trial until they have been softened up with long, arduous spells of solitary confinement.[1]

In some cities, the RAF support scene that had developed around the Committees Against Torture overlapped with the *sponti* left, though the two were never coterminous. It was far less close to the K-groups, for these remained overwhelmingly hostile to any guerilla politics. Even the KPD/ML, which had provided such unprecedented support during the third hunger strike, remained dead set against the guerilla's politics; its activity on behalf of the prisoners had simply been a case of nonsectarian solidarity with victims of state repression. As for people on the undogmatic left other than the *spontis*, they generally remained uneasy with the level of violence employed and hostile to much of the RAF's politics, though this did not rule out their feeling outraged at how the prisoners were treated.

---

1 Jacobson, "Show Trial," 17.

It was horror at the way its prisoners were treated that was the main factor drawing people into the RAF's support scene in this period, and the prisoners themselves became potent symbols, both of the violence of the system they were fighting against and of the possibility of resistance. Despite the risks and the human toll, the strategic use of hunger strikes had proven a useful tactic capable of rallying these supporters, as well as important sections of the liberal left.

In some cases, concern with liberating or protecting the prisoners would serve as an impetus for further armed actions. From the very beginning, low-level attacks—smashed windows, slashed tires, even firebombings—were carried out by members of the support scene and others on the radical left without much fanfare and often on a one-off or ad hoc basis. Eventually, other guerilla groups also took action on behalf of the captured combatants.

As we have seen, in 1974, the 2nd of June Movement had killed Judge von Drenkmann in an attempted kidnapping meant to support the RAF prisoners' hunger strike. Most people considered the RAF to be operationally finished, and many assumed that the 2JM—which had always kept a much lower profile than the RAF—might be a successor organization.

Then, much to the surprise of many, on February 2, 1975, a communiqué was released from the RAF outside of prison—the first such communiqué since the May Offensive almost three years previously. More surprisingly still, this "new" RAF was ordering the prisoners to call off their third hunger strike. It disparaged the "legal left"—a category which was clearly meant to include the *spontis* and other supporters who fell shy of carrying out guerilla-level actions—stating that this left,

> as a result of their defensiveness and helplessness in the face of the new fascism, has not developed the capacity to organize solidarity as a weapon, and has failed to develop in a way that corresponds to the construction of the guerilla and the politics of the RAF.[2]

Finally, the new reconstituted guerilla promised to carry out its own action on behalf of the prisoners, announcing that "the prisoners' struggle... is now something that we must settle with our weapons."

---

2 Letter from the RAF to the RAF prisoners, reprinted on page 338.

Barely three weeks later, on February 27, 1975, the 2nd of June Movement kidnapped prominent West Berlin Christian Democrat Peter Lorenz, a candidate for mayor in the upcoming West Berlin city elections. Given the timing, it is not surprising that some may have mistaken this for a RAF action, but in fact it was not.

The 2JM commando demanded the release of six prisoners being held in West Berlin's Moabit prison: Ingrid Siepmann, Verena Becker, Gabriele Kröcher-Tiedemann, Rolf Pohle, Rolf Heißler, and Horst Mahler. They further demanded that each prisoner be given 20,000 DM[1] and safe passage out of the country.

All six prisoners on the 2JM's list had been active in the APO, and all except Mahler could trace their roots to the antiauthoritarian scene. The women were all members of the 2nd of June Movement, and the men were all accused of being members of the RAF (a charge which Pohle denied, all the while expressing his solidarity with the other prisoners). There was, nevertheless, some criticism of this action, as the kidnappers did not demand the release of Meinhof, Ensslin, Raspe, or Baader, whom RAF supporters considered to be not only the heart of the resistance, but also those most likely to be targeted by the state.

Horst Mahler let it be known that he would not go with the others and remained in prison. He used this opportunity to reaffirm his new anti-guerilla position, releasing a public statement to this effect:

> The kidnapping of the enemy of the people Peter Lorenz as a means of freeing political prisoners is an expression of politics disconnected from the struggle of the working class, and can only lead to a dead-end. The strategy of individual terror is not the strategy of the working class. During the show trial of Bäcker, Meinhof, and myself in September of last year, in an open critique, which was simultaneously a self-criticism, I clearly stated that my place is at the side of the working class. I am of the firm conviction that the prison gates will be thrown open for all political prisoners through the struggle of the working class and that the terror verdicts passed against me will be wiped away—for that reason, I decline to have myself removed from the country in this way... Onward with the KPD.[2]

---

1 At the time, a little more than $8,000.
2 Ralf Reinders and Ronald Fritzch, *Die Bewegung 2. Juni*, (Berlin, Amsetrdam: ID-Archiv, 1995), 86.

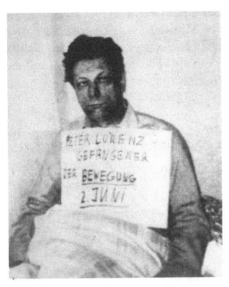

"Peter Lorenz—Prisoner of the 2nd of June Movement": *of his ordeal he would later recall, "I could always wash, was well fed, they didn't harass me. I was afraid primarily of what the police might do... The food was simple food like everyone eats. They were intelligent people, and I was well treated." According to 2JM's Ronald Fritzsch and Ralf Reinders, upon his release Lorenz shook hands with his captors and expressed the hope that they would meet again under better circumstances, perhaps at one of his garden parties.*

In a stunning victory for the guerillas, the state chose to acquiesce. There was just one sticking point: one radical regime after another refused to accept the prisoners.[3] Finally, it was decided that the FRG itself would try and entice the People's Democratic Republic of Yemen to offer them sanctuary.

The only self-described Marxist-Leninist country in the Arab world at the time, the PDRY (or South Yemen) was a staunch opponent of Western imperialism, and had earned the admiration of many progressive people for its far-reaching social and economic reforms.[4] (Saudi Arabia's King Faisal, on the other hand, described it as a "satanic citadel of subversion,"[5] while to the Associated Press it was "a radical Arab backwater regarded as the Cuba of the Red Sea.")[6] Nevertheless, in the real political world, the Cold War notwithstanding, even anti-American states would rather not be associated with guerilla actions in the First World—there was simply too much to lose and too little to gain.

---

3 The FRG approached Libya, Syria, and Ethiopia; all refused to take the prisoners.
4 Joe Stork, "Socialist Revolution in Arabia: A Report from the People's Democratic Republic of Yemen," *MERIP Reports* 15 (March, 1973): 1-25. See also Maxine Molyneux, Aida Yafai, Aisha Mohsen, and Noor Ba'abad, "Women and Revolution in the People's Democratic Republic of Yemen," *Feminist Review* 1 (1979): 4-20.
5 Stork, 23.
6 Associated Press, "Kidnaped Berlin Political Figure is Released Unhurt," *Wisconsin State Journal*, March 5, 1975.

Yet, the West German establishment was adamant that it wanted this exchange to work, and so Foreign Minister Hans-Dietrich Genscher promised that if South Yemen accepted the prisoners, the FRG would provide 10 million DM in development aid. The deal was sealed, and the PDRY agreed to accept the six prisoners.[1]

On March 3, a Lufthansa plane left Frankfurt airport for Aden. On board were the five newly freed revolutionaries (Mahler having opted to remain behind), along with former West Berlin Mayor Albertz, whom the 2JM had stipulated must accompany the prisoners to confirm that all went as planned.

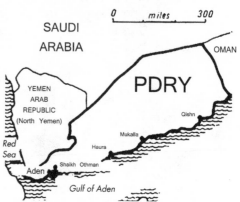

On March 4, Peter Lorenz was released unharmed. Within minutes, the police sealed off sections of West Berlin, raiding left-wing hangouts and homes which had been identified as possible targets beforehand. Two hundred people were caught up in the police sweeps, but none of the guerillas could be found, and all those detained had to be released with no charges laid.[2]

The People's Democratic Republic of Yemen, or South Yemen. Note that in 1990, at a time of worldwide retreat for "real existing socialism," the PDRY agreed to unification with North Yemen, creating the Republic of Yemen.

The Lorenz kidnapping was a perfectly planned and executed action. While the 2nd of June Movement would be criticized for not demanding freedom for leading RAF cadre, most observers agreed that the exchange only worked because none of the prisoners requested had a particularly notorious profile. The 2JM timed its action well, abducting the mayoral candidate just seventy-two hours before the city elections.

---

1 Fred Halliday, *Revolution and Foreign Policy: The Case of South Yemen 1967-1987* (Cambridge: Cambridge University Press, 1990), 76-77. The aid had in fact been promised in 1967, but had been frozen when the Marxist-Leninist National Liberation Front had out-maneuvered the Front for the Liberation of Occupied South Yemen (favoured by the imperialist countries) for power, and, in line with the Soviet position, refused to recognize West Berlin as part of the FRG.

2 *Time Magazine* [online], "The Lorenz Kidnaping: A Rehearsal?" March 17, 1975.

Finally, the group managed to take control of the media, insisting that the government respond to its demands on television. As one television editor put it:

For 72 hours we just lost control of the medium, it was theirs, not ours... We shifted shows in order to meet their timetable. Our cameras had to be in position to record each of the released prisoners as they boarded their plane to freedom, and our news coverage had to include prepared statements at their dictate... There is plenty of underworld crime on our screens but... now it was the real thing and it was the gangsters who wrote the script and programmed the mass media.[3]

The successful liberation of political prisoners, with negotiations carried out through the media itself, constituted a serious blow to the government's prestige. Going slightly over the top, the *Frankfurter Allgemeine Zeitung* waxed poetic as to how, "The humiliation of the state was completed in the nation's electronic Valhalla."[4] CDU politician Alfred Dregger understood what was at stake:

Citizens have the impression that alongside the legitimate civil power there now also exists an illegitimate power, which, at least on occasion, can make the power of the state submit to it, an illegitimate power which has become a negotiating partner of the state power in the full glare of television publicity. This means we must expect further attempts at kidnapping and blackmail.[5]

Nor was Dregger the only one to understand that the 2JM's success would beckon to others. On March 7, Chancellor Schmidt acknowledged that the government was expecting there to be more abductions.[6] The CIA-funded *Encounter* magazine suggested that all it would take for the RAF to be free would be "if Lufthansa can find another open Arab air-strip on which to disembark them,"[7] while *Time* magazine entitled its article on the subject, "The Lorenz Kidnaping: A Rehearsal?"

---

3 Quoted in Richard Clutterbuck, "Terrorism and Urban Violence," *Proceedings of the Academy of Political Science* 34, no. 4, The Communications Revolution in Politics (1982): 173.

4 Cobler, 193.

5 Ibid.

6 *European Stars and Stripes*, "Hunt for anarchists stepped up," March 7, 1975.

7 Melvin J. Lasky, "Ulrike Meinhof & the Baader-Meinhof Gang," *Encounter* 44 no. 6 (June, 1975): 23.

This was a bitter pill for the state to swallow and contributed to future reticence to negotiate with "terrorists."

The context in which the Lorenz kidnapping occurred only made it all the more impressive. In the early seventies, there had been a rash of hostage-takings around the world to secure the release of political prisoners, but these had mostly been the work of Palestinian groups, and by 1975 this tactic was proving ever less successful. The police intervention against Black September at the Munich Olympics in 1972, for example, did not bode well for guerillas taking hostages in the FRG.

In fact, it is possible that the state intended a double-cross: subsequent to Lorenz's release pressure was put on South Yemen to detain the five freed prisoners and to send them back to the FRG. The Aden government refused, pointing out that it had never agreed to be party to such a ruse. Bonn cancelled the promised development aid package, but there was nothing else it could do apart from complaining loudly and hypocritically about how the PDRY was "harboring terrorists."[1]

Whether the RAF's February communiqué to the prisoners indicates that there were already plans for what came next, or whether the new guerillas were inspired by the 2JM's success—or both—remains a matter of conjecture. It has been said that key RAF prisoners felt that the 1974 busts were due to people spending too much time on preparation when they should have been going into action.[2] Following the death of Holger Meins, there was intense pressure to act, and certain departures from the Committees Against Torture were certainly a sign that something was afoot. Indeed, as one such new recruit to the RAF later recalled, it was Baader himself who specified what should be done next.[3]

On April 25, almost two months after the 2JM's operation, the RAF's "Holger Meins Commando"—consisting primarily of former SPK members, most of whom had been active in the Committees Against Torture—seized the top floor of the West German embassy in Stockholm, Sweden, taking twelve hostages. They demanded the release of twenty-six West German political prisoners—not only Ensslin, Meinhof, Raspe, Baader, and the rest of the RAF, but also Annerose Reiche of the 2JM, and various "independent" political prisoners, such

---

1 Halliday, 77. Roughly $3 million DM were eventually released as "emergency food aid" and pumps for Aden's water supply.

2 Dellwo, 93.

3 Ibid., 10.

as Wolfgang Quante (a squatter who had been arrested in 1974 after a bomb went off in his house), and Sigurd Debus and Wolfgang Stahl, Hamburg-based independent Maoists who had been robbing banks to fund guerilla operations.

If the 2JM had measured their demands against what the state might be likely to concede, the RAF seemed intent on avoiding any such limits.

Swedish police rushed in, occupying the embassy's ground floor. They were repeatedly told to leave the building, and the guerilla threatened to execute the FRG's Military Attaché if they did not do so. When the police failed to heed these warnings, Lieutenant Colonel Baron Andreas von Mirbach was shot through the head.

Thus convinced that the guerillas meant business, the police quickly vacated the premises and set up their perimeter outside. A special intervention team was flown in from Hamburg,[4] telephone lines to the embassy were cut, and the surrounding area was evacuated.

Chancellor Helmut Schmidt summoned a special Crisis Management Team (*Krisenstab*), consisting of his ministerial cabinet and the House Speaker of each parliamentary party, in order to facilitate communication and provide the government with cross-party backing.[5] Thus united, the West German government refused to give in to any of the commando's demands. For its part, the Swedish government tried to defuse the situation, offering the hostage takers safe passage out of the country, but this was rejected out of hand: "It's useless, we're not negotiating," a guerilla spokesperson is alleged to have replied. "If our demands aren't met, we shall shoot a hostage every hour. Victory or death!"[6]

Slightly more than one hour later, at 10:20 PM, the commando shot dead Economic Attaché Heinz Hillegaart.

Shortly before midnight, as police were preparing to storm the building, the explosives the guerilla had laid detonated.[7] Police rushed in, and

---

4 The MEK, or *Mobiles Einsatz Kommando*—similar to an American SWAT team.
5 Karrin Hanshew, "Militant Democracy, Civil Disobedience, and Terror: Political Violence and the West German Left during the 'German Autumn,' 1977" in *War and Terror in Contemporary Historical Perspective*, Harry and Helen Gray Humanities and Program Series 14, American Institute for Contemporary German Studies Humanities Volume 14, Johns Hopkins University 2003: 28.
6 Aust, 291.
7 The state and media claimed that the explosives went off due to some error on the part of the commando; the guerilla suggested that the MEK intentionally triggered the explosion.

Subsequently, certain RAF prisoners would claim that Hausner's efforts to save Wessel and Rössner suggested that his initial injuries were not so serious; instead, they would assert that he had been beaten by the Swedish police, and that this is how his skull was fractured, leading to his death. This was part of a conspiracy theory that the police had purposefully set off the guerilla's

Siegfried Hausner

explosives, and that Hausner was the only one who had enough knowledge about how the explosives had been laid to prove this. In this regard, they would accuse the state pathologist Rauschke of covering up evidence of a beating. While Hausner's death would always be attributed to the state, these particular claims faded from RAF statements, which eventually framed the murder as the state having withheld medical care. *(Prisoners' testimony in Stammheim, July 9, 1975, in Texte des prisonniers de la "fraction armée rouge" et dernières lettres d'Ulrike Meinhof, 72.)*

RAF members Siegfried Hausner, Hanna Krabbe, Karl-Heinz Dellwo, Lutz Taufer, and Bernd Rössner were all captured. One RAF member, Ulrich Wessel, had been killed on the spot, not by the explosives themselves, but by his own hand grenade which he dropped as the blast went off. In spite of severe burns to his own body, Siegfried Hausner tried unsuccessfully to revive Wessel and single-handedly dragged Bernd Rössner out of the building.

It would subsequently be said that the embassy occupation had been organized by Hausner, who had been released from prison in 1974. Trained as a welder, and already suspected of building some of the bombs used in the RAF's May Offensive, it was Hausner who had rigged the explosives that were used in Stockholm. Despite the fact that he had a fractured skull and burns over most of his body, he was only hospitalized for a few days, then, over objections from doctors in Sweden and Germany, flown to Stammheim Prison.

He died soon after.

The other captured combatants would be brought to trial in the city of Düsseldorf, and on July 20, 1977, each received double life sentences.[1]

Coming right after the Lorenz kidnapping, the embassy takeover prompted Chancellor Schmidt to announce that "anarchist guerillas" posed the worst threat West Germany had faced in its twenty-six-year history.[2] Yet the action was clearly a failure: no one was freed, two RAF members were dead, and four more in prison.

In contrast with the Lorenz kidnapping, the state now emerged victorious, and capitalized on the situation to enlist the people's support in its campaign against the guerilla. Gas stations received a circular from the BKA, explaining to attendants that, "Your knowledge puts you in a special position to help the police. The enclosed checklist will help you to notice suspicious features when attending to vehicles; please report them."[3] A similar plan was discussed to enlist hair stylists—who would be asked to report who had their hair cut, dyed or restyled, who bought wigs, etc.—but did not pass.[4]

While it may have helped solidify public opinion behind the state, the Stockholm action in no way represented an end to far-left support for the guerilla. Indeed, defeat or no defeat, the fact that people had been willing to lay their lives on the line impressed many, and this itself served as an inspiration to struggle. According to Karl-Heinz Dellwo,

> Actually the Stockholm action also encouraged some people to go underground. Before Stockholm, we were only about ten comrades, of whom not all were sure how far they were prepared to go. Afterwards, the RAF was rebuilt with many more people. Stockholm as such also established a new reality on our side. The embassy said: the RAF is still there and has the capacity to carry out such an attack—imagine what would be possible if it was organized on a larger scale.[5]

---

1 Associated Press, "4 get life for attack at embassy," *European Stars and Stripes,* July 21, 1977.
2 Thaddeus Kopinski, "From barroom brawls to bombings," *Post Herald and Register,* April 27, 1975.
3 Cobler, 168.
4 Ibid.
5 Dellwo, 124.

The Holger Meins Commando has been described as a new "generation" of the RAF, a term which some supporters felt was promoted by
the state and counterinsurgency forces to suggest that successive waves
of combatants were in fact members of different organizations. This
was seen by these supporters as part of an ongoing strategy to divide the
prisoners from one another in order to break solidarity.

This terminology was resisted, and the RAF line was always that
all actions claimed by the various RAF commandos were the work of
one single, unified organization for which all members bore collective
responsibility.

While we acknowledge the sentiment in this position, we nevertheless
note that during the guerilla's history there were clearly different waves
of fighters with different priorities which led to an evolving praxis. The
captured combatants always had the moral authority to sanction or
repudiate the guerilla's activities, so one can certainly talk of organizational continuity. Nevertheless, given the clearly distinct waves of fighters, we think it makes more sense to talk about an emerging tradition of
armed resistance in which the choice to identify with the RAF's praxis
had real political significance, rather than to regard the RAF as a standing army or corporate body which retained a frozen identity even as its
own members changed.

Regarding the guerilla in 1975, it is clear that the Holger Meins
Commando consisted of former members of the prisoner support scene
who felt the state was intent on exterminating the prisoners, and that it
would not think twice before crushing any legal or semi-legal solidarity
movement. As Dellwo stated decades later,

> Stockholm was also an endorsement and reaffirmation for the
> prisoners. People they didn't know at all carried out such an action
> to get them out. That proved there was a desire on the outside for
> "the dividing line" and the revolutionary struggle.[1]

Yet, the focus for the revolutionary struggle had changed, as can be
seen in the communiqué accompanying the Stockholm action, and
with subsequent actions in the 1970s. During the 1970-72 period, the
RAF had been preoccupied with things like radical subjectivity, workers' alienation, the exploitation of the Third World, police violence, a

---

1 Ibid. In terms of how the prisoners themselves felt about this action on their
behalf, Dellwo recounts that during his first visit from Klaus Croissant, the lawyer
passed on a thankful greeting from Meinhof: "Stockholm is the Diên Biên Phu of
social democracy."

left wing out of touch with rebel youth, and a "new fascism" exemplified by social democratic corporatism and general repression. In statements like *The Urban Guerilla Concept*, *Serve the People*, and *Black September*, the RAF had attempted to grapple with these questions while dialoguing with the rest of the left.

This initial openness now gave way to a single-minded focus on a "new fascism" defined as attacks on the prisoners and their legal team, and hardly anything else.

Clearly, the prisoners' struggle was not only guiding the RAF, drawing in almost all of it new recruits: it was now defining its very politics.

On May 9, 1975, seven months after Holger Meins's death and within a month of the Stockholm action, Meins's former lawyer Siegfried Haag, along with Elisabeth von Dyck, herself a former SPK member[2] and assistant to RAF lawyer Klaus Croissant, were caught trying to smuggle guns out of Switzerland.[3] They were released and immediately went underground, Haag issuing a letter in which he accused Attorney General Buback of trying to frame him.[4]

It has been claimed that Haag had a direct hand in recruiting members of the Holger Meins Commando. Whatever the truth of the matter, his decision to join the guerilla has been noted as a key point in the development of armed activity to free the prisoners.[5]

Despite the heavy losses, the Stockholm action would not be the last attempt to replicate the successful Lorenz kidnapping.

---

2 Aust, 149.

3 Rote Armee Fraktion, 197.

4 Defense Attorney Siegfried Haag Goes Underground, see page 341.

5 Varon, 231, 268.

Letter from the RAF
to the RAF Prisoners

To the RAF prisoners:

We are asking you to call off your hunger strike now even though the demand for an end to isolation has not been met. This demand has not been met because of the powerful reactionary mobilization and the class offensive from above, the subjective conditions of an underdeveloped class struggle, the corruption of the proletariat's class organizations, and the weakness of the revolutionary left.

Understand that this is an order.

The fact is that the legal left, as a result of their defensiveness and helplessness in the face of the new fascism, has not developed the capacity to organize solidarity as a weapon, and has failed to develop in a way that corresponds to the construction of the guerilla and the politics of the RAF.

The strike has brought them face-to-face with reality: the weakness of political strategies that ignore the need to establish and develop the capacity to act from the underground, the necessity for armed politics as the concrete expression of proletarian internationalism here. Our massive mobilization in 68 was followed by a series of setbacks: the splits, the sects, and the corruption that forced us onto the defensive.

We are saying that the prisoners' strike has done everything it could to mediate, mobilize, and organize anti-imperialist politics here. Its escalation would not contribute anything qualitative to the struggle.

The state has calculated that it will be able to create propaganda from the execution of guerilla prisoners—who struggle, always struggle, in spite of everything struggle—that would make resistance seem hopeless. Allowing you to continue in this situation would amount to sacrificing you.

We are taking this weapon away from you, because the prisoners' struggle—given the existing balance of power—is now something that we must settle with our weapons.

VICTORY WILL BE OURS!

RAF

February 2, 1975

Occupation of the
West German Embassy in Stockholm

To the governments of the Federal Republic of Germany
and the Kingdom of Sweden:

On April 24, 1975, at 1:50 PM, we occupied the embassy of the
Federal Republic of Germany in Stockholm and took 12 embassy
employees prisoner, including Ambassador Dieter Stoecker, Military
Attaché Andreas von Mirbach, Economic Advisor Heinz Hillegaart,
and Cultural Advisor Anno Elfgen, in order to free 26 political prisoners in the Federal Republic of Germany, namely:

Gudrun Ensslin, Stuttgart	Ali Jansen, Berlin
Andreas Baader, Stuttgart	Brigitte Mohnhaupt, Berlin
Ulrike Meinhof, Stuttgart	Bernhard Braun, Berlin
Jan Raspe, Stuttgart	Ingrid Schubert, Berlin
Carmen Roll, Stuttgart	Annerose Reiche, Berlin
Werner Hoppe, Hamburg	Ilse Stachowiak, Hamburg
Helmut Pohl, Hamburg	Irmgard Möller, Hamburg
Wolfgang Beer, Hamburg	Sigurd Debus, Hamburg
Eberhard Becker, Hamburg	Christa Eckes, Hamburg
Manfred Grashof, Zweibrücken	Wolfgang Stahl, Hamburg
Klaus Jünschke, Zweibrücken	Margrit Schiller, Lübeck
Wolfgang Quante, Bremen	Monika Berberich, Berlin
Ronald Augustin, Bückeburg	Johannes Weinrich, Karlsruhe

1. Within 6 hours, by 9:00 PM, the imprisoned comrades must be
brought to the Rhine-Main airport in Frankfurt. There, they must be
allowed to speak freely amongst themselves and with their lawyers.
They must be allowed to broadcast information by radio and television
concerning the course of events.

Contact between ourselves and the prisoners must be provided, first
by telephone, and later by radio, and must be maintained until their arrival in whatever country agrees to receive them.

A Lufthansa Boeing 707, fully fueled, with a 3-man crew, must be
held at the ready at the Rhine-Main airport.

Within 10 hours, by 1:00 AM, the prisoners must be flown out of the
FRG. They must be accompanied only by Backlund, the Kingdom of

Sweden's Ambassador in the FRG, and one of their lawyers. We will tell you the destination once the flight is underway.

The federal government must give each of the prisoners 20,000 dollars.

2. Our statement and statements from the prisoners or their lawyers must be immediately distributed to the international press agencies and broadcast unedited over radio and television in the FRG.

Throughout the entire process, the government must announce its decisions through the mass media. The departure of the comrades must be broadcast live by television in the FRG and Sweden.

3. Our demands are not negotiable, nor will we extend the period of time in which they are to be fulfilled. If the Federal Republic tries to delay the freeing of the prisoners, we will shoot one official from the FRG's foreign office for each hour that the time limit of the 1st or 2nd ultimatum is exceeded. Any attempt to storm the embassy will result in the death of everyone in the building. In the case of an attack, 15 kg of TNT will detonate in the embassy enclosure.

After they land, the freed comrades will confirm by radio that they have been granted permission to stay. We will then free some of the embassy employees and announce our means of departure.

We will be human beings—freedom through armed anti-imperialist struggle.

Responsibility for the shooting of Military Attaché Andreas von Mirbach lies with the police, who, despite repeated warnings, failed to vacate the embassy building.

Holger Meins Commando
April 24, 1975

Defense Attorney
Siegfried Haag Goes Underground

Attorney General Buback and the state security police are attempting to have me imprisoned on the basis of a series of totally fabricated allegations.

During the search of my home and my offices, with the participation of Federal Prosecutor Zeis, who was also armed, state security police seized a large number of files concerning my clients' defense, notes from discussions regarding the preparation of their defense, as well as correspondence. At the same time, they seized my personal notes for the impending trial against Andreas Baader, Gudrun Ensslin, Ulrike Meinhof, and Jan-Carl Raspe.

Given the gravity of what has happened here, the intentional destruction of the last place where the accused prisoner might still place some trust—the trust a defendant places in his lawyer—this can be qualified as an openly fascist act of violence.

This is a state where the extermination of revolutionaries is part of the program, with legislation and the justice system mobilized towards this end, a state that tortures political prisoners by subjecting them to systematic isolation for extended periods and to brainwashing in special units created for this purpose within the prisons. This is a state where functionaries have executed Holger Meins and Siegfried Hausner. This is a state that slanders its lawyers using the entire arsenal of psychological warfare—using the media to conduct its malicious campaign—that excludes them, treats them like criminals, and finally imprisons them. In a state like this, I will not allow my freedom to be threatened any longer, nor will I be exercising my profession as a lawyer any more.

It is time for those of us who are struggling against imperialism to move on to more important tasks.

Siegfried Haag
May 11, 1975

■ ■ ■ ■ ■ ■ ■ ■ ■ ■ 9

Shadow Boxing:
Countering Psychological Warfare

WHILE THE OVERWHELMING MAJORITY OF Germans never approved of the RAF or their declared strategy, there was a small but not insignificant base of support and sympathy for the guerilla amongst young people and the radical left.

Apart from the undeniable pleasure many felt at seeing certain targets physically attacked, there was widespread outrage at the brutal and seemingly excessive repression the state indulged in. Despite capture, the prisoners from the guerilla were managing to beat the odds and turn this repression to their advantage in a way that was consistent with their strategy of bringing out the violence inherent in the system.

"The position of citizens in a powerful state—Don't forget, Berlin has a Social Democratic tradition." (Police action in West Berlin on the night of March 4/5, 1975)

Even before this strategy had won the new recruits who carried out the Stockholm action, countering this rise in sympathy had been designated a top priority for all sections of the political establishment. In the words of Interior Minister Hans-Dietrich Genscher of the FDP, "The sympathizers are the water in which the guerilla swims: we must prevent them from finding that water."[1]

Or as the CDU opposition leader Helmut Kohl put it, "We need to drain the swamp... in which the flowers of Baader-Meinhof have grown."[2]

To this end, a variety of propaganda maneuvers, described by the prisoners as psychological warfare, combined with renewed efforts to isolate and neutralize those who were considered to be sympathizers and supporters, often through use of the *Berufsverbot*, §129, and specially crafted legislation. Such repression took on new dimensions under Siegfried Buback, who succeeded Ludwig Martin as Attorney General on May 31, 1974, just weeks after the SPD's Helmut Schmidt replaced Willy Brandt as Chancellor. (Brandt had been forced to step down following a spy scandal known as the Guillaume Affair.)

The guerilla's lawyers were among the first to be targeted.

On October 16, 1974, the Federal Supreme Court filed to seize defense correspondence between attorney Kurt Groenewold and the RAF prisoners, alleging that he and other lawyers were at the core of the prisoners' communication network, known as *Info*. This move came in the midst of the third hunger strike, and constituted the first foray in the state's newest offensive against the prisoners' supporters.

Info was a system of prison communication devised with the help of lawyers from the Committees Against Torture, whereby messages would be passed between the prisoners. It represented a covert means of breaking through the isolation conditions, of maintaining group identity, sharing political opinions, and coordinating hunger strike activities. As we shall see, because it was so vital to the prisoners' survival, it was severely repressed.

An explosion of rage and rebellion swept across West Germany following the death of Holger Meins in November 1974. On November 26, the state responded with Operation Winter Trip, which according to Attorney General Buback was specifically aimed at "the sympathizers'

---

1 Speech to the *Bundestag*, June 7, 1972, quoted in *Texte des prisonniers de la "fraction armée rouge" et dernières lettres d'Ulrike Meinhof*, Draft version, A3.

2 Television interview, April 25, 1975, quoted in Ibid., A6.

scene,"[3] both through direct repression and by preparing public opinion to accept new restrictions on civil liberties.

On December 13, the Attorney General filed to seize legal correspondence between the prisoners and defense attorneys Klaus Croissant and Hans-Christian Ströbele. Buback accused Croissant of belonging to a "criminal association" with his clients, a claim he based on Croissant's use of the "terminology of left extremism, such as isolation torture, extermination conditions, brainwashing units, and the like."[4] Buback also pointed to Croissant's public statements in support of the prisoners' hunger strike and regarding the death of Holger Meins.

On December 30, Second Senate Judge Theodor Prinzing ruled that Croissant was indeed acting as "supporter" and "mouthpiece" for the prisoners and, as such, for a "criminal association." Ströbele was also alleged to be a member of a criminal association for referring to himself as a "socialist and a political lawyer," and for expressing "solidarity with the thinking of the prisoners," whom he referred to as "comrades."[5]

(Ströbele's wife, Juliana Ströbele-Gregor, was for a time banned from her job as a schoolteacher, subject to the *Berufsverbot* due to her husband's work on the prisoners' behalf. Although she succeeded in forcing the Administrative Court in Berlin to withdraw the ban, she remained stigmatized as the wife of a "terrorist lawyer.")[6]

On January 1, 1975, all of this was given added legal significance as legislation known as the *Lex Baader-Meinhof*, or "Baader-Meinhof Laws," became constitutional amendments to the Basic Law. This solidified the attacks on the defense, §§138a-d allowing for the exclusion of any lawyers deemed to be "forming a criminal association with the defendant." §231a and §231b allowed for trials to continue in the absence of a defendant if the reason for this absence was found to be of the defendant's own doing—a stipulation directly aimed at the prisoners' effective use of hunger strikes.[7] Under §146, joint defenses were now prohibited, even though the Stammheim prisoners were facing a joint trial. This paragraph was used to forbid Otto Schily from speaking to those of the accused whom he was not defending, even when he

---

3 Croissant, "Le procès de Stuttgart," 17.

4 Bakker Schut, *Stammheim*, 157.

5 Ibid., 158.

6 Jacobs, "Civil Rights and Women's Rights," 168.

7 It should be noted that even as they condemned this as a transparent move to bar them from proceedings, the prisoners also insisted that they were unfit to stand trial because of the isolation conditions, not the hunger strikes themselves.

saw them every day in court. Surveillance of defense correspondence was sanctioned by §148 and §148a, while the previously held right of the accused and defense lawyers to issue statements under §275a was withdrawn.[1]

On March 17, 1975, Prinzing approved Buback's motion and Croissant was barred from representing Baader. The court listed three reasons for this decision. First, in November 1974, Croissant had refused to share information that the lawyers were circulating amongst the prisoners with his client Bernhard Braun because of Braun's decision to break off his hunger strike. Second, Croissant had spoken at a solidarity event for the hunger strikers on November 8, 1974, the day before the death of Holger Meins. Third, Croissant had represented the prisoners in their negotiations with *Spiegel* regarding an interview conducted in January 1975.[2]

All three acts were deemed to constitute punishable offenses under §129.

On May 5, 1975, Groenewold was barred from representing Baader on the basis of allegations that his office served as an "information central" to allow prisoners to communicate between themselves. What this likely meant was that he had passed letters from one prisoner to another, and may have photocopied letters meant to be shared with several prisoners, all as part of the *Info* system.

The next day, on May 6, Ströbele was similarly excluded, again on the basis of accusations that he was key to an "information central."

It is clear that this series of exclusions, as well as those that followed, were meant to serve several functions.

The most apparent objective was to prevent the prisoners from adequately defending themselves in the Stammheim trial which was about to begin on May 21.

Croissant argued that by facilitating the prisoners' interview with *Spiegel*, and making public statements on their behalf, he was merely doing what any good lawyer was supposed to do: presenting his clients' version of events and their motivations to the public. Yet, it would seem the prisoners were not supposed to have lawyers who did their job properly, for as Croissant observed, "By this court decision, just a few weeks before his trial, Andreas Baader is being denied a lawyer who has spent several years preparing his defense..."[3]

---

1 Cobler, 207.

2 "Wir waren in den Durststreik treten," *Spiegel* 4/1975: 52-57. Cf 300-318.

3 Croissant, "Le procès de Stuttgart," 18.

Indeed, as the pretrial hearing began, Baader no longer had a single attorney of his choosing.

These exclusions also served a second, and in some ways more insidious function. The prisoners had come to depend on their attorneys, and the role they played in facilitating communication. The lawyers' visits and the *Info* communication system provided a form of human contact, a source of information regarding developments outside of the prison, and a modicum of political discussion.

As RAF prisoner Brigitte Mohnhaupt explained:

> *Info... was the only possibility—that is how we conceived of and understood it—the only possibility, in general, of social interaction between isolated prisoners. Even if it was only a surrogate for communication, only letters and paper, it was, nonetheless, the only option for discussion, for political discussion, for political information and, obviously, for orientation.*

Such communication, besides constituting a basic human need, was also a form of resistance. Again, according to Mohnhaupt:

> *The sense of Info, its entire purpose, as we understood it, was as a means to resist isolation. We have said that every sentence that a prisoner writes in Info is like an act, every sentence is an action—that's how it was for the prisoners.*[4]

The state would allege that *Info* was used as a form of discipline between prisoners, by which the "ringleaders" coerced the others into participating in hunger strikes. There were also allegations that the prisoners used the system to communicate with active commandos on the outside, a claim which has never been substantiated. As Mohnhaupt explained, what seems far more likely is that *Info* was threatening precisely because it opened a hole in the brutal isolation conditions the government was attempting to perfect. By clamping down on the lawyers and putting an end to this contact, the courts were able to further isolate the prisoners.[5]

Finally, the vendetta against the lawyers can be seen as part of

---

4 Brigitte Mohnhaupt's Testimony at the Stammheim Trial, July 22, 1976.

5 In 1987, RAF lawyer Pieter Bakker Schut published the entire *Info* collection in a book entitled *Das Info: brief von gefangen aus der raf aus der discussion 1973-1977*. It is available online at the site maintained by his former client, ex-RAF prisoner Ronald Augustin, at http://labourhistory.net/raf/search.php?search=das+info+bakker+schut&field=o&word=o&btn=Search#

the state's broader repressive approach intended to intimidate those who might stand with the guerilla. Groenewold was subjected to the *Berufsverbot* on June 12[1] and later that month, RAF lawyers found their offices and homes targeted as police carried out simultaneous raids in Hamburg, Heidelberg, Stuttgart, and West Berlin.

Over the next several years, the lawyers were repeatedly arrested and in some cases sentenced to considerable prison terms. They were openly followed by police; in some cases, agents were stationed outside their offices, taking photos of everyone, political or not, who entered.

On June 18, 1976, in a period of incredible tension in the movement, the office of Klaus Jürgen Langner, Margrit Schiller's attorney, was fire-bombed; seven people on the premises were injured.[2] Not long after-wards, Axel Azzola resigned his mandate, explaining that "In this trial, one cannot speak without fear, and without freedom of speech there can be no defense... I am terribly afraid."[3]

These attacks on the lawyers came at the same time as a new volley of legislation, aimed at the entire radical left, was being passed through the legislature.

In the summer of 1976, §129a became law, a more intimidating sub-section of §129 specifically related to "support for a terrorist organiza-tion": the maximum penalty for "ringleaders" and "chief instigators" was increased to ten years.[4] At the same time, civil rights protections were loosened so that mere suspicion that an individual was supporting a criminal organization, even where no criminal act had been commit-ted, became sufficient grounds to issue search and arrest warrants.[5]

This came after §88a had been passed in January 1976, providing for a maximum three-year jail sentence for those who "produce, distrib-ute, publicly display, and advertise materials that recommend unlawful acts—such as disturbing the peace in special (e.g. armed) cases, murder, manslaughter, robbery, extortion, arson, and the use of explosives."[6]

It was not long before §88a was being used to prosecute not only radical newspapers which reprinted the guerilla's communiqués, but also the bookstores which carried such publications. On August 18, the

---

1 Bakker Schut, *Stammheim*, 519.

2 Ibid., 630.

3 Ibid., 419.

4 Varon, 256.

5 Cobler, 117-118.

6 Braunthal, 160-161.

police carried out predawn raids on the homes of booksellers in seven cities, as well as ten bookstores and a book distribution center, confiscating many volumes that they deemed subversive.[7]

Beyond the legal chill, a variety of dirty tricks and lies were also used to try to undercut public sympathy for the guerilla.

False flag attacks like the ones threatened in Stuttgart in 1972 were now actually carried out, taking aim at random bystanders. A bomb placed in the Bremen Central Station in December 1974 injured five people. Then, in 1975, there was a spate of such attacks: on September 13, four people were hurt when a bomb went off in the Hamburg train station,[8] claimed by a phantom "RAF Ralf Reinders Commando."[9] (The next day, a fake bomb threat was called in to the Munich Central Station: an anonymous caller directed police to a locker, where they found a communiqué from the RAF, the 2nd of June Movement, and the Revolutionary Cells denouncing the previous day's attack.) In October, a bomb was discovered and defused in the Nuremberg train station, claimed by a phantom "Southern Fighting Group of the RAF." Finally, in November 1975, a similar bomb went off in the Cologne train station.

As with the Hamburg attack, the RAF denounced all these as false flag actions, and released its own communiqués disavowing them, insisting that "the urban guerilla cannot resort to terrorism as a weapon."[10] Instead, it suggested that they were the work of either a CIA unit or else a neofascist group controlled by state security: this is not as farfetched a theory as it may seem, such scenarios having played themselves out elsewhere in Europe in the 1970s.[11]

Nor was the media neglected as a weapon to be wielded against the guerilla.

In May 1975, within a month of the Stockholm action and the start of the Stammheim pretrial hearings, the government announced that

---

7 Ibid., 161.

8 Associated Press, "Terrorist Bomb Racks Train Station," *Modesto Bee,* September 14, 1975.

9 Reinders was a 2nd of June Movement member arrested in September 1975, in connection with the Lorenz kidnapping. The 2JM also disclaimed responsibility for this attack.

10 The Bombing of the Hamburg Train Station, cf 378-79.

11 Most notoriously in Italy. For several examples, see: Stuart Christie, *Stefano Della Chaie: Portrait of a Black Terrorist,* (Black Papers, No 1) (London: Anarchy Magazine/Refract, 1984).

the RAF had "possibly" managed to steal mustard gas from an army depot.[1] One German newspaper warned the public that:

> Terrorists are planning a poison attack. The Federal Criminal Investigation Bureau informed the speaker of the German Bundestag on Thursday that members of the Baader-Meinhof gang are planning a poison attack on the German parliament. According to the Bureau's reports, substantial quantities of poison gas which disappeared a few weeks ago from an army depot have fallen into the hands of members of the Baader-Meinhof gang... Health departments and hospitals have been prepared for the possibility of a terrorist attack with the chemical weapon."[2]

It was later revealed, though less widely reported, that only two litres were missing, and that they might in fact have simply been misplaced. A few months later, it was admitted that this was in fact the case, and that they had since been found.

Nor was the phantom mustard gas scare an isolated case.[3]

An almost humorous example occurred in Munich when a judge taking the subway home from a party thought he recognized one of the RAF fugitives riding along with him: Rolf Pohle, who had been freed during the exchange for Lorenz earlier that year. *Spiegel* got wind of this and another ominous fact: a plan of the subway system had been reported missing from a telephone cabinet, clearly a newsworthy item in fastidious Bavaria. The magazine declared that all this pointed to a possible impending RAF attack, and a full-scale manhunt was launched throughout the *Land*.

Nothing came of this, and government officials were later forced to admit that the judge in question had been "no longer quite sober" on the night in question.[4]

On top of such scaremongering news stories, an additional component of the state's psychological warfare strategy was the trial of Ensslin, Baader, Raspe, and Meinhof—the Stammheim show trial.

The accused had never denied that they bore responsibility for the attacks in May 1972, establishing what would become the standard

---

1 Associated Press, "W. Germans fear possible gas attack by terrorists," *Reno Evening Gazette*, May 16, 1975.
2 Cobler, 46.
3 Ibid.
4 Ibid., 47.

practice of all RAF members accepting responsibility for all RAF actions. Yet, this trial was no formality; rather, it was used as a forum for the state to "expose" the captured combatants as monsters and the RAF as something monstrous.

Although the defendants had been apprehended in 1972, the trial was not scheduled to begin until 1974; it was then postponed for an additional year to avoid any unpleasant publicity during the World Cup held in Stuttgart that summer.[5] Next, its very location was turned into a propaganda statement about the danger posed by the accused: having the trial in the regular Stuttgart court house was deemed out of the question, and instead a special "terrorist-proof" facility was ordered built especially for the RAF's alleged ringleaders.

As a journalist from the *Sunday Times* wrote in 1975:

> *That remarkable building is now almost complete in a sugar beet field near Stammheim prison. A concrete and steel fortress that will cost about £3 million, it includes among the features not normally found in courthouses, anti-aircraft defense against helicopter attack, listening devices sown in the ground around the building, scores of closed-circuit TV cameras, and an underground tunnel linked to Stammheim so that the defendants can be smuggled in and out of court without showing their noses in the open. The five judges (no jury), the accused and all witnesses will sit behind bullet-proof glass security screens.*
>
> *Photographing the new court-house is strictly forbidden. The site workmen were, literally, sworn to secrecy. Plain-clothes police patrol it constantly, and local farmers, to their disgust, must carry passes to get to their fields.*[6]

In this already Orwellian setting, the prisoners were confronted with the testimony of those few of their former comrades who had agreed to cooperate in return for leniency, new identities, or simply as a result of being psychologically broken by isolation.

Karl-Heinz Ruhland, who had proven an embarrassment to the state in the first RAF trials, was now reinforced by a slightly more convincing turncoat: Gerhard Müller, a former SPK member, who had been captured along with Meinhof in 1972. After two-and-a-half years of

---

5 Jacobson, 21.
6 Ibid.

hunger strikes and isolation, Müller could take no more and finally broke during the third hunger strike, in the winter of 1974/75. Tempted with offers of leniency and threatened with a murder charge going back to Hamburg police officer Norbert Schmid in 1971, he agreed to work for the prosecution.

The murder case was dropped, and the charges relating to the May Offensive—for which he could have received life—culminated in a ten-year sentence, of which he was only required to serve half.[1] The deal was further sweetened with offers of a new identity and the possibility of selling his story for a considerable sum.[2] He eventually received 500,000 DM and was relocated to the United States.[3]

In exchange, Müller painted a nightmare picture of the RAF as brutal killers, accusing Baader in particular of having executed one member, Ingeborg Barz, simply because she wished to opt out of the guerilla struggle.

Barz had joined the RAF in 1971 along with Wolfgang Grundmann; they had both been previously active in the anarchist prisoner support group Black Aid.[4] While she is known to have participated in the Kaiserslautern bank robbery during which police officer Herbert Schoner was killed, she was never apprehended, nor did she ever surface from the underground. Disputing Müller's claims, witnesses subsequently came forward testifying that they had met with Barz after this supposed execution, and when Müller brought police to the place where she was supposedly buried, they found nothing there.[5]

Brigitte Mohnhaupt took the witness stand to refute this story, describing in detail the various ways in which people might leave the guerilla, and insisting that, even in the case of traitors, the RAF had not carried out any executions. Given the growing list of former members who worked with the media and Buback's prosecutors against the RAF and the glaring fact that none of them had been killed, Mohnhaupt's statements were far more credible than Müller's.

Another somewhat less important witness for the prosecution was Dierk Hoff, a metalworker and former SDS member from the Frankfurt

---

1 Aust, 164.

2 Ibid., 360.

3 Christiane Ensslin and Klaus Jünschke, "Stimmen aus Stammheim: Isolationshaft ist kein Mythos," *Neue Rheinische Zeitung* [online], August 8, 2007.

4 Becker, 273.

5 Aust, 362-363.

scene. Hoff, who had built bombs and other weapons for the guerilla, testified that he had not realized what he was doing at the time. He claimed that Holger Meins, the conveniently dead former film student, had put him up to it with a story about how they were to be used as realistic props in a movie about terrorism. By the time he realized what was what, it was too late: the guerilla warned him that he was too deeply involved to be able to go to the police.

In exchange for his cooperation, Hoff's somewhat incredible story was not challenged by the prosecution, and he received only a short prison term.[6] Despite this, his testimony was not felt to be particularly damaging.

Supporters' claims that all these broken witnesses were being paraded out not to secure a conviction (of which there was never any doubt) but to discredit the guerilla were vindicated at the eleventh hour as the trial was wrapping up. In January 1977, Otto Schily received a tip that Federal Judge Theodor Prinzing, who was in charge of the trial and was thus supposed to pretend to be impartial, had been passing on court documents and evidence to a judge from the appeals court. Copies of these documents had then been making their way to the press, accompanied by suggestions as to how they could be used to discredit the guerilla.

In his eagerness to exploit the testimony of Müller and the others, Prinzing had miscalculated, and in so doing provided the defense with one of its few legal victories: the Federal Judge was forced to recuse himself.[7] He was replaced by associate judge Eberhard Foth, and the circus continued.

Nevertheless, the point had been made: this was a propaganda exercise, coordinated by either the BKA or the BAW, with a purely political goal. In other words, it was a show trial.

The prisoners defended themselves against all this as best they could: they may have accepted collective responsibility for all of the attacks the RAF had carried out, but they were far from indifferent about what was said in court. It was of great importance for them to counter allegations that could easily undermine what support they enjoyed on the left.

---

6 Associated Press, "Baader-Meinhof Armourer Testifies," *European Stars and Stripes*, January 28, 1976; "Handelsgeschäfte mit der 'Wahrheit' Kronzeugen als Sonder- Beweismittel der Anklage," http://www.freilassung.de/div/texte/kronzeuge/goe1.htm.

7 Aust, 384-386.

In her 1974 statement to the court regarding the liberation of Baader, Ulrike Meinhof had already attempted to refute the state's slanders, and to place the guerilla's actions within their proper political context. But the smears continued, and during the years of trials to come, the prisoners repeatedly felt compelled to defend not only their politics, but also their internal structure in the face of accusations of authoritarianism and cold inhumanity.

Quoted out of context, the prisoners' attempts to defend their past practice can seem exaggerated, even shrill. The desire to paint one's own experiences in the most favorable light can easily backfire, making one appear to be an uncritical enthusiast, dewy-eyed, if not fanatical, which is precisely what we are told to expect from self-styled revolutionaries. Nevertheless, it is difficult to see what else they could have done, as the state moved to use their various trials as so many opportunities to present its cockamamie stories and slanders.

In this context, the prisoners had little choice but to do what they could to affirm their political identity and continuing solidarity with one another.

"We know why he's saying it"

These are excerpts from Brigitte Mohnhaupt's testimony at Stammheim; a cruder but more complete translation is available at http://www.germanguerilla.com/red-army-faction/ documents/76 _0708 _mohnhaupt_pohl.html. (M. & S.)

ON MÜLLER'S CLAIMS
REGARDING THE "LIQUIDATION" OF COMRADES
Of course there were people who left. It would be untrue to say otherwise. Contradictions develop within a group engaged in the process that this one is engaged in. In the course of the struggle, there are obviously contradictions, and there are people who decide at a certain point to no longer do the job, because they no longer want to.

They decide to return to their previous lives, to go back, or they do other things, even though everyone knows perfectly well that it isn't possible, that it is a lie, when one has already been engaged in a practice such as ours. Such a decision can only be a step backwards, which always signifies a step backwards into shit.

There were departures like that, but there was obviously never a question of liquidation at any point or regarding any departure. There were departures involving people who, as I've already said, could no longer do the work, who no longer wanted to do it, because they understood that it meant going underground, which is what armed struggle always means. It was a completely free decision on their part. Leaving was the right thing for them to do. It would be stupid for them to stay, because there wouldn't, in any case, be any way to engage in a shared practice.

There were also departures that we ourselves decided upon. There were people who knew that we were ending relations with them for clear reasons, basically for the same reason, because, at a given point, it was no longer possible to have a shared practice, because contradictions had developed. And, yeah, they're all still alive, that's all complete nonsense—it unfolded completely normally. They do other things, conscious that they can never again engage in this practice.

Maybe it should be explained how things would happen when someone decided to stop. It always happened in the course of a discussion in which everyone participated, or at least a good number of people, everyone who could participate, given the circumstances.

This took place in the context of discussions. It wasn't done in a heavy-handed way. Each time there was an evolution which allowed the person concerned—along with all the others, each person in the group—to understand that the point had been reached where it was no longer possible to work together, the time had come for him to make a decision: to change, if he still wanted to, if he could manage it, if he could, obviously, with the help of all the others—or else he can leave.

At that point, he is free to leave, and there is no pressure, because it's his decision, because he understands this, and because throughout it all there is no loss of self-respect, he is not rejected. It could not possibly have been handled any other way given the structure.

That is what makes this Hausner story of Müller's absolutely impossible. Under certain specific circumstances, liquidation is obviously an option. But within the context of what the group was doing in 72, it would have been an error in that situation.

It is absolutely untrue that Hausner wanted to leave, and it is also completely untrue that we had said he should leave. There was absolutely no reason, given who he was, given what he had done, that would have led us to force him to leave or to have liquidated him. It's absolutely ridiculous. It never happened. Obviously, everyone makes mistakes, but nobody had the arrogance or the absolutism to say, "Me, I don't make mistakes."

In any case, given the situation within the group, it is a swinish lie that we would have said, "Now he must leave, and if he doesn't leave, then..."—what Müller said was, "If he couldn't go to Holland, if he couldn't be sent to a foreign country, then it was necessary, as an emergency solution, to simply liquidate him."

If such a thing could have happened, it would have weakened and destroyed the structure, destroyed the group, destroyed the individuals who had struggled as part of the group, rather than strengthening them, because if something like that could happen in the group how would it remain possible for individuals to struggle, to be courageous, and above all to find their identities?

I maintain that it is impossible, even as an emergency solution or because there was no more place for someone, for things to have functioned in the way Müller described. It's complete nonsense.

Is this clear yet?

I can give another example: the story of the woman in Berlin, Edelgard Graefer, I believe—in any case it was Graefer—who denounced a half a dozen people. She betrayed the people and gave away safehouses. And what happened? What was done? She got a slap in the mouth and was hit in the throat with a placard. So, I think these facts speak for themselves: when someone betrays people, in effect lines them up against the wall, because you never know what could happen when the cops break into an apartment, and this person only receives a slap in the head, then it is all the more absurd to think that someone who has never betrayed anyone could, as the result of a situation where everything culminates, as Müller describes it, in searches and whatever, in arrests, could simply be shot down. It's absolutely out of the question.

And, of course, the strongest evidence, I would say, that this story can't be true is simply that Siegfried Hausner led the Holger Meins Commando, and it would have been out of the question for it to be otherwise. Quite simply, he made the arrangements, he did it himself, which clarifies the nature of the structure that existed at the time. I believe this clarifies everything. Why would he have done it? Why would he have struggled in a situation like the one Müller described?

ON MÜLLER'S CLAIMS
REGARDING THE SPRINGER BOMBING

For instance, the statement which suggests that Ulrike carried out the attack against the Springer Building over the objections of Andreas or Gudrun or in opposition to a part of the group, and the claim that this led to a split, or, at least, to conflict between members, terror, or whatever it was that the pig said.

The truth is that when the Hamburg action was carried out—and this was already clarified during this trial—we knew nothing because of the structure of our groups: decisions were made autonomously, and actions were carried out autonomously. After the action against Springer, there was a lot of criticism from other groups. As a result, Ulrike went to Hamburg to find out what had happened, because the RAF never considered actions if there was a risk that civilians could be hurt. It was an essential principle in all discussions and in the criticism addressed to the Hamburg group, that they carried out the action without clearly considering that Springer, of course, wouldn't evacuate the building. So given this, it had not been well prepared. That was the criticism made of the group that had carried out the action.

That is why Ulrike went to Hamburg at that time, to clarify this, to find out what had happened. After doing this, she formulated the statement about this action, in which everything was explained, the entire process, the warnings, Springer not evacuating, etc.

Which shows that what Müller said, yeah, we know that already, and we know why he's saying it. What he claims now, regarding Ulrike, that she had or could have intended to carry out actions that the others objected to, it is completely absurd, but it fits in perfectly with the current line: "the tensions." Its purpose is to legitimize Ulrike's murder. The claim that there were tensions is a story that goes back—according to what Müller has said here—to Hamburg, to the organization of the group in 71-72. It is purely and simply a fabrication, presented here with the sole objective of legitimizing the murder...

Brigitte Mohnhaupt
Stammheim Trial
July 22, 1976

On the Liberation of Andreas Baader

The following text was read by Ulrike Meinhof at her trial alongside Hans-Jürgen Bäcker and Horst Mahler. (M. & S.)

This trial is a tactical maneuver, a part of the psychological war being waged against us by the BKA, the BAW, and the justice system:

- with the goal of obfuscating both the political ramifications of our trials and the BAW's extermination strategy in West Germany;
- with the goal of using separate convictions to create the appearance of division, by putting only a few of us on display at any one time;
- with the goal of erasing the political context of all the RAF prisoners' trials from the public consciousness;
- with the goal of forever eliminating from the people's consciousness the fact that on the imperialist terrain of West Germany and West Berlin there is a revolutionary urban guerilla movement.[1]

We—the Red Army Faction—will not participate in this trial.

THE ANTI-IMPERIALIST STRUGGLE

If it is to be more than just an empty slogan, the struggle against imperialism must aim to annihilate, to destroy, to smash the system of imperialist domination—on the political, economic, and military planes. It must aim to smash the cultural institutions that imperialism uses to bind together the ruling elites and the communications structure that ensures their ideological control.

In the international context, the elimination of imperialism on the military plane means the elimination of U.S. imperialism's military alliances throughout the world, and here that means the elimination of NATO and the *Bundeswehr*. In the national context it means the elimination of the state's armed formations, which embody the ruling class's monopoly of violence and its state power: the police, the BGS, the secret service. On the economic plane, it means the elimination of the power

---

1 The preceding points appeared in the German as one long paragraph; they have been reformatted here for added readability.

structure that represents the multinational corporations. On the political plane, it means the elimination of the bureaucracies, organizations, and power structures, whether state or non-state (parties, unions, the media), that dominate the people.

PROLETARIAN INTERNATIONALISM

The struggle against imperialism here is not and could not be a national liberation struggle. Socialism in one country is not its historical perspective. Faced with the transnational organization of capital and the military alliances with which U.S. imperialism encircles the world, the cooperation of the police and the secret services, the way the dominant elite is organized internationally within U.S. imperialism's sphere of power—faced with all of this, our side, the side of the proletariat, responds with the struggle of the revolutionary classes, the people's liberation movements in the Third World, and the urban guerilla in imperialism's metropole. That is proletarian internationalism.

Ever since the Paris Commune, it has been clear that a people who seek to liberate themselves within the national framework in an imperialist state attract the vengeance, the armed might, and deadly hostility of the bourgeoisie of all the other imperialist states. That is why NATO is currently putting together an intervention force, to be stationed in Italy, with which to respond to internal difficulties.

Marx said, "A people who oppress another cannot themselves be free." The military significance of the urban guerilla in the metropole—the RAF here, the Red Brigades in Italy, and the United Peoples Liberation Army[1] in the U.S.A.—lies in the fact that it can attack imperialism here in its rear base, from which it sends its troops, its arms, its instructors, its technology, its communication systems, and its cultural fascism to oppress and exploit the people of the Third World. This is because it operates within the framework of the Third World liberation struggles, struggling in solidarity with them. That is the strategic starting point of the guerilla in the metropole: to unleash the guerilla, the armed struggle against imperialism, and the people's war in imperialism's rear bases, to begin a long-term process. Because world revolution is surely not an affair of a few days, a few weeks, or a few months, because it is not an affair of a few popular uprisings, it will not be a short process. It is not

---

1 Klaus Croissant indicated that Meinhof misspoke, intending to refer to the Symbionese Liberation Army (SLA), a guerilla group active in the California between 1973 and 1975.

a question of taking control of the state as the revisionist parties and groups imagine—or, more correctly, as they claim, for they don't really have any imagination.

THE NOTION OF THE NATION STATE

In the metropole, the notion of the nation state has become a hollow fiction, given the reality of the ruling classes, their policies, and their structure of domination, which no longer has anything to do with linguistic divisions, as there are millions of immigrant workers in the rich countries of Western Europe. The current reality—given the globalization of capital, given the new media, given the mutual dependencies that support economic development, given the growth of the European Community, and given the crisis—while remaining subjective, greatly encourages the formation of European proletarian internationalism, to the point that the unions have worked for years to box it in, to control it, to institutionalize it, and to repress it.

The fiction of the nation state, to which the revisionist groups are attached with their organizational form, is in keeping with their fetish for legality, their pacifism, and their massive opportunism. We are not reproaching the members of these groups for coming from the petit bourgeoisie, but for reproducing, in their politics and in their organizational structure, the ideology of the petit bourgeoisie, which has always been hostile to proletarian internationalism—their class position and conditions of social reproduction cannot be seen otherwise. They are always organized within the state as a complement to the national bourgeoisie, to the dominant class.

As for ourselves—we of the RAF, revolutionary prisoners detained in isolation, in special units, subjected to highly structured and completely illegal brainwashing programs in prison, as well as those underground— the argument that the masses are not yet sufficiently advanced just reminds us of what the colonialist pigs have been saying about Africa and Asia for the past seventy years. According to them, blacks, illiterates, slaves, colonized peoples, torture victims, the oppressed, and the starving, who suffer under the yoke of colonialism and imperialism, are not yet advanced enough to control their own administration like human beings. According to them, they are not yet advanced enough to control their own industrialization, their own education, their own future. This is the argument of people concerned with their own positions of power, those who want to rule the people, not to emancipate them or to help them in their struggle for liberation.

THE GUERILLA IN THE METROPOLE

Our action on May 14, 1970, was and remains an exemplary action for the guerilla in the metropole. It contained all of the elements required for a strategy of armed struggle against imperialism. It served to free a prisoner from the grip of the state. It was a guerilla action, an action of a group that, in deciding to carry it out, organized itself as a politico-military cell. They acted to free a revolutionary, a cadre who was and remains indispensable for organizing the guerilla in the metropole. And not only indispensable like every revolutionary is indispensable in the ranks of the revolution, for already at this stage, he embodied everything that made the guerilla possible, that made possible the politico-military offensive against the imperialist state. He embodied the determination, the will to act, the ability to orient himself solely and exclusively in terms of the objectives, while leaving space for the collective learning process, and practicing leadership collectively right from the start, mediating between each person's individual experience and the collective as a whole.

This action was exemplary, because in the struggle against imperialism it is necessary above all to liberate the prisoners, to liberate them from prison, which has always been an institution used against all of the exploited and oppressed, historically leading only to death, terror, fascism, and barbarism. To liberate them from their imprisonment within the most complete and utter alienation, from their self-alienation, from the state of political and existential disaster in which the people are obliged to live while in the grip of imperialism, of consumer society, of the media, and of the ruling-class structures of social control, where they remain dependent on the market and the state.

The guerilla—and not only here: it is the same in Brazil, in Uruguay, in Cuba, and, for Che, in Bolivia—always starts from point zero, and the first phase of its development is the most difficult. Neither the bourgeois class prostituted to imperialism, nor the proletariat colonized by it, provide anything of use to us in this struggle. We are a group of comrades who have decided to act—to break with the stage of lethargy, of purely rhetorical radicalism, of increasingly vain discussions about strategy—and to struggle. We are lacking in everything, not only the capacity to act: it is only now that we are discovering what sort of human beings we are. We are uncovering the metropolitan individualism that comes from the system's decay, the alienated, false, poisonous relationships that it creates in our lives—in the factories, the offices, the schools, the universities, the revisionist groups, during apprenticeships, or at part time jobs. We are discovering the effects of the division between professional life and private life, the division between intellectual labor and manual labor, the childishness of the hierarchical labor process, all of which reflect the psychic distortions produced by consumer society, by this degenerate metropolitan society, fallen into decay and stagnation.

But that is who we are, that is where we come from. We are the offspring of metropolitan annihilation and destruction, of the war of all against all, of the conflict of each individual with every other individual, of a system governed by fear, of the compulsion to produce, of the profit of one to the detriment of others, of the division of people into men and women, young and old, sick and healthy, foreigners and Germans, and of the struggle for prestige. Where do we come from? From isolation in individual row-houses, from the suburban concrete cities, from prison cells, from the asylums and special units, from media brainwashing, from consumerism, from corporal punishment, from the ideology of nonviolence, from depression, from illness, from degradation, from humiliation, from the debasement of human beings, from all the people exploited by imperialism.

We must find, in our distress, the need to liberate ourselves from imperialism and to struggle against it. We must understand that we have nothing to lose by destroying the system, but everything to gain from armed struggle—collective liberation, life, human dignity, and our identity. We must understand that the cause of the people, the masses, the assembly line workers, the lumpen proletariat, the prisoners, the apprentices—the lowest of the masses here and the liberation movements in the Third World—is our cause. Our cause—armed struggle against imperialism—is the masses' cause and vice versa, even if it can only become a reality through a long-term process whereby the politico-military offensive develops and people's war breaks out.

That is the difference between true revolutionary politics and politics that only seem revolutionary, but are in fact opportunist. It is necessary that we start from the objective situation, from the objective conditions, from the actual situation of the proletariat and the masses in the metropole, from the fact that all layers of society are in all ways under the system's control. The opportunists base themselves on the alienated consciousness of the proletariat; we start from the fact of their alienation, which indicates why their liberation is necessary.

In 1916 Lenin responded to the colonialist, renegade pig Kautsky:

> No one can seriously think it possible to organise the majority of
> the proletariat under capitalism. Secondly—and this is the main
> point—it is not so much a question of the size of an organisation,
> as of the real, objective significance of its policy: does its policy
> represent the masses, does it serve them, i.e., does it aim at their
> liberation from capitalism, or does it represent the interests of the
> minority, the minority's reconciliation with capitalism?
>
> Neither we nor anyone else can calculate precisely what portion of
> the proletariat is following and will follow the social-chauvinists
> and opportunists. This will be revealed only by the struggle, it
> will be definitely decided only by the socialist revolution. And it
> is therefore our duty, if we wish to remain socialists to go down
> lower and deeper, to the real masses; this is the whole meaning
> and the whole purport of the struggle against opportunism.[1]

THE GUERILLA IS THE GROUP

The role of the guerilla leadership, the role of Andreas in the RAF, is
to provide orientation. It is not only a matter of distinguishing what is
essential from what is secondary in each situation, but also of knowing
how to connect each situation to the greater political context by elabo-
rating its particularities, while never losing sight of the goal—revolution—as a result of details or specific technical or logistical problems,
never losing sight of the overall tactical or strategic politics of the alliance, the question of class. This means never falling into opportunism.

This, said Le Duan,[2] is "the art of dialectically connecting firm principles with flexibility in action, the art of applying the law of development that seeks to see incremental changes transformed into qualitative leaps within the revolution."[3] It is also the art of "never shrinking

---

1 With minor omissions, this is a quote from Lenin's *Imperialism and the Split
in Socialism* written in October 1916 and available at http://www.marxists.org/
archive/lenin/works/1916/oct/x01.htm.

2 Le Duan became the first Secretary of the Communist Party in North Vietnam in
1960. After the death of party founder and leader Ho Chi Minh in 1969, Le took
over the leadership of the government. He remained General Secretary of the CP
and head of the government until his death in 1986 at the age of seventy-nine.

3 This quote is from Le Duan's *Principles and Methods of Revolutionary Action*,
written on the occasion of the 40th Anniversary of the establishment of the
Indochinese Communist Party (1970). A slightly different translation appears in

from the unimaginable enormity of your goals," but of pursuing them stubbornly and without allowing yourself to be discouraged. It is the courage to draw lessons from your errors and the general willingness to learn. Every revolutionary organization and every guerilla organization knows that practice requires that it develop its capabilities—at least any organization applying dialectical materialism, any organization that aims for victory in the people's war and not the edification of a party bureaucracy and a partnership with the imperialist power.

We don't talk about democratic centralism because the urban guerilla in the metropole of the Federal Republic can't have a centralizing apparatus. It is not a party, but a politico-military organization within which leadership is exercised collectively by all of the independent sections, with a tendency for it to be subsumed by the group as part of the collective learning process. Tactically, the goal is to always allow for an autonomous orientation towards militants, guerillas, and cadres. Collectivity is a political process that functions on all levels: in interaction and communication and in the sharing of knowledge that occurs as we work and learn together. An authoritarian leadership structure would find no material basis in the guerilla, because the real (i.e., voluntary) development of each individual's productive force is necessary for the revolutionary guerilla to make an effective revolutionary intervention from a position of weakness, in order to launch the people's liberation war.

PSYCHOLOGICAL WARFARE

Andreas, because he is a revolutionary, and was one from the beginning, is the primary target of the psychological war that the cops are waging against us. This has been the case since 1970, since the first appearance of the urban guerilla with the prison break operation.

The guiding principle of psychological warfare is to set the people against the guerilla, to isolate the guerilla from the people, to distort the real, material goals of the revolution by personalizing events and by presenting them in psychological terms. The goals of the revolution are freedom from imperialist domination, from occupation, from colonialism and neocolonialism, from the dictatorship of the bourgeoisie, from military dictatorship, from exploitation, from fascism, and from

---

This Nation and Socialism Are One: Selected Writings of Le Duan First Secretary, Central Committee Vietnam Workers Party available at http://leninist.biz/en/1976/ NSO261/05-Principles.and.Methods.of.Revolutionary.Action#forw1page17.

imperialism. Psychological warfare uses the tactic of mystifying that which is easy enough to understand, presenting as irrational that which is rational, and presenting the revolutionaries' humanity as inhumanity. This is carried out by means of defamation, lies, insults, bullshit, racism, manipulation, and the mobilization of the people's unconscious fears and reflexes inculcated over decades or centuries of colonial domination and exploitation—knee-jerk existential fear in the face of incomprehensible and hidden powers of domination.

Through psychological warfare, the cops attempt to eliminate revolutionary politics and the armed anti-imperialist struggle in the German metropole, as well as its effect on the consciousness of the people, by personalizing it and turning it into a psychological issue. In this way, the cops attempt to present us as what they themselves are, they attempt to present the RAF's structure as similar to their own, a structure of domination mimicking the organizational form and functioning of their own structures of domination, a structure like that of the Ku Klux Klan, the mafia, or the CIA. And they accuse us of the tactics that imperialism and its puppets use to impose themselves: extortion, corruption, competition, privilege, brutality, and the practice of stepping over corpses to achieve their goals.

In their use of psychological warfare against us, the cops rely upon the confusion of all those who are obliged to sell their labor simply to survive, a confusion born of the obligation to produce and of the fear for one's very existence that the system generates within them. They rely on the morbid practice of defamation, which the ruling class has directed against the people for decades, for centuries; a mixture of anticommunism, antisemitism, racism, sexual oppression, religious oppression, and an authoritarian educational system. They rely on consumer society brainwashing and the imperialist media, re-education and the "economic miracle."

What is shocking about our guerilla in its first phase, what was shocking about its first actions, is that they showed that people could act outside of the system's limits, that they didn't have to see through the media's eyes, that they could be free from fear—that people could act on the basis of their own very real experiences, their own and those of the people. Because the guerilla starts from the fact that— despite this country's highly advanced technology and immense wealth—every day people have their own experiences with oppression, media terrorism, and insecure living conditions, which lead to mental illness, suicide, child abuse, indoctrination, and housing shortages.

That is what the imperialist state finds shocking about our actions: that the people can understand the RAF for what it is: a practice, a cause born in a logical and dialectical way from actual relationships. A practice which—insofar as it is the expression of real relationships, insofar as it expresses the only real possibility for reversing and changing these relationships—gives the people their dignity and makes sense out of struggle, revolution, uprisings, defeats, and past revolts—that is to say, it returns to the people the possibility of being conscious of their own history. Because all history is the history of class struggle, a people who has lost a sense of the significance of revolutionary class struggle is forced to live in a state in which they no longer participate in history, in which they are deprived of their sense of self, that is to say, of their dignity.

The guerilla allows each person to determine where he stands, to define, often for the first time, his overall situation and to discover his place within class society, within imperialism: to determine this for himself. Many people think they are on the side of the people, but the moment the people start to confront the police and start to struggle, they cut and run, issue denunciations, put the brakes on, and side with the police. This is a problem that Marx often addressed: that one is not what one believes oneself to be, but what one is in one's true functions, in one's role within class society. That is to say, if one doesn't decide to act against the system, doesn't take up arms and fight, then one is on the system's side and effectively serves as an instrument for achieving the system's goals.

With psychological warfare, the cops attempt to turn the achievements of the guerilla's actions back against us: the knowledge that it isn't the people who are dependent on the state, but the state that is dependent on the people—that it isn't the people who need the investment firms or the multinationals and their factories, but it is the capitalist pigs who need the people—that the goal of the police isn't to protect the people from criminals, but to protect the imperialist order of exploitation from the people—that the people don't need the justice system, but the justice system needs the people—that we don't need the American troops and installations here, but that U.S. imperialism needs us. Through personalization and psychological rationalization, they project the clichés of capitalist anthropology onto us. They project the reality of their own facade, of their judges, of their prosecutors, of their screws, and of their fascists, pigs who take pleasure in their alienation, who only live by torturing, by oppressing, and by exploiting others, pigs for whom the whole point of their existence is their career, success, elbowing their way to the top, and taking advantage of others, pigs who take pleasure from the hunger, the misery, and the deprivation of millions of human beings in the Third World and here.

What the ruling class hates about us is that despite a hundred years of repression, of fascism, of anticommunism, of imperialist wars, and of genocides, the revolution once again raises its head. In carrying out psychological warfare, the bourgeoisie, with its police state, sees in us everything that they hate and fear about the people, and this is especially so in the case of Andreas. It is he who is the mob, the street, the enemy. They see in us that which menaces them and will overthrow them: the determination to provoke the revolution, revolutionary violence, and political and military action. At the same time they see their own powerlessness, for their power ends at the point when the people take up arms and begin to struggle.

The system is exposing itself, not us, in its defamation campaign. All defamation campaigns against the guerilla reveal something about those who carry them out, about their piggishness, about their goals, their ambitions, and their fears.

And to say we are "a vanguard that designates itself as such" makes no sense. To be the vanguard is a role that we cannot assign ourselves, nor is it one that we can demand. It is a role that the people give to the guerilla in their own consciousness, in the process of developing their consciousness, of rediscovering their role in history as they recognize themselves in the guerilla's actions, because they, "in themselves," recognize the necessity to destroy the system "for themselves" through guerilla actions. The idea of a "vanguard that designates itself as such" reflects ideas of prestige that belong to a ruling class that seeks to dominate. But that has nothing to do with the role of the proletariat, a role that is based on the absence of property, on emancipation, on dialectical materialism, and on the struggle against imperialism.

THE DIALECTIC
OF REVOLUTION AND COUNTERREVOLUTION
That is the dialectic of the anti-imperialist struggle. The enemy unmasks itself by its defensive maneuvers, by the system's reaction, by the counterrevolutionary escalation, by the transformation of the political state of emergency into a military state of emergency. This is how it shows its true face—and by its terrorism it provokes the masses to rise up against it, reinforcing the contradictions and making revolution inevitable.

As Marighella said:

> *The basic principle of revolutionary strategy in conditions of permanent political crisis is to develop, in the city as well as in the countryside, such a breadth of revolutionary activity that the enemy finds himself obliged to transform the political situation in the country into a military situation. In this way dissatisfaction spreads to all layers of the population, with the military alone responsible for all of the hatred.*

And as a Persian comrade, A.P. Puyan,[1] said:

> *By extending the violence against the resistance fighters, creating an unanticipated reaction, the repression inevitably hits all other oppressed milieus and classes in an even more massive way. As a result, the ruling class augments the contradictions between the oppressed classes and itself and creates a climate which leads of necessity to a great leap forward in the consciousness of the masses.*

And Marx said:

> *Revolutionary progress is proceeding in the right direction when it provokes a powerful, unified counterrevolution, which backfires by developing an adversary that cannot lead the party of the insurrection against the counterrevolution except by becoming a truly revolutionary party.*[2]

In 1972, the cops mobilized 150,000 men to hunt the RAF, using television to involve the people in the manhunt, having the Federal Chancellor intervene, and centralizing all police forces in the hands of the BKA. This makes it clear that, already at that point, a numerically insignificant group of revolutionaries was all it took to set in motion all of the

---

1 Amir Parviz Puyan was a prominent member of the Organization of the People's Fedayeen Guerillas, a Marxist-Leninist guerilla group established in 1971. By the time of the 1979 revolution, the OPFG was the most significant guerilla group operating in Iran.

2 Probably quoted from memory, this is a mangled paraphrasing of an argument from Marx's "The Class Struggles in France." The full passage as it appears in Marx and Engels, *Selected Works II*, ed. V. Adoretsky (London: Lawrence and Wishart, 1942), 192: "revolutionary advance made headway not by its immediate tragi-comic achievements, but on the contrary by the creation of a powerful, united counter-revolution, by the creation of an opponent, by fighting which the party of revolt first ripened into a real revolutionary party."

material and human resources of the state. It was already clear that the state's monopoly of violence had material limits, that their forces could be exhausted, that if, on the tactical level, imperialism is a beast that devours humans, on the strategic level it is a paper tiger. It was clear that it is up to us whether the oppression continues, and it is also up to us to smash it.

Now, after everything they have carried out against us with their psychological warfare campaign, the pigs are preparing to assassinate Andreas. As of today, we political prisoners, members of the RAF and other anti-imperialist groups, are beginning a hunger strike.[1] We must add the fact that for some years now—in keeping with the police objective of liquidating the RAF, and consistent with their tactic of psychological warfare—most of us have found ourselves detained in isolation. Which is to say, we have found ourselves in the process of being exterminated. But we have decided not to stop thinking and struggling: we have decided to dump the rocks the state has thrown at us at its own feet.

The police are preparing to assassinate Andreas, as they attempted previously during the summer 1973 hunger strike when they deprived him of water. At that time, they attempted to have the lawyers and the public believe that he was allowed to drink again after a few days: in reality he received nothing, and the pig of a doctor at the Schwalmstadt prison, after nine days, when he had already gone blind, said, "If you don't drink some milk, you'll be dead in ten hours." The Hessen Minister of Justice came from time to time to have a look in his cell, and the Hessen prison doctors' group was at that time meeting with the Wiesbaden Minister of Justice. There exists a decree in Hessen that anticipates breaking hunger strikes by withholding all liquids. The complaints filed against the pig of a doctor for attempted murder were rejected, and the procedure undertaken to maintain the complaint was suspended.

We declare today that if the cops attempt to follow through with their plans to deprive Andreas of water, all RAF prisoners participating in the hunger strike will immediately react in turn by refusing all liquids. We will react in the same way if faced with any attempted assassination through the withholding of water, no matter where it occurs or against which prisoner it is used.

Ulrike Meinhof
September 13, 1974

---

1 This signaled the third of the RAF prisoners' hunger strikes; see page 253.

The Bombing of the Bremen Train Station

RAF actions are never directed against the people. Given the choice of target, the bomb that exploded in the Bremen Central Station on Saturday bears the mark of the ongoing security police operation. To intimidate and control the people, they are no longer restricting themselves to the fascist tactic of threats:

- of bombings, as in Stuttgart in June 1972;
- of rocket attacks against the millions of spectators at the Soccer World Cup in March 1974;
- of poisoning the people's drinking water in Baden-Württemberg in August 1974.[2]

The state security police have now escalated to provocative actions, with the risk of unleashing a bloodbath upon the people.

The RAF prisoners
December 9, 1974

---

2 These are actions the police and media claimed the RAF was planning.

The Nature of the
Stammheim Trial:
The Prisoners Testify

All there is to say regarding our identity is that which remains of the moral person in this trial: nothing. In this trial, the moral person—this concept created by the authorities—has been liquidated in every possible way—both through the guilty sentence Schmidt has already pronounced and through the Federal Supreme Court decision relative to §231a[1] of the Penal Code in the recent hearing before the Federal Administrative Court, which, by ratifying the Federal Supreme Court decision, has done away with the legal fictions of the Basic Law.

Given that the prisoners do not have any recognized rights, our identity is objectively reduced to the trial itself. And the trial is—this much one should perhaps say about the indictment—about an offense committed by an organization. The charges of murder and attempted murder are based on the concept of collective responsibility, a concept which has no basis in law. The entire indictment is demagogy—and this has become clear, just as it has become clear (ever since his outburst during the evidentiary hearing) why Prinzing must exclude us. As a result, it must be demagogically propped up with perjury and restrictions on our depositions. And we see how Prinzing sees things in a way that allows for a verdict even though there is no evidence; and so it becomes clear why he previously, and now for a second time, felt obliged to decimate the defense with a volley of legislation and illegal attacks.

We have been amused by this for some time now.

We consider what is going on here to be a masterpiece of reactionary art. Here, in this "palace of freedom" (as Prinzing calls these state security urinals), state security is pitifully subsumed within a mass of alienated activities. Or in other words, it's as if the same piece is being played out on three superimposed levels of the same Renaissance stage—the military level, the judicial level, and the political level.

The indictment is based on a pack of lies.

---

1 §231a and §231b allowed for trials to continue in the absence of a defendant, if the reason for this absence was found to be of the defendant's own doing—a stipulation directly aimed at the prisoners' effective use of hunger strikes.

After state security suppressed nine-tenths of the files—and, as Wunder stated, it wasn't the BAW, but the BKA: the BAW itself, according to Wunder, is only familiar with a fraction of these files—they have been obliged to work with lies.

One of the lies is the claim that one can, using §129, construct an indictment that can allow for a "normal criminal trial"—even though this paragraph, since it inception, that is to say since the communist trials in Cologne in 1849,[2] has been openly used to criminalize political activity, assimilating proletarian politics into criminality. So as to not disrupt normal criminal proceedings, they use the concept of "criminal association," a concept that historically has only come into play when dealing with proletarian organizations.

It is a lie to say that the goal of a revolutionary organization is to commit reprehensible acts.

The revolutionary organization is not a legal entity, and its aims—we say, its goals and objectives—cannot be understood in dead categories like those found in the penal code, which represents the bourgeoisie's ahistorical view of itself. As if, outside of the state apparatus and the imperialist financial oligarchy, there is anyone who commits crimes that have as their objective oppression, enslavement, murder, and fraud—which are only the watered down expressions of imperialism's goals.

Given the role and the function that §129 has had in class conflicts since 1848, it is a special law. Ever since the trial of the Cologne Communists, since the Bismarck Socialist Laws, since the "law against participation in associations that are enemies of the state" during the Weimar Republic, its legacy and essence has been to criminalize the extra-parliamentary opposition by institutionalizing anticommunism within parliament's legal machinery.

In and of itself, bourgeois democracy—which in Germany has taken form as a constitutional state—has always found its fascist complement to the degree that it legalizes the liquidation of the extra-parliamentary opposition, with its tendency to become antagonistic. In this sense, justice has always been class justice, which is to say, political justice.

In other words, bourgeois democracy is inherently dysfunctional given its role in stifling class struggle when different factions of capital come in conflict with each other within the competitive capitalist

---

2 Following the 1848 working-class uprising in Germany in which prominent communists including Karl Marx and Friedrich Engels played an important role, a series of trials in Cologne was used in a partially successful attempt to destroy the Communist League, also known as the First International.

system. In the bourgeois constitution, it anticipates the class struggle as class war. Communists have always been outlaws in Germany, and anticommunism a given.

That also means that Prinzing—with his absurd claim that this is a "normal criminal trial" despite the fact that the charges are based on this special law—is operating in an absolute historical vacuum, which explains his hysteria. The BAW operates in a legal vacuum situated somewhere between the bourgeois constitutional state and open fascism. Nothing is normal and everything is the "exception," with the objective of rendering such a situation the norm. Even the state's reaction—which of course this judge fails to grasp—places our treatment in the historical tradition of the persecution of extra-parliamentary opposition to the bourgeois state. Prinzing himself, with §129, establishes the historical identity this state shares with the Kaiser's Reich, the Weimar Republic, and the Third Reich. The latter was simply more thorough in its criminalization and destruction of the extra-parliamentary opposition than the Weimar Republic and the Federal Republic.

Finally, this paragraph conveys the conscious nature of this political corruption of justice, as it violates the constitutional idea that "Nobody can be deprived of…" and because today, just as in the 50s, it lays the basis for trials based on opinions, that is to say, for the criminalization of opinions.

It is a paragraph that is dysfunctional, given that the bourgeois state claims that the bourgeoisie is by its very nature the political class. Within the bourgeois state's system of self-justification, it reflects the fact that the system—capitalism—is transitory, as their special law against class antagonism undermines the ideology of the bourgeois state.

As a special law, it cannot produce any consensus, and no consensus is expected. It equates the monopoly of violence with parliamentarianism and private ownership of the means of production. Clearly, this law is also an expression of the weakness of the proletariat here since 45. They want to legally safeguard the situation that the U.S. occupation forces established here, by destroying all examples of autonomous and antagonistic organization.

The entire construct, with its lies, simply reveals the degree to which the imperialist superstructure has lost touch with its own base, has lost touch with everything that makes up life and history. It reveals the deep contradiction found at the heart of the break between society and the state. It reveals the degree to which all the factors that mediate between real life and imperialist legality are dispensed with in this, the most advanced stage of imperialism. They are antagonistic. The relationship is one of war, within which maintaining legitimacy is reduced to simply camouflaging nakedly opportunist calculations.

In short, we only intend to refer to the concept of an offense committed by an organization, which forms the entire basis for Buback's charge, and which—as it is the only way possible—has been developed through propaganda.

But we also do this in the sense of Blanqui: the revolutionary organization will naturally be considered criminal until the old order of bourgeois ownership of the means of production that criminalizes us is replaced by a new order—an order that establishes the social appropriation of social production.

The law, as long as there are classes, as long as human beings dominate other human beings, is a question of power.

The RAF Prisoners
August 19, 1975

In order to create greater publicity for this statement from the guerilla regarding the right-wing attacks, on September 14, 1975, we announced that a bomb would explode in Munich Central Station at 6:50 PM. At 6:55 PM, we telephoned to direct the search to locker 2005, in which, rather than a bomb, the following statement was found:

No Bomb in Munich Central Station

Disappointed that once again there is no "bloodbath" to blame on "violent anarchists," as was the case in Birmingham,[1] in Milan,[2] and most recently here at home, in Bremen in December 74, and yesterday in Hamburg?

This is to make something perfectly clear to you cops and those of you on the editorial staffs of the newspapers and the radio stations:

The guerilla's statements and practice show that their attacks are directed against the ruling class and their resistance is against the system's oppression.

- In June 72, the police tried to create panic in Stuttgart with bomb threats. They used the World Cup to threaten thousands with claims that the guerilla planned rocket attacks against football stadiums. As part of their intimidation, they spoke of a plan to poison the drinking water in Baden-Würrtemberg. In Bremen, in December 74, and yesterday in Hamburg, provocateurs acted for real: explosives were set off in the midst of large groups of people. Without any consideration for the health and wellbeing of the people, they turned their threats into deeds, doing everything they can to increase the agitation against the radical left and the guerilla.

---

1 On November 21, 1974, bombs in two pubs in Birmingham, England claimed twenty-one lives. These bombings were denounced by the left as a counterinsurgency action meant to discredit the Irish nationalist movement, but the IRA acknowledged its responsibility some years later.

2 On December 12, 1969, a bomb exploded in a public square in Milan killing a large number of people. Initially blamed on anarchists, the action was subsequently proven to be the work of fascists supported by the Italian security services and NATO.

- The guerilla in Germany has attacked the U.S. Army, which was engaged in a war against the Vietnamese people. The guerilla has bombed the Federal Constitutional Court, the capitalist associations, and the enemies of the Chilean and Palestinian people. They kidnapped the CDU leader Lorenz to gain the freedom of political prisoners. They struggle against rising prices and the increased pressure brought to bear on the people, e.g., the Berlin transit price actions.[3]

We demand that the press, the radios, and TV broadcast this statement!
We are the urban guerilla groups

> Red Army Faction
> 2nd of June Movement
> Revolutionary Cells

And above all struggle against those who are responsible for planning and carrying out the attacks in Bremen and Hamburg. The choice of targets shows who the culprits are. [...][4]

> Red Army Faction
> 2nd of June Movement
> Revolutionary Cells
> September 14, 1975

---

3 Many of the actions listed here were carried out by the Revolutionary Cells. For more on this guerilla organization, see pages 436-41.
4 This was the most complete version of this document available to us.

The Bombing of the
Hamburg Train Station

In the face of the state propaganda effort to tie the attack at the Hamburg Central Station to the RAF, we state clearly: the nature of this explosion speaks the language of reaction. It can only be understood as part of the psychological war that state security is waging against the urban guerilla. The method and objective of this crime against the people bear the mark of a fascist provocation.

The political-military actions of the urban guerilla are never directed against the people. The RAF's attacks target the imperialist apparatus, its military, political, economic, and cultural institutions and its functionaries in the repressive and ideological state structures.

In its offensive against the state, the urban guerilla cannot resort to terrorism as a weapon. The urban guerilla operates in the rift between the state and the masses, working to widen it and to develop political consciousness, revolutionary solidarity, and proletarian power against the state.

In opposition to this, this intelligence service-directed terrorist provocation against the people is meant to increase fear and strengthen the people's identification with the state. At the Hessen Forum, Wassermann, the President of the Braunschweig Court of Appeals explained the state security countertactic—in his words, one must "increase citizens' feelings of insecurity" and "act on the basis of this subjective feeling of fear."

In the meantime, the *Frankfurter Rundschau* report (September 9) confirmed that the state security counter-operations conducted since 72 (bomb threats against Stuttgart, threats to poison drinking water, stolen stocks of mustard gas, SAM rocket attacks on football stadiums, the bomb attack on Bremen Central Station and now in Hamburg) were developed from programs created by the CIA. The FR is only substantiating what has been known for a long time now, that the use of poison in subway tunnels and the contamination of drinking water in large cities is a special warfare countertactic, a "psychological operation" of intelligence services and counterguerilla units.

At this point, the question to be answered is whether the attack in Hamburg was the act of a lone criminal, of the radical right-wing Bremen group under intelligence service control, of state security itself, or of the special CIA counterinsurgency unit established at the American embassy in Bonn after Stockholm.

What is certain is that state security works within the reactionary structures through a network of state security journalists who use the media conglomerates and public institutions to attack the urban guerilla. High profile figures in this network close to the BKA's press office and the BAW press conferences are Krumm of the *Frankfurter Rundschau,* Busche of the *Frankfurter Allgemeine Zeitung,* Leicht and Kuchnert of the *Süddeutsche Zeitung,* and Rieber and Zimmermann, who are published in many national newspapers. Zimmermann's article about the alleged connection between the attack, the RAF, the 2nd of June Movement, and Siegfried Haag was simultaneously published in eight national newspapers.

The incredible fact that state reaction is now resorting to such measures against the weak urban guerilla here simply indicates the strategic importance of this instability for the Federal Republic as part of the U.S. imperialist chain of states. In the North-South and East-West conflicts, the FRG is a central base of operations for U.S. imperialism; militarily in NATO, economically in the European Community, politically and ideologically through the Social Democrats and their leadership role in the Socialist International.

The state's attempt to use its intelligence services to provoke a reactionary mass mobilization is not a response to the guerilla, but is rather a reaction to strategic conditions; namely, the economic and political weakness of the U.S. chain of states. They are responding to the future potential and current reality of revolutionary politics. The objective and function of psychological warfare, in the way it is being waged against every democratic initiative, is to cause splits, isolation, withdrawal, and eventually extermination.

Marx said, "Revolutionary progress disrupts the course of a closed and powerful counterrevolution by producing rebels who convert the party of resistance into a truly revolutionary party."[1]

The urban guerilla has shown that the only way to resist state terror is through armed proletarian politics.

The RAF Prisoners
Stammheim
September 23, 1975

---

1 Probably quoted from memory, this is a very mangled version of a phrase from Marx's "Class Struggles in France." See page 367, fn 2.

The Bombing of the
Cologne Train Station

On the night of November 11-12, state security agents and/or fascists again set off a bomb in a train station—first Hamburg and Nuremberg, and now Cologne.

The federal government's Terrorism Division and the cops hoped to create a bloodbath with this pointless act of terrorism. In Bremen and Hamburg, the bombs exploded on Federal Football League game days. In Cologne, the Carnival began on November 11, certainly a night when many people would be out; it was only by chance that no one was injured. [...]

The urban guerilla has often stated, and has proven through its practice since 1970, that its actions are never and have never been directed against the people. [...][1]

Red Army Faction
2nd of June Movement
Revolutionary Cells
November 1975

---

1 This was the most complete version of this document available to us.

10

The Murder of Ulrike Meinhof

O N MAY 9, 1976, THE state announced that Ulrike Meinhof had committed suicide.

Government officials claimed that the guerilla leader had hanged herself following a period of extreme depression provoked by tension with her co-defendants, particularly Andreas Baader.

The prisoners' lawyers responded to the alleged suicide almost immediately. One of her attorneys, Michael Oberwinder, challenged the claim that Meinhof had been suffering from extreme depression:

> *I myself talked with Frau Meinhof... last Wednesday... regarding the suits. There was not the least sign of disinterest on her part, rather we had an animated discussion in the context of which Frau Meinhof explained the group's point of view.*[2]

He further added:

> *If Federal Prosecutor Kaul, as it says here, speaks of a certain coldness between Ulrike Meinhof and Andreas Baader, that is a monstrous claim that doesn't correspond to reality.*

---

2 Commission internationale d'enquête sur la mort d'Ulrike Meinhof, 9.

Defense attorney Otto Schily further posed some interesting questions:

> *Why didn't they allow a trusted doctor chosen by (Meinhof's) sister to assist in the autopsy? Why the suspicious haste regarding the autopsy?*[1]

Her attorney Axel Azzola dismissed the theory out of hand:

> *The authorities are responsible for her death. There is no such thing as suicide. There are only the pursuers and the pursued.*[2]

The defense attorneys called for an independent investigation. As a result, on July 16, 1976, an International Investigatory Commission into the Death of Ulrike Meinhof was formed;[3] its findings, delivered on December 15, 1978, revealed compelling evidence that Meinhof had been murdered, with some suggesting that it also pointed to the possibility that she had been raped beforehand.

In examining the autopsy report, the Commission uncovered a series of medical contradictions. A group of English doctors noted the absence of usual signs of asphyxiation, the normal cause of death in a suicide by hanging:

> *The report mentions neither bulging of the eyes or tongue, nor a cyanosis (bruising) of the face, habitual signs of death by asphyxiation. In spite of the fracture of the hyoid bone at the base of the tongue, there is no swelling of the neck in the area of the mark left by the "rope made from a bath towel" from which the prisoner was hanging. The negative results are irregular for a death by asphyxiation, that is the least we can say. On the other hand, they fit a death by pneumo-cartic compression very well, that is to say a death by pressure on the carotid artery, which can provoke death by a reflexive cardiac arrest.*

---

1 Ibid., 10.

2 United Press International, "German rebel hangs herself," *Pharos Tribune,* May 10, 1976.

3 The commissioners were: Michelle Beauvillard (a lawyer from Paris), Claude Bourdet (a journalist from Paris), Georges Casalis (a theologian from Paris), Robert Davezies (a journalist from Paris), Joachim Israel (a sociology professor from Copenhagen), Panayotis Kanelakis (a lawyer from Athens), Henrik Kaufholz (a journalist from Denmark), John McGuffin (a writer from Belfast), Hans-Joachim Meyer (a neuropsychiatrist from the FRG), and Jean-Pierre Vigier (a doctor from Paris).

To many supporters, this evidence seemed to indicate that Meinhof was strangled to death before being hanged.

Furthermore, the autopsy results suggested to some that Meinhof had been raped before she was murdered:

> *The two autopsy reports mention a marked edema in the external genital area and swelling of the two calves. The two reports mention an abrasion covered with clotted blood on the left buttock. The Janssen report also mentions an ecchymosis on the right hip. The chemical analysis for sperm had, according to the official statement, a positive result, in spite of the absence of spermatozoa.*[4]

A letter from Dr. Klaus Jarosch, a professor at the University of Linz, to defense attorney Michael Oberwinder, dated August 17, 1976, concurred with the opinion of the English doctors: "It certainly does not appear to be a typical death by asphyxiation due to hanging...."[5]

There were several problems with the claim that Meinhof had used her prison towel to fashion a rope for hanging herself. Both the report of West German neuropsychiatrist Hans-Joachim Meyer[6] and that of the Stuttgart-based Technical Institute of Criminology[7] noted discrepancies in the width and length of the towel-rope found in Meinhof's cell, and the other towels in Stammheim. Furthermore, the TIC noted that neither Meinhof's scissors nor the table knife in her cell had any traces of fiber on them, raising the question of how the towel would have been cut.[8] Finally, RAF prisoner Ingrid Schubert declared that the prisoners had carried out a series of tests with their own prison issue towels, and

---

4 Commission internationale d'enquête sur la mort d'Ulrike Meinhof, 25. It should be noted that Stefan Aust, the most intelligent defender of the state's version of events, objects that "the 'sperm test' was a phosphatase test customarily carried out to establish the presence of certain yeasts. There are many of these, found not only in sperm but in all proteins, also occurring as a result of bacterial contamination. Thus, such a test will be positive in the majority of cases. Only if it gives a negative result are further specialized tests unnecessary. In Ulrike Meinhof's case, further microchemical and microscopic tests were carried out, and clearly showed that the protein traces were not spermatic filaments." (Aust, 346-7) The editors of this volume are highly skeptical of the state's story, and yet feel readers are best situated to make up their own minds on the matter.

5 Commission internationale d'enquête sur la mort d'Ulrike Meinhof, 28.

6 Ibid., 32-34.

7 Ibid., 45-46.

8 Ibid., 46.

that neither new nor old towels had managed to bear a weight of more than fifty kilos without tearing out of the window grating.[1]

There were also significant contradictions regarding a chair allegedly used in the hanging. The report of the legal doctor and that of the criminal police claimed that the chair placed on top of a mattress was supporting Meinhof's left leg. The chair is not mentioned in the report of Schreitmüller, a prison functionary, who explicitly stated, "I did not see a chair." When questioned by Croissant, he even went so far as to state that the report of a chair, published in *Spiegel*, was false. Prison doctor Henck stated in his report, "The feet were 20 cm from the floor." Police reports mentioned neither the chair nor the mattress. The prisoners, in their statement, noted that a chair on such an unstable base would surely have tipped as a result of reflex motions, and that such reflex motions would have caused severe bruising of the legs.[2]

Important objects were missing in the inventory of her cell taken following her death. A blanket she always used, on which Andreas Baader's name was sewn, had gone missing, and was never found. Similarly, Meinhof was found dead wearing black pants and a grey shirt, whereas that day she had been wearing blue jeans and a red shirt. The Commission posed the question as to why a woman intent on committing suicide would change before doing so, and noted that investigators never made any effort to examine the clothing she had been wearing earlier that day.[3]

On the evening of her death, the duty guard removed the light bulbs from Meinhof's cell, as was standard procedure. However, the May 10 inventory turned up a light bulb in Meinhof's desk lamp. A test for fingerprints produced some partial prints, insufficient for positive identification, but in no way matching those of Ulrike Meinhof. The Commission further noted that the result of these fingerprint tests was only sent to the investigators after the investigation had been closed.[4]

The way in which the autopsy was conducted also raised serious concerns. Neither the prisoners nor their lawyers were permitted to see the body before the autopsy. Professor Rauschke, the specialist in legal medicine appointed by the state to conduct the autopsy, failed to carry out skin tests that could have established whether or not Meinhof was

---

1 Ibid., 42-43.
2 Ibid., 46.
3 Ibid., 47-49.
4 Ibid., 47-48.

Ulrike's Brain

A gruesome postscript to Ulrike Meinhof's death and the subsequent cover-up surfaced decades later.

In 2002, it came to light that the BAW had arranged for Meinhof's brain to be surreptitiously removed during her autopsy and delivered to the neurologist Jürgen Peiffer at Tübingen University. The state was still curious as to whether "left-wing terrorism" might in fact be the result of some kind of neurological disorder. Peiffer was happy to oblige, and after carrying out his tests claimed that Meinhof did indeed suffer from brain damage, which "undoubtedly gives cause to raise questions in court about how responsible she was for her action."[1]

Following this, Meinhof's brain was stored away in a cardboard box where it remained untouched for twenty years, until 1997 when it was transferred to the Psychiatric Clinic in Magdeburg. There, Dr. Bernhard Bogerts, a psychiatrist, studied it for five years, coming to a similarly totalitarian conclusion, namely that "The slide into terror can be explained by the brain illness."[2]

At the demand of her daughters, Meinhof's brain was interred at her burial place on December 22, 2002.

In 2002, it was also revealed that Andreas Baader, Jan-Carl Raspe, and Gudrun Ensslin—who had all been similarly "suicided" in Stammheim—had all had their brains removed prior to burial in 1977, without their relatives' knowledge or consent.

The whereabouts of their brains remains unknown today.[3]

---

[1] Roger Boyles, "Daughter Defies State Over Ulrike Meinhof's Brain," *The Times* [online], November 9, 2002.

[2] *BBC News* [online], "Meinhof Brain Study Yields Clues," November 12, 2002.

[3] *Spiegel* [online], "Gehirne der toten RAF-Terroristen verschwunden," November 16, 2002.

dead prior to being hanged.[1] Rauschke had also performed the autopsy on Siegfried Hausner, and some supporters and members of the guerilla would point to this as further evidence of a cover-up, given the theory some held at that time that Hausner's autopsy had been used to camouflage the fact that he had been beaten to death by the Swedish police.[2]

There were also problems regarding the inspection of the cell. Klaus Croissant, Meinhof's sister Inge Wienke Zitzlaff, and her step-daughter Anja Röhl were all denied the right to attend the inventory, while attorney Michael Oberwinder was only permitted to stay in the hallway outside of the cell as the Criminal Police searched it for five hours.[3] Two days after her death, the entire cell, including the window grating, was painted. This is not standard procedure. It was not until after this that lawyers and relatives were permitted inside the cell.[4]

Given the mass of evidence, the Commission concluded:

> *The totality of the medical and legal contradictions, facts, and evidence that we have uncovered and proven, rule out the possibility of suicide as the cause of Meinhof's death.*[5]

At a conference in May 1975, Dr. Hans Josef Horchem, at the time head of the *Verfassungsschutz*, had underscored Meinhof's importance in the eyes of the state. "Through the lack of new ideologues of Ulrike Meinhof's quality," the head of the political police had mused, "the continuation of the phenomenon of terror could be curtailed."[6]

Noting this, the Commission concluded:

> *It is not impossible that Ulrike Meinhof's death was part of a secret service strategy to combat the RAF. In which case, her "suicide" would have been meant to show everyone how her politics and those of the RAF had failed, and how, by her "suicide," she herself had recognized this failure.*[7]

---

1 Ibid., 62-64.

2 This theory regarding Hausner's death disappeared from RAF statements before the end of the decade. For a synopsis, see sidebar, page 334.

3 Ditfurth, 440.

4 Commission internationale d'enquête sur la mort d'Ulrike Meinhof, 64-65.

5 Ibid., 50.

6 Ibid., 81.

7 Ibid., 81. For instance, immediately after Meinhof's death, one UPI article was claiming that "Acquaintances said Mrs. Meinhof may have killed herself because she despaired of achieving her goal of overthrowing what she called the 'repressive capitalist bourgeois system.'" (United Press International, "German Rebel Hangs

The Commission further noted that the murder of Ulrike Meinhof would be far from inconsistent with past treatment of RAF prisoners. Andreas Baader, Ronald Augustin, and Ali Jansen had been deprived of water for extensive periods during hunger strikes.[8] They also noted that Holger Meins, Katharina Hammerschmidt, and Siegfried Hausner had all died as a result of medical mistreatment.[9]

The timing of Meinhof's death was also taken by some as evidence of a counterinsurgency operation. On May 4, the prisoners had filed demands for the production of evidence. The demands were aimed at unmasking specific political and union figures, and, in particular, at revealing that both the current SPD Chancellor, Helmut Schmidt, and his predecessor, Willy Brandt, had ties to the CIA.

According to the Commission, "It is clear that the confrontation would have reached its climax at this point in the trial."[10]

These demands, as it turns out, were based on Meinhof's work. Documents pertinent to this subject, as well as those pertinent to other work she was doing, documents that she always kept with her, were never seen again after her death.

As far as the Commission was concerned, the question was not whether Meinhof's strategy might have damaged well-known politicians. Rather, the Commissioners noted that Meinhof's plan risked

---

Herself"). *Bild* was, of course, more crude, implying Meinhof was jealous of Ensslin's relationship with Baader: after stating that the guerilla leader had "made herself look beautiful one more time," it claimed that she killed herself because she "could see how it was not only their shared convictions that united Andreas Baader and Gudrun Ensslin but also recollections of their shared pleasures in the bedroom." (Quoted in Clare Bielby, "'Bonnie und Kleid': Female Terrorists and the Hysterical Feminine.")

8 Komitees gegen Folter, 28, 30.

9 Commission internationale d'enquête sur la mort d'Ulrike Meinhof, 74-75.

10 Ibid., 80-81.

dealing a serious blow to the Attorney General's use of the Stammheim trial to depoliticize the defendants and the actions for which they were being held accountable.

The prisoners would subsequently insist that even the concept of institutional murder regarding Meinhof's death was not precise enough. Rather, it was the execution of a revolutionary in the context of a military conflict.[1] As Meinhof herself had said in court the day before she was found dead, "It is, of course, a police tactic in counterinsurgency conflicts, in guerilla warfare, to take out the leaders."[2]

Meinhof's sister, Inge Wienke Zitzlaff, similarly rejected the state's version of events. "My sister once told me very clearly she never would commit suicide," she remembered. "She said if it ever were reported that she killed herself then I would know she had been murdered."[3]

Not only members of the RAF support scene, but also many in the undogmatic left and the K-groups, agreed that Meinhof's death must have been a case of murder.

An open letter signed by various intellectuals—including Jean-Paul Sartre and Simone de Beauvoir—compared it to the worst crimes of the Nazi era.[4] Left-wing poet—and former anti-Nazi resistance fighter—Erich Fried described the fallen guerilla as "the most important woman in German politics since Rosa Luxemburg."[5]

There was a wave of low-level attacks against German targets across Europe. In Paris, the offices of two West German steel companies were bombed, as was the German

---

1 Interview with Le Monde Diplomatique, see page 408.

2 *Deutsche Welle* [online], "Journalists Unearth Rare Terrorism Trial Tapes from 1970s," July 31, 2007.

3 United Press International, "Urban Guerilla Leader Hangs Herself in Cell," *Hayward Daily Review*, May 10, 1976.

4 NEA/London Economist News Service, "Friends Mourn Meinhof's Tragic Death," *Pharos Tribune*, May 23, 1976.

5 *Frankfurter Allgemeine Zeitung*, May 17, 1976, quoted in Kramer, 195.

Cultural Center in Toulouse[6] and Daimler-Benz in Nimes. In Italy, the German Academy and the West German Travel Bureau in Rome were firebombed;[7] in Milan, targets associated with Bosch and Volkswagen were attacked. The West German consulate in Venice was similarly firebombed. On May 11, the West German consulate in Copenhagen was firebombed.

Meanwhile, back in the FRG, bombs went off in Munich outside the U.S. Armed Forces radio station and in a shopping center in the middle of the night,[8] and a molotov cocktail was thrown at the *Land* Courthouse in Wuppertal.

Thousands reacted with sorrow and rage, demonstrations took place across the country, and both social and political prisoners in Berlin-Tegel Prison held a three-day hunger strike, as did thirty-six captives at the Hessen Women's Prison.

Fighting was particularly fierce in Frankfurt; according to one police spokesperson, it was "the most brutal in the postwar history of the city."[9] Following a rally organized by the *sponti* left,[10] with the watchword that "Ulrike Meinhof is Dead—Let's Rescue the Living," hundreds of people rampaged through the downtown area, breaking the windows at American Express and the America House cultural center, setting up barricades and defending them against police water cannons with molotov cocktails. Twelve people were arrested and seven cops were injured, one of them seriously when his car was set ablaze as he sat in it.[11]

As we shall see in Section 11, this demonstration and the reaction to it constituted a turning point for the *sponti* scene.

On May 15, some 7,000 people, many with their faces blackened and heads covered to avoid identification by the police, attended Meinhof's funeral in West Berlin.[12] Wienke Zitzlaff requested that in lieu of flowers,

---

6 United Press International, "German Terrorist Dies Violent Death in Prison," *Coshocton Tribune*, May 10, 1976.

7 NEA/London Economic News Service, "Tragic Death is Mourned," *Uniontown Morning Herald*, May 27, 1976.

8 *Corpus Christi Times*, "Bombing seen as protest," May 14, 1976.

9 *Winnipeg Free Press*, "Uneven contest," May 19, 1976.

10 Roger Cohen, "Germany's Foreign Minister is Pursued by his Firebrand Self," *New York Times* [online], January 15, 2001.

11 *Lincoln Star*, "Anarchist's Death Causes Bombings," May 11, 1976.

12 Varon, 234.

Meinhof, described as "the most important woman in German politics since Rosa Luxemburg," would not be forgotten by future generations.

left: "Ulrike Meinhof, murdered 9.5.1976 in Stammheim prison—Protest is when I say I don't like this and that. Resistance is when I see to it that things that I don't like no longer occur."

right: "Because freedom is only possible in the struggle for liberation; Lesbian demostration at Ulrike's grave on October 7, 1995; Internationalist Feminists will celebrate Ulrike Meinhof's 61st birthday; Build a Revolutionary Women's Movement"

donations be made to the prisoners' support campaign.[1] When they left the cemetery, mourners joined with demonstrations in downtown West Berlin and at the Moabit courthouse where Meinhof had been sentenced two years earlier in her trial with Horst Mahler and Hans-Jürgen Bäcker.[2]

That same day, there were bomb attacks in Hamm in North Rhine-Westphalia, and also in Rome, Seville, and Zurich.

Three days later, there was another demonstration of 8,000 people in West Berlin, during which several police officers were injured. Bombs continued to go off in France, and cars with German license plates and

---

1 Associated Press, "Anarchist Buried," *Waterloo Courier,* May 16, 1976.
2 United Press International, "Funeral to demonstration," *Playground Daily News,* May 16, 1976.

the offices of a right-wing newspaper were targeted.[3] On June 2, the Revolutionary Cells bombed the U.S. Army Headquarters and U.S. Officers' Club in Frankfurt, carrying out the attack under the banner of the "Ulrike Meinhof Commando."[4] That same day, just outside the city, two fully loaded military trucks at a U.S. airbase were blown up.

Claims that Meinhof had committed suicide were interpreted by the RAF as part of the state's psychological warfare campaign, a horrible escalation intended to discredit the guerilla in general and Meinhof's participation in particular.

In an attempt to refute claims that there had been a falling out between Meinhof and the others, or that she was weakening in her resolve, the prisoners opted to release several documents she had written just before her death.

These documents were accompanied by the following stipulation by Jan-Carl Raspe:

> *This is a fragment about the structure of the group, which Ulrike insisted on presenting in Stammheim, in order to destroy the leadership theory around which the BAW wanted to build this trial. Andreas was opposed, and we all wanted to write it differently.*
>
> *It is not very important, but I have put it out today anyway because it refutes Buback's filthy lies—"the conflict"—and because this is what Ulrike was working on last.*
>
> *It must only be published in its entirety, accompanied by the two letters to Hanna Krabbe and the one to the Hamburg prisoners.*

These documents were intended to refute allegations that Meinhof had committed suicide by showing her to be as committed and determined as ever. Ironically, this makes them amongst the least interesting of the statements from the captured combatants. Meinhof's praise for the RAF's collective process and for Baader as an individual, taken out of context, may seem naïve, while her letters to other prisoners, which were not written for broad publication, would strike many as unduly harsh.

---

3 Associated Press, "Bombs damage building in Paris," *Oxnard Press Courier,* May 19, 1976.
4 United Press International, "Army Headquarters Hit by Terrorist Bombs," *Valley Morning Star,* June 2, 1976.

The prisoners were aware of this, and their reticence is noted by Raspe, but countering the suicide story was clearly viewed as being of greater importance. After all, the state had shown that it was prepared to incorporate the death or even murder of prisoners into its psychological warfare campaign. How could countering this campaign *not* assume the highest priority?

Apart from releasing Meinhof's last documents, the defense attorneys arranged for a collective interview with the prisoners, meant to be published in *Le Monde Diplomatique*, one of France's most important newspapers. Here, the prisoners put forward their view of the murder, the state's propaganda campaign, and the way in which their broken former comrades were used against them. (Although this interview was widely circulated within the radical left, to the best of our knowledge it was never in fact published in *Le Monde Diplomatique,* although the information was parsed into a series of articles that appeared at that time.)

The state's psychological warfare campaign failed in its attempt to turn Meinhof's death against the prisoners. The story it floated—that she had had a "falling out" with the others, supposedly as a result of the Springer bombing four years earlier[1]—was simply not credible.

Meinhof's death may have traumatized the RAF and its prisoners, but it certainly did not lessen their resolve. The stakes now seemed higher than ever, and West Germany's "fascist drift" seemed well nigh indisputable.

As never before, circumstances cried out for action.

The cry would not go unanswered.

---

1 The state would claim that Meinhof had organized this bombing, which the others disagreed with because of the risk posed to innocent bystanders. This version of events was flatly contradicted by Brigitte Mohnhaupt's testimony in Stammheim (see pages 357-58). Not to mention that since the Springer bombing, Meinhof and the others had continued to struggle together through isolation and three brutal hunger strikes.

Meinhof: The Suicide-Murder Debate

As strongly as we can, the editors of this book are putting forth the thesis that Ulrike Meinhof was murdered, while in no way presenting any information that we do not firmly believe to be true.

The history of the RAF and its support scene is only comprehensible if one appreciates that there was—and is—real evidence with which to dispute the state's suicide thesis. The belief that the state had murdered a revolutionary leader is based on neither paranoia nor flakey conspiracy theories, but on an abundance of inconsistencies and irregularities in how it dealt with her death, and on its culpability in the deaths of several other RAF combatants—Katharina Hammerschmidt, Holger Meins, and Siegfried Hausner.

In the years immediately following her death, progressive commentators would always refer to Meinhof's death as having occurred "under suspicious circumstances," a phrase which indicated skepticism regarding the state's claims that she had committed suicide. The radical left was in near unanimity about her murder, despite the lack of hard proof one way or the other.

It was enough that the government's story simply did not add up, and the onus was felt to be on the state to explain these inconsistencies.

Over the years, this position has reversed itself in scholarly, historical, and journalistic accounts. Although the many inconsistencies in the state's story remain, it continues to be said that these are more likely evidence of "incompetence" or "mistakes" than of a cover-up. As Meinhof's biographer Jutta Ditfurth explains it,

> The suspicion that Ulrike Meinhof might have been murdered continues to this day, and this has much to do with the careless, unprofessional, and hasty way that the responsible authorities mishandled the corpse.[2]

According to most people, including many on the left, the onus now lies with those who disbelieve the suicide theory to come up

---

2 Ditfurth, 444.

with incontrovertible evidence—perhaps a signed confession or a secret service memo—proving that Meinhof was murdered.

This principle of trusting the state and being skeptical of its adversaries says far more about the political culture in which we are living today, than about any proof or evidence of suicide that has ever come to light, for the essential facts known remain the same now as they were thirty-some years ago.

Without a shadow of a doubt, the decline of the murder thesis is a direct consequence of the decline of the RAF and its support scene. It is a chilling example of how, once a revolutionary tendency disappears, the state's version simply wins the contest by acclamation, no actual facts required.

Unlike the state, we do not claim there is a "correct position" on a question of fact that has yet to be proven. But we find it singularly unhealthy—and dishonest—when authors boldly state that "special investigations... amassed overwhelming evidence that Meinhof committed suicide,"[1] all the while failing to provide any of this "overwhelming evidence."

To understand the RAF's history, it is necessary to appreciate the shadowy and bizarre behavior of the state's functionaries in this matter, behavior for which the easiest explanation remains that they had something to hide.

As a matter of respect to a fallen revolutionary, it is necessary to remember that this question remains on the table.

---

1 Hockenos, 119.

Jan-Carl Raspe:
On the Murder of Ulrike Meinhof

I don't have much to say.

We believe Ulrike was executed. We don't know how, but we understand the reasoning behind the method chosen. I recall Herold's statement, "Actions against the RAF must primarily be developed in such a way as to undermine the positions held by sympathizers."

And Buback said, "State security is given life by those who are committed to it. People like Herold and myself, we always find a way."

It was a cold, calculated execution, just like with Holger, just like with Siegfried Hausner. If Ulrike had decided to end it all, to die, because she saw this as her last chance to save herself—to save her revolutionary identity—from the slow destruction of her will in isolation—then she would have told us—or at least she would have told Andreas: that was the nature of their relationship.

I believe that the execution of Ulrike now, at this moment, is a result of developments—an initial political breakthrough in the conflict between the international guerilla and the imperialist state in the Federal Republic. To say anything more about this would require getting into things I don't wish to discuss.

This murder is consistent with all of the state's attempts to deal with us over the past six years—the physical and psychological extermination of the RAF—and it is aimed at all of the guerilla groups in the Federal Republic, for whom Ulrike played an essential ideological role.

Now I want to say that as long as I've been witness to the relationship between Ulrike and Andreas—and I've witnessed it for the past seven years—it was marked by intensity and tenderness, sensitivity, and clarity.

And I believe that it was precisely because of this relationship that Ulrike was able to survive the eight months in the dead wing.

It was a relationship like that which can develop between siblings, oriented around a common objective and based on shared politics.

And she was free, because freedom is only possible in the struggle for liberation.

There was no breakdown in their relationship during these years. There couldn't have been, because it was based on the politics of the RAF, and when there were fundamental contradictions within the group, they were addressed concretely through praxis. No reason for such a breakdown can be found in the course of our theoretical work, the only kind that remains possible in prison—nor can it be found in the shared nature of our struggle or the history of the group.

This can be clearly seen in the discussions and Ulrike's letters and manuscripts in the period leading up to Friday evening. They show what this relationship was really like.

It is a crude and sinister smear, a bid to use Ulrike's execution for psychological warfare purposes, to now claim that "tensions" and "estrangement" existed between Ulrike and Andreas, between Ulrike and us. This is Buback in all his stupidity.

So far all such efforts have simply further exposed the fascist nature of the reactionary forces in the Federal Republic.

Jan-Carl Raspe
May 11, 1976

*This is a fragment about the structure of the group, which Ulrike
insisted on presenting in Stammheim, in order to destroy the
leadership theory around which the BAW wanted to build this trial.
Andreas was opposed, and we all wanted to write it differently.
It is not very important, but I have put it out today anyway
because it refutes Buback's filthy lies—"the conflict"—and
because this is what Ulrike was working on last.
It must only be published in its entirety, accompanied by the two
letters to Hanna Krabbe and the one to the Hamburg prisoners.*

*Jan
May 11, 1976*

Fragment Regarding Structure

Concepts developed by Habermas provide a starting point, from which
we can draw conclusions about proletarianization in the metropole: isolation resulting from the alienation which exists throughout the entire
system of production. Isolation is the basis for manipulation.

Freedom in the face of this system is only possible through its total
negation, that is to say, through an attack on the system as part of a
fighting collective, the guerilla, a guerilla that is necessary if a genuine
strategy is to be developed, if victory is to be had.

The collective is a key part of the guerilla's structure, and once subjectivity is understood as the basis of each person's decision to fight,
the collective becomes the most important element. The collective is a
group that thinks, feels, and acts as a group.

The guerilla leadership consists of the individual or individuals who
maintain the open and collective functioning of the group and who
organize the group through their practice—anti-imperialist struggle,
based on each individual's self-determination and decision to be part of
the intervention, understanding that he can only achieve what he wants
to achieve collectively, meaning within the group in all its dimensions,
military and strategic, and as the embryo of the new society, developing and conducting the anti-imperialist struggle through the group
process.

The line, which is to say a rational and logical strategy geared towards a single purpose—action—is developed collectively. It is the result of a process of discussion informed by everyone's experiences and

knowledge, and is therefore collectively formulated and serves to draw people together. In other words, the line is developed in the course of practice, through an analysis of conditions, experiences, and objectives. Coordination is only possible because there is unanimity regarding the goal and the will to achieve it.

Once the line has been developed and understood, the group's practice can be coordinated according to a military command structure. Its execution requires absolute discipline, and, at the same time, absolute autonomy, that is to say, an autonomous orientation and decision-making capacity regardless of the circumstances.

What unites the guerilla at all times is each individual's determination to carry on the struggle.

Leadership is a function that the guerilla requires. Leadership cannot be usurped. It is exactly the opposite of what psychological warfare describes as the RAF's leadership principle. Andreas has stated that if he had in fact acted in the way described by the BAW, there would be no RAF and the political events of the past five years would not have occurred. Simply stated, we would not exist. If he assumed leadership of the RAF, it is because from the beginning he has always had that which the guerilla needs most: willpower, an awareness of the goals, determination, and a sense of collectivity.

When we say that the line is developed in the course of practice, through an analysis of conditions, experiences, and objectives, what we mean is that leadership falls to the individual who has the broadest vision, the greatest sensitivity, and the greatest skill for coordinating the collective process.

Leadership must have as its goal the independence and autonomy of each individual—militarily speaking, of each combatant.

This process can't be organized in an authoritarian way. No group can work this way. The idea of a ringleader is out of the question.

The goal of the BAW's smear campaign against Andreas is clear: they are laying the groundwork for the pacification of public opinion in the event he is murdered. They present the entire issue as if it is only necessary to snuff out this one guy, Andreas, and that would solve the whole problem the urban guerilla poses this state—according to Maihofer, the only problem this state does not have under control.

We doubt that. Over these past five years, we have learned from Andreas—because he was the example we needed—specifically, someone from whom one could learn to struggle, struggle again, always struggle.

What he and we are doing is in no way irrational, involves no compulsion, and is not evil.

One reason that the BAW hates Andreas in particular is because he makes effective use of all available weapons in the struggle. It was from him that we learned that the bourgeoisie has no weapons that we can't turn against them—a tactical principle drawn from the observation that revolutionary contradictions can be developed within capitalism. So Andreas is the guerilla about whom Che said, "He is the group."

Of us, he is the one who has consistently and for a long time now made the function of rejecting individual possessions clear. It was he who anticipated the role of the guerilla and of the group and who was able to direct the process, because he understood that it was necessary. It was he who understood the complete dispossession implicit in proletarianization as it exists in the metropole. It was he who understood that the guerilla's isolation required the development of strength, subjectivity, and willpower in order to build a guerilla organization in the Federal Republic.

Once again, we must not forget that all revolutionary initiatives are initially instinctive processes—for us, the massive wave of strikes in Russia in 1905 and the October Revolution come to mind—direction, coherence, continuity, and political power encouraged individuals to develop their resolve and willpower.

For Gramsci, willpower was the sine qua non; strength of will as the motor force of the revolutionary process in which subjectivity plays an important role.

Ulrike Meinhof
1976

Two Letters To Hanna Krabbe

Krabbe, along with the other members of the Holger Meins Commando, was to go on trial in May 1976 on charges relating to the Stockholm action. (M. & S.)

FIRST LETTER (MARCH 19, 1976)

The politicians' drivel is not what the people think, but what the politicians need them to think. And when they say "we," they are only trying with their drivel to mold what the people think and how they think it. The state wouldn't need opinion polls, nor would it need the *Verfassungsschutz*, if indoctrination by psychological warfare was as simple as that.

As Gramsci said, the legal country is not the real country; or more plainly stated: the dominant opinion is not the opinion of the dominated. What you say is bullshit. You reason in the realm of the imaginary, as if the enemy is the ideology which he sputters, the drivel, the platitudes that they've drummed into you from their bag of tricks with the politicians' cadence of consensus, as if the media and the people whom they pour all this shit on were one and the same thing. It is not real; it is the product of the counterinsurgency machine constructed by the BKA, the BAW, the *Verfassungsschutz*, the government, the media, the secret services, etc.

Just as the enemy is non-material, rather than material.

You don't ask yourself what the condition that Brandt calls "normal" really is—and you don't recognize in Buback's statement that he has determined the conflict—war and its dimensions—to be international, and that he speaks as a representative of U.S. capital's international interests. You only find it "absurd," and instead of analyzing it, you offer a single word—"CIA"—which is a metaphor for Buback's morally decadent policy—and which is gratuitous. You thereby incriminate yourself, because, in practice, you whine about the fact that this is war, after having clearly stood on our side in this war and having begun to struggle.

Your text resembles that of the legal American civil rights movement, which begs the question, if that is how you see things, why are you in here and not out there?

In any event, you are here.

The internationalism that you have struggled for and which the RAF represents is not that of international, inter-state organizations like the United Nations or Geneva; it is the internationalism of the war against imperialism being waged by the liberation movements in the Third World and in the metropole.

War—that is all. You won't find your bearings here by relying on rumors, but only by studying the facts and their connection to the class struggle.

If in isolation you do not make an effort to persistently and continuously analyze reality by understanding it on a material basis, in the context of the struggle—class struggle understood as war—it is because you've lost touch, you're coming apart, you are sick, which means you are starting to have a sick relationship with reality. That constitutes a betrayal in the face of the reality of torture and the effort that resistance demands if it is to be more than just a word.

It is not acceptable—in isolation you can't permit yourself, on top of everything else, to torment yourself. That, as Andreas has said, doesn't mean that you can avoid certain experiences in the process of liberation from alienation. But it is one thing to be destroyed because of trying to understand politics, the facts and how they relate to each other, to understand the group so as to act—and quite another to be destroyed because isolation strips you of all illusions about yourself, which can be a very hard pill to swallow.

And if it is the case that your capacity to act is based on socialization through fear and despair, then struggle on the basis of that.

Eventually you may understand—I can't say for sure—that we can only achieve something with words if they lead to a correct understanding of the situation in which each of us finds ourselves under imperialism, that it is senseless to want to fight with words, when one can only fight with clarity and truth.

Given the environment in which we are struggling—the postfascist state, consumer culture, metropolitan chauvinism, media manipulation of the masses, psychological warfare, and social democracy—and faced with the repression that confronts us here, indignation is not a weapon. It is pointless and empty. Whoever is truly indignant, that is to say, is concerned and engaged, does not scream, but instead reflects on what can be done.

That's the SPK—replacing the struggle with screams. It is not simply distasteful: in isolation it will destroy you, because it means opposing brutal, material repression with nothing more than ideology, instead of opposing it with a psychological effort, which also implies a physical effort.

Arm the masses—even now, capital is doing this much more quickly: the cops, the army, and the radical right. So before you give up on the West German masses, or "the masses" in general, think about what it's really like here. Ho[1] wrote in *l'Humanité*,[2] in 1922, "The masses are fundamentally ready for rebellion, but completely ignorant. They want to liberate themselves, but they don't know how to begin."

That is not our situation.

In our situation here and now, the most pressing issue we must address is how to explain the at times gruesome experiences we have had in isolation—which are intended to foster betrayal, capitulation, self-destruction, and de-politicization—so that you will not have to experience them any more. For if it is true that in the guerilla each individual can learn from every other individual, then it must be possible to communicate our experiences—the condition for which is understanding the collective as a process—a process for which the institutionalization of people in authoritarian boxes is anathema.

Understanding the collective as a process means struggling together against the system, which is very real and not at all imaginary.

Ulrike Meinhof
March 19, 1976

---

1 Ho Chi Minh was a founder and the leading figure in the Vietnamese Communist Party from 1941 until his death in 1969 at the age of seventy-nine.

2 *l'Humanité* is the newspaper of the French Communist Party.

SECOND LETTER (MARCH 23, 1976)

It's bullshit: the "psychiatric" section.

The objective at Ossendorf, like everywhere else, is extermination, and the psychiatrists participate, developing the methods which are applied by state security—psychiatry as a thoroughly imperialist science is a means, not an end.

Psychiatric treatment is a front in the psychological war; it is intended to persuade broken fighters of the absurdity of revolutionary politics, to deprive the fighters of their convictions. It is also a police tactic for destruction through "forced liberation," as Buback calls it, and its military interest is in recruitment—establishing control.

What Bücker[3] does isn't psychiatric treatment—it's terror. He wants to wear you down. Using terms like therapy, brainwashing leaves you absolutely twisted. You must raise a shield against this frontal assault.

The Ossendorf method is the typical prison method, but at Ossendorf its design and application have been perfected, and are epitomized by Bücker and Lodt.[4] It is aseptic and total. They deprive the prisoner of air until he finally loses his dignity, all sense of self, and all perception of what terror is. The goal is extermination. Psychiatric treatment is only one aspect, only one instrument among others. If you allow yourself to be paralyzed by it, like a deer in the headlights, if you fail to resist it, what else can be expected.

"No windows"—obviously. But there are even more unimaginable things about isolation—the sadism with which it is developed, the perfection of its application, the totality of the extermination pursued by the Security Group, and the shock we experience when we realize the intensity of the antagonism within which we have chosen to struggle, and when we recognize the nature of the fascism that rules here. This is not simply rhetoric that we are using, but is in fact an accurate description of the repression one encounters if one starts to engage in revolutionary politics in this country.

They cannot use psychiatry against someone who doesn't accept or want it. Your shrieks about psychiatry mystify the realities of isolation. It is effective—it must be struggled against, and, naturally, you must engage in war against Bücker's bullying.

So demand an end to acoustic surveillance; accept only visual surveillance, like in Stammheim. Naturally, it was also a struggle here to get

---

3 Georg Bücker was, at this time, the warden at Ossendorf penitentiary.

4 Lodt was, at this time, the Inspector for Security at Ossendorf penitentiary.

rid of the cop who came to listen to us, to be allowed to sit on the floor, etc. For you, only repression exists. That's perfectly clear.

Also, you are a pig. You pull the demand for association and the line on "prisoners of war" out of your bag of tricks, as if they are a threat—against Müller.[1] That is nonsense. We must have association and the application of the Geneva Convention, but what do you expect from Müller?

We struggle against them and the struggle never ends, and they won't make the struggle any easier for us. Obviously, if you only think in terms of bourgeois morality, you will soon run out of ammunition. It's idiotic. So, take care of yourself, because nobody else can do it for you in isolation.

Not even Bernd.[2]

Ulrike Meinhof
March 23, 1976

---

1 Herman-Josef Müller was the chief judge in the trial of the Holger Meins Commando.

2 Bernd Rössner, another member of the Holger Meins Commando.

Letter to the Hamburg Prisoners

*This letter was written to RAF prisoner Werner Hoppe,
who came to the RAF out of the communist section
of the student movement. (M. & S.)*

We are beginning to find you truly insufferable—the class perspective with which you puff yourselves up. And it's not because of a question of definition, but because the *struggle*, meaning what is essential, doesn't exist in it. There is nothing there. It is a showpiece that has very little in common with what *we* want. What we want is revolution. That is to say, there is a goal, and, with regards to the goal, there isn't a position, but *only* the movement, the struggle, the relationship to *being*, which, as you say, means struggling.

There is the class reality: proletariat, proletarianization, declassing, humiliation, abuse, expropriation, servitude, poverty.

Under imperialism, the complete penetration of all relationships by the market and the nationalization of society by repressive and ideological state structures leave no place and no time about which you can say: this is my starting point. There is only illegality and liberated territory. Furthermore, you will not achieve illegality as an offensive position for revolutionary intervention until you yourself are on the offensive; without that it is nothing.

The class position is Soviet foreign policy presented as the class position of the international proletariat, and the USSR's accumulation model presented as socialism.

It is the line—the apology—for socialism in one country. Meaning, it is an ideology that aims to secure the domination of a dictatorship that does not proceed offensively against imperialism, but which instead responds defensively to the encirclement it now faces.

You can say that Soviet domestic and foreign policy was historically necessary, but you can't claim that makes it absolute as the class position. The class position—that is to say, class interests, class needs, the class obligation to struggle for communism so as to be able to live—is curbed through such politics. I would actually say it is abolished, which is nonsense. Position and movement are mutually exclusive. It is a construct geared towards creating a safety net and self-justification—a facade.

It is a reframing of class politics as economic interests, which is incorrect. Class politics are the result of the confrontation with the politics of capital, and the politics of capital are a function of its economy. I think Poulantzas[1] correctly addressed this when he said that the economic activities of the state are part of its repressive and ideological activities—they are part of the class struggle.

Class politics are a struggle against the politics of capital and not against the economy, which, directly or by way of the state, proletarianizes the class. The class position of the proletariat is war. It is a *contradictio in adjecto*—it is nonsense. It is nonsense from a class point of view, because the Soviet Union attempts to promote its state policy under the cover of class struggle. What I am saying is that it is the expression of Soviet foreign policy.

Which is to say, they can be allies in the process of liberation, but not protagonists. The protagonist has no position—the protagonist has a goal. The "class position" is always a cudgel. It is always the claim to possess and bestow, by way of the party apparatus, a conception of reality different from reality as it is perceived and experienced. Specifically, it is a claim to a class position without class struggle. As you say, it is "on this basis" that we should act, rather than on the basis of how we have been acting up to now.

In 1969, it was the MLs, the KSV, and the AO groups who, with the "class position," depoliticized the movement in the universities by supporting policies that no student could relate to emotionally. It is a position for the liquidation of the anti-imperialist protest movement. And I think that that is the horrible thing about this concept and what it represents, the fact that it rules out any emotional identification with proletarian politics—it is a kind of catechism.

We do *not* act on the basis of a class position, no matter what its class perspective may be, but on the basis of class *struggle*, which is the principle of all history, and on the basis of class *war* as the reality within which proletarian politics are realized—and, as we have discovered, only in and by war.

The class position can only be the class *movement* within the class war, the world proletariat engaged in armed struggle, the true vanguard, the liberation movements.

---

1 Nicos Poulantzas was a Greek Marxist philosopher who was very influential in New Left intellectual circles in the sixties and the seventies.

Or, as Jackson[2] said, "connections, connections, connections." As such: movement, interaction, communication, coordination, common struggle—strategy.

All of this is paralyzed by the concept of "class position"—and that is how you used it when you attempted to win over Ing.[3] You must know by now that there is not much worse than being fed complete nonsense.

Which is all to say, the class position is a triumphalist position.

Certainly, there is also something heroic about it. However, we're not concerned with that. We are, instead, concerned with its consequences.

But that's enough. I have the impression that I'm talking to a wall, and that is not the point of all of this. The goal is to have you climb down from your pedestal.

So, come on down. You're boasting.

Ulrike Meinhof
April 13, 1976

---

2 George Jackson was a young Black social prisoner politicized in prison in the U.S. in the late 60s. He was the author of *Blood in My Eye*, a strategic manual for Black revolution, and *Soledad Brother*, a collection of writings consisting primarily of letters. He joined the Black Panther Party while in the prison. He was killed by guards during an alleged escape attempt on August 21, 1971.

3 Apparently an abbreviated pseudonym; translated as Ilse in the French version published by Maspero in 1977.

Interview with
Le Monde Diplomatique

This interview originated from questions presented to the lawyers by Le Monde Diplomatique. The political parts of the questions were answered by the prisoners. While we are not aware of the interview ever being published by the liberal French newspaper, copies were distributed by the prisoners' supporters. The date normally given for this document is June 10, 1976.

A somewhat expanded version of the interview addressing supplementary questions exists. However, the only version of that text available to us was an extremely poorly translated and badly organized English-language version. Faced with this problem, we decided to base our translation on the German-language version available on a website maintained by former RAF member Ronald Augustin. The English-language translation of the longer version available to us indicates that little of substance was added to what is presented here. (M. & S.)

Q.: The alleged suicide of Ulrike Meinhof is seen overwhelmingly by the left and critical observers as an institutional murder, the culmination of 4 years of soul-destroying solitary confinement.

A: The concept of institutional murder is not precise enough. It is more accurate to say that, in a military conflict, imprisoned revolutionaries will be executed. We are certain that, as with Holger Meins and Siegfried Hausner, it was murder—a premeditated execution following the years of psychological warfare. We are trying to find out the details of how this murder was committed. It is clear that the state has done everything possible to hide the facts, while state security and the state security journalism organized by the BAW attempt to exploit the situation for propaganda purposes. Nothing indicates suicide, but there are many facts that suggest murder:

The prisoners were not allowed to see their dead comrade. Her corpse was rushed out of the prison as the first lawyer arrived to visit Gudrun

Ensslin. The corpse underwent an autopsy by order of the BAW, without the lawyers or relatives having an opportunity to see her, in spite of their demands to do so. Her sister was denied the right to bring in a pathologist of her choosing. The corpse was so mangled after the autopsy that the second pathologist could not deliver any precise findings—for example, a 25 cm long caesarean scar from the birth of her children could not be located.

Her brain and internal organs were removed.

Nevertheless, the effects of numerous injuries from blunt objects were visible on her legs.

And the injuries to the organs in her throat (a broken hyoid bone and the damage to the thyroid cartilage) virtually rule out "death by hanging."

The request to have the cell inspected by her lawyer, her executor, or a relative was denied. The cell was "renovated," totally repainted, two days after her death, even though the wing in which she died is not occupied. So far, neither the lawyers nor the relatives have received any answers from the authorities, besides the terse assertion that it was "suicide by hanging."

In the press statements from the political judiciary, there are five contradictory versions regarding how the rope was secured. The one that ultimately became the official version and which was published was that she had rolled a hand towel into a 5 cm thick rope and fastened it tightly around her neck. Then she climbed onto a chair and threaded and fastened this 5 cm thick rope through the mesh of a screen, through which not even the small finger of a child would fit (for this an instrument would be needed, and none was found). Then she is supposed to have turned herself around and jumped.

Before this version was decided upon, the prison warden, who was one of the first in the cell, stated that there was no chair near the corpse, and the prison doctor who examined her first declared that her feet were 20 cm from the floor.

In the statements from the political judiciary, one finds only contradictions. Nonetheless, there has been no inspection of the files, and they have adamantly refused to share information with the relatives, the lawyers or neutral authorities. Regarding the possibility of an international committee of inquiry, which has been demanded throughout Europe, the Ministry of Justice declared, "There is neither the grounds nor the scope for any international body."

Q: Against which background is deliberate murder to be seen?

A: The story behind this murder is documented in the files. On the government's behalf, and using all available political and moral means, the Attorney General has tried for six years to "exterminate" the RAF prisoners, especially Ulrike and Andreas, and to "wipe out" the example they set in resisting the new fascism's institutional strategy, as formulated by Schmidt in government statements and programs.

For as long as the RAF has existed, the Attorney General's plan for Ulrike was to use her to personalize and pathologize revolutionary politics. Therefore, after her arrest, she was to be broken in the dead wing and psychiatrically restructured before her trial. After her arrest, she was imprisoned, by order of the BAW, from June 16, 1972, until February 9, 1973—that is 237 days—in a dead wing, which means total acoustic isolation. That is the prison in which state security houses prisoners during the phase of interrogation and "preparation for trial." It is an extreme form of torture. No human can endure a lengthy period in an acoustic and social vacuum. One's sense of time and one's physical equilibrium are destroyed. One aspect of white torture is that the prisoner's agony is magnified, not reduced, as the torture continues. The ultimate result is irreversible brainwashing, which, to begin with, dissolves the control the tortured person has over what he says, over his speech; he babbles.

And his ability to grasp even a single thought is destroyed. What is left is a body, which on the outside shows hardly any sign of injury.

The program was at all times under the control of the BAW and the state security psychiatrist, Götte. But Ulrike endured the 237 days, because she fought. All of us could see that her mind and her will remained unbroken.

Another RAF prisoner, Astrid,[1] who had previously spent three months in the dead wing, never recovered—not even after her release three years ago. Even today she is seriously ill.

The BAW assumed that Ulrike would be broken by the dead wing. On January 4, 1973, Buback—the Attorney General—wrote that Ulrike was to be committed "to a public sanitarium—or a nursing home—so that a report on her mental health could be prepared." The public, which the defense lawyers were able to mobilize, just barely managed to prevent this. But the BAW tenaciously pursued their goal of having

---

1 Astrid Proll, a founding member of the RAF.

Ulrike declared mentally ill. On April 18, 1973, Buback directed the justice system psychiatrist Witter to deliver an opinion on Ulrike's sanity. In his letter, he said:

> On the basis of Frau Meinhof's conduct to date, it seems doubtful she would cooperate regarding particular examinations or consent to surgical treatment. If professional opinion suggests that certain interventions are necessary, I would ask you to report to me with detailed information on the examination considered necessary, so that, under §81 of the Criminal Code, the pertinent court order can be obtained. Should it be necessary to involve a neurologist, I would suggest making arrangements to obtain the cooperation of the Director of the University Neurological Clinic in Homburg, Professor Dr. Loew.

At this point the attempt to gain control of Ulrike's brain became obvious. Loew is one of the most notorious neurosurgeons in Germany. He experiments with "adaptive surgery" on prisoners.

Witter, in his answer, initially requested an x-ray of the skull and a scintigraphy.[2] But in the same letter, he explains to the BAW that the examination could be carried out under anesthesia, should Ulrike, to quote, "refuse to cooperate."

The objective of this intervention is made clear in an August 28, 1973, letter to the Attorney General. It says, "Above all, proof of a brain tumor could be an important indication of the need for a therapeutic operation."

"Important indication" here means that permission for cretinization is not required from either the prisoner or the prisoner's relatives. The psychiatrist decides "after consideration" about whether to proceed with stereotactical[3] mutilation. The BAW then files a petition with the investigating judge and after receiving the decision orders the intervention, with the proviso that "These measures can be undertaken against the will of the accused, and if necessary by use of direct force and under anesthesia."

---

2 According to the MedicineNet.com, scintigraphy is "A diagnostic test in which a two-dimensional picture of a body radiation source is obtained through the use of radioisotopes."

3 According to the *American Medical Heritage Dictionary*, stereotactical pertains to stereotaxis, which is "A surgical technique that uses medical imaging to precisely locate in three dimensions an anatomical site to which a surgical instrument or a beam of radiation is directed."

The whole thing eventually failed as a result of massive international protest, including that of many doctors.

Striving for an orderly retreat, the BAW declared that they had only at this point become aware of Ulrike's medical history, which had been published in the *Zentralblatt für Neorochirurgie* in 1968 and in *Stern* in 1972. That is a stupid lie, as, according to the files, Ulrike was identified by state security after her arrest in 72 by referring to the x-rays in her medical files.

After that, Ulrike was placed in the dead wing on two more occasions—alone from December 21, 1973, until January 3, 1974, and together with Gudrun from February 5, 1974, until April 28, 1974.

But the incarceration of the two prisoners in the dead wing met with such strong international protests that the SPD government had to drop their plan to pathologize Ulrike in order to depict fundamental opposition to the Federal Republic as constituting an illness. The project, a "quiet and determined assertion of normality," was an attempt to present, through torture and neurosurgery, a destroyed mind at a political show trial. It failed. That is the back story.

All the facts, which are gradually becoming known, suggest that on the night of May 8-9, 1976, Ulrike was murdered by state security, because the years of torture had failed to destroy her political identity, her revolutionary consciousness, and her will to fight.

The staging of the suicide follows the exact psychological warfare line that state security has followed since 1970. Physical liquidation and the political extermination of the RAF were the objectives of the massive hate and counterinsurgency campaign. Two months ago, Buback, the Attorney General, held that the second package of special legislation that had been rushed through was no longer needed for this trial, because, "We do not need any legal provisions. State security is given life by those who are committed to it. People like Herold and myself, we always find a way. If there are statutory provisions that must from time to time be stretched, they will for the most part be ineffective."

While Herold, the President of the BKA, said at a meeting regarding the problem of these prisoners, "Actions against the RAF must primarily be developed in such a way as to undermine the positions held by sympathizers."

As an example, four hours after her death, the BAW disseminated rumors through the press regarding the motive: "tensions within the group," "far-reaching differences," etc., and the BAW's statement was nothing new. It is a word for word repetition of a formulation published in 1971, five years ago, as part of a state security disorientation campaign. Then it was: Ulrike Meinhof has created "tensions" and "far-reaching differences" within the RAF.

But Ulrike's last letters and the experiences of everyone who knows the group—and the experiences of all the lawyers who have seen the group over the past twelve months—prove that the relationships within the group were intense, loving, disciplined, and mutually open.

Everyone could see this.

Five years ago, in 1971, the state was unable to get at Ulrike. She was free, because she was underground. So as part of the psychological warfare campaign, state security claimed she was dead.[1] Now she was defenseless and imprisoned, so she was killed, because she continued to struggle in prison and at the trial.

One must understand at what point in time this murder was staged: four days earlier, the prisoners had filed evidentiary petitions, for which Ulrike had done the essential work.

These petitions addressed:

> *1) the fact that, in violation of international law, since its foundation the territory of the Federal Republic of Germany has been a strategic base for the aggressive, expansionist policies of the U.S.A. against third states, against the constitutional governments of third states, and against the anticolonial, national, and anti-imperialist liberation movements in the Third World,*
>
> *in the course of which, amongst other things, all relevant overt and covert military and secret service operations against the Warsaw Pact states and against legitimate parliamentary changes of government in the West European states, against anti-imperialist liberation movements in the Middle East, in Africa, and in South-East Asia, were planned, organized, orchestrated, supported, and overseen by U.S. intelligence services based on the territory of the Federal Republic of Germany,*
>
> *specifically*

---

1 In early 1972, the BKA lost all trace of Meinhof (according to Stefan Aust, she was in Italy at the time). Rumours began to be spread, *Bild* publishing an article under the headline, "Has Ulrike Meinhof Committed Suicide?" and the *Frankfurter Allgemeine Zeitung* quoting unnamed government sources to the effect that she had been dead for months, either from a tumor or from suicide. See: Aust, 200.

a) that the IG Farben building in Frankfurt am Main functioned as the headquarters of several U.S. secret service organizations throughout the entire duration of the illegal aggression of the U.S.A. in Indochina;

b) that these U.S. agencies in the IG Farben building in Frankfurt am Main carried out strategic military planning, management, coordination, and control functions for both the operations and logistics of the U.S. military forces in Indochina and secret operations of U.S. intelligence agencies in Indochina;

2) that the structuring of the Federal Republic of Germany as a state after 1945 was carried out and developed by the U.S.A. as part of their expansionist strategy directed towards world power— particularly

that after the Second World War, the CIA, founded as an illegal arm of American foreign policy, directly controlled all relevant political, economic, and cultural institutions in the Federal Republic during the Cold War, through civilian front organizations, or through the businesses, unions, cultural organizations, and student organizations that they controlled, and later through the financing of political parties and trade unions, as well as by educating, financing, and sponsoring politicians and officials;

3) that through overt and covert, direct and indirect pressure, in the form of illegal interference in the internal affairs of the Federal Republic, and through the complete economic, military, and political hegemony of the U.S.A. over the Federal Republic, the Kiesinger/Brandt and Brandt/Scheel governments were involved in the overt and covert, aggressive, genocidal strategy against the Third World liberation movements, particularly in Indochina,

a) in that they supported the aggression politically, economically, and through propaganda, and allowed the U.S. Army to use military bases on the Federal Republic's territory;

b) in that they, as a sub-center of U.S. imperialism, developed a policy of illegal interference in the internal affairs of the Third World, particularly in regards to Indochina and the European periphery. This was done using their own intelligence services and through the export of police and military, weapons, training, technology, and logistics, through the financing of political parties, politicians, etc., as well as through economic pressure;

4) that the Federal Republic of Germany

a) on the basis of its origins as a product of the dictatorship of the Allied military powers led by the U.S.A.,

b) on the basis of conditions and requirements assuring the rights of the occupying powers under the leadership of the U.S.A., control was handed over to the German authorities,

c) on the basis of the provisions of the German Treaty of 1956 and later modifications of the Treaty,

particularly

the CIA-controlled dependence of the Federal Republic on the U.S.A., without it being a colony under international law, but with no declared national sovereignty in relationship to the U.S.A.

That was an extract.

One line in the petitions, for example, dealt with how social democracy and the trade unions, with the help of CIA-bought politicians like Willy Brandt and Rosenberg,[1] used career "advancement" and "positions" in the party and the trade union leadership, etc. to win support for the aggression and the consolidation of U.S. imperialism in Europe and in the Third World. This was established through extremely well documented investigations by comrades and friends, using witnesses who were directly involved.

The BAW coordinates matters between the domestic and foreign intelligence services—that is to say, between the CIA, BND, *Verfassungsschutz*, Military Counter-Intelligence Service, etc.—and is also the point of intersection between the propaganda and ideological functions of the political judiciary. With these petitions, the BAW was confronted with the problem that the crude theatrics with which they had hoped to depoliticize the trial—four years of torture, hate campaigns, psychological warfare, special legislation, a special court, the liquidation of the defense, etc.—were all crumbling in full public view. And at exactly this point, Ulrike would give up? It is absurd: the prisoners knew that the confrontation would come to a head here, and Ulrike was determined to fight to establish the facts during the trial, as were we all. Her letters and manuscripts, her speeches, and her work for the trial, for example, are proof of this right up until the very last day.

---

1 Ludwig Rosenberg was, at this time, the Chairman of the *Deutschen Gewerkschaftsbund* (DGB—German Union Association).

She was murdered once it became clear to the BAW that the fascist example of the victory of the political judiciary and the Federal Republic over the guerilla—the show trial in Stammheim—might collapse despite all the repression.

Stammheim was meant to demonstrate the hopelessness of any and all resistance within the Federal Republic.

In this regard, for four years, "all possible means" were used—as had been expressly sanctioned by Schmidt and the Federal Constitutional Court. One can now say that they were unsuccessful.

What the struggle of the Stammheim prisoners established and communicated is the necessity, the possibility, and the logic of politics based on revolutionary action in the Federal Republic.

Q: The accused have fought with their last remaining means, the hunger strike, against the prison conditions. Has this achieved a change in the conditions of solitary confinement? Does the court take the state of health of the accused into account?

A: No.

At the time the prisoners broke off their hunger strike, after five months, it had become clear that the legal left could not manage a second mass mobilization like the one that followed the murder of Holger Meins. Furthermore, it had become clear that the BAW and Buback were determined to use the hunger strike to kill even more prisoners from the RAF, accompanying this with a bombastic display of medical window dressing. At this point, the RAF on the outside issued a statement ordering the prisoners to end the strike, even though their demand, the end of solitary confinement, had not been achieved. The statement said:

> We are saying that the prisoners' strike has done everything it could to mediate, mobilize, and organize anti-imperialist politics here. Its escalation would not contribute anything qualitative to the struggle.
>
> The state has calculated that it will be able to create propaganda from the execution of guerilla prisoners—who struggle, always struggle, in spite of everything struggle—that would make resistance seem hopeless. Allowing you to continue in this situation would amount to sacrificing you.

We are taking this weapon away from you, because the prisoners'
struggle—given the existing balance of power—is now something
that we must settle with our weapons.[1]

This was a realistic appraisal of the balance of power.

The court had arrived at the conclusion that the prisoners, weakened by years of isolation, were only capable of attending the trial for two or three hours a day, which effectively excluded them from the trial. Disagreeing with the court-appointed doctors (no expert for the defense was accepted), whose involvement the defense finally succeeded in obtaining after months of fighting, the court maintained that the prisoners' inability to appear was a result of the hunger strike, and as such was deliberate and self-inflicted.[2]

In their expert opinion, the doctors clearly state that the prisoners' miserable state of health is caused by their prison conditions. Eight other expert opinions from public health agency doctors, etc. in RAF trials reached an identical conclusion: years of solitary confinement equals extermination.

The Federal Supreme Court has used disinformation to stretch the definition of "self-inflicted". Unlike the court, they do not claim that the inability to appear is due to the hunger strike—extracts from the expert opinions, which refute this claim, have been published since then. Instead, the Federal Supreme Court claims that the prisoners have, through their behavior in custody, forced the authorities to impose these prison conditions. The Federal Supreme Court eventually adopted this position and declared torture constitutional. In fact the custodial judge has already asked the prison warden to make sure that such prisoners are held in isolation. The Federal Supreme Court and the Federal Supreme Court judge who arrived at this decision know what they are doing. The judge consciously supported the objectives of the police and the Bonn Security Group's "Terrorism" Section—they and the BAW dictate prison conditions. Political justice in the Federal Republic is a function of the counterinsurgency campaign.

The rulings clearly state that the prison conditions can and will be changed if the prisoners renounce their politics, provide evidence, and place themselves at the disposal of the psychological warfare campaign

---

1 Letter from the RAF to the RAF prisoners, cf 338

2 According to §§231-231b, passed in June 1975, trials could proceed in the absence of defendants if this was due to self-inflicted health concerns.

against the urban guerilla. As regards such rulings, torture is clearly defined in international conventions as those means employed to destroy the prisoner with the objective of extorting statements that can be used in propaganda. It is in just this way that the West German justice system has legalized extermination imprisonment, so as to use the prisoners' state of health against the political prisoners.

Q: Has a political defense of the RAF been possible at any time during the Stuttgart-Stammheim proceedings? Are the accused free to explain their political motives and objectives at this trial?

A: So far, the prisoners have seldom been able to utter a sentence without being interrupted by Prinzing, or else the BAW intervenes. Bobby Seale was at least publicly gagged.[1] Here the court just switches off the prisoners' microphones, and if the prisoners still continue to speak, it bars them from the proceedings for at least four weeks. This method of interruption is effective. If one's thought process is interrupted ten times, then it is derailed. The spectators get the impression of mental redundancy. The trial's political significance is blocked. Every minute of the proceedings is simply psychological warfare.

There was an attempt to present a political defense, that is to say, to reconstruct the defense after the lawyers who had prepared it were barred shortly before the trial began. The court reacted by barring six more lawyers. Using challenges, denials, and, above all, court-appointed public defenders, the BAW has established Disciplinary Committees,[2] with the aim of applying the *Berufsverbot*. And it works. The Bar Association's Disciplinary Committee has a new staff made up of lawyers who specifically represent the interests of the BAW.

The Chairman of the Law Society admitted this openly during a radio interview a few months ago. Now the circle of special legislation will be closed. In June, the SPD presented parliament with a new "package" of special legislation that would perfect the existing ones. Now a prosecution motion will be sufficient to begin Disciplinary Committee proceedings against a lawyer so as to disbar him and initiate *Berufsverbot* proceedings against him, etc.

---

1 A founding member of the Black Panther Party, Seale was tied to a chair and gagged during the Chicago 8 trial, at which he and seven white codefendants (none of whom were tied or gagged in spite of disruptive behaviour) were charged in connection with violent protests during the Chicago 1968 Democratic Convention.
2 Literally, "Courts of Honor," or *Ehrengericht* in German.

The law will also be applied to trials that are already underway—in effect retroactively.

It is the second wave of special legislation, all for a single trial. As the trial was underway, Ströbele and Croissant were arrested and all of the defense material on which they were working was seized, and this after the BAW had already confiscated all of the prisoners' defense materials in three cell raids.

A detail worth adding is that the office of Andreas Baader's last remaining lawyer, Haag, who avoided arrest, was searched by Zeis, one of the federal prosecutors from Stammheim. This means that the BAW—by having the same federal prosecutor carry out both the persecution of the lawyers and the prosecution of the prisoners—does not even feel the need to hide why it is criminalizing the lawyers. That is the whole problem in the Federal Republic. Fascism is open, but there is no consciousness of it, and hardly any resistance.

Q: In a petition for a stay of proceedings, one of the defense lawyers described the trial as a military-political conflict rather than a legal one. What measures did the ruling class use to ensure that this conflict would be carried out with unequal weapons?

A: Special legislation, a judge illegally pushed into the head position, a 16 million DM³ bunker built just for this trial on the outskirts of town far away from any public transportation, the confiscation of 90% of the files by the BAW and the BKA, witnesses coached by the police and presenting testimony that has been structured for propaganda purposes, the persecution of lawyers, which of course handicaps the remaining lawyers at the trial.

Lawyers depend on a minimum of constitutional consistency. If, as in these proceedings, it is totally absent due to blatant repressive measures, then the lawyers are helpless. Special legislation for these big trials has reduced the number of defense counsel for each prisoner to three, and the successive banning of lawyers and the ban on the collective defense of the accused precludes any division of labor between the lawyers.

The despotic, secret administrative exclusions, which are effected with random, arbitrarily constructed accusations, including the *Berufsverbot* executed by the Bar Association—and one must say it—resemble the state security orgies of 1933. The arrests; the terrorism against the

---

3 Roughly $6.25 million at the time.

lawyers' offices, with the confiscation of all of their files, including files from other proceedings, which a political lawyer depends on to make a living; the terrorism through open surveillance; the open intimidation of former clients, who are sought out, questioned, and pressured by the BKA squads; the loss of mandates; the criminal charges; the convictions based on defense arguments presented in court, etc., etc.—all of this leaves the lawyers helpless. The lawyers were confronted with false documents fabricated by the BAW, documents which were published with false quotes in the propaganda magazines of the Federal Ministry of the Interior, and which were distributed to schools, etc. in their millions; they are encircled by the police and by propaganda.

The prisoners say that in the legal vacuum of these proceedings, the lawyers are like chickens with their heads cut off. They are no match for the pragmatism, military in its precision, which extends over the whole repressive legal structure, from the government to the lawless terror of state security—just as was the case in 1933.

Either one sides with the prisoners' politics, the anti-imperialist struggle—because the persecution of the lawyers is also part of the struggle to eliminate these politics—or one succumbs to the repression. Some become opportunists, submitting themselves to the directives and threats that are present in each of these trials, where they function to prevent attempts to clarify the facts and organize solidarity. Others pull back, take flight, or fall silent, sometimes going so far as to no longer present the line that was developed by the defense team long ago.

Jan's lawyer, in a state of psychological distress, resigned from his mandate in the current Stammheim trial at the very moment when the key defense motion was to be presented—the basis for resistance in human rights law and for the application of prison conditions as mandated for prisoners of war in the Geneva Convention.[1] He had worked on it for three years. The evidentiary motion had as its theme the opposition to the Vietnam War between 67 and 72 and the political conclusions the RAF had arrived at as a result.

This means that the threat of the Disciplinary Committee, that is to say, the threat of the *Berufsverbot*, has caused these lawyers to abandon their professional principles and duties, it has prevented them from struggling to assure the minimum level of human rights for their clients, all in order to avoid risking their own position within the legal profession. The heightened repression has brought them back in line;

---

1 For more on this defense motion, see pages 455-56.

they accept the dismantling of the defendants' rights. It's grotesque. As political lawyers, they are, therefore, completely corrupt.

Besides the barriers with which the BAW has institutionally—through parliament, the courts, the board of the Bar Association, the LAWs, the law schools, etc.—made it difficult to accept a mandate in these proceedings, it has become almost impossible to find lawyers who are prepared to come to Stammheim. Fear reigns.

The confiscation of 90% of the files—over 1,000 file folders—is part of this mix of terror and fear. The suppression of the evidentiary files was necessary in order to be able to actually charge the prisoners. It is part of determining the outcome. Besides, the selective use of files is necessary for the BAW's ringleader construct. But, above all, the publication of the files would shed light on the manhunt that occurred between 1970 and 1972, the extent of the police investigation, and the size of the police apparatus, of which one is aware—the government continually crows about it—but which one cannot visualize.

"One thinks away from it," filmmaker Kluge[2] recently said, and rightly so. The Bonn Security Group, with the *Verfassungsschutz*, the BND, the Military Counter-Intelligence Service, and the CIA, investigated the entire West German left, which, as a result, is now fully identified and within the grasp of state security. They have monitored telephones all the way to the top of the ministerial bureaucracy,[3] spied on people, and sown suspicion. Trade unions, party youth sections, writers, journalists, and ministers were spied on. Were the files to become public, people would see how much control the police have over society and the state, the degree of mistrust and insecurity, the massive lack of legitimacy. Seeing this, they would see how fragile the consensus is within the state, this state that lacks national identity and legitimacy, this state inflamed by its chauvinism and its dependency on the U.S.A. It would be public incitement to resistance.

Q: The mass media in the FRG more or less ignores the trial. Before the trial began, there were a series of press campaigns against the RAF, the defense attorneys, and sympathizers. Is this the result of psychological warfare?

---

2 Alexander Kluge of *Gruppe 47* was a lawyer, filmmaker, television producer, screenplay writer, and author, best known for pioneering the New German Film style of the sixties and seventies.

3 Earlier in 1976, Klaus Traube, one the highest placed men in the nuclear industry, had had his home and office bugged by the BND. See Aust, 387-388.

A: The total synchronization of the mass media is a prerequisite for this police trial. Buback prepared a judicial press conference for the BAW in Karlsruhe; institutional press conferences are normally only held by the federal government and *Länder* bodies. They are an instrument for what is called "offensive information," which is another expression of information policy making use of police tactics. At the same time, Buback also has a network of state security journalists at his disposal in the media, in the corporate editorial boards, and in the public institutions, who ensure that the trial is not simply ignored. The reports that appear are all similarly structured. Never a word of what the prisoners say. The defense line is falsified, with the result that witnesses' testimony is twisted around to mean the opposite of what was said.

For example, the fact that the witness Hoff is completely discredited doesn't appear in the newspapers. Hoff's appearance had been trumpeted by the BAW in a press campaign that lasted months, his testimony was described as crucial to establishing the facts. What was published was that he, speaking for the government, denied the testimony of another witness who unmasked him. Hoff was a militant from the Frankfurt scene who was involved in the SDS at the time of the student movement between 67 and 71, and who had worked for the Algerian liberation movement in the early 60s. In prison he was bribed with promises and turned. Now he stammers exactly what state security has trained him to say, none of which confirms what the BAW has been claiming through press headlines for the past six months. The joke was that he really couldn't incriminate Andreas. But on that day when he admitted in Stammheim that he could not even identify Andreas, all the German press printed that he had identified him.

There are also a couple of dozen other examples from significant points during the trials. For example, it was reported in the media that the prisoners had taken responsibility for the attack on the Springer Building. In fact, they had, in their explanation about the attacks against the U.S. Headquarters in Frankfurt and Heidelberg, expressly stated that they didn't know about the attack on the Springer Building and did not approve of it conceptually.[1] But these are only details. What

1 The explanation referred to here is not the communiqué which accompanied the Springer action and which is reprinted in this volume, but rather a court statement Gudrun Ensslin presented during in the Stammheim trial. Those who believe Meinhof committed suicide often point to this court statement as a motivating factor, as they claim Meinhof had been involved in organizing the Springer action and that Ensslin was rebuking her. These claims were vehemently denied by the

one had with Hoff was a programmed, brainwashed police recording, not a high point, but a pile of shit.

One must understand what happened. Hoff had so thoroughly memorized the testimony that had been formulated by the investigating judge that every time the word "pause" appeared in the transcript, because his dinner came or whatever, he came to a standstill. On the other hand, he could not repeat a single sentence from the transcript. He did not understand the content of his testimony. One could read along and see how he got stuck in a passage and was only able to get past the pauses with his lawyer's help, and at other times had to be stopped. A macabre spectacle. Prinzing treated him obsequiously and assiduously. He was accompanied 24 hours a day by a "psychological caretaker" from the BKA, and during the breaks in the trial he went over his lines with his BKA interrogators. On the other hand, the BAW immediately threatened witnesses who disputed Hoff's story with the complete disruption of their lives: *Berufsverbot* and the withdrawal of their passports. The trial is a government operation, and so the coverage is seamless propaganda, completely structured by the government.

A comparison to the Third Reich's *Reichsschrifttumkammer*[2] or the *Volksgerichtshof*[3] reporting is accurate. The only difference is that the forms of manipulation have now been perfected; the instruments of psychological warfare are more difficult to see through than the fascist propaganda of that time.

Q: What attitude do the democratic and anticapitalist forces in the FRG have towards the RAF trial?

A: The left is afraid. The small, subversively-inclined groups push away the trial. They know it's their trial, that in the end it's the Vietnam opposition of the 60s which is to be liquidated. They know that state security's psychological war against the RAF, in which the trials play a role and Stammheim is the key, is directed against all opposition, and, as such, against them as well. And the terror is effective. They agonize. They are angry, but stick their heads in the sand.

---

prisoners themselves; see Brigitte Mohnhaupt's Testimony at the Stammheim Trial, July 22, 1976, cf 357-8.

2 *Reichsschrifttumkammer* (Reich Writers Chamber): a legal body responsible for classifying literature during the Third Reich.

3 *Volksgerichthof* (People's Court): the Nazi puppet court that hounded opponents, usually sentencing them to death on the basis of coerced and falsified testimony.

It's gone so far that *Informationsdienst,* which published, in the Federal Republic, the names of a few CIA agents from the U.S. embassy in Bonn, does not dare to publish prisoners' texts that have already been read in public. Of the Maoist groups, the KBW has at least criticized the trial from a legal point of view. They don't understand that the violations of the law, the legalization of isolation torture by the Federal Supreme Court and the Federal Constitutional Court are signs of war and fascism. With their stupid dogmatism, they misrepresent the prisoners' politics and defend democratic rights, which were never real in the Federal Republic, and which are embedded in the Constitution only as a vehicle for anticommunism. But that doesn't work for the state apologists who define themselves according to Lenin's organizational model or according to the pre-party formation model.

The KPD and the KPD/ML, as Maoists, are entirely submissive to Peking. They openly support the U.S. military strategy; the strengthening of NATO and the *Bundeswehr* so as to entrench the hegemony of West German imperialism in Western Europe. Defense of the Fatherland. The RAF thinks otherwise: they attacked the U.S. presence in the Federal Republic and the politics of the Brandt/Scheel and Schmidt/Genscher governments, which served the interests of U.S. capital in the Federal Republic, that strategic sub-center of U.S. imperialism. One cannot regret the fact that these sects ignore the trial, given that the reactionary content of their political practice makes their anti-imperialist rhetoric purely abstract.

For as long as it has existed, the DKP has been licking the boots of social democracy. They are doubtless the most corrupt communist party, at least in Western Europe. As far as I know, one thing that has contributed to this—and this is why, for example, Ulrike, who had previously fulfilled important functions for the illegal KPD, broke with them—is the way in which this party began to adjust its political line to accommodate the SPD so as to facilitate its legalization.

The problem is the overall depoliticization of the left. In fact, at no time during the campaign against the *Berufsverbot* was the question of the state addressed; what sort of state it is and whose state it is that the left is publicly sanitizing. The left, claiming a strategic perspective, began the march through the institutions in 68—although the ambivalence as to whether "a revolutionary career perspective" was not simply another term for "an official's salary" was already apparent at the time. The hue and cry about the *Berufsverbot* disguised their objective.

State security must preserve the entire civil service so as to—and this is the case in the trials—shift the whole institution to the right. The extremely aggressive way in which they pursue this objective, without running up against any resistance, is a function of the postfascist state in the Federal Republic. Part of this is the structure of the state and its unbroken continuity with the Third Reich, which includes the political hygiene practiced through the eradication of opposition between 33 and 45, and after 45 the gagging, paralyzing, and integrating of the groups emerging from illegality, groups which had been corrupted in exile and which were eventually brought under the control of the U.S. occupying power, the CIA, etc. during the Cold War.

The qualitative leaps which take place as fascism develops have not been grasped. Not so long ago even Amnesty International, an active anti-communist organization, or anti-Soviet in any event, that acts primarily in a way that is supportive of the FRG, complained that people no longer dare to sign petitions opposing torture in Latin America and South East Asia out of fear of being registered with the *Verfassungsschutz*. And they will be registered. The fear is well founded.

The full extent of the problem is apparent in the process of adopting a new *Verfassungsschutz* law in Lower Saxony. Almost all other *Länder* already have such a law, in accord with the principles issued centrally by the Interior Ministers Conference. The law decrees that all employees and officials of the civil service and radio and TV corporations have a duty to provide information to the *Verfassungsschutz*. At the same time, the BKA, equipped with the largest database in the world, is screening the entire left. What is taking place is, in practice, the almost complete control and registration of the political scene in the Federal Republic, which is a more far-reaching process than the physical internment that has taken place in Chile. The political climate resembles that which follows a fascist putsch. Accordingly, panic rules.

The fact that the guerilla and the prisoners from the RAF do not have this problem of fear is the result of having a political coherence that has its political history, but not its political center, in the Federal Republic. Its identity is international.

If the fascist drift is to be understood at all in the Federal Republic, then it will be understood through the guerilla struggle. The guerilla struggle tempers the demoralization of the left, allowing one to develop a self-critical relationship with one's own corruption; and it does that through Stammheim, through the prisoners' struggle, and through resistance. However, within this state, the fact that the enormous repression in the prisons has not broken the prisoners has very little impact on the overall depoliticization of this left.

Q: What is the significance of the RAF trials in the current political and economic situation in the FRG?

A: The prisoners say the trials are irrelevant. State security is in total control of the terrain. The trials are thoroughly preprogrammed. One must fight because one must always fight, but the machine demonstrates that nothing can be achieved at this level. But the procedural measures, including the dressing up of military methods and goals as the rituals of normal criminal proceedings, are an organic expression of the break in U.S. capital's strategy since its defeat in Vietnam. The intensity of the whole thing indicates the defensive position of U.S. capital and the resistance to its strategy since Vietnam.

Within the FRG, the trials are meant to accustom the population to the State of Emergency, so that it is accepted as normal and those who resist can be destroyed. That is the lesson state security hopes to impart with these trials. And at home, it works. Abroad, it doesn't. Abroad, the exceptional character of repression in the FRG has been recognized, and the government's domestic policies, which in the FRG are always a function of U.S. foreign policy—that has been the strategic function of the FRG for American capital since 45, or at least since its founding in 1949—are recognized as dysfunctional.

This is exactly what social democracy is meant to hide: the fact that today, serving the interests of international U.S. capital, West German imperialism is no different than the old fascism—this time without a reactionary mass mobilization, but rather as an institutional state strategy (over which U.S. capital has total control). This only became clear in the state's reaction to the politics of the RAF.

The prisoners say the preventive counterrevolution only makes sense when its relationship to the global system is considered: the repression within the state is a function of the strategic role the FRG plays for American capital. Just as its strategic operations in Europe and in the Common Market are a function of U.S. capital's defensive action in the Third World, as are those in the Mediterranean states of Europe and North Africa which are meant to secure military control of Middle Eastern oil—by assuring the existence of counterrevolutionary forces, which they control in these states. In this global system, the legal attacks on anti-imperialist politics in the FRG have political relevance, because they completely unmask social democracy. The RAF was clear that this was how it would unfold and that the SPD was the transmission belt of the new fascism. The RAF analyzed and anticipated this development long before it became obvious to world opinion in Portugal.[1]

Brandt wrote in a letter to Palme:[2] "Social democratic politics anticipate catastrophe so as to prevent it."

The RAF says that the strategic project of U.S. imperialism that is carried through by German social democracy and the Socialist International[3] represents the smooth unfolding of the fascist drift within civilian state structures. This is the "unique nature" of their relationship. Here in a social democratic police state, that with socialist rhetoric and through the usurping of the old antifascism is celebrated as *Modell Deutschland*, this policy was forced to take an extremely developed form. That this was due to a social revolutionary guerilla representing positions held by a tiny minority has nothing to do with provocation. The armed struggle here has a tactical quality—it is a factor which clarifies reality and represents the only option for proletarian resistance to the reactionary integration of Western Europe, which the U.S. is pushing through using West German social democracy.

On this topic, a statement from the prisoners:

> *The entire discussion turns on this perspective. Mediated by the political-military attack, the repressive structuring of the entire capitalist machine becomes central to the system, and in this way the response to its decisive crisis is already anticipated.*
>
> *Through the attack, capital's internal strategy is certainly and simultaneously disrupted by the obligation to react. They must mobilize their forces and dialectically this provokes an*

---

1 An antifascist military coup heralded an end to the Portuguese Salazar dictatorship in 1974, setting off a popular but limited upheaval during which people occupied factories and seized land, while demanding retribution for the crimes of the fascist regime. The Portuguese Socialist Party (later the Social Democrat Party) was instrumental in reining in this revolt, and within a few years, the PS's Mario Soares was subjecting Portugal to IMF dictates and entering into a coalition with the ultra-right Democratic and Social Center Party.

2 Olaf Palme was the Social Democratic Prime Minister of Sweden from 1969 until his assassination in 1986.

3 The Second International, the international organization of social democratic parties.

overall understanding of resistance that includes the concept of revolution. An experience and an understanding of imperialism in the metropole reveals the clear necessity for fundamental opposition, both nationally and internationally. And it also develops a strategic line: the internationalism of the guerilla as the form of proletarian politics that is antagonistic to capitalist development in the context of the class war.

This is the case because of two coinciding factors:

Nationally, it is the tactic of resistance against fascism in the form of the terrorist national security state.

Internationally, in the strategic sub-centre of the U.S.A.—the Federal Republic—it serves an offensive function on behalf of the anti-imperialist liberation struggles.

Naturally, this tactical understanding is also the line the prisoners are asserting at the trial, about which it is still possible to say:

It is not enough to talk loudly about fascism—but presenting a defense at this trial makes sense if it clarifies the necessity and the possibility for armed resistance as a factor in political opposition here in the FRG—and this must be the case if it needs to be smashed as brutally as is the case in Stammheim.

And one must add—if it weren't for the RAF, what would anyone in France, Italy, Holland, or the Scandinavian states know about the reactionary role of social democracy in the Federal Republic?

Q. Is there not a danger of a collective conviction of the accused, as the prosecution evidently has difficulty proving the guilt of each individual on the basis of the evidence? And how is your concept of the "principal guiding function" for the Stammheim trial to be understood?

A. They were already convicted before the trial began, by the media hate campaign, by the prison conditions, by isolation, by sensory deprivation, by deprivation of water, by the attempt at a stereotactical intervention, by drugging during interrogation, etc.—and by statements made by the Chancellor during the parliamentary debates after the Stockholm action. State security murdered four prisoners in a single year: Holger Meins, Katharina Hammerschmidt, Siegfried Hausner, and Ulrike Meinhof. Meanwhile, isolation units have been built in about 15 prisons. There are not four, but about 120 prisoners who, in this context, are subjected to the same prison conditions, and, out of these 120, 4 have been selected to support the "ringleader" construct.

In the last weeks before Ulrike's murder, this treatment was focused on two of the prisoners, Andreas and Ulrike, as part of the psychological warfare strategy of personalizing revolutionary politics, and the policy of the intelligence services in all counterrevolutionary projects of cutting off the head.

Andreas is the prisoner against whom state security concentrated their hate campaign, because he organized both the collective politics of the group, even in the situation of complete isolation in prison, and the all-out defensive strategy. When the trial began, he no longer had a lawyer and he faced three counts of attempted murder.

Since 65, Ulrike had played a guiding ideological role for the revolutionary left in the Federal Republic. She was to be broken in the dead wing through white torture, pathologized, and eventually turned into a cretin with a brain operation, so as to be used in the trial as evidence against the RAF's politics and against the broader anti-imperialist struggle in the FRG. Because the group struggled as a group, and we could still mobilize public opposition, this project had to be abandoned.

Then Ulrike was killed—as on each previous occasion when a conflict with the prisoners came to a head and became public knowledge, a RAF cadre was executed:

- Holger Meins, to break the hunger strike.
- Siegfried Hausner, during the action in Stockholm to free the prisoners, when the embassy was blown up by the Hamburg MEK to conceal their entry. Siegfried led the group and laid the explosives. He could have proved that the explosion was caused by West German state security. State security knew this when they removed him from the hospital in Stockholm. In order to liquidate him, they chose not to bring him to a hospital, but rather to keep him completely out of the public eye—for example, a visit from his lawyer, which he had demanded— they brought him to Stammheim's hermetically-sealed hospital ward—where, without qualified medical attention, he died.
- Ulrike Meinhof, before the decisive intervention in the trial, by which the whole doctrine of the show trial was in danger of being turned against the BAW and the government.

Since the latest guerilla attack against the U.S. Headquarters in Frankfurt,[1] every day we must be prepared for the possibility that a prisoner may be murdered.

All of the legal proceedings against RAF prisoners are part of one single focused operation. The decision of the BAW to organize the trials separately reflects the information they have. In a regional trial, in which the BAW had no business, a former federal prosecutor suddenly appeared to organize the prosecution's strategy along the lines of the BAW's principal guiding function. There is the example of the former Federal Prosecutor Kirsch, who turned the trial in Kaiserslautern into a vehicle for the hate campaign against Andreas.

Stammheim's principal guiding function is to set the tone for the entire judiciary. The Stammheim measures establish a legal vacuum in which all trials are expected to run smoothly, even those with less propaganda value, less manipulation of the facts, and less witness preparation.

The Stammheim measures have a bottom-up effect. The court can and does proceed with the assumption that the higher authorities will sanction each of its measures. There is no appellate authority. The entire state—a monstrous counterinsurgency machine—stands behind the court.

The prisoners do not deny their responsibility for the RAF's attacks against the U.S. military installations in the Federal Republic or their policy of using military means against the U.S. genocide in Vietnam; not one RAF prisoner denies this. The defense strategy is to expose the role of the Federal Republic as a strategic sub-centre, and the fact that this role is both a necessary condition for and a function of the aggressive human rights violations and the belligerence of the U.S. war machine in Vietnam.

The Federal Republic is totally integrated into U.S. foreign policy and military strategy, both actively and passively. The Federal Republic is a supply base, a training center, a troop transfer point, a centre for the U.S. electronics and logistics used in Vietnam, a staging point, and rear base area in the war against Vietnam. From this it follows conclusively that, since the failure and disintegration of the opposition to the Vietnam War, everyone in the Federal Republic had and has, under human rights law, the right to armed resistance. These prisoners are

---

1 On June 2, 1976, the Revolutionary Cells bombed the U.S. Army Headquarters and U.S. Officers' Club in Frankfurt, carrying out the attack under the banner of the "Ulrike Meinhof Commando." That same day, two fully loaded military trucks at a U.S. airbase were blown up just outside of the city.

prisoners of war. Furthermore, when all means of protest against isolation torture available within this state have been exhausted, we must do what is necessary so that the prisoners are recognized as prisoners of war by the United Nations and the International Red Cross, and that, as a result, the prison conditions established in the Geneva Convention are applied.

Naturally, the prisoners don't deny that they were and are organized in the RAF, that they have struggled and still struggle as part of the RAF—if one can put it that way at this point—and that they have contributed to its analysis and strategy both conceptually and in practice.

What the national security state hopes to achieve with Stammheim, false witnesses, the manipulation of files, and the totally obscure charges—because "joint responsibility" does not exist in the Criminal Code here—is a blatantly farcical conviction, in which the true dimensions of the confrontation are meant to be overshadowed by proving concrete participation in the actions. The goal of neutralizing the politics of the conflict in an underwater ballet of thousands of BKA experts is also, therefore, absurd, because, given the documents and the facts that are known to us, no criminal indictments are possible.

Because the conflict is political, the state insists on understanding it in military terms: the moral, psychological, and physical extermination of "the enemy"—as Prinzing once let slip—at the level of criminalistics. What would be best in the view of the BAW would be one big high treason trial against all RAF prisoners. The clichéd elements of high treason—threatening the existence of the Federal Republic and its constitutional order by violence or threat of violence—are present in all the court decrees, charges, etc. against this group. But to do so would mean admitting that there exists fundamental political opposition within the Federal Republic and that revolutionary politics are possible even in this state.

That would not fit into the concept developed by social democracy. Their plan is to "quietly" and "decisively" maintain that the State of Emergency is the "normal state of affairs," and they do this by all manner of manipulation, psychological warfare, repression, control, registration, police penetration of society and its social neutralization, and covert police actions. The normal state of affairs in the Federal Republic should be one in which there is no opposition to the presence of the U.S. military machine, U.S. capital, the state, or social democracy. That is wishful thinking, given that the RAF is a result of the politicization of the Vietnam opposition and of the proletarianization and declassing that occurred in the 60s, and which led to an offensive break with the legality of the imperialist state.

Stammheim, where a mass of falsified and fabricated criminal details are meant to undermine the political content of the confrontation, makes it clear what the issue is in the Federal Republic: fascism. The filthy, old political machine we know so well, in a new and more monstrous form—no longer as a function of national monopoly capitalism, but as part of the globalization of U.S. capital.

The prisoners say that it is because of the strategic function that the Federal Republic plays for U.S. capital that the urban guerilla can destabilize things here—and it makes no difference how small a minority they are. Their strategy clarifies why it is extremely difficult to develop a revolutionary position in the Federal Republic, as well as why it is necessary to do so. That it is possible has been proven in the six years since the first action.

Meanwhile, Elsewhere on the Left...
(an intermission of sorts)

I N 1976, THE RAF REMAINED a recognized part of the revolutionary left. Years of psychological operations may have seriously compromised it in the eyes of liberals and the general public, but the state had failed to completely isolate it despite all its efforts to do so. The group benefited from sympathy in some quarters, and a smaller number of people even found its struggle inspirational.

Yet, the left itself was changing; the RAF, with its core cadre in prison and its supporters focused almost solely on their release, was not in a position to follow these developments as closely as it should have.

With the collapse of the APO, many leftists turned towards the Social Democrats, the SPD acquiring over 200,000 new members between 1969 and 1974.[1] For all the youthful exuberance of the sixties movement, in the end, many students had been integrated into the system. The situation only worsened, the SPD's drift to the right accelerating in 1974 when an espionage scandal forced Brandt to relinquish the Chancellor's office to Helmut Schmidt.

Nevertheless, throughout the 1970s, the numbers of people organizing politically outside of the establishment continued to grow, albeit in a less culturally spectacular way than in the preceding decade.

---

1 Hülsberg, 45.

THE K-GROUPS

As we have already seen, the APO as it had existed was incapable of rising to the challenge posed by the Social-Liberal Coalition, and many of those who retained their radical opposition to capitalism found themselves joining one of the many newly-founded Marxist-Leninist organizations, the K-groups. These had much in common with other new communist parties which sprang up throughout the Western world at this time, combining an enthusiastic (if somewhat unhealthy) *esprit de corps* with a more conservative approach to political organizing. As elsewhere, Maoism in the FRG peaked in the first half of the 1970s, declining rapidly near the end of the decade.

As the years wore on, some of these Marxist-Leninist organizations would develop positions reminiscent of the postwar KPD's "patriotic communism." The Bavaria-based *Arbeiterbund*, for instance, held that the German nation was divided and oppressed by both U.S. imperialism and Soviet "social imperialism," and thus advanced the troublesome slogan, "Germany to the Germans."

The RAF's insistence that West Germany was itself an oppressor nation, and that even its working class constituted a labor aristocracy, would contrast sharply with this.

"Forward in the
struggle for the rights
of the working class
and the people—
Forward in the
struggle for the victory
of socialism"

The K-groups could not be expected to offer any substantial support to the RAF given their opposition to guerilla activities in the First World, which most of them perceived as adventurist and even counterrevolutionary. Perhaps of equal importance, their "anti-revisionist" trajectory and uncritical support for China's foreign policy led many Maoists to oppose those national liberation movements in the Third World which received aid from the East Bloc countries. Eventually, some K-groups would even go so far as to support the same anticommunist guerillas that the United States was backing at the time.

Despite these differences, certain K-groups—notably the KPD/ML—did offer important and much appreciated support to the prisoners during their third hunger strike in 1974.

If the K-groups represented one answer to the APO's shortcomings, other militants, especially those who remained based in the universities and the counterculture, had set out on a very different trajectory. Anarchism, anti-vanguardist Marxism, and even simple "actionism" revealing a bias against any political theory, combined and fed into the *sponti* scene. These activists placed great store in the politicization of everyday life, and one's personal liberation from authoritarian institutions—a process which they felt could only be made possible in spaces freed from capitalist domination. Later in the decade, parts of this scene would be instrumental in spreading the ideas of autonomist communism from Italy to the Federal Republic.

In the early seventies, the *spontis* lead militant squatters' movements in Frankfurt and Hamburg, although these were unfortunately unable to survive repeated police attacks. More than one RAF member came out of these squatting scenes[1] that during their brief existence played a role similar to that of the communes in the APO days, providing spaces where people could create their own cultures and relationships while being pulled in a militant direction by the very fact that they were living in illegal conditions.

In 1974, the movement acquired its own national newspaper, *Info-BUG*,[2] based in West Berlin. The other important newspaper associated with the *spontis* was Daniel Cohn-Bendit's *Pflasterstrand*, founded in 1976 and based in Frankfurt. *Informationsdienst*, more radical than *Pflasterstrand* and also with a broader appeal, was yet another regular movement publication that had been coming out of that city since 1973.

The *spontis* formed the radical edge of the undogmatic left, and of all the various non-guerilla scenes, they were closest to

WIDER DIE UNTERTANENFABRIK
Kampf dem LHG

DEMONSTRATION
12. Dez. um 13.30 h ab Audi - Max / Uni

Poster for a sponti demonstration: "The LHG Struggles Against the Education Factory"

---

1 For instance, Karl-Heinz Dellwo and Bernd Rössner of the RAF's Holger Meins Commando had both been active in the Hamburg squatters' scene, as had Susanne Albrecht, Silke Maier-Witt, and Siegrid Sternebeck who would all be involved in events in 1977.

2 An acronym for "Info Berlin Undogmatic Groups."

the RAF. As a result of their squatting experiences, the Frankfurt scene in particular had had to develop a capacity to defend itself from the police, and had even built up a fighting squad, the Putz Group,[1] whose job it was to take on the cops at demos. In regular training sessions, the Putz members practiced stone-throwing, one-on-one combat, unarresting comrades, and, according to some accounts, the use of molotov cocktails. As one former member recalled, "We had the complete gear that the cops had, except for guns."[2]

According to one historian of the period, there was a great deal of overlap and cross-pollination between the *spontis* and squats and the circles in which the guerillas and their supporters moved.[3] Perhaps for this precise reason, the most acrimonious debate over armed politics occurred within this scene.

Shortly after Holger Meins's death in 1974, the organization Revolutionary Struggle, led by Cohn-Bendit and his friend Joschka Fischer, had joined with the squatting council and other *sponti* groups to issue a declaration of unambiguous solidarity with the guerilla.[4] Shortly afterwards, however, Revolutionary Struggle issued another statement, "Mass-Militancy vs. the Guerilla," meant to initiate debate over the most appropriate use of political violence in the scene and questioning the logic of clandestine armed struggle.[5]

At the same time, another guerilla organization had formed which represented the politics and practice of the *sponti* scene far better than the RAF: this was the Revolutionary Cells, or RZ.

The RZ's first actions were carried out in November 1973, two months after a CIA-backed coup had toppled the socialist Allende government in Chile. On the weekend of November 16 and 17, bombs went off at the offices of an ITT subsidiary in both West Berlin and Nuremberg, causing over $200,000 in damages.[6]

---

1 As author Paul Hockenos explains, "In German, *auf den Putz hauen* is slang for having a wild, rowdy time. Perhaps 'to raise hell' fits the meaning best." (117).

2 Hans-Joachim Klein quoted in Hockenos, 124.

3 Ibid., 114-115.

4 Cf 264-5.

5 Geronimo, *Feuer und Flamme: Zur Geschichte der Autonomen.* (Berlin: ID-Archiv, 1990). An English translation of this book was published by PM Press in 2012.

6 Associated Press, "W. German ITT Offices Bombed," *Des Moines Register,*

A communiqué explained:

> *The Revolutionary Cells claim responsibility for the attack on the ITT branches in Berlin and Nuremberg on November 16 and 17, 1973. We attacked the ITT branches, because ITT is responsible for the torture and murder of women, workers, and peasants.*
>
> *As early as 1971, ITT wanted, with the help of the then head of the CIA, McCone, who also sat on ITT's Board of Directors, to prevent Allende's electoral victory, using ITT's own domestic politics section, the news services, and the counterintelligence services, while, of course, supported by the mass murderer Nixon. Towards this end, ITT provided the CIA with 1 million dollars. ITT allowed the assassination of the much-loved General Schneider, so as to provoke a putsch. This was unsuccessful, because the Chilean people knew that they had to fight for their freedom and that the ruling class would use all the means at its disposal to oppress the people—the capitalist system—they don't give a shit how many people must die in the process.[7]*

These were the opening salvos of one of West Germany's most interesting, and least known, guerilla groups.

Dubbed "the after work guerillas," the RZ adopted a very different approach from either the RAF or the 2JM. Anybody could carry out an action within the context of the RZ's politics—defined as anti-imperialism, anti-Zionism, and "supporting the struggles of workers, wimmin and youth"[8]—and claim it as an RZ action. In line with this, the Cells did not field underground militants, but rather advised comrades to maintain their "legal" existence while carrying out clandestine armed activities. Finally, the group's domestic wing purposefully stopped short of carrying out lethal attacks, the sole fatality during their entire nineteen-year existence being a politician who bled out when an RZ cell knee-capped him in 1981. (The group subsequently issued a communiqué explaining that they had not meant to kill him.)

November 19, 1973; Associated Press, "Bomb rips ITT subsidiary office in Berlin," *European Stars and Stripes*, November 18, 1973.

7 "Aktionen gegen ITT Berlin und Nürnberg (November 73)," http://www.freilassung.de/div/texte/rz/zorn/Zorn12.htm.

8 Autonome Forum, "A Herstory Of The Revolutionary Cells And Rote Zora—Armed Resistance in West Germany," http://www.etext.org/Politics/Autonome. Forum/Guerrilla/Europe/Rote.Zora/mini-herstory.1988.

The RZ would suffer few arrests, and even fewer casualties, all the while carrying out far more attacks than the RAF and 2JM combined. It should, however, be noted that many of these attacks were of a limited nature similar to those carried out by RAF supporters who were likewise living and working in the legal movement. Apart from bombing the Chilean consulate, the offices of El Al, police stations, U.S. army bases, government buildings, and bosses' cars, for years the RZ also forged transit passes which were widely distributed, and food vouchers which were passed out to homeless families. Starting on May Day 1975, the Cells issued an annual newspaper, *Revolutionärer Zorn* (Revolutionary Rage), explaining their positions and actions; it was immediately banned under §88a, but broadly distributed and widely read in the scene regardless.

Eventually, an autonomous women's guerilla group, Rote Zora (named after a Pippy Longstocking-type character from a children's book) would emerge from the Cells, bombing the Federal Doctors' Association in Karlsruhe on April 29, 1977, as payback for the association's opposition to abortion reform.[1] While Rote Zora was independent of the RZ, the two organizations always worked closely together in both theoretical and practical matters.

Some militants from the founding generation of the RZ felt they would best serve the international anti-imperialist revolution by literally fighting alongside the Third World guerilla in joint commandos. In practical terms, this meant working under the direction of a PFLP splinter faction operating out of South Yemen, lead by Waddi Haddad: the PFLP (External Operations).[2] While the RZ tendency concerned is often described as the "international wing," it actually represented a very small number of militants and only participated in a handful of actions, none of which were particularly succesful, while one constituted a decisive military and political defeat.

The first of these occurred on December 24, 1975, with Hans-Joachim Klein and former 2JM member Gabriele Kröcher-Tiedemann participating in a joint German-Palestinian commando under the control of the Venezuelan adventurer Ilich Ramírez Sánchez, better known as

---

1 "Interview mit der Roten Zora Juni 1984" at http://www.freilassung.de/div/texte/ rz/zorn/Zorn50.htm. The first Rote Zora action is often dated 1975, which, while understandable, is technically incorrect, as previous bombings were claimed simply by "Women of the Revolutionary Cells."

2 For more on this see Appendix VI—The German Guerilla's Palestinian Allies: Waddi Haddad's PFLP (EO), pages 559-61.

"Carlos." Klein had moved from the Committees Against Torture and the Putz Group to the RZ following Holger Meins's death.[3] Given that Klein was the only RZ member to have participated, and that he subsequently broke from the guerilla, some people do not consider the RZ's international wing to have been involved. (As for Kröcher-Tiedemann, she was certainly acting independently of 2JM in this operation.)

The so-called "December 21st Movement of the Arabic Revolution" delivered a bloody nose to the Organization of Petroleum Exporting Countries as it met in Vienna. Sixty oil ministers from around the world were taken hostage, and both an Austrian police officer and a Libyan diplomat were killed in the process. In exchange for the ministers' release, the guerilla demanded—and received—a $5 million ransom, and all were flown to Algeria from whence they returned to the underground.

The operation had been meant to punish OPEC for its recent decision to lift its embargo against Israel. Yet, it was not considered a success: the plan had been for the Carlos-led guerilla to execute diplomats from Saudi Arabia and Iran, both of which were important American allies; instead, Carlos negotiated a ransom for their freedom. Many reports claim that he was in fact excluded from Haddad's organization for this breach.

Not that this less bloody outcome assuaged the operation's many critics: officials from the PLO accused Carlos of having orchestrated a "criminal act" designed to "undermine the nature of the Palestinian struggle," claiming that the raid was such a disaster it could have been an imperialist false flag operation—which it wasn't.[4] Nevertheless, all of the guerillas had survived (though Klein had been seriously wounded), and so it could not be considered an unmitigated failure.

The same could not be said for the next operation to include members of the RZ's international wing.

On June 27, 1976, a joint commando made up of members of the PFLP(EO) and members of the RZ[5] hijacked an Air France airliner traveling from Tel Aviv to Paris, diverting it to Entebbe, Uganda. The

---

3 Imre Karacs, "After 25 years Carlos the Jackal gets his revenge," *(London) Independent* [online], October 18, 2000. Klein later recalled that with Meins's death, "It became clear to me that we must do something more than support people in prison. In an emergency, we had to participate in armed actions ourselves."

4 *Time Magazine* [online], "Kidnaping in Vienna, Murder in Athens," Jan. 5, 1976.

5 Wilfried Böse and Brigitte Kuhlmann, both founding members from the Frankfurt scene.

guerillas demanded the release of 53 political prisoners held by Israel, West Germany, France, Switzerland, and Kenya. The West Germans demanded were RAF members Werner Hoppe, Jan-Carl Raspe, and Ingrid Schubert, and 2JM members Ralf Reinders, Fritz Teufel, and Inge Viett.

The hostage taking was a drawn out affair, in part because so many governments were involved. After a week of holding all 260 passengers and crew, the guerillas arranged to release the non-Jewish passengers: the Jews were to be held back so that they would be the ones killed if the commando's demands were not met.

On July 4, an Israeli commando raided the airport, killing forty-seven Ugandan soldiers who were guarding the area, and all of the guerillas. Over one hundred Jewish hostages were saved and quickly flown out of the country.

Entebbe was a fiasco, doing so much harm to the Palestinian cause that British diplomats at the time even considered the possibility that it might be a Mossad false flag attack—but it wasn't.[1]

Some observers eventually concluded that the singling out of Jews for execution represented a political defeat far greater than any military failure. Certainly, Entebbe provides a stark example of the inability some leftists had in recognizing or rejecting antisemitism.

At the time, however, it is unclear how this racist selection was actually viewed. Many German gentiles failed to understand why the separation of Jews was antisemitic, and *Spiegel* went so far as to describe it as a sophisticated tactic.[2] Detlev Claussen, a member of the *Sozialistisches Büro*, was one of the few to tackle the question head on, arguing that Entebbe represented the "continuity of German antisemitism."[3]

Within the radical scene, the issue was hardly debated. With very few exceptions, the revolutionary left would only repudiate the operation years later, looking back on it with some shame. Finally, in a 1992 self-criticism that very much marked the end of the organization, the

---

1 Fran Yeoman, "Diplomats suspected Entebbe hijacking was an Israeli plot to discredit the PLO," *Times Online*, June 1, 2007.

2 *Spiegel*, "Härte bedeutet Massaker," July 5, 1976, quoted in Annette Vowinckel, "Der kurze Weg nach Entebbe oder die Verlängerung der deutschen Geschichte in den Nahen Osten," http://www.zeithistorische-forschungen.de/site/40208212/default.aspx#pgfId-1033195a.

3 Jeffrey Herf, "The 'Holocaust' Reception in West Germany: Right, Center and Left," *New German Critique* 19, special issue, Germans and Jews (Winter, 1980): 44.

RZ explained how they had experienced and failed to react to the facts around the antisemitic selection:

> *It took years for us to absorb this setback. As a result of the impact of the loss of our friends, we were initially unable to assess the political dimensions of the catastrophe that Entebbe was for us. Instead of appreciating what confronted us, specifically that we as an organization had taken part in an operation in which Israeli citizens and Jewish passengers of other nationalities were singled out and taken hostage, we occupied ourselves above all with the military aspects of the action and its violent conclusion... Our understanding of solidarity prevented criticism of the comrades; we rejected a discussion about the mistakes, as if solidarity did not in principle include the truth that some comrades make mistakes.[4]*

Horrible as it was, in 1976, Entebbe was just another disaster hitting the already shell-shocked *sponti* scene.

The "Mass Militancy vs. the Guerilla" debate had taken on a sense of urgency with the May 10, 1976, Frankfurt protests, the day after Meinhof's death in prison. During the Frankfurt riots, a cop was nearly killed when persons unknown lobbed several molotov cocktails at his car. One bounced in through the window exploding on top of him: the twenty-three-year-old police officer, Jürgen Weber, sustained burns over 60% of his body. His survival remained uncertain for several days.[5]

A $20,000 reward was posted for information leading to Weber's assailants. Then, on May 14, police raided a dozen collective houses, arresting fourteen people on suspicion of attempted murder, first-degree assault, and membership in a criminal organization under §129.[6]

The fourteen were all released the next day, but the night in jail had momentous ramifications. Whether out of fear or introspection, one of the arrestees—Joschka Fischer, the alpha male of the *sponti* scene—decided that night that militant protest had gone too far. Upon his release, he broached the subject with his friend Cohn-Bendit, who agreed, and the two men set upon planning how to win over the rest of the scene.

---

4 "Gerd Albartus ist tot," http://www.freilassung.de/div/texte/rz/zorn/Zorn04.htm
5 Cohen; see also: Hockenos, 120.
6 "Festnahmen nach Frankfurter Ausschreitungen," *Frankfurter Allgemeine Zeitung.* See also Hockenos, 120, though note that his assertion that the arrests occurred in June seems incorrect.

The first opportunity to present their new position was an Anti-Repression Conference organized by the *Sozialistisches Büro* over the weekend of June 5-7. There, Fischer addressed a rally of over 10,000 people, many of them militants and street fighters like himself. Arguing that political violence had hit a brick wall, he warned that the *sponti* scene risked falling into the same trap as the guerilla, which he described as "lashing out blindly" due to its own "hopelessness." Directing his comments at the guerilla itself, he beseeched them:

> *For the very reason that our solidarity belongs with our comrades in the underground and because we feel so closely linked with them, we call upon them to end this death trip at once, to return from their "armed self-isolation." We call upon them to put down the bombs and to pick up stones again.[1]*

According to several contemporaries, only Fischer, who had credibility as a seasoned activist and a Putz Group leader, could have gotten a hearing for such views. As it happens, he reportedly received wild applause.

Why Fischer adopted a hard line against the guerilla is not clear. In later years, he pointed to the horror of Entebbe—like many Frankfurt militants, he had known the RZ fighters who died there—and also to the fear he had seen in a policeman's eyes as he beat him up a year previously.

Obviously, the Meinhof demonstration, and the realization that continued militancy might lead to prison, played a very large part in the equation. Years later, Cohn-Bendit would explain:

> *The Meinhof demonstration was a decisive experience. One was faced with the fact that a dynamic could lead to a fatal outcome. That was the beginning of the radical dissociation of the entire scene from the terrorists and of a new discussion about the state and our resistance to it.[2]*

Despite this reference to "resistance," and Fischer's words at the Anti-Repression Conference about "picking up stones," what was soon being

---

1 Hockenos, 121-122. Please note that a large excerpt of Fischer's speech, or else a text closely based on it, is credited "anonymous" and reprinted in *semiotext(e): The German Issue* [Anonymous, "To Have Done with Armed Isolation," translated by Wynn Gunderson. *semiotext(e)* 4, no. 2 (1982): 130-133].

2 Daniel Cohn-Bendit, interviewed by Stefan Aust, Gunther Latsch, Georg Mascolo and Gerhard Spörl, "Ein Segen für dieses Land," *Spiegel* [online], May 2001.

put forth was that militancy altogether should be toned down, if not cut out. The Putz Group was disbanded, *Pflasterstrand* began pushing the anti-violence line, and by 1977 Fischer had repudiated revolution as a goal. As former *sponti* Wolfgang Kraushaar has suggested:

> When confronted with a crisis, which [Fischer] had until then understood as revolutionary violence, he began to question the whole notion of proletarian revolution. The fact that his existential experience with violence resulted in his reassessment of the entire revolutionary process being in a state of crisis was probably due to his own lack of political self-understanding.[3]

While not everyone followed Fischer in this retreat, many did, and the *sponti* scene's inability to cope with escalation as it occurred indicated that it had indeed reached its limits. A long period of decline ensued.

By the winter of 1977-78, as the postwar generation lay besieged by the worst repression they had ever experienced, *Pflasterstrand* would be focusing on male anxieties about non-penetrative sex,[4] and, by the early 1980s, Fischer and Cohn-Bendit were leading former *spontis* and other leftists into the Green Party, where they coalesced in a "realo" faction opposing the Greens' more radical grassroots wing.[5] By 1998, the former street fighter had become Germany's Green Foreign Minister, who was instrumental in formulating the country's decision to take part in NATO's war against Serbia in 1999.[6]

As a somewhat Shakespearian postscript to Fischer's colorful career, in 2001, Ulrike Meinhof's daughter Bettina Röhl came into possession of photographs of the Foreign Minister in his Putz Group days beating up a cop. Clearly marked by her mother's larger than life experiences, Röhl is a woman with an axe to grind against anyone and everyone connected to the seventies radical left. She published the photos on her website, provoking a furor in Germany, but failing to really damage Fischer's reputation in any way, though greatly raising his profile internationally.

It was not that the man was untouchable; rather, his own life arc was simply a more vivid version of that of countless men and women of his generation.

---

3 Geronimo.
4 Herzog, 429-430.
5 Hockenos, 167, 169.
6 Ibid., 258, 267-268.

WOMEN'S LIBERATION

Dwarfing the *spontis* and the K-groups, the strongest movements in the 1970s in West Germany were clearly the women's liberation movement and the *Bürgerinitiativen* (Citizens Initiatives). At the same time, these movements remained far more interesting than the SPD or its left-wing, the *Jusos*. Of course, the comparison is not really fair, for both these were broad movements which could, and did, overlap with each other, with the various strains of the radical left, and with sections of the mainstream political spectrum.

While both of these movements drew on the legacy of the APO, neither one fit comfortably within the categories of the left, New or Old, nor were they preoccupied with doing so. This provided the basis for very different reactions from the different guerilla groups.

While the significance of the "women's question" had obviously been recognized in Germany since well before the time of the Federal Republic, the 1960s saw the emergence of a new feminism there, as in many other countries. This new wave was born of the insights and rebellious spirit of the anticolonial revolutions and the students' movement, but even more so as a result of the frustration radical women experienced when the left failed to live up to its promise, proving itself as mired in sexism as the rest of society.

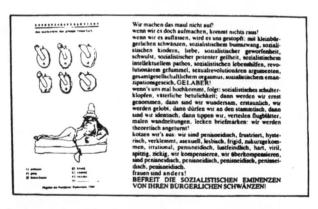

Famous leaflet produced by the "Broad's Council" of the SDS in 1968: "Liberate the Socialist Men from their Bourgeois Dicks." The men whose six penises were mounted on the wall above the axe-wielding woman had their names listed below: Helmut Schauer, Peter Gäng, Dieter Kunzelmann, Hans-Jürgen Krahl, Bernd Rabehl, and Reimut Reiche were all leading men in the APO. A space for a seventh name was left blank.

As the APO declined, the women's liberation movement entered a period of rapid advance. While many feminists continued to work within the male-dominated left, others separated themselves from its campaigns and organizations to a degree greater than what occurred in most other countries at that time.[1] These women had no lack of areas in which to put their energies, areas which had often been neglected by their male "comrades": opposing violence against women, organizing collective childcare, struggling for reproductive rights, and much more. This work was often based in autonomous women's centers, the first ones being established in Frankfurt and West Berlin in 1972, but others soon appearing in cities across the country.

If the contours of the West German women's movement were similar to those in other imperialist countries in the seventies, they were not identical. Most observers agree, for instance, that the West German experience was marked by the lack of an official national organization, such as the American National Organization of Women, and also by less contact with professional political women's organizations in the main parties. These differences allowed the West German movement to develop a far greater emphasis on autonomy, not only from men, but also from the political establishment and the political left.[2]

A variety of issues, ranging from sexism in the media to wages for housework, attracted political action, which in turn ranged from petitions to demonstrations to disruptive "go-ins." However, by far the most important and unifying struggle was the campaign to repeal §218 of the Basic Law, the paragraph of the constitution banning abortion under any circumstances. Under §218, a woman who had an abortion was liable to a five-year prison term; anyone who performed such a procedure was liable to a ten-year term.[3] It was estimated that 1,000,000 abortions were nevertheless performed every year, either in often perilous conditions or else necessitating travel to Holland or England where the procedure was not illegal.[4]

The movement against §218 stormed its way onto the public stage on June 2, 1971, when feminist journalist Alice Schwarzer arranged

---

1 Edith Hoshino Altbach, "The New German Women's Movement," *Signs* 9, no. 3 (Spring, 1984): 462.

2 Hoshino Altbach, "The New German Women's Movement," 456, 462; Katsiaficas, 75.

3 K.C. Horton, "Abortion Law Reform in the German Federal Republic," *International and Comparative Law Quarterly* 28, no. 2 (April 1979): 288-289.

4 Ibid., 290.

to have 374 women publicly "confess" to having had abortions in the pages of the mainstream magazine *Stern*. Two months later, Schwarzer had collected thousands more "confessions" and tens of thousands of solidarity signatures.[1]

Within a year, the sensation had become a movement, putting its feet on the ground in Frankfurt in March 1972 at the first National Women's Conference of the postwar period. It was here that an "Aktion 218" working group established plans for a renewed campaign to decriminalize abortion, the beginning of what one German feminist would call "a children's crusade against the patriarchy."[2]

The movement grew by leaps and bounds, bringing together women from a variety of political perspectives, including many radicals. A national day of action was called by the Berlin Women's Center, and on March 16, 1974, thousands of women took to the streets against §218, while 329 doctors gambled their professional licenses by declaring in *Spiegel* that they had helped women to obtain illegal abortions. At the same time, a current affairs television program prepared a show in which thirteen doctors were all to assist in an illegal abortion. Following protests from the Churches and the CDU ("[the telecast would be] an unheard of offense to the moral sense of millions of citizens and an acme of tastelessness"[3]), the show was banned, and all that appeared during the prime time slot was a blank screen.[4]

Poster for demonstration against the antiabortion §218.

1 Katsiaficas, 69. It should be noted that this tactic had been inspired by a similar action in France, where 343 women had "confessed" in like manner in the pages of *le nouvel Observateur* in 1971, at a time when Schwarzer was living in Paris. (Hoshino Altbach (ed.), "German Feminism," 103.)

2 Gunhild Feigenwinter quoted in Hoshino Altbach, "The New German Women's Movement," 456.

3 Associated Press, "German TV cancels film showing abortion," *European Stars and Stripes*, March 13, 1974.

4 Katsiaficas, 72.

The campaign seemed to have made a breakthrough, and the *Bundestag* passed an SPD bill in April permitting abortion in the first trimester, which most considered to be a real victory. When the bill became law in July of that year, though, the CDU and CSU immediately appealed to the Federal Constitutional Court, which voted six to two in February 1975 that the legislation violated the Constitution.[5] The movement had been dealt a major blow.[6]

One week later, bombs went off in the court's chambers in Karlsruhe. As a communiqué explained:

> *On March 4, 1975, the women of the Revolutionary Cells carried out an attack against the Federal Constitutional Court.*
>
> *Not to "defend the constitution from the Federal Constitutional Court"... but to defend ourselves from the constitution. A constitution that provides the legal framework for the daily exploitation, grinding down, and psychological destruction of millions of women and men. A constitution that criminalizes women—many driven to their deaths—if they do not allow the doctors' mafia and the judges' mafia to control their sexuality, as well as decisions regarding their own bodies and the number of children they will have.[7]*

From informal conversations, we gather that this was a well-received action, serving to galvanize militant feminism and strengthen the struggle for free and accessible abortion for all women.

This was one of three bombings carried out by the Women of the Revolutionary Cells in 1975; there were no similar attacks until Rote Zora's appearance in 1977. Clearly there was room to experiment with feminist armed politics, and some militants were taking up this challenge. This was not the case with the RAF.

---

5 Horton, 291.

6 In 1976, abortion was decriminalized for women who agreed to undergo counseling beforehand. (Katsiaficas, 72)

7 "Aktion gegen das Bundesverfassungsgericht (März 75)," http://www.freilassung.de/div/texte/rz/zorn/Zorn12i.htm

Later in the decade, a number of efforts would be made to define, or at least explore, the relationship between feminism and armed anti-imperialism. This was as a result of developments on the ground, as certain women attempted to grapple with the meaning of the guerilla's politics, and with the prominence of so many women in the RAF. The process received added impetus as activists from both milieux were brought together within the peace and antinuclear movements that emerged from the other trend the RAF was ignoring: the rise of the Citizens Initiatives.

BÜRGERINITIATIVEN: THE CITIZENS INITIATIVES

The Citizens Initiatives had developed from the least radical section of the APO in combination with segments of the SPD. The term itself covers what is described in North America as "civil society," with the proviso that the groups involved tended to be based in one locality and focused on one single issue. This varied wildly from opposition to nuclear power, highway expansion, or deforestation, to promotion of the rights of guest workers, tenants, or the elderly, or work around some particular government policy or piece of legislation, for instance the *Berufsverbot*.[1]

It is difficult to draw a hard and objective line between the Citizens Initiatives and various left or feminist projects, and indeed there was always overlap. However, the explicitly non-ideological and reformist approach that characterized the Initiatives makes the term a meaningful one in examining the struggle in the 1970s. While individuals might work with a Citizens Initiative for their own ideological reasons (i.e., against the *Berufsverbot* because they were communists), the idea behind the Initiative itself was the issue being tackled, not how it fit into some greater political scheme. At least initially, the campaigns were ends in themselves, not aspects of some broader strategy.

As such, the Citizens Initiatives were always consciously reformist, even system-supportive, often firmly anchored in the SPD and hoping to win over politicians so that they could enact the changes deemed necessary.

From about a thousand such groups in 1972, the numbers grew several fold by 1975 to an estimated 60,000 to 160,000 people; by the end of the seventies, the total membership has been estimated as anywhere

---

1 Michal Y. Bodemann, "The Green Party and the New Nationalism in the Federal Republic of Germany," *Socialist Register* (1985-86): 142.

between 300,000 and a half million,[2] all the way up to two or three million people.[3]

Initially, these citizens' groups may have been based in the SPD, but as the Schmidt administration carried out a series of massive public investments in new highways, nuclear plants, and heavy industries, those involved became more susceptible to radical ideas, especially those which questioned the logic of capitalist development and environmental destruction.[4]

West Germany's ecology movement grew directly out of these Initiatives, and opposition to nuclear power became the common denominator binding it together. Even people committed to strictly reformist goals began to find themselves standing against the state, and in certain circumstances were radicalized by the force of events. In this way, the Initiatives defied the skepticism of many on the revolutionary left, who had not thought them capable of overcoming their reformist origins and moving beyond their limited goals.

It was only a bit of a stretch to tie the German nuclear program to relations with the global South, given that atomic energy was proposed as a salve following the OPEC "oil shock" in 1973; some would even try to conceptualize the antinuclear movement as part of the resistance to imperialism.

This new antinuclear movement first showed its promise in February 1975, when news spread that police had attacked a small protest outside a nuclear power plant: within days, tens of thousands of people had descended on the Wyhl plant.[5] Over the years to come, similar rallies outside nuclear power stations mobilized greater and greater numbers as protests evolved into occupations, and police attacks were met with increasingly sophisticated tactics and mass militancy. The BKA eventually responded by opening files on "all persons who take part in the preparation for and/or carrying out of violent demonstrations, especially against the building or operation of atomic energy plants."[6]

Most of the left took note of the growing antinuclear movement, and of the more general spread of the Citizens Initiatives, and reacted

---

2 Katsiaficas, 63.

3 Hockenos, 134.

4 Bodemann, 142.

5 Katsiaficas, 81-82.

6 *The Atomic State and the People Who Have to Live In It,* (D-Bochum: Campaign against the Model West Germany, 1979). Reprinted in "German war machine targets anti-nukers," *Open Road* 11 (Summer 1980).

with varying measures of interest and support. Many in the feminist movement discovered a synergy with the new concern with peace and environmentalism, easily framed as women's issues. To the K-groups, such single-issue campaigns could serve as hunting grounds for new recruits, though by a twist of the dialectic, it was eventually they who were often recruited. Sections of the undogmatic left, more enthusiastic about movementism, found a hospitable home in these increasingly militant protests and the communities of resistance which developed around them. Previous misgivings notwithstanding, as the *sponti* scene entered its period of decline, the antinuclear movement provided a convenient home for many, including not a few erstwhile street fighters.

But the RAF and its support base were focused on the prisoners and did not respond to these new developments. Guerilla anti-imperialism was by definition illegal, and the only supporters the RAF felt it needed were those who were already prepared to support its actions. In the mid-seventies, at least, it showed little interest in reaching out to people who would have to be struggled with on this point.

While there are plenty of good reasons to be wary of tailing popular mobilizations, such a strategy also comes with an inevitable cost when there is no large revolutionary movement from which to draw strength. The founding members of the RAF had almost all been politically active in the sixties APO, a youth rebellion against the stifling postwar culture, which drew strength and inspiration from the anticolonial revolutions sweeping the world at the time. While they looked to the Third World as the most important theater in the global revolution, the first RAF members were all firmly rooted in the German radical left.

Scene from Wyhl protests, February 1975. Note the police armored personnel carrier is graffitied "KKW Nein": "No Nuclear Power Plant".

In the intervening years, though, the group and its support scene had acquired two paradoxes which made this connection difficult to maintain.

On the one hand, the guerilla continued to view imperialism as the defining problem of their time, and in theory this could have—and normally should have—meant supporting the struggles of the millions of people in the Third World. In practice, however, the RAF's anti-imperialism was solely expressed through struggles around prison conditions in the Federal Republic, and even then only with regards to political prisoners. Karl-Heinz Dellwo tells of how the Hamburg Committee Against Torture was approached by an Eritrean comrade who asked for help in an occupation of the Ethiopian Embassy: "We were so involved in supporting the prisoners that we declined, explaining that we had to deal with freeing our prisoners first," he recalls.[1]

At the same time, the RAF prisoners continued to condemn campaigns based on humanitarian concern, or mere solidarity against repression, even as almost all of their recruits since 1973 had joined for precisely these reasons. Emotional identification with the prisoners, and anguish at their torture were by far the most traveled road into the guerilla or its support scene. Yet the prisoners rejected this appeal as "bourgeois antifascism."

Neither of these paradoxes constituted errors, or hypocrisy. The gap between theory and practice was not that wide. But they did not make it easy for activists from the broader radical left to get involved in the guerilla's struggle. The intellectual and emotional leap required was such that the support scene began to assume an identity distinct from all the other tendencies of the radical left. It was becoming a tendency in its own right.

The comparison with the Revolutionary Cells is telling. The RZ pioneered a strategy of reaching out to activists where they were at, and in doing so managed to pull several movements—even those based on the Citizens Initiatives—to the left. They specialized in bombings in solidarity with these reformist campaigns, encouraging others to follow suit. With their slogan "Create one, two, many Revolutionary Cells!" they meant to show people that they themselves could step beyond the lines of legal protest established by the state.

This strategy had its drawbacks, but one of its undeniable strengths was its ability to make armed struggle seem accessible, all the while

---

1 Dellwo, 95.

ensuring that the combatants—who did not go underground—would remain connected to the rest of the radical left.

The RAF's single-minded focus on the prisoners in this period may be a testament to the stature and unflinching resistance of its founding members, who had established the first armed clandestine organization in postwar Germany, repeatedly risked their own lives struggling behind bars, and inspired new waves of guerillas. Yet in retrospect, this focus also appears to represent a setback; if not a temporary defeat, then, certainly, a retreat from the RAF's initial impulse, as the guerilla became locked in on the prisoners to the exclusion of all other social contradictions.

The RAF would doggedly follow this trail as long as it could, and barely survive the consequences.

& Back to the RAF...

NINETEEN SEVENTY SIX WAS A difficult year for the radical left, and especially for the RAF. Losing Ulrike Meinhof was certainly the hardest blow, and it was accompanied by another wave of repressive legislation and renewed attacks on the prisoners' legal team.

To top it off, several RAF members were captured that year, including two outside of Germany.

On July 21, 1976, Rolf Pohle—one of the prisoners exchanged for Peter Lorenz a year earlier—was arrested in Athens. German "super cop" Werner Mauss[1] had learned that the fugitive was hiding in the Greek capital; he also knew that Pohle was a regular reader of the *Süddeutsche Zeitung* newspaper. Mauss "borrowed" two hundred Athens police officers for a few hours, arranging to have eighty different newspaper stands staked out: when Pohle went to buy the paper, he walked right into the trap.[2]

---

1 The legends that surround Mauss are more fantastic than most spy thrillers. A "plausibly deniable" agent for the German state, newspapers were forbidden to publish his photograph in the 1970s for fear that this would compromise his operations. According to Olivier Schmidt, Mauss was deeply involved in coordinating counterinsurgency operations against the RAF in this period and allegedly arranged for certain leading businessmen to pay the secret services for additional protection. ("Free Agent 'Werner Mauss' Gets Caught," *Intelligence* 50, December 16, 1996).

2 Karl-Ludwig Günsche and Hans Werner Loose, "Werner Mauss 40 years of fighting against criminality," *Die Welt* July 31, 1998.

Pohle's capture made headlines around the world, not because he was a particularly high profile target (he had even denied being a member of the RAF), but because on August 20, an Athens court turned down Bonn's request for extradition on the grounds that the crimes in question had been politically motivated. Helmut Schmidt was not amused, and under intense diplomatic pressure, including threats that West Germany would block its entry into the European Economic Community, the Greek government quickly, and successfully, appealed this ruling.

Pohle was extradited to the Federal Republic on October 1: on top of his original conviction dating from 1973, he was also sentenced to three years and three months for extortion, as police claimed that during the Lorenz exchange he had threatened that the captive would be killed if the authorities did not hand over all the money that had been demanded.[1]

The kerfuffle around the initial Greek refusal to extradite Pohle provided a convenient backdrop to a meeting of eighteen European heads of state in Strasbourg, France, in late September. The summit was called specifically to pass a draft treaty that would close any "loopholes" that might allow guerillas to seek refuge in any of the countries concerned.[2] This laid the basis for what would become the European Convention on the Suppression of Terrorism in 1977.

Pohle's extradition and the new antiterrorist convention underscored the increasing amount of time West German guerillas were spending in neighboring countries. Unlike South Yemen or the Palestinian camps in Lebanon, these were not safe havens, but still they afforded a measure of anonymity and breathing room to those in the underground.

Almost two months after Pohle was returned to the FRG, Siegfried Haag was arrested along with Karlsruhe activist Roland Mayer, driving on the autobahn between Frankfurt and Kassel. The former lawyer had received guerilla training in South Yemen earlier that year, and since his return had been busy recruiting new members for future actions. In hindsight it seems that papers he was carrying when arrested were in

---

1 Associated Press, "Terrorist kidnapper jailed for extortion," *European Stars and Stripes*, March 12, 1978. Pohle was finally released in 1982, at which point he did not rejoin the guerilla, but returned to Greece. He eventually found a job at the Athens daily *Eleftherotypia*, where he worked until his death from cancer in 2004. (Associated Press, "Deaths: Rolf Pohle," *The Daily Globe*, February 10, 2004).
2 Craig R. Whitney, "Treaty Seen to Block Asylum for Terrorists," *Salt Lake Tribune*, September 3, 1976.

fact coded notes, listing many of the next year's targets. He was charged with a variety of offenses related to the Stockholm action, and in 1978 he was sentenced to fifteen years in prison. Mayer received twelve years.

The next arrest did not occur in the Federal Republic, but in neighboring Austria. On December 14, 1976, Waltraud Boock was caught following a bank robbery in Vienna, while two of her comrades managed to get away with 100,000 shillings. In solidarity with Boock, a bomb exploded in a Vienna police building a few days later, another being disarmed just before it went off in the police headquarters.[3] Boock would be sentenced to fifteen years, to be served in Austrian prisons. The unusually heavy prison sentence for a crime in which no one was hurt was probably meant as a message to West German guerillas, especially after the 1975 OPEC raid, letting them know that crimes committed in this country would be dealt with harshly.

While these arrests did constitute setbacks, none of them was decisive. As would become clear in due time, the guerilla had managed to regroup, to attract new members, and had plans for the future.

At the same time, the prisoners also had plans. A new hunger strike was in the works, and a new strategy had been discussed, one which represented a further refinement of the RAF's demand for association, and which would have serious implications for some of its supporters.

The captured guerillas were going to demand to be treated as prisoners of war, as outlined by the Geneva Convention. This was based on a strategy Meinhof had developed in the year before she was murdered, with help from attorney Axel Azzola, a professor of Public Law at Darmstadt Technical University. The RAF was going to argue that because it had carried out its attacks in solidarity with the anticolonial movements, especially in the context of the Vietnam War, its prisoners were themselves POWs.

When Azzola had filed a motion to this effect in January 1976, it had publicly signaled an important shift in the RAF's trial strategy, one which seems to have enjoyed the support of the entire defense team.

Andreas Baader would later admit that the prisoners had little hope of seeing the government agree to their new line:

> *We don't believe that this demand on the part of the prisoners will be achieved. We've never said that we did. What will be achieved is that the demand will raise awareness and resistance against the*

---

3 *Corpus Christi Times,* "Police building hit by bomb," December 17, 1976.

*international counterinsurgency line in West Europe, which has
now become government policy: the criminalization of the urban
guerilla ...*[1]

Baader was arguing that regardless of its success, the very process of
struggling for POW status would provide supporters with an opportunity to promote the RAF's politics, all the while exposing the inhumane
conditions to which the prisoners were subjected. However, it was also
clear that the very process of claiming a special status also alienated
some supporters, especially (but not only) those from the *sponti* scene,
which was already splitting over the question of militancy.

These left-wing critics considered the RAF's new line to be a stretch,
muddying the waters of legitimate resistance to the FRG's "fascist drift"
by confusing it with the national liberation struggles in the Third World.
Not only that, but by claiming a special status for themselves, it was felt
the RAF was engaging in an arrogant form of vanguardism, elevating
itself above other prisoners, including some other political prisoners.

In the winter of 1976-77, this criticism would provide the basis for
an unprecedented exchange of letters in the pages of *Info-BUG*, the undogmatic left's magazine in West Berlin. The Revolutionary Cells sent
in an open letter to the RAF, in which it took them to task not only for
their new POW strategy, but also for their growing distance from the
radical left. They were voicing a number of concerns and complaints
probably shared by many others, activists who were trying to avoid the
flight from militancy exemplified by *Pflasterstrand*, but who also continued to disagree with key elements of the RAF's politics.

It was a dramatic move, and the only time the RZ would engage in
such public criticism. Perhaps not surprisingly, it provoked an angry
and defensive reply from RAF prisoner Monika Berberich. In turn, this
led to a series of letters as readers took positions for or against the
RAF's practice to date.

Some activists remember this debate as having been acrimonious, and
weakening the prisoners' support scene. While this may be so, events
over the next year showed that the prisoners, whether because of or despite their new strategy, remained capable of rallying impressive levels
of support from both the legal left and the guerillas in the field.

---

1 Andreas Baader on the Geneva Convention, cf 467-8.

RZ Letter to the RAF Comrades

This letter is addressed to all RAF comrades.
It is an open letter.
We are a section of the Revolutionary Cells (RZ). However, many
arguments from the undogmatic movement are integrated into
this letter, both because we consider these arguments to be correct
and because we feel ourselves to be a part of this movement.

We request that all groups and all comrades (for example, the publishing houses, undogmatic groups from various areas, newspapers, unaffiliated comrades, the 2nd of June Movement...) discuss this letter.

Truth be told, we have wanted to pose some questions to you—the comrades of the RAF—for some time now. The reason is the rumor that the RAF prisoners are planning a 4th hunger strike, with the demand that the Geneva Convention be applied and their status as prisoners of war be recognized.

Now, you might ask us why we feel the need to hold an "open discussion." Comrades, the reason is that we are afraid we might receive an unreasonably hostile response from you. Something suggesting that we are at least objectively acting as cops, or that our letter is a state security initiative. However, we recognize that we must not allow the possibility of such reproaches to cause us to shrink from a discussion with you.

What is important for us now (!) is that we come to an understanding with you. In the context of this discussion, it will become clear just how far we have drifted from each other and the need we feel for you to discuss with us our perspective, our actions, our evolution, and our lives. We proceed from the belief that you must feel a similar need! Likewise, you must feel the need to more clearly enter into discussion with the broader undogmatic movement. Otherwise, you are elevating yourselves to an arbitrary vanguard position.

The 71/72 RAF actions were an important development for many comrades. They shook many people, including us, out of our slumber. As this resonated in different areas, a hopeful joy arose regarding the impotence of the entire state apparatus and the guerilla's capacity to carry out actions, even in the FRG. At the time, these actions drew the widespread anti-imperialist movement together, causing the further development of an idea that had been rattling around in the heads of thousands of people. We saw that what had long been thought about was in fact possible. Without the RAF, there wouldn't be an RZ today, there wouldn't be groups that understand that resistance doesn't stop where the criminal code starts. The texts you issued clearly demonstrated the meaning of "no compromise," "draw a clear dividing line between the enemy and yourself," and "freedom in the face of this system requires its complete negation"; that is to say, they demonstrated that it is possible to attack this system in a fighting collective and that we must choose to struggle if we are to remain human.

However, what we now want you to tell us is whether you still stand by what the RAF said in 71/72? What do you think about the Stockholm liberation action? What errors do you think you've made in the interim? What do you hope to achieve with your trials?—People, we're asking you these things, because we are no longer clear about your politics. We recognize little of the RAF's original orientation.

Another important point: address the change. Better yet: rejuvenate the clearly significant impact of the information you provided, the statements you made, and the mobilization that resulted from the way you "made use of the trials." For instance the way Brigitte Mohnhaupt clarified your structure for that rat Prinzing—using that as the key venue—so as to expose the bought-off witness Müller as a liar.[1] Why did it take Müller, Prinzing, Buback & Co. to get you to say something about your structure, while we and others have waited since 72 for precisely such information and so much more?

Comrades, we have a completely practical problem with you. We have considered you comrades for a long time now, but many people on the outside don't feel that they are your comrades. We and others have been and will be used and subordinated to your trial strategy, for example, and for other mobilizations and campaigns as well. It is not possible to develop or discuss a common strategy with you. Obviously it is extremely difficult to do that through the prison walls. But we have the impression that that is not the only obstacle. Much more important

---

1 On July 22, 1976, Brigitte Mohnhaupt used her trial testimony to rebut claims about the RAF's allegedly hierarchical structure. Short excerpts from this statement are reprinted in this volume on pages 173 and 355-8. A less refined translation of the entire statement is available online at http://www.germanguerilla.com/red-army-faction/documents/76_0708_mohnhaupt_pohl.html.

is the fact you were much too quick to judge us. All too often you have indicated that you have no faith in our strength or that of others; in those on the outside, who also want to and must struggle, and who also hope to make decisions for themselves. They don't, however, want to offer you the wrong kind of support, blindly praying that they meet your rigid demands. Rather, they first want to think things over for themselves. That also goes for a large part of the undogmatic movement.—Yes comrades, we appear to be nothing more to you than a tool to be discarded when it is worn out. You don't ask why it's worn out. You simply assume we are weak and (massively) opportunistic, that we are completely at peace in this corrupt, man-eating system. And that's depressing. Enough of the category of comrade or pig!

And now listen carefully: it is simply complete, defeatist nonsense to claim that the entire left is on the defensive. Your disgusting fantasy about us and our strength is really a sign that you are on the defensive... How did you arrive at the decision to break off the last hunger strike, incorrectly claiming that we (the RZ, the 2nd of June Movement, the undogmatic groups, and and and...) were on the defensive??? You achieved absolutely nothing with your last hunger strike, while your defense attorneys and the Committees Against Torture gave everything they had to support your demands. Professors, doctors, writers (Sartre[2]), clergy (Scharf[3]), Amnesty (Austria), many undogmatic and even dogmatic groups (KPD/ML) supported your hunger strike. The murder of Holger was immediately answered by the shooting of von Drenkmann. Many people understood clearly that torture occurred even in German prisons. Is that really nothing? Do you really see that as a sign of the entire left being on the defensive?[4]

Besides the broad-based solidarity during the hunger strike, things have developed and are developing that are far from discouraging, things that you have only partially grasped. Recent history clearly shows that the masses here have not been completely bought off. It also shows how fruitful this terrain can be: the Nordhorn-Range, the September

---

2 The French playwright and existentialist philosopher had visited Baader in Stammheim during the third hunger strike, decrying the isolation conditions as torture which "provokes deficits in the prisoner; it leads him to stupefaction or to death." See "The Slow Death of Andreas Baader by Jean-Paul Sartre" http://www.marxists.org/reference/archive/sartre/1974/baader.htm.

3 Karl Scharf was at this time the Lutheran Bishop of West Berlin.

4 This paragraph is very much directed at the arguments made in the Letter from the RAF to the RAF prisoners, cf 338.

strikes of 73, the RZ attacks on ITT, Wyhl, Brokdorf, women's groups, the attack by the women of the RZ against the Federal Constitutional Court due to §218, forged public transit passes,[1] increasing struggle and politicization in the prisons, foreigners' committees and groups, Lorenz and his vacation, riots in Frankfurt against public transit fare increases, squats, etc. That is also partially the result of your practice. Comrades, do these movements simply not exist in your minds? Or do you think they are of no importance? Are they not important enough for you in the context of internationalism? Or do you consider them irrelevant because they don't have the same political practice as the RAF?

And now to the particulars: we cannot accept the complete lack of solidarity with which you treat some comrades from these movements:

For example, the *Informationsdienst* writer who reported on your trial. You accused him of objectively being a cop, because he didn't quote Andreas Baader word for word. When this "objective cop" responded in a way that showed solidarity, you broke off all communication. Does that mean that you found his criticism to be accurate or that from this point onward, he is simply objectively a cop? This ID writer subsequently stopped his reporting...

Also, we can't accept some of your denunciations of individual lawyers. You certainly know what we mean! These lawyers are comrades!

How did it happen that the attorney Croissant came to be the executor of Ulrike's "estate"? Ulrike isn't a file. She struggled alongside you! As you know, since then Klaus Croissant has gone so far as to accuse Klaus Wagenbach[2] of working hand in hand with state security, and has used the justice system (that wants to exterminate you) to request a legal decision to have Peter Brückner's[3] book about Ulrike Meinhof withdrawn from circulation. Via Klaus Croissant, §88a[4] will be imple-

---

1 The RZ and Rote Zora regularly distributed forged public transit passes.

2 Klaus Wagenbach is a prominent left-wing publisher with his roots in the APO. He read the eulogy at Ulrike Meinhof's funeral.

3 Peter Brückner was a left-wing psychologist loosely connected to the Frankfurt School. In 1972, he was suspended from his position at the Technical University in Hannover for allegedly lending the RAF material support (most likely shelter), a charge based on Karl-Heinz Ruhland's questionable testimony (Varon, 239-240). In 1978, he was once again suspended for taking a public stand against the repressive atmosphere the state was attempting to engender through its suppression of *Buback: In Memoriam* (see pages 534-35). He died in 1982 while still appealing the details of this suspension. (Braunthal, 98)

4 §88a, which criminalized literature which "glorifies violence," passed into law on January 16, 1976.

mented from the left. Nothing like that has ever happened before! Why don't you just talk to Klaus Wagenbach—a comrade? How do you feel about the new §88a?

You've maintained complete silence about a very important article from the Red Aid/West Berlin Prisoners' Collective (published in *Info-BUG* #III) regarding the problems faced by POWs. We think that's bullshit.

Your silence regarding the Committees Against Torture (they primarily supported the RAF prisoners) must finally end. Start with their activities up until the persecution through surveillance, raids, and Winter Trip. After that the committees dissolved themselves. Did you agree to this? Were they quickly replaced by a defense committee/support fund?

These are only some examples. What we're trying to say to you is that in the future you can't continue to abuse important comrades in the movement. You can't continue to denounce them as objective cops, state security agents, or BKA members. It is not only a disgrace, it is extremely dangerous! We will not allow you to continue to do this in the future. Period!

You, that is to say the RAF comrades, have drawn attention to an important point. Yet again. Specifically, the problem of psychological warfare. Since you first decided to point it out, we have begun to consider the press and interviews and their function in Buback's strategy much more seriously. So we really don't understand why you've effectively left the field to this regimented media. In the near future an RZ interview will address this.

We usually first learn of your statements from the *Frankfurter Rundschau*, *Süddeutsche Zeitung*, *Berliner Zeitung*, etc. Initially, their meaning is only clear to comrades "in the know." The same is true with regards to the Geneva Convention. It is extremely common that we get our first information about you from random newspapers and news shows. It must be clear to you that as a result rumors and incorrect reports circulate as news about you. It is only very seldom that we get the information from you first. It usually comes too late to correct false reports. As a result many comrades can only then be mobilized for whatever campaign. Often without understanding what it is they're doing. When you howl about that—without doing anything about it either on the outside or from within prison—how do you make yourselves look? You're reaction is out of proportion. We cannot in any way accept your treating us or others with scorn.

Now a few basic questions:

What's your position regarding the politics of the Revolutionary Cells and the 2nd of June Movement? For instance, the Lorenz kidnapping, forged public transit passes, the attack of the women of the RZ against the Federal Constitutional Court, forged food vouchers for Berlin's homeless...?

How do you support your lawyers, who are directly or indirectly subjected to the *Berufsverbot*? Who suffer constant persecution? How do you help them keep their COURAGE up, besides railing against Buback & Co.? We're asking, because at this point there aren't many left lawyers remaining to defend revolutionary prisoners.

Why, at this point, do you only seek the support of prominent personalities? Is it because they're in the forefront of the legal movement? We see this as a huge mistake.

What's your position on a common discussion of all political prisoners and all prisoners that have been politicized in prison? We don't mean by this that you should demand that they all be placed together in the same concentration camp, which is Buback's idea. That's a mistake. Rather we mean the mutual strengthening of all prisoners who struggle inside the prisons.

Don't you think that the Stockholm action should be criticized? And certainly not only because the action failed to achieve its demands. That's not the point. Rather, because the whole action was an unpleasant example of how a few comrades totally overshadowed your relationships and experiences. They did not mediate anything of a long-term nature. Even the demands themselves bore no relationship to the action. Two comrades paid for the action with their lives. The timeframe for fulfilling the demands was far too short.—Mistakes were made that must be completely avoided the next time. So mistakes were made. Turn every defeat into victory!...

What, for example, is your position regarding the powerful movements in Brokdorf, Wyhl etc.? And what is your overall position regarding the antinuclear movement?

We think that state security has reinforced your isolation from each other, and you have completely isolated yourselves from the broader left-wing movement. You must make contact with them again: a fish out of water will die of thirst! Even if you think you don't need water to swim. We think that the tactics that you share with us are not primarily based on causing criminal damage. Even communiqués must be written in West German so that everybody can understand them. Your communiqués can no longer be understood by the general public. They can only be understood by insiders. So now mobilizations are the result of psychological pressure, not of objective necessity.

And now, RAF comrades, we arrive at the possibility of a 4th hunger strike:

We think that there is too much ambiguity and contradiction between you and those who should and could support the hunger strike. We have attempted to identify some of these issues. So this letter should be taken as the beginning of a long discussion. Now you have to put your cards on the table. Otherwise this isn't going to work anymore. Otherwise what you want is blind solidarity. You can no longer avoid clarifying whether we and others on the left are your comrades. Whether we're nothing more than your instrument, now defined as the "left on the defensive."

Will you choose the Geneva Convention, the closed concentration camp, and with that take a position against us, or will you choose equality with other prisoners, will you choose to break through your isolation, and thereby decide in favor of unity with us? Previously, you demanded the abolition of special conditions and equality with other prisoners. Now, you insist upon a piece of paper, specifically the Geneva Convention. However, POW status implies [illegible in the version provided]. With your demand you overlook the interests of other prisoners. You must be prepared to withdraw your denunciations! Do you really want to throw away your lives for a foolish demand like POW status? Is it because you think you are no longer necessary? Is it because you think you can no longer rely on the movement?

Should you decide, in spite of everything, to just blow this letter off and—as has been the case before—to greet it with silence, and should you decide, in spite of everything, to gamble with your lives for the application of the Geneva Convention, our solidarity will be more a torment than a given.

A Revolutionary Cell
December 1976

Monika Berberich Responds
to the Alleged RZ Letter

Only one thing is clear about this letter: its state security function, its function for Buback's extermination strategy against us in the form it is now taking: psychological warfare to destroy the RAF's politics.

That is to say, what is clear in it is the treachery of a section of the undogmatic left, their capitulation to Buback, and their total subservience to his objectives. Even if the letter doesn't come from the RZ, *Info-BUG* published and distributed it and nobody from that section of the left did anything to prevent it. The lies, falsehoods, and denunciations in this letter are nothing new, nor is the fact that *Info* published it. But this letter is different, because it doesn't come from a prisoner support group, but from the RZ (in any event, that's where it claims to come from)—an organization that struggles—and this gives it a totally different kind of credibility and authority.

The function of this letter is to disorient those people in the undogmatic scene who want something other than the private, insubstantial screwing around of the *sponti* groups, those who really want to know something about us, who want to orient themselves around us, to struggle or to support us. It also serves to let Buback know that the section of the left that wrote this letter and those who find it accurate will not resist his efforts to liquidate the RAF's politics and the prisoners, to kill Andreas, to completely seal the holes, etc. But not just that: it also tells him that this left is not prepared to support a hunger strike that we believe is necessary; rather it is ready to support and is already supporting the creation of propaganda to justify his countermeasures.

The disorientation campaign unfolds following the pattern of psychological warfare—through allegations and lies about us. They don't talk about the state's repression, just like when the bourgeois media publish state security information about us: "there aren't many left lawyers remaining to defend revolutionary prisoners"; the support groups disband because of police repression; the *Informationsdienst* writer can only respond to criticism like the ultimate bourgeois journalist—aggrieved and offended, as if his article was a favor to us.

Info-BUG demands we respond to an insignificant Red Aid/Prisoners Collective article. The *sponti* left, as a result of its many splits and its totally defensive posture, is incapable of grasping the objective and subjective circumstances of the struggle, and is incapable of drawing on the facts and coming to an accurate appraisal of the balance of power. Instead it acts on the basis of a blind, narrow-minded, apolitical self-assessment, or else in an undifferentiated and ill-conceived way on the basis of various concepts and forms of struggle and mobilization. Then there's the claim that it's our job to offer revolutionary commentary and assessments of other groups and popular mobilizations. ("What's your position regarding the politics of the action...") Solidarity is not a question of politics and consciousness, but of feelings ("don't feel that they are your comrades"), etc.

All of this has the objective of telling the comrades being written about that they don't need to start struggling, to start figuring things out for themselves, or to support us as long as we "greet it with silence" and "don't put our cards on the table." It has the objective of preventing the potential mobilization and radicalization that could develop as a result of a new hunger strike. The support for Buback's extermination strategy is based on the complete acceptance of all the state's allegations about us, which make up the core of the psychological warfare being waged against us: that the RAF has a gang structure, that we are hierarchically structured, "tools" and of course "those at the top"—that is implicit in all the bullshit in this document, in which they characterize their relationship to us in this way: "to all RAF comrades" (in italics); "We will be used and subordinated..."; "...blindly praying that they meet your rigid demands..."; "...we appear to be nothing more to you than a tool to be discarded..."; "... as a result many comrades can only then be mobilized..."; "...mobilizations are the result of psychological pressure..."; "our solidarity will be more a torment..."; etc..

Then, with teeth bared: we're "mistaken," with "foolish ideas," which have "totally overshadowed our relationships and experiences"—this is the babble of psycho-cops; we have only ourselves to blame if we're isolated ("...you have isolated yourselves...")—the Federal Constitutional Court said the same thing in their ruling, in which they legally sanctioned torture; and finally—and this is consistent—we are "throwing away our lives"—which is an endorsement of the state's claim that Ulrike committed suicide—as with the deaths of Holger, Siegfried, and Katharina, who are "themselves responsible."

In Müller's case, it took state security three years using isolation, torture, and brainwashing to bring him to the point where he presented this idiotic SS[1] construct as his own experience—also precisely on the theme chosen here: the structure of the group. These leftists arrive at these conclusions on their own, facing no concrete threat, just their own naked fear. Their solidarity with us could cost them the ridiculous privileges that they cultivate in their idyllic counterculture.

One must also understand the method adopted in this letter, with its introduction and explanation about why it was written now, or rather why it wasn't written sooner ("an unrealistically hostile response—objective cop/state security action") which is meant to suggest that this letter can in no way be that, and which thereby pre-empts any critique which says that that is in fact exactly what it is.

Given the way the letter is constructed, precisely following the pattern and techniques of psychological warfare, it is possible that it is not only objectively a state security product.

Monika Berberich
January 10, 1977

---

1 Berberich is purposefully using the acronym for the Nazi SS to indicate state security, or *Staatsicherheit*.

Andreas Baader:
On the Geneva Convention

The demand for the application of the Geneva Convention is a necessary vehicle for our politics, because the dead wings, isolation, and stress manipulation are being used to break the group in prison, to prepare for show trials, and to gain information, or more accurately, to gain informants. It has been clear since 72, when, for example, Schmidt said in a government statement that the goal of the countertactic is to use prisoners who have been turned to infiltrate the illegal structures. It is clear that this is easier in prison, where state security and the state security psychiatrists have total control over our living conditions, and where electronic surveillance is easier than it is in the scene, which can respond to repression with semi-conspiratorial measures and a system of filters, which set in motion a process of polarization.

There is a history of illegal resistance groups and there is a history of police tactics. If we don't understand the latter, and if we don't recognize them in the measures against us, we will be defeated by the old reality that the police apparatus has a linear learning process and the illegal groups learn by acting, learning in leaps and bounds.

We don't believe that this demand on the part of the prisoners will be achieved. We've never said that we did. What will be achieved is that the demand will raise awareness and resistance against the international counterinsurgency line in West Europe, which has now become government policy: the criminalization of the urban guerilla (ISC Report[2]). In any event, what the guerilla is addressing here and what it is struggling for is international awareness. Everything must be concentrated on exposing and disrupting the American strategy in West Europe, which is being carried through by the scripted domestic and foreign policies of the FRG.

None of that is new. The weapons used against the prisoners aren't all bad, because the aggressive way in which they use special laws, special courts, special handling, all the special measures in this trial to destroy us, while at the same time denying that they are doing so, will expose the system internationally and will isolate it.

---

2 Institute for the Study of Conflict, an "antiterrorist" thinktank based in London, England.

By publicizing these measures, which are forbidden by the Geneva Convention (because it is a set of rules for emergency situations that establishes how human rights should be understood in intra-state conflicts, which the discourse no longer addresses) people will be mobilized and radicalized around the critical issue: that the state is at war (which Maihofer made very clear in Karlsruhe) and, therefore, is in a dialectic that—because war frames the question of legitimacy along military lines—destroys the ideological justification of the constitutional state itself.

All of this is about this process and not just a tattered piece of paper. Through it runs the horizontal and vertical learning and polarization process, which is necessary for the struggle to develop. It is the terrain on which we can very concretely organize our logistics, our information, and the defense of our underground members and the prisoners.

POW status on its own will never be enough to protect against the coercive psychological and spiritual destruction of the "irregulars"— and if it is ever forced through, it will not be because the prisoners can force the state to exercise its monopoly of violence according to the legal rules of civil war, but as a result of the international character and concrete reality of the liberation wars, which also address these demands.

Andreas Baader
June 2, 1977

Daring to Struggle, Failing to Win

NINETEEN SEVENTY SEVEN IS OFTEN described as the moment of truth in the RAF's battle against the West German state—for better or for worse. In fact, most histories of the RAF actually stop after this point, or mention all that came afterwards as a barely interesting epilogue.

Such a perspective is mistaken, and amounts to closing the book before the story is even half done. Nevertheless, it cannot be denied that 1977 was a year like no other, representing an attempt to push things to a qualitatively higher level. As events reached their climax in a bloody series of events known as "The German Autumn," every sector of society was shaken to the core.

As debate over the RAF's struggle played itself out in the pages of *Info-BUG*, state psychological operations continued unabated in the corporate press. Newspapers repeated police allegations that RAF supporters had murdered a banker, his wife and three children, and also that the guerilla was planning to kidnap the Canadian ambassador.[1] In January, police claimed they found and defused a bomb at the Weisbaden train station, presumably another false flag attack.[2]

---

1 Reuters, "Envoy Gets Kidnap Threat," *Winnipeg Free Press*, January 22, 1977.
2 United Press International, "Explosive device defused in Wiesbaden," *European Stars and Stripes*, January 26, 1977.

Then, on February 9, Brigitte Mohnhaupt, who had been captured following the May Offensive, was released from prison: her four-and-a-half-year sentence for illegal possession of firearms[1] and membership in a criminal association had come to an end. She immediately went underground, rejoining the guerilla.

On March 29, prisoners from the RAF and the 2nd of June Movement began their fourth hunger strike, demanding POW status, association in groups of no less than fifteen, an end to isolation, an international investigation into the deaths of Holger Meins, Siegfried Hausner, and Ulrike Meinhof, and an end to false flag actions and communiqués. Initially, thirty-five prisoners participated, but soon the number refusing food surpassed one hundred, and some even began refusing liquids.

The irony was that the hunger strike for POW status, which the RZ had feared would limit itself to an elite group, managed to rally more prisoners than any previous hunger strike. This was grim testimony to the number of combatants who had been captured, along with the number of supporters who were now serving time under §129.

At the same time, the guerilla was not going to let the prisoners wage this battle on their own.

On April 7, as Attorney General Buback was waiting at a traffic light in Karlsruhe, two individuals pulled up on a motorcycle alongside his Mercedes. One of them then pulled out a submachine gun and fired, riddling the Attorney General's car with bullets.

Siegfried Buback, the man who had come to personify the judicial attacks against the guerilla, had been assassinated.

The RAF immediately issued a communiqué claiming responsibility in the name of the "Ulrike Meinhof Commando" explaining Buback's responsibility for the deaths of Meinhof, Hausner, and Meins.

Along with the Attorney General, his chauffeur Wolfgang Göbel and bodyguard Georg Wurster were also killed. Even some of the prisoners' own lawyers were shocked, Otto Schily declaring on their behalf that they viewed "this senseless and brutal murder with the utmost horror and revulsion."[2]

Within a day, police announced that Günter Sonnenberg, Christian Klar, and Knut Folkerts (all of whom were formerly active in the prisoner support scene) were being sought in connection to the attack, and

---

1 United Press International, "4 W. German Terrorists Arrested," *Pacific Stars and Stripes*, May 31, 1978.
2 Aust, 401.

a bounty of 200,000 marks[3] was being offered for information leading to their capture.[4]

This assassination occurred not only in the context of Buback's continuing attacks against the lawyers, but also two weeks before the end of the Stammheim show trial in which Baader, Ensslin, and Raspe were found guilty of various offenses relating to the May Offensive of 1972.

As has been noted elsewhere:

> *This attack marked a shift to a strategy that would be marked by an overwhelming focus on assassinations of key members of the state apparatus and the business elite. Although this might not have been recognized at the time, it was a shift to an entirely new phase in the RAF's practice.*[5]

Or, as Knut Folkerts later testified, the assassination "showed that we knew who they were, that we could attack them, and that there was nothing they could do to stop us."[6]

The hunger strike continued, the prisoners consolidating their support. Soon relatives of the prisoners began a solidarity hunger strike, and on April 17, Peter's Church in Frankfurt was occupied and turned into a hunger strike information center. As the number of prisoners refusing food reached one hundred and twenty, more outside supporters began a second solidarity hunger strike in a Bielefeld Church. On April 27, relatives of political prisoners held a demonstration at the United Nations headquarters in Switzerland demanding the application of the Geneva Convention. The next day, Amnesty International added its voice to that of eighty clergymen and two hundred and forty-five lawyers, all urging the government to abandon its hard line.

Finally, on April 30, it was announced that the prisoners would be granted limited association. Years of struggle seemed to have finally paid off. In response to this victory the prisoners agreed to call off their hunger strike.

The seventh floor of Stammheim prison—where Baader, Raspe, and Ensslin were held along with Irmgard Möller, who had been transferred

---

3   Roughly $88,000.

4 Associated Press, "3 Sought In Slaying Of Official," *Press Courier*, April 8, 1977.

5 Arm the Spirit, "A Brief History of the Red Army Faction."

6 "Déclaration de Knut Folkerts dans le procèes contre Brigitte Schulz et Christian Klar (5-6-84) à Stuttgart-Stammheim, concernant l'action contre Buback," *Ligne Rouge* 11, (December 1984).

there in January of that year—was soon being renovated to allow up to sixteen prisoners to be housed together.

At the same time, the hunt for the guerillas in the field continued.

On May 3, Günter Sonnenberg and Verena Becker were captured in the German-Swiss border town of Singen. (In the two years since she had been freed in exchange for Lorenz, Becker had moved from 2JM to the RAF.) A woman had tipped off the police after spotting the two as they sat in a café: she recognized Sonnenberg from the wanted posters that had gone up throughout Western Europe following the Buback assassination.

When the police arrived on the scene, the guerillas tried to play it cool, innocently pretending to have left their ID papers in their car. While being escorted from the café—presumably to retrieve these phantom ID papers—they drew their weapons and shot the two cops, commandeered a car, and took off.[1] Pursued by squad cars alerted to the incident, they took a wrong turn and ended up in a field. This forced them to ditch their vehicle and try to escape on foot.

At this point, one of the guerillas dropped a submachine gun—as it would turn out, the same weapon that had been used to kill Buback. A cop picked the weapon up and fired: Becker was hit in her leg, while Sonnenberg was critically injured, struck by bullets in his torso and head. His wounds were such that it took several hours before he could be positively identified, and days later it was still unclear if he would survive.[2]

As a result of his injuries, Sonnenberg suffered brain damage, and is prone to epileptic seizures to this day. Years later, he would recall his condition following capture:

> I didn't know anything except my name. I could neither read nor write, nor formulate things in any form. Words and concepts were utterly foreign to me. Even things having to do with daily life—like plate and spoon, bed and sink, book and radio—I no longer knew these words and concepts.[3]

Two days later, on May 5, Uwe Folkerts (Knut's brother) and Johannes Thimme were both arrested in Holland, the police claiming that they

1 Reuters, "Suspects shot in gun battle," *Winnipeg Free Press,* May 4, 1977.
2 United Press International, "Captured Gun confirmed as Buback Murder Weapon," *European Stars and Stripes,* May 5, 1977.
3 Letter from Günter Sonnenberg in *Angehörigen Info 87,* January 18, 1992.

had been involved in the Buback assassination, as well as with alleged plans to seize hostages to exchange for the prisoners.[4]

Throughout the summer, different RAF prisoners would go back on hunger strike for various periods of time, demanding the association they had been promised.

At the same time, the state was not letting up on its attacks against the lawyers. In one particularly incredible move, attorneys Armin Newerla and Arndt Müller were charged with attempted murder on the grounds that they did not discourage their clients Verena Becker and Sabine Schmitz[5] from hunger striking.[6] On July 8, Klaus Croissant fled the country: on June 26 he had been subjected to a partial *Berufsverbot*, and there were signs he might be arrested at any time. Pieter Bakker Schut, Ronald Augustin's Dutch attorney, suggested he go to the Netherlands, but Croissant chose Paris, where he held a press conference four days later, requesting political asylum.[7] The lawyer pointed to the years of harassment he had endured, and noted that with the ongoing confrontation things were getting worse: he was facing a third arrest and, as he was now subjected to the *Berufsverbot*, could neither defend himself nor continue to defend his clients except from outside the country. His home, office, and telephone had all been bugged, and surrounding buildings were used for physical surveillance, which included state agents openly photographing everyone who entered his office. On December 15, 1976, one of his secretaries had been offered several thousand DM by the *Verfassungsschutz* in exchange for copies of legal notes and a list of his clients. Finally, he pointed to the fact that he was followed to and from his office by uniformed police, which he described as a form of psychological terrorism.[8]

---

4 United Press International, "Germans seize brother of Buback case suspect," *European Stars and Stripes*, May 6, 1977. In late 1978, Uwe Folkerts was found guilty of lending his car to RAF members Adelheid Shultz and Sabine Schmitz, and was sentenced to sixteen months in prison; as he had already served eighteen months by that point, he was immediately released. Thimme eventually received a similar sentence; upon release, he remained active within the guerilla's semi-clandestine support scene until he blew himself up trying to plant a bomb in 1985. (Associated Press, "New Blast in Germany," *Syracuse Herald-Journal*, January 21, 1985)

5 Schmitz had been arrested in December 1976 and charged under §129. See: United Press International, "German police hunt Haag helpers," *European Stars and Stripes*, December 8, 1976.

6 Bakker Schut, *Stammheim* 465-473.

7 Ibid., 532.

8 *Actualité de la Résistance Anti-Impérialiste*, no. 3, Paris, June 6, 1978: 8, 10.

As we shall see, while Croissant's plea would raise international awareness about what was happening in the Federal Republic, it would not be sufficient to keep him safe. Nevertheless, for the time being he was allowed to remain in Paris, as the French authorities tried to decide how to handle the affair.

The next attack occurred on July 30 in the wealthy Frankfurt suburb of Oberursel. Three RAF members, including a young woman named Susanne Albrecht, came with red roses to the door of a thirty-room villa belonging to Jürgen Ponto.[1] One of the most important businessmen in West Germany, Ponto had direct ties to many Third World governments and had served as an advisor to South Africa's infamous apartheid regime. He was also godfather to Albrecht's sister and a close friend of her parents.

The guerillas attempted to abduct the businessman, but when he resisted they opened fire, shooting him five times. He died on his kitchen floor.

As Albrecht had been recognized by Ponto's wife, she signed her name to the guerilla's communiqué for this action. She was sought for this attack along with Angelika Speitel, Silke Maier-Witt, and Siegrid Sternebeck. With the exception of Speitel, who had been underground for some years now, the women had all been active together since 1974, meeting through the Hamburg squats, Red Aid, and the Committees Against Torture. They had all known members of the Holger Meins Commando who had carried out the ill-fated Stockholm action in 1975. All four went underground immediately.

(A political storm ensued when it was learned that Ponto had never been warned that police knew Albrecht was close to the RAF. This led the FDP Federal Minister of the Interior Werner Maihofer to famously state that, "There is no capitalist who does not have a terrorist in his own intimate circle of friends or relations.")[2]

On August 8, Helmut Pohl, Wolfgang Beer, and Werner Hoppe, who had been moved to be with the others in Stammheim just a month earlier, were transferred back to Hamburg. The precise excuse used was a "fight" with guards—essentially a set up whereby the guards provoked an incident and used it as an excuse to attack and beat all of the prisoners on the floor.[3] It appeared that Buback's replacement,

---

1 Associated Press, "Terror Suspect Nabbed," *The Times*, August 2, 1977.
2 Aust, 418.
3 Ibid., 411-412.

Kurt Rebmann, had moved to reverse his previous agreement for association.

In reaction to these shenanigans and to the attack on Ponto, all RAF prisoners went on hunger strike, some escalating to a thirst strike almost immediately.

It was only days before the force-feeding began.

Defense attorneys Newerla and Müller began organizing public support for the striking prisoners, and became subject to even heavier levels of harassment and outright repression. On August 15, the lawyers' offices were bombed, almost certainly with the collusion of the police who had the premises under surveillance twenty-four hours a day. Müller and assistant Volker Speitel were there at the time, but were not injured.[4] Newerla was subsequently arrested when multiple copies of the left-wing magazine *MOB* which supported the prisoners were found in his car: he was charged with "supporting a terrorist organization" under §129a.[5]

The new Attorney General staked out the "hard-line" position for which he would be remembered. "I know that the population is not at all interested if these people go on hunger and thirst strikes," Rebmann told the press. "The population wants these people to be hit hard, just as hard as they have earned with their brutal deed."

He was asked about the possibility of prisoners dying. "That is always a bad thing," he answered, "but it would be the consequence which has been made clear to them and their lawyers and which is clear to them. The conditions of imprisonment don't justify such a strike; they are doing very well considering the circumstances."[6]

On August 25, the RAF responded by targeting Rebmann's offices. Peter-Jürgen Boock (the husband of Waltraud Boock) set up an improvised rocket launcher aimed at the Attorney General's headquarters, but the timing device was not set properly, and it failed to fire. Boock later broke with the RAF and claimed that he had purposefully sabotaged this attack, as his conscience would not allow him to risk the lives of the secretaries and office workers in the building.[7] (The editors of

---

4 Associated Press, "Radical lawyer's office bombed," *Oakland Tribune,* August 15, 1977.

5 Bakker Schut, *Stammheim,* 472.

6 *Frankfurter Rundschau,* August 15, 1977, quoted in "The Stammheim Deaths," *Cienfuegos Press Anarchist Review,* no. 4.

7 Aust, 414-5.

this volume assume this statement to be false, along with almost everything else Boock has said.)

Whatever the truth of the matter, the RAF attempted to put this mishap in the best possible light, issuing a communiqué a week later in which they pretended that the entire exercise had merely been intended as a warning. The guerilla went on to promise that it was more than willing to act should it prove necessary to save the prisoners:

> *Should Andreas, Gudrun, and Jan be killed, the apologists for the hard line will find that they are not the only ones with weapons at their disposal. They will find that we are many, and that we have enough love—as well as enough hate and imagination—to use both our weapons and their weapons against them, and that their pain will equal ours.*[1]

Following Meinhof's murder, and in the context of the recent hunger strikes and Rebmann's bloodthirsty statements, the guerilla was clearly concerned that the state might move to kill Baader, Ensslin, and Raspe. This fear was shared by the prisoners themselves, who knew that they might suffer reprisals for the guerilla's actions.

Indeed, anticipating such reprisals, and following the breakdown of negotiations between Amnesty International and the Federal Government, the prisoners called off their hunger and thirst strike on September 2. In a short statement, Jan-Carl Raspe explained that the attacks on Ponto and Rebmann had created an environment in which the prisoners had become hostages and the state was ready and willing to kill them to set an example.[2]

The failed Ponto kidnapping had been intended to be the first of a two-pronged action to put pressure on the West German bourgeoisie to force the state to free the prisoners. Despite their failure to take Ponto alive, it was decided to follow through on the second part of this plan.

On September 5, the RAF's "Siegfried Hausner Commando" kidnapped Hanns Martin Schleyer. His car and police escort were forced to a stop by a baby stroller that was left out in the middle of the road, at which point they were ambushed by guerillas who killed his chauffeur, Heinz Marcisz, and three police officers—Reinhold Brändle, Helmut Ulmer, and Roland Pieler—before making their getaway.

---

1 The Attack on the BAW, see pages 496-97.
2 Statement Calling Off the Fifth Hungerstrike, see page 495.

A note received soon after warned that, "The federal government must take steps to assure that all aspects of the manhunt cease—or we will immediately shoot Schleyer without even engaging in negotiations for his freedom."

Schleyer was the most powerful businessman in West Germany at the time. Like Ponto, he was a frequent figure on television representing the ruling-class point of view. He was the president of both the *Bundesverband der Deutschen Industrie* (Federal Association of German Industrialists) and the *Bundesvereinigung der Deutschen Arbeitgeberverbände* (Federal Association of German Employers), and had a reputation as an aggressive opponent of any workers' demands.[3] As a veteran of Hitler's SS, he was a perfect symbol of the integration of former Nazis into the postwar power structure.[4]

Hanns Martin Schleyer in captivity. The RAF had considered having him hold a sign with his SS number and the caption "A Prisoner of His Own History," but quickly rejected this idea. Not only did the guerillas have no wish to inflict needless humiliation, but they were also aware that their captive was already unpopular in West Germany and feared he would have less exchange value if he was debased further.

---

3 Associated Press, "Schleyer No Friend of Socialists, Unions," *Abilene-Reporter News*, October 20, 1977.

4 Schleyer had joined the SS in 1933, just two months after his eighteenth birthday. A committed fascist, he held several important positions in the Nazi Student Association before and during the war. In 1943, he began working for the Central Federation of Industry for Bohemia and Moravia, where he was in charge of "Germanizing" the economy of Czechoslovakia. Following the Nazi defeat, he was captured by French forces and imprisoned for three years, classified as a "fellow traveler" by the denazification authorities. He was released in 1949 and used his experience during the Nazi occupation of Czechoslovakia to get hired to the foreign trade desk in the Baden-Baden Chamber of Commerce and Industry. (Heike Friesel, "Schleyer, a German Story," Litrix.de: German Literature Online, translated by Philip Schmitz, http://www.litrix.de/buecher/sachbuecher/jahr/2004/schleyer/enindex.htm)

As the guerilla would later explain:

> *We hoped to force the SPD to decide whether to exchange these two figures who embodied the global power of West German capital in a way that no more than ten other individuals do: Ponto for international financial policy (revealing how all the German banks, especially his own Dresdner Bank, work to support reactionary regimes in developing countries, as well as the role of the FRG's financial policy as a tool in the institutional strategy to control the way in which European integration unfolds)—and Schleyer for national economic policy (the large corporations, concerted action, the FRG as an international model of social peace). They embodied the power within the state that the SPD, as the ruling party, must respect if it wishes to stay in power.*[1]

The attempted Ponto kidnapping may have ended in failure, yet it was felt that the plan could not be called off, that lives were at stake: "the prisoners had reached a point where we could no longer put off an action to liberate them. The prisoners were on a thirst strike and Gudrun was dying."[2]

Within a day of Schleyer's kidnapping, the commando demanded the release of eleven prisoners—including Ensslin, Raspe, and Baader—and safe passage to a country of their choosing. This demand was reiterated on September 6, as the guerilla suspected state security of not relaying their first communiqué to the proper authorities.

Pastor Martin Niemöller and the Swiss human rights advocate Denis Payot (whom the RAF mistakenly thought held a position in the United Nations) were to accompany the prisoners to their final destination. The commando further demanded that the prisoners be given 100,000 DM each ($44,000), and that their entire communiqué be read on *Tagesschau*, a nightly current affairs television program.

In discussions with state representatives, the prisoners promised that they would not return to the FRG or participate in future armed actions if exiled. Nevertheless, the government issued a statement indicating that it would not release them under any circumstances.

Government officials declared a "supra-legal state of emergency,"

---

1 Moncourt and Smith Vol. II, 246..
2 Ibid.

and Schmidt convened the Crisis Management Team, which had first been established in 1975 during the Lorenz action and then during the RAF's Stockholm siege. Over the next weeks, this team served to concentrate all decision-making powers in the hands of the executive:

> *Arguing that each party was represented on the committee, the need to consult parliament in matters of national importance was effectively curtailed. For the length of the "German Autumn" the crisis management team was the ruling body, responsible for all negotiations with the terrorists and the enactment of security measures.*[3]

One of the first measures taken was a "voluntary" news ban, immediately followed by a total *Kontaktsperre* (Contact Ban) against all political prisoners. As its name implies, the Contact Ban deprived the prisoners of any contact with each other, as well as with the outside world. All visits, including those with lawyers and family members, were forbidden. The prisoners were also denied any access to mail, newspapers, magazines, television, or radio. In short, they were placed in 100% individual isolation,[4] in what has been described as a case of "counter-kidnapping" by the state.[5]

While the Contact Ban was initially not sanctioned by law, parliament obliged by rushing through the appropriate legislation in record time (just three days) and with only four votes against.[6] The justification offered was a claim that the prisoners had directed the kidnapping from within their cells with the help of the lawyers. As evidence, police claimed to have found a hand drawn map used in the kidnapping in Armin Newerla's car on September 5.[7]

On September 9, *Agence France Presse*'s Bonn office received an ultimatum from the Siegfried Hausner Commando, setting a 1:00 PM deadline for the release of the prisoners. The state countered with a proposal that Denis Payot act as a go-between.

Secret negotiations began the same day, the RAF repeatedly—and less and less convincingly—warning of dire consequences if the prisoners were not immediately released, while the state very successfully

---

3 Hanshew, 28.
4 Cobler, 144.
5 Ibid., 145.
6 Hanshew, 26, 43.
7 Bakker Schut, *Stammheim*, 490.

stalled for time. The SPD's Minister in Charge of Special Affairs, Hans-Jürgen Wischnewski, who had a good reputation from having acted as a go-between with various Third World liberation movements,[1] began to travel to various foreign capitals looking for a "progressive regime" which might take the prisoners. Or so the RAF was meant to believe: according to political scientist (and former counterinsurgency expert) Richard Clutterbuck, Wischnewski's trips were a careful ploy, picked up by the media as a sign that the government was willing to give in despite Schmidt's official "no-deals" policy. Clutterbuck credits the media reports to this effect for the fact that the RAF did not kill Schleyer when their first ultimatums expired.[2]

The Minister in Charge of Special Affairs traveled first to Algeria and Libya, then South Yemen and Iraq, and finally to Vietnam. Though their refusal was not immediately made public, none of these countries would accept the prisoners—a decision that in the case of the PDRY was informed by the way the FRG had reneged on its promises following the Lorenz prisoner exchange.[3]

Meanwhile, the hunt for the guerilla and their captive continued.

On September 19, Knut Folkerts and another RAF member narrowly escaped from Dutch police after the manager of a car rental agency in Utrecht became suspicious of their identification papers. They got away and managed to rent a car at another agency, but when they returned it four days later, the police were lying in wait. By the time the bullets had stopped flying, Folkerts was in custody, two cops were wounded and a third, officer Arie Kranenburg, was dead. Mohnaupt managed to get away.[4]

The search for Schleyer was extended to Holland, but to no avail.

On September 30, defense attorney Ardnt Müller was arrested. Accused of having worked with Newerla and defense attorney Klaus Croissant to recruit for the RAF, he was imprisoned under Contact Ban

---

1 While sitting in the *Bundestag* for the SPD, Wischnewski had acted as an interlocutor with the Algerians during the National Liberation Front's war for independence from France, and had been a public critic of Adenauer's hardline pro-French policy in that conflict. He later negotiated the release and free transit of Germans arrested during the Pinochet coup in Chile, as well as free transit out of the country for Chileans who had taken refuge in foreign embassies.

2 Richard Clutterbuck, 173.

3 Halliday, 77-78.

4 Associated Press, "Dutch capture German terrorist," *Lima News,* September 23, 1977.

conditions. The arrest was buttressed by the claim that on September 2, Müller had used Newerla's car, in which the aforementioned map had been found.

On October 7, the thirty-second day of the kidnapping, newspapers in France and Germany received a letter from Schleyer, accompanied by a photo, decrying the "indecisiveness" of the authorities.

On October 13, with negotiations deadlocked, a new development moved the already intense confrontation to an entirely different level, as a Palestinian group intervened in solidarity with the RAF. The "Struggle Against World Imperialism Organization"—also known as the Martyr Halimeh Commando—hijacked a Lufthansa airliner traveling from Majorca, Spain to Frankfurt, West Germany. This was actually a PFLP (EO) commando, led by Zohair Youssef Akache.[5]

Eighty-five passengers and five crew members were taken hostage.

At 4:00 PM, the airliner landed in Rome to refuel and to issue the commando's demands. These were the release of the eleven RAF prisoners, and also two Palestinians being held in Turkey, Mahdi Muhammed and Hussein Muhammed al Rashid, who were serving life sentences for an attempted hijacking at Istanbul airport in 1976, in which four people had been killed.

Led by Waddi Haddad, the PFLP (EO) had split from the more well known PFLP in the early seventies. It was the PFLP (EO) that had worked with the RZ's international wing during the Entebbe hijacking a year earlier, and during the attack on the OPEC oil ministers in Vienna in 1975.[6] Both of these actions had been viewed negatively by the RAF prisoners, and yet they had never criticized them publicly.

It remains unclear how the Palestinian guerillas came to be involved in the RAF's 1977 campaign. Haddad was killed by the Mossad soon afterwards, and all accounts seem to come solely from the German side; in evaluating them, it should be kept in mind that this entire operation was later seen as a serious error by the RAF and its supporters.

---

5 Akache had already cut his teeth as a guerilla earlier that year in London, England. On April 10, 1977, he had assassinated Qadi Abdullah Amhen al Hijri, the former Prime Minister of North Yemen, along with his wife Fatima and senior diplomatic official Abdullah Ali Al Hammami (Aust, 510). Al Hijri, who had had dozens of political dissidents put to death and thousands more imprisoned during his brief reign, was a traditionalist who strongly opposed any rapprochement with South Yemen. (*News Journal*, "Leftists suspected: Former Yemen Premier Killed," April 11, 1977)

6 See pages 438-441. Also see, Appendix VI—The German Guerilla's Palestinian Allies: Waddi Haddad's PFLP (EO), on pages 559-61.

Some say that faced with the increasingly unpromising situation in the FRG, with the government obviously stalling for time while negotiating in bad faith, Brigitte Mohnhaupt and Peter-Jürgen Boock had flown to Baghdad to enlist Haddad's aid; according to some versions, they agreed to pay $15 million for it.[1] According to other reports, it was Haddad who contacted the RAF, using the RZ international wing's Johannes Weinrich as a go-between.[2] According to Stefan Wisniewski, one of those involved in the Schleyer kidnapping,

> The Palestinians had their own interest in such an action. Of course, getting the prisoners out, there was also the issue of two Palestinian prisoners who were sitting in a Turkish prison, but there was also something else altogether. They said to themselves, "When a country like the Federal Republic, the most important country in the European Community, is involved in a confrontation that the entire world is watching, then we have an opportunity to introduce our concerns."[3]

Regardless of these details, it was a plan agreed to by the RAF in the field, several of whose members had spent time in a PFLP (EO) training camp in South Yemen.[4] The 1976-1977 wave of combatants had moved to the international terrain, in a way the RAF had never done before.[5]

Not only that, but they had sanctioned an action in which civilians were being used as hostages—another unprecedented step which the guerilla would eventually see an error.[6] Suddenly, it was not just one

---

1 Butz Peters, "Landshut-Befreiung: Die RAF erleidet ihre größte Niederlage," *Welt Online*, October 14, 2007.

2 Oliver Schröm "Im Schatten des Schakals. Carlos und die Wegbereiter des internationalen Terrorismus," 9.
http://www.lavocatdelaterreur.com/pdf/Im%20Schatten%20des%20Schakals.pdf.

3 Wisniewski, 26.

4 One far-right anti-RAF source claims that Siegfried Haag and Elisabeth von Dyck had first entered into contact with the PFLP (EO) in 1976, after being rebuffed by both Arafat's Fatah and Habash's PFLP. While we do not share this source's perspective, this version of events seems credible. 2008-World Journal, untitled, at http://soc.world-journal.net/18sept2008spywars2.html.

5 "Terrorism expert" and *Stern* journalist Oliver Schröm states that cooperation between the PFLP (EO) and the RAF had been made difficult in the past specifically by Andreas Baader, who opposed carrying out attacks outside of the Federal Republic. (Schröm, 9)

6 While hostages were taken during the Stockholm occupation in 1975, only government representatives, not civilians, were killed. While the distinction may seem to be a fine one, it was considered important by the RAF and its supporters.

man, a former Nazi and current representative of the West German ruling class, who was being held hostage, but a plane full of ordinary people. A quiet horror descended, not only on many supporters of the guerilla, but on some RAF prisoners, too. As Karl-Heinz Dellwo recalls:

> This hostage-taking completely threw aside what Gudrun had called "the moral ticket." Holger Meins's last letter closed with the appeal "Serve the People," and here the people were being attacked.[7]

Furthermore, the SAWIO was a Palestinian commando acting primarily to demand the release of First World revolutionaries, providing more evidence that the events of 77 were no longer even orbiting the realities of the West German left, and that the organic relationship the RAF founders had enjoyed with the broader movement in 72 was now far in the past. Andreas Baader is reported to have said as much to government representatives at Stammheim, stating that the prisoners did not condone operations like the skyjacking which target innocent civilians, but that the "brutality" of the latest wave of combatants had been made inevitable by the government's attacks.[8]

It is horrible to note that the Palestinians were risking their lives—and as we shall see, most of them would pay that price—for West German prisoners who disapproved of the whole operation in the first place. This was a sign that the guerillas in the field had miscalculated in more ways than one.

Nevertheless, none of the RAF prisoners publicly disavowed this action, any misgivings tempered with the hope that this might swing the balance in their favor. Indeed, previous opinion polls had shown 60% opposed and 22% in favor of yielding to the RAF's demands; once the airliner was seized, opinion became evenly split on the matter.[9]

The plane flew to Cyprus and from there to the Gulf, where it landed first in Bahrain and then, at 6:00 AM on October 14, in Dubai.

Within a few hours, Denis Payot announced receipt of a communiqué setting a deadline of 8:00 AM October 16 for all the demands to be met, "if a bloodbath was to be avoided."[10] The communiqué, signed by both

---

7 Dellwo, 133.

8 Aust, 525.

9 Richard L. Strout, "Countdown to a Crisis: Is Nuclear Terrorism Next?" *Fresno Bee*, October 26, 1977.

10 Mike Ryan, "The Stammheim Model—Judicial Counter-Insurgency," *New Studies on the Left* 14, no. 1 & 2 (1989).

the SAWIO and the Siegfried Hausner Commando, was accompanied by a videotape of Schleyer.

At 5:47 PM, the West German government released a statement specifying that they intended to do everything possible to find "a reasonable and humanitarian solution," so as to save the lives of the hostages. That evening Wischnewski left Bonn for Dubai: he was no longer traveling to arrange sanctuary for the prisoners, or even to pretend to do so, but rather to negotiate the terms of an intervention.

On October 15, Denis Payot announced that he had an "extremely important and urgent" message for the Siegfried Hausner Commando from the federal government in Bonn. Wischnewski, on site in Dubai, announced that there would be no military intervention. That evening, West German television broke its self-imposed silence (which had been requested by the state) for the first time since the kidnapping, showing a thirty second clip from the Schleyer video received the day before.

As another day drew to an end, the West German government publicly announced that Somalia, South Yemen, and Vietnam had all refused to accept the RAF prisoners and the two Palestinians held in Turkey.

At 8:00 AM on October 16, the forty-first day since the kidnapping of Schleyer, the deadline established in the October 14 ultimatum passed. In Geneva, Payot once again announced that he had received an "extremely important and urgent" message from Bonn. At 10:43 AM, the Turkish Minister of Finance and Defense announced that Turkey was prepared to release the two Palestinians should the West German government request it.

At 11:21 AM, the airliner left Dubai.

At noon, the second ultimatum passed.

At 2:38 PM, government spokesman Klaus Bölling declared that a "realistic" solution was still being sought. Seven hours later, a plane landed in the Saudi Arabian city of Jiddah, carrying Wischnewski and the GSG-9, the special operations unit that had been established just four years earlier following the Black September attack at the Munich Olympics.

That night, the plane carrying the hijackers and their hostages was forced to make an emergency landing in South Yemen to refuel. The PDRY's military had blocked off the airstrip with tanks, not wanting anything to do with the skyjacking, but the plane set down on a sand track beside the runway itself.[1]

---

1 Fred Halliday states that the PDRY's reticence to get involved was due to the fallout from their having agreed to provide refuge to the prisoners exchanged for

Finally refueled the next morning, the plane took off, landing in Mogadishu, Somalia at 3:20 AM German time on October 17. An hour later the dead body of Flight Captain Jürgen Schumann, who had been sending out coded messages about the situation on board, was pushed out the door.[2]

The hijackers announced they were extending their deadline to 2:00 PM, German time.

At 1:30 PM Bölling held a press conference, during which he insisted that the goal of the authorities, "has been and remains saving the lives of the hostages."[3]

At 2:00 PM, yet another deadline passed. Minutes earlier, the plane carrying Wischnewski and the GSG-9 had landed in Mogadishu.

At the same time, in the Federal Republic, Schleyer's family released a statement announcing their willingness to negotiate directly with the kidnappers.

At 8:20 PM, Bölling issued a statement that the "terrorists" had no option but to surrender. Twenty minutes later, the West German government requested an international news blackout of developments at the airport in Mogadishu.

At 11:00 PM on October 17, sixty GSG-9 agents stormed the airliner: guerilla fighters Zohair Youssef Akache, Hind Alameh, and Nabil Harb were killed, and Souhaila Andrawes was gravely wounded. All of the hostages were saved, and the operation was considered a great success. All the more so, as it was the GSG-9's first officially acknowledged mission.

The next morning, at 7:00 AM, a government spokesperson publicly announced the resolution of the hijacking.

One hour later, Bölling announced the "suicides" of Gudrun Ensslin and Andreas Baader, and the "attempted suicides" of Jan-Carl Raspe and Irmgard Möller. Raspe died of his wounds soon after.

The following day, almost as a statement of victory, the government lifted the Contact Ban.

To all appearances, the prisoners had been killed in retaliation for the guerilla's actions. The Siegfried Hausner Commando issued a com-

---

Lorenz in 1975. Stefan Wisniewski has a very different view of the matter: given the PDRY's good relations with the Palestinian resistance, he feels that the only reason Aden could have had to refuse the hijackers permission to land would have been foreign pressure, either from the GDR or the Soviet Union. (Wisniewski, 27)

2 Aust, 520.

3 Ryan, 64.

muniqué announcing that it, in turn, had executed Schleyer. On the evening of October 19, police recovered his body in the trunk of a car in the border town of Mulhouse, just where the RAF had said it would be.

After forty-three days, the most violent clash between the anti-imperialist guerillas and the West German state had come to its bloody conclusion.

As the RAF would later acknowledge: "We made errors in 77, and the offensive was turned into our most serious defeat."[1]

It would take some time for the guerilla to formulate the lessons to be drawn from this unprecedented defeat.

18.10.77—Gudrun, Andreas, and Jan were murdered in Stammheim— Solidarity with the Political Prisoners' Struggle

---

1 Moncourt and Smith, 232.

Fourth Hunger Strike

"THOSE WHO UNDERSTAND THEIR SITUATION
ARE UNSTOPPABLE."

Given the fact that the state has turned treatment outside of the legal norms into a permanent exception

and

that six years of state security justice has proven that when it comes to us, whether in manhunts or in prison, human and constitutional rights aren't worth the paper they're written on,

we demand

on behalf of the prisoners from the anti-imperialist groups struggling in the Federal Republic, treatment under the minimum guarantees of the 1949 Geneva Convention, specifically Articles 3, 4, 13, 17, and 130.[2]

Which, for the political prisoners in Hamburg, Kaiserslautern, Cologne, Essen, Berlin, Straubing, Aichach, and Stammheim would mean, at a minimum, and in keeping with the testimony of all expert witnesses at RAF trials, that the prisoners be brought together in groups of at least 15 and that they be allowed to interact freely with one another.

Concretely, we are demanding:

1. The abolition of isolation and group isolation in the prisons of the Federal Republic and the closing of special isolation wings, which are meant to destroy prisoners, and where any communication is recorded and analyzed.

2. Investigations into the deaths of Holger Meins, Siegfried Hausner, and Ulrike Meinhof by an International Commission of Inquiry, support for the work of this Commission, and the publication of its findings in the Federal Republic.

---

2 See Appendix IV—The Geneva Convention: Excerpts, pages 554-56.

3. The government must publicly and clearly acknowledge that the claims that:

- the RAF planned to set off three bombs in downtown Stuttgart (June 72);
- the RAF planned to poison the drinking water in a large city (Summer 74);
- the RAF stole mustard gas and planned to use it (Summer 75);
- the Holger Meins Commando set off the explosives in Stockholm themselves (April 75);
- the RAF planned to contaminate Lake Constance with atomic waste (September 75);
- the RAF planned attacks against nuclear power plants and planned to make use of nuclear, chemical, and bacteriological weapons (since January 76);
- the RAF planned a raid on a playground to take children hostage (March 75).

are psychological warfare fabrications, used to legitimize an aggressive police force and state security apparatus, to disrupt solidarity with the resistance groups, and to isolate and destroy them; that all of these claims are false and that the statements released by the police, intelligence agencies, and the judiciary in this regard are baseless.

The hunger strike
is an example of our solidarity

- with the hunger strike of prisoners from the Palestinian resistance for prisoner of war status;[1]
- with the hunger strike for political status of the IRA prisoners in Irish and English prisons, status they are denied on the basis

---

1 Starting with a few dozen prisoners in February, within a month hundreds of Palestinian prisoners had joined a hunger strike throughout Israel's prisons, and outside support was offered by left-wing Arab and Jewish organizations. The basic demands were better conditions and an end to racist discrimination within the prisons, whereby Jewish prisoners received preferential treatment in regards to food and visits. [Journal of Palestine Studies, "Strike of Arab Prisoners in Israel," *Journal of Palestine Studies* 7, no. 1 (Autumn, 1977): 169-171].

of a European antiterrorism law put forward by the Federal Republic;[2]

- with the demand of the ETA prisoners and other antifascist forces in Spain for an amnesty;[3]
- with all those taken prisoner in the struggle for social revolution and national self-determination;
- with all those who have begun to fight against the violation of human rights, the miserable conditions, and the brutal repression in the prisons of the Federal Republic.

ARM THE RESISTANCE!
ORGANIZE THE UNDERGROUND!
CARRY OUT THE ANTI-IMPERIALIST OFFENSIVE!

The RAF prisoners
March 29, 1977

---

2 Twenty IRA prisoners were hunger striking at the time against brutal conditions at Ireland's Maximum Security Portlaoise prison. The strike lasted forty-seven days before it was ended by the intervention of the Catholic hierarchy.

3 The ETA was a Basque separatist guerilla. At the time, there was a mass militant movement demanding amnesty for hundreds of Basque and antifascist political prisoners in Spain, many of whom had been incarcerated due to their activities against the fascist Franco dictatorship.

The Assassination
of Attorney General
Siegfried Buback

For "protagonists of the system" like Buback, history always finds a way.

On April 7, 1977, the Ulrike Meinhof Commando executed Attorney General Siegfried Buback.

Buback was directly responsible for the murders of Holger Meins, Siegfried Hausner, and Ulrike Meinhof. In his function as Attorney General—as the central figure connecting and coordinating matters between the justice system and the West German news services, in close cooperation with the CIA and the NATO Security Committee—he stage-managed and directed their murders.

Under Buback's regime, Holger was intentionally murdered on November 9, 1974, by systematic undernourishment and the conscious manipulation of the transportation schedules from Wittlich to Stammheim. The BAW calculated that they could use the execution of a cadre to break the prisoners' collective hunger strike against exterminationist prison conditions, after the attempt to kill Andreas through the manipulation of force-feeding failed due to the mobilization of public pressure.

Under Buback's regime, Siegfried, who had led the Holger Meins Commando, was murdered on May 5, 1975, as the MEK (*Mobiles Einsatzkommandos*) detonated the explosives at the German Embassy in Stockholm. While he was under the exclusive jurisdiction of the BAW and the BKA, he was delivered to the FRG and his life was put in danger as he was transported to Stuttgart-Stammheim, thereby assuring his death.

Under Buback's regime, Ulrike was executed in a state security action on May 9, 1976. Her death was staged as a suicide to make the politics that Ulrike had struggled for seem senseless.

The murder was an execution; it followed the BAW's attempt to render Ulrike a cretin through a forced neuro-surgical operation, after which she was to be presented—destroyed—at the Stammheim trial, so as to condemn armed resistance as an illness. This project was prevented by international protests.

The timing of her murder was precisely calculated:

- before the decisive initiative in the trial, the defense motion that would have explained the 1972 RAF attacks against the U.S. Headquarters in Frankfurt and Heidelberg in light of the FRG's participation in the U.S.A.'s aggressive human rights violations in Vietnam;
- before Ulrike could be called as a witness in the Holger Meins Commando's Düsseldorf trial, where she would have testified about the very extreme form of torture that they used against her for 8 months in the dead wings;
- before her sentencing—at which point critical international public opinion, which had developed as a result of the Stammheim show trial and the cynical use of imperialist violence, would have been informed of the role of the federal government and its executive organs. This would have caused all of this to rebound against them.

Ulrike's history, in a way that is clearer than that of many combatants, is a history of resistance. For the revolutionary movement, she embodied an ideological vanguard function, which was the target of Buback's showpiece, the simulated suicide: her death—which the BAW used in propaganda to show the "failure" of armed struggle—was meant to destroy the group's moral stature, its struggle, and its impact. The BAW's approach, which they have followed since 71 with manhunts and operations conducted against the RAF, follows the counterinsurgency strategy of the NATO Security Committee: criminalization of revolutionary resistance—for which the tactical steps are infiltration, disrupting solidarity, isolating the guerilla, and eliminating its leadership.

Within the imperialist FRG's anti-guerilla counterstrategy, the justice system is a weapon of war—used to pursue the guerilla operating underground and to exterminate the prisoners of war. Buback—whom Schmidt called "an energetic combatant" for this state—understood the conflict with us as a war and engaged in it as such: "I have lived through the war. This is a war using different means."

We will prevent the BAW from murdering our fighters in West German prisons, which it intends to do simply because the prisoners will not stop struggling and the BAW sees no solution except their liquidation.

We will prevent the BAW and the state security organs from retaliating against the imprisoned fighters for the actions of the guerilla outside.

We will prevent the BAW from using the prisoners' fourth collective hunger strike for minimum human rights as an opportunity to murder Andreas, Gudrun, and Jan, which psychological warfare since Ulrike's death has been openly promoting.

ORGANIZE THE ARMED RESISTANCE AND THE ANTI-IMPERIALIST FRONT IN WESTERN EUROPE.

WAGE WAR IN THE METROPOLE AS PART OF THE INTERNATIONAL WAR OF LIBERATION.

Ulrike Meinhof Commando
April 7, 1977

Statement Calling Off
the Fourth Hunger Strike

In recent days, all efforts to break the hunger strike of the remaining 100 prisoners through force-feeding—with extreme brutality in the case of Hamburg-Holstenglacis—have failed. After the prison doctor in Stammheim and the anaesthetist they brought in refused to forcibly administer psychiatric drugs or narcotics to the prisoners, the prison warden, today, April 30, 1977, at 12 o'clock, read us a "Binding Declaration from the Ministry of Justice" to the effect that, "after considering the opinion of medical advisors, there will be an immediate centralization in Stammheim of all political prisoners—i.e., §129a prisoners—including those from other *Länder* in the Federal Republic, and that to this end work will be done to create the prison space necessary."

This decision is based on a cabinet resolution.

This fulfils the major demand of the hunger strike.

The RAF prisoners are calling off their strike.

"Whoever is not afraid of being drawn and quartered will pull the emperor off his horse."

Gudrun Ensslin
for the RAF prisoners
April 30, 1977

The Assassination of Jürgen Ponto

In a situation where the BAW and state security are scrambling to massacre the prisoners, we haven't got a lot of time for long statements.

Regarding Ponto and the bullets that hit him in Oberursel, all we can say is that it was a revelation to us how these people, who launch wars in the Third World and exterminate entire peoples, can stand dumbfounded when confronted with violence in their own homes.

The "big money" state security smear campaign is bullshit, as is everything that has been said about the attack.

Naturally, it is always the case that the new confronts the old, and here that means the struggle for a world without prisons confronting a world based on cash, in which everything is a prison.

Susanne Albrecht
on behalf of a RAF Commando
August 14, 1977

Statement Breaking Off
the Fifth Hunger Strike

Over the past week, we learned from a member of Amnesty International that the International Executive Committee's mediation process—to establish more humane prison conditions, in line with the doctors' demands, and to bring the hunger strike to an end—had broken down, because "the situation had hardened." And, "following the attacks against the BAW and Ponto, the authorities had received instructions from above to make an example of the prisoners."

That is in keeping with Rebmann's announcement.

As a result, the prisoners have broken off their strike on the 26th day—so as not to facilitate the murderous plan. They arrived at this decision after they were openly made hostages of state security, and taking into account the federal government's efforts—arrests, raids, and detentions at the borders—to disrupt the grievance at the Human Rights Commission in Strasburg regarding human rights violations in the Federal Republic.

Jan-Carl Raspe
for the RAF prisoners
September 2, 1977

The Attack on the BAW

All the theories about the apparatus which we used to prevent the federal prosecutors from sitting comfortably in their offices musing about how to arrange the next murder of a political prisoner, or planning a manhunt or a show trial or raids against citizens and lawyers who sympathize with us, or fabricating all of the lies and the hatred of the "information offensive"—are false.

It wasn't used to create a bloodbath—in this nest of reactionary violence, which already during the communist trials of the fifties sided with the ongoing fascism—or as part a "new strategy" or the "arms race between rival guerilla groups" that we read about.

Nor was it used to attack Rebmann, although he appears to be even more unscrupulous, more brutal, and a more loathsome demagogue than Buback.

It was simply meant as a warning, in a situation where over forty political prisoners were on hunger strike, because when he was Undersecretary for the Ministry of Justice in Baden-Wurttemburg, Rebmann promised to allow the prisoners' association in groups of 15. As Attorney General, he has reversed himself and broken this promise.

The group that previously existed in Stammheim is now smaller instead of larger, and the prisoners are now—after five years of isolation—once again totally segregated from one another, despite the fact that doctors, Amnesty International, the World Council of Churches, the League for Human Rights, and the Association of Democratic Jurists have all demanded that they be granted association, because isolation causes illness and, with time, death—that is to say, as a form of imprisonment, isolation constitutes torture and is a violation of human rights.

We proceeded from the view that following Buback's removal from office because of the murders of Holger, Ulrike, and Siegfried, and given the complete isolation the hunger strike provoked, Rebmann felt a need to distinguish himself by using the situation to execute Andreas, Gudrun, and Jan.

We agree with the prisoners' decision to break off their hunger and thirst strike, and we ask them to not resume it for the time being, not until we know whether the sanctimonious gang of murderers—the Ministers of Justice, judges, prosecutors, and cops—will choose to remain as arrogant in the face of our weapons, which we can use, as they do in the face of the weapons the prisoners have at their disposal.

The moral appeal of a hunger strike is useless, because this state's political violence is not in danger of becoming "fascistoid" or of showing "fascist tendencies," but is transforming itself into a new fascism, one that differs from National Socialism only inasmuch as it represents American and German monopolies, and can therefore proceed more aggressively, more powerfully, and more subtly than German capital during its barbaric nationalist period.

Whether they are part of the justice system, the executive, the political parties, the corporations, or the media, the greasy elite understand only one language: violence.

The misery and humiliation in the state security wings and the barbarism of force-feeding is for them no more than their own sick in-joke for the lunchroom.

Should it be taken up again, they intend to use the strike to kill you, just like now, because we need you, and they want to take every trace of morality and solidarity that the sacrifice of your struggle has produced and bury them under a mountain of shit, a mountain of cynical rumor-mongering and propaganda.

They'd like to have a good long laugh at our expense. Those who understand the struggle in the isolation holes (the dungeons, the torture of force-feeding)—those who understand the prisoners' determination, know that it is possible to be free. We will not make any further demands, and the ongoing activity and solidarity of the RAF will not be limited to communiqués.

We repeat: should a prisoner be murdered—and death in an isolation cell is nothing other than murder—we will respond immediately, both inside and outside of Germany.

Should Andreas, Gudrun, and Jan be killed, the apologists for the hard line will find that they are not the only ones with weapons at their disposal. They will find that we are many, and that we have enough love—as well as enough hate and imagination—to use both our weapons and their weapons against them, and that their pain will equal ours.

"THE SOLIDARITY OF THE PEOPLE
IS GROUNDED IN REVOLT."

RAF
September 3, 1977

The Schleyer Communiqués

MONDAY, SEPTEMBER 5, 1977

The federal government must take steps to ensure that all aspects of the manhunt cease—or we will immediately shoot Schleyer without even engaging in negotiations for his freedom.

TUESDAY, SEPTEMBER 6, 1977

On Monday September 5, 1977, the Siegfried Hausner Commando took Hanns Martin Schleyer, the President of the Federal Association of German Industries and the President of the Employers Association, captive. Regarding the conditions for his release, we will repeat our first communiqué to the federal government, which we have learnt has been suppressed since yesterday by the security staff. That is, all aspects of the search for us must be immediately discontinued or Schleyer will be shot immediately. As soon as the manhunt stops, Schleyer will be released under the following conditions:

RAF prisoners: Andreas Baader, Gudrun Ensslin, Jan-Carl Raspe, Verena Becker, Werner Hoppe, Karl-Heinz Dellwo, Hanna Krabbe, Bernd Rössner, Ingrid Schubert, and Irmgard Möller must be released in exchange for Schleyer, and must be free to travel to a country of their choosing. Günter Sonnenberg, who is unfit for imprisonment due to a gunshot injury he suffered during his arrest, must be immediately released. The warrant for his arrest must be lifted. Günter will leave with the 10 other prisoners, with whom he must immediately be placed so they can talk. The prisoners must be assembled at 8:00 AM on Wednesday at the Frankfurt Airport. Between then and their departure at 12:00 noon, they must be allowed to talk freely and unimpeded amongst themselves. At 10:00 AM, one of the prisoners will enter into direct communication with the commando via German television to inform us that their departure is unfolding according to plan.

For purposes of public oversight and to safeguard the prisoners' lives between takeoff and landing, we propose that the prisoners be accompanied by Payot, the General Secretary of the United Nations' International Federation of Human Rights, and Pastor Niemöller. We request that they accept this role to ensure that the prisoners arrive at their chosen destination alive. Naturally, we would agree to any alternative proposal from the prisoners.

Each prisoner will be given 100,000 DM. This communiqué, which can be authenticated by Schleyer's photo and his letter, must be broadcast unedited and unaltered on the *Tagesschau* this evening at 8:00 PM. We will establish the concrete details for freeing Schleyer as soon as we receive confirmation that the prisoners have been freed, that they won't be extradited, and when the federal government releases a statement guaranteeing that it won't pursue extradition. We are assuming that Schmidt, who demonstrated in Stockholm how quickly he can make decisions, will be equally quick this time given his personal connection to this greasy magnate of the cream of the national business world.

Siegfried Hausner Commando

WEDNESDAY, SEPTEMBER 7, 1977

We presume that the decision not to broadcast our demands and ultimatum on yesterday's 8:00 PM *Tagesschau*, as we had stipulated, is the result of a decision taken behind closed doors by the Crisis Management Team and reflects a decision by the federal government to resolve the situation militarily. The BKA's ploy, demanding proof that Schleyer is alive, even though they received Schleyer's handwritten letter yesterday and are also in possession of a photo of him taken yesterday, has the same function of buying time. We will only respond to the questions the BKA published today, when it is clear that the federal government is holding up its end of the deal—and we are running out of patience repeating this:

The manhunt must be stopped immediately. The prisoners must be gathered together in one place. The confirmation that this has been done will be delivered by one of the prisoners on German television today. As a clear gesture, we demand that the video recording, in which Schleyer reads his letter attached here, be broadcast on every television news show that airs at 6:00 PM tonight.

Siegfried Hausner Commando

THURSDAY, SEPTEMBER 8, 1977

There will be no further communiqués from us until the prisoners are flown out. The federal government has enough proof to assure them that Schleyer is alive: his letter and the videotape, as well as the recording with his answer to both questions. Go-betweens are unnecessary, as are all other stalling tactics. A resolution which includes Schleyer's release depends on the departure of the prisoners: otherwise it is not happening. For the last time, we demand:

That the federal government publicly announce its decision by 8:00 PM this evening. By Friday at 10:00 AM, proof that preparations have been made for the prisoners' departure. By 12:00 noon, the prisoners' departure on a fully fueled Lufthansa long haul aircraft must be broadcast live on television. The remaining demands are known to you from the previous communiqués.

Siegfried Hausner Commando

MONDAY, SEPTEMBER 12, 1977

We will wait until 12:00 AM for a decision from the federal government as to whether they want to make the exchange or not, and that decision should come in the form of obvious preparations for assembling the prisoners. The way in which this should occur has already been established. One of the prisoners must confirm that preparations are underway. The prisoners themselves will inform the federal government of possible destinations. The federal government will receive no further response from us to BKA messages transmitted via Payot. Should the federal government decide to once again allow our ultimatum to pass in silence, they will be responsible for the consequences.

Siegfried Hausner Commando

TUESDAY, SEPTEMBER 13, 1977

We have nothing to add to our statement of September 12, 1977. We request that Monsieur Payot play the role that the federal government assigned him, that role and that role only, and that he stop participating in the delays and postponements, which reflect a decision in favor of creating space to maneuver for a military solution.

The tactic of the so-called secret negotiations is absurd given the action's goal: freeing the prisoners. We have responded to the federal government's contemptible maneuvers for 9 days with multiple extensions of our ultimatum—they face a dilemma in that agreeing to the demands would contradict the institutionalized hate-driven civil war mentality they have whipped up against the RAF, and would require resisting the American thumbscrews. On the federal government's side, during these 9 days there has not been a single concrete development to indicate a willingness to exchange Schleyer. The BKA's claim that the manhunt was called off is a joke. Every newspaper carries photos of highway checkpoints and reports of homes raided. We are giving the federal government one last extension until 12:00 AM tonight to fulfil our demands.

Siegfried Hausner Commando

MONDAY, SEPTEMBER 26, 1977

If the federal government still wants to save Schleyer's life, they must immediately call off the manhunt in Germany, as well as arranging a halt to those that have begun in France, Holland, and Switzerland. Our demand that all aspects of the search cease remains unchanged.

We are also warning the federal government not to tap our telephone conversations with Payot or attempt to use them in any other way in the search. We will only conduct further negotiations with the federal government through the lawyer Payot if they discontinue their tactic of attempting to prolong telephone calls with senseless conversation, and if it is made clear that measures are being taken to prepare the release of the 11 prisoners specified.

Further signs of life from Schleyer will only be forthcoming if there is concrete evidence that the exchange is being prepared.

Also, if the federal government continues to withhold information from us about the results of Wischnewski's negotiations, all we have to say is that we know for certain that there are countries willing to take the 11 prisoners.

Siegfried Hausner Commando

THURSDAY, OCTOBER 13, 1977

We have given Helmut Schmidt enough time to choose between the American strategy for the extermination of liberation movements in Western Europe and the Third World, and the interests of the federal government in seeing that the most important industrialist alive today not be sacrificed to this imperialist strategy. The ultimatum of the

"Martyr Halimeh" Commando's Operation Kofr Kaddum and the ultimatum of the RAF's "Siegfried Hausner" Commando are identical.

The ultimatum expires on Sunday, October 16, 1977, at 8:00 AM GMT. If, at that time, the eleven prisoners specified have not arrived at their destination, Hanns Martin Schleyer will be shot. After holding Schleyer for forty days, there won't be another extension of the ultimatum or any further contact. Any delay will mean Schleyer's death.

To save time, it won't be necessary for Pastor Niemöller or the lawyer Payot to accompany the prisoners. We will receive confirmation of the prisoners' arrival even without confirmation from escorts. Hanns Martin Schleyer will be freed within 48 hours of our having received confirmation. Freedom through armed anti-imperialist struggle!

Siegfried Hausner Commando

Operation Kofr Kaddum

To all revolutionaries in the world

To all free Arabs

To the Palestinian masses

Today, Thursday, October 13, 1977, a Lufthansa 737 leaving Palma de Majorca en route to Frankfurt, flight number LH 181, passed into the complete control of the Commando "Martyr Halimeh".

This operation has as a goal the liberation of our comrades in the prisons of the imperialist-reactionary-zionist alliance. This operation reinforces the goals and demands of the Commando "Siegfried Hausner" of the RAF, which commenced on 05-09-77.

Revolutionaries and freedom fighters of the entire world are confronted with the monster of world imperialism, the barbaric war against the peoples of the world, under the hegemony of the U.S.A.

In this imperialist war, the sub-centers like Israel and the FRG have the executive function of oppressing and liquidating all revolutionary movements in and on their specific national territory.

In our occupied land, the imperialist-zionist-reactionary enemy demonstrates the very high level of their hostility, of their bloody aggressivity, against our people and our revolution, against all the Arab masses and their progressive and patriotic forces. The expansionist and racist nature of Israel is, with Menachem Begin at the summit of this ensemble of imperialist interests, clearer than it has ever been.

On the basis of these same imperialist interests West Germany was constructed as a U.S. base in 1945. Its function was the reactionary integration of the countries of West Europe via economic oppression and blackmail. As far as the underdeveloped countries of the world are concerned. West Germany gives financial, technical, and military support to reactionary regimes in Tel-Aviv, Pretoria, Salisbury, Santiago de Chili, etc...

There is a close and special cooperation between the two regimes in Bonn and Tel-Aviv in the military and economic fields, as well as in the area of shared political positions. The two enemy regimes work together against patriotic and revolutionary liberation movements in the world in general and in Arab, African, and Latin American regions in particular. This is manifested by their providing racist and minority regimes in Pretoria and Salisbury with arms and atomic and military technology, by delivering mercenaries and credits to them, by opening markets for their products, by breaking boycotts and economic embargos surrounding them.

A significant example of the close cooperation between the Mossad, the German Secret Services, the CIA, and the DST is the filthy piracy of the imperialist-reactionary alliance: the Zionist invasion of Entebbe.

Actually, the identical character of Neo-Naziism in West Germany and Zionism in Israel is in the process of becoming clearer in the two countries:

- reactionary ideology is dominant.
- fascist, discriminatory, and racist labor laws are enforced.
- the worst methods of psychological and physical torture and murder are used against fighters for freedom and national liberation.
- forms of collective punishment are practiced.
- all guarantees of international law, such as laws governing the humane treatment of prisoners, a just trial, and a defense are completely abolished.

While the Zionist regime is the most authentic and practical continuation of Naziism, the government in Bonn and the Parties in parliament do their best to revive Naziism and expansionist racism, especially amongst military personnel and within the other State institutions.

Economic circles and the magnates of multinational corporations play an effective role in these efforts. Ponto, Schleyer, and Buback are blatant examples of persons who have effectively served old Naziism and who now, in practice, execute the goals of the Neo-Nazis in Bonn and the Zionists in Tel-Aviv, both locally and internationally.

Part of the anti-guerilla strategy of the enemies is non-acquiescence to the legitimate demands with the goal of freeing our imprisoned revolutionaries, who suffer the most cruel forms of torture with the silent awareness of the international public. We declare that this will not succeed. We will force the enemy to free our prisoners, who daily defy them by fighting oppression, even in prison.

VICTORY FOR THE UNITY OF ALL REVOLUTIONARY
STRENGTH IN THE WORLD

Struggle Against World Imperialism Organization
October 13, 1977

SAWIO Ultimatum

To the Chancellor of the Federal Republic of West Germany

this is to inform you that the passengers and the crew of the LH 737 plane, flight no. 181 leaving from Palma to Frankfurt, are under our complete control and responsibility. the lives of the passengers and the crew of the plane as well as the life of Mr. Hanns-Martin Schleyer depends on your fulfilling the following—

1. Release of the following comrades of the RAF from prisons in West Germany—Andreas Baader, Gudrun Ensslin, Jan-Carl Raspe, Verena Becker, Werner Hoppe, Karl-Heinz Dellwo, Hanna Krabbe, Bernd Roessner, Ingrid Schubert, Irmgard Moeller, Guenter Sonnenberg—and with each the amount of DM 100,000.

2. Release of the following Palestinian comrades of PFLP from prison in Istanbul—Mahdi and Hussein.

3. The payment of the sum of $15 million U.S. dollars according to accompanying instructions.

4. Arrange with any one of the following countries to accept to receive all the comrades released from prison:
   1. Democratic Republic of Vietnam
   2. Republic of Somalia
   3. People's Democratic Republic of Jemen

5. The german prisoners should be transported by plane, which you should provide, to their point of destination. they should fly via Istanbul to take in the two Palestinian comrades released from Istanbul prison.

   the turkish government is well informed about our demands.

   the prisoners should all together reach their point of destination before Sunday, 16th of Oct. 1977, 8.00 o'clock a.m. GMT.

   the money should be delivered according to accompanying instructions within the same period of time.

6. If all the prisoners are not released and do not reach their point of destination, and the money is not delivered according to instructions, within the specified time, then Mr. Hanns-Martin Schleyer, and all the passengers and the crew of the LH 737 plane, flight no. 181 will be killed immediately.

7. If you comply with our instructions all of them will be released.

8. We shall not contact you again. This is our last contact with you. You are completely to blame for any error or faults in the release of the above mentioned comrades in prison or in the delivery of the specified ransom according to the specified instructions.

9. Any try on your part to delay or deceive us will mean immediate ending of the ultimatum and execution of Mr. Hanns-Martin Schleyer and all the passengers and the crew of the plane.

S.A.W.I.O.
October 13, 1977

Final Schleyer Communiqué

After 43 days, we have put an end to Hanns Martin Schleyer's pitiful and corrupt existence. From the moment he began his power play, Herr Schmidt gambled with the possibility of Schleyer's death: he can find him on rue Charles Peguy in Mulhouse in a green Audi 100 with Bad Homburg license plates.

As compensation for our pain and suffering over the massacres in Mogadishu and Stammheim, his death is meaningless. Andreas, Gudrun, Jan, Irmgard, and ourselves, we are not surprised by the dramatic and fascist methods the imperialists use to exterminate the liberation movements. We will never forget Schmidt and the alliance that participated in this bloodbath.

THE STRUGGLE HAS ONLY BEGUN.
FREEDOM THROUGH ARMED ANTI-IMPERIALIST STRUGGLE

Siegfried Hausner Commando
October 19, 1977

77: Living With The Fallout

The movement was under total observation—the BKA thought that Schleyer was hidden outside of Germany, so they wanted to follow any thread and not arrest people. I don't think that movement people were at all involved in the kidnapping, but the state knew that the third generation came out of the prison support movement so they watched every move.

They were looking all over Europe. I was in the United States at the time and they raided the house of friends I was staying with. A friend of mine was traveling in Italy on his motorcycle and was followed by Italian cops from village to village. Every time we crossed the border going to Switzerland, for example, they would stop the car three kilometers before the border on the autobahn and wait for us with machine guns.

We were anti-imps visiting prisoners, leafleting, spray-painting, etc. Often when I left the prison after a visit, I would be searched, as would my car, by very nervous young cops with machineguns. When I went to political meetings, they followed us openly. But they didn't arrest us. It scared people away, of course. It split the movement, and it pushed others underground. It made me personally feel very determined and hateful.

The state built an enormous data bank. Cases came to light where people were listed as "terrorists" because of who they were sitting next to on the train. There were street controls of cars, and people had to show their passports all the time.

Publishers and bookstores had a very hard time, were raided. Although they did not agree with the RAF, they did it for freedom of speech. Trials and more trials. For every leaflet there was a big debate. Did you put it on the counter or not. New laws: §88a and §130 made it impossible to publish anything, for instance like the book you are planning now. You had to hide the typewriter, get it published in Holland, bring it back across the border—really hard—distribute it illegally.

Homes were raided to take away typewriters and papers. Trials and more trials. With §129a, everything counted as support. So the left had to spend a lot of energy on defense stuff. But only individuals were arrested not whole groups or meetings...

I moved quite often during those years, and every single time the cops went to my neighbors or landlords and asked them to take note of the people who visited me. My neighbors always told me this—smile.

We never spoke on the phone, not about politics, and especially not about love affairs, friends etc., because we didn't want to help them complete their psychological profiles. This is part of why I was so shocked when later all the letters from the prisoners, showing their fights, were published. We tried not to visit non-political friends in order to protect them, and then that led to our isolation, and it definitely added to the hate we felt.

It was very hard on the lawyers. When Croissant fled to France and asked for political asylum, it was a great propaganda coup, but also very real—they wanted to bury him in prison. When I visited him in Stammheim prison, he told me that he was scared because he found a razor blade in his cupboard, which he took as a hint that he should kill himself.

510

14

The Stammheim Deaths

Murder would make the better story. I looked under every rock. I spent weeks and months following up every lead, and the simple truth is there is nothing that allows you to truly maintain that it was clearly either a murder or a suicide.

Stefan Aust[1]

It remains for me a suicide under state surveillance. There are enough reasons to believe that someone in the state apparatus knew about the weapons and the suicide plan. This doubtless indicates the hope that they would die. And so I say: there is no clear distinction in this case between murder and suicide.

Karl-Heinz Dellwo[2]

---

1 Agnes Steinbauer, "Tod in Stammheim," *Deutschlandradio* [online], May 9, 2006.
2 Karl-Heinz Dellwo, interview by Axel Vornbäumen, "Ich bin kein Pazifist," *tagespiegel* [online], March 26, 2007.

Today, thirty years later, just as before, I don't in any way believe the suicide version. Not because I've never had doubts. Not because I've never permitted myself to speculate in various ways. Not because I never despaired in the face of the unlimited pressure of the campaign that I, like the other prisoners, experienced from the outset: not supported by facts, but rather continuously bringing it in line with the official versions, insinuations, misrepresentations, lies. No, what always made me skeptical of every new "incontravertible proof" was that I knew them—the dead—better than to be affected by everything that was produced.

Ronald Augustin[1]

Irmgard Möller stated: at no time was there a suicide pact between Andreas Baader, Gudrun Ensslin, Jan-Carl Raspe, and herself. She did not attempt suicide. The four stab wounds on the left side of her chest were not self-inflicted. Her last recollection before losing consciousness was two distant bangs and a high-pitched noise. This occurred Tuesday, October 18, 1977, at 4:30 AM.

Jutta Bahr-Jentges, Irmgard Möller's attorney[2]

WITHIN FIVE MONTHS OF THEIR deaths, a government commission of inquiry ruled that Gudrun Ensslin, Jan-Carl Raspe, and Andreas Baader had killed themselves in a "collective suicide."[3]

Much as in the case of Meinhof's death, in time the available historical sources would come to almost unanimously parrot the state's suicide story, generally with a dismissive reference to "conspiracy theories" some extremists might hold to the contrary. In both cases, evidence which points to state murder is simply never mentioned, leaving casual readers with the impression that any such claims must indeed be evidence of the irrationality or cultishness of the guerilla's supporters.

---

1 Ron Augustin, "Der zweite Tod," *Junge Welt* [online], September 10, 2007.
2 Text from an untitled movement flier widely distributed in the years following the Stammheim deaths. Möller has repeated these facts numerous times since.
3 Associated Press, "3 Terrorist Deaths Ruled 'a Collective Suicide,'" *European Stars and Stripes*, February 25, 1978.

Gudrun Ensslin,
Jan-Carl Raspe,
and Andreas Baader

One sign of how far removed we are today from the RAF's heyday is that for some years now, certain former guerillas have been echoing the state's claims of suicide. While these former guerillas were themselves not held at Stammheim, and so have no more direct knowledge than we do about what happened, such claims are deeply disturbing to those who supported the RAF for many years. As we have seen, outrage at the treatment of the prisoners, the torture and abuse which seemed to culminate in these murders, was the key factor bringing in new supporters throughout the seventies. Many of these people are now confronted with the painful possibility that the guerilla was willing to so cynically manipulate their feelings.

The editors of this volume cannot be certain of what happened that night in Stammheim. Nevertheless, as in the case of Ulrike Meinhof's death in that prison, we feel there is compelling evidence pointing to state murder. While we keep an open mind, what follows are some of the reasons why we remain unconvinced by the state's suicide story. As in the case of Meinhof, we consider the way in which accounts of these latter Stammheim deaths gloss over these inconsistencies to be a sign of the unhealthy political culture we live in today.

Andreas Baader and Jan-Carl Raspe died as a result of gunshot wounds, Gudrun Ensslin as a result of hanging, and the sole survivor, Irmgard Möller, suffered repeated stab wounds inflicted with a kitchen knife.

As the two men were alleged to have shot themselves, some explanation as to where the guns had come from was required. On October 27, a spokesperson for the administration at Stammheim offered the necessary story. He stated that it was "not out of the question... that one of the prisoners' lawyers passed the contraband articles to a prisoner during a visit."[4]

---

4 *Der Stammheimtod: Kampagne gegen das Modell Deutschland*, no. 4, Bochum, December 1977, 5.

This claim was met with widespread incredulity. Before entering the visiting area, lawyers had to empty their pockets and give their jackets to an employee for verification; they were body searched physically and with a metal detector. Prisoners were strip searched and given a new set of clothes both when entering and when leaving visits with lawyers. Further, due to the Contact Ban, the lawyers had been unable to see their clients since September 6.

In the case of Andreas Baader, several other irregularities were apparent. There were three bullet holes in the cell. One bullet lodged in the wall, one in the mattress, and the third, the cause of death, lodged in the floor: this scenario seemed indicative of a struggle, not a suicide.

Baader was supposed to have shot himself in the base of the neck in such a way that the bullet exited his forehead. Repeated tests indicated that it was not easy for an individual to position a gun against his or her own body in such a way. Making the feat well nigh impossible, according to fluorescent x-ray analysis, there were thirty to forty centimeters between the pistol's barrel and the point of entry at the time the fatal shot was fired.

To top it all off, Baader had powder burns from the recoil on his right hand. Baader, however, was left-handed, and would almost certainly have used his left hand to shoot himself.

The newspaper of the KBW: "One Way—Or Another— These are Concentration Camp Methods! Down with the Contact Ban Law!"

In the case of Raspe, no powder burns were found at all. Powder burns always occur when firing a weapon.

The gun smuggling theory relied on the testimony of Hans-Joachim Dellwo, brother of RAF prisoner Karl-Heinz Dellwo, and Volker Speitel, the husband of RAF member Angelika Speitel. They had both been arrested on October 2, 1977, and charged with supporting a criminal organization under §129.

Speitel had been an important figure in the Committees Against Torture, and both men would later admit to having acted as couriers for the guerilla. They testified that they were aware of lawyers smuggling items to the prisoners during the

Stammheim trial that had ended in April 1977, specifically claiming that guns had been smuggled in. The plot sketched by the state was that these guns were then hidden away in the prisoners' belongings and in the cell walls when work was done to renovate the seventh floor that summer.[1]

Guerilla supporters were quick to note that Speitel and Dellwo's testimony was tainted by the fact that they each received reduced sentences and new identities in exchange for these allegations.[2] It has been further claimed that the police threatened Speitel with Youth Court action against his eight-year-old son if he refused to cooperate.[3]

Besides conveniently explaining two of the Stammheim deaths, the gun smuggling story served several additional purposes. From that point on, all lawyers' visits with RAF prisoners were through a screen, a process which facilitated auditory surveillance, as well as depriving the prisoners of one of their last direct human contacts. Furthermore, from that point on, the guards were permitted to look through lawyers' files "to prevent smuggling." Finally, as a result of Dellwo and Speitel's testimony, both Armin Newerla and Arndt Müller were brought to trial, and in 1980 the two attorneys were convicted of smuggling in weapons and explosives, receiving respective sentences of three-years-and-six-months and four-years-and-eight-months.

In the case of Gudrun Ensslin, who was found hanged, contradictions similar to the case of Ulrike Meinhof present themselves. The chair she allegedly stood on to hang herself was too far away from her body to have been used, and the torn sheets supporting her would not likely have tolerated the weight of a falling body. Nor did her cell contain the fibers one would have expected from her tearing up a sheet. As was the case with Meinhof, the skin test that would have established whether Ensslin was dead before she was hanged was never undertaken.

In search of a motive for this mass suicide, the state suggested that the prisoners realized there was no hope for their liberation following the storming of the hijacked airliner in Mogadishu, and consequently chose to kill themselves rather than face life in prison. This theory raises three questions. How would the prisoners, given the Contact Ban, have

---

1 Aust, 379-380.
2 Peter Henkel, "Milde Urteile für Volker Speitel und Hans-Joachim Dellwo," *Frankfurter Rundschau* [online], December 15, 1978; Martin Knobbe, "Der Ankläger und sein Informant," *Stern* [online], April 27, 2007.
3 Augustin, "Der zweite Tod."

known about these developments? How would they have organized a group suicide under such conditions? And further, why would they have made their deaths look like murders?

On October 20, authorities claimed to have "discovered" a radio in Raspe's cell, a cell that he had only occupied since October 4. The state alleged that, using the wall sockets and tools stolen when the prison was being renovated, the prisoners constructed an elaborate communication system that allowed them to monitor radio broadcasts and to communicate with each other.

This was only the first in a series of very convenient discoveries. On October 22, two hundred and seventy grams of explosives were "discovered" in the prisoners' wing. On November 12, a razor blade and three detonators were "found" in Baader's cell. Finally, on December 12, a gun and ammunition were "found" in a cell formerly occupied by RAF prisoner Helmut Pohl. It is worth noting that the government's Commission of Inquiry was unclear about whether this gun was a Smith & Wesson or a Colt .38, the model used by special police units.

In such an atmosphere, with the state alleging incredible feats of Houdini-like derring-do on the part of the prisoners, people understandably began to believe anything could be possible. For instance, Baader's lawyer, Hans-Heinz Heldmann, in the October 1977 issue of the KB's *Arbeiterkampf*, pointed to a new mystery. At the time of his death, there was a large quantity of fine, light-colored sand on and in Baader's shoes: according to Heldmann, the quality and quantity of the sand suggested that Baader had been flown to Mogadishu and then returned to Stammheim.[1] As has been noted elsewhere, this theory simply cannot be true: there would have been no time to fly to Mogadishu and back, even in the supersonic Concorde airplane. Indeed, Irmgard Möller, the sole survivor of the Stammheim events, has explained that this sand was more likely picked up in the prison, part of the building materials left over from renovations earlier that year.[2]

Even taken at face value, the state's claims do not point to "simple suicide": in the final analysis, the evidence indicates that *if* prisoners would have had access to guns and radios then someone in a position of authority would have known it. Former *Spiegel* editor Stefan Aust, for instance, has suggested that the prisoners may have been allowed to believe they had established a "secret" communication system so that

---

1 *Der Stammheimtod*, 13-14.
2 Aust, 549.

what they said to each other could be monitored. What emerges then is a picture of the prisoners being allowed to have weapons and to communicate with each other, while the authorities listened in as a suicide pact was agreed acted on, all the while doing nothing to interfere.[3]

As evidenced by the quote at the beginning of this chapter, Karl-Heinz Dellwo, a former member of the Holger Meins Commando that seized the Stockholm embassy in 1975, now holds this view and indeed claims to have held it for years while he publicly backed the murder theory. (It should be noted that Dellwo was held in Hamburg, not Stammheim, at the time, and so could have no direct knowledge of the events in question.)

If this scenario were true, it would be a particularly stark elaboration of an old SPK slogan, namely that "suicide = murder." Indeed, a section of the radical left has always held that even if the prisoners did commit suicide, they would have done so only as a consequence of the harsh prison conditions in which they were held, and that in such a case, the government would still be culpable.

One of the biggest problems with the suicide story is that not all of the prisoners died.

On October 27, Irmgard Möller, the sole survivor from the alleged group suicide, issued a statement claiming that she had not attempted to kill herself. She stated that the last thing she heard before going to sleep on the night in question was two muffled explosive sounds. She was not aware of anything until she awoke some hours later, feeling intoxicated, disoriented, and having difficulty concentrating.

She had been stabbed repeatedly in the chest, the blade penetrating down to her heart sac. The state later claimed that she had done this to herself, using a prison-issue butter knife she had squirreled away. She has always denied this claim.

Möller has further stated that the prisoners had no contact with one another except by shouting through the air vents in their cells or when

---

3 In this regard see Aust, 432, 482-483, 487-488, 496-497, 550-552. Regarding the possibility that police might have learned of guns in Stammheim from Volker Speitel as early as October 4, see Aust, 484. It should be noted that although Aust claims to believe the prisoners committed suicide, he emphasizes that there remain serious inconsistencies in the official version of events, including evidence pointing to the possibility that Baader was shot by a gun with a silencer on it, which would mean that the murder weapon was removed after he was killed (Aust, 547), and also that guards lied when they claimed Möller had lifted her sweater before allegedly stabbing herself (Aust, 548), a "fact" which the state claimed proved suicide as an assassin would not have tried to spare the victim's clothing.

going by each other's cells on the way to or from the yard. Finally, she insists the prisoners had absolutely no idea of developments in Mogadishu.

To this day, she maintains that Ensslin, Baader, and Raspe were murdered.

Of course, following Meinhof's death, the prisoners knew that murders might be disguised as suicides. On October 7, Andreas Baader had sent his lawyer the following letter:

> As a result of the measures of the last 6 weeks and a few remarks from the guards, one can draw the conclusion that the Administration of State Security, which—as a guard who is now permanently on the 7th floor has said—hopes to provoke one or more suicides here, or, in any case, create the plausible appearance of such. In this regard, I stress: none of us—this is clear from the few words that we have been able to exchange at the doors in the last few weeks and from the years of discussion—have the intention of killing ourselves. Should we—again a guard—"be found dead," we have been killed, as is the procedure, in keeping with the tradition of legal and political measures here.[1]

Gudrun Ensslin had also written to her lawyers, stating:

> I am afraid of being suicided in the same way as Ulrike. If there is no letter from me and I'm found dead; in this case it is an assassination.[2]

Her father, the pastor Helmut Ensslin, had been similarly warned. As he would tell the Italian magazine *Lotta Continua*:

> I am convinced that she was murdered. She was always afraid that she would be murdered, even in the case of being liberated and going out of the country. After the death of Ulrike, she told me that it might end that way. And, for her, a suicide was absolutely out of the question. Gudrun had never lied, just as the others from the RAF have never lied; they always took responsibility for their deeds.[3]

---

1 Aust, 489.

2 Ryan, 66.

3 *Informationsdienst*, no. 202, November 5, 1977, quoted in *Cienfuegos Press Anarchist Review*, "The Stammheim Deaths."

In conversation with two prison chaplains on the afternoon of October 17, Ensslin had explained that there were three sheets of paper kept in a file in her cell, containing important information.

"They should be sent to the head of the Chancellery if they do away with me, or if I'm executed," she had said. "Please would you see that they get there? I'm afraid that otherwise the Federal Prosecutor will suppress or destroy them."[4]

Needless to say, according to the official account, these three sheets of paper were never found.[5]

Although no independent body was ever formed to investigate the Stammheim deaths, the International Investigatory Commission into the Death of Ulrike Meinhof was still sitting at the time. They had several interesting comments. They noted that on both nights, May 8/9, 1976, and October 17/18, 1977, an auxiliary was in charge of surveillance rather than the usual person. They also noted that, in both incidents, the autopsies posed similar problems.

Regarding the incriminating evidence "turned up" by prison authorities during the cell searches, they approvingly quoted from the press release of Irmgard Möller's lawyer, Jutta Bahr-Jentges, of October 25, 1977:

> Why these inventories of the cells without neutral witnesses, without lawyers, these inventories which have produced receivers, radios, Morse code apparatuses, quantities of plastic explosives— might as well find atomic bombs?[6]

The Commission further noted the existence of an uncontrolled entrance to the seventh floor that opened into the cell area, and which was not visible from the guard's office. This entrance was not acknowledged by authorities until November 4, 1977. The Commission observed:

> This indicates that—as citizens have been saying for some time— the functionaries of the BKA, the BND, and the secret services have constant, uncontrolled access to the cells.[7]

---

4 Aust, 526.
5 Ibid., 528.
6 Commission internationale d'enquête sur la mort d'Ulrike Meinhof, 67.
7 Ibid., 55-58.

The cover-up was so glaring that the *Frankfurter Rundschau* remarked, in reference to the official investigation:

> The Parliamentary Commission is faced with... three sorts of witnesses: those who know nothing, those who don't want to know anything, and those who aren't allowed to make a statement.[1]

As a macabre postscript to all this, RAF prisoner Ingrid Schubert was moved into isolation in Munich-Stadelheim prison on November 11, 1977. One hour later, she was found hanged dead.[2] As in the case of Meinhof and Ensslin, the autopsy failed to find the usual signs of death by hanging.[3]

On the Thursday before her death, she had assured her lawyer that she had no intention of committing suicide.

---

1 Ibid., 68.

2 *Internazionale Kommission zum Schutz der Gefangenen une Gegen Isolationshaft*, 4.

3 Ryan, 66.

15

On the Defensive

Nᴇᴡs ᴏғ ᴛʜᴇ sᴛᴀᴍᴍʜᴇɪᴍ ᴅᴇᴀᴛʜs electrified, astounded, and horrified the European left, provoking an outpouring of rage. Security experts and government officials warned that more "terrorist" attacks would follow, and braced themselves accordingly. City streets were flanked with sandbagged gun emplacements and miles of barbed wire stretched through the capital.[4]

The wave of protest and violence was not long in coming, though in the end it subsided well short of the "100,000 bombings" that one group promised would avenge the events of October 18.

In the week immediately following the deaths, West German and right-wing targets were attacked in over twenty Italian cities. Simultaneous explosions rocked the Siemens, BMW, and Opel auto buildings in Rome,[5] car showrooms were firebombed in Bologna, Milan, Livorno, and Turin, and West German consulates were attacked in Genoa and Venice.[6] A police officer in the Northern town of Brescia lost his hand while trying to defuse a bomb, and club-wielding demonstrators sent

4 Mary Campbell, "History's coldest winter wrote top story for '77," *Lima News,* December 27, 1977.
5 United Press International, "Italian Leftists Continue Their Reign of Terror," *El Paso Herald-Post,* October 26, 1977.
6 Associated Press, "Schleyer Found Dead," *Danville Register,* October 20, 1977.

dozens of cops to the hospital in Sicily. In Milan, city councillor Carlo Arienti, a Christian Democrat, miraculously survived being shot eight times in an action claimed by the Red Brigades to "honor our West German comrades."[1]

A telephone caller in Milan threatened, "We are also ready to 'suicide' the German Ambassador."[2] As a result, the FRG embassy was ringed with riot police and armored personnel carriers. Left-wing students demonstrating on the Rome University campus engaged police in a three-hour gun battle, leaving five police and three students wounded and twenty-five people in custody on charges of possessing weapons and firebombs.[3] At the same time, windows were smashed on the upper class Via Veneto and molotov cocktails were thrown at cops, the protesters denouncing "German Nazis for the cold blooded murder of our comrades."

In Paris and Nice, molotov cocktails were thrown at German tourist buses,[4] as well as at the Franco-German Bank and a car showroom.[5] The offices of the progressive *Libération* newspaper were occupied[6] in an effort to force its journalists to launch an investigation into the Stammheim deaths, as bombs went off in Toulouse, Versailles,[7] and Le Havre.[8]

In France, neofascists retaliated against the wave of protest by bombing the offices of the left-wing *Syndicat de la Magistrature*,[9] leaving behind papers that simply read "Baader Murderer."[10] In a public state-

---

1 Associated Press, "Extremists Protest Deaths of 3 German Prisoners," *Amarillo Globe Times,* October 19, 1977.

2 United Press International, "Leftist Terrorists Vow to Foul German Economy," *Coshocton Tribune,* October 22, 1977.

3 United Press International, "Deaths of W. German Terrorists Protested with Bombings, Student Riot," *Valley News,* October 21, 1977.

4 Associated Press, "Industrialist's Killers Sought," *Wisconsin State Journal,* October 21, 1977.

5 United Press International, "Terrorists Bomb German Property," *Ruston Daily Leader,* October 24, 1977.

6 United Press International, "Leftists Continue Terror Reign," *Salina-Journal,* October 24, 1977.

7 United Press International, "Leftist terrorists vow to foul German economy."

8 United Press International, "Terrorists Bomb German Property."

9 United Press International, "Protests Sweep Three Nations," *Valley News,* October 27, 1977.

10 United Press International, "Italian Radicals Say Suicide Squad Will Kill West German Ambassador," *Galveston Daily News,* October 26, 1977.

ment, one self-styled "Anti-Terrorist Brigade" claimed to have captured and killed a member of the guerilla; as no body was ever found, this was likely bluster. Nevertheless, police used the spectre of further escalation and counter-escalation as an excuse to ban all protests outside the West German embassy in Paris.[11]

Violent protests also broke out in Athens, and Greek police engaged in a firefight with reported anarchists who were driving a car full of explosives, presumably to attack a nearby factory owned by a West German corporation.[12] Around the same time, three people were injured when the West German Cultural Center in Istanbul was firebombed during two days of anti-German demonstrations in Turkey.[13]

In Holland, several men abducted real estate tycoon Maurits Caransa, pushing him struggling into an automobile after he left a club where he had been playing bridge. The press reported that a German-speaking man had called the newspaper *Het Parool*: "We are the Red Army Faction," he apparently said. "We have Caransa. You will hear from us." Another newspaper claimed to receive a call demanding that Queen Juliana abdicate and that Knut Folkerts, still awaiting extradition, be freed.[14] Despite these reports, when Caransa was released three days later after haggling with his captors over a four million dollar ransom, it was revealed to have been a "normal" kidnapping unrelated to the RAF or any other guerilla group.[15]

At the same time, another kidnapping, one which was not reported as being politically motivated, was in fact the work of the guerilla: in a defiant act, on November 9, the anti-authoritarian 2nd of June Movement snatched lingerie magnate Walter Palmers in Vienna, dragging him from his car as he arrived home for dinner. He was released unharmed four days later, after his son delivered a ransom of $3.1 million.[16] Nobody was arrested, and the 2JM took the money and divided it three ways, giving badly needed funds to the RAF and an unspecified Palestinian group.

---

11 Ibid.

12 United Press International, "Deaths of W. German Terrorists Protested with Bombings, Student Riot."

13 United Press International, "Protests Sweep Three Nations."

14 United Press International, "Gang Kidnaps Dutch Millionaire," *Kingsport Times News*, October 29, 1977.

15 United Press International, "Caransa Released After Ransom Paid," *Coshocton Times*, November 2, 1977.

16 *Bridgeport Telegram*, "Large ransom frees Viennese millionaire," Nov. 14, 1977.

As far away as Seattle, in the United States, the George Jackson Brigade bombed a Mercedes-Benz dealership in solidarity with the RAF. "We chose Mercedes-Benz as a target," they explained, "because it is a German luxury car which is a favorite item of conspicuous consumption for ruling-class bosses, and because of its association with Hans Martin Schleyer."[1]

Meanwhile, newspapers reported that they had received threats that three Lufthansa planes would be blown up on November 15, prompting massive cancellations,[2] though in the end there were no attacks on the airline.

The flames of protest spread quickly, but by the end of the year, the violence had clearly been contained. The strongest reaction had been from the Italian left, where a tradition of militancy and a keen awareness of the realities of postfascist state repression provided the basis for the fierce fightback, giving rise to 147 documented anti-German attacks between October 18 and December 31 of 1977.[3] The massive offensive by the revolutionary movement in Italy, including militant strikes and numerous armed actions, certainly contributed to the impressive show of solidarity.

In the Federal Republic itself, courthouses were bombed in Hannover,[4] Zweibrucken,[5] and Hamburg,[6] but these were isolated acts. This meek reaction, especially when compared to what was happening in other countries, was a measure of the extent to which the visible might of the state and vicious anticommunist hysteria had put the left on the defensive. Rage had been muted by despair, as many people now felt that the level of conflict had exceeded their capacities. They recoiled in shock as the country seemed to be transforming itself into a police state.

---

1 George Jackson Brigade, "You Can Kill a Revolutionary But You Can't Kill the Revolution," November 1, 1977. http://www.gjbip.org/comm_teeth.htm.

2 Associated Press, "Lufthansa Airlines Flying Anti-Missile Patterns," *Florence Morning News,* November 15, 1977.

3 Vittorfranco S. Pisano, "Terrorism in Italy, March 27, 1978," Heritage Foundation, http://www.heritage.org/Research/Europe/bg56.cfm.

4 *Kingsport-Times,* "West Germans Take Seriously Terrorist Threat on Schmidt," October 22, 1977.

5 United Press International, "Terrorist Bomb Blasts Building in W. Germany," *Ogden Standard-Examiner,* October 31, 1977.

6 Associated Press, "Bonn: terrorist death was suicide," *Modesto Bee,* November 14, 1977.

The cream of the West German establishment gathered at Schleyer's state funeral on October 24, surrounded by 750 police, with snipers in place on the surrounding rooftops.

In this paramilitary setting, President Walter Scheel declared:

> *The fight against terrorism is the fight of civilization against a barbarism trying to destroy all order... They are the enemies of every civilization... The nations of the earth are beginning to realize this. They realize with horror that not this or that order is being attacked, but all order.*

Specifically referring to anyone who dared protest following the Stammheim deaths, he remarked that, "They too share the guilt."[7]

It should be noted that while this lynch mob atmosphere met with broad support from the West German public, for many—including people who had no truck with revolutionary politics—things seemed to be going too far. The new "muscular" social democracy seemed to find appropriate expression on the cover of *Stern* magazine around this time, where Chancellor Schmidt posed wearing the uniform of the BGS. This government reaction to the events of 1977 demonstrated the degree to which the SPD could act as repressively as the CDU, and has been identified as the starting point of yet another split between the party's leadership and its more left-wing members, a development that accelerated over the next few years, giving rise to the Green Party.[8]

Police set up special phone numbers in eighteen cities where one could hear taped recordings of the RAF members' voices; in Bonn, the line was so jammed with calls that a second number had to be set up. Over 100,000 police were mobilized, and alleged terrorist hideouts were raided. In West Berlin, thirty-eight apartments, bookstores, and printing shops were searched and forty people taken into custody, prompting a protest outside of police headquarters, which was met by cops swinging rubber truncheons.[9] *Info-BUG* and its printers Firma Agit-Druck were amongst those targeted, and the radical newspaper found itself banned.

---

7 United Press International, "Crusade against terrorism urged," *Newport Daily News*, October 25, 1977.

8 Hanshew, 29-30

9 Associated Press, "German Leftists, Police Battle after Paper Raided," *Waterloo Courier*, October 24, 1977.

At the same time, in France, attorney Klaus Croissant was being publicly referred to as "a central figure in international terrorism." The lawyer was supported by philosophers Michel Foucault and Jean-Paul Sartre,[1] as well a number of professional associations, including the *Syndicat de la Magistrature*, the *Confédération Syndicale des Avocats*, the *Jeunes Avocats*, the *Mouvement d'action judicaire*, and the *Association Francaise des Juristes Democrates*.[2] There was also a Committee for the Immediate Liberation of Klaus Croissant, which made its point

by mailing one thousand crescent-shaped pastries to government officials, each one accompanied by a note which read, "If a croissant can circulate freely in the marketplace, why not a lawyer?"[3]

Croissant's persecution by an authoritarian state across the Rhine brought back memories that added weight to the entire affair. As one defense lawyer put it:

> When I see this hunted lawyer on the one side, and on the other Prosecutor Shuller, a former stormtrooper and member of the old National Socialist party, I know where I stand.[4]

But to no avail: on November 2, extradition hearings began in Paris, and two weeks later, the court ruled that Croissant could be handed over to the Germans. By November 19, he was sitting in a cell in Stammheim.[5]

The RAF was on the defensive, and initial reports indicated that members had fled the country. Reportedly, one million handbills and posters went out across Europe and as far away as Japan,[6] identifying the suspects as Susanne Albrecht, Rolf Heißler, Christian Klar, Friederike Krabbe, Silke Maier-Witt, Brigitte Mohnhaupt, Adelheid

---

1 François Dosse, *History of Structuralism* (Minneapolis: University of Minnestota Press, 1998), 337.

2 Bakker Schut, *Stammheim*, 533-534.

3 *Libération*, "1000 croissants pour un avocat," October 10, 1977.

4 *Libération*, "Klaus Croissant et la raison d'État," October 10, 1977.

5 Bakker Schut, *Stammheim*, 532-533.

6 United Press International, "Germans Ask Japan Help Tracking Killers," *Newport (R.I.) Daily News*, November 12, 1977.

Schulz, Angelika Speitel, Sigrid Sternebeck, Willy Peter Stoll, Christof Wackernagel, Rolf Clemens Wagner, Elisabeth von Dyck, Juliane Plambeck, Inge Viett, and Jörg Lang. The equivalent of $19,200 was offered for information leading to the arrest of each of these suspects, for a total of over $300,000. (Plambeck and Viett were not actually members of the RAF, but of the 2nd of June Movement, and as such the two would dissolve their organization and join the RAF in 1980.)[7]

The first RAF members arrested after the Stammheim deaths were Christof Wackernagel and Gert Schneider. The two men were in Amsterdam, but their safehouse had been identified during the Caransa investigation, and the police had it under constant observation. On November 11, the two men were followed as they left the apartment; when they realized that police were surrounding them, they drew their weapons and began to fire, even throwing a hand grenade. Sharpshooters took them out: one guerilla was hit in the chest and stomach, the other received a bullet in the head.[8]

Schneider was being sought in connection with the Schleyer kidnapping, Wackernagel in connection with the recent Zweibrucken courthouse bombing. Both men were extradited to the Federal Republic.

One name that did not immediately appear on the wanted posters was that of Peter-Jürgen Boock, the husband of RAF prisoner Waltraud Boock, and yet it was later revealed that this man had in fact been central to the events of 77.

Boock had wanted to join the RAF ever since he was a teenaged runaway, one of the kids Baader and Ensslin had worked with in Frankfurt back in 1970. They had rejected him as a member at the time, not least because of his drug habit, a curse which only worsened as the years went on. Nevertheless, by the mid-seventies, with the original leadership largely removed

Peter-Jürgen Boock

---

7   Moncourt and Smith Vol. II, 131-2.
8 Associated Press, "West German Terrorists Lose Shootout," *Brainerd Daily*, November 11, 1970.

from the field, Boock became a trusted recruit and was sent to South Yemen for training in 1975.[1]

In the wake of 77, Boock and other RAF fugitives had found shelter in Baghdad, but he remained plagued by his addiction, and when he began going through withdrawal, some of his comrades became desperate. On January 21, 1978, Christine Kuby was arrested following a shootout with police in a Hamburg drugstore; she had been attempting to use a forged prescription to buy narcotics for Boock.[2]

Shortly afterwards, the *Verfassungsschutz* tried to carry out an ambitious false flag action, meant to entrap the guerillas. Dynamite was set off in the wall of Celle prison with the goal of allowing Sigurd Debus to escape. Debus, while not a member, was a political prisoner who had participated in hunger strikes with the RAF: the hope was that he would unwittingly lead the *Verfassungsschutz* to the underground guerillas. (As it turned out, Debus did not escape. When the details of this operation came to light in the mid-eighties it caused some consternation.)[3]

In March, the prisoners went on an unsuccessful and uneventful sixth collective hunger strike, demanding association, an international inquiry into the Stammheim deaths and that of Ingrid Schubert, and a return of all documents that had been seized from the dead prisoners' cells. This time, Klaus Croissant was not able to organize support on the outside: his trial on charges of supporting a terrorist organization had just begun on March 9.[4] Refusing to distance himself from his former clients, he now joined them in their hunger strike.

As progressive journalist Oliver Tolmein wrote years later, "Klaus Croissant was a lawyer who had a political understanding of justice and, as a result, never drew a firm line between defending his

---

1 In 1988, RAF prisoners Knut Folkerts, Rolf Heißler, Sieglinde Hofmann, Christian Klar, Christine Kuby, Roland Mayer, Brigitte Mohnhaupt, Adelheid Schulz, Günter Sonnenberg, and Rolf Clemens Wagner signed a joint declaration about Boock, his drug habit and his lies. They explained that when he joined the guerilla he claimed to have been diagnosed with intestinal cancer, and that he only had a short while to live. He explained away his drug use, insisting it was to deal with the pain from his cancer. It was only when he was examined by doctors in Yugoslavia in mid-1978 that it came to light that he had never had cancer, he was simply a junkie lying to manipulate his friends into getting him dope. See Moncourt and Smith Vol. II, 328-332.

2 Jan-Eric Lindner, "Es begann wie ein Routine-Einsatz - dann fielen Schüsse," *Hamburger Abendblatt* [online], March 3, 2006.

3 Braunthal, 159-160.

4 Bakker Schut, *Stammheim*, 532-537.

clients and political engagement."[5] As a result of such commitment, on February 16, 1979, the tireless advocate was found guilty of supporting a terrorist organization and sentenced to two-and-a-half years in prison, plus four years of *Berufsverbot*.[6]

On May 11, 1978, Stefan Wisniewski was apprehended at the Paris airport as he was waiting to board a flight to Yugoslavia. Not only was Wisniewski carrying drugs, police also found a letter from Karl-Heinz Dellwo that had been smuggled out of prison, in which the RAF prisoner strongly criticized the hijacking that ended in the Mogadishu debacle.[7]

On June 30, four RAF members—Brigitte Mohnhaupt, Sieglinde Hofmann, Peter-Jürgen Boock, and Rolf Clemens Wagner—were arrested in Zagreb. The Yugoslav government entered into negotiations with the FRG, hoping to exchange the RAF combatants for eight members of the Croatian far right being held by West Germany. When this crass attempt at a trade broke down, the RAF prisoners were ferreted out of Yugoslavia to an undisclosed third country.

On September 6, RAF member Willy Peter Stoll was shot dead by police in a Chinese restaurant in Düsseldorf. A few days later, the cops located his apartment, where they found a coded diary, an arsenal of weapons (including a homemade "Stalin Organ" capable of firing primitive missiles), and fingerprints of six other suspected RAF members.[8]

Later that month, police surprised three people engaged in target practice in the woods outside of Dortmund. Michael Knoll and Angelika Speitel were both shot, police officer Hans-Wilhelm Hansen was killed while another RAF member managed to escape with his submachine gun. Knoll died of his wounds on November 25.[9]

Also in September, a figure from the earliest days of the guerilla once again made the headlines: Astrid Proll, who had fled from a medical clinic in 1974, was identified and arrested in England. Proll had not been involved in armed struggle since her escape, but had rather found a place for herself in the feminist and squatting communities in London, where the former getaway car driver worked as a mechanic and ran an

---

5 Oliver Tolmein, "Beharren: Freundfeind", *Freitag* 17 [online], April 19, 2002.
6 Bakker Schut, 534.
7 *Spiegel* 44, 2007.
8 *Time Magazine* [online], "Closing in on an elusive enemy," October 9, 1978.
9 United Press International, "Cops ambush terror courier," *Newport Daily News*, September 25, 1978.

right: Demonstration organized by the Friends of Astrid Proll campaign in London, England.

Astrid Proll

auto maintenance class for women. It would later be said that *Gruppe 47* poet Erich Fried had been one of those who secretly helped her get by while she was in hiding.[1]

A campaign took shape, largely at the initiative of radical feminists, to support Proll and attempt—unsuccessfully—to fight against her extradition, for in the fugitive's own words, "I do not expect to survive if I am returned to Germany."[2] Nevertheless, once she was returned, the state quickly agreed to drop the most serious charges: the main evidence against her was that of the discredited Karl-Heinz Ruhland, and the memo from state security that proved her innocence had come to light.

Meanwhile, on November 1, 1978, Rolf Heißler and Adelheid Schulz were identified as they were attempting to cross into Holland. A firefight ensued and border guards Dionysius de Jong and Johannes Goemans were both shot dead.

The guerilla was still regrouping, and yet there would be more casualties before it was operational again.

In the midst of the prisoners' seventh hunger strike, Elisabeth von Dyck was identified by police while entering a suspected RAF safehouse in Nuremberg on May 4, 1979. She was shot in the back, and died on the spot.[3]

A month later, Rolf Heißler was captured after he miraculously survived being shot in the head as he entered a Frankfurt apartment.[4]

---

1 Goettle, "Die Praxis der Galaxie."

2 Friends of Astrid Proll.

3 "ai-168" http://www.nadir.org/nadir/periodika/angehoerigen_info/ai-168.html.

4 Associated Press, "Nab murder suspect in Frankfurt," *Pacific Stars and Stripes,* June 12, 1979.

ON THE DEFENSIVE (15)

Heißler's capture would actually go down in history as one of the first public successes of computer data mining in defense of the state. As an engineering magazine explains:

> Much was already known about the terrorists. "The police knew that they rented apartments to conduct their crimes," recalls Hansjürgen Garstka, the State of Berlin's commissioner for data protection and freedom of information. "But they used them only a couple days before the event. Also, the police knew these people paid their electricity and rent only in cash." The terrorists preferred high-rise apartments with underground garages and direct access to the highway, and they were primarily young and German.
>
> Profile in hand, the police contacted electricity companies, to find out which apartments used no or little electricity, and apartment complexes, to find out which people paid in cash; they also combed through household registrations (German citizens are required to register with the state). "The results were all merged, and in the end, they found one flat which fit absolutely absolutely this profile," Garstka says. Police put the apartment under surveillance and soon nabbed RAF member Rolf Heißler.[5]

While such law enforcement techniques might not raise an eyebrow today, it must be remembered how advanced—as if from science fiction—such levels of surveillance seemed to most people just a generation ago. There was a public outcry when it was learned how the bust had been carried out, and that Horst Herold's BKA, with its massive computers, was behind it. (Learning a lesson from this, legislation was passed in the mid-eighties allowing such data mining in the FRG.)[6]

While the guerilla were the only ones actually being gunned down, 1977 and the years that followed challenged an entire society, as the state unleashed a wave of repression, and anyone to the left of Helmut Schmidt felt they might be a potential target:

> A virtual war atmosphere was created in the country in mid-October: hundreds of thousands of motorists were pulled off the road and searched; constant appeals to the population were issued to encourage their reporting any suspicious types or activities to

---

5 J. Kumagai, "The German Solution," *IEEE Spectrum*, April 11, 2003.
6 Ibid.

the police—such as sudden change of address, of hair cut or any
other cosmetic changes, unusual mailings or publications.[1]

That September and October, as Schleyer was being held in captivity, one hundred and fifty agents were on duty round the clock at the special headquarters set up in Cologne. Every day, over 15,000 phone calls were monitored, as 3,000 other police officers took part in the hunt.[2]

Conservatives took advantage of the frenzied atmosphere to settle scores with the progressive intelligentsia, the overwhelming majority of whom were firmly opposed to the guerilla and the revolutionary left. The Hessen CDU Chair Alfred Dregger accused the Frankfurt School academics of contributing to terrorism, a sentiment echoed by the CDU Prime Minister of Baden-Württemberg, Hans Filbinger.[3] At the same time, in September 1977, CSU representative Dietrich Spranger issued a list of public figures whom he held responsible for "terrorism" in the Federal Republic, an unlikely collection which included Willy Brandt, Peter Brückner, Pastor Helmut Gollwitzer, and authors Günter Grass and Heinrich Böll.[4] The fact that two of those on this list—Böll and Gollwitzer—had recently joined pastor Heinrich Albertz and Bishop Kurt Scharf in a public appeal for the release of Schleyer did not seem to make a difference.[5]

Böll in particular remained tarred by the Springer Press as a "terrorist sympathizer" no matter what he did. This could have dramatic

---

1 Margit Mayer, "The German October of 1977," *New German Critique* 13 (Winter 1978): 155.

2 Hockenos, 124.

3 Rolf Wiggershaus, *The Frankfurt School: Its History, Theories and Political Significance*. Translated by Michael Robertson (Cambridge, Mass. : MIT Press, 1994), 656. Fittingly enough, it was revealed within a year of these accusations that several weeks after the war, while sitting in a British internment camp, Filbinger had acted in his capacity as a judge to sentence a sailor to death for calling an officer a "Nazi pig." After briefly denying the story and accusing his accusers of being terrorist sympathizers, Filbinger admitted it was true, but defended himself saying that "What was right in the Third Reich cannot be wrong today." [Jeffrey Herf, "The 'Holocaust' Reception in West Germany: Right, Center and Left," *New German Critique* 19, special issue, Germans and Jews (Winter, 1980): 34]

4 Heinrich Böll, interviewed by Gert Heidenreich (Bavarian Radio), September 28, 1977, "This Type of Cheap Propaganda is Extremely Danegrous," translated by Martin Black, in *Stories, Political Writings and Autobiographical Works*, Martin Black (ed.), (New York: Continuum International Publishing Group, 2006), 293.

5 Associated Press, "Wife of seized industrialist pleas for terrorists' trade," *Modesto Bee*, September 12, 1977.

consequences; for instance, an anonymous call was received stating that armed men had been seen entering the home of the famous author's son. As a result, forty heavily armed cops from the special antiterrorist unit raided the house; of course, there were no guerillas there. When the elder Böll complained of this in an interview the next day, Bavarian radio refused to broadcast it on the grounds that it was "inflammatory."[6]

Most people stood behind the government, not only in its hunt for the RAF, but also in its general crackdown on the radical left. In one poll, 62% of respondents stated that they were willing to accept restrictions on their personal freedoms through controls and house searches, while only 21% were opposed.[7] At the same time, politicians and the press became ever more bloodthirsty. Years later, RAF member Christian Klar recounted that:

> On September 8, 1977, the Crisis Management Team allowed Die Welt to demand that Rebmann's plan [that the prisoners be killed] be carried out. On September 10, the Suddeutsche Zeitung published the same thing as reflecting a discussion within the CSU Land group, which wanted a prisoner shot at half-hour intervals until Schleyer was released. A day later, Frühschoppen demanded the introduction of bloody torture, noting that the guerilla groups in Latin America had been defeated in that way. The next day, Spiegel provided a platform for the CSU's Becher and Zimmermann to express their longing for the deaths of the Stammheim prisoners. On September 13, the same idea was put forward by the SPD through Heinz Kühn, but in a more delicate way: "The terrorists must be made to understand that the death of Hanns Martin Schleyer will have grave consequences for the fate of the violent prisoners they are hoping to free through their disgraceful actions."[8]

Indeed, following the Stammheim deaths, even allowing Ensslin, Raspe, and Baader to be buried in a common grave in the Stuttgart cemetery was enough to earn one the sobriquet of being "soft on terrorism." Stuttgart's moderate CDU mayor, Manfred Rommel—the son of the famed Field Marshal—refused to forbid such a burial, insisting that "Death must end all animosity." As a result, he found himself

---

6 Braunthal, 162.

7 Ibid., 174.

8 *A Statement Regarding 77*. See Moncourt and Smith Vol. ii, 297-303.

marginalized within the *Land* party organization, and telephone calls flooded in from angry citizens demanding that the RAF dead be cremated and their ashes poured into the city sewers.[1]

Little wonder that, commenting on the political climate that autumn, Heinrich Böll would remark:

> *I am gradually beginning to wonder whether it's even necessary to—to put it bluntly—do away with democracy. People are intimidated to such an extent—the media have become so cautious—that laws would hardly need to be changed. The whole thing occurs on a "fantastic" plane... Even the liberal newspapers are becoming extremely conformist and cautious—they hardly need to lift a finger.[2]*

While this reactionary atmosphere reached its crescendo in the days of autumn, the state clampdown had begun well before the Schleyer kidnapping.

On April 25, 1977, just a few weeks after the RAF had killed Siegfried Buback, a student newspaper in the picturesque university town of Göttingen published an article entitled *Buback: In Memoriam*, in which the anonymous author admitted his "secret joy" at the Attorney General's assassination, while nevertheless condemning such armed attacks as counterproductive. Within the context of the split occurring in the *sponti* scene at the time, the article actually represented a move away from political violence:

> *Our force cannot be Al Capone's force, a copy of street terror, and constant terror; not authoritarian, but rather antiauthoritarian and therefore more effective. Leftists shouldn't be killers, shouldn't be ruthlessly brutal people, shouldn't be rapists, but also not saints or innocent lambs. Our daily objective is to formulate a concept and modus operandi of force and militancy which are fun and have the blessings of the masses, so that the left doesn't acquire the same face as the Bubacks.[3]*

Obviously the writer was hostile to the RAF's politics, but such subtleties were lost on the state, and police seized upon the opportunity

---

1 Wellington Long, "Germany has second Rommel," *Sunday Sun*, April 16, 1978.
2 Böll, 295.
3 Anonymous, "Buback: In Memoriam," *semiotext(e)* 4, no. 2, the German Issue, (1982): 129.

to clamp down on the undogmatic left and sympathetic academics. *Buback: In Memoriam* was banned under §88a and raids were carried out against student and alternative publishers suspected of knowing the author's identity.[4]

The women's movement, which had no organic ties at all to the RAF, similarly found itself the target of the same antiterrorist hype. The Women's Center in Frankfurt was raided by police, and members were charged under §129a—the antiterrorist subsection of §129—for having provided women with the names of doctors willing to perform abortions.[5]

Male politicians and clergymen lost no time in sharing their opinions of the RAF's female combatants. As an article in *New German Critique* explained:

> *The fact that 60% of the terrorists sought by the police are women has not gone unnoticed by those conducting what has been referred to in the European press as the "witch-hunt" against dissenters. Blame for the predominance of women terrorists has been placed at the feet of the nascent German women's movement. Former Director of the Office for the Protection of the Constitution[6] Günther Nollau sees in female terrorists "an excess in the liberation of women." Conservative academic sectors speak of the "dark side of the movement for total equality." The Christian Socialist newspaper Bayern Kurier claims, "Observers of the scene view the newly established feminism, which is preached by the left, as an essential reason for the recent change in sex roles on the terror front." Women's publishing houses have been invaded by police, assuming that the owners were aiding and abetting terrorism, and the Women's Vacation House in Gaiganz was subject to such constant surveillance and so many raids by police looking for hidden persons, that the lease was revoked by intimidated landlords.[7]*

This was all the more galling, for in the years since the APO, the West German women's movement had moved away from its socialist roots, to such a point that at the time it could be said that many women "would

---

4 Mayer, 156; Hanshew, 33.
5 Jacobs, 170-171.
6 The *Verfassungsschutz*.
7 Ibid., 166-167.

prefer no politics at all to leftist politics."[1] As Georgy Katsiaficas has written about feminism in the FRG in the late seventies:

> *As many women turned further inward, limiting themselves to their private spheres of lovers and close friends, radicals felt that the slogan "The personal is political" had been turned on its head—to the point where the political was irrelevant.[2]*

On the other side of the equation, nothing but silence had ever emanated from the RAF and its support organizations on questions of feminism and women's liberation. This was all the more remarkable given the large proportion of RAF members who were women, and the hackneyed sexist terms in which counterinsurgency writers often attacked their politics.

This silence was certainly a consequence of the RAF's particular brand of anti-imperialism, which zeroed in on this one contradiction as being primary to the exclusion of all others. One comrade who was active doing prisoner support work during this period remembers visiting a female political prisoner and asking her about this, only to be informed that, "If you carry a gun, it does not matter if you are a man or a woman."

A similar sentiment was expressed by Inge Viett, who would move from the 2nd of June Movement to the RAF in 1980:

> *None of us came out of the feminist movement... We had no conscious need to live through that kind of process of women's liberation... We simply made a decision, and then we struggled, doing all the same things as the men. For us, there was no Man-Woman question. For us living in the underground, that old concept of roles didn't exist.[3]*

Feminists might have objected that for most people—even some who do carry guns, and even some who do live in the underground—being a man or a woman does matter, both in terms of one's relationship to imperialism and one's perspectives for resisting it. During the 1970s, it seems not to have occurred to the women or men in the RAF that

---

1 Hilke Schlaeger, "West German Women's Movement," *New German Critique* 13 (Winter 1978): 64.

2 Katsiaficas, 78-9.

3 Ute Kätzel, "Die Mädchen fielen aus ihrer Rolle," *die tageszeitung* [online], October 25-26, 1997.

gender made a difference as to how imperialism was experienced by its victims, or that anti-imperialism might benefit from an explicit connection to women's liberation.

Despite this unpromising background, the Stammheim trauma sparked a process of change, both within the support scene and amongst a minority of feminists, too. The consensus against violence that existed in the women's movement was by no means complete, and despite the loud protestations of those who insisted that all violence was "male," others felt that nonviolence in a sexist society was of limited value. Referring specifically to the Stammheim deaths, French feminist Françoise d'Eaubonne pointedly suggested that there was something positive to be learned from the women of the RAF, even when their choices had tragic consequences. Writing in 1978, in a text which was discussed both in France and in the Federal Republic, she asked:

> *Is it not better for a woman to be beaten to death by a prison guard at Stammheim than to be humiliated by the blows of a husband's fists? Is it not better to endure insults before a court of law which one can denounce as "Nazi pigs!" than to endure in silence the insults of an employer? And is it not better, ultimately, to meet death having fought back than to die in resignation and defeat? If we must die, then better with weapon in hand.*[4]

Women Against Imperialist War: in the early eighties, as sections of the women's movement attempted to bridge the distance that had separated them from the RAF support scene, this became one of the most important anti-imperialist groups in the FRG.

---

4 Françoise D'Eaubonne, *Feminismus und "Terror,"* (Munich: Trikont, 1978) quoted in Sibylle Plogstedt, "Has Violence Arrived in the Women's Movement," in *German Feminism: Readings in Politics and Literature*, ed. Edith Hoshino Altbach (Albany, NY: State University of New York Press, 1984), 337.

The lurch to the right, the Stammheim deaths, the rampant police repression, and the terrorist-baiting of the women's movement all worked to push certain women to explore the possibilities of renewed solidarity. A conference on women and repression was organized in Frankfurt in 1978 and a women's solidarity committee was formed to support Irmgard Möller. Slowly but surely, small groups took the first steps out of their isolation, and the reaction provoked by the anti-RAF repression would once again cause some to rally to the anti-imperialist camp.

At the same time, the antiterrorist hysteria provided the state with an opportunity to move against the K-groups that had been reinforcing the increasingly militant antinuclear movement ever since 1976. After Schleyer was seized, the opposition CDU called for a ban against the three largest Maoist parties, the KBW, the KPD,[1] and the KPD/ML, with ludicrous claims that they had some connection to "terrorism." In response, all three organizations called for a joint demonstration in Bonn on October 8, 1977, under the slogan "Marxism-Leninism Cannot Be Outlawed!" Twenty thousand people marched under red flags in one of the very few common activities these three organizations would mount during the decade.

Just as most of these Maoist K-groups imploded over the next few years, hemorrhaging members to the new Green Party, 1977 would also exacerbate divisions on the undogmatic left. The anti-guerilla positions that Joschka Fischer, Daniel Cohn-Bendit, and others had been pushing since 1976 now appeared to carry even more weight, and several important intellectuals, including Rudi Dutschke and Herbert Marcuse, made public declarations in the popular press denouncing the RAF's struggle against the Federal Republic.[2]

While much of the undogmatic left was retreating from militancy, this was by no means a homogenous phenomenon. In a very different vein, in January 1978, other radicals drew on the strengths of the counterculture to break through the crisis. The idea for a mass gathering originated with a dozen Berlin *spontis* who knew each other from playing soccer and from the bar scene.[3] "Tunix"—a play on words meaning "Do Nothing"—created a rallying point for those who wished neither to return to the system nor to simply retreat into themselves.

---

1 The Maoist party, not to be confused with the pro-Soviet party of the 1950s.
2 Hanshew, 37.
3 Michael Sontheimer, "Soziale Bewegungen Auf zum Strand von Tunix!" *Spiegel* [online], January 25, 2008.

As three of the organizers ("Quinn the Eskimo," "Frankie Lee," and "Judas Priest") explained in their call out:

> When our identity is under attack, like during the situation in the fall of 77, then we need to take the initiative and state openly what it is we want. Political taboos and appeals to the constitution won't save us.[4]

With thousands of people attending, the Tunix gathering marked the dawn of a new era for the antiauthoritarian left.[5] Participants took to the streets in Berlin, throwing bricks and paint-filled eggs at the courthouse, the America House, and the Women's Prison, carrying banners which read "Free the prisoners!", "Out With the Filth," and "Stammheim is Everywhere."[6]

This renewed antiauthoritarian left expressed itself in diverse ways, including the birth of an autonomist scene which drew direct inspiration from the Italian Marxist current of the same name, remaining committed to radical politics. Another product of this period was the newspaper *tageszeitung* (Daily News), a national radical left daily. Radical weekly newspapers had existed in almost every city previously, but *Info-BUG* had been the only one with a truly national circulation. Even then, it had been focused on West Berlin, and had been banned the day of the Stammheim deaths. *taz* became the voice of the Tunix generation, establishing a national circulation dwarfing *Info-BUG* or any other publication in the scene.[7] (However, like much of this "alternative" effervescence, *taz* accompanied the Greens back into the system over the next ten years.)[8]

The first issue of *tageszeitung* appeared September 27, 1978.

---

4 Geronimo.

5 Estimates for the number of people who attended range from 5,000 (Michael Sontheimer, "Soziale Bewegungen Auf zum Strand von Tunix!") to 20,000 (Katsiaficas, 65).

6 Geronimo.

7 Michael Sontheimer, interviewed by Rainer Berthold Schossig, "25 Jahre taz" *Deutschlandradio* [online], April 12, 2004.

8 Katsiaficas, 179.

Basing itself both in the Tunix scene and in the Citizens Initiatives—ever more swollen by disaffected Social Democrats unhappy with Schmidt's continuing march to the right—the Green Party was founded in 1980. In the same way that Willy Brandt's "Let's Dare More Democracy!" had spelled the end to the APO, the Greens eventually came to represent the end for many seventies radicals, and the avenue that more than one former militant would follow right into the establishment. As one snide *Spiegel* writer put it on their 25th anniversary, "It was not the 68ers and their Green offshoots who civilized Germany, but Germany which civilized them."[1] (But this is a story best left for our next volumes.)

The undogmatic left had been polarized by the RAF's struggle, splitting to the left and to the right. This is unremarkable in itself, as is the fact that those who veered rightwards into the Greens were also those who found the RAF's politics uninspirational, to say the least. What is noteworthy is that those who veered to the left, the autonomists, were often similarly unimpressed with the RAF and its legacy. Certainly, nobody would be inspired by 1977 to set up an armed group, in the way that the RAF's early actions had inspired the RZ and others.

Indeed, it is striking how much the RAF's legacy and credibility were damaged by 1977; it took years to recover, even while most of the guerillas remained uncaptured. Most popular and even scholarly works about the group act as if it disbanded afterwards, while in fact it remained active until the 1990s.

Compare this to 1972, when practically the entire guerilla had been wiped out by arrests, and yet the actions of the May Offensive inspired renewed resistance throughout the spectrum of the revolutionary left.

One part of the equation was the distance that had grown between the RAF and the rest of the left, both as a result of its own paradoxes and of the vicious state repression and psychological operations. The other factor, in its own way an expression of the first, was the level of confrontation in which the 1977 commandos had chosen to engage, well beyond the capacity of any other segment of the left to imitate or even support.

While the RAF was in crisis, the Revolutionary Cells and Rote Zora continued to score successes, and carried out approximately eighty actions over the next decade, suffering hardly any arrests. There were also

---

1 Claus Christian Malzahn, "Happy 25th Birthday Greens. What's the Plan Now?" *Spiegel* [online], January 13, 2005.

many low-level attacks carried out by one-off groups, most of which have left no record, yet which nevertheless contributed to an overall armed orientation remarkably different from that which existed in North America at the time.

In a significant way, these developments indicate the degree to which the RAF's armed strategy had marked revolutionary politics in West Germany, even while its ideology was rarely accepted.

Not that the RAF itself had been removed from the battlefield.

Though it looked broken by defeat and repression, the RAF would once again manage to regroup and draw in new members, establishing the basis for renewed campaigns of revolutionary violence in the 1980s.

In a few years, events would reveal that the tradition of armed resistance, and the legacy of the first guerillas to emerge from the APO, had beaten the odds and survived the devastating blows of the seventies.

APPENDICES

Excerpts from the
Frankfurter Allgemeine Zeitung

As detailed in Section 6, Black September: A Statement from Behind Bars, much has been made of an article which appeared in the *Frankfurter Allgemeine Zeitung* on December 15, 1972, entitled "Ulrike Meinhof läßt sich nur die Stichwort geben."

In order to allow readers to judge the rendition in the CIA-funded *Encounter* magazine, we have reprinted the last section of this article in German, alongside our own version and George Watson's:

FRANKFURTER ALLGEMEINE ZEITUNG

Freitag, 15. Dezember 1972 / Nr. 291

Ulrike Meinhof läßt sich nur die Stichworte geben

Heftiger Ausbruch der Zeugin vor Gericht · Mahler trägt aus seinem „Dokument" vor · Bericht von Peter Jochen Winters

Die Kritik an Löwenthal im Hessischen Landtag

„Ohne dass wir das deutsche Volk vom Faschismus freisprechen—denn die Leute haben ja wirklich nicht gewußt, was in den Konzentrationslagern vorging –, können wir es nicht für unseren revolutionären Kampf mobilisieren", sagt sie. Die Linke sei nach dem Krieg in bezug auf den Faschismus „fahrlässig dumm und dreist vorgegangen. Man habe die Personen in den Vordergrund gerückt, aber nicht tiefer geblickt. „Wie war Auschwitz möglich, was war Antisemitismus?" Das hätte man damals klären müssen, anstatt gemeinsam Auschwitz als Ausdruck des Bösen zu verstehen, meint Ulrike Meinhof.

„Das Schlimmste ist, dass wir uns alle Kommunisten und andre, darin einig waren." Doch jetzt hat sie erkannt, dass Antisemitismus in seinem Wesen antikapitalistisch sei. Er mache sich den Haß der Menschen auf ihre Abhängigkeit vom Geld als Tauschmittel, ihre Sehnsucht nach dem Kommunismus zu eigen.

„Auschwitz heißt, daß sechs Millionen Juden ermordet und auf die Müllkippen Europas gekarrt wurden als das, als was man sie ausgab—als Geldjuden." Finanzkapital und Banken, „der harte3 Kern des Systems" des Imperialismus und Kapitalismus, Hätten den Haß der Menschen auf das Geld und die Ausbeutung von sich ab und auf die Juden gelenkt. Diese Zusammenhänge nicht deutlich gemacht zu haben, sei das Versagen der Linken, der Kommunisten gewesen.

Die Deutschen waren antisemitisch, also sind sie heute Anhänger der RAF. Sie wissen es nur nicht, weil man vergessen hat, sie vom Faschismus, vom Judenmord, freizusprechen und ihnen zu sagen, dass Antisemitismus eigentlich Haß auf Kapitalismus ist. In der Tat eine bemerkenswerte Erklärung für das Scheitern der „Baader-Mahler-Meinhof-Gruppe", die sich Ulrike Meinhof da zurechtgezimmert hat. Dadurch ist es möglich, auch den Münchener Anschlag des „Schwarzen September" zu preisen. Sie fühle eine „historische Identität" mit den Juden im Warschauer Getto, die waffenlos einen Aufstand versuchten und sich hinschlachten ließen, bekennt sie. „Wir haben das ganze Blabla durchbrochen. Wir haben eine gewisse Ermutigung für die Linke dargestellt, die freilich wieder den Bach 'runtergegangen ist, weil sie uns alle verhaftet haben."

In December, 1972, for example, Ulrike Meinhof of the West German "Red Army Faction" appeared between a judicial hearing and spoke up publicly for the Good Old Cause of revolutionary extermination. "How was Auschwitz possible, what was anti-Semitism?" she asked from the dock. According to a newspaper account:

> People should have explained that, instead of accepting Auschwitz collectively as an expression of evil. The worst of it is that we were all agreed about it, Communists included. But now she [Meinhof] had recognized that anti-Semitism was essentially anti-capitalist. It absorbed the hatred of men for their dependence on money as a means of exchange, and their longing for communism...

How much was socialism, and how much national-socialism in her passionate defense?

> Auschwitz meant that six million Jews were killed, and thrown on the waste-heap of Europe, for what they were: money-Jews (Geldjuden). Finance capital and the banks, the hard core of the system of imperialism and capitalism, had turned the hatred of men against money and exploitation, and against the Jews. The failure of the Left, of the Communists, had lain in not making these connections plain...

And so Marxism and racialism could be proposed once more as philosophical comrades, in our own times, and the link yet again made plain:

> Germans were anti-Semitic, and that is why they nowadays support the Red Army Fraction. They have not yet recognised all this, because they have not yet been absolved of fascism and the murder of the Jews. And they have not yet been told that anti-Semitism is really a hatred of capitalism.

"Unless we absolve the German people of fascism—that the people really didn't know what was going on in the concentration camps—they can't be mobilized for our struggle," she said. After the war, the left, in dealing with fascism, were "negligent, stupid, and insolent." They dealt with the people in the foreground, but didn't look any deeper. "How was Auschwitz possible; what was antisemitism?" That is something that someone should have clarified at the time. Instead of collectively understanding Auschwitz as an expression of evil, Meinhof stated.

"The worst thing is that all of us, communists as well as others, were united in this." However, she now recognizes that antisemitism can in it's own way be anticapitalist. It separates the hatred of people about their dependency on money as a means of exchange from their desire for communism.

"Auschwitz meant that six million Jews were murdered and carted off to Europe's garbage heap, dispensed with as money Jews." Finance capital and banks, "the hard core of the system" of imperialism and capitalism deflected the hate of the people for money and oppression from itself and transferred it to the Jews. Not having made this connection clear was the failure of the left and the communists.

Germans were antisemitic, therefore they are today RAF supporters. Only they don't know it, because they've forgotten that they must be absolved of fascism and murdering Jews, and that antisemitism is in reality hatred of capitalism. In this regard Ulrike Meinhof ably constructed a remarkable statement about the failure of the Baader-Meinhof Group. With it, it is also possible to praise the Black September attack in Munich. She claimed to feel an "historical identity" with the Jews of the Warsaw Ghetto, who attempted an unarmed uprising leading to their defeat. "We have broken through the entire blah blah. We have provided the left with obvious encouragement, which they have voluntarily allowed to dissipate, because we've all been arrested."

The European Commission of Human Rights and the RAF Prisoners

In its July 8, 1978 decision, the European Commission of Human Rights noted the following effects on the health of Gudrun Ensslin, Jan-Carl Raspe, and Andreas Baader as a result of their prolonged imprisonment under conditions of single or small-group isolation:

(i)   *State of health*

In September 1975:
19. The applicants are in a state of physical and mental exhaustion (Dr. Mende). Their blood pressure is low. Their weight is about 70% of that of a normally healthy person of the same age and build (Dr. Müller). They present the following symptoms in varying degrees: problems of concentration, marked fatigue, difficulties of expression or articulation, reduced physical and mental performance, instability, diminished spontaneity and ability to make contacts, depression (especially noted by Dr. Rasch).

In April 1977:
20. The decline in both physical and mental health is very pronounced in Ensslin (concurring opinion by Dr. Rasch, Dr. Müller, and Dr. Schröder): loss of weight, very low blood pressure, premature aging, severe difficulties of expression and lack of concentration, motor disturbances. The deterioration in the condition of Baader and Raspe is perceptible, though less spectacular: decrease in activity and spontaneity, emotional regression, problems of articulation, hesitancy in speech. They are nevertheless fit for detention.

21. *The experts ascribe the applicants' state of health to a series of factors and circumstances: the particular conditions of their imprisonment, the length of the detention on remand, hunger strikes, tension generated by the trial and the applicants' wish to defend themselves, etc.. The importance attached to these different factors varies from one report to another.*

The particular conditions of imprisonment

22. *There is no sensory isolation strictly speaking, such as can be brought about by a substantial reduction in stimulation of the sensory organs. On the other hand, the applicants are subjected to evident social isolation. The international literature on criminology and psychology indicates that isolation can be sufficient in itself to gravely impair physical and mental health. The following conditions may be diagnosed: chronic apathy, fatigue, emotional instability, difficulties of concentration, diminution of mental faculties, disorders of the neuro-vegetative system. Opinions differ on the precise scale of these phenomena. There are no reports in the literature of situations comparable to that of the applicants (Dr. Rasch), affording a better assessment of the psychiatric effects. From the standpoint of internal medicine, certain analogies can be found in case-studies of elderly and isolated persons, persons kept alive artificially in intensive care units, and long-term prisoners (Dr. Müller and Dr. Schröder). However, certain experts state that they have little personal experience of the physical and mental effects of normal imprisonment (Dr. Müller and Dr. Schröder).*

From: European Commission of Human Rights, *Decisions and Reports* 14 (Strasbourg: June 1979), 96-97. As wikipedia tells us, "From 1954 to the entry into force of Protocol 11 of the European Convention on Human Rights, individuals did not have direct access to the European Court of Human Rights; they had to apply to the Commission, which if it found the case to be well-founded would launch a case in the Court on the individual's behalf. Protocol 11 which came into force in 1998 abolished the Commission, enlarged the Court, and allowed individuals to take cases directly to it."

The FRG and the State of Israel

In order to appreciate the relationship between the West German radical left and the Palestinian resistance, it may be helpful to take a brief look at the history of West German support for Israel.

Although the two countries did not exchange embassies until the mid-1960s, there had been contact and cooperation well before then. Throughout this period, this contact was understandably marked by the recent genocide that had almost ended Jewish civilization in Europe, and had led to the creation of the Israeli colonial state in 1949. Contrary to expectations, however, the two countries would quickly become close allies, for regardless of the feelings of many citizens, each one had its own reasons to use the Holocaust as a stepping-stone to future goals.

The first official agreement between the two governments came about in 1952, when the FRG signed the Luxembourg Agreement, promising to deliver a total of three billion marks worth of reparations (mainly in the form of goods) to Israel over a period of fourteen years.[1] The FRG was literally building the Israeli economy, helping to provide the West with its beachhead in the Middle East.

By the end of the decade, the Luxembourg Agreement was supplemented by a plan to give—not sell—arms and materiel to the Israeli military. What started as motor vehicles, training aircraft, and helicopters was soon extended to include anti-tank rockets and other shooting weapons.[2] By the mid-sixties, the FRG was delivering "aircraft including Noratlas transporters, Dornier DO-27 communication planes and French 'Fouga Magister' jet trainers, anti-aircraft guns with electronic homing devices, helicopters, howitzers, submarines, and speedboats."[3] Some claimed that 5,000 Israeli officers and soldiers had been trained by the *Bundeswehr* in West Germany.[4]

---

1 George Lavy, *Germany and Israel: Moral Debt and National Interest* (London: Frank Cass, 1996), 11.

2 Ibid., 53.

3 Ibid., 56.

4 Deutsche-Arabische Gesellschaft der DDR, *Friend and enemy of the Arabs: facts on the attitude of the GDR and of West Germany on the imperialist aggression of*

Right from its inception, Israel was engaged in ethnic cleansing: harassing, terrorizing, and murdering Palestinians in order to free up more land for Jewish settlers. Through its financial and military assistance, the FRG was directly complicit with this process, almost right from the start.

Unlike the reparations payments, the military aid and training was kept strictly secret. The Israeli government feared that its own population, which included a large number of Holocaust survivors, would vote them out of office if they learned that they were being armed and trained by the very Germans who so recently had carried out genocide against their people. The West German government was also wary of domestic repercussions, as the idea of getting involved in an international flashpoint like the Middle East was expected to be unpopular so soon after the Second World War. But much more importantly, the West German government was worried that such military support would alienate Arab governments, especially Egypt, perhaps even pushing them closer to the Soviet Bloc.

As it turns out, this is exactly what happened.

On October 26, 1964, the *Frankfurter Rundschau* broke the story. Despite initial denials from both Bonn and Tel Aviv, within days, both governments were forced to admit that military arms and training had been provided since 1959. Reaction across the Arab world was quick in coming, one Egyptian journalist observing that "Germany, who wants to make up for the sins of the Nazi regime, makes the Arabs pay with their security."[5] Within a year, Egypt's Nasser had arranged for the East German leader Walther Ulbricht to visit Cairo, and the FRG's contacts throughout the Arab world suffered greatly.

Nevertheless, though the arms shipments were cut off in 1965, the FRG remained Israel's staunchest European ally. The opportunity to prove this came soon enough.

On June 5, 1967, Israel attacked Egyptian forces in the Sinai and the Gaza Strip with air strikes and tanks, beginning what became known as the Six Day War. (Just two weeks previously, the FRG had delivered a final shipment of 800 troop transports.)[6] Soon, both Syria and Jordan entered the conflict in support of Egypt. Nevertheless, thanks

---

Israel against the Arab States, (Dresden, German Democratic Republic: German-Arab Society of the GDR, 1967), 20.

5 Muhammad Heikal in Lavy, 100.

6 Deutsche-Arabische Gesellschaft der DDR, 21.

to its far greater military capacity, Israel quickly routed all three Arab armies, seizing the Golan Heights, the Sinai Peninsula, the West Bank, and the Gaza Strip. As a measure of the military imbalance, barely 1,000 Israeli soldiers lost their lives in this conflict, compared to over 11,000 Egyptians, 700 Jordanians, and 2,500 Syrians.

Hundreds of thousands of Palestinians fled the newly occupied territories, swelling the numbers in the hellish Jordanian refugee camps, while over 600,000 remained as newly colonized subjects of the racist Israeli state.

Back in the FRG, the Six Day War provided the occasion for a strangely unhealthy—but highly revealing—identification with the Israeli aggressors. The SPD, the CDU, and the Springer Press all went into overdrive, whipping up war frenzy throughout the country, even as Bonn professed that it would not intervene. As Chancellor Kiesinger, the former Nazi, explained it, "our non-intervention, i.e. neutrality in the sense of international law, cannot mean moral indifference or indolence of the heart."[1]

City governments sent hundreds of thousands of marks in donations, and hundreds of thousands more were contributed by individual citizens to the German-Israeli Society,[2] while the West German Federation of Trade Unions invested three million marks in Israeli bonds, "as a visible expression of solidarity with and confidence in Israel."[3] Parallel to this, development aid credits to Israel's Arab neighbors were frozen and German development aid workers were flown home.[4]

Hundreds of volunteers were recruited and flown from Munich and the NATO Rhine-Main Airport to support Israel in the war zone.[5] While the West German government insisted that these volunteers were only engaged in "non-military" activities, East German newspapers claimed that many were in fact serving as soldiers.[6]

In newspapers and magazines, most especially the Springer Press, the Israeli attack was described in eerily nostalgic terms. Defense Minister Moshe Dayan was praised as a new "desert fox,"[7] a term that had previ-

---

1 Lavy, 150.

2 Deutsche-Arabische Gesellschaft der DDR, 32

3 Lavy,153.

4 Deutsche-Arabische Gesellschaft der DDR, 34.

5 Lavy, 150; Deutsche-Arabische Gesellschaft der DDR, 31.

6 Deutsche-Arabische Gesellschaft der DDR, 31.

7 Lavy, 155.

ously been reserved for Erwin Rommel, Hitler's Commander-in-Chief in North Africa. Israel was now the "brother nation," with the Israelis dubbed the "Prussians of the Middle East," and Jerusalem being "the Berlin of the Middle East."[8] The Israeli offensive was approvingly referred to as a "Blitzkrieg," and in *Spiegel* it was announced that "Jews are not as anti-Semites wanted to see them. On the contrary, danger seems not to develop the evil but the noble qualities"—which is the kind of compliment that isn't one, when you think about it. A *Die Welt* writer was similarly forthright, admitting that Israel had "overcome our anti-Semitism."[9]

Other than actual neo-nazis, the only German support for the Palestinian side at this time came from the APO. The SDS was already pro-Palestinian,[10] but it was this war frenzy that pushed the entire New Left to become anti-Zionist.[11] This fact, along with the odd identification with Israel on the part of the militaristic German right-wing, should be remembered when considering the assertion comrades would soon make that Israel represented the "new Nazism": while obviously incorrect, such a claim was at least partly a reaction against a reinvigorated German chauvinism projecting itself onto the racist Jewish state.

As such, anti-Zionism became a defining element of the radical left, and, as the 1970s dawned, it was shared by the K-groups, the *spontis*, and most certainly the guerilla.

---

8 Ibid., 154.

9 Ibid.,155.

10 Ibid.,156.

11 Jessica Benjamin and Anson Rabinbach, "Germans, Leftists, Jews," *New German Critique* 31, West German Culture and Politics (Winter 1984): 184.

The Geneva Convention: Excerpts

Art. 3. In the case of armed conflict not of an international character occurring in the territory of one of the High Contracting Parties, each Party to the conflict shall be bound to apply, as a minimum, the following provisions:

1. (1) Persons taking no active part in the hostilities, including members of armed forces who have laid down their arms and those placed hors de combat by sickness, wounds, detention, or any other cause, shall in all circumstances be treated humanely, without any adverse distinction founded on race, colour, religion or faith, sex, birth or wealth, or any other similar criteria.

    To this end the following acts are and shall remain prohibited at any time and in any place whatsoever with respect to the above-mentioned persons:
    (a) violence to life and person, in particular murder of all kinds, mutilation, cruel treatment and torture;
    (b) taking of hostages;
    (c) outrages upon personal dignity, in particular humiliating and degrading treatment;
    (d) the passing of sentences and the carrying out of executions without previous judgment pronounced by a regularly constituted court, affording all the judicial guarantees which are recognized as indispensable by civilized peoples.

    (2) The wounded and sick shall be collected and cared for.
    An impartial humanitarian body, such as the International Committee of the Red Cross, may offer its services to the Parties to the conflict.
    The Parties to the conflict should further endeavour to bring into force, by means of special agreements, all or part of the other provisions of the present Convention.
    The application of the preceding provisions shall not affect the legal status of the Parties to the conflict.

Art. 4. Persons protected by the Convention are those who, at a given moment and in any manner whatsoever, find themselves, in case of a conflict or occupation, in the hands of a Party to the conflict or Occupying Power of which they are not nationals.

Nationals of a State which is not bound by the Convention are not protected by it. Nationals of a neutral State who find themselves in the territory of a belligerent State, and nationals of a co-belligerent State, shall not be regarded as protected persons while the State of which they are nationals has normal diplomatic representation in the State in whose hands they are.

The provisions of Part II are, however, wider in application, as defined in Article 13.

Persons protected by the Geneva Convention for the Amelioration of the Condition of the Wounded and Sick in Armed Forces in the Field of 12 August 1949, or by the Geneva Convention for the Amelioration of the Condition of Wounded, Sick and Shipwrecked Members of Armed Forces at Sea of 12 August 1949, or by the Geneva Convention relative to the Treatment of Prisoners of War of 12 August 1949, shall not be considered as protected persons within the meaning of the present Convention.

Art. 13. The provisions of Part II cover the whole of the populations of the countries in conflict, without any adverse distinction based, in particular, on race, nationality, religion or political opinion, and are intended to alleviate the sufferings caused by war.

Art. 17. The Parties to the conflict shall endeavour to conclude local agreements for the removal from besieged or encircled areas, of wounded, sick, infirm, and aged persons, children and maternity cases, and for the passage of ministers of all religions, medical personnel and medical equipment on their way to such areas.

Art. 130. The detaining authorities shall ensure that internees who die while interned are honourably buried, if possible according to the rites of the religion to which they belonged and that their graves are respected, properly maintained, and marked in such a way that they can always be recognized.

Deceased internees shall be buried in individual graves unless unavoidable circumstances require the use of collective graves. Bodies may be cremated only for imperative reasons of hygiene, on account of the religion of the deceased or in accordance with his expressed wish to this effect. In case of cremation, the fact shall be stated and the reasons given in the death certificate of the deceased. The ashes shall be retained for safe-keeping by the detaining authorities and shall be transferred as soon as possible to the next of kin on their request.

As soon as circumstances permit, and not later than the close of hostilities, the Detaining Power shall forward lists of graves of deceased internees to the Powers on whom deceased internees depended, through the Information Bureaux provided for in Article 136. Such lists shall include all particulars necessary for the identification of the deceased internees, as well as the exact location of their graves.

APPENDIX V

Strange Stories:
Peter Homann and Stefan Aust

A former *Spiegel* journalist, Peter Homann was amongst those who traveled to Jordan for training in 1970. According to his friend Stefan Aust, also a friend of Ulrike Meinhof when she worked at *konkret*, Homann had become estranged from the RAF at this time, and the group had even threatened to execute him.

Even more outrageously, upon his return Homann claimed to have learned of a harebrained plan to send Ulrike Meinhof's seven-year-old twin daughters to be raised as orphans in Al Fatah's Children's Home in Amman.

Homann apparently informed Aust of this bizarre plan, and the two men set about tracking down the Meinhof twins, eventually finding them in the care of some Italian hippies. The twins were rescued and sent back to live with their father Klaus Rainer Röhl in the FRG. According to Aust, the RAF subsequently tried to kill Homann as revenge for this intervention.

This story became quite well known following the publication of Aust's book *Der Baader-Meinhof Komplexe* in 1985, a massive tome that quickly became the standard reference for the RAF's history up to 1977.[1] By that time, many of those who could either confirm or deny these allegations were no longer alive.

As such, and with some consternation, even sympathizers were left with no choice but to believe this version of events. Whether one supported the RAF or not, it seemed clear that the group had embarked upon a very bad childcare strategy to say the least. Even those who did not like Aust's politics could nevertheless be glad that he and Homann had acted when they did.

Indeed, one of Meinhof's daughters, Bettina Röhl, clearly accepts this story as true. Her own anger at what her mother allegedly planned

---

1 With some hesitation, we ourselves have used this book as a major source in our own research. While Aust is no sympathiser, his work is unparalleled in its detail.

for her has fueled a vendetta she wages to this day against all those she suspects of having colluded with the guerilla struggle.

However, in 2007, new information was brought to light by historian Jutta Ditfurth. In a sympathetic biography of Meinhof, Ditfurth claims that Homann and Aust's entire story was nothing but an elaborate lie.[1]

According to Ditfurth, the fate of the Meinhof-Röhl children was still before the family courts at the time of this alleged rescue, and there was a strong chance custody would be granted to Meinhof's older sister Inge Wienke Zitzlaff, a school principal in Hessen who had two daughters of her own.

Ditfurth claims this plan had been made before Ulrike Meinhof ever went underground in 1970, and that as a backup, were the family court to rule in Röhl's favor, some thought had been given to sending the twins to East Germany.

As Ditfurth points out, at the time of this alleged plot to send the children to Jordan, it was clear to all concerned that that country was on the brink of civil war. Indeed, within a month of the guerillas' return to the FRG, war did break out, leading to the slaughter of between 4,000 and 10,000 Palestinians. The Children's Home—where Homann and Aust claim the girls would have been sent—was one of the targets bombed by the Jordanian air force, leaving no survivors.

Obviously, Ditfurth's research does more than simply show Ulrike Meinhof in a very different and far more human light. It also provides a far more credible explanation as to why, in early 1972, the RAF would castigate Homann for turning against them: if Meinhof was not in fact planning to abandon her children, then Homann's intervention amounted to an actual kidnapping, one which wrecked Meinhof's carefully laid plans for her daughters.

We do not know the truth of this matter. We have always been aghast at this story of the RAF planning to exile two young children to dangerous and unfamiliar surroundings. We have no desire to whitewash such a plan if it did in fact exist. That said, Ditfurth's recent research makes a lot more sense than the previous Aust-Homann story, and while this does not itself prove its accuracy, it certainly gives us occasion for pause and consideration.

As with so much in this story, readers will have to make up their own minds.

---

1 Ditfurth, 290-292.

The German Guerilla's Palestinian Allies: Waddi Haddad's PFLP (EO)

Though many accounts of the Entebbe and Mogadishu skyjackings claim that they were carried out by the Popular Front for the Liberation of Palestine, led at the time by Dr. George Habash, this is not the case.

Rather, they, as well as the 1975 attack on the OPEC Conference in Vienna, were all organized by Dr. Waddi Haddad and carried out by members of Haddad's PFLP (External Operations)[2] group. While many observers assume the PFLP (EO) and PFLP were the same organization, this belief is not supported by most serious histories.

Along with Habash, Waddi Haddad had been a founding member of the Popular Front for the Liberation of Palestine, and the Arab National Movement before it. As the PFLP moved rapidly leftwards in the period following the Six Day War, Haddad came to represent old guard hostility to the Front's new Marxist-Leninist orientation.[3] At the same time, he was the politburo member charged with establishing the PFLP's External Operations branch, responsible for armed activities outside of Israel/Palestine.[4] Such activities took on great importance in the wake of Israel's 1967 victory.

Thus, one possible source of confusion is that the PFLP (EO) was originally part of the PFLP and acted with its approval.

The External Operations branch, acting under the authority of the PFLP, carried out the Dawson's Field skyjackings in 1970, precipitating the civil war in Jordan.[5] Given the disaster this ended up inflicting on the Palestinians—thousands of civilians killed, and the expulsion of the guerilla from the country—"external operations" fell into disfavor.

---

2 Also known as PFLP (Special Operations Group) and PFLP-COSE.

3 Yezid Sayigh, *Armed struggle and the Search for State: the Palestinian National Movement, 1949-1993* (Oxford: Clarendon Press 1997), 232.

4 Ibid.

5 Cf 56.

In this moment of retreat and demoralization, many militants urged that skyjackings and attacks on civilians be repudiated: a PFLP "conference of the leftist phenomenon" argued in February 1972 that hijackings in particular represented "a fundamental point of dispute between the Left and Right in the PFLP... not only because they contradicted adherence to Marxist-Leninist theory, but also because they invited much damage to the Palestinian revolution."[1]

For Haddad, however, operations in Europe and elsewhere, whether against military or civilian targets, remained legitimate and useful weapons in the war against Zionism and imperialism.

According to some accounts, Haddad left or was ejected from the PFLP in 1972, taking the External Operations branch with him.[2] According to others, he remained a PFLP member for a number of years despite being marginalized, keeping the External Operations group active as an unsanctioned, rogue outfit.[3]

Authors who claim the PFLP (EO) post-72 was simply a deniable but unofficially sanctioned PFLP section do not appear credible, as they never seem able to provide any proof with which to substantiate their allegation. Rather, they exploit the two group's lack of hostility toward one another, stretching this to imply that they remained one and the same. Examples of these good relations include Haddad's continued contributions to the PFLP,[4] and the fact that Habash spoke at Haddad's funeral in 1978.

As a splinter group, the PFLP (EO) was deprived of the logistical and practical support it had previously enjoyed from the broader Palestinian national movement. This new situation was compensated for by the support Haddad subsequently received from various anti-American Arab governments—Iraq, Algeria, Libya, and the PDRY[5]—and eventually from the KGB, which was secretly supporting his activities by 1975.[6]

---

1 Sayigh, 300-301. Also: Helena Cobran, *The Palestinian Liberation Organization: People, Power and Politics* (Cambridge: Cambridge University Press, 1984), 148.

2 Cobran, 148.

3 For instance, Mongrel Media "Magnolia Pictures & Wild Bunch / Yalla Films Present Terror's Advocate, a Film by Barbet Schroeder," 9.
http://www.mongrelmedia.com/press/Terrors_Advocate/press_kit.pdf.

4 Sayigh, 305.

5 Ibid.

6 John Follain, *Jackal: The Complete Story of the Legendary Terrorist, Carlos The Jackal* (New York: Arcade Publishing, 1998), 281.

As part of the strategy of attacking targets outside of the Middle East, Haddad soon forged ties with a number of European anti-Zionist organizations, both legal and illegal. The Venezuelan adventurer Carlos who had joined Haddad's network in 1970, was prominent in this process, and was personally responsible for recruiting several activists from the Frankfurt radical scene, including Wilfried Böse, Brigitte Kuhlmann, and Johannes Weinrich, all founding members of the RZ.[7]

While both popular and left-wing accounts tend to attribute the Entebbe and Mogadishu skyjackings to the PFLP, the accounts attributing these operations to Haddad and the PFLP (EO) seem far better documented. We are convinced of this by simply cross-referencing various facts, and examining reports of Haddad's activities in this period.

While there is a frustrating dearth of English-language material examining the relations between the two groups, and the PFLP proper may have chosen not to dispel this confusion at the time, this does not change the fact that by 1972, the "regular" PFLP and Haddad's PFLP (EO) were two distinct organizations.

In late 1977, Waddi Haddad suddenly became afflicted with what seemed to be an aggressive type of leukemia. Despite the best efforts of doctors in Algeria and the German Democratic Republic, he died on March 28, 1978.

His funeral in Baghdad was attended by leaders from all sections of the Palestinian resistance.

In the thirty years since his death, it has been revealed that the controversial Palestinian guerilla commander was in fact poisoned by Mossad, the Israeli secret service. While the timing coincided with the Mogadishu skyjacking, it would seem that this assassination had been decided upon in the wake of Entebbe.[8]

As a publication of the U.S. Special Operations Command's Joint Special Operations University approvingly notes, "Upon his death, the organization he had headed dissolved, and attacks on Israel and Israeli interests declined precipitously."[9]

---

7 Schröm, 1-3.

8 Graham H. Turbiville, Jr., *Hunting Leadership Targets in Counterinsurgency and Counterterrorist Operations: Selected Perspectives and Experience* (Hurlburt Field, Florida: Joint Special Operations University Press, 2007),16.
https://jsoupublic.socom.mil/publications/jsou/
JSOU07-6turbivilleHuntingLeadershipTargets_final.pdf.

9 Ibid.

Dramatis Personae

Adenauer, Konrad: 1876-1967; 1945, founding member of CDU; 1949, Federal Chairman of the CDU; 1949-1963, Chancellor; 1951-1955, also Minister of Foreign Affairs.

Akache, Zohair: 1954-1977; member of the PFLP-EO; killed during the Mogadishu action.

Albertz, Heinrich: 1915-1993; clergyman; 1966-1967, Mayor of West Berlin, forced to resign in wake of Benno Ohnesorg killing; as requested by 2JM, accompanied the guerillas released in exchange for Peter Lorenz in 1974.

Albrecht, Susanne: b. 1951; 1977, joined the RAF; 1980, left the RAF and received asylum in the GDR; 1990, arrested and cooperated with police and prosecutors; 1996, released from prison.

Allnach, Kay-Werner: Member of the RAF; 1974, arrested.

Andrawes, Souhaila: b. 1953; 1977, injured and arrested during the Mogadishu action; 1978, sentenced to twenty years in prison in Somalia; 1980, pardoned; 1991, moved to Norway; 1994, arrested; 1995, extradited to Germany and sentenced to twelve years; 1997, transferred to Norway to complete her sentence; 1999, released from prison on health grounds.

Asdonk, Brigitte: b. 1949; founding member of the RAF; 1970, arrested; 1982, released from prison.

Augustin, Ronald: b. 1949; Dutch citizen; 1971, joined RAF; 1973, arrested; 1980, released from prison.

Aust, Stefan: b. 1946; journalist; 1994-2008, Editor-in Chief of *Spiegel*.

Azzola, Axel: lawyer for RAF prisoners; in 1976, following Meinhof's murder, he resigned his mandate claiming he feared for his life.

Baader, Andreas: 1943-1977; participated in the 1968 Frankfurt department store arsons; founding member of the RAF; 1972, arrested following May Offensive; 1977, killed in prison during the events of the German Autumn.

Bäcker, Hans-Jürgen: b. 1939; founding member of the RAF; 1970, suspected of acting as a police informant, broke with the RAF; 1971, arrested, charged with the 1970 liberation of Baader; 1974, acquitted.

Barz, Ingeborg: b. 1948; founding member of the RAF; 1972, left the RAF, but was never seen again; presumed dead.

Baumann, Michael "Bommi": b. 1948; founding member of the 2JM; 1975, broke with guerilla politics in his autobiography *Wie alles Anfing* (*Terror or Love?* in English translation); 1981, arrested in London and extradited to West Germany, sentenced to five years.

Becker, Eberhard: SPK attorney arrested at RAF safehouse in Hamburg on February 4, 1974.

Becker, Verena: b. 1953; 2JM member, received a six year sentence in 1974; 1975, released from prison as part of a prisoner exchange for CDU politician Peter Lorenz who had been kidnapped by the 2JM, joined the RAF before 1977; 1977, arrested, broke with the RAF in prison and cooperated with police and prosecutors; 1989, pardoned.

Beer, Henning: b. 1959; brother of Wolfgang Beer; 1979, joined the RAF; 1982, left the RAF and received asylum in the GDR; 1990, arrested and cooperated with police and prosecutors; 1995, released from prison.

Beer, Wolfgang: 1953-1980; brother of Henning Beer; RAF member; 1974, arrested; 1978, released from prison; 1980, died in a car accident while living underground.

Berberich, Monika: b. 1942; founding member of the RAF; 1970, arrested; 1976, escaped from prison, recaptured two weeks later; 1988, released from prison.

Böll, Heinrich: 1917-1985; novelist and *Gruppe 47* member; 1970-1972, President of the PEN Club of the FRG; 1972, won the Nobel Prize for Literature.

Bölling, Klaus: b. 1928; SPD member; 1974-1981, Speaker of the House and head of the Federal Press Service; federal government contact person with Mogadishu hijackers during the German Autumn.

Boock, Peter-Jürgen: b. 1951; c. 1975, joined RAF; 1980, broke with RAF; 1981, arrested, cooperated with police and prosecutors; 1998, pardoned.

Boock, Waltraud: RAF member; 1976, arrested in Vienna following a bank robbery, sentenced to fifteen years.

Böse, Wilfried: 1949-1976; founding member of the RZ; 1976, killed during the Entebbe hijacking.

Brändle, Reinhold: 1936-1977; Schleyer's bodyguard; 1977, killed by the RAF.

Brandt, Willy: 1913-1992; SPD politician; 1964, Federal Chairman of the SPD; 1966-1969, Minister of Foreign Affairs and Vice Chancellor; 1969-1974, Chancellor, 1974, Chairman of the Socialist International (Second International).

Braun, Bernhard: b. 1946; Associated with the SPK and subsequently with both the 2JM and the RAF; 1972, arrested following May Offensive.

Buback, Siegfried: 1920-1977; 1974-1977, Attorney General; 1977, assassinated by the RAF.

Buddenberg, Wolfgang: b. 1911; Federal Supreme Court Judge; 1972, targeted by a RAF car bomb that injured his wife Gerta.

Carlos (Ilich Ramírez Sánchez): b. 1949; guerilla mercenary closely tied to the Palestinian movement; 1994, arrested in Sudan and extradited to France; 1997, sentenced to life in prison; 2003, aligned himself with fundamentalist Islam, stating his support for Osama bin Laden and the 9/11 attacks; 2005, adopted the name Salim Muhammad.

Cohn-Bendit, Daniel: b. 1945; 1968, leader of the French student uprising known as the May Revolution, expelled to West Germany; leading figure in the *sponti* movement in the seventies, and an early backer of the Green Party.

Croissant, Klaus: 1931-2002; lawyer for RAF prisoners; 1977, arrested and sentenced to two and a half years for supporting a terrorist organization; upon his release he would begin working for the *Stasi*, while running (unsuccessfully) on the Alternative List in the 1980s.

Dellwo, Hans-Joachim: brother of Karl-Heinz Dellwo; arrested 1977 on charges of supporting a criminal organization; cooperated with police and prosecutors; moved to Canada upon his release from prison.

Dellwo, Karl-Heinz: b. 1952; 1974, joined RAF; part of the Holger Meins Commando that carried out the failed Stockholm embassy hostage taking in 1975; received two life sentences in 1977; 1995, released from prison.

Drenkmann, Günter von: 1910-1974; social democratic president of West Berlin Supreme Court; killed during an attempted kidnapping by the 2JM, meant to avenge the death of Holger Meins.

Dyck, Elisabeth von: 1951-1979; member of the SPK, assistant to RAF lawyer Klaus Croissant and subsequently suspected RAF member; 1975, went underground; 1979, shot dead by police.

Dregger, Alfred: 1920-2002; CDU member; 1956-1970, Mayor of Fulda; 1982-1991, Chairman of the CDU/CSU Federal Parliamentary Faction.

Dümlein, Christine: b. 1949; 1975, joined the RAF; 1980, left the RAF and received asylum in the GDR; 1990, arrested and cooperated with police and prosecutors, released after one day as the only crime she was guilty of was membership in a terrorist organization, and the statute of limitations had expired.

Dutschke, Rudi: 1940-1979; leading theorist for the SDS and the APO; 1968, victim of an assassination attempt; 1979, founding member of the Green Party, drowned the same year when he had a seizure while taking a bath.

Eckes, Christa: 1950-2012; RAF member; arrested February 4, 1974; 1984, arrested.

Eckhardt, Hans: 1922-1972; police officer; 1972, killed in an exchange of fire with RAF members.

Ensslin, Gudrun: 1940-1977; participated in the 1968 Frankfurt department store arsons; founding member of the RAF; 1972, arrested following May Offensive; 1977, killed in prison during the events of the German Autumn.

Epple, Richard: 1954-1972; 1972, killed by police who believed he was a RAF member when he ran a police checkpoint.

Filbinger, Hans: 1913-2007; former hardline Nazi judge; 1966-1978, CDU President of Baden-Württemberg.

Fischer, Joschka: b. 1948; leading figure in the *sponti* movement in the seventies; 1983-1985, Green Party member of parliament; 1991-1994, Minister of the Environment in Hessen; 1998-2005, Federal Minister of Foreign Affairs.

Folkerts, Knut: b. 1952; RAF member; 1977, arrested; 1995, released from prison.

Folkerts, Uwe: b. 1948; brother of Knut Folkerts, arrested May 4, 1977, found guilty of supporting a criminal organization and released after eighteen months.

Fried, Erich: 1921-1988; Austrian poet, *Gruppe 47* member.

Friedrich, Ralf Baptist: b. 1946; 1977, joined the RAF; 1980, left the RAF and received asylum in the GDR; 1990, arrested and cooperated with police and prosecutors.

Genscher, Hans-Dietrich: b. 1927; FDP politician; 1969-1974, Federal Minister of the Interior; 1974-1992, Federal Minister for Foreign Affairs.

Gnädinger, Fritz-Joachim: b. 1938; Federal Prosecutor; 1969-1975, SPD member of parliament.

Göbel, Wolfgang: 1947-1977; Buback's chauffeur; 1977, killed by the RAF.

Goemans, Johannes: 1954-1978; Dutch customs officer; 1978, killed in exchange of fire with RAF members.

Goergens, Irene: b. 1951; founding member of the RAF; 1970, arrested; 1977, released from prison.

Grashof, Manfred: b. 1946; 1970, joined RAF; 1972, arrested prior to the May Offensive, broke with the RAF in prison; 1988, pardoned.

Groenewold, Kurt: b. 1937; lawyer for RAF prisoners; 1975, subjected to the *Berufsverbot.*

Grundmann, Wolfgang: b. 1948; founding member of the RAF; 1972, arrested prior to the May Offensive; 1976, released from prison.

Grustadt, Eric: b. 1936; 1970, joined the RAF, arrested the same year.

Haag, Siegfried: b. 1944; 1972, served as lawyer for Andreas Baader; 1975, went underground; 1976, arrested, alleged to have organized both the 1975 Stockholm action and the 1977 offensive; broke with the RAF in prison; 1987, released from prison.

Haddad, Waddi: 1927-1978; 1967-1970, leading figure in the PFLP's military wing; expelled from the PFLP at some point in the 1970s; at some point between 1970 and 1972 established the PFLP (EO) as a body separate from the PFLP; 1977, poisoned by the Mossad, succumbs in 1978.

Hammerschmidt, Katharina: 1943-1975; 1970, RAF supporter; 1972, turned herself in following May Offensive; 1974, released from prison for health reasons; 1975, died of cancer.

Hansen, Hans-Wilhelm: police officer killed in 1978 in a firefight with RAF members.

Harb, Nabil: 1954-1977; member of the PFLP (EO); killed during the Mogadishu action.

Hausner, Siegfried: 1952-1975; SPK member, joined RAF; 1972, arrested following May Offensive and sentenced to three years; 1974, released from prison; 1975, led the Holger Meins Commando's hostage taking at the FRG embassy in Stockholm; died as a result of injuries sustained during this action.

Heinemann, Gustav: 1899-1976; 1949-1950, Federal Minister of the Interior for the CDU; 1952, left the CDU to co-found the GVP; 1957, joined the SPD; 1966-1969, Federal Minister of Justice; 1969-1974, President.

Heißler, Rolf: b. 1948; 1970-971, member of the Tupamaros-Munich; 1975, joined the RAF after release from prison as part of a prisoner exchange for CDU politician Peter Lorenz who had been kidnapped by the 2JM; 1979, arrested; 2001, released from prison.

Helbing, Monika: b. 1953; 1977, joined the RAF; 1980, left the RAF and received asylum in the GDR; 1990, arrested and cooperated with police and prosecutors; 1995, released from prison, living under a new name.

Heldmann, Hans-Heinz: Lawyer for RAF prisoners.

Herold, Horst: b. 1923; 1967-1971, President of the Nuremberg Police; 1971-1981, President of the BKA.

Hillegaart, Heinz: 1911-1975; Foreign Service Diplomat; 1975, killed during the Stockholm action.

Hoff, Dierk: b. 1948; 1971-1972, built items the RAF used in bombings, claimed to believe they were movie props; 1975, arrested and turned state evidence in exchange for the charges against him being dropped.

Hofmann, Sieglinde: b. 1945; 1976, joined the RAF; 1980, arrested in Paris and extradited to West Germany; 1999, released from prison.

Homann, Peter: b. 1936; founding member of the RAF; 1970, broke with the RAF.

Hoppe, Werner: b. 1949; 1970, joined the RAF; 1971, arrested; 1979, released from prison on grounds of ill health.

Jansen, Ali: b. 1948; 1970, joined RAF, arrested the same year and sentenced to ten years in prison.

Jendrian, Günter: taxi driver; 1974, killed by police who believed he was a RAF member.

Jong, Dirk "Dionysius" de: 1959-1978; Dutch customs officer; 1978, killed in exchange of fire with RAF members.

Jünschke, Klaus: b. 1947; member of the SPK; 1972, joined RAF, arrested following May Offensive; broke with the RAF in prison; 1988, pardoned.

Kiesinger, Kurt Georg: 1904-1988; CDU politician; 1958-1966, President of Baden-Württemberg; 1966-1969, Chancellor; 1967-1971, Federal Chairman of the CDU.

Klar, Christian: b. 1952; 1976, joined the RAF; 1982, arrested; 1985, received five life sentences plus fifteen years in prison; 2007, denied clemency; 2008, released from prison.

Klein, Hans-Joachim: b. 1947; 1974, joined the RZ; 1975, seriously injured participating in the Vienna OPEC action, left the guerilla, issuing a critical assessment and mailing it with his weapon to *Spiegel*; 1979, released a book critically assessing the guerilla struggle; 1998, arrested in France and extradited to Germany, acted as a crown witness to avoid a life sentence and was sentenced to nine years; 2003, pardoned.

Knoll, Michael: 1949-1978; Member of the RAF; 1978, killed in an exchange of fire with the police.

Krabbe, Friederike: b. 1950; younger sister of Hanna Krabbe; SPK member; allegedly joined RAF prior to 1977 and participated in Schleyer kidnapping; never captured.

Krabbe, Hanna: b. 1945; sister of Friederike Krabbe; SPK member; 1974, joined RAF; part of the Holger Meins Commando that carried out the failed Stockholm embassy hostage taking in 1975; received two life sentences in 1977; 1996, pardoned and released from prison.

Krahl, Hans-Jürgen: 1943-1970; leading theorist in the SDS and the APO; 1970, died in a car accident.

Kranenburg, Arie: 1931-1977; Dutch customs officer; 1977, killed in an exchange of fire with RAF members.

Kröcher-Tiedemann, Gabriele: 1951-1995; 2JM member; 1973, arrested; 1975, released from prison as part of a prisoner exchange for CDU politician Peter Lorenz who had been kidnapped by the 2JM; 1975, participated in the Vienna OPEC action; 1977, arrested in Switzerland for the shooting of two Swiss customs agents; 1987, extradited to West Germany; 1990, acquitted on charges related to the 1975 Vienna OPEC action; 1991, released from prison; 1995, died of cancer.

Kuby, Christine: RAF member, arrested in 1978; released 1995.

Kuhlmann, Brigitte: 1949-1976; founding member of the RZ; 1976, killed during the Entebbe action.

Kunzelmann, Dieter: b. 1939; Kommune 1 member, 1969, founding member of the Tupamaros-West Berlin; 1970, arrested; 1975, released from prison; 1983-1985, Alternative List member of parliament in West Berlin.

Kurras, Karl-Heinz: The undercover police officer who shot Benno Ohnesorg on June 2, 1967.

Lang, Jörg: b. 1950; lawyer who was arrested in 1972 on charges that he had helped recruit for the RAF; went underground in 1974; at one time accused, perhaps spuriously, of helping to organize the events of 1977; to the best of our knowledge, never captured.

Langhans, Rainer: b. 1940; Kommune 1 member.

Langner, Klaus Jürgen: lawyer for Margrit Schiller; his offices were firebombed in 1976.

Linke, Georg: Librarian; shot and seriously injured during the Baader breakout.

Lorenz, Peter: 1922-1987; 1969-1981, Berlin Chairman of the CDU; 1975, kidnapped by the 2JM and exchanged for five political prisoners.

Luther, Angela: b. 1940; 2JM member; worked with the RAF during 1972 May Offensive; participated in successful kidnapping of Peter Lorenz and prisoner exchange in 1975; never captured.

Mahler, Horst: b. 1936; founding member of the RAF; 1964, began acting as lawyer for the SDS and the APO; 1969, co-founded the Socialist Lawyers Collective; 1970, arrested; 1974, acrimoniously parted ways with the RAF in prison, affiliating himself with the KPD/AO; 1975, refused to leave prison as part of the Lorenz exchange; 1980, released from prison; 1997, publicly acknowledged his ties to the neo-nazi NPD; 2000, joined the NPD; 2003, founded the Holocaust denial organization, the VRBHV.

Maier-Witt, Silke: b. 1950; 1977, joined the RAF; 1980, left the RAF and received asylum in the GDR; 1990, arrested and cooperated with police and prosecutors; 1995, released from prison.

Maihofer, Werner: 1918-2009; FDP politician; 1972-1974, Federal Minister for Special Affairs; 1974-1978, Federal Minister of the Interior.

Marcisz, Heinz: 1936-1977; Schleyer's chauffeur; 1977, killed by the RAF.

Martin, Ludwig: 1909-2010; 1963-1974, Attorney General.

Mayer, Roland: RAF member; 1976, arrested.

McLeod, Ian: Scottish businessman, suspected of working as British intelligence agent; 1972, shot dead by police who believed he was a RAF member.

Meinhof, Ulrike: 1934-1976; founding member of the RAF; 1959, joined the illegal KPD; 1959-1969, *konkret* journalist, 1960-1964, Editor-in-Chief of *konkret*; 1964, left the KPD; 1972, arrested following May Offensive; 1976, killed in prison.

Meins, Holger: 1941-1974; 1969, joined Kommune 1, worked on *883*; 1970, joined RAF; 1972, arrested following May Offensive; 1974, died on hunger strike in prison.

Meyer, Till: b. 1944; founding member of the 2JM; 1972, arrested; 1973, escaped from prison; 1975, arrested; 1978, broken out of prison, arrested by West German police in Bulgaria the same year; 1986, released from prison; 1992, exposed as a *Stasi* agent.

Mirbach, Andreas von: 1931-1975; Military Attaché at the West German Embassy in Stockholm; 1975, killed during the Stockholm action.

Mohnhaupt, Brigitte: b. 1949; 1971, joined the RAF; 1972, arrested following May Offensive; 1977, released from prison, went back underground; 1982, arrested; 2007, released from prison.

Möller, Irmgard: b. 1947; 1971, joined the RAF; 1972, arrested following May Offensive; 1977, the only survivor of the Stammheim killings; 1994, released from prison.

Müller, Arndt: lawyer for RAF prisoners, 1977, arrested and charged with supporting a terrorist organization; 1980, sentenced to four years and eight months in prison.

Müller, Gerhard: b. 1948; SPK member; 1971, joined the RAF; 1972, arrested following May Offensive; 1974, served as a crown witness against RAF prisoners; served a six-and-a-half year sentence, upon his release was relocated to the U.S.A.

Negt, Oskar: b. 1934; Frankfurt School philosopher and social theorist; 1972, as a representative of the New Left and the APO developed a bitter critique of the RAF.

Newerla, Armin: Lawyer for RAF prisoners; 1977, arrested and charged with supporting a terrorist organization; 1980, sentenced to three years and six months in prison.

Oberwinder, Michael: lawyer for RAF prisoners.

Ohnesorg, Benno: 1940-1967; shot dead by an undercover police officer at an anti-Shah demonstration in West Berlin on June 2, 1967.

Payot, Denis: Swiss lawyer; 1977, acted as the intermediary between the RAF and the West German government during the German Autumn.

Pieler, Roland: 1957-1977; Schleyer's bodyguard; 1977, killed by the RAF.

Plambeck, Juliane: 1952-1980; founding member of the 2JM; 1975, arrested; 1976, broke out of prison; 1980, joined the RAF, died in a car accident the same year.

Pohl, Helmut: b. 1943; 1970, associated with the RAF; 1973, joined the RAF; 1974, arrested; 1979, released from prison and went back underground; 1984, arrested; 1998, pardoned after he suffered a stroke in prison.

Pohle, Rolf: 1942-2004; associated with both the RAF and the 2JM; 1971, arrested; 1975, released from prison as part of an prisoner exchange for CDU politician Peter Lorenz who had been kidnapped by the 2JM; 1976, arrested in Greece and extradited to West Germany; 1982, released from prison; 1984, returned to Greece.

Ponto, Jürgen: 1923-1977; chairman of the board of the Dresdner Bank; 1977, shot dead by the RAF during a bungled kidnapping attempt.

Prinzing, Theodor: b. 1923; 1974-1977, main judge in the Stammheim trial of RAF prisoners; 1977, forced to recuse himself when it was discovered he had been leaking classified trial documents.

Proll, Astrid: b. 1947; founding member of the RAF; 1971, arrested; 1973, released to a prison hospital for health reasons; 1974, escaped and fled to England where she lived under the name Anna Puttick; 1978, arrested in London and extradited to West Germany; 1980, sentenced to five-and-a-half years, but immediately released on the basis of time served.

Proll, Thorwald: b. 1941; brother of Astrid Proll; 1968, participated in the Frankfurt department store arsons, went underground when released awaiting the outcome of an appeal, but later turned himself in and served out his sentence.

Rabehl, Bernd: b. 1938; leading theorist for the SDS and the APO; 2005, began a public association with the neo-nazi NPD.

Raspe, Jan-Carl: 1944-1977; 1967, founding member of Kommune 2; 1970, joined the RAF; 1972, arrested following May Offensive; 1977, killed in prison during the events of the German Autumn.

Rauch, Georg von: 1947-1971; 1968, founding member of the Roaming Hash Rebels; 1970, arrested; 1971, killed in an exchange of fire with the police.

Rebmann, Kurt: 1924-2005; 1977-1990, Attorney General.

Reinders, Ralf: b. 1948; founding member of the 2JM; 1975, arrested; 1990, released from prison.

Röhl, Klaus Rainer: b. 1928; 1953, joined KPD; 1957, founded *konkret*; 1961, married Ulrike Meinhof; 1964, left the KPD; 1974, left *konkret*; 1981, took over *Spontan*; 1995, joined the FDP.

Roll, Carmen: SPK member, 1972, joined the RAF, arrested the same year prior to the May Offensive; 1976, released from prison, moved to Italy.

Rössner, Bernd: b. 1946; 1974, joined the RAF; part of the Holger Meins Commando that carried out the failed Stockholm embassy hostage taking in 1975; received two life sentences in 1977; 1992, released from prison on health grounds; 1994, pardoned.

Ruhland, Karl-Heinz: b. 1938; 1970, became close to the RAF, arrested the same year, becoming the first RAF associate to serve as a crown witness.

Scheel, Walter: b. 1919; Chairman of the FDP, 1968-1974; Vice-Chancellor and Foreign Minister during Willy Brandt's Social-Liberal Coalition (1969-1974); President during the first five years of Helmut Schmidt's administration (1974-1979).

Schelm, Petra: 1951-1971; 1970, joined RAF; 1971, killed in an exchange of fire with the police.

Schiller, Karl: 1911-1994; SPD politician; 1966-1972, Minister of the Economy; 1971-1972, Minister of Finance.

Schiller, Margrit: b. 1948; SPK member; 1971, joined the RAF, arrested; 1973, released from prison and went back underground; 1974, arrested; 1979, released from prison; 1985, moved to Cuba; 1993, moved to Uruguay; 2003, returned to Germany.

Schily, Otto: b. 1932; lawyer for RAF prisoners; 1980, founding member of the Green Party; 1989, left the Green party to join the SPD; 1994-1998, Chairman of the SPD Parliamentary Faction; 1998-2005, Federal Minister of the Interior; 2005, joined the boards of two biometric security firms.

Schleyer; Hanns Martin: 1915-1977; former SS member and leading West German industrialist; 1977, kidnapped and executed by the RAF during the German Autumn.

Schmid, Norbert: 1938-1971; police officer; 1971, killed in an exchange of fire with RAF members.

Schmidt, Helmut: b. 1918; SPD politician; 1967-1969, Chairman of the SPD Parliamentary Faction; 1969-1972, Federal Minister of Defense; 1972, Federal Minister of Economics; 1972-1974, Federal Minister of Finance; 1974-1982, Chancellor.

Schmitz, Sabine: b. 1956; joined RAF sometime in 1976, arrested that same year and charged under §129.

Schneider, Gert: Member of the RAF, 1977, arrested in Amsterdam and extradited to West Germany, sentenced to fifteen years in prison.

Scholze, Uli: b. 1947; 1970, joined the RAF, but left shortly thereafter.

Schoner, Herbert: 1939-1971; police officer; 1971, shot dead by RAF members robbing a bank.

Schubert, Ingrid: 1944-1977; founding member of the RAF; 1970, arrested; 1977, killed in prison.

Schulz, Adelheid: b. 1955; 1976, joined the RAF; 1982, arrested; 1998, released from prison on health grounds; 2002, pardoned.

Schumann, Jürgen: 1940-1977; pilot; 1977, killed during the Mogadishu action.

Siepmann, Ingrid: b. 1944; member of the 2JM; 1974, arrested; 1975, released from prison as part of a prisoner exchange for CDU politician Peter Lorenz who had been kidnapped by the 2JM; 1982, believed killed by Israeli airstrike in Lebanon.

Söhnlein, Horst: b. 1943; 1968, participated in the Frankfurt department store arsons, released while awaiting an appeal; 1969, turned himself in when the appeal was denied.

Sonnenberg, Günter: b. 1954; member of the RAF; 1977, arrested; 1992, released from prison.

Speitel, Angelika: b. 1952; RAF member; 1978, arrested; 1989, pardoned.

Speitel, Volker: b. 1950; RAF supporter; 1977, arrested, cooperated with police and prosecutors; 1979, released from prison.

Springer, Axel: 1912-1985; media magnate, owner of the Springer Press.

Stachowiak, Ilse "Tinny": b. 1954; 1970, joined the RAF; 1971, arrested, released the same year and went back underground; 1974, arrested.

Sternebeck, Sigrid: b. 1949; 1977, joined the RAF; 1980, left the RAF and received asylum in the GDR; 1990, arrested and cooperated with police and prosecutors.

Stoll, Willy Peter: 1950-1978; member of the RAF; 1978, shot dead by police.

Strauß, Franz Josef: 1915-1988; CSU politician; 1953-1955, Federal Minister for Special Affairs; 1955-1956, Federal Minister for Atomic Issues; 1956-1962, Federal Minister of Defense; 1966-1969, Federal Minister of Finance; 1978-1988, President of Bavaria.

Ströbele, Hans-Christian: b. 1939; lawyer for RAF prisoners; 1969, co-founder of the Socialist Lawyers Collective; 1978, founding member of the Alternative List; 1978, co-founder of the *taz*; 1985, joined the Green Party.

Sturm, Beate: b. 1950; 1970, joined the RAF; 1971, left the RAF, subsequently gave a number of interviews about the organization.

Taufer, Lutz: b. 1944; member of the SPK; 1975, joined the RAF; part of the Holger Meins Commando that carried out the failed Stockholm embassy hostage taking in 1975; received two life sentences in 1977; 1995, released from prison; 1999, moved to Brazil.

Teufel, Fritz: b. 1943; founding member of Kommune 1; founding member of the 2JM; 1975, arrested, sentenced to five years in prison.

Thimme, Johannes: 1956-1985; 1976, affiliated himself with the RAF support scene, served several prison sentences; 1985, killed when a bomb he was helping to plant exploded prematurely.

Ulmer, Helmut: 1953-1977; Schleyer's bodyguard; 1977, killed by the RAF.

Urbach, Peter: b. 1941; police infiltrator working in the milieu of the SDS and the APO in the late sixties, particularly close to members of Kommune 1, the 2JM, and the RAF; 1970, facilitated the arrest of Andreas Baader, after which he was provided with a new identity and relocated outside of West Germany.

Viett, Inge: b. 1944; founding member of the 2JM; 1972, arrested; 1973, broke out of prison; 1975, arrested; 1976, broke out of prison; 1980, joined the RAF; 1982, left the RAF and received asylum in the GDR; 1990, arrested, the only refugee in the GDR who would not provide evidence against other guerillas; 1997, released from prison.

Vogel, Andreas: 2JM member; 1976, arrested, sentenced to ten years in prison.

Wackernagel, Christof: b. 1951; 1977, joined the RAF, arrested the same year; 1983, broke with the RAF; 1987, released from prison.

Wagenbach, Klaus: b. 1930; founder of influential left press Wagenbach Publishers; 1976, read the eulogy at Ulrike Meinhof's funeral.

Wagner, Rolf Clemens: b. 1944; member of the RAF; 1979, arrested in Zurich, Switzerland and extradited to Germany; 2003, pardoned on health grounds; 2007, subject to investigation after stating in a interview that the Schleyer kidnapping was a legitimate action.

Weinrich, Johannes: b. 1947; founding member of the RZ; by the late seventies part of the Carlos group; 1995, arrested in Aden, Yemen and extradited to Germany, sentenced to life in prison.

Weissbecker, Thomas: 1949-1972; associated with Kommune 1, the Roaming Hash Rebels, the Tupamaros-West Berlin, the 2JM, and the RAF; 1971, arrested and acquitted; 1972, shot dead by police during a manhunt for the RAF.

Wessel, Ulrich: 1946-1975; member of the SPK; member of the RAF; 1975, killed during the Stockholm action he was participating in as a member of the Holger Meins Commando.

Wischnewski, Hans-Jürgen: 1922-2005; member of the SPD; 1959-1961, Chairman of the *Jusos*; 1966, Federal Minister for Economic Cooperation; 1970, member of the SPD's Executive Committee; 1974, Secretary of State; 1974-1976; Minister of State at the Department of Foreign Affairs; 1976-1979, Minister of State at the Federal Chancellery; 1977, government envoy to Third World countries during the German Autumn; 1979-1982, Deputy Chairman of the SPD; 1982, Minister of State at the Federal Chancellery.

Wisniewski, Stefan: b. 1953; 1975, joined the RAF; 1978, arrested at Orly Airport in Paris; 1999, released from prison.

Witter, Hermann: 1916-1991; Director of the Institute for Forensic Medicine and Psychiatry at University of Homburg/Saar.

Wurster, Georg: 1944-1977; Buback's bodyguard; 1977, killed by the RAF.

Zeis, Peter: Federal Prosecutor involved in the Stammheim trial against Andreas Baader, Gudrun Ensslin, Ulrike Meinhof, Holger Meins, and Jan-Carl Raspe.

Zitzlaff, Inge Wienke: b. 1931; Ulrike Meinhof's sister.

Armed Struggle in West Germany: A Chronology

1958

Leadership of the *Sozialistischer Deutscher Studentenbund* (Socialist German Students Federation, or SDS) won by activists significantly to the left of the SPD.

1961

The SDS and left-wing Society for the Promotion of Socialism are purged from the SPD.

1964

December 18, 1964
400 demonstrators greet Congolese President Moise Tschombe at the West Berlin airport. 150 protestors clash with the police in the streets of West Berlin. Rudi Dutschke will later claim this demonstration marked the beginning of the APO.

1966

April 9–11, 1966 (Easter Weekend)
Demonstrations against the Vietnam War occur throughout West Germany.

May 22, 1966
The SDS organizes a conference against the Vietnam War. Participants include Conrad Ahlers, Oskar Negt, Herbert Marcuse, and Jürgen Habermas. As a result of this conference, the SDS emerges as the key organization in the antiwar movement.

May 30, 1966
Student organizations hold a conference in Bonn against the *Notstandsgesetze* (Emergency Laws) being proposed by the government.

October 8, 1966
8,000-9,000 participate in a national congress to oppose the proposed Emergency Laws. 24,000 people participate in the closing demonstration.

December 1, 1966
The CDU/SPD Grand Coalition is formed.

December 10, 1966
In a closing speech at the Vietnam Weeks, SDS leader Rudi Dutschke proposes the formation of an extra-parliamentary opposition, which will become known as the APO. A demonstration at the close of the conference is brutally attacked by police.

1967

January 1, 1967
Kommune 1 founded in West Berlin. The first commune to come out of the student movement, it represents the anarchist tendency.

**March 25–27, 1967
(Easter Weekend)**
Demostrations occur throughout West Germany against the government's antidemocratic measures and against the Vietnam War.

April 5, 1967
Kommune 1 carries out a pudding attack on U.S. Vice President, Hubert Humphrey, in West Berlin, which is followed by arrests and an intense media smear campaign.

April 19, 1967
2,000 students participate in a sit-in at the Free University in West Berlin to protest the university's disciplinary measures against FU students arrested with Kommune 1 members in connection with the pudding attack against Hubert Humphrey on April 5.

April 21, 1967
With support from NATO, a coup establishes a far-right military junta in Greece.

May 12, 1967
Kommune 1 is expelled from the SDS.

May 20, 1967
The Republican Club, a meeting place for leftists, opens in West Berlin. Horst Mahler is a founding member.

May 24, 1967
Two days after a fire levels a Brussels department store, Kommune 1 members pass out a leaflet suggesting that burning department stores might not be such a bad way to advance the revolution. Fritz Teufel and Rainer Langhans are arrested and charged with inciting arson.

June 2, 1967
Student Benno Ohnesorg is shot and killed by undercover police officer Karl-Heinz Kurras during a demonstration against a visit by the Shah of Iran to West Berlin. Initially acquitted, Kurras is retried, convicted, and spends four months in jail. He is allowed to retain his job.

June 3–4, 1967
Protests of the killing of Benno Ohnesorg on June 2 are held at almost every university in West Germany. Violent clashes with the police occur in Hamburg.

June 5–11, 1967
Israel attacks Egyptian forces in Sinai and the Gaza Strip—Syria and Jordan soon enter the conflict in support of Egypt. Nevertheless, due to its greater military capacity, Israel routes all three Arab armies, in what is known as the Six Day

War. Hundreds of thousands
of Palestinians flee the newly
Occupied Territories, finding
their way to neighboring Jordan.
The Six Day War establishes anti-
Zionism as a key element of the
West German left.

September 5, 1967
At an SDS congress Rudi Dutschke
and Hans-Jürgen Krahl raise the
idea of the urban guerilla. This is the
first time the idea has been openly
discussed in the SDS or the APO.

October 21, 1967
10,000 people demonstrate in West
Berlin against the Vietnam War on
the same day as similar protests
take place around the world. There
are clashes with police in West
Berlin. Following the demonstration,
Andreas Baader and Astrid Proll lay
a bomb at America House. It fails to
detonate due to a technical failure.

1968
January 30, 1968
The Tet Offensive begins in Vietnam.
The offensive, which lasts two
months, is a turning point in the war,
forcing the U.S. into a defensive
position from which it will never
recover.

February 1–7, 1968
A week of violent student
demonstrations against the Vietnam
War sweeps West Germany.

February 2, 1968
At the Springer Tribunal at the
Critical University, Holger Meins
shows a film about how to make a
molotov cocktail. The Springer Press
refers to the Tribunal as an act of
fascist terror, comparing students to
Hitler's SA.

February 17–18, 1968
The International Congress on
Vietnam is held at the Technical
University in West Berlin. 12,000
people attend the closing
demonstration.

February 21, 1968
A demonstration organized by the
West Berlin Senate, the Federation
of Trade Unions, and the Springer
Press against the student movement
and in support of the U.S. war
against Vietnam draws 80,000. Many
participants carry placards reading
"Rudi Dutschke: Public Enemy
Number One" and "Berlin Must Not
Become Saigon."

April 1968
Georg von Rauch, Michael "Bommi"
Baumann, and others form the
Wieland Kommune in West Berlin.

April 3, 1968
Andreas Baader, Gudrun Ensslin,
Thorwald Proll, and Horst Söhnlein
firebomb 2 Frankfurt department
stores to protest the escalation of
the Vietnam War.

April 4, 1968
Andreas Baader, Gudrun Ensslin, Thorwald Proll, and Horst Söhnlein are arrested for the arsons of the previous day.
Martin Luther King is assassinated in Memphis, Tennessee.

April 11, 1968
Student leader Rudi Dutschke is shot three times, including once in the head, and seriously injured in West Berlin. The shooter, Josef Bachmann, is a young right-wing worker from Munich, who claims to have been inspired by the *Bild Zeitung*. The shooting sparks weeks of violent unrest, primarily directed against the Springer Press. In Munich, two demonstrators are killed in clashes with the police. Demonstrations and clashes occur for the rest of the month in cities throughout West Germany.

May 1968
Student mass demonstrations happen around the world: West Germany, France, Austria, Italy, Yugoslavia, England, Turkey, Brazil, Japan, the USA…

May 3–June 30, 1968
A student strike in Paris, France sets in motion events that will last until August, including widespread workers' strikes, mass demonstrations, street confrontations, and factory occupations, almost bringing down the Charles De Gaulle government.

May 5, 1968
Ulrike Meinhof argues in her weekly column in the influential left magazine *konkret* that the time has come to escalate from protest to resistance.

May 15–30, 1968
A wave of demonstrations against the proposed Emergency Laws sweeps West Germany.

May 30, 1968
In West Germany, the Emergency Laws become law. Student protests erupt all over the country. Police forcibly clear Frankfurt University.

May 31, 1968
80,000 people in more than 50 cities demonstrate to protest the adoption of the Emergency Laws.

June 28, 1968
The Emergency Powers Act is passed. A riot occurs at the Free University in West Berlin.

September 12–16, 1968
At the 23rd Delegates Conference of the SDS in Frankfurt, Heike Sanders of the Steering Committee for Women's Liberation intervenes to denounce the male authoritarian nature of the SDS and is booed down. When SDS leader Hans-Jürgen Krahl refuses to address the issue, women attack him with tomatoes, marking a fundamental first step in the development of the women's movement in West Germany and West Berlin.

October 14, 1968

The trial of Andreas Baader, Gudrun Ensslin, Thorwald Proll, and Horst Söhnlein for the April 3 department store arsons in Frankfurt begins.

October 30, 1968

Daniel Cohn-Bendit, who had been expelled from France for his leading role in the protests there earlier in the year, is arrested for disrupting the arson trial of Andreas Baader, Gudrun Ensslin, Horst Söhnlein, and Thorwald Proll.

October 31, 1968

The Frankfurt LG sentences Andreas Baader, Gudrun Ensslin, Thorwald Proll, and Horst Söhnlein to three years in prison for the April department store arsons in Frankfurt.

November 4, 1968

Following threats to disbar left-wing attorney Horst Mahler because of his participation in anti-Springer protests, students and police clash violently in an incident that will, after the name of the street it occurs on, become known as the Battle of Tegeler Weg.

1969

February 27, 1969

Richard Nixon visits West Berlin and is met with massive demonstrations and an unsuccessful bombing attempt against his motorcade. Kommune 1 members Dieter Kunzelmann and Rainer Langhans

are arrested for the attempted bombing. The bomb was supplied by *Verfassungsschutz* infiltrator Peter Urbach.

April 1, 1969

The *Sozialistisches Büro* is founded in Offenbach.

May 7, 1969

Because of political differences with her husband, *konkret* publisher Klaus Rainer Röhl, Ulrike Meinhof, at that time a *konkret* columnist, leads a group of thirty people who demolish the inside of his suburban Hamburg villa.

June 7, 1969

Young workers and apprentices demonstrate in Cologne. Their slogan is "Self-determination and class struggle instead of co-management and union crap."

June 13, 1969

Andreas Baader, Gudrun Ensslin, Thorwald Proll, and Horst Söhnlein, who had been sentenced for the April, 1968, department store arson, are released while their case is appealed.

Fall 1969

The urban guerilla groups Tupamaros-West Berlin and Tupamaros-Munich are formed. Dieter Kunzelmann and other members of the Tupamaros-West Berlin receive training in an Al Fatah (PLO) training camp in Jordan. There are six bombings in West Berlin.

September 2–19, 1969
Wildcat strikes occur in the mining, metal, energy, and car industries.

October 21, 1969
A new Social-Liberal coalition government of the SPD and the FDP is formed. Willy Brandt (SPD) is Chancellor, Gustav Heinemann (SPD) is President, and Walter Scheel (FDP) is Foreign Minister.

1970

February 12, 1970
Fifty-two psychiatric patients form the *Sozialistisches Patientenkollektiv* (SPK—Socialist Patients' Collective) in Heidelberg. The group's motto is "Turn Illness Into a Weapon."

March 21, 1970
At a meeting in Frankfurt the SDS Federal Association is dissolved by acclamation. A few local groups carry on for a short period.

April 4, 1970
Andreas Baader is arrested in West Berlin. While it first appears this was a "routine traffic stop", it is later revealed that he was in fact set up by police spy Peter Urbach.

May 14, 1970
An armed group breaks Andreas Baader out of the library of the Institute for Social Research, where he had obtained permission to work with Ulrike Meinhof on a book about juvenile detention centres. An Institute employee, Georg Linke,

is shot and seriously injured. This marks the beginning of the Red Army Faction (RAF).

May 20, 1970
In an amnesty, the new Social-Liberal Coalition pardons thousands of students who had been sentenced to up to nine months in prison for various offences committed at demonstrations.

June–August 1970
Twenty members of the RAF receive training in an Al Fatah (PLO) training camp in Jordan.

June 2, 1970
The West German press receives a communiqué claiming credit for breaking Baader out of prison on May 14.

June 5, 1970
In a statement entitled *Die Rote Armee aufbauen* (Build the Red Army), sent to the radical left magazine *883*, the RAF effectively announces its existence.

June 11, 1970
The so-called "Hand Grenade Law" is passed arming police with hand grenades, machineguns, and semi-automatic pistols.

September 17, 1970
Following a series of daring skyjackings by the PFLP's External Operations section, civil war breaks out in Jordan. The massacre of Palestinians at the hands of the

Jordanian forces will be known as Black September, different estimates placing Palestinian deaths at between 4,000 and 10,000. As a result of this defeat, the PFLP (EO) will eventually be ejected from the PFLP.

September 29, 1970
Three simultaneous bank robberies, carried out in cooperation with the Blues, an amorphous organization including members of the Tupamaros-West Berlin and the Roaming Hash Rebels, mark the RAF's first action. The robberies net 220,000 DM.

October 8, 1970
Acting on a tip-off, police raid two West Berlin apartments and arrest RAF members Horst Mahler, Irene Goergens, Ingrid Schubert, Monika Berberich, and Brigitte Asdonk. These are the first arrests of RAF members.

October 10, 1970
Hans-Jürgen Bäcker, suspected of being the snitch who gave away the location of the safehouses raided two days earlier, leaves the group. Shortly thereafter Uli Scholze, Ilse "Tinny" Stachowiak, Beate Sturm, and Holger Meins join the group.

November 16, 1970
City Hall in Neustadt is broken into, thirty-one official stamps, fifteen passports, and eleven ID cards are stolen.

November 21, 1970
City Hall in Lang-Gons is broken into; 166 ID cards, a bottle of cognac, and more than 430 DM are stolen.

December 4, 1970
RAF associate Eric Grustadt is arrested.

December 20, 1970
RAF associate Karl-Heinz Ruhland is arrested. He begins to cooperate immediately. Although he only knows RAF members by their code names, he will become a key witness in a series of RAF trials.

December 21, 1970
RAF members Ali Jansen and Uli Scholze are arrested in Nuremberg shortly after stealing a car. Astrid Proll and Ulrike Meinhof escape. Scholze is released the next day and leaves the RAF.

1971
January 15, 1971
Two banks in Kassel are simultaneously robbed by the RAF, netting an estimated 114,000 DM.

January 28, 1971
Minister of the Interior, Hans-Dietrich Genscher, announces a major manhunt for the RAF.

February 2, 1971
Hans-Jürgen Bäcker, who had left
the group after being accused
of being a snitch, is arrested and
charged with participating in the
Baader jailbreak.

February 10, 1971
RAF members Astrid Proll and
Manfred Grashof are shot at by
police in Frankfurt, but escape.
The Springer Press declares the RAF
to be "Public Enemy #1."

February 25, 1971
A seven year-old child is kidnapped,
and the media float the story that
his abductors are demanding
Mahler's freedom—it turns out this
is a lie, and young Michael Luhmer is
released two days later unharmed.

February 28, 1971
The BAW (Federal Prosecutors
Office) assumes responsibility for all
RAF-related cases.

April 1971
The RAF releases its foundational
manifesto, *Das Konzept
Stadtguerilla* (The Urban
Guerilla Concept).

April 12, 1971
RAF member Ilse "Tinny"
Stachowiak is arrested at the
Frankfurt train station.

April 13, 1971
RAF member Rolf Heißler is arrested
during a bank robbery in Munich.

April 25, 1971
Letters received from alleged
"left-wing kidnappers" claim
that Professor Berthold Rubin
and Rudolph Metzger had been
abducted, and demand Horst
Mahler's release from prison.
This later turns out to be a hoax
masterminded by far-right lawyer
Jürgen Rieger.

May 1971
*Über den bewaffneten Kampf
in Westeuropa* (Regarding the
Armed Struggle in West Europe),
a document signed The RAF
Collective, but entirely the work of
Horst Mahler, is released. The rest
of the RAF reject the document, and
the pursuant tension will eventually
lead to Horst Mahler being expelled
from the group.

May 6, 1971
RAF founding member Astrid Proll is
arrested in Hamburg.

May 18, 1971
The trial of Horst Mahler, Ingrid
Schubert, and Irene Goergens for
breaking Andreas Baader out from
the Institute for Social Reserach
Library begins. The trial will last
less than one month and Schubert
will receive a six-year sentence,
Goergens four years, and Mahler
will be acquitted though held in
custody as the state prepared other
charges.

June 24, 1971

SPK members exchange fire with the police at a traffic checkpoint, injuring one police officer. The SPK's office is raided that evening. The SPK dissolves itself, many of its members going underground and joining the RAF.

July 1971

RAF members meet with the Blues and Tupamaros-West Berlin members to discuss the possibility of organizational fusion. Thomas Weissbecker and Angela Luther express an interest and begin working with RAF members.

July 8, 1971

Blues members Thomas Weissbecker, Michael "Bommi" Baumann, and Georg von Rauch go to trial for beating *Quick* journalist Horst Rieck. Baumann and Weissbecker are released on bail. Von Rauch, facing other charges, with a possible ten year sentence, pretends to be Weissbecker (the two men strongly resemble each other) and leaves with Baumann. Weissbecker is later released by the embarrassed authorities. All three go underground. This marks the beginning of the process leading to the formation of the 2nd of June Movement (2JM), a West Berlin-based anarchist guerilla group.

July 15, 1971

During *Aktion Kobra* (Operation Cobra), a manhunt involving 3,000 police officers, RAF member Petra Schelm is shot and killed by the police at a Hamburg roadblock. Werner Hoppe is arrested and charged with attempted murder of a police officer.

July 25, 1971

The respected Allensbach Institute publishes a poll indicating that 20% of West Germans younger than thirty feel a certain sympathy for the RAF and 10% of the population in the North of West Germany would shelter a RAF member for a night.

September 1971

Respected left publisher Rotbuch releases Mahler's *Über den bewaffneten Kampf in Westeuropa* (Regarding the Armed Struggle in West Europe) in booklet form. It is promptly banned by the state.

September 1, 1971

Horst Herold is named head of the *Bundeskriminalamt* (Federal Criminal Bureau—BKA). He immediately begins centralizing the bureau and constructing what will become the most extensive police computer database in the world.

September 25, 1971

RAF members Margrit Schiller and Holger Meins exchange fire with the police in Freiburg. Police officer Friedrich Ruf is shot through the hand, and police officer Helmut Ruf (not related) is seriously injured.

October 21, 1971

During a routine traffic stop in West Berlin, a shootout occurs between Georg von Rauch and police officer Peter Mäker. Mäker is shot in the thigh, and von Rauch makes his escape.

Policeman Norbert Schmid is killed in a shootout with RAF members in Hamburg. RAF member Margrit Schiller is arrested in connection with the shooting in the early hours of the following morning. The shooter Gerhard Müller will later serve as a state witness in order to avoid being charged with murder.

November 1971

RAF prisoner Astrid Proll becomes the first prisoner to be held in the dead wing at Cologne-Ossendorf.

November 1, 1971

A bank robbery in Kiel is presumed to be the work of the RAF.

November 16, 1971

The BKA sets up the Baader-Meinhof Special Commission.

December 4, 1971

During a massive manhunt in West Berlin, following the discovery of a RAF safehouse, three Blues members are involved in a shootout with the police. Georg von Rauch is shot in the head and killed. Michael "Bommi" Baumann and another guerilla escape.

December 5, 1971

An estimated five to seven thousand people demonstrate in West Berlin to protest von Rauch's killing.

December 8, 1971

A vacant nurse's residence in West Berlin is occupied and named the Georg von Rauch House. It exists to this day, housing up to forty youth at any time.

December 17, 1971

Rolf Pohle is arrested while trying to buy guns in Neu-Ulm—the police claim the weapons were intended for the RAF.

December 22, 1971

RAF members Klaus Jünschke, Ingeborg Barz, and Wolfgang Grundmann rob a bank in Kaiserslautern, netting an estimated 134,000 DM. Police officer Herbert Schoner is shot dead when he stumbles upon the robbery.

December 1971–January 1972

In a series of meetings held at the Georg von Rauch House, members of the Blues, Tupamaros-West Berlin, the Roaming Hash Rebels, and the *Rote Ruhr Armee* decide upon fusion, forming the 2nd of June Movement (2JM).

1972

January 10, 1972

Spiegel publishes a letter from noted West German author Heinrich Böll in which he describes the

Springer Press coverage of the RAF as "naked fascism," making him a target of the right-wing media and the police for years to come.

January 28, 1972
The Interior Ministers Conference passes the *Radikalenerlass* (Anti-Radical Act), generally known as the *Berufsverbot* (Professional Ban), barring people with left histories from working at any level of the civil service, including in the field of public education.

February 21, 1972
RAF members dressed in full Carnival regalia rob a bank in Ludwigshafen, making off with 285,000 DM.

March 1, 1972
Richard Epple, a seventeen-year-old apprentice, who is driving without a license, is mowed down when he runs a police checkpoint.

March 2, 1972
An unarmed Thomas Weissbecker is shot and killed by police in Augsburg. RAF member Carmen Roll is arrested while trying to flee. In Hamburg, police raid a RAF safehouse. When RAF members Manfred Grashof and Wolfgang Grundmann arrive, a police officer opens fire. Grundmann surrenders immediately, but Grashof returns fire. Police Superintendent Hans Eckhardt is seriously wounded and subsequently dies of his injuries, and Grashof is seriously injured.

Judge Wolfgang Buddenberg, who is in charge of all RAF arrests, nonetheless orders Grashof removed from the hospital to a prison cell.

March 3, 1972
Demonstrations throughout West Germany to protest the murder of Weissbecker.
2JM bomb the Berlin *Landeskriminalamt* (*Land* Criminal Bureau—LKA) in retaliation for the killings of RAF members Petra Schelm and Thomas Weissbecker.

March 15, 1972
Former RAF associate turned state witness Karl-Heinz Ruhland is sentenced to four-and-a-half years.

March 22, 1972
The Social-Liberal coalition government passes the *Schwerpunktprogramm Innere Sicherheit* (Priority Program for Internal Security), increasing and upgrading security measures overall and expanding the powers of the *Verfassungsschutz*.

April 1972
The RAF issues a major document entitled *Dem Volk dienen: Stadtguerrilla und Klassenkampf* (Serve the People: The Urban Guerilla and Class Struggle). *Spiegel* prints extracts.
The not-guilty sentence against Horst Mahler in the Baader jailbreak trial is overturned on appeal.

May 1972

The RAF responds to the carpet-bombing of Vietnam with a bombing offensive known as the May Offensive.

May 11, 1972

The RAF's Petra Schelm Commando bombs the Headquarters of the U.S. Army's V Corps in Frankfurt. One officer is killed and thirteen soldiers are injured.

May 13, 1972

The RAF's Thomas Weissbecker Commando bombs the police headquarters in both Augsburg and Munich to avenge Thomas Weissbecker's killing.

May 14, 1972

The RAF release a communiqué *For the Victory of the People of Vietnam* claiming responsibility for the May 11 bombing.

May 15, 1972

The RAF's Manfred Grashof Commando plants a bomb in Judge Buddenberg's car. His wife Gerta is seriously injured, when she, instead of Judge Buddenberg, uses the car.

May 16, 1972

The RAF releases a communiqué claiming responsibility for the May 13th bombing.

May 19, 1972

The RAF's 2nd of June Commando bombs the Springer Building in Hamburg. Despite three warnings, the building is not cleared and seventeen workers are injured.

May 20, 1972

The RAF release a communiqué addressing the May 15 attack on Judge Buddenberg, and another regarding the May 19 attack on the Springer Building.

May 24, 1972

The RAF's July 15th Commando bombs the Headquarters of the U.S. Army in Europe in Heidelberg. Three soldiers are killed.

May 25, 1972

The RAF releases a communiqué addressing the attack of the previous day.

May 28, 1972

The RAF issues a communiqué to the West German press demanding that they print the communiqués explaining the May Offensive. A false communiqué is issued claiming that the RAF will place three random car bombs in Stuttgart on June 2, the anniversary of the killing of Benno Ohnesorg.

May 29, 1972

The RAF issues a communiqué addressing the false communiqué regarding the attacks threatened against Stuttgart.

May 31, 1972

A recorded message from Ulrike Meinhof is played at the Red Aid Teach-In in Frankfurt.
The BKA initiates a massive manhunt for RAF members, known as Operation Washout.

June 1, 1972

RAF members Andreas Baader, Holger Meins, and Jan-Carl Raspe are arrested in Frankfurt. Baader is shot in the thigh. Three hundred cops and a tank are used to make the arrests.

June 3–4, 1972

Close to 10,000 people attend the Angela Davis Congress in Frankfurt, organized by the *Sozialistisches Büro*. Oskar Negt, an important New Left intellectual, uses the occasion to launch an attack on the RAF, arguing that leftists should not show the guerilla any solidarity.

June 7, 1972

RAF member Gudrun Ensslin is arrested in a boutique in Hamburg after a shop attendant notices a gun in her purse.

June 9, 1972

RAF members Brigitte Mohnhaupt and Bernhard Braun are arrested in West Berlin.

June 15, 1972

RAF member Ulrike Meinhof and supporter Gerhard Müller are arrested in an apartment outside of Hannover. Police are tipped off by a left-wing trade unionist who had agreed to shelter them for the evening. Meinhof will be held in the dead wing at Cologne-Ossendorf, where she will remain without respite for eight months.

June 22, 1972

The constitution is amended to increase prison sentences and to increase the powers of the police and to better arm them, particularly in the case of the *Bundesgrenzschutz* (Federal Border Patrol—BGS) and the *Verfassungsschutz*.

June 25, 1972

Scottish businessman Ian McLeod is shot and killed by police who believe him to be a RAF member. At the time he is standing naked, unarmed, in his bedroom.

June 29, 1972

On the advice of her attorney, Otto Schily, Katharina Hammerschmidt, who is wanted for supporting the RAF, surrenders to the police.

July 7, 1972

Recent RAF recruit Hans-Peter Konieczny is cornered by the police in Offenbach. He is persuaded to cooperate in exchange for leniency. He agrees to set up Klaus Jünschke and Irmgard Möller, who are arrested two days later. Konieczny is released two months later.

July 13, 1972
Attorney Jörg Lang, who is believed to have introduced Konieczny to the RAF, is arrested and charged with acquiring safehouses for the group.

July 9, 1972
RAF members Irmgard Möller and Klaus Jünschke are arrested in Offenbach, set up with the help of Konieczny.

July 26, 1972
The Hamburg LG sentences RAF member Werner Hoppe, who was captured on July 15, 1971, to ten years in prison for attempted murder.

September 5–6, 1972
Palestinian guerilla group Black September takes eleven Israeli athletes hostage at the Olympic Games in Munich. Offered safe passage out of the country, they are ambushed by police at Fürstenfeldbruck Airport. During the ensuing shootout, the eleven athletes are executed, one cop is killed, and five of the eight Black September members are killed.

September 12, 1972
The Interior Ministers Conference establishes the GSG-9, a special counterterrorism police unit.

October 3, 1972
The West German government bans the General Union of Palestinian Workers and the General Union of Palestinian Students. Approximately one hundred Palestinians are expelled from West Germany.

October 29, 1972
The Palestinian guerilla group Black September hijacks an airplane and demands the release of the three Palestinians who survived the September 6 shootout. This time West Germany acquiesces.

November 1972
The RAF releases a major document entitled *Die Aktion des Schwarzen September in München—Zur Strategie des antiimperialistischen Kampfes* (The Black September Action in Munich: Regarding the Strategy for Anti-Imperialist Struggle). In it, they use the Black September attack in Munich as a starting point for a sweeping discussion of anti-imperialist resistance in West Germany and throughout the world.

1973
Jan. 17–Feb. 16, 1973
Forty RAF prisoners participate in the 1st collective hunger strike, demanding access to independent doctors and transfer to the general population. Andreas Baader announces the hunger strike while testifying at Horst Mahler's trial in West Berlin.

February 1973
RAF member Margrit Schiller is released from prison and immediately goes back underground.

February–October 1973
Tens of thousands of workers participate in wildcat strikes in the steel and auto industries.

April 1973
The Committees Against Torture are formed by attorneys representing the RAF prisoners; their express purpose is to focus public attention on the struggle of the RAF prisoners against destructive prison conditions.

May 8–June 29, 1973
Sixty RAF prisoners participate in the 2nd collective hunger strike, demanding an end to special treatment and free access to political information.

July 13, 1973
Federal Supreme Court Judge Knoblich rules that the state can proceed with x-rays and a scintigraphy (a radiographic procedure used to determine if brain surgery is necessary) on RAF prisoner Ulrike Meinhof, even against her will, and with the use of restraining devices or anesthesia if necessary. This decision is based on the proposition that Meinhof's behaviour may be the result of a brain abnormality. Massive protest in West Germany and internationally, including the protest of many doctors, prevents the government from proceeding with its plan.

July 16, 1973
For the first time, the BKA raids the cells of RAF prisoners.

July 24, 1973
RAF member Ronald Augustin is arrested in Lingen. Augustin is a Dutch citizen who met RAF members when they were in Amsterdam.

November 22, 1973
The West Berlin LG sentences RAF member Ali Jansen to ten years in prison on two counts of attempted murder.

1974
January
Katharina Hammerschmidt, who has been denied medical care while in prison, is released to a clinic and her trial adjourned. She is suffering from cancer.

January 3, 1974
RAF prisoner Ulrike Meinhof is released from the Cologne-Ossendorf dead wing. Shortly thereafter she releases a document describing the physical and psychological impact of sensory deprivation torture.

February 4, 1974

In simultaneous predawn actions, RAF safehouses are raided by police in Hamburg and Frankfurt. RAF members and supporters Helmut Pohl, Ilse Stachowiak, Christa Eckes, and Eberhard Becker are arrested in Hamburg, while Margrit Schiller, Kay-Werner Allnach, and Wolfgang Beer are arrested in Frankfurt. Astrid Proll is released from prison for health reasons; she later flees to London, England, where she lives under the name of Anna Puttick.

April 25, 1974

In Portugal, the Caetano dictatorship is overthrown in a left-wing military coup, known as the Carnation Revolution. By the end of the year, all Portuguese colonies will receive their independence.

April 28, 1974

RAF prisoners Ulrike Meinhof and Gudrun Ensslin transferred from Cologne-Ossendorf prison to Stammheim.

May 16, 1974

SPD Chancellor Willy Brandt, under constant fire since it became known in late April that one of his personal assistants was an East German spy, steps down, handing power to Helmut Schmidt.

May 21, 1974

Taxi driver Günter Jendrian is killed by police in Munich when they mistake him for a RAF member.

May 31, 1974

Siegfried Buback succeeds Ludwig Martin as Attorney General.

July 23, 1974

In the wake of a failed coup, the Greek military junta collapses.

September 1974

The RAF prisoners release *Provisorisches Kampfprogramm für den Kampf um die politischen Rechte der gefangenen Arbeiter* (Provisional Program of Struggle for the Political Rights of Imprisoned Workers), the only document they will ever release addressing prisoners in general.

Sept. 13, 1974–Feb. 5, 1975

Ulrike Meinhof announces the RAF prisoners' 3rd collective hunger strike while testifying at the trial where she, Horst Mahler, and Hans-Jürgen Bäcker face charges related to Baader's breakout from the Institute for Social Reserach Library. For the first time, the prisoners demand association with one another, rather than integration into general population. At least thirty-one prisoners, including 2JM prisoners and others, participate.

September 27, 1974

Monika Berberich reads a statement expelling Horst Mahler from the RAF during the Bäcker-Mahler-Meinhof trial at which she is testifying. Mahler has by this time joined the Maoist KPD (previously known as the KPD/AO).

October 2, 1974
The perceived leadership of the RAF, Andreas Baader, Ulrike Meinhof, Gudrun Ensslin, Jan-Carl Raspe, and Holger Meins are indicted on dozens of charges.

October 16, 1974
The BAW files for seizure of the correspondence between defense attorney Kurt Groenewold and the RAF prisoners on the basis of a claim that attorneys form the core of an illegal RAF communication system.

November 9, 1974
RAF member Holger Meins dies after almost two months on hunger strike against isolation. Demonstrations break out all over West Germany.

November 10, 1974
Günter von Drenkmann, President of the West Berlin Supreme Court, is killed during an attempted kidnapping by the 2JM. A communiqué is issued claiming the action in retaliation for the death of Holger Meins.

November 18, 1974
Holger Meins is buried in the family grave in Hamburg. Five thousand people attend the funeral, amongst them Rudi Dutschke, who, standing over Meins's casket, famously gives the clenched fist salute, crying, "Holger, the fight goes on!"

November 26, 1974
With *Aktion Winterreise* (Operation Winter Trip), the BKA searches dozens of houses and offices in twelve cities, including the West Berlin office of attorneys Klaus Eschen, Henning Spangenberg, and Hans-Christian Ströbele. Roughly forty people are arrested.

November 29, 1974
The West Berlin LG sentences Ulrike Meinhof to eight years in prison for her role in the Baader jailbreak. Recently expelled RAF member Horst Mahler is sentenced to 14 years. Hans-Jürgen Bäcker, who testified against the guerilla, is acquitted.

December 4, 1974
Philosopher and Nobel Prize winner Jean-Paul Sartre visits RAF prisoner Andreas Baader in prison.

December 7, 1974
A bomb explodes in Bremen Central Station, and five people are injured.

December 9, 1974
The RAF issues a communiqué denouncing the Breman train station bombing as a police action.

December 13, 1974
Attorney General Siegfried Buback files for seizure of the correspondence between RAF prisoners and defense attorneys Klaus Croissant and Hans-Christian Ströbele.

December 30, 1974

Second Senate Judge Theodor Prinzing rules that defense attorney Klaus Croissant is acting as supporter and spokesman for the RAF prisoners and, as such, for a criminal association.

1975

January 1, 1975

The *Lex Baader-Meinhof* (Baader-Meinhof Laws) come into effect. Amongst other things, the laws allow the court to exclude defense attorneys who are suspected of forming a criminal association with their clients, and allows trials to continue without the accused present if the reason for the absence is deemed to be the fault of the prisoner, e.g., the result of illness due to hunger striking.

January 20, 1975

Spiegel prints an interview with RAF prisoners Andreas Baader, Gudrun Ensslin, Ulrike Meinhof, and Jan-Carl Raspe.

The Federal Supreme Court alleges that defense attorney Hans-Christian Ströbele is a member of a criminal association for referring to himself as a "socialist and a political attorney" and for expressing "solidarity with the thinking of the prisoners," whom he refers to as comrades.

February 2, 1975

The RAF on the outside writes a letter to the hunger striking prisoners ordering them to call off their hunger strike and promising to carry out an action on their behalf.

February 27, 1975

The 2JM kidnap Peter Lorenz, CDU candidate for mayor in West Berlin, from his automobile, beating his chauffer Werner Sowa. Sowa identifies Angela Luther, who has been underground for three years, as one of the kidnappers. Luther, who was also alleged to be involved with the RAF's 1972 May offensive, disappears without a trace.

February 28, 1975

The Lorenz kidnappers demand the release of six imprisoned guerillas: Rolf Pohle, Rolf Heißler, Gabriele Kröcher-Tiedemann, Verena Becker, Ingrid Siepmann, and Horst Mahler.

March 1–3, 1975

The *Verfassungsschutz* surreptitiously plants bugs in the cells of five RAF prisoners.

March 3, 1975

Rolf Pohle, Rolf Heißler, Verena Becker, Ingrid Siepmann, and Gabrielle Kröcher-Tiedemann with former West Berlin Mayor, Heinrich Albertz acting as insurance, are flown to Aden, South Yemen. Horst Mahler declines to go with them.

March 4, 1975

Peter Lorenz is released unharmed, and police raid suspected left-wing safehouses throughout West Berlin and West Germany.

March 8, 1975
Facing pressure from the West German government, the government of South Yemen refuses to extradite the recently released prisoners, but does ask them to leave the country.

March 17, 1975
Defense attorney Klaus Croissant is barred from representing Andreas Baader.

April 15, 1975
American attorneys Ramsey Clark, the former Attorney General of the United States, William Kunstler, Peter Weiss, and William Schaap file a formal protest against the *Lex Baader-Meinhof* at West Germany's Constitutional Court. The court bars attorneys Klaus Croissant, Kurt Groenewold, and Hans-Christian Ströbele from the RAF's defense team.

April 22, 1975
A Stuttgart court bars attorney Klaus Croissant from defending RAF prisoner Andreas Baader.

April 24, 1975
The RAF's Holger Meins Commando occupies the West German Embassy in Stockholm, Sweden and demands the release of twenty-six political prisoners. During a tense standoff, the guerilla executes the Military and Economic Attachés. Police storm the building, detonating explosives the guerilla had laid. RAF member Ulrich Wessel is killed, and RAF member Siegfried Hausner is seriously injured.
All RAF prisoners' cells are searched and newspapers, radios, etc. confiscated.

May 1975
Interpol declares the RAF a criminal organization and places fifteen West German citizens on its wanted list.

May 1, 1975
The *Verfassungsschutz* bugs two additional cells occupied by RAF prisoners.

May 4, 1975
RAF member Siegfried Hausner, who was seriously injured during the April 24 action at the German Embassy in Stockholm, dies in Stammheim Prison.

May 5, 1975
Defense attorney Kurt Groenewold is excluded as Andreas Baader's attorney on the basis of allegations that his office served as an "information central" to allow prisoners to communicate amongst themselves.

May 9, 1975
Elisabeth von Dyck and Siegfried Haag are arrested on charges of smuggling weapons out of Switzerland. They are released soon after.

May 10, 1975
All of Siegfried Haag's files related to the Stammheim trial are seized.

May 11, 1975
Attorney Siegfried Haag goes underground, joining the RAF.

May 13, 1975
Attorney Hans-Christian Ströbele is barred from defending Andreas Baader.

May 16, 1975
Rumors are spread in the media that the RAF is planning a poison gas attack on parliament.

May 21, 1975
The pretrial hearing for Ulrike Meinhof, Gudrun Ensslin, Jan-Carl Raspe, and Andreas Baader begins in Stammheim. Defense attorneys Otto Schily, Marielouise Becker, Rupert von Plottnitz, and Helmut Riedel, as well as several court-appointed attorneys, are present, but Andreas Baader is still without an attorney.

May 23, 1975
Federal Minister of the Interior Werner Maihofer claims there are two hundred to three hundred terrorist sympathizers in West Germany, with a hardcore of about thirty.

June 5, 1975
RAF prisoner Andreas Baader reminds the court that he is still without legal representation and claims that the prisoners' cells are bugged. He is dismissed as paranoid in the media. Two years later the government will admit to

the bugs, but claim they were only used during the Stockholm crisis and briefly in 1976, after which the tapes were immediately erased.

June 12, 1975
Kurt Groenewold, one of the attorneys representing RAF prisoners, is subjected to the *Berufsverbot* for his alleged role in the RAF prisoners' *Info* system.

June 23, 1975
Defense attorneys for the RAF prisoners in Hamburg, Heidelberg, Stuttgart, and West Berlin have their offices and homes searched. Hans-Christian Ströbele and Klaus Croissant are arrested. Files relating to the Stammheim trial are seized.

June 29, 1975
RAF member Katharina Hammerschmidt dies of cancer in a West Berlin hospital.

August 9, 1975
RAF prisoners Andreas Baader, Ulrike Meinhof, Gudrun Ensslin, and Jan-Carl Raspe are jointly charged with four murders and fifty-four attempted murders.

September 2, 1975
The trial of RAF members, Manfred Grashof, Wolfgang Grundmann, and Klaus Jünschke begins in Kaiserslautern under heavy security.

September 13, 1975

A bomb explosion in Hamburg Central Station injures eleven people. Although the RAF is blamed by police and the media, the RAF, the 2JM, and the RZ all distance themselves from the action.

September 14, 1975

A false bomb threat at the Munich train station leads police to a communiqué signed by the RAF, the 2JM, and the RZ denouncing the recent train station bombings as counterinsurgency actions.

October 6, 1975

A bomb is discovered in the Nuremberg train station. Although the RAF is blamed by police and the media, the RAF, the 2JM, and the RZ all distance themselves from the action.

November 12, 1975

A bomb explodes in the Cologne Central Station. The RAF, the 2JM, and the RZ issue a common statement denouncing the bombing as a police counterinsurgency action.

December 16–24, 1975

Police carry out raids of left bookstores, publishers, printing presses, and housing collectives throughout West Germany.

December 21, 1975

An OPEC Conference in Vienna, Austria is raided by a mixed Palestinian/West German commando calling itself the *Bewegung 21. Dezember der arabischen Revolution* (December 21st Movement of the Arabic Revolution), under the leadership of the Venezuelan Carlos. They take the Oil Ministers hostage. One guerilla, RZ member Hans-Joachim Klein, is severely injured in an exchange of fire in the OPEC office, which also leaves Austrian police officer Anton Tichler, Iraqi guard Khalifi, and a Libyan Oil Ministry representative Yousef Ismirili dead. 2JM member Gabriele Kröcher-Tiedemann is identified as the shooter. In exchange for the hostages the guerillas receive a $5 million ransom and are flown to Algeria.

1976

January 13, 1976

The trial of RAF prisoners Andreas Baader, Ulrike Meinhof, Gudrun Ensslin, and Jan-Carl Raspe begins.

January 16, 1976

The West German parliament passes §88a, a censorship law, under which, effective May 1 of that year, writing, producing, publishing, distributing, advertising, selling, or displaying materials "glorifying acts of violence" is a criminal offense subject to a maximum three year jail sentence.

January 20, 1976

RAF prisoner Ulrike Meinhof's attorney Axel Azzola puts forward a motion that the defendants in the Stammheim trial be recognized as POWs.

March 16, 1976

The Hamburg LG sentences RAF member turned state witness Gerhard Müller to ten years in prison. In exchange for his cooperation, Müller is never charged with the murder of police officer Norbert Schmid. Instead, he is released after six-and-a-half years, paid 500,000 DM, and relocated to the U.S.A.

RAF member Irmgard Möller is sentenced to four-and-a-half years.

May 4, 1976

Attorneys for RAF prisoners Andreas Baader, Ulrike Meinhof, Gudrun Ensslin, and Jan-Carl Raspe petition to have Richard Nixon, Willy Brandt, Helmut Schmidt, Georg Kiesinger, and Walter Scheel called as witnesses in an attempt to prove that U.S. activity in Southeast Asia violated international law, making the RAF attacks legitimate and legal under international law. The petition is rejected.

May 6, 1976

The trial of the members of the RAF Holger Meins Commando, Hanna Krabbe, Lutz Taufer, Karl-Heinz Dellwo, and Bernd Rössner begins.

May 7, 1976

Police Chief Fritz Sippel is shot in Sprendlingen. It is believed that RAF members Peter-Jürgen Boock and Rolf Clemens Wagner are the shooters.

May 9, 1976

RAF member Ulrike Meinhof is found hanged in her cell. The state claims it is a suicide. Fellow prisoners and supporters assert that it is murder. An International Commission will eventually rule that the evidence indicates murder.

May 10, 1976

In response to Ulrike Meinhof's murder there are riots in West Berlin and a molotov cocktail attack on the *Land* Courthouse in Wuppertal.

May 11, 1976

RAF prisoner Jan-Carl Raspe makes a brief statement during the Stammheim trial and releases a package of documents that indicate Meinhof's state of mind at the time of her death and the unlikelihood that she committed suicide.

In response to Ulrike Meinhof's murder, there is rioting in Frankfurt, during which a police officer is severely burned when a molotov cocktail explodes in his car.

May 14, 1976

In response to Ulrike Meinhof's murder, the Stachus Shopping Centre in Munich is bombed.

Police raid a dozen collective houses in Frankfurt, arresting fourteen people on a variety of charges relating to the May 11 riot, including attempted murder. All are released the next day.

May 14–16, 1976
Thirty-six women hunger strike in Hessen prison in response to Meinhof's murder.

May 16, 1976
Ulrike Meinhof is buried in West Berlin. Following the funeral, there is a massive demonstration.

May 18, 1976
Eight thousand demonstrate in West Berlin against the murder of Meinhof. Clashes with the police lead to numerous arrests.

June 2, 1976
The RZ's Ulrike Meinhof Commando bombs the Headquarters of the U.S. Army and U.S. Officers Club in Frankfurt.
A group calling itself the Friends of the 2nd of June firebombs two fully loaded military trucks at the U.S. Air Force Base in Frankfurt.

June 5–7, 1976
The *Sozialistisches Büro* organizes an Anti-Repression Congress in Frankfurt. Twenty thousand people take part. Attorney Klaus Croissant is among the speakers, as is *sponti* leader Joschka Fischer, who makes a historic speech urging the radical left to reject the armed struggle.

June 10, 1976
The Interior Ministers Conference gives the police the right to shoot to kill when dealing with suspected terrorists.

June 14, 1976
Twenty-four attorneys for political prisoners release a statement protesting the murder of Ulrike Meinhof, as well as isolation and torture.

June 16, 1976
Five former intelligence agents, including Winslow Peck (National Security Agency - Air Force), Gary P. Thomas (Military Intelligence), and Philip Agee (CIA), testify in Stammheim about the use of West German territory by the U.S. for the Vietnamese War effort.

June 18, 1976
The office of Klaus Jürgen Langner, Margrit Schiller's attorney, is firebombed. Seven people are injured.

June 24, 1976
The West German parliament passes legislation integrating §129a, which illegalizes "supporting or participating in a terrorist organization," into the Basic Law.

June 30, 1976
Attorney Klaus Croissant is banned from taking on any more political cases.

July 1976

The influential French monthly newspaper *Le Monde Diplomatique* interviews the RAF prisoners and their attorneys.

July 7, 1976

RAF member Monika Berberich and 2JM members, Juliane Plambeck, Gabriele Rollnik, and Inge Viett overpower a guard and scale the wall, escaping from the Lehrter Straße Women's Prison in West Berlin.

July 16, 1976

Attorney Klaus Croissant is arrested and charged with supporting a criminal organization after he announces the formation of an International Commission into the Death of Ulrike Meinhof.

July 21, 1976

Rolf Pohle, one of the prisoners exchanged for Peter Lorenz in 1975, is arrested by West German police in Athens, Greece.

RAF member Monika Berberich, who escaped from a West Berlin prison with three other women on July 7, is rearrested.

July 22, 1976

RAF prisoner Brigitte Mohnhaupt testifies at the Stammheim trial refuting most of Gerhard Müller's testimony.

August 18–19, 1976

Left bookstores and publishers in West Berlin, Hamburg, Bochum, Essen, Cologne, Heidelberg, Tübingen, and Munich are raided in connection with §88a. Books and magazines are seized and a Bochum book dealer is arrested and held for a week.

October 1, 1976

In spite of protests, Greece, under extreme pressure including threats of economic sanctions, extradites Rolf Pohle to West Germany.

November 10, 1976

Ministers from nineteen EEC countries establish the European Convention on the Suppression of Terrorism.

November 30, 1976

RAF members Siegfried Haag and Roland Mayer are arrested on the Frankfurt-Kassel highway. Chief Federal Prosecutor Siegfried Buback claims that they were in possession of a variety of weapons at the time of the arrest. Attorney Klaus Croissant is denied the right to represent Haag.

December 1976

A section of the RZ releases an open letter criticizing the RAF's strategy and dogmatism.

December 8, 1976

Attorney Brigitte Tilgener is denied the right to represent RAF prisoner Siegfried Haag.

December 10, 1976

The BAW accuses attorney Hans-Christian Ströbele of supporting a terrorist organization and applies for a *Berufsverbot* against him.

December 13, 1976

Attorneys Klaus Croissant and Hans-Christian Ströbele are denied the right to represent RAF prisoner Brigitte Mohnhaupt.

December 14, 1976

RAF member Waltraud Boock is arrested in Vienna, Austria following a bank robbery.

December 15, 1976

One of attorney Klaus Croissant's secretaries is offered several thousand DM by the *Verfassungsschutz* for copies of legal notes and clients' names.

December 17, 1976

There is a bomb attack against the Vienna, Austria Police Information Centre demanding the release of RAF member Waltraud Boock. This is followed by two bomb threats with the same demand.

December 21, 1976

Attorney General Siegfried Buback requests that attorney Jürgen Laubacher be denied the right to represent RAF prisoner Siegfried Haag, because he has previously represented political prisoners.

1977

January 10, 1977

RAF prisoner Monika Berberich responds critically to the RZ's open letter of December 1976, which criticized the RAF's strategy and dogmatism.

January 12, 1977

Defense attorney Otto Schily launches a motion of non-confidence against Theodor Prinzing, the judge in the Stammheim trial, when it is discovered that he has leaked the trial tapes to the media, in spite of the fact that it is illegal to make them public.

January 23, 1977

Chief Judge Theodor Prinzing is expelled from the Stammheim trial for partiality following eighty-five legal requests for his removal.

January 27, 1977

Seventeen states sign the European Convention on the Suppression of Terrorism in Strasbourg, France, committing them to a common struggle against terrorism.

February 4, 1977

In Vienna, RAF member Waltraud Boock is sentenced to fifteen years.

February 8, 1977

RAF member Brigitte Mohnhaupt is released from prison and immediately goes back underground.

March 17, 1977

The state admits to having bugged the cells of seven RAF prisoners, and to having listened in on the prisoners' conversations with their attorneys. They claim, however, to have only used the bugs briefly on two occasions, during the Stockholm crisis of 1975, and briefly on one occasion in 1976. They also claim to have destroyed the tapes immediately afterwards.

The media spreads rumors that the RAF is planning to kidnap children from playgrounds.

March 29–April 30, 1977

RAF and 2JM prisoners begin the 4th collective hunger strike, demanding POW status under the Geneva Convention, association in groups of no less than fifteen, abolition of isolation, an international investigation into the deaths of Holger Meins, Siegfried Hausner, and Ulrike Meinhof, and an end to psychological warfare through false actions and communiqués. Thirty-five prisoners participate from the outset, including Waltraud Boock in Vienna, but soon one hundred prisoners are hunger striking against brutality and force-feeding.

April 7, 1977

The RAF's Ulrike Meinhof Commando assassinates Attorney General Siegfried Buback, riddling his car with submachine gun fire, also killing his driver, Wolfgang Göbel, and a bodyguard, Georg Wurster.

All RAF prisoners' cells are searched and newspapers, radios, etc. confiscated.

April 14, 1977

The head of the BKA, Horst Herold, claims that there are between 400 and 500 terrorists with 4,000 to 5,000 sympathizers in West Germany.

April 26, 1977

Attorneys Otto Schily and Hans-Heinz Heldmann temporarily halt their pleas in the Stammheim trial to protest the bugging of their meetings with witnesses.

April 28, 1977

The Stuttgart OLG finds RAF members Gudrun Ensslin, Jan-Carl Raspe, and Andreas Baader guilty of six murders and thirty-four attempted murders in connection with six bomb attacks. They are sentenced to life plus fifteen years. The so-called Stammheim trial lasts two years, including 192 days of testimony, and costs $15 million.

April 30, 1977

The Minister of Justice for Baden-Wurttemburg rules that the RAF prisoners' demands for association must be met. In response to this gesture, the prisoners end their hunger strike. Shortly thereafter work begins on the seventh floor of Stammheim to allow the association of sixteen prisoners.

May 2, 1977

The weekly news magazine *Spiegel* prints poll results claiming 50% of West German citizens want the reinstatement of the dead wing in prisons. Thirty-five thousand people sign a petition to this effect.

May 3, 1977

RAF members Günter Sonnenberg and Verena Becker, formerly of the 2JM, are arrested in the German-Swiss border town of Singen. Sonnenberg is shot in the head and Becker in the leg. Sonnenberg is suspected in the Buback assassination and Becker has been wanted ever since she was freed through the Lorenz kidnapping.

May 5, 1977

RAF supporters Uwe Folkerts and Johannes Thimme are arrested in connection with the Buback assassination.

May 13, 1977

RAF member Irene Goergens is released from prison.

June 2, 1977

The Kaiserslautern LG sentences RAF members Manfred Grashof and Klaus Jünschke to life in prison. Wolfgang Grundmann is sentenced to four years.
RAF members Verena Becker and Sabine Schmitz start a hunger strike for association with prisoners in Stammheim.

June 22, 1977

RAF prisoners Hanna Krabbe, Bernd Rössner, Karl-Heinz Dellwo, and Lutz Taufer begin a hunger strike for association with the prisoners in Stammheim.
RAF members Sabine Schmitz and Verena Becker break their hunger strike when they are assured that they will be allowed association with other RAF prisoners.

June 27, 1977

The Stuttgart OLG bars attorney Klaus Croissant from representing defendants in trials related to state security.

July 1, 1977

RAF members Willy Peter Stoll and Knut Folkerts rob a gun store in Frankfurt, making off with fifteen revolvers and three pistols.
Kurt Rebmann becomes Siegfried Buback's successor as Attorney General.

July 7, 1977

RAF prisoners Helmut Pohl, Wolfgang Beer, and Werner Hoppe are moved to Stammheim.

July 8, 1977

Attorney Klaus Croissant, facing increasing harassment, flees to Paris, and holds a press conference at which he requests political asylum.

July 12, 1977

Attorney Klaus Croissant files a formal request for political asylum in France.

July 16, 1977
West Germany requests that France extradite Klaus Croissant.

July 20, 1977
The Düsseldorf OLG sentences RAF members Hanna Krabbe, Karl-Heinz Dellwo, Lutz Taufer, and Bernd Rössner to two life sentences for their respective roles in the April 24, 1975, Stockholm Embassy action.

July 27, 1977
RAF prisoner Waltraud Boock begins a hunger strike for application of the Geneva Convention governing POWs and for association with RAF prisoners in Stammheim.

July 30, 1977
Jürgen Ponto, the President of West Germany's largest bank, the Dresdner Bank, is shot and killed in his home. Susanne Albrecht, who is the sister of Ponto's goddaughter, is recognized. She goes underground along with Angelika Speitel, Silke Maier-Witt, and Siegrid Sternebeck. Immediately following the shooting RAF prisoners are searched and the Contact Ban is applied.

August 8, 1977
A special unit brutally breaks up the month-old Stammheim group, marking the renewal of draconian prison conditions.

August 9–September 2, 1977
RAF prisoners participate in the 5th collective hunger strike in response to the attack on the Stammheim prisoners and the Ponto assassination. Some of the prisoners escalate to a thirst strike almost immediately.

August 12, 1977
RAF member Elisabeth von Dyck is named as a suspect in connection with the Ponto assassination.

August 13, 1977
Berufsverbot is requested against attorney Kurt Groenewold.

August 14, 1977
Susanne Albrecht issues a communiqué on behalf of the RAF regarding the July 30 assassination of Ponto.

August 15, 1977
The office of attorneys Arndt Müller and Armin Newerla (previously Klaus Croissant's office, which they have taken over) is firebombed while under 24-hour-a-day police surveillance.

August 20, 1977
Attorney Armin Newerla is arrested along with six other people.

August 22, 1977
Attorney Armin Newerla and the six other people arrested are released, but charges of supporting a terrorist organization are laid against Newerla and one other person.

August 25, 1977
A RAF commando carries out a failed missile attack against the BAW office in Karlsruhe. The rocket failed to ignite due to a technical failure.

August 30, 1977
Attorney Armin Newerla is re-arrested and his office is searched and documents are seized.

September 2, 1977
Following the breakdown of negotiations between Amnesty International and the Federal Government, the prisoners call off their hunger and thirst strike.

September 5, 1977
West Germany's top Industrialist, and former SS officer, Hanns Martin Schleyer is kidnapped from his limousine in Cologne, by the RAF's Siegfried Hausner Commando. His chauffeur and three bodyguards are killed.

September 6, 1977
A total Contact Ban is instituted against all political prisoners.

September 13, 1977
At the funeral of Schleyer's driver in Cologne, North Rhein-Westphalia Prime Minister Heinz Kühn delivers a speech warning the kidnappers that Schleyer's death will have repercussions for the prisoners.

September 19, 1977
RAF member Angelika Speitel is involved in a shootout with police in Den Haag, Holland.

September 22, 1977
RAF member Knut Folkerts, a suspect in the Buback assassination, is arrested with a large sum of money and a false passport in Utrecht, Holland, following a shoot-out in which police officer Arie Kranenburg is killed. Brigitte Mohnhaupt manages to get away.

September 28, 1977
The Hamburg LG sentences RAF members Christa Eckes, Helmut Pohl, and Wolfgang Beer to seven years, five years, and four-and-a-half years in prison, respectively.

September 29, 1977
Parliament votes 371 to 4, with 17 abstentions, ratifying the Contact Ban.
The editors of *Arbeiterstimme* (Workers' Voice), the newspaper of the KBW, are sentenced to six months in prison for publishing an anonymous article entitled "Buback Shot—Enough Reasons, But What's The Purpose."

September 30, 1977
The BKA, through attorney Denis Payot, states that all of the countries visited by Hans-Jürgen Wischnewski declined to accept the prisoners. Attorney Ardnt Müller is arrested and the documents remaining in his office are seized.

A representative from the BAW flies to Paris with information he claims proves defense attorney and political exile Klaus Croissant's role in the RAF. Croissant is arrested.

October 2, 1977
Volker Speitel and Rosemarie Prieß, workers in Klaus Croissant's office, are arrested on a train in Puttgarden.

October 8, 1977
Twenty thousand people participate in a demonstration in Bonn to protest the state's threat to ban three Maoist organizations, the KBW, the KPD, and the KPD/ML.

October 13, 1977
A four person PFLP (EO) group calling itself the Struggle Against World Imperialism Organization, hijack a Lufthansa airliner en route from Majorca to Paris, taking it first to Rome, then to Cyprus. They issue a communiqué saying their action is meant to reinforce the demands of the Siegfried Hausner Commando. Attorney Hans-Christian Ströbele's home and office are raided.

October 16, 1977
Denis Payot receives a communiqué from the SAWIO demanding the release of the eleven prisoners demanded by the RAF's Siegfried Hausner Commando, as well as the release of two Palestinians held in Turkey, and fifteen million U.S. dollars, to be delivered by Schleyer's son Eberhard.

October 17, 1977
The hijacked jetliner arrives at Mogadishu, Somalia.
Hans-Jürgen Wischnewski and the GSG-9 fly to Mogadishu.
The trial of Rolf Pohle begins in Munich.

October 18, 1977
The jetliner in Mogadishu is stormed and three of the four hijackers are killed, the fourth is badly injured, but all of the hostages are rescued. Shortly thereafter a state official announces the "suicides" of Andreas Baader and Gudrun Ensslin and the attempted "suicides" of Jan-Carl Raspe and Irmgard Möller. Raspe subsequently dies of his wounds. Only Möller survives to refute the state's suicide contention. In West Berlin, thirty-eight apartments, bookstores, and printing shops are searched and forty people taken into custody. *Info-BUG* and its printers Firma Agit-Druck are amongst those targeted, and the radical newspaper now finds itself banned.

October 19, 1977
The DPA News Agency in Stuttgart receives the final communiqué from the kidnappers, saying that Schleyer has been executed. His body is found in the trunk of a green Audi 100 in the border town of Mulhouse, France, just where the RAF said it would be.
Attorneys Otto Schily and Hans-Heinz Heldmann hold a press conference to denounce the

state's suicide story regarding the prisoners.

October 20, 1977
The Contact Ban is lifted.

October 27, 1977
Ensslin's parents bury Gudrun Ensslin, Jan-Carl Raspe, and Andreas Baader in Stuttgart. Several hundred supporters attend the funeral.

November 2, 1977
At Klaus Croissant's extradition trial in Paris, fifteen attorneys from all over West Europe plead that he not be extradited.

November 9–13, 1977
The 2JM kidnaps industrialist Walter Palmers in Vienna. He is released in exchange for a ransom of thirty-one million shillings, which was divided amongst the 2JM, the RAF, and a Palestinian group.

November 11, 1977
RAF members Christof Wackernagel and Gert Schneider are arrested in Amsterdam. A year later they will be extradited to West Germany.

November 12, 1977
RAF prisoner Ingrid Schubert, one of eleven prisoners demanded in exchange for Schleyer, is found hanged in her cell in Munich. The state claims it is suicide but supporters believe it is a murder.

November 16, 1977
The French Court of Appeals rules that Klaus Croissant be extradited to West Germany.

November 17, 1977
Klaus Croissant is extradited from France to West Germany and immediately imprisoned in Stammheim.

November 19, 1977
RAF prisoner Irmgard Möller begins a hunger strike for association with RAF prisoner Verena Becker.

November 28, 1977
The trial of RAF member Verena Becker begins. She is charged with attempted murder, robbery, and membership in a terrorist organization.

December 20, 1977
In Utrecht, Holland, RAF member Knut Folkerts is sentenced to twenty years in prison. He is later extradited to West Germany.

December 28, 1977
The Stuttgart OLG sentences RAF member Verena Becker to life in prison.

1978

January 18, 1978
The trial of attorney Kurt Groenewold on charges of helping organize the RAF prisoners' illegal communications system begins in Hamburg.

January 21, 1978

RAF member Christine Kuby is arrested in a shootout with police in a Hamburg drugstore. Kuby and a police officer are injured. Kuby was attempting to use a forged prescription to buy narcotics for fellow RAF member Peter-Jürgen Boock, a drug addict.

January 28, 1978

The Tunix Congress is held in West Berlin. A broad cross section of the left meets to discuss how to proceed after the German Autumn.

February 1, 1978

RAF prisoners held in Holland begin a hunger strike, demanding an end to isolation and bans on visits, free access to literature, and to be flown to a country of their choice.

February 9, 1978

RAF prisoners in Hamburg begin a hunger strike, demanding POW status, association, the return of the confiscated writings of Gudrun Ensslin, Jan-Carl Raspe, and Andreas Baader, and an independent investigation into the murders of the RAF prisoners.

March 3, 1978

Deutschland im Herbst (Germany in Autumn), a film examining the events surrounding the Schleyer kidnapping and the Stammheim deaths, with segments by several West German directors, including Alexander Kluge, Volker Schlöndorff, and Rainer Werner Fassbinder,

premieres. The events will thereafter be known as the *Deutscher Herbst* (German Autumn).

March 9, 1978

Former defense attorney Klaus Croissant's trial begins. Croissant refuses to distance himself from his former clients, but, rather, publicly identifies himself with them ideologically.

March 10–April 2, 1978

RAF prisoners participate in the organization's sixth collective hunger strike, demanding POW status, association, the release of seriously ill RAF prisoner Günter Sonnenberg, and an end to the psychological warfare against the RAF.

April 26, 1978

The Stuttgart OLG sentences Günter Sonnenberg to two life prison sentences.

May 11, 1978

RAF member Stefan Wisniewski is arrested at Orly Airport in Paris. He is in possession of a letter from RAF prisoner Karl-Heinz Dellwo criticizing the Schleyer kidnapping, along with forty capsules of narcotics for RAF member Peter-Jürgen Boock, a drug addict.

June 30, 1978

RAF members, Sieglinde Hofmann, Brigitte Mohnhaupt, Rolf Clemens Wagner, and Peter-Jürgen Boock are arrested in Yugoslavia.

July 10, 1978

The Hamburg OLG sentences attorney Kurt Groenewold to two years probation and a fine of 75,000 DM for supporting a criminal organization.

September 6, 1978

RAF member Willy Peter Stoll is shot dead by police in a Düsseldorf restaurant.

September 15, 1978

Former RAF member Astrid Proll, who has been living under the name of Anna Puttick in London, is arrested by British police. She is extradited less than a year later to West Germany.

September 24, 1978

RAF members Angelika Speitel and Michael Knoll are wounded and arrested in a shoot-out in which police officer Hans-Wilhelm Hansen is killed. RAF member Werner Lotze escapes. Michael Knoll subsequently dies of his injuries.

November 1, 1978

RAF members Rolf Heißler and Adelheid Schulz shoot and kill Dutch border guards Dionysius de Jong and Johannes Goemans at the Kerkade border crossing into Holland.

November 6, 1978

Former RAF prisoner Wolfgang Beer along with supporters Peter Alexa, Mathias Böge, Simone Borgstedde, Ingrid Jakobsmeier, Rosemarie Prieß, Helga Roos, and four other people, occupy the offices of DPA, demanding that the newswire run something about the life threatening prison conditions in which Karl-Heinz Dellwo and Werner Hoppe are being held. They are all arrested and sentenced to a year in prison.

November 17, 1978

When the West German government refuses to exchange them for eight exiled Croat fascists, Yugoslav authorities release RAF members Sieglinde Hofmann, Brigitte Monhaupt, Rolf Clemens Wagner, and Peter-Jürgen Boock, who were arrested on June 30. They are flown to an undisclosed third country.

December 14, 1978

The Stuttgart OLG sentences RAF supporters Volker Speitel and Hans-Joachim Dellwo to three years and two months, and two years in prison, respectively, for supporting a terrorist organization. Both had agreed to cooperate with the police in exchange for reduced sentences and new identities.

December 15, 1978

The International Investigatory Commission into the Death of Ulrike Meinhof releases its findings, which indicate that Meinhof was murdered.

Mid-December 1978

RAF members Susanne Albrecht, Sieglinde Hofmann, Christian Klar, Werner Lotze, Silke Maier-Witt, Brigitte Mohnhaupt, Adelheid Schulz, and Rolf Clemens Wagner seek refuge at a Palestinian training camp in South Yemen.

1979

February 1979

RAF members Susanne Albrecht, Sieglinde Hofmann, Christian Klar, Werner Lotze, Silke Maier-Witt, Brigitte Mohnhaupt, Adelheid Schulz, and Rolf Clemens Wagner return from South Yemen and begin preparations for a new offensive.

February 8, 1979

Werner Hoppe, whose health has been seriously damaged by years of isolation, is released from prison on compassionate grounds.

February 16, 1979

The Stuttgart LG sentences attorney Klaus Croissant to two-and-a-half years in prison and four years of *Berufsverbot* for supporting a terrorist organization.

April 20–June 26, 1979

More than seventy prisoners participate in the RAF prisoners' seventh collective hunger strike, demanding the end of isolation, the application of the Geneva Convention, and the release of Günter Sonnenberg.

May 2, 1979

The Hamburg OLG sentences RAF member Christine Kuby to life in prison.

May 4, 1979

RAF member Elisabeth von Dyck is shot dead by the police in Nuremberg.

May 31, 1979

The Heidelberg LG sentences Irmgard Möller to life in prison for her role in the RAF's May 1972 offensive.

June 9, 1979

RAF member Rolf Heißler is shot in the head without warning as he enters an apartment in Frankfurt. He survives and is placed under arrest.

June 25, 1979

The RAF's Andreas Baader Commando attempts to assassinate the NATO Chief of Staff, U.S. General Alexander Haig.

July 11, 1979

The Stuttgart OLG sentences Siegfried Haag and Roland Mayer to fourteen years and twelve years in prison, respectively.

November 19, 1979

RAF members Christian Klar, Rolf Clemens Wagner, Henning Beer, and Peter-Jürgen Boock rob a bank in Zurich of an estimated 548,000 Swiss francs. Making their getaway, they shoot two police officers, and passer-by

Edith Kletzhändler is killed by a ricocheting bullet. Rolf Clemens Wagner is arrested in Zurich later the same day.

1980

January 31, 1980
On the basis of testimony supplied by former RAF supporters Volker Speitel and Hans-Joachim Dellwo, the Stuttgart OLG sentences attorneys Arndt Müller and Armin Newerla to four years and eight months, and three years and six months respectively for smuggling weapons and explosives into Stammheim.

February 22, 1980
Astrid Proll is sentenced to five-and-a-half years for bank robbery and using a forged ID, but is immediately released on the basis of time already served.

May 5, 1980
2JM members Ingrid Barabas and Regine Nicolai, RAF member Sieglinde Hofmann, and two supporters (Karola Magg and Karin Kamp-Münnichow) are arrested in Paris.

June 1980
Der Minister und der Terrorist (The Minister and the Terrorist), a book-length conversation between Federal Minister of the Interior Gerhart Baum (FDP) and former RAF member Horst Mahler is released.

June 2, 1980
The 2JM releases a communiqué announcing its dissolution and merger with the RAF. Some 2JM members in prison will release a document distancing themselves from this fusion later in the month, but the 2JM will never claim responsibility for another action.

July 25, 1980
RAF members Juliane Plambeck, formerly of the 2JM, and Wolfgang Beer are killed in a traffic accident outside of Bietigheim-Bissingen.

July 31, 1980
The Düsseldorf OLG sentences RAF member Knut Folkerts to a life sentence for three murders.

September 5, 1980
The Düsseldorf OLG sentences RAF members Christof Wackernagel and Gert Schneider to fifteen years in prison for attempted murder and membership in a terrorist organization.

September 26, 1980
The Düsseldorf OLG sentences RAF member Rolf Clemens Wagner to life in prison.

October 1980
RAF members Susanne Albrecht, Werner Lotze, Christine Dümlein, Monika Helbing, Ekkehard von Seckendorff, Sigrid Sternebeck, Ralf Baptist Friedrich, and Silke Maier-Witt leave the RAF. They are provided with new identities and

sanctuary in East Germany. Two years later, Inge Viett and Henning Beer will join them.

1981

January 22, 1981
RAF member Peter-Jürgen Boock is arrested in Hamburg. He soon renounces the RAF.

February 2–April 16, 1981
More than 100 political prisoners participate in the RAF prisoners' eighth collective hunger strike, demanding association and the release of seriously ill prisoner Günter Sonnenberg.

April 16, 1981
Political prisoner Sigurd Debus, who is participating in the hunger strike although he is not a RAF member, dies of a brain hemorrhage that is the result of being force-fed. The Federal Minister of Justice agrees to association of prisoners in groups of four and an end to solitary isolation. As a result, the hungerstrike is called off.

August 4, 1981
French police officer Francis Violleau is shot and seriously injured in an exchange of fire with RAF member Inge Viett in Paris. Viett is one of the 2JM members who joined the RAF when the organizations fused.

August 31, 1981
The RAF's Sigurd Debus Commando bombs the Headquarters of the U.S. Air Force in Ramstein injuring seventeen people and causing 7.2 million DM in damage.

September 15, 1981
The RAF's Gudrun Ensslin Commando attacks the car carrying the head of the U.S. Army in Europe, General Frederick Kroesen, with a bazooka. The armour-plated vehicle survives the attack, and Kroesen and his wife suffer only minor injuries.

October 10, 1981
265,000 march in antiwar demonstration in Bonn, the largest demonstration in West German history.

December 4, 1981
The Düsseldorf OLG sentences RAF member Stefan Wisniewski to life in prison for his role in the Schleyer kidnapping, among other things.

1982

Inge Viett and Henning Beer leave the RAF and are provided with new identities and sanctuary in East Germany.

Early 1982
RAF prisoner Verena Becker begins cooperating with the *Verfassungsschutz*, naming Stefan Wisniewski as the shooter in the Buback assassination. Other RAF

members have already been convicted for this murder, and the *Verfassungsschutz* does not pursue this lead. Twenty-five years later, in 2007, a political crisis will develop around exactly this question.

May 1982
The RAF releases a major theoretical text re-evaluating their practice and opening a new phase in their discussion with the legal movement. This paper, *Guerilla, Widerstand und antiimperialistische Front* (The Guerilla, The Resistance, and the Anti-Imperialist Front), calls for a broad-based front involving the guerilla, the semi-legal movement, and the legal anti-imperialist movement. It becomes known as the May Paper and is hotly debated amongst supporters, some of whom see it as showing a bold new way forward, while others see it as a betrayal of some of the guerilla's key tenets.

June 16, 1982
The Frankfurt OLG sentences RAF member Sieglinde Hofmann to fifteen years in prison for her role in planning the attempted kidnapping that led to the Ponto assassination.

October 1, 1982
The CDU proposes a constructive vote of no confidence which is supported by the FDP: the motion is carried, and two days later the *Bundestag* votes in a new right-wing CDU/CSU-FDP coalition cabinet, with Helmut Kohl as the chancellor.

November 10, 1982
The Düsseldorf OLG sentences RAF member Rolf Heißler to two life terms plus fifteen years in prison for the murder of a police officer and membership in a terrorist organization.

November 11, 1982
RAF members Brigitte Mohnhaupt and Adelheid Schulz are arrested at the RAF's Heusenstamm arms depot.

November 16, 1982
RAF member Christian Klar is arrested at the RAF's Anmühle arms depot.

December 14, 1982
The neo-nazi Hexel-Hepp Group bombs the U.S. Army Base in Hessen. Two GIs are seriously injured. Many people on the left originally applaud the action, believing it was carried out by the RZ. The RZ issues a statement pointing out operational indicators that the action came from the right and criticize the superficiality of the left's analysis of the action, establishing the difference between anti-Americanism and anti-imperialism.

1984

May 7, 1984

The Stuttgart OLG sentences RAF member Peter-Jürgen Boock to three times life plus fifteen years for his role in the murders of Ponto and Schleyer.

Summer 1984

Members of the "anti-imperialist resistance" including Birgit Hogefeld and Wolfgang Grams go underground, rejuvenating the RAF.

July 2, 1984

RAF members Helmut Pohl, Christa Eckes, Stefan Frey, Ingrid Jakobsmeier, Barbara Ernst, and Ernst-Volker Staub are arrested in Frankfurt after one of them accidentally discharges a gun into the apartment below their safehouse. Police find a document entitled *Acktionspapier* (Action Paper), directed to members of the "anti-imperialist resistance" working within the context of the Front concept, as spelled out in the RAF's 1982 May Paper.

November 5, 1984

The RAF robs a gun shop in Maxdorf for weapons, making off with twenty-two handguns and 2,800 rounds of ammunition.

December 1984

The first issue of the illegal RAF support newspaper *Zusammen Kämpfen* (Struggling Together) comes out.

December 4, 1984

RAF prisoners begin their ninth collective hunger strike, demanding association in large groups and uncensored mail and visits. Within the context of the anti-imperialist Front, dozens of armed attacks will be carried out by supporters during the seventy-nine days that the prisoners will be on hunger strike.

December 18, 1984

The RAF's Jan-Carl Raspe Commando attempts to bomb the SHAPE School, the NATO Officers' School, in Oberammergua. The bomb is discovered and defused.

1985

1985 sees an ambitious offensive by the anti-imperialist resistance, within the framework of the RAF's Front concept as spelled out in the 1982 May Paper. Within the first half of the year alone, there are one hundred eleven firebombings and thirty-nine bombings reported by the Minister of the Interior, and for periods of time, daily low- and medium-level attacks.

January 15, 1985

The RAF issue a bilingual joint statement with the French anti-imperialist guerilla group *Action Directe* entitled *Pour l'unité des revolutionaires en Europe de l'ouest / Für die Einheit der Revolutionäre in Westeuropa* (For the Unity of

Revolutionaries in West Europe) calling for united guerilla action in West Europe.

January 20, 1985

RAF supporter Johannes Thimme is killed and Claudia Wannersdorfer is seriously injured when a bomb they are planting at the Association for the Development of Air and Space Industries in Stuttgart explodes prematurely.

January 25, 1985

Action Directe's Elisabeth von Dyck Commando assassinates General René Audran, ambushing him as he parked his car outside his suburban Paris home. Audran was in charge of arms sales for the French Ministry of Defense.

February 1, 1985

The RAF's Patsy O'Hara Commando assassinates arms manufacturer Ernst Zimmerman, Chairman of the MTU Board of directors. The murder remains unsolved.

February 2, 1985

The RAF sends a letter to the prisoners asking them to call off their hunger strike, saying that the mobilization it has achieved is as much as can be expected in the existing conditions.

March 13, 1985

The Düsseldorf OLG gives RAF member Adelheid Schulz 3 life sentences for her role in the Schleyer kidnapping and

for membership in a terrorist organization. Rolf Clemens Wagner receives 2 life sentences, largely as a result of Peter-Jürgen Boock's testimony.

April 1985

The illegal RAF support newspaper *Zusammen Kämpfen* releases an interview with the RAF addressing their common actions with *Action Directe* and the Front concept in general.

April 2, 1985

The Stuttgart OLG sentences RAF members Brigitte Mohnhaupt and Christian Klar to 5 life sentences each in connection with every RAF action from 1977 until 1981.

August 8, 1985

In Wiesbaden, RAF members abduct 20-year-old American GI Edward Pimental in order to steal his ID card, and then execute him with a single shot to the back of the head. The joint RAF and *Action Directe* George Jackson Commando uses his ID card to gain entrance to the Rhein-Main U.S. Air Force Base in Frankfurt, where they then plant a bomb which causes 1 million DM in damage and kills a soldier, Frank Scarton, and a civilian employee, Becky Jo Bristol.

August 25, 1985

In a second communiqué regarding the Rhein-Main Air Base action, the RAF claims responsibility for the killing of U.S. GI Edward Pimental, whose ID card they used to gain access to the Air Base for the August 8, 1985 action. Prior to the release of this communiqué, many supporters had denounced the killing as a false flag action. The execution of Pimental, which was clearly unnecessary, will provoke much criticism from the support scene.

September 1985
The illegal RAF support newspaper *Zusammen Kämpfen* releases an interview with the RAF entitled *An die, die mit uns kämpfen* (To Those Who Struggle Alongside Us), addressing questions and criticisms that have arisen on the left in the wake of the Pimental killing.

December 6, 1985
The Stuttgart OLG sentences RAF supporter Claudia Wannersdorfer to eight years in prison.

1986
January 1986
The RAF releases *Die revolutionäre Front aufbauen* (Build the Revolutionary Front), an assessment of their 1984-1985 offensive and a call for the further development of the revolutionary front in West Germany and West Europe.

January 31–February 4, 1986
The Anti-Capitalist and Anti-Imperialist Resistance in Western Europe Conference in Frankfurt, organized by RAF supporters to advance the Front concept, draws thousands from all over West Europe and around the world.

March 1986
All over West Germany there are actions against the Reinhard Hauff film, *Stammheim,* based on the Stefan Aust book, *Der Baader-Meinhof Komplex.* Both are seen as counterinsurgency pieces.

July 9, 1986
The RAF's Mara Cagol Commando assassinates Karl Heinz Beckurts, the President of Siemens and a key figure in Strategic Defense Initiative (Star Wars) development, and his chauffer Eckhard Groppler.

October 10, 1986
The RAF's Ingrid Schubert Commando assassinates Foreign Department Director Gerold von Braunmühl in Bonn for his role in restructuring West Europe into a unified imperialist bloc geared towards destabilizing the Eastern Bloc and rolling back the anti-imperialist movement in the Third World. The murder has never been solved.

November 28, 1986
Peter-Jürgen Boock, who has broken with the RAF, has his sentence of three times life plus fifteen years reduced to a single life sentence.

1987

February 25, 1987

Action Directe members Nathalie Ménigon, Joëlle Aubron, Jean-Marc Rouillan, and Georges Cipriani are arrested in a farmhouse outside Orleans.

1988

June 17, 1988

An attempted bombing of a discotheque popular with U.S. military personnel in Rota, Spain is disrupted when a police patrol happens upon the scene. The would-be bombers escape following a firefight. Alleged former RAF members Horst Meyer and Andrea Klump are sought in connection with the action.

September 1988

The RAF releases a joint statement with Italy's Red Brigades calling for greater cooperation between guerilla groups in West Europe. Within days, there are raids across Italy, with six Red Brigades safehouses being discovered and twenty militants arrested.

September 20, 1988

The RAF's Khaled Aker Commando attempts to assassinate Secretary of State for the Minister of Finance, Hans Tietmeyer, but their automatic pistol jams.

November 30, 1988

President Bernhard Vogel pardons former RAF members Klaus Jünschke and Manfred Grashof, both of whom have publicly distanced themselves from the RAF.

1989

February 1–May 14, 1989

Political prisoners participate in the RAF's 10th collective hunger strike, demanding improved prison conditions and the right to communicate between themselves.

November 9, 1989

The Berlin Wall falls.

November 30, 1989

The RAF's Wolfgang Beer Commando assassinates Deutsche Bank Chairman Alfred Herrhausen in Bad Homburg. His chauffer is also injured. The murder is never solved, and the sophistication of the bomb, containing armour piercing projectiles and triggered by a laser, leads many to suspect the involvement of the East German *Stasi*.

1990

June 6, 1990

Susanne Albrecht is arrested in East Berlin, in the GDR.

June 12, 1990

Inge Viett is arrested in Magdeburg, in the GDR.

June 14, 1990

Werner Lotze and Christine Dümlein are arrested in Seftenbeck, in the GDR.

Ekkehard von Seckendorff and Monika Helbing are arrested in Frankfurt an der Oder, in the GDR.

June 15, 1990

Sigrid Sternebeck and Ralf Friedrich are arrested in Schwedt, in the GDR.

June 18, 1990

Silke Maier-Witt and Henning Beer are arrested in Neubrandenberg, in the GDR.

Of the above listed arrestees, Dümlein and von Seckendorf are quickly released, the charges against them being moot due to the statute of limitations. Nonetheless, they, like all of the arrestees, with the exception of Viett, provided prosecutors with testimony against other former guerillas. All those charged, with the exception of Viett, would, as a result, receive relatively short sentences. Their testimony would be used to increase the sentences of Eva Haule, Christian Klar, Adelheid Schulz, and Sieglinde Hofmann during trials in 1994 and 1995.

July 27, 1990

The RAF's José Manuel Sévillano Commando fails in an assassination attempt against State Secretary of the Minister of Interior Affairs, Hans Neusel. The attempted murder has never been solved.

August 1990

The final issue of the illegal RAF support newspaper *Zusammen Kämpfen* comes out.

October 3, 1990

Germany is officially reunited, with the German Democratic Republic being absorbed into the Federal Republic of Germany, again collectively known simply as Germany.

1991

January 16–April 12, 1991

Following the occupation of Kuwait by Iraq, the U.S. Air Force and ground troops attack Iraq, in what will become known as the first Gulf War.

February 13, 1991

The RAF machineguns the U.S. Embassy in Bonn. First they call the commando the Vincenzo Spano Commando. In a statement released on February 24, they will call it the Ciro Rizatto Commando.

April 1, 1991

The RAF's Ulrich Wessel Commando assassinates Karsten Rohwedder, the Chairman of the *Treuhandstalt*, the organization responsible for privatizing industry in the former East Germany. He is shot through the window of his home in Düsseldorf by a sniper. His wife is injured by one of the three shots. In 2001, DNA evidence from hair found at the scene will implicate Wolfgang Grams, but by that time Grams is dead.

June 3, 1991
The Stuttgart OLG sentences former RAF member Susanne Albrecht, arrested in the former GDR, to twelve years in prison.

July 3, 1991
The Koblenz OLG sentences former RAF member Henning Beer, arrested in the former GDR, to 6 years in a minimum-security prison.

October 8, 1991
The Stuttgart OLG sentences Silke Maier-Witt, arrested in the former GDR, to 10 years in prison.

November 30, 1991
President Richard von Weizsäcker pardons former RAF member Verena Becker. She began cooperating shortly after her arrest.

December 23, 1991
A bus carrying Russian Jewish refugees on their way Israel is bombed in Budapest, Hungary. Alleged former RAF members Horst Meyer and Andrea Klump are sought in connection with the action, carried out by a fringe Palestinian guerilla group, the Movement for the Freedom of Jerusalem.

December 26, 1991
The U.S.S.R. is dissolved.

1992
January 6, 1992
The Kinkel Initiative, a government proposal for the gradual decarceration of RAF prisoners, is launched. By September of 1993, eight prisoners from the RAF and its support movement have been released: Günter Sonnenberg, Bernd Rössner, Karl-Friedrich Grosser, Claudia Wannersdorfer, Thomas Thoene, Angelica Goder, Barbel Hofmeier, and Christian Kluth. The initiative is harshly criticized by Chancellor Helmut Kohl, the BAW, the *Verfassungsschutz*, and the BKA Terrorism Unit.

February 24, 1992
The Stuttgart OLG sentences former RAF member Monika Helbing, arrested in the former GDR, to 7 years in prison.

March 11, 1992
The Bavaria OLG sentences former RAF member Werner Lotze, arrested in the former GDR, to 11 years in prison.

April 10, 1992
The RAF issues the *Zäsurerklarung* (Ceasefire Statement), also known as the April Paper, announcing a unilateral de-escalation, indicating that it will no longer assassinate leading figures of the state or industry. The paper calls for the decarceration of RAF prisoners who have already served lengthy

sentences and for all who are ill. This paper is generally seen as a response to the Kinkel Initiative.

April 15, 1992
RAF prisoner Irmgard Möller, who has been in prison since 1972, issues a statement voicing her support to the RAF's ceasefire decision and calling for the immediate release of two seriously ill RAF prisoners, Günter Sonnenberg and Bernd Rössner.

May 15, 1992
RAF prisoner Günter Sonnenberg is released from prison.

May 18, 1992
Spiegel publishes an interview with RAF prisoner Irmgard Möller.

June 1992
konkret publishes an interview with RAF prisoners being held in Celle, Lutz Taufer, Karl-Heinz Dellwo, and Knut Folkerts.

June 22, 1992
The Stuttgart OLG sentences former RAF members Sigrid Sternebeck and Ralf Baptist Friedrich, arrested in the former GDR, to eight-and-a-half and six-and-a-half years in prison, respectively.

June 29, 1992
The RAF releases a statement expressing their solidarity with protests being planned for the IMF World Economic Summit to take place in Munich from July 6

to July 8. In the document, also sometimes known as the June Paper, the RAF also reaffirms its April de-escalation.

July 6–8, 1992
Extremely violent protests involving tens of thousands of people greet the IMF World Economic Summit in Munich.

August 1992
The RAF releases a statement, sometimes known as the August Paper, pronouncing the end of the Front concept first developed in the May Paper of 1982 and calling for a broad-based discussion to determine the next step to be taken by the movement.

August 26, 1992
The Koblenz OLG sentences former RAF member Inge Viett, arrested in the former East Germany, to thirteen years in prison.

September 30, 1992
The RAF writes a letter to *konkret* regarding the June interview with the RAF prisoners in Celle.

November 3, 1992
The Stuttgart OLG reduces RAF prisoner Christian Klar's sentence to a single life sentence.

1993

Early 1993

Attorney Hans-Christian Ströbele mediates a meeting between RAF prisoners in Celle, Karl-Heinz Dellwo, Lutz Taufer, and Knut Folkerts and the President of Daimler-Benz, Edzard Reuter and Chairman of the Central Council of Jews, Ignatz Bubis, to explore ways of preventing a new upsurge of violence in Germany. The RAF prisoners request that Reuter put pressure on the federal government.

March 9, 1993

The Düsseldorf OLG decides that as a result of the extreme gravity of his crimes, RAF prisoner Stefan Wisniewski will only be eligible for parole after twenty years.

March 30, 1993

The RAF's Katharina Hammerschmidt Commando detonates thirty-four 200 kg bombs at a new High Security prison outside of Darmstadt shortly before it is to open, causing 123 million DM in damages and setting back the opening four years.

June 27, 1993

RAF members Wolfgang Grams and Birgit Hogefeld are lured into an ambush in Bad Kleinen by police infiltrator Klaus Steinmetz. Following a shootout, both GSG-9 agent Michael Newrzella and Wolfgang Grams lie dead. As evidence mounts of gross irregularities in all aspects of the operation, including eyewitness reports that Grams was executed on site after he had been subdued, Minister of the Interior Rudolph Seiters resigns and Attorney General Alexander von Stahl is fired.

October 18, 1993

The Stuttgart OLG sentences former RAF member Ingrid Jakobsmeier to fifteen years in prison.

October 28, 1993

RAF prisoner Brigitte Mohnhaupt, speaking for herself and fellow RAF prisoners Hanna Krabbe, Irmgard Möller, Christine Kuby, Sieglinde Hofmann, Rolf Heißler, Rolf Clemens Wagner, Eva Haule, Adelheid Schulz, Christian Klar, and Helmut Pohl, releases a statement announcing a split with the Celle prisoners and the RAF on the outside.

November 2, 1993

The RAF releases statement responding to Brigitte Mohnhaupt, requesting that the prisoners she represented reconsider their decision to break with the RAF.

November 24, 1993
The Düsseldorf OLG sentences RAF member Rolf Clemens Wagner to 12 years for the attempted assassination of Alexander Haig, largely on the basis of testimony by Werner Lotze.

1994
March 6, 1994
The RAF releases a statement assessing their relationship with police infiltrator Klaus Steinmetz and the killing of RAF member Wolfgang Grams. They again reiterate their decision not to carry out attacks against representatives of the state and industry and call for a broad-based debate to determine the next step to be taken by the movement. They also demand association for political prisoners.

April 28, 1994
The Frankfurt OLG sentences RAF member Eva Haule to life in prison.

April 29, 1994
RAF prisoner Bernd Rössner is pardoned by President Richard von Weizsäcker.

July 27–August 3, 1994
RAF prisoners Manuela Happe, Eva Haule, Rolf Heißler, Sieglinde Hofmann, Christian Klar, Hanna Krabbe, Christine Kuby, Irmgard Möller, Brigitte Mohnhaupt, Helmut Pohl, Adelheid Schulz, Rolf Clemens Wagner, and Birgit Hogefeld engage in a limited hunger strike demanding the release of Irmgard Möller who has been imprisoned since 1972. Although they refer to it as the RAF's 11th collective hungerstrike, a number of prisoners do not participate, a further sign of the gravity of the split in the group.

December 1, 1994
RAF prisoner Irmgard Möller is released from prison.

1995
February 21, 1995
RAF prisoner Christine Kuby is released from prison.

April 25, 1995
RAF prisoner Manuela Happe is released from prison.

April 26, 1995
RAF prisoner Lutz Taufer is released from prison.

May 10, 1995
RAF prisoner Karl-Heinz Dellwo is released from prison.

September 5, 1995
On the basis of testimony from former RAF members arrested in the former GDR, the Düsseldorf OLG sentences RAF member Adelheid Schulz to life in prison in connection with the attack on U.S. General Frederick Kroesen.

September 26, 1995

On the basis of testimony from former RAF members arrested in the former East Germany, the Stuttgart OLG sentences RAF member Sieglinde Hofmann to life in prison for her role in the Schleyer kidnapping and execution.

November 13, 1995

RAF prisoner Knut Folkerts is released from prison.

1996

May 10, 1996

RAF prisoner Hanna Krabbe is released from prison.

November 5, 1996

Birgit Hogefeld is sentenced to life in prison, with no possibility of parole for fifteen years.

November 19, 1996

The Frankfurt OLG sentences PFLP (EO) member Souhaila Andrawes, the sole survivor of the Mogadishu hijacking, to twelve years in prison. After serving a year in prison in Somalia, Andrawes had moved to Oslo with her husband and daughter. Tracked down by German police in 1994, she was arrested and extradited to Germany in 1995. She serves six years of her sentence before being released due to ill health.

December 9, 1996

The left-wing daily newspaper *junge Welt* prints a letter from the RAF addressing the split in the RAF.

1997

January 1997

RAF prisoner Inge Viett is released from prison.

1998

March 13, 1998

Former RAF member Peter-Jürgen Boock is released from prison.

April 20, 1998

The RAF issues a document entitled *Die Stadtguerilla in Form der raf ist nun Geschichte* (The Urban Guerilla in the Form of the RAF is Now History) announcing its dissolution. The document is dated March 1998.

June 1, 1998

RAF prisoner Helmut Pohl, who had suffered as stroke in May, is pardoned by President Roman Herzog and released from prison.

October 19, 1998

RAF prisoner Adelheid Schulz is released from prison due to ill health.

October 27, 1998

The SPD/Green Party coalition government is formed with former *Jusos* leader Gerhard Schröder (SPD) as Chancellor, former *sponti* leader Joschka Fischer (Green Party) as Minister of Foreign Affairs, and former RAF lawyer Otto Schily (SPD) as Minister of the Interior.

1999
March 1, 1999
RAF prisoner Stefan Wisniewski is released from prison. He continues to be subjected to parole conditions.

May 5, 1999
RAF prisoner Sieglinde Hofmann is released from prison. She continues to be subjected to parole conditions.

July 20, 1999
In Duisburg, an armored car is attacked with a bazooka and robbed of an estimated one million DM. DNA evidence ties Daniela Klette and Ernst Volker Staub, former RAF members still living underground, to the robbery. Another alleged RAF member still at large, Burkhard Garweg, is also sought in connection with the robbery. The three remain at large.

September 15, 1999
In a shootout with police in Vienna, Alleged former RAF member Horst Meyer is shot and killed and Andrea Klump is arrested.

2001
May 15, 2001
The Stuttgart OLG sentences Andrea Klump to nine years in prison in connection with an action in Spain and an action in Hungary, neither of which were carried out by the RAF. She remains in prison, but is not generally considered a RAF prisoner.

October 26, 2001
RAF prisoner Rolf Heißler is released from prison. He continues to be subjected to parole conditions.

2002
February 26, 2002
President Johannes Rau pardons RAF member Adelheid Schulz. Schulz, who was released from prison in 1998 for health reasons, remains in poor health.

2003
December 10, 2003
RAF prisoner Rolf Clemens Wagner is released from prison.

2007
January 13, 2007
Clergyman Heinrich Fink reads a message from RAF prisoner Christian Klar to the Rosa Luxemburg Conference in Berlin. In his message, Klar calls for

the continuing struggle against capitalism and for a more humane society.

February 26, 2007

The television news magazine *Report Mainz* (The Mainz Report) reports on RAF prisoner Christian Klar's application for a presidential pardon, setting off a media debate.

March 25, 2007

RAF prisoner Brigitte Mohnhaupt is released from prison. She remains subject to parole conditions.

April 25, 2007

Attorney General Monika Harms launches an investigation into the allegations of former RAF members Peter-Jürgen Boock and Verena Becker that Stefan Wisniewski was the shooter in the Buback assassination.

May 7, 2007

Following a personal conversation with RAF prisoner Christian Klar, President Horst Köhler turns down Klar's clemency request. He will also turn down a similar request from Birgit Hogefeld.

August 27, 2007

RAF prisoner Eva Haule is released from prison. She remains subject to parole conditions.

September 9–10, 2007

Special programming on ARD commemorates the 30th anniversary of the Schleyer kidnapping. Former

RAF member Peter-Jürgen Boock claims in an interview that Stefan Wisniewski and Rolf Heißler executed Schleyer in a wooded area in Alsace. He also claims that there were plans to kidnap then Chancellor Helmut Schmidt.

October 18, 2007

In an interview with *junge Welt*, Rolf Clemens Wagner expresses the opinion that even in retrospect, many RAF actions still seemed correct. *Bild Zeitung* and former Federal Minister of Defense (CDU) Rupert Scholz call for charges to be laid for "speech encouraging criminality" and "disparaging the memory of the dead," but nothing comes of it.

2008

January 3, 2008

The Federal Supreme Court orders coercive detention for former RAF members Brigitte Mohnhaupt, Knut Folkerts, and Christian Klar to apply pressure to have them provide information regarding the assassination of Attorney General Siegfried Buback in 1977. The order is subsequently reversed. The case has been reopened on the basis of claims by former RAF members Peter-Jürgen Boock and Verena Becker that Stefan Wisniewski and not Knut Folkerts, who was convicted for the crime, was the shooter.

September 25, 2008

The German release of *Der Baader-Meinhof Komplex*, a film based on Stefan Aust's book of the same name, and directed by Uli Eidel. Ronald Augustin criticizes the film for portraying Baader as a madman and all of the female guerillas as cold blooded killers.

December 19, 2008

Christian Klar is released from prison after 26 years. Birgit Hogefeld, who will reach her mandatory release date in 2011, remains the only RAF member in prison. A newspaper article reporting on a welcome home party held for Klar in Berlin a week after his release, quoted Inge Viett asserting that the guerrilla was "a reasonable expression of our resistance to capitalism" and that, in retrospect, she wishes they had carried out the guerilla struggle with more know-how, intelligence, patience, and support.

Note on Sources and Methodology

Obviously, many of the challenges in working on this book have stemmed from the nature of the organization we have chosen to study.

The Red Army Faction was not just a clandestine organization, but also a revolutionary communist one. As such, it faced not just state repression, but also actual historical suppression, not merely through "regular" police and paramilitary action, but also more subtly, through ideological attrition. The latter has sometimes taken the form of outright lies with their origin in psychological warfare, but just as insidious has been the unanimous, unexamined rejection of the group's core beliefs on the part of all those who have studied it. As to those authors writing from an explicitly anti-left perspective, they have often been skeptical about the group's political beliefs even being germane to its activities or history; for them the political verbiage simply provided cover for deranged crimes.

All works must at times rely on unverifiable assumptions or guesses. This is especially so when studying a clandestine organization, and some authors have clearly felt entitled to make a virtue of necessity, crafting the RAF's narrative to suit their own political bias, which is more often than not the bias of those who pretend to have no bias at all.

Of course, we too have been forced to make guesses where there is no way of knowing for sure. We have tried, however, to always indicate where we are unsure, and our somewhat excessive use of footnotes is intended to give the reader an opportunity to see on what we are basing our assertions.

A further, at times bewildering, challenge in recovering the RAF's history has been the fact that many authors seem to feel entitled to play very loose with facts both critical and incidental to this story. This kind of shoddy scholarship is a defining feature of the "real crime" and espionage genres, and in the case of a revolutionary organization, it is often compounded by fabrications planted by the state, which liberal scholars often seem unwilling to subject to the same hermeneutic of suspicion as claims made by the movement. We have found almost all of the state's psychological warfare stories repeated in some place or another as if they were fact. In some cases, "plans" the state accused the RAF of having actually get promoted to actual events, i.e. we found one mention of a RAF commando attacking a nuclear power plant in 1977—despite the fact that no such attack ever took place, as should be easy to verify from available public sources.

This basic intellectual corruption seems to come with a free pass to be less than rigorous regarding other facts as well; on several occasions, we found that authors would get people's names wrong, dates wrong, and the basic facts about various actions wrong. Siegfried Hausner becomes "Wolfgang Hausner", Andreas Baader dies on a hunger strike, supporters become members, the RZ and 2JM become the RAF... these are just some of the "facts" we have found in various "reputable" works.

In fairness, some authors seem to have sincerely tried to do their best. Others have done very well in general, only to falter when certain subjects are broached. And while almost all works we consulted start from assumptions that we eventually rejected, we nevertheless continued to consult, and to rely on, these works. That is to say, one or many errors, or an open right-wing bias, have not been enough to rule out our consulting a book or article, providing we could not find any other source contradicting it.

The internet is widely considered an unreliable source of information, and yet we have found it to be an excellent tool with which to cross-reference the various "facts" found in most accounts of the RAF story. Even such inherently problematic sources as Wikipedia have served as a crucial warning system to indicate where the extant narrative is missing information, or is in error. In many such cases, we would later find authoritative material indicating that the "unreliable" internet had in fact been correct where some "reputable" work had erred.

Finally, while we have been open about our bias, we should also admit that there are most likely errors and omissions in our work. We have tried our hardest to weed them out, but both as a result of the murky and often contradictory existing record, and as a result of our own inevitable mistakes, chances are, some have snuck in.

We hope, however, to have succeeded in providing a fair and accurate representation of the first part of the RAF saga.

Any note on sources would be remiss without pointing all readers to the incredible Rote Armee Fraktion Collection of the International Institute of Social History, Amsterdam, maintained as an online archive by former RAF member Ronald Augustin. The collection includes tens of thousands of pages related to the RAF, including several books; while most of the documents are in German, some are in other languages, including English:

http://www.labourhistory.net/raf/index.php

A far more modest collection of RAF-related documents in English is available on the German Guerilla website:

http://www.germanguerilla.com

Bibliography

BOOKS

Abendroth, Wolfgang, Helmut Ridder and Otto Schonfeldt, eds. *KPD Verbot oder mit Kommunisten leben*. Hamburg: Rororo Taschenbuch Verlag, 1968.

Afro-Asian Solidarity Committee of the German Democratic Republic. *The Neo-colonialism of the West German Federal Republic*. Berlin: Afro-Asian Solidarity Committee of the German Democratic Republic, 1965.

Alexander, Robert J. *International Maoism in the developed world*. Westport, Conn.: Praeger,1999.

Ali, Tariq. *Street fighting Years: An Autobiography of the Sixties*. New York, NY: Verso, 2005.

Aly, Götz. *Hitler's Beneficiaries: Plunder, Racial War, and the Nazi Welfare State*. Translated by Jefferson Chase. New York: Metropolitan, 2007.

Aust, Stefan. *The Baader-Meinhof Group: The Inside Story of a Phenomenon*. Translated by Anthea Bell. London: The Bodley Head Ltd., 1987.

Bakker Schut, Pieter, ed. *Das Info: brief von gefangen aus der raf aus der discussion 1973-1977*. Kiel: Neuer Malik Verlag, 1987.

---------- *Stammheim*. Kiel: Neuer Malik Verlag, 1986.

Baumann, Bommi. *Terror or Love? The Personal Account of a West German Urban Guerilla*. Translated by Helene Ellenbogen and Wayne Parker. London: John Calder Publications, 1979.

Becker, Jillian. *Hitler's Children: The Story of the Baader Meinhof Gang*. London: Panther Granada Publishing, 1978.

Berman, Paul. *Power and the Idealists: Or, The Passion of Joschka Fischer, and Its Aftermath.* Brooklyn, NY: Soft Skull Press, 2005.

Bewegung 2. Juni (2nd of June Movement). *Der Blues: Gesammelte Texte der Bewgung 2. Juni, Vol. 1.* self-published illegally in West Germany, no date (1982?).

---------- *Der Blues: Gesammelte Texte der Bewgung 2. Juni, Vol. 2.* self-published illegally in West Germany, no date (1982?).

Böll, Heinrich. Interview by Gert Heidenreich (Bavarian Radio), September 28, 1977. "This Type of Cheap Propaganda Is Extremely Danegrous." Translated by Martin Black, in Martin Black, ed. *Stories, Political Writings and Autobiographical Works.* New York: Continuum International Publishing Group, 2006.

Braunthal, Gerard. *Political Loyalty and Public Service in West Germany: the 1972 Decree Against Radicals and Its Consequences.* Amherst: University of Massachusetts Press, 1990.

Butz, Peters. *RAF Terrorismus in Deutschland.* Stuttgart: Deutsche Verlags Anstalt, 1991.

Cattan, Henry. *The Palestine Question.* London: Croom Helm, 1987.

Childs, David. *From Schumacher to Brandt: The Story of German Socialism 1945-1965.* New York: Pergamon Press, 1966.

Christie, Stuart. *Stefano Della Chaie: Portrait of a Black Terrorist. (Black Papers, No 1).* London: Anarchy Magazine/ Refract, 1984.

Cobler, Sebastien. *Law, Order and Politics in West Germany.* Harmondsworth, Eng.: Penguin Books, 1978.

Cobran, Helena. *The Palestinian Liberation Organization: People, Power and Politics.* Cambridge: Cambridge University Press, 1984.

Croissant, Klaus, ed. *à propos du procès Baader-Meinhof, Fraction Armée Rouge : de la torture dans les prisons de la RFA.* Paris: Christian Bourgeois Éditeur, 1975.

Dellwo, Karl-Heinz. *Das Projektil sind wir.* Hamburg: Nautilus, 2007.

Deutsche-Arabische Gesellschaft der DDR. *Friend and Enemy of the Arabs: Facts on the Attitude of the GDR and of West Germany on the Imperialist Aggression of Israel against the Arab States.* Dresden, German Democratic Republic: German-Arab Society of the GDR, 1967.

Ditfurth, Jutta. *Ulrike Meinhof: Die Biografie.* Berlin: Ullstein, 2007.

Dobson, Christopher. *Black September: Its Short, Violent History.* New York: Macmillan, 1974.

Dosse, François. *History of Structuralism.* Minneapolis: University of Minnesota Press, 1998.

Dutschke, Gretchen. *Wir hatten ein barbarisches, schones Leben.* Rudi Dutschke. Ein Biographie. Köln: Koln, Kiepenheuer & Witsch, 1996.

European Commission of Human Rights. *Decisions and Reports.* 14. Strasbourg: ECHR, 1979.

Follain, John. *Jackal: The Complete Story of the Legendary Terrorist, Carlos The Jackal.* New York: Arcade Publishing, 1998.

Friends of Astid Proll. *Astrid Proll: The case against her extradition.* London: Friends of Astrid Proll 1978.

Ganser, Daniel. *NATO's Secret Army: Operation Gladio and Terrorism in Western Europe.* London: Frank Cass, 2005.

Geronimo, *Feuer und Flamme: Zur Geschichte der Autonomen.* Berlin: ID-Archiv, 1990.

Hadawi, Sami. *Crime and No Punishment: Zionist-Israeli Terrorism 1939-1972.* Beirut: Palestine Research Centre, 1972.

Halliday, Fred. *Revolution and Foreign Policy: The Case of South Yemen 1967-1987.* Cambridge: Cambridge University Press, 1990.

Hanshew, Karrin. "Militant Democracy, Civil Disobedience, and Terror: Political Violence and the West German Left during the 'German Autumn,' 1977" in *War and Terror in Contemporary Historical Perspective,* Harry and Helen Gray Humanities and Program Series 14, Washington DC: American Institute for Contemporary German Studies Humanities, Johns Hopkins University, 2003.

Herminghouse, Patricia A. and Magda Mueller, eds. *German Feminist Writing.* New York: Continuum, 2001.

Higham, Charles. *Trading with the Enemy: An Exposé of the Nazi-American Money Plot, 1933-1949.* New York: Delacorte Press, 1983.

HKS 13. *vorwärts bis zum nieder mit: 30 Jahre Plakate unkontrollierter Bewegungen.* Berlin: Verlag Assoziation A, 2001.

Hockenos, Paul, *Joschka Fischer and the Making of the Berlin Republic: an Alternative History of Postwar Germany.* Oxford: Oxford University Press, 2008.

Holderberg, Angelika ed., *Nach dem bewaffneten Kampf.* Gießen: Psychsozial-Verlag, 2007.

Hoshino Altbach, Edith, ed. *German Feminism: Readings in Politics and Literature.* Albany, NY: State University of New York Press, 1984.

Hülsberg, Werner. *The German Greens: A Social and Political Profile.* Translated by Gus Fagan. London: Verso, 1988.

Kalb, Madeleine G. *The Congo Cables: The Cold War in Africa from Eisenhower to Kennedy.* New York: Macmillan, 1982.

Kallam, Mahmud Abdallah. *Sabra wa Shatila: dhakirat ad-Damm.* Beirut: Beisan Publishing.

Katsiaficas, Georgy. *The Subversion of Politics: European Autonomous Social Movements and the Decolonization of Everyday Life.* Oakland: AK Press, 2006.

Klein, Aaron J. *Striking Back: the 1972 Munich Olympics Massacre and Israel's Deadly Response.* New York: Random House, 2005.

Komitees gegen Folter. *Der Kampf Gegen die Vernichtungshaft.* (n.p., n.d.)

Kramer, David. "Ulrike Meinhof: An Emancipated Terrorist?" in *European Women on the Left: Socialism, Feminism, and the Problems Faced by Political Women, 1880 to the Present.* Jane Slaughter and Robert Kern, eds. Contributions in Women's Studies. Westport Conn.: Greenwood Press 1981.

Krippendorf, Ekkert and Volker Rittberger, eds. *The Foreign Policy of West Germany: Formation and Contents.* London: SAGE Publications, 1980.

Commission internationale d'enquête sur la mort d'Ulrike Meinhof. *La Mort d'Ulrike Meinhof: Rapport de la Commission international d'enquête.* Paris: Librairie François Maspero, 1979.

Langer, Bernd. *Art as Resistance.* Translated by Anti-Fascist Forum. Göttingen: Aktiv-Dr. und Verl., 1998.

Lavy, George. *Germany and Israel: Moral Debt and National Interest.* London: Frank Cass, 1996.

Lee, Butch. *Jailbreak Out Of History: The Re-Biography of Harriet Tubman.* Montreal: Kersplebedeb Publishing, 2000.

Lee, Martin. *The Beast Reawakens.* Boston: Little, Brown and Company, 1997.

Metz, Helen Chapin. Library of Congress Federal Research Division. *Israel, A Country Study.* Whitefish, Montana: Kessinger publishing, 2004.

MacDonald, Eileen. *Shoot the Women First.* London: Arrow Books Ltd., 1991.

Major, Patrick. *The Death of the KPD: Communism and Anti-Communism in West Germany, 1945-1956.* Oxford: Clarendon Press, 1997.

Marcuse, Herbert. *Counterrevolution and Revolt*. Boston: Beacon Press, 1989.

Meyer, Matt, ed. *Let Freedom Ring: A Collection of Documents from the Movements to Free U.S. Political Prisoners*. Montreal/Oakland: Kersplebedeb Publishing/PM Press, 2008.

Murphy, Anthony, ed. and trans. *The Urban Guerilla Concept*. Montreal: Kersplebedeb Publishing, 2003.

O'Balance, Edgar. *Arab Guerilla Power*. London: Faber and Faber, 1974.

O'Neill, Brad E. *Armed Struggle in Palestine: A Political-Military Analysis*. Boulder, Colorado: Westview Press, 1978.

Pittman, Avril. *From Ostpolitik to Reunification: West German-Soviet Political Relations Since 1974*. New York: Cambridge University Press, 1992.

Prairie Fire Organizing Committee. *War on the War Makers: Documents and Communiqués from the West German Left*. San Francisco: John Brown Book Club, n.d.

Proll, Astrid. *Baader Meinhof: Pictures on the Run 67-77*. Zurich: Scalo, 1998.

Reeve, Simon. *One Day in September: The Full Story of the 1972 Munich Olympics Massacre*. New York: Arcade Publishing, 2000.

Rose, Paul Lawrence. *Revolutionary Antisemitism in Germany from Kant to Wagner*. Princeton: Princeton University Press, 1990.

Rote Armee Fraktion. *Texte und Materialien zur Geschichte der RAF*. Berlin: ID-Verlag, 1997.

Roth, Karl Heinz. *L'autre movement ouvrier en Allemagne 1945-78*. Translated by Serge Cosseron. Paris: Christian Bourgois Editeur, 1979.

Sayigh, Yazid. *Armed struggle and the Search for State: the Palestinian national movement, 1949-1993*. Oxford: Clarendon Press, 1997.

Scalzo, Salvator, Steffi de Jong, and Joost van den Akker. *Terror, Myth and Victims: The Historical Interpretation of the Brigate Rosse and the Rote Armee Fraktion.* October 26, 2007. http://www.brigaterosse.org/brigaterosse/documenti/ archivio/DocApprBRandRAF.pdf.

Socialist Patients' Collective. *SPK - Turn Illness into a Weapon.* Preface by Jean-Paul Sartre. Translation by Huber. KRRIM, 1993.

Texte des prisonniers de la "fraction armée rouge" et dernières lettres d'Ulrike Meinhof. Draft Version, Cahiers Libres 337 / François Maspero.

Texte des prisonniers de la "fraction armée rouge" et dernières lettres d'Ulrike Meinhof. Cahiers Libres 337 / François Maspero, 1977.

Thomas, Nick. *Protest Movements in 1960s West Germany: A Social History of Dissent and Democracy.* New York: Berg, 2003.

Tse-Tung, Mao. *Quotations from Chairman Mao Tse Tung.* Peking: Foreign Languages Press, 1966.

Turbiville, Graham H. Jr. *Hunting Leadership Targets in Counterinsurgency and Counterterrorist Operations: Selected Perspectives and Experience.* Hurlburt Field, Florida: Joint Special Operations University Press, 2007. https://jsoupublic.socom.mil/publications/jsou/JSOU07-6turbivilleHuntingLeadershipTargets_final.pdf.

Vague, Tom. *Televisionaries: The Red Army Faction Story, 1963-1993.* Oakland: AK Press, 1994.

Varon, Jeremy. *Bringing the War Home: The Weather Underground, the Red Army Faction, and Revolutionary Violence in the Sixties and Seventies.* Berkeley: University of California Press, 2004.

Von der Zwangernährung zur "Koma-Losung." West Germany, September 1985.

Wiggershaus, Rolf. *The Frankfurt School: Its History, Theories and Political Significance.* Translated by Michael Robertson. Cambridge, Mass.: MIT Press, 1994.

Wisniewski, Stefan. *We were so terribly consistent... A Conversation About the History of the Red Army Faction.* Montreal: Kersplebedeb, 2008.

Wolf, Markus, and Anne McElvoy. *Man without a Face: The Autobiography of Communism's Greatest Spymaster.* New York: Times Books, 1999.

FILM

Conradt, G., and H. Jahn. *Starbuck Holger Meins.* Directed by G. Conradt. Germany: Hartmut Jahn Filmproduktion, 2002.

Lewis, B., director. *Baader Meinhof: In Love With Terror.* United Kingdom: A Mentorn Production for BBC FOUR, 2002.

JOURNALS

Anonymous. "Buback: In Memoriam," in "The German Issue," special issue, *semiotext(e)* 4, no. 2 (1982): 124-133.

Anonymous. "To Have Done with Armed Isolation," in "The German Issue," special issue. Translated by Wynn Gunderson. *semiotext(e)* 4, no. 2 (1982): 130-133.

Benjamin, Jessica, and Anson Rabinbach. "Germans, Leftists, Jews." *New German Critique* 31 (Winter 1984): 183-193.

Bier, Jean-Paul. "The Holocaust and West Germany: Strategies of Oblivion 1947-1979," in "Germans and Jews," special issue, *New German Critique* 19 (Winter 1980): 9-29.

Billig, Otto. "The Lawyer Terrorist and his Comrades." *Political Psychology* 6, no.1 (March 1985): 29-46.

Bodemann, Michal Y. "The Green Party and the New Nationalism in the Federal Republic of Germany." *Socialist Register* (1985-86): 137-157.

Busuttil, James J. "The Bonn Declaration on International Terrorism: A Non-Binding International Agreement on Aircraft Hijacking." *The International and Comparative Law Quarterly* 31, no. 3. (July 1982): 474-487.

Candar, Cengiz. "A Turk in the Palestinian Resistance." *Journal of Palestine Studies* 30, no. 1 (Autumn, 2000): 68-82.

Clutterbuck, Richard. "Terrorism and Urban Violence." in *Proceedings of the Academy of Political Science* 34, no. 4 (1982). The Communications Revolution in Politics (1982): 165-175.

de Boer, Connie. "The Polls: Terrorism and Hijacking." *The Public Opinion Quarterly* 43, no. 3 (Autumn, 1979): 410-418.

Evans, Alona E. "Aircraft Hijacking: What is Being Done?" *American Journal of International Law* 67 (1973): 641-671.

"Federal Constitutional Court Issues Temporary Injunction in the NPD Party Ban Case." *German Law Journal* 2, no. 13 (August 1, 2001.) http://www.germanlawjournal.com/ past_issues.php?id=74.

Graf, William D. "Anti-Communism in the Federal Republic of Germany." *Socialist Register* (1984): 164-213.

---------- "Beyond Social Democracy in West Germany?" *Socialist Register* (1985/86): 98-136.

Herf, Jeffrey. "The 'Holocaust' Reception in West Germany: Right, Center and Left," in "Germans and Jews," special issue, *New German Critique* 19 (Winter 1980): 30-52.

Herzog, Dagmar. "'Pleasure, Sex, and Politics Belong Together': Post-Holocaust Memory and the Sexual Revolution in West Germany," in "Intimacy," special issue, *Critical Inquiry* 24, no. 2 (Winter 1998): 393-444.

Horton, K.C. "Abortion Law Reform in the German Federal Republic." *The International and Comparative Law Quarterly* 28, no. 2 (April 1979): 288-296.

Hoshino Altbach, Edith. "The New German Women's Movement." *Signs* 9, no. 3 (Spring, 1984): 454-469.

Hudson, Michael C. "Developments and Setbacks in the Palestinian Resistance Movement 1967-1971." *Journal of Palestine Studies* 1, no. 3 (Spring 1972): 64-84.

Jacobs, Monica. "Civil Rights and Women's Rights in the Federal Republic of Germany," in Special Feminist Issue, *New German Critique* 13 (Winter 1978): 164-174.

Koopmans, Ruud. "The Dynamics of Protest Waves: West Germany, 1965 to 1989." *American Sociological Review* 58, no. 5 (October 1993): 637-658.

Kumagai, J. "The German Solution." *IEEE Spectrum* (April 11, 2003): 30.

Lasky, Melvin J. "Ulrike Meinhof & the Baader-Meinhof Gang." *Encounter* 44, no.6: 9-23.

Mayer, Margit. "The German October of 1977." *New German Critique*13 (Winter 1978): 155-163.

Mazrui, Ali A. "The Third World and International Terrorism: Preliminary Reflections." *Third World Quarterly* 7, no. 2. (April 1985): 348-364.

Mewes, Horst. "The German New Left." *New German Critique*1 (Winter 1973): 22-41.

Molyneux, Maxine, Aida Yafai, Aisha Mohsen, and Noor Ba'abad "Women and Revolution in the People's Democratic Republic of Yemen." *Feminist Review* 1 (1979): 4-20.

Monson, Robert A. "Political Toleration versus Militant Democracy: The Case of West Germany." *German Studies Review* 7, no. 2 (May 1984): 301-324.

"The Palestinian Resistance and Jordan." *Journal of Palestine Studies*, 1, no. 1. (Autumn 1971): 162-170.

Paul, Diane. "'In the Interests of Civilization': Marxist Views of Race and Culture in the Nineteenth Century." *Journal of the History of Ideas* 42, no. 1 (January-March, 1981): 115-138.

"Recent Emergency Legislation in West Germany." *Harvard Law Review* 82, no. 8. (June 1969): 1704-1737.

Ryan, Mike. "The Stammheim Model—Judicial Counter-Insurgency."
    New Studies on the Left 14, no. 1 & 2 (1989): 45-68.

Schlaeger, Hilke and Nancy Vedder-Shults. "West German Women's
    Movement." *New German Critique* 13 (Winter 1978):
    59-68.

Schmidtke, Michael A. "Cultural Revolution or Cultural Shock?
    Student Radicalism and 1968 in Germany," in
    "Rethinking 1968: The United States & Western
    Europe," special issue. *South Central Review* 16, no. 4,
    (Winter, 1999 - Spring, 2000): 77-89.

Schweitzer, C. C. "Emergency Powers in the Federal Republic of
    Germany." *The Western Political Quarterly* 22, no. 1
    (March 1969): 112-121.

Shell, Kurt L. "Extraparliamentary Opposition in Postwar Germany,"
    in "West German Election of 1969." special issue.
    Comparative Politics 2, no. 4 (July 1970): 653-680.

Stork, Joe. "Socialist Revolution in Arabia: A Report from the People's
    Democratic Republic of Yemen." *MERIP Reports* 15
    (March, 1973): 1-25.

"Strike of Arab Prisoners in Israel." *Journal of Palestine Studies* 7, no.
    1 (Autumn 1977): 169-171.

Watson, George. "Race and the Socialists." *Encounter* 47
    (November 1976): 15-23.

Webler, Wolff-Dietrich. "The Sixties and the Seventies: Aspects of
    Student Activism in West Germany." *Higher Education*
    9, no. 2 (March 1980): 155-168.

MOVEMENT PUBLICATIONS

Actualité de la Résistance Anti-Impérialiste. no. 3, Paris,
    June 6, 1978.

"Déclaration de Knut Folkerts dans le procèes contre Brigitte Schulz et Christian Klar (5-6-84) à Stuttgart-Stammheim, concernant l'action contre Buback." Ligne Rouge #11 décembre 1984.

Der Stammheimtod: Kampagne gegen das Modell Deutschland. no. 4, Bochum, December 1977.

"German war machine targets anti-nukers." *Open Road* 11, Summer 1980.

Internazionale Kommission zum Schutz der Gefangenen une Gegen Isolationshaft. October 1980.

"Les democraties face à la violence." *la Lanterne Noire* 5, decembre 1975.

"The Stammheim Deaths." *Cienfuegos Press Anarchist Review* 4, http://www.katesharpleylibrary.net/stammheim.htm.

WEBSITES

Unless otherwise noted, websites were accessed on May 3, 2008.

"24-Punkt-Haftstatut." http://www.nadir.org/nadir/archiv/ PolitischeStroemungen/Stadtguerilla+RAF/RAF/ brd+raf/053.html.

"ai-168." http://www.nadir.org/nadir/periodika/angehoerigen_info/ ai-168.html.

"Aktion gegen das Bundesverfassungsgericht (März 75)." http://www. freilassung.de/div/texte/rz/zorn/Zorn12i.htm.

"Aktionen gegen ITT Berlin und Nürnberg (November 73)." http:// www.freilassung.de/div/texte/rz/zorn/Zorn12.htm.

"Die Integration der Bundesrepublik ins westliche Bündnissystem." http://www.kssursee.ch/schuelerweb/kalter-krieg/kk/ integration.htm.

"Gerd Albartus ist tot." http://www.freilassung.de/div/texte/rz/zorn/ Zorn04.htm.

"Handelsgeschäfte mit der 'Wahrheit' Kronzeugen als Sonder-
Beweismittel der Anklage." http://www.freilassung.de/
div/texte/kronzeuge/goe1.htm.

"Interview mit der Roten Zora Juni 1984."
http://www.freilassung.de/div/texte/rz/zorn/Zorn50.htm.

"Kurt Groenewold." http://www.literaturhaus.at/autoren/F/fried/
gesellschaft/mitglieder/groenewold/.

"Terrorism 101-Counter-Terrorism Organizations: Germany-GSG-9."
http://www.terrorism101.org/counter/Germany.html.

2008-World Journal. untitled.
http://soc.world-journal.net/18sept2008spywars2.html.

Amayreh, Khaled. "Christians, too, suffer the evilness of the
occupation." at http://www.thepeoplesvoice.org/cgi-bin/
blogs/voices.php/2007/12/26/christians_too_suffer_the_
evilness_of_th.

Arm the Spirit. "A Brief History of the Red Army Faction."
http://www.hartford-hwp.com/archives/61/191.html.

Autonome Forum. "A Herstory Of The Revolutionary Cells And Rote
Zora—Armed Resistance in West Germany." http://
www.etext.org/Politics/Autonome.Forum/Guerrilla/
Europe/Rote.Zora/mini-herstory.1988.

Bielby, Clare. "'Bonnie und Kleid': Female Terrorists and the
Hysterical Feminine." Forum: University of Edinburgh
Postgraduate Journal of Culture and Arts no. 2.
http://forum.llc.ed.ac.uk/issue2/bielby.html.

Datenbank des deutschsprachigen Anarchismus. "Agit 883
(Datenbank des deutschsprachigen Anarchismus:
Periodika)."
http://projekte.free.de/dada/dada-p/P0000921.HTM.

Elter, Andreas. "Die RAF und die Medien: Ein Fallbeispiel für
terroristische Kommunikation, Andreas Elter."
Bundeszentrale für politische Bildung (August, 20, 2007.)
http://www.bpb.de/themen/XNP7ZG,0,0,Die_RAF_
und_die_Medien.html.

Frank Bärmann, Frank. "Nachruf auf Rolf Pohle." Freie
    Arbeiterinnen- und Arbeiter-Union (March 8, 2004.)
    http://www.fau.org/artikel/art_040308-182546.

George Jackson Brigade, "You Can Kill a Revolutionary But You
    Can't Kill the Revolution." November 1, 1977. http://
    www.gjbip.org/comm_teeth.htm.

Hannover, Heinrich. "Terrorsitenprozessen."http://www.freilassung.
    de/div/texte/kronzeuge/heinhan1.htm.

in bewegung bleiben. "Wer Gewalt sät."
    http://www.bewegung.in/mate_saehen.html.

L'Avocat de la terreur. "Oliver Schröm : Im Schatten des Schakals.
    Carlos und die Wegbereiter des internationalen
    Terrorismus." http://www.lavocatdelaterreur.com/pdf/
    Im%20Schatten%20des%20Schakals.pdf.

Linksnet. "Rede zum Angela-Davis-Kongress 1972."
    http://www.linksnet.de/artikel.php?id=374.

Freisel, Heike "Schleyer, a German Story." Litrix.de: German
    Literature Online. Translated by Philip Schmitz,
    http://www.litrix.de/buecher/sachbuecher/jahr/2004/
    schleyer/enindex.htm.

Marxists Internet Archive. "Lenin's What is to be Done? Trade-
    Unionist Politics and Social Democratic Politics."
    http://www.marxists.org/archive/lenin/works/1901/
    witbd/iii.htm#v05fl61h-397-GUESS.

-------------- "Minimanual of the Urban Guerilla-Chapter 28."
    http://www.marxists.org/archive/marighella-
    carlos/1969/06/minimanual-urban-guerrilla/ch28.htm.

Materialien zur Analyse von Opposition. "USA Black Panther Party
    (BPP) und Angela Davis Materialien zur Analyse von
    Opposition, Von Jürgen Schröder, Berlin, 8.8.2005."
    http://www.mao-projekt.de/INT/NA/USA/USA_Black_
    Panther_Party_und_Angela_Davis.html.

MIPT Terrorism Knowledge Base. "Black September attacked
    Business target (Feb. 8, 1972, Federal Republic of
    Germany)." http://www.tkb.org/Incident.jsp?incID=790.

Mongrel Media. "Magnolia Pictures & Wild Bunch / Yalla Films Present Terror's Advocate, a Film by Barbet Schroeder." http://www.mongrelmedia.com/press/Terrors_Advocate/press_kit.pdf.

Nobel Foundation. "Saul Bellow—Nobel Lecture." http://nobelprize.org/nobel_prizes/literature/laureates/1976/bellow-lecture.html.

Pisano, Vittorfranco S. "Terrorism in Italy." (March 27, 1978). Heritage Foundation. http://www.heritage.org/Research/Europe/bg56.cfm.

Reinders, Ralf, Klaus Viehmann, and Ronald Fritzsch. "Zu der angeblichen Auflösung der Bewegung 2. Juni im Juni 1980." in bewegung bleiben. http://www.bewegung.in/mate_nichtaufloesung.html.

Rote Hilfe e.v. "Zwischen RAF-Solidarität und „linker Caritas" - Teil 1 / 1 / 2007 / Die Rote Hilfe Zeitung / Publikationen / Rote Hilfe e.V. - Rote Hilfe e.V." http://www.rote-hilfe.de/publikationen/die_rote_hilfe_zeitung/2007/1/zwischen_raf_solidaritaet_und_linker_caritas_teil_1.

Sartre, Jean-Paul. "The Slow Death of Andreas Baader." (1974). Translated by Mitch Abidor. Marxists Internet Archive. http://www.marxists.org/reference/archive/sartre/1974/baader.htm.

Schulz, Jan-Hendrik. "Zur Geschichte der Roten Armee Fraktion (RAF) und ihrer Kontexte: Eine Chronik, Jan-Hendrik Schulz." Zeitgeschichte Online. May 2007. http://www.zeithistorische-forschungen.de/site/40208730/default.aspx.

Soligruppe, Christian S. "Der *Spiegel*, 1975, BAADER/MEINHOF Müdes Auge." http://www36.websamba.com/Soligruppe/data/spiegel1975.htm.

Untitled. http://soc.world-journal.net/18sept2008spywars2.html.

Vowinckel, Annette. "Der kurze Weg nach Entebbe oder die Verlängerung der deutschen Geschichte in den Nahen Osten." http://www.zeithistorische-forschungen.de/site/40208212/default.aspx#pgfId-1033195a.

OTHER NEWSPAPERS & PERIODICALS

Ascherson, Neil. "Leftists Disturbed by Violence of Berlin Gunmen." *Winnipeg Free Press*, July 4, 1970.

Associated Press. "Schleyer Found Dead." *Danville (Virginia) Register*, October 20, 1977.

------------- "2 German terrorists given life." *European Stars and Stripes*, June 3, 1977.

------------- "3 Sought In Slaying Of Official." *Press Courier (Oxnard, California)*, April 8, 1977.

------------- "3 terrorist deaths ruled 'a collective suicide.'" *European Stars and Stripes*, February 25, 1978.

------------- "4 get life for attack at embassy." *European Stars and Stripes*, July 21, 1977.

------------- "Anarchist Buried." *Waterloo Courier*, May 16, 1976.

------------- "Baader-Meinhof Armourer Testifies." *European Stars and Stripes*, January 28, 1976.

------------- "Bay Area Service for Slain Jews." *Daily Review (Hayward, California)*, September 8, 1972.

------------- "Berlin Cops, Leftists Clash for 2nd Night." *European Stars and Stripes*, May 17, 1971.

------------- "Bomb rips ITT subsidiary office in Berlin." *European Stars and Stripes*, November 18, 1973.

------------- "Bombers Threaten 3 Blasts Friday in Stuttgart Area." *European Stars and Stripes*, May 29, 1972.

------------- "Bombs damage building in Paris." *Press Courier (Oxnard, California)*, May 19, 1976.

------------ "Bonn fears more violence." *Syracuse (New York) Post-Standard*, Nov. 12, 1974.

------------ "Bonn: terrorist death was suicide." *Modesto (California) Bee*, November 14, 1977.

------------ "Cohn-Bendit Jailed; Court Brawl Follows." *European Stars and Stripes*, November 1, 1968.

------------ "Deaths: Rolf Pohle." *Daily Globe (Ironwood, Michigan)*, February 10, 2004.

------------ "Dutch capture German terrorist." *Lima (Ohio) News*, September 23, 1977.

------------ "Extremists protest deaths of 3 German prisoners." *Amarillo (Texas) Globe Times*, October 19, 1977.

------------ "German Draws 10-year term." *European Stars and Stripes*, July 27, 1972.

------------ "German Leftists, Police Battle after Paper Raided." *Waterloo Courier*, October 24, 1977.

------------ "German TV Cancels Film Showing Abortion." *European Stars and Stripes*, March 13, 1974.

------------ "Hit Kiesinger; Term Suspended." *European Stars and Stripes*, August 26, 1969.

------------ "Industrialist's Killers Sought." *Wisconsin State Journal*, October 21, 1977.

------------ "Kidnaped Berlin Political Figure is Released Freed Unhurt." *Wisconsin State Journal*, March 5, 1975.

------------ "Kidnaped German Boy, 7, Freed After Ransom." *European Stars and Stripes*, February 29, 1971.

------------ "Lufthansa Airlines Flying Anti-Missile Patterns." *Florence (South Carolina) Morning News*, November 15, 1977.

------------ "Nab murder suspect in Frankfurt." *Pacific Stars and Stripes*, June 12, 1979.

\-\-\-\-\-\-\-\-\-\-\-\-\- "New Blast in Germany." *Syracuse (New York) Herald-Journal,* January 21, 1985.

\-\-\-\-\-\-\-\-\-\-\-\-\- "New Terror Ring Smashed By Raids in German Cities." *European Stars and Stripes,* February 5, 1974.

\-\-\-\-\-\-\-\-\-\-\-\-\- "Paper Reports Plot to Kidnap Willy Brandt." *European Stars and Stripes,* February 13, 1971.

\-\-\-\-\-\-\-\-\-\-\-\-\- "Police Hunting SS Member's Son in Kidnapings." *European Stars and Stripes,* March 2, 1971.

\-\-\-\-\-\-\-\-\-\-\-\-\- "Radical Lawyer's Office Bombed." *Oakland (California) Tribune,* August 15, 1977.

\-\-\-\-\-\-\-\-\-\-\-\-\- "Raids in German Cities Smash New Terror Ring." *European Stars and Stripes,* February 5, 1974.

\-\-\-\-\-\-\-\-\-\-\-\-\- "Schleyer No Friend of Socialists, Unions." *Abilene (Texas)-Reporter News,* October 20, 1977.

\-\-\-\-\-\-\-\-\-\-\-\-\- "Student 'Army' Battles With Berlin Police." *Fresno (California) Bee,* November 4, 1968.

\-\-\-\-\-\-\-\-\-\- "Terror Suspect Nabbed." *The Times (San Mateo, California),* August 2, 1977.

\-\-\-\-\-\-\-\-\-\- "Terrorist Bomb Racks Train Station." *The Modesto Bee (Modesto, California),* September 14, 1975.

\-\-\-\-\-\-\-\-\-\- "Terrorist kidnapper jailed for extortion." *European Stars and Stripes,* March 12, 1978.

\-\-\-\-\-\-\-\-\-\- "Terrorists Take Child as Hostage." *The Troy Record (Troy, New York),* February 25, 1971.

\-\-\-\-\-\-\-\-\-\- "Trial starts in Munich for accused Meinhof-gang munitions supplier." *European Stars and Stripes,* September 26, 1973.

\-\-\-\-\-\-\-\-\-\- "W. German ITT Offices Bombed." *Des Moines Register (Des Moines, Iowa),* November 19, 1973.

\-\-\-\-\-\-\-\-\-\- "W. Germans fear possible gas attack by terrorists." *Reno Evening Gazette (Reno, Nevada),* May 16, 1975.

---------- "W. Germans sentence 3 guerrillas to life for bomb deaths." *Tri-City Herald (Pasco, Kennewick, Richland, Washington)*, April 28, 1977.

---------- "West Berlin Publisher is Sentenced." *The Danville Bee (Danville, Va.)*, February 16 1970

---------- "West German police round up anarchist groups." *Greeley Tribune (Greeley, Colorado)*, November 27, 1974.

---------- "West German Terrorists Lose Shootout." *The Brainerd Daily (Brainerd, Minnesota)*, November 11, 1970.

---------- "Wife of seized industrialist pleas for terrorists' trade." *Modesto Bee (Modesto, California)*, September 12, 1977.

---------- "Woman gets Jail for Slapping Bonn Chief." *The Fresno Bee (Fresno, California)*, November 8, 1968.

---------- "Wrong Boy Kidnaped, Released; Ransom Paid." *Panama City News Herald (Panama, Florida)*, February 27, 1971.

Augustin, Ron. "Der zweite Tod." *Junge Welt*, Sept. 10, 2007. https://www.jungewelt.de/loginFailed.php?ref=/2007/09-10/006.php.

BBC News. "Meinhof Brain Study Yields Clues." November 12, 2002. http://news.bbc.co.uk/1/hi/world/europe/2455647.stm.

Binder, David (New York Times Service). "'Republic of West Berlin' suggested by radical group." *The Charleston Gazette (West Virginia)*, November 7, 1968.

Boyles, Roger. "Daughter Defies State Over Ulrike Meinhof's Brain." *The Times*, November 9, 2002. http://www.timesonline.co.uk/tol/news/world/article825312.ece

The Bridgeport (Connecticut) Telegram. "Large ransom frees Viennese millionaire." November 14, 1977.

Busch, Jürgen. "Die letzte Waffe des Anarchisten." *Frankfurter Allgemeine Zeitung*, November 11, 1974.

---------- "Viele Gruppen—viele führende Leute." *Frankfurter Allgemeine Zeitung*, November 14, 1974.

Campbell, Mary (Associated Press). "History's coldest winter wrote top story for '77." *The Lima News (Lima, Ohio)*, December 27, 1977.

Cohen, Roger. "Germany's Foreign Minister is Pursued by his Firebrand Self," *New York Times*, January 15, 2001. http://query.nytimes.com/gst/fullpage.html?res=9C00EE DD123DF936A25752C0A9679C8B63

Cohn-Bendit, Daniel. Interview by Stefan Aust, Gunther Latsch, Georg Mascolo and Gerhard Spörl "Ein Segen für dieses Land." *Spiegel*, May 2001. http://wissen.spiegel.de/ wissen/dokument/dokument.html?id=18370264

The Corpus Christi (Texas) Times. "Bombing Seen as Protest." May 14, 1976.

---------- "Police building hit by bomb." December 17, 1976.

Dellwo, Karl-Heinz. Interview by Axel Vornbäumen. "Ich bin kein Pazifist." *Tagespiegel*, March 26, 2007. http://www. tagesspiegel.de/zeitung/Sonntag;art2566,2208178

Deutsche Presse Agentur "Soziale Bewegungen Auf zum Strand von Tunix!" *Spiegel*, January 25, 2008.

---------- "Stasi soll RAF über Razzien informiert haben," September 29, 2007. http://www.monstersandcritics. de/artikel/200739/article_31643.php/*Stasi*-soll-RAF- %C3%BCber-Razzien-informiert-haben.

---------- "Wieder Anschlag auf einen Richter." *Frankfurter Allgemeine Zeitung*, November 21, 1974.

Deutsche Welle. "Journalists Unearth Rare Terrorism Trial Tapes from 1970s." July 31, 2007. http://www.dw-world.de/dw/ article/0,,2715909,00.html.

---------- "My Mother, The Terrorist." March 14, 2006. http://www. dw-world.de/popups/popup_printcontent/0,,1933629,00. html

die tageszeitung. "30 Jahre Deutscher Herbst 'Die RAF war nicht ganz so schlicht.'" October 17, 2007.

Ditfurth, Jutta. Interview by Arno Luik. "Ditfurth über Meinhof: 'Sie war die große Schwester der 68er'." *Stern* 46/2007. http://www.stern.de/politik/historie/:Ditfurth-%FCber-Meinhof-Sie-Schwester-68er/602814.html

Ensslin, Christiane and Klaus Jünschke. "Stimmen aus Stammheim: Isolationshaft ist kein Mythos." *Neue Rheinische Zeitung,* August 8, 2007. http://www.nrhz.de/flyer/beitrag.php?id=11287.

European Stars and Stripes. "General Pearson seeks community help in solving Frankfurt bombings." May 16, 1972.

------------- "German Facilities Struck by Bombs." May 13, 1972.

------------- "German terrorist is hospitalized." November 14, 1974.

------------- "Hunt for anarchists stepped up." March 7, 1975.

------------- "Meinhof." November 30, 1974.

------------- "Meinhof: Female German Guerrilla Leader gets 8-year term for role in murder plot." November 30, 1974.

------------- "New Violence Hits Frankfurt." November 2, 1968.

------------- "Released from Custody." February 11, 1973

Fichter, Tilman. Interview by Philipp Gessler and Stefan Reinecke. "The anti-semitism of the 68ers." *tageszeitung,* Oct. 31, 2005. http://www.signandsight.com/features/434.html.

Frankfurter Allgemeine Zeitung. "Berliner CDU ruft zu einer Demonstration." November 16, 1974.

------------- "Bescheidene Mitgleiderzahlen radikaler Organisation." June 7, 1972.

------------- "Beshuldigungen nach dem Tod von Holger Meins." November 10, 1974.

------------- "Die Vollzuganstalt Wittlich." November 10, 1974.

------------- "DKP verurteilt anarchistische Demonstrationen in Frankfurt." May 26, 1972.

------------- "Empörung nach den tödlichen Schüsssen von Berlin." November 12, 1974.

\-\-\-\-\-\-\-\-\-\-\-\-\- "Erklärung der Kirche gegen Terorismus."
November 29, 1974.

\-\-\-\-\-\-\-\-\-\-\-\-\- "Erst nach Stunden identifiziert." June 19, 1972.

\-\-\-\-\-\-\-\-\-\-\-\-\- "Festnahmen nach Frankfurter Ausschreitungen."
May 15, 1976.

\-\-\-\-\-\-\-\-\-\-\-\-\- "Keine Solidarisierung mit Abenteurern." May 29, 1972.

\-\-\-\-\-\-\-\-\-\-\-\-\- "Maihofer: 'Brutale Strategie' der Baader-Meinhof-
Bande." November 14, 1974.

\-\-\-\-\-\-\-\-\-\-\-\-\- "Todesfälle eingeplant?" November 14, 1974.

\-\-\-\-\-\-\-\-\-\-\-\-\- "Verdacht der Unterstützung von Terroristen beunruhigt
die Berliner evangelische Kirche." November 12, 1974.

\-\-\-\-\-\-\-\-\-\-\-\-\- "Verstärkte Sicherheitsmaßnahmen im gesamtem
Bundesgebiet." November 12, 1974.

\-\-\-\-\-\-\-\-\-\-\-\-\- "Zweihundert Studenten der Freien Universität im
Hungerstriek Demonstrationen und Krawalle in Berlin."
November 13, 1974.

The Fresno (California) Bee. "Plane is Offered Lorenz Kidnappers."
February 22, 1975.

Goettle, Gabriele. "Die Praxis der Galaxie." die tageszeitung, July 28,
2008. http://www.taz.de/1/leben/koepfe/artikel/1/die-
praxis-der-galaxie/

Günsche, Karl-Ludwig and Hans Werner Loose. "Werner Mauss 40
years of fighting against criminality." Die Welt, July 31,
1998. http://www.werner-mauss.com/index1339.html.

Haworth, David. "Why German Workers Don't Ask For Raises."
Winnipeg Free Press, December 11, 1968.

Henkel, Peter. "Milde Urteile für Volker Speitel und Hans-Joachim
Dellwo." Frankfurter Rundschau, December 15, 1978.
http://www.fr-online.de/in_und_ausland/politik/
zeitgeschichte/der_deutsche_herbst/das_ende/40164_
Milde-Urteile-fuer-Volker-Speitel-und-Hans-Joachim-
Dellwo.html

Intelligence. "Free Agent 'Werner Mauss' Gets Caught." Dec. 16, 1996. http://www.blythe.org/Intelligence/readme/50Maus.

Jacobson, Philip. "Show Trial." *Sunday Times Magazine,* Feb. 23, 1975: 12-23.

Karacs, Imre. "After 25 years Carlos the Jackal gets his revenge." *The (London) Independent,* October 18, 2000. http://www. independent.co.uk/news/ world/europe/after-25-years-carlos-the-jackal-gets-his-revenge-635028.html

Kätzel, Ute. "Die Mädchen fielen aus ihrer Rolle." *die tageszeitung,* October 25-26, 1997.

The Kingsport (Tennessee) Times. "West Germans Take Seriously Terrorist Threat on Schmidt." October 22, 1977.

Kirn, Thomas. "Bombendrohungen werden schnell geahndet." *Frankfurter Allgemeine Zeitung,* June 9, 1972.

Knobbe, Martin. "Der Ankläger und sein Informant." *Stern,* April 27, 2007. http://www.stern.de/politik/ deutschland/:Ehemaliger-RAF-Helfer--Der-Ankl%E4ger-Informant/588020.html

Kopinski, Thaddeus. "From barroom brawls to bombings." *Post Herald and Register (Beckley, W. Va.),* April 27, 1975.

LA Times—Washington Post Service. "West Germany's 'Bonnie and Clyde' Have Country in an Uproar." *The Lawton Constitution,* December 3, 1972.

Lams, Dave. "Police Trace Leads in V Corps Blasts." *European Stars and Stripes,* May 13, 1972.

Libération. "1000 croissants pour un avocat." October 10, 1977.

------------- "Klaus Croissant et la raison d'État." October 10, 1977.

Lincoln Star. "Anarchist's Death Causes Bombings." May 11, 1976.

Lindner, Jan-Eric. "Es begann wie ein Routine-Einsatz - dann fielen Schüsse." *Hamburger Abendblatt,* March 3, 2006. http:// www.abendblatt.de/daten/2006/03/03/539507.html

Long, Wellington. "Germany has second Rommel." *The Sunday Sun (Lowell, Mass.),* April 16, 1978.

Malzahn, Claus Christian. "Happy 25th Birthday Greens. What's the Plan Now?" *Spiegel,* January 13, 2005. http://www.spiegel.de/international/0,1518,336623,00.html

McCarty, Patricia (United Press International). "The terrorist war." *European Stars and Stripes,* August 9, 1973.

NEA/London Economic News Service. "Tragic Death is Mourned." *Uniontown Morning Herald (Uniontown, Pennsylvania),* May 27, 1976.

---------- "Friends Mourn Meinhof's Tragic Death." *The Pharos Tribune (Logansport, Indiana),* May 23, 1976.

News Journal (Mansfield, Ohio). "Leftists suspected: Former Yemen Premier Killed." April 11, 1977.

Newsweek. "The Angela Davis Case." October 26, 1970: 18-24. http://www.itsabouttimebpp.com/News_Media/pdf/Angela_Davis.pdf

Peters, Butz. "Landshut-Befreiung: Die RAF erleidet ihre größte Niederlage." *Welt Online,* October 14, 2007. http://www.welt.de/politik/article1263664/Die_RAF_erleidet_ihre_groesste_Niederlage.html

Reuters. "Envoy Gets Kidnap Threat." *Winnipeg Free Press,* Jan. 22, 1977.

---------- "Suspects shot in gun battle." *Winnipeg Free Press,* May 4, 1977.

Roth, Andrew. "Obituary: Melvin Lasky, Cold Warrior who Edited Encounter Magazine." *The Manchester Guardian,* May 22, 2004. http://www.guardian.co.uk/news/2004/may/22/guardianobituaries

Sontheimer, Michael. Interview by Rainer Berthold Schossig, "25 Jahre taz." *Deutschlandradio,* April 12, 2004, http://www.dradio.de/dlf/sendungen/interview_dlf/256035/

Sontheimer, Michael. "Soziale Bewegungen Auf zum Strand von
        Tunix!" *Spiegel,* January 25, 2008. http://einestages.
        spiegel.de/static/authoralbumbackground/1287/auf_zum_
        strand_von_tunix.html

Spaemann, Robert. "Kaffee, Kuchen und Terror." *Die Zeit,* 19/1998.
        http://www.zeit.de/1998/19/Kaffee_Kuchen_und_Terror

Spiegel. "Gehirne der toten RAF-Terroristen verschwunden."
        November 16, 2002. http://www.spiegel.de/
        panorama/0,1518,druck-223109,00.html

Steinbauer, Agnes. "Tod in Stammheim," *Deutschlandradio,*
        May 9, 2006. http://www.dradio.de/dlf/sendungen/
        kalenderblatt/496823/.

Strout, Richard L (TRB From Washington). "Countdown to a Crisis:
        Is Nuclear Terrorism Next?" *The Fresno Bee (Fresno,
        California),* October 26, 1977.

Synovec, Dan. "Anarchist gang blamed," *European Stars and Stripes,*
        May 27, 1972.

---------- "Bombs kill 3 at USAREUR Hq." *European Stars and
        Stripes,* May 25, 1972.

---------- "Security beefed up at U.S. installations." *European Stars
        and Stripes,* May 13, 1972.

---------- "Terrorists: odd solidarity prompts aid to the Baader-
        Meinhof gang." *European Stars and Stripes,*
        June 3, 1972.

Tersteegen, Wolfgang. "Mit der Bombe im Handgepäcke."
        Frankfurter Allgemeine Zeitung, June 19, 1972.

Thomson, George (Associated Press). "Berlin police, leftists battle."
        The Lowell Sun (Lowell, Mass.), November 4, 1968.

Time Magazine. "Battle of Berlin." July 3, 1972. http://www.time.
        com/time/magazine/article/0,9171,877839,00.html.

---------- "Closing in on an elusive enemy." October 9, 1978. http://
        www.time.com/time/magazine/article/0,9171,919863,00.
        html.

---------- "Guerrillas on Trial." December 9, 1974. http://www.time. com/time/magazine/article/0,9171,908968,00.html.

---------- "Kidnaping in Vienna, Murder in Athens." January 5, 1976 http://www.time.com/time/magazine/ article/0,9171,947609,00.html.

---------- "The Lorenz Kidnaping: A Rehearsal?" March 17, 1975. http://www.time.com/time/magazine/ article/0,9171,912980,00.html

---------- "Return of Black September." November 13, 1972. http:// www.time.com/time/magazine/article/0,9171,910445,00. html

Tolmein, Oliver. "Beharren: Freundfeind." *Freitag* 17, April 19, 2002. http://www.freitag.de/2002/17/02170125.php.

United Press International. "4 W. German Terrorists Arrested." *Pacific Stars and Stripes,* May 31, 1978.

---------- "8 Terrorist gang suspects still sought." *European Stars and Stripes,* July 10, 1972.

---------- "Army Headquarters Hit by Terrorist Bombs." *Valley Morning Star (Harlingen, Texas),* June 2, 1976.

---------- "Baader-Meinhof lawyer praises guerillas." *European Stars and Stripes,* October 10, 1972.

---------- "Captured Gun confirmed as Buback Murder Weapon." *European Stars and Stripes,* May 5, 1977.

---------- "Caransa Released After Ransom Paid." *The Coshocton Times (Coshocton, Ohio),* November 2, 1977.

---------- "Cops ambush terror courier." *Newport Daily News (Newport, Rhode Island),* September 25, 1978

---------- "Crusade against terrorism urged." *Newport Daily News (Newport, Rhode Island),* October 25, 1977.

---------- "Deaths of W. German terrorists protested with bombings, student riot." *Valley News (Van Nuys, Calif.),* October 21, 1977.

---------- "Ends French Stay: Member of Gang Turns Self In." *European Stars and Stripes,* July 1, 1972.

---------- "Explosive device defused in Wiesbaden." *European Stars and Stripes,* January 26, 1977.

---------- "Funeral to demonstration." *Playground Daily News (Fort Walton Beach, Florida),* May 16, 1976.

---------- "Gang Kidnaps Dutch Millionaire." *Kingsport Times News (Kingsport, Tennessee),* October 29, 1977.

---------- "German police hunt Haag helpers." *European Stars and Stripes,* December 8, 1976.

---------- "German rebel hangs herself." *The Pharos Tribune (Logansport, Indiana),* May 10, 1976.

---------- "German Terrorist Dies Violent Death in Prison." *The Coshocton Tribune (Coshocton, Ohio),* May 10, 1976.

---------- "Germans Ask Japan Help tracking killers." *Newport (R.I.) Daily News,* November 12, 1977.

---------- "Germans seize brother of Buback case suspect." *European Stars and Stripes,* May 6, 1977.

---------- "Gunmen kill German judge." *Morning Herald (Hagerstown, Maryland),* November 11, 1974.

---------- "Italian Leftists Continue Their Reign of Terror." *El Paso Herald-Post (El Paso, Texas),* October 26, 1977.

---------- "Italian Radicals Say Suicide Squad Will Kill West German Ambassador." *Galveston Daily News (Galveston, Texas),* October 26, 1977.

---------- "Leftist terrorists vow to foul German economy." *The Coshocton Tribune (Coshocton, Ohio),* October 22, 1977.

---------- "Leftists Continue Terror Reign." *The Salina-Journal (Salina, Texas),* October 24, 1977.

---------- "Meinhof-Al Fatah Ties Described." *European Stars and Stripes,* October 19, 1972.

---------- "Other Arab guerrilla demand told." *Daily Review (Hayward, California)*, September 8, 1972.

---------- "Paper Says Macleod was a British Spy." *European Stars and Stripes*, July 3, 1972.

---------- "Parting shots." *European Stars and Stripes,* October 4, 1980.

---------- "Professor endangered by kidnapper's threat." *The Dominion Post (Morgantown, W. Va.)*, April 25, 1971.

---------- "Protests Sweep Three Nations." *The Valley News (Van Nuys, Calif.)*, October 27, 1977.

---------- "Raided Flat is Suspected Anarchist Hq." *European Stars and Stripes*, October 28, 1971.

---------- "Suicide Victim Died of Despair—Comrade." *Raleigh Register (Beckley, West Virginia)*, November 14, 1977.

---------- "Terrorist Bomb Blasts Building in W. Germany." *Ogden Standard-Examiner (Ogden, Utah)*, October 31 1977.

---------- "Terrorists Bomb German Property." *Ruston Daily Leader (Ruston, Louisiana)*, October 24, 1977.

---------- "U.S. Hunts German Terrorists." *Pacific Stars and Stripes*, July 23, 1978.

---------- "Urban Guerilla Leader Hangs Herself in Cell." *The Daily Review (Hayward, California)*, May 10, 1976.

---------- "West W. German Professor Admits Kidnaping Hoax." *European Stars and Stripes*, April 27, 1971.

Whitney, Craig R. (New York Times Writer) "Treaty Seen to Block Asylum for Terrorists." *Salt Lake Tribune,* September 3, 1976.

Winnipeg Free Press. "Uneven contest." May 19, 1976.

Winters, Peter Jochen. "Die Verquickung in Machenschaften der Meinhof-Bande began mit einer Kirschenbetzung." *Frankfurter Allgemeine Zeitung*, November 25, 1974.

---------- "Ulrike Meinhof läßt sich nur die Stichwort geben." *Frankfurter Allgemeine Zeitung,* December 15, 1972.

---------- "Unklarheit über die Rolle der verhafteten Pfarrersfrau." *Frankfurter Allgemeine Zeitung,* November 23, 1974.

Wolff, Alexander "Thirty years after he helped plan the terror strike, Abu Daoud remains in hiding -- and unrepentant." *Sports Illustrated,* August 26, 2002. http://sportsillustrated.cnn.com/si_online/news/2002/08/20/sb2/

Yeoman, Fran "Diplomats suspected Entebbe hijacking was an Israeli plot to discredit the PLO." Times Online, June 1, 2007. http://www.timesonline.co.uk/tol/news/world/middle_east/article1867995.ece

INDEX

anti-Americanism 185, 615. *See also* Federal Republic of Germany: considered a colony

antiauthoritarianism 28, 43, 46, 244, 245, 328, 534, 539. *See also* RAF ideas on: anarchism and antiauthoritarianism; *See also* anarchists and anarchism; *See also* spontis; mentioned by Thorwald Proll 70, 75, 77

Anti-Capitalist and Anti-Imperialist Resistance in Western Europe Conference (1986) 618

anticommunism 33–34, 36, 313, 373–374, 544–547. *See also* anarchists and anarchism: as a slander; *See also* Springer Press; Adenauer era 6, 8–9, 13–16, 14–15, 16, 21

antinuclear movement 22–23, 26, 449–451; mentioned by RZ 460, 462

Anti-Repression Conference (1976) 442, 601

antisemitism 26, 46, 195–196, 553. *See also* Meinhof, Ulrike: accusations of antisemitism; selection at Entebbe 440–441

Anti-Terrorist Brigade 523

anti-Zionism. *See* Revolutionary Cells: anti-Zionism; *See* APO (Außerparlamentarische Opposition): anti-Zionism

APO (Außerparlamentarische Opposition) 29–44, 97, 108, 111, 168–169, 200, 328, 448, 460, 579. *See also* RAF ideas on: the APO; *See also* youth culture (1960s-70s); *See also* protests; anticolonialism 23, 26, 27, 31–32, 34–35; anti-Notstandsgesetze campaign 38–39, 90, 226, 579, 582; anti-Springer campaign 37, 90, 91, 97, 147, 150, 177, 180, 182, 226, 581, 582, 583; anti-Vietnam war 35, 42, 48, 579, 580, 581; anti-Zionism 34, 46, 553, 581; apprentices' collectives 50, 118, 583; Bundeswehr campaign 90, 91; Carbora Bassa campaign 97, 149; decline 42–44, 46, 50, 433–434, 435, 445, 540; fear of fascism 36, 39; GDR 27, 28, 30, 58;

guerilla 35, 37–38, 45–49, 51, 65, 118, 450, 581; sexual revolution 25–26, 44, 51; West Berlin 29–30; women 31, 42, 44, 444–445; and working class 29, 37, 44

Arafat, Yassir 56. *See also* Fatah; *See also* PLO (Palestine Liberation Organization)

Arbeiterbund 434

Arbeiterkampf 168, 516

Arbeiterstimme 607

Arienti, Carlo 522

Armut in der Bundesrepublik 143–144

Asdonk, Brigitte 60, 149, 563, 585

Association for the Development of Air and Space Industries 617

Association Francaise des Juristes Democrates 526

Aubron, Joëlle 619

Audran, René 617

Augstein, Rudolph 11, 232

Augustin, Ronald 258, 473, 512, 563, 593, 628; dead wing 285; released (1980) 258–259; release demanded 339; water deprivation 258, 387; website XVIII, XX, 408

Auschwitz trials 26–27

Australia 210

Austria 455, 603. *See also* Revolutionary Cells: OPEC raid in Vienna (1975); *See also* 2nd of June Movement: Palmers kidnapping (1977)

Aust, Stefan 161, 563, 618, 628; and Meinhof's daughters 118, 557–558; on Meinhof's death 383; on Stammheim deaths (1977) 511, 516

Authoritarian Personality 84

autonomists 435, 539–540

Azzola, Axel 348, 382, 455, 563, 600

Interpol 597

IRA (Irish Republican Army) 305, 311, 376; Portlaoise prison hunger strike 488–489

Iran 369, 439; and FRG 124–125, 125–126, 131; and imperialism 31, 210, 211, 212; mentioned in passing 149, 183, 213

Iraq 209, 620; and Waddi Haddad 482, 560, 561; and RAF 480, 527

Ireland 489

Irish Republican Army. *See* IRA (Irish Republican Army)

Ismirili, Yousef 599

isolation torture. *See also* prison conditions: as "extermination"; applied to RAF prisoners 238, 252, 428, 520; as experienced by victims 242–243, 249; discussed by RAF 249, 281, 286–287, 300–302, 320–323, 401–402, 403; health effects 244, 267, 345, 417, 548–549; methods 241–242, 515; resistance to 286–287, 344, 347, 370, 401–402, 403–404, 487, 493, 497, 604, 610, 614; sensory deprivation 238–240, 249, 271–273, 285, 302, 319, 410, 428, 491, 605

Israel 439, 440. *See also* Federal Republic of Germany—Imperialism: and Israel; *See also* New Left: Anti-Zionism; *See also* undogmatic left: Anti-Zionism; *See also* Revolutionary Cells: anti-Zionism; *See also* Zionism; and Entebbe 440; mentioned by Black September 204; mentioned by RAF 206, 214, 228, 229, 231–232; Mossad 561; reaction to Munich Olympics 191–192; considered "Nazi" 215, 231, 504; Palestinian prisoners' hunger strike (1977) 488; Six Day War 34, 56, 580–581; Yom Kippur War 199

Israel, Joachim 382

Italy 87, 254, 435, 508; mentioned by RAF 311, 360; and RAF 50, 389, 413, 521–522, 524, 529, 619; strategy of tension 62, 349

Jackson, George 407

Jakobsmeier, Ingrid 611, 616, 623

James, Daniel 178

Jansen, Ali 59, 113, 569; captured (1970) 60, 86, 585; release demanded 339; trial (1973) 593; water deprivation 258, 387

Japan 207, 526

Jarosch, Klaus 383

Jendrian, Günter 569, 594

Jeunes Avocats 526

Jishshi, Sammar 'Adnan 'abd al-Ghani al- 191

Jochimsen, Luc 145

Jong, Dirk "Dionysius" de 530, 569, 611

Jordan 557, 558. *See also* Black September (massacre); Black September, targeted by 188, 193; rear base area 56–57, 583; Six Day War 34, 551–552, 581

Juliana (queen) 523

junge Welt 625

Jünschke, Klaus 569; captured (1972) 172, 591; Kaiserslautern bank robbery 588; pardoned (1988) 619; release demanded 339; trial (1975-77) 598, 605

Jusos 256, 444, 625; mentioned by RAF 102, 147, 148

K.1. *See* Kommune 1

Kamp-Munruchow, Karin 613

Kanelakis, Panayotis 382

Kappel (judge) 72

Karlek med forhinder 319

Katsiaficas, Georgy 117

Kaufholz, Henrik 382

Kaul (federal prosecutor) 381

Kautsky, Karl 364

KB (Kommunistischer Bund) 168, 183, 516. *See also* K-groups

KBW (Kommunistischer Bund West-
deutschland) 434, 514, 607; Stam-
mheim trial 424; threat to ban 538,
608
Kent State killings 153, 207
Kenya 440
KGB 560
K-groups 42–43, 118, 434, 538, 553,
608. See also KB (Kommunistischer
Bund); See also KPD (Kommunistische
Partei Deutschlands) [Maoist]; See
also KPD/ML (Kommunistische Partei
Deutschland/Marxisten-Leninisten);
and antinuclear movement 450, 538;
antisemitism 198; attitude towards the
RAF 168, 245, 255, 258, 263, 326,
328, 388, 424, 434
Khalifi (guard) 599
Kiesinger, Kurt Georg 29, 41, 552, 569,
600. See also Grand Coalition
Kilgore Commission 5
Kim Il Sung 151
King, Martin Luther 36, 582
Kinkel Initiative 621
Klar, Christian 526, 569, 612, 615, 626,
627; Boock's Lies (1988) 527; Buback
assassination 470; captured (1982)
615; Committees Against Torture 253;
prison 624; released (2008) 628;
release denied 627; split in the RAF
623; Statement Regarding 77 533;
trials 617, 620, 623; Zurich bank rob-
bery (1979) 612
Klarsfeld, Beate 41
Klau Mich 75
Klee, August 72–73
Klein, Hans-Joachim 201, 439, 569;
OPEC raid (1975) 438–439, 599; Putz
Group 436
Klett, Arnulf 181
Klette, Daniela 626
Kletzhändler, Edith 613
Kluge, Alexander 25, 421, 610
Klump, Andrea 619, 621, 626
Kluth, Christian 621
Knoblich (judge) 241, 593

Knodler-Bunte, Eberhard 27
Knoll, Michael 529, 570, 611
Knutz, Siegfried 301
Köhler, Horst 627
Kohl, Helmut 344, 615, 621
Komitees gegen Folter. *See* Committees
Against Torture
Kommune 1 31, 45, 49, 53, 237, 580,
583; mentioned by Thorwald Proll 69,
75; sexual politics 51
Kommune 2 59
Kommunistische Volkszeitung 434, 514
Konieczny, Hans-Peter 591
konkret 26, 28, 557, 583, 622; and KPD
26, 28; Meinhof's columns 32, 38, 41,
48–49, 53, 582; mentioned by RAF
84, 155
Kontaktsperre. *See* prison conditions:
Contact Ban
KPD/AO (Kommunistische Partei
Deutschlands/Aufbauorganisation).
See KPD (Kommunistische Partei
Deutschlands) [Maoist]
KPD (Kommunistische Partei
Deutschlands) [Maoist] 245. *See
also* KSV (Kommunistische Student-
verband); criticized by RAF 289, 424;
Horst Mahler 255, 256, 328, 594;
threat to ban 538
KPD (Kommunistische Partei
Deutschlands) [pro-Soviet] 15, 17–18;
anti-rearmament movement 20–21;
as DKP 42, 88, 102. *See also* DKP
(Deutsche Kommunistische Partei);
banning of 15–16; criticized by RAF
225, 228, 309, 424; konkret 26, 28
KPD/ML (Kommunistische Partei
Deutschland/Marxisten-Leninisten)
42; criticized by RAF 424; support
for prisoners 245, 258, 263, 326, 434,
459; threat to ban 538, 608
Krabbe, Friederike 526, 570

Kurt Groenewold 247; and Gustav Heinemann 41; *konkret* 26, 28, 557; *konkret* columns 32, 37–38, 41, 48–49, 582; and KPD (1959-64) 26, 28, 424; Letter to the Prisoners in Hamburg (1976) 405–407; library break-out 54, 55, 584; mentioned by the state 117, 172, 386; neurological abuse 241, 319, 322, 384, 409–412, 490, 593; On the Dead Wing (1972-73) 271–273; psychological warfare 413; and Jan-Carl Raspe 59, 395–396; Regarding the Liberation of Andreas Baader (1974) 359–370; release demanded 189, 192, 328, 332, 339; and Klaus Rainer Röhl 26, 48, 583; role in the left 53, 388, 390, 395, 429; *Spiegel* interview (1975) 300, 596; Springer bombing 357–358, 422–423; Stammheim trial 388, 455, 598, 600. *See also* Stammheim trial (1976-77); Statement to the Red Aid Teach-In (1972) 169, 200, 591; sued by Franz Josef Strauß (1961) 41; third hunger strike (1974-75) 253, 594; trial (1974) 255, 595; Two Letters to Hanna Krabbe (1976) 400–402; underground 258, 413, 585

Meinhof, Ulrike—death in Stammheim 381–387, 600, 611. *See also* protests: death of Ulrike Meinhof (1976); *See also* International Investigatory Commission into the Death of Ulrike Meinhof; *See also* Meinhof, Ulrike—death in Stammheim: psychological warfare; demand for international investigation 470, 487, 604; "estate" 460; funeral 389, 460; historiography 393–394; Jan-Carl Raspe: On the Murder of Ulrike Meinhof (1977) 395–396; psychological warfare 358, 381, 386–387, 391–392, 396, 412–413, 413, 430, 491; discussed by the RAF 395–396, 408–409, 412–413, 416, 490–491; mentioned by RAF 428, 428–429, 465, 496; rape 382–383

Meins, Holger 238, 572. *See also* Meins, Holger—death in Cologne-Wittlich; Agit 883 46, 55; in APO 31; captured (1972) 170, 171, 200, 591; force-feeding 259, 259–260, 292–295; isolation 238; Last Letter (1974) 296–299, 483; Molotov Cocktail film 150, 581; Report on Force-Feeding (1974) 292–295; underground 59, 353, 585, 587

Meins, Holger—death in Cologne-Wittlich 260–261, 595. *See also* protests: death of Holger Meins (1974); demand for international investigation 487, 604; effect on prisoners supporters 262, 332, 345, 439; psychological warfare 263; discussed by RAF 303–305, 304, 307, 429; mentioned by RAF 341, 395, 408, 428, 465, 470, 490, 496

Meir, Golda 189; mentioned by RAF 206, 231

Ménigon, Nathalie 619

Merck, Bruno 190; mentioned by RAF 231, 233

Metzger, Rudolph 586

Meyer, Hans-Joachim 382, 383

Meyer, Horst 619, 621, 626

Meyer, Till 242, 254, 572

Milberg, Peter 273

Militant Black Panther Aunties 51

military bases, U.S. 11–13, 316, 367, 414. *See also* RAF (Red Army Faction): attack on U.S. Army V Corps (1972); *See also* RAF (Red Army Faction): attack on USAREUR in Heidelberg (1972); *See also* RAF (Red Army Faction): attack on U.S. Air Force in Ramstein (1981); *See also* RAF (Red Army Faction): attempted bombing of SHAPE School (1984); *See also* RAF (Red Army Faction): Rhein-Main Air Base bombing (1985)

Military Counter-Intelligence Service 415, 421

Minimanual of the Urban Guerilla. *See* Marighella, Carlos

677

252–253, 260, 292–295, 304, 334–335, 370, 387, 493; mentioned by Thorwald Proll 72–77; neurosurgery and psychiatry 241, 242, 276, 280, 282, 286, 301, 306, 319, 403, 410–412, 490; 24-Point Program 242; United States 239; water deprivation 250, 258–259, 259, 285, 304, 370, 387, 428

prisons. *See also* Stammheim deaths; *See also* Meinhof, Ulrike—death in Stammheim; *See also* Meins, Holger—death in Cologne-Wittlich; *See also* prison conditions; Aichach 487; Baden-Rastatt 238; Berlin 286, 487; Berlin-Lehrter Strasse 285; Berlin-Moabit 285, 286; Berlin-Tegel 285, 302; Bruchsal 285, 302; Celle 528, 622, 623; Cologne 238, 285, 487; Cologne-Ossendorf 238, 240, 286, 403, 591, 594; Cologne-Wittlich 238; Düsseldorf-Schwalmstadt 238, 304, 370; Essen 238, 285, 487; Frankfurt-Preungesheim 273, 275, 285; Fuhlsbüttel 285; Hamburg 238, 286, 487; Hamburg-Holstenglacis 493; Hamburg remand centre 285; Hannover 285, 302; Hessen 601; Hessen-Ziegenhain 250; Kaiserslautern 487; Lehrter Women's Prison 602; Lübeck 286; Mannheim 285; Munich-Stadelheim 520; Plötzensee 81; Stammheim 471–472, 474, 487, 493, 509, 594, 604, 605, 606, 609, 613; Straubing 285, 302, 487; Stuttgart 286; West Berlin-Moabit 238; West Berlin Women's Prison 250; Zweibrücken 302, 304, 320

Proll, Astrid 573; alleged firefight (1971) 60, 86, 586; before RAF 48, 50, 51, 581; captured (1971) 64, 586; captured (1978) 529, 611; dead wing 238, 239–240, 302, 410, 588; escapes to England (1974-8) 240, 529–530, 594; library break-out 55; in RAF 161, 585; trials 113, 613

Proll, Thorwald 50, 573; Closing trial statement (1968) 66–78; Frankfurt department stores 48–49, 582, 583

propaganda. *See* psychological warfare

Protestants 20, 257–258

protests; peace (1952) 21; nuclear weapons (1956) 22–23; Moise Tschombe (1964) 27–28, 579; Vietnam War (1964-) 35–36, 579, 581; Shah of Iran (1967) 31–32, 226; shooting of Benno Ohnesorg (1967) 33–34, 580; anticommunist (1968) 36, 581; anti-Notstandsgesetze (1968) 38–39; attempted assassination of Dutschke (1968) 36–37, 111, 207, 307; Battle of Tegeler Weg (1968) 40, 288, 583; Nixon (1969) 583; shooting of Georg von Rauch (1971) 110, 588; for abortion rights (1974) 446; death of Holger Meins (1974) 261–262, 263–265, 344, 416, 459, 595; Wyhl (1975) 449, 450; death of Ulrike Meinhof (1976) 388–391, 441, 442, 600, 601; anti-communist ban (1977) 538, 608; Stammheim deaths (1977) 521–524; peace (1981) 614; IMF World Economic Summit (1992) 622

Psychiatric Clinic in Magdeburg 384

psychological warfare 61, 237–238, 429, 461, 464–466. *See also* false flag actions; *See* Baader, Andreas: hate campaign, target of; *See* Meinhof, Ulrike—death in Stammheim: psychological warfare; *See also* news media; anarchist smear 315–316; BAW 379, 381, 398, 400, 412, 422–423, 430; BKA 232, 290, 304, 350, 379, 400, 412; Bonn Security Group 232, 286, 290; former guerillas 113, 154–155, 263, 352; Ulrike Meinhof on 354, 359, 365–366, 367–368; use of RAF 117, 140–141, 142, 233

Public Service, Transport, and Communication Union 22, 169

South Africa 11, 132, 474, 503

Southern Fighting Group of the "RAF" 349

Soviet Union 28, 485, 621. *See also* Sino-Soviet split; *See also* KPD (Kommunistische Partei Deutschlands) [pro-Soviet]; *See also* DKP (Deutsche Kommunistische Partei); mentioned by RAF 88, 308–309, 405–406; occupation of Germany 4, 17

Sowa, Werner 596

Sozialistische Hochschulinitiative 264

Sozialistisches Büro 199–200, 440, 583. *See also* Angela Davis Congress (1972); Anti-Repression Conference (1976) 442, 601

Spain 125, 183; prison amnesty movement (1977) 489

Spangenberg, Henning 595

Spartacus Youth 140

SPD (Sozialdemokratische Partei Deutschlands) 63, 312, 525. *See also* Social-Liberal Schmidt-Genscher Government (1974-1982); *See also* Social-Liberal Brandt-Scheel Government (1969-1974); *See also* Brandt, Willy; *See also* Schmidt, Helmut; abortion rights 447; anti-rearmement movement 20, 21–22; benefits from collapse of APO 433; and Citizens Initiatives 448, 449; class base 9, 10, 29; functionaries mentioned by RAF 81, 88, 134, 147, 181, 233, 303, 322; Grand Coalition 29, 38; Hans-Christian Ströbele 246; mentioned by RAF 102, 126, 148–149, 225, 228–229, 229–230, 275, 305, 379, 418, 427, 533; movement against nuclear weapons (1950s) 23; Otto Schily 247; repression 237–238, 265–266, 267, 418, 533; and SDS 23–24, 579; Zionism 552

Speitel, Angelika 514, 527, 576, 607; captured (1978) 529, 611; Ponto assassination 474, 606

Speitel, Volker 475, 576; arrested (1977) 608; informant 514–515, 613; trial (1978) 611

Spiegel; abortion rights campaign 446; on Entebbe 440; mentioned by RAF 83–84, 155, 313; and RAF 54, 65, 118, 350, 557, 588, 605, 622; on rearmement 11; "Wir waren in den Durststreik treten" interview 300–323, 346, 596; Zionism 553

SPK (Socialistiches Patientenkollektiv) 108, 517, 584, 587; and Committees Against Torture 245; and RAF 108, 114, 118, 171, 172, 250, 325, 332, 337, 351, 587; mentioned by RAF 147, 401

spontis 43, 169, 435–436; attitude towards antinuclear movement 450; anti-Zionism 553; Meinhof demonstration (1976) 389, 441–442, 600; attitude towards RAF 201, 326, 435–436, 456, 534–535; mentioned by RAF 464; third RAF hunger strike (1974-75) 254, 257, 264–265; Tunix (1978) 538

Spranger, Dietrich 532

Springer, Axel 576

Springer Press 33, 581. *See also* APO (Außerparlamentarische Opposition): anti-Springer campaign; and Heinrich Böll 112, 532, 589; anticommunism 33–34, 36, 581; bombed by RAF 165, 177, 179, 180. *See also* RAF (Red Army Faction): attack on Springer Building (1972); mentioned by RAF 71, 83, 86, 93, 99, 101, 103, 146, 150–151, 206, 207, 232, 235, 274, 303; on the RAF 112, 586; Zionism 207, 552, 552–553

Springer Tribunal 581

squats 147, 184, 333, 460; Frankfurt 435, 436; Hamburg 435, 474; Hannover 148; Kassel 148

Stachowiak, Ilse 59, 576, 585; captured (1971) 64, 586; captured (1974) 325–326, 594; release demanded 339

THE AUTHORS

André Moncourt is the pseudonym of a writer with his political roots in the movements of the seventies and eighties.

J. Smith is the pseudonym of an activist who has been involved in the radical left for over twenty years.

Both feel very lucky to have had a chance to tell this story.

THE TYPE

The title heads for the introductory sections of this book, as well as the text in sidebars, is set in Avenir, a geometric sans-serif typeface designed by Adrian Frutiger in 1988. The title heads for RAF documents have been set in ITC American Typewriter Std.

The textface chosen for the body of this book is Sabon, a Garamond face designed by Jan Tschichold in 1964.

As a young typographer in the 1920s, Tschichold was a fan of the Bauhaus style, and had quite the collection of posters from the Soviet Union. For these sins he was arrested by the gestapo in 1933 and all copies of his books were banned "for the protection of the German people." Unlike so many others, he managed to be released, and fled to Switzerland, where he lived for the rest of his life.

KERSPLEBEDEB PUBLISHING AND DISTRIBUTION

CP 63560
CCCP Van Horne
Montreal, Quebec,
Canada, H3W 3H8
http://www.kersplebedeb.com
http://www.leftwingbooks.net
info@kersplebedeb.com

Since 1998 Kersplebedeb has been an important source of radical literature and agit prop materials.

The project has a non-exclusive focus on anti-patriarchal and anti-imperialist politics, framed within an anticapitalist perspective. A special priority is given to writings regarding armed struggle in the metropole, and the continuing struggles of political prisoners and prisoners of war.

KER
SPL
EBE
DEB

GERMANGUERILLA.COM

Many of the texts in this book—as well as supporting documents providing added contextualization—were first published to this website, devoted to archiving documents and analysis about the urban guerilla in the Federal Republic of Germany.

Come by and visit to see as our work proceeds on our second volume.

About PM Press

politics • culture • art • fiction • music • film

PM Press is an independent, radical publisher of books and media to educate, entertain, and inspire. Founded in 2007 by a small group of people with decades of publishing, media, and organizing experience, PM Press amplifies the voices of radical authors, artists, and activists. Our aim is to deliver bold political ideas and vital stories to all walks of life and arm the dreamers to demand the impossible. We have sold millions of copies of our books, most often one at a time, face to face. We're old enough to know what we're doing and young enough to know what's at stake. Join us to create a better world.

PM Press • PO Box 23912 • Oakland, CA 94623
510-703-0327 • info@pmpress.org • www.pmpress.org
PM Press in Europe • europe@pmpress.org • www.pmpress.org.uk

FOPM: MONTHLY SUBSCRIPTION PROGRAM

These are indisputably momentous times—the financial system is melting down globally and the Empire is stumbling. Now more than ever there is a vital need for radical ideas.

In the many years since its founding—and on a mere shoestring—PM Press has risen to the formidable challenge of publishing and distributing knowledge and entertainment for the struggles ahead. With hundreds of releases to date, we have published an impressive and stimulating array of literature, art, music, politics, and culture. Using every available medium, we've succeeded in connecting those hungry for ideas and information to those putting them into practice.

Friends of PM allows you to directly help impact, amplify, and revitalize the discourse and actions of radical writers, filmmakers, and artists. It provides us with a stable foundation from which we can build upon our early successes and provides a much-needed subsidy for the materials that can't necessarily pay their own way. You can help make that happen—and receive every new title automatically delivered to your door once a month—by joining as a Friend of PM Press. And, we'll throw in a free T-shirt when you sign up.

Here are your options:
- **$30 a month:** Get all books and pamphlets
- **$40 a month:** Get all PM Press releases (including CDs and DVDs)
- **$100 a month:** Superstar—Everything plus PM merchandise & free downloads

For those who can't afford $30 or more a month, we have **Sustainer Rates** at $15, $10 and $5. Sustainers get a free PM Press T-shirt and a 50% discount on all purchases from our website.

Your Visa or Mastercard will be billed once a month, until you tell us to stop. Or until our efforts succeed in bringing the revolution around. Or the financial meltdown of Capital makes plastic redundant. Whichever comes first.

RECOMMENDED FROM PM PRESS

Fire and Flames: A History of the German Autonomist Movement

by Geronimo

Introduction by George Katsiaficas and afterword by Gabriel Kuhn

ISBN: 978-1-60486-097-9

Published by PM Press

208 pages • paperback • $19.95

Fire and Flames was the first comprehensive study of the German autonomous movement ever published. Released in 1990, it reached its fifth edition by 1997, with the legendary German *konkret* journal concluding that "the movement had produced its own classic." The author, writing under the pseudonym of Geronimo, has been an autonomous activist since the movement burst onto the scene in 1980-81. In this book, he traces its origins in the Italian Autonomia project and the German social movements of the 1970s, before describing the battles for squats, "free spaces," and alternative forms of living that defined the first decade of the autonomous movement. Tactics of the "Autonome" were militant, including the construction of barricades or throwing molotov cocktails at the police. Because of their outfit (heavy black clothing, ski masks, helmets), the Autonome were dubbed the "Black Bloc" by the German media, and their tactics have been successfully adopted and employed at anti-capitalist protests worldwide.

Fire and Flames is no detached academic study, but a passionate, hands-on, and engaging account of the beginnings of one of Europe's most intriguing protest movements of the last thirty years.

 PM PRESS, PO Box 23912, Oakland, CA, 94623
www.pmpress.org

RECOMMENDED FROM PM PRESS

The Angry Brigade

A History of Britain's First Urban Guerilla Group

by Gordon Carr

Prefaces by John Barker
and Stuart Christie

PM Press 2008
ISBN: 978-1-60486-049-8

280 pages • paperback

$24.95

Based on extensive research, this book remains the essential study of Britain's first urban guerilla group in the revolutionary ferment of the 1960s, following their armed campaign and the police investigation. Extensively researched—among both the libertarian opposition and the police—this remains the essential study of Britain's first urban guerilla group.

Maroon the Implacable

The Collected Writings of Russell Maroon Shoatz

Edited by Fred Ho and Quincy Saul

Foreword by Chuck D; Afterword by Matt Meyer and Nozizwe Madlala-Routledge

PM Press 2013
ISBN 978-1-60486-059-7

312 pages paperback

$20.00

Russell Maroon Shoatz is a political prisoner who has been held unjustly for over thirty years, including two decades in solitary confinement. He was active as a leader in the Black Liberation Movement in Philadelphia, both above and underground. This is the first published collection of his accumulated written works, and also includes new essays written expressly for this volume.

PM PRESS, PO Box 23912, Oakland, CA, 94623
www.pmpress.org

RECOMMENDED FROM PM PRESS

CREATING A MOVEMENT WITH TEETH

A Documentary History of the George Jackson Brigade

edited by Daniel Burton-Rose
preface by Ward Churchill

Creating a Movement with Teeth

A Documentary History of the George Jackson Brigade

edited by Daniel Burton-Rose
Preface by Ward Churchill
PM Press 2008
ISBN 978-1-60486-223-2
320 pages • paperback

$24.95

Bursting into existence in the Pacific Northwest in 1975, the George Jackson Brigade claimed 14 pipe bombings against corporate and state targets, as many bank robberies, and the daring rescue of a jailed member. In more than a dozen communiqués and a substantial political statement, they explained their intentions to the public while defying the law enforcement agencies that pursued them.

Love and Struggle

My Life in SDS, the Weather Underground, and Beyond

by David Gilbert
Foreword by Boots Riley
PM Press 2012
ISBN 978-1-60486-319-2
352pages paperback

$22.00

From the early anti-Vietnam War protests to the founding of SDS, from the Columbia Strike to the tragedy of the Townhouse, Gilbert was on the scene: as organizer, theoretician, and above all, activist. In this extraordinary memoir, written from the maximum-security prison where he has lived for almost thirty years, he tells the intensely personal story of his own Long March from liberal to radical to revolutionary.

PM PRESS, PO Box 23912, Oakland, CA, 94623
www.pmpress.org

Kersplebedeb
Publishing and Distribution

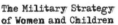

The Red Army Faction
A Documentary History
Volume 2: Dancing with Imperialism

by André Moncourt and
J. Smith

Introduction by Ward Churchill

ISBN: 978-1-60486-030-6

Published by PM Press and
Kersplebedeb

480 pages • paperback • $26.95

"With material like this at our disposal, not only should it prove possible to overcome the current inertia evidenced by those claiming to oppose imperialism from within the metropoles, but maybe this time we'll get it right."
from the Introduction
by Ward Churchill

The long-awaited Volume 2 of the first-ever English-language study of the Red Army Faction covers the period immediately following the organization's near-total decimation in 1977. This work includes the details of the guerilla's operations, and its communiqués and texts, from 1978 up until the 1984 offensive.

This was a period of regrouping and reorientation for the RAF, with its previous focus on freeing its prisoners replaced by an anti-NATO orientation. The possibilities and perils of an armed underground organization relating to the broader movement are examined, and the RAF's approach is contrasted to the more fluid and flexible practice of the Revolutionary Cells. At the same time, the history of the 2nd of June Movement (2JM), an eclectic guerilla group with its roots in West Berlin, is also evaluated, especially in light of the split that led to some 2JM members officially disbanding the organization and rallying to the RAF. Finally, the RAF's relationship to the East German Stasi is examined, as is the abortive attempt by West Germany's liberal intelligentsia to defuse the armed struggle during Gerhart Baum's tenure as Minister of the Interior.

Dancing with Imperialism *will be required reading for students of the First World guerilla, those with interest in the history of European protest movements, and all who wish to understand the challenges of revolutionary struggle.*

CPSIA information can be obtained
at www.ICGtesting.com
Printed in the USA
JSHW030830140223
375763JS00002B/3